ENCYCLOPEDIA OF ARMS CONTROL AND DISARMAMENT

RICHARD DEAN BURNS

Editor in Chief

Volume III

CHARLES SCRIBNER'S SONS • NEW YORK
Maxwell Macmillan Canada • TORONTO
Maxwell Macmillan International • NEW YORK   OXFORD   SINGAPORE   SYDNEY

Charles Scribner's Sons   Maxwell Macmillan Canada, Inc.
Macmillan Publishing Company   1200 Eglinton Avenue East
866 Third Avenue   Suite 200
New York, New York 10022   Don Mills, Ontario M3C 3N1

Macmillan Publishing Company is part of the Maxwell Communication Group of Companies.

Library of Congress Cataloging-in-Publication Data

Encyclopedia of arms control and disarmament / Richard Dean Burns,
    editor in chief.
      p.   cm.
    Includes bibliographical references and index.
    ISBN 0-684-19281-0 (set : alk. paper) : $280.00. — ISBN
0-684-19603-4 (vol. 1 : alk. paper). — ISBN 0-684-19604-2 (vol. 2 :
alk. paper). — ISBN 0-684-19605-0 (vol. 3 : alk. paper)
    1. Arms control—Encyclopedias.   2. Disarmament—Encyclopedias.
I. Burns, Richard Dean.
JX1974.E57   1993
327.1′74′03—dc20   92-36167
                                            CIP

1   3   5   7   9   11   13   17   19   V/C   20   18   16   14   12   10   8   6   4   2

PRINTED IN THE UNITED STATES OF AMERICA

The paper used in this publication meets the minimum requirements
of American National Standard for Information Sciences—Permanence
of Paper for Printed Library Materials. ANSI Z3948-1984. ∞™

CONTENTS

SOURCES AND ACKNOWLEDGMENTS

Several excellent collections of arms control and disarmament documents were useful sources for this volume. The following four were especially helpful:

Subcommittee on Disarmament, Pursuant to Senate Resolution 93, and Continued by Senate Resolution 185, Eighty-fourth Congress, *Disarmament and Security: A Collection of Documents, 1919–55* (Washington, D.C.: Government Printing Office, 1956).

United States Arms Control and Disarmament Agency, *Arms Control and Disarmament Agreements: Texts and Histories of the Negotiations* (Washington, D.C.: Arms Control and Disarmament Agency, 1990).

Trevor N. Dupuy and Gay M. Hammerman, eds., *A Documentary History of Arms Control and Disarmament* (New York: R. R. Bowker Company, 1973).

Leon Friedman, ed., *The Law of War: A Documentary History* (New York: Random House, 1972).

In addition, the editor is indebted to several organizations for granting permission to reprint documents protected by copyright:

Excerpt from *The Odyssey of Homer* translated by Richmond Lattimore. Copyright 1965, 1967 by Richmond Lattimore. Reprinted by permission of HarperCollins Publishers Inc.

Approximately 202 words from *The War with Hannibal* by Livy, translated by Aubrey de Sélincourt (Penguin Classics, 1965), copyright © the estate of Aubrey de Sélincourt, 1965.

League of Nations Draft Convention (9 December 1930) and Resolution Proposing a One-Year Armament Truce (29 September 1931) from John W. Wheeler-Bennett, ed., *Documents on International Affairs, 1931* (London: Humphrey Milford, 1932). Reprinted by permission of Humphrey Milford and The Royal Institute of International Affairs.

Gay Hammerman's translations of Treaty Concluded at Paris Between France and Prussia (8 September 1808), Act Signed by the Plenipotentiaries of Austria, France, Great Britain, Prussia, and Russia (20 November 1815), and Treaty Between the Emperor and Spain and Great Britain, and the Netherlands (15 November 1715) in Trevor Dupuy and Gay Hammerman, eds., *A Documentary History of Arms Control and Disarmament* (New York and London: R. R. Bowker and Company, 1973).

Extracts from Convention II of 1899 and Convention IV of 1907 in James Brown Scott, ed., *The Hague Conventions and Declarations of 1899 and 1907* (New York: Oxford University Press, 1918), pp. 116–118; original copyright held by Carnegie Endowment for International Peace, 1915.

Convention for the Control of the Trade in Arms and Ammunition (10 September 1919) and Convention for the Supervision of the International Trade in Arms and Ammunition and in Implements of War, (17 June 1925) from *International Conciliation: Documents for the Year, 1929* (Carnegie Endowment for International Peace, 1929), pp. 300–310 and 312–238.

Excerpts from Peace of Westphalia, Treaty of Utrecht, Treaty of Paris, and Treay of Versailles from Fred L. Israel, ed., *Major Peace Treaties of Modern Times, 1648–1967* (New York: Chelsea House in association with McGraw-Hill, 1967), 4 vols. Reprinted by permission of Chelsea House.

Turko-Soviet Naval Treaty (Protocol Supplementing Article II of the Protocol of 17 December 1929), as reprinted in Leonard Shapiro, ed., *Soviet Treaty Series*, vol. 2, 1929–1939 (Washington, D.C.: Georgetown University Press, 1955), Doc. no. 374.

Excerpt from Treaty between Great Britain and Spain (28 August 1814), reprinted in Clive Parry, *Consolidated Treaty Series,* vol. 63 (Dobbs Ferry, N.Y.: Oceana Publications, 1969).

CHRONOLOGY
OF TREATIES
IN VOLUME III

Where a treaty has been excerpted more than once, the page number of its principal entry has been listed.

5

TREATIES

Limitation of Weapons and Personnel

○

See also The Proliferation of Nuclear Weapons. *Entries that are the subjects of essays in Volumes I and II are marked with asterisks.*

Limitation of weapons and personnel is a technique that involves placing specific limits on the mobilization, possession, or construction of military forces and equipment; it may, additionally, result in the reduction of existing military forces and equipment. These restrictions on matériel may be "qualitative," regulating weapons design, as well as "quantitative," limiting numbers of weapons.

The extracts that are reproduced below include the more prominent arms control treaties and the arms control portions of various other treaties. It should be noted that some of these treaties also carry provisions dealing with other techniques, such as demilitarization or prohibition of specific weapons.

Early Examples

Rome-Carthage Treaty of Peace (202 B.C.)

This treaty, popularly known as the "Treaty of Zama," ended the Second Punic War between the two warring Mediterranean commercial powers. Hannibal's defeat at the battle of Zama forced Carthage to sue for peace. While many of the victorious Romans spoke of burning Carthage to the ground, the task of besieging and capturing the heavily fortified city persuaded Roman leaders to instead impose harsh unilateral military terms on the vanquished.

Essentially, Rome's imposed military terms (1) required the destruction of all warships, except ten; (2) outlawed Carthage's training and possession of trained war elephants; (3) limited Carthage's use of mercenary soldiers; (4) limited possession of armaments in general; and (5) prevented Carthage from making war without Rome's permission.

Terms of peace were put to them [the envoys of Carthage]: they were to live as free men under their own laws, and to continue to hold the cities and territories which they had held before the war; the Romans from that day on would cease their raiding attacks. All deserters, runaway slaves, and prisoners-of-war were to be delivered to the Romans, all warships to be surrendered, with the exception of ten triremes, and all the trained elephants in their possession were to be handed over and no more to be trained. They were not to make war on anyone inside or outside Africa without permission from Rome; they were to make restitution to Masinissa [the Numidian prince] and draw up a treaty with him; they must supply grain and pay to the allied troops until their own envoys had returned from Rome. They were to pay 10,000 talents of silver spread by equal instalments over fifty years, and to hand over 100 hostages of [the victorious Roman general] Scipio's choosing between the ages of fourteen and thirty years. An armistice would be granted, provided that the transport ships captured during the previous time of peace were returned, together with their crews and cargoes: otherwise there would be no armistice nor any hope of peace. [Livy, *The War With Hannibal,* Book 30, trans. by Aubrey de Sélincourt (Baltimore, Md.: Penguin Classics, 1965), pp. 36–37, copyright © the Estate of Aubrey de Sélincourt, 1965.]

In 150 B.C., Carthage rearmed—to punish the Numidians for attacking the Carthaginian city of Oroscopa—without the permission of Rome, in violation of the Treaty of Zama. The Romans used this treaty violation as an excuse to eliminate Carthage as a threat permanently. After an extended siege, the Romans captured the city, burned it, plowed under all remaining signs of the city, and scattered the remaining Carthaginians.

Peace of Apamea (188 B.C.)

Polybius has described in some detail a Roman peace treaty which, not uncommonly, imposed stiff military restrictions upon a defeated enemy. The edited text of this imposed treaty appears below.

There shall be friendship between Antiochus and the Romans for all time if he fulfils the conditions of the treaty:

King Antiochus and his subjects shall not permit the passage through their territory of any enemy marching against the Romans and their allies or furnish such enemy with any supplies: the Romans and their allies engage to act likewise towards Antiochus and his subjects: Antiochus shall not make war on the inhabitants of the islands or of Europe: he shall evacuate all cities, lands, villages, and forts on this side of Taurus as far as the river Halys and all between the valley of Taurus and the mountain ridges that descend to Lycaonia: from all such places he is to carry away nothing except the arms borne by his soldiers, and if anything has been carried away, it is to be restored to the same city: he shall not receive either soldiers or others from the kingdom of Eumenes: if there be any men in the army of Antiochus coming from the cities which the Romans take over, he shall deliver them up at Apamea: if there be any from the kingdom of Antiochus dwelling with the Romans and their allies, they may remain or depart at their good pleasure: Antiochus and his subjects shall give up the slaves of the Romans and of their allies, both those taken in war and those who deserted, and any prisoners of war they have taken, if there be such: . . . he shall surrender all the elephants now in Apamea and not keep any in [the] future: he shall surrender his long ships with their gear and tackle and in future he shall not possess more than ten decked ships of war, nor shall he have any galley rowed by more than thirty oars, nor a moneres [a ship with one bank of oars] to serve in any war in which he is the aggressor: his ships shall not sail beyond the Calycadnus and the Sarpedonian promontory unless conveying tribute, envoys or hostages: Antiochus shall not have permission to hire mercenaries from lands under the rule of the Romans, or to receive fugitives. . . .

[*Polybius: The Histories,* 6 vols., trans. by W. R. Paton (New York: G. P. Putnam's Sons, 1922): Book XXI, 41.4–42.22]

Anglo-French Naval Limitation Pact (1787)

The 1780s were a turbulent decade in Europe. In particular, France was undergoing severe internal dislocations and, at the same time, was roiling the international waters by seeking to woo Holland away from its English connection with the Franco-Dutch Alliance of December 1785. The Dutch were a major maritime power, who by allying their fleets with French warships in the East Indies, could threaten England's Indian territories and commerce. Closer at home, Holland's strategic location—controlling the mouths of such important rivers as the Rhine, Meuse, and Schledt—posed a potentially more serious security problem. Meanwhile, Great Britain was in the midst of a rearmament program aimed at revitalizing its military and naval strength, which had been dissipated during its recent ill-fated struggle—also involving France—to retain its American colonial empire. In order to accomplish this, the British needed time.

When civil war broke out in Holland during June 1787, which ultimately involved Prussia, France, and Britain, the British prime minister, William Pitt, proposed that France and England discontinue "warlike preparations . . . until such time as notice might be given for their renewal." This was not Pitt's first such attempt to get France to agree to limit its military activities; during the 1785–1786 negotiations for a commercial treaty, he had attempted a first step toward the limitation of armaments, by suggesting that the two powers reduce their warships in the East Indies, but the French foreign minister declined. However, Pitt's second suggestion was accepted by the new foreign minister, Count Montmorin, on 4 August 1787.

As a result of subsequent negotiations, the British and French each agreed (1) to limit active naval forces to six ships-of-the-line; (2) to maintain naval armaments at a peacetime level; and, should the situation change, (3) to resist augmenting their naval strength until the other party had been notified of their impending action.

Reciprocal Declaration Between the Courts of Versailles and London to Maintain Active Only Six Ships-of-the-Line

His Very Christian Majesty and Serene Britannic Majesty wishing to consolidate more and more the good harmony which exists between them, have decided, opportunely, in the current position of affairs, to agree that no one on either side will prepare any naval armaments beyond the peacetime establishment; and that neither will make any attempt to place in the water a greater number of ships-of-the-line than the six whose armaments have already been reciprocally communicated; and that in a situation where one of the two sovereigns should find it necessary to make some different arrangement, it would not take place until after preliminary notification.

[Signatures]

[G. F. de Martens, *Recueil de Traites,* 2d ed. (n.p.: À Gottingue, Dans La Librairie de Dieterich, 1818), vol. 4, p. 279]

Although the arms limitation treaty was the product of the sanguine hope of creating and extending a sense of harmony between the two nations, in less than three weeks after its signing, both countries were on the verge of war with the other because of events in Holland. Neither nation at this time, however, wanted to become embroiled in a foreign war, as each was wrestling with deep internal political divisions. Consequently, following further negotiations three separate declarations aimed at firming up the initial agreement were signed at Versailles on 27 October 1787.

Declaration

The events which have taken place in the republic of the United Provinces [Holland], appearing no longer to leave any subject of discussion, and still less of contest, between the two courts, the undersigned are authorized to ask, whether it is the intention of his Most Christian Majesty to carry into effect the notification, made on the 16th of September last, by his Most Christian Majesty's minister plenipotentiary, which, by announcing that succours would be given in Holland, has occasioned the naval armaments on the part of his Majesty; which armaments have become reciprocal?

If the court of Versailles is disposed to explain itself on this subject, and upon the conduct to be adopted towards the republic, in a manner conformable to the desire which has been expressed on both sides, to preserve the good understanding between the two courts; and it being also understood, at the same time, that there is no view of hostility towards any quarter, in consequence of what has passed, his Majesty, always anxious to concur in the friendly sentiments of his Most Christian Majesty, would agree with him, that the armaments, and in general all warlike preparations should be discontinued on each side, and that the navies of the two nations should be again placed upon the footing of the peace establishment, as it stood on the 1st of January of the present year.

[Signatures]

Counter-Declaration

The intention of his Majesty not being, and never having been, to interfere by force in the affairs of the republic of the United Provinces, the communication made to the court of London, on the 16th of the last month, by Monsieur Barthelemy, having had no other object than to announce to that court an intention, the motives of which no longer exist, especially since the King of Prussia has imparted his resolution, his Majesty makes no difficulty to declare, that he will not give any effect to the Declaration above mentioned; and that he retains no hostile view towards any quarter, relative to what has passed in Holland.—His Majesty, therefore, being desirous to concur with the sentiments of his Britannic Majesty, for the preservation of the good harmony between the two courts, agrees with pleasure with his Britannic Majesty, that the armaments, and in general all warlike preparations, shall be discontinued on each side; and that the navies of the two nations shall be again placed upon the footing of the peace establishment, as it stood on the 1st of January of the present year.

[Signatures]

Joint-Declaration

In consequence of the Declaration, and Counter-Declaration, exchanged this day, the undersigned, in the name of their respective sovereigns, agree, that the armaments, and in general all warlike preparations, shall be discontinued on each side; and that the navies of the two nations shall be again placed upon the footing of the peace establishment, as it stood on the 1st of January of the present year.

[Signatures]

[*The Parliamentary History of England: From the Earliest Period to the Year 1803* (London: T. C. Hansard, 1816), XXVI, cols. 1264–1265]

In early December 1787, Britain and France exchanged figures on what had constituted the naval home fleet of each as of 1 January 1787. Pitt suggested a simple on-site inspection system to verify that the mutually agreed-to reduction of navies had taken place. He proposed to the reluctant French "that an officer on each side will be admitted in the principal ports, who may have a private letter stating who he is, from the Secretary of State, the Marine Minister, or whomever is thought best." As the French showed no interest in the idea, it was abandoned. It should also be noted that the declarations implied a reduction of land as well as naval forces, yet apparently only the navy was returned to peacetime status.

Political and martial forces soon overwhelmed arms control efforts as revolutionary France declared war against Britain and Holland in 1793. Yet the 30 August 1787 agreement and subsequent declarations marked the high point in diplomatic attempts to maintain peace between Great Britain and France during an unusually turbulent decade.

Franco-Prussian Treaty (1808)

Treaty Concluded at Paris Between France and Prussia for the Regulation of War Contributions, the Occupation of Three Fortified Places, and the Recognition of the Kings of Spain and of Naples, 8 September 1808

Article 1. His Majesty the King of Prussia, wishing to avoid everything that could give umbrage to France, assumes the obligation of not maintaining for ten years, starting on January 1, 1809, more than the number of troops specified below, namely:

- 10 infantry regiments, forming at most an effective force of 22,000 men;

- 8 cavalry regiments or 32 squadrons, forming at most an effective force of 8,000 men;
- A corps of artillery miners and sappers, at most 6,000 men;
- not including the King's Guard, which is estimated, infantry and cavalry, to have at most 6,000 men.
- Total.. 42,000 men

Article 2. When the ten years have elapsed, His Majesty the King of Prussia will again come under the common law, and will maintain the number of troops that seems proper to him under the circumstances.

Article 3. There shall not be, during these ten years, any extraordinary calling up of militia or of civil guards, nor any mustering activities tending to augment the force specified above.

Article 4. His Majesty the King of Prussia undertakes not to keep in service any subject belonging to the provinces that he has ceded.

Article 5. In return for the guarantee stipulated in the treaty of this date, and as security for the alliance contracted with France, His Majesty the King of Prussia promises to make common cause with His Majesty the Emperor of the French if war should be declared between him and Austria and, in that case, to put at his disposition a division of 16,000 men, including infantry, cavalry, and artillery.

This obligation will last for ten years. However, since the King of Prussia has not yet been able to form his military establishment, he will not be obligated for any contingent during the present year, and will only have to furnish a contingent of 12,000 men, including infantry and cavalry, during the year 1809, if war should break out, a possibility which the friendly relations existing between France and Austria give no reason to fear.

Article 6. These separate articles shall be ratified, and the ratifications exchanged, within the same period as those of the treaty of this date.

[France, Ministry of Foreign Affairs, *Recueil des traités de la France* (Paris, 1864–1907), vol. 2, pp. 270–273; trans. by Gay Hammerman in Trevor Dupuy and Gay Hammerman, eds., *A Documentary History of Arms Control and Disarmament* (New York and London, 1973), p. 37]

Limitation of Egyptian Arms (1841–1879)

The Ottoman Turks sought to employ arms control techniques during the nineteenth century to maintain their rule over the empire's most prized province, Egypt, at a time that local governors, or Pashas, sought not only independence but also their own empire. During the two previous decades, Muhammad [Mehemet] Ali had employed French assistance to enlarge and train his army and acquire a substantial naval squadron. The Firman of 1841 established Muhammad Ali's hereditary rule of Egypt, but in return he and his family were to accept the restrictions imposed by the sultan on Egypt's army and navy—the latter to prevent him from building ironclad warships. These measures were encouraged by Britain, Austria, and Russia, and they were moderated by France.

The Firman of 27 May 1866 allowed Ismail (ruler, 1863–1879), grandson of Muhammad Ali, to increase the number of his troops to 30,000. Again in the Firman of 1873, Ismail was allowed to increase his army to the extent he thought was necessary; however, the restriction against his building of ironclads was not lifted.

The Firman of 2 August 1879 reimposed the original restrictions on Egyptian military forces. The number of troops allowed in peacetime was limited to 18,000 and the construction of ironclads was prohibited unless otherwise instructed by the sultan.

Firman from the Ottoman Sultan to Mehemet Ali, Pasha of Egypt, 1 June 1841

In time of peace, 18,000 men will suffice for the internal service of the province of Egypt; it shall not be allowed to increase their numbers. But as the land and sea forces of Egypt are raised for the service of my Sublime Porte [the Sultan], it shall be allowable, in time of war, to increase them to the number which shall be deemed suitable by my Sublime Porte.

. . . . .

The Governor of Egypt shall appoint the officers of the land and sea forces up to the rank of Colonel. With regard to the appointments to ranks higher than that of Colonel, that is to say, of Pashas Miri livi (Brigadier-Generals), and of Pashas Ferik (Generals of Division), it will be absolutely necessary to apply for permission for them, and to take my orders thereupon.

Henceforth the Pashas of Egypt shall not be at liberty to build vessels of war without having first applied for the permission of my Sublime Porte, and having obtained from it a clear and positive authority.

[Thomas E. Holland, *European Concert in the Eastern Question* (Oxford: Clarendon Press, 1885), pp. 112–113]

Black Sea Naval Limitation (1856)

Convention Between Russia and Turkey, Limiting Their Naval Forces in the Black Sea, 30 March 1856

1. The High Contracting Parties mutually engage not to have in the Black Sea any other vessels of war than those of which the number, strength, and size are hereafter stipulated.

2. The High Contracting Powers reserve to themselves each to maintain in that sea six steamships having a length of 50 meters in length at the line of flotation, of a tonnage of eight hundred tons at the maximum, and four light steam or sailing vessels of a tonnage not to exceed two hundred tons each.

[Ratification]

[Signatures]

[Thomas E. Holland, *European Concert in the Eastern Question* (Oxford, 1885), pp. 257–258]

Argentine-Chilean Naval Limitation (1902)

Convention Between Chile and the Argentine Republic Respecting the Limitation of Naval Armaments, 28 May 1902

The Minister for Foreign Affairs, Don José Francisco Vergara Donoso, and Dr. José Antonio Terry, Envoy Extraordinary of the Argentine Republic, having met together in the Ministry for Foreign Affairs of Chile, have agreed to include in the following Convention the various decisions arrived at for the limitation of the naval armaments of the two Republics, decisions which have been taken owing to the initiative and the good offices of His Brittanic Majesty's Government, represented in Chile by their Envoy Extraordinary and Minister Plenipotentiary, Mr. Gerard Lowther, and in the Argentine Republic by their Envoy Extraordinary and Minister Plenipotentiary, Sir William A. C. Barrington:

Article I. With the view of removing all motive for uneasiness or suspicion in either country, the Governments of Chile and of the Argentine Republic desist from acquiring the vessels of war now building for them, and from henceforth making new acquisitions.

Both Governments agree, moreover, to reduce their respective fleets, with which object they will continue to exert themselves until they arrive at an understanding which shall establish a just balance between the said fleets.

This reduction shall take place within one year, counting from the date of the exchange of ratifications of the present Convention.

Article II. The two Governments bind themselves not to increase their naval armaments during a period of five years, without previous notice; the one intending to increase them shall give the other eighteen months' notice.

It is understood that all armament for the fortification of the coasts and ports is excluded from this Agreement, and any floating machine, such as submarine vessels, etc., destined exclusively for the defence of these, can be acquired.

Article III. The two Contracting Parties shall not be at liberty to part with any vessel, in consequence of this Convention, in favour of countries having questions pending with one or the other.

Article IV. In order to facilitate the transfer of pending contracts, both Governments bind themselves to prolong for two months the term stipu-lated for the delivery of the vessels building, for which purpose they will give the necessary instructions immediately this Convention has been signed.

[Ratification]

[Signatures]

[*American Journal of International Law,* vol. 1 (1907), *Supplement: Official Documents,* pp. 294–295]

Germany Disarmed

Treaty of Versailles (1919)

Treaties disarming the defeated nations other than Germany are not reprinted here; however, the disarmament clauses were similiar in design. The texts of the Treaty of St. Germain-en-Laye (1919), Treaty of Neuilly (1919), and Treaty of Trianon (1920) may be found in several treaty collections; for example, see U.S. Senate, Committee on Foreign Relations, Subcommittee on Disarmament, Disarmament and Security: A Collection of Documents, 1919–55 *(Washington, D.C.: G.P.O., 1956).*

The Treaty of Versailles: Sections Dealing with German Disarmament, 28 June 1919

Part V: MILITARY, NAVAL AND AIR CLAUSES

In order to render possible the initiation of a general limitation of the armaments of all nations, Germany undertakes strictly to observe the military, naval and air clauses which follow.

SECTION 1: MILITARY CLAUSES

CHAPTER 1: EFFECTIVES AND CADRES OF THE GERMAN ARMY

Article 159. The German military forces shall be demobilised and reduced as prescribed hereinafter.

Article 160

1. By a date which must not be later than March 31, 1920, the German Army must not comprise more than seven divisions of infantry and three divisions of cavalry.

After that date the total number of effectives in the Army of the States constituting Germany must not exceed one hundred thousand men, including officers and establishments of depots. The Army shall be devoted exclusively to the maintenance of order within the territory and to the control of the frontiers.

The total effective strength of officers, including the personnel of staffs, whatever their composition, must not exceed four thousand.

2. Divisions and Army Corps headquarters staffs shall be organised in accordance with Table No. I annexed to this Section.

The number and strengths of the units of infantry, artillery, engineers, technical services and troops laid down in the aforesaid Table constitute maxima which must not be exceeded.

The following units may each have their own depot:

> An Infantry regiment;
> A Cavalry regiment;
> A regiment of Field Artillery;
> A battalion of Pioneers.

3. The divisions must not be grouped under more than two army corps headquarters staffs.

The maintenance or formation of forces differently grouped or of other organisations for the command of troops or for preparation for war is forbidden.

The Great German General Staff and all similar organisations shall be dissolved and may not be reconstituted in any form.

The officers, or persons in the position of officers, in the Ministries of War in the different States in Germany and in the Administrations attached to them, must not exceed three hundred in number and are included in the maximum strength of four thousand laid down in the third sub-paragraph of paragraph (1) of this Article.

Article 161. Army administrative services consisting of civilian personnel not included in the number of effectives prescribed by the present Treaty will have such personnel reduced in each class to one-tenth of that laid down in the Budget of 1913.

Article 162. The number of employees or officials of the German States, such as customs officers, forest guards and coastguards, shall not exceed that of the employees or officials functioning in these capacities in 1913.

The number of gendarmes and employees or officials of the local or municipal police may only be increased to an extent corresponding to the increase of population since 1913 in the districts or municipalities in which they are employed.

These employees and officials may not be assembled for military training.

The reduction of the strength of the German military forces as provided for in Article 160 may be effected gradually in the following manner:

Within three months from the coming into force of the present Treaty the total number of effectives must be reduced to 200,000 and the number of units must not exceed twice the number of those laid down in Article 160.

At the expiration of this period, and at the end of each subsequent period of three months, a Conference of military experts of the Principal Allied and Associated Powers will fix the reductions to be made in the ensuing three months, so that by March 31, 1920, at the latest the total number of German effectives does not exceed the maximum number of 100,000 men laid down in Article 160. In these successive reductions the same ratio between the number of officers and of men, and between the various kinds of units, shall be maintained as is laid down in that Article.

CHAPTER II: ARMAMENT, MUNITIONS AND MATERIAL

Article 164. Up till the time at which Germany is admitted as a member of the League of Nations the German Army must not possess an armament greater than the amounts fixed in Table No. II annexed to this Section, with the exception of an optional increase not exceeding one-twentyfifth part for small arms and one-fiftieth part for guns, which shall be exclusively used to provide for such eventual replacements as may be necessary.

Germany agrees that after she has become a member of the League of Nations the armaments fixed in the said Table shall remain in force until they are modified by the Council of the League. Fur-

thermore she hereby agrees strictly to observe the decisions of the Council of the League on this subject.

Article 165. The maximum number of guns, machine guns, trench-mortars, rifles and the amount of ammunition and equipment which Germany is allowed to maintain during the period between the coming into force of the present Treaty and the date of March 31, 1920, referred to in Article 160, shall bear the same proportion to the amount authorized in Table No. III annexed to this Section as the strength of the German Army as reduced from time to time in accordance with Article 163 bears to the strength permitted under Article 160.

Article 166. At the date of March 31, 1920, the stock of munitions which the German Army may have at its disposal shall not exceed the amounts fixed in Table No. III annexed to this Section.

Within the same period the German Government will store these stocks at points to be notified to the Governments of the Principal Allied and Associated Powers. The German Government is forbidden to establish any other stocks, depots or reserves of munitions.

Article 167. The number and calibre of the guns constituting at the date of the coming into force of the present Treaty the armament of the fortified works, fortresses, and any land or coast forts which Germany is allowed to retain must be notified immediately by the German Government to the Governments of the Principal Allied and Associated Powers, and will constitute maximum amounts which may not be exceeded.

Within two months from the coming into force of the present Treaty, the maximum stock of ammunition for these guns will be reduced to, and maintained at, the following uniform rates:—fifteen hundred rounds per piece for those the calibre of which is 10.5 cm. and under: —five hundred rounds per piece for those of higher calibre.

Article 168. The manufacture of arms, munitions, or any war material, shall only be carried out in factories or works the location of which shall be communicated to and approved by the Governments of the Principal Allied and Associated Powers, and the number of which they retain the right to restrict.

Within three months from the coming into force of the present Treaty, all other establishments for the manufacture, preparation, storage or design of arms, munitions, or any war material whatever shall be closed down. The same applies to all arsenals except those used as depots for the authorised stocks of munitions. Within the same period the personnel of these arsenals will be dismissed.

Within two months from the coming into force of the present Treaty German arms, munitions and war material, including anti-aircraft material, existing in Germany in excess of the quantities allowed, must be surrendered to the Governments of the Principal Allied and Associated Powers to be destroyed or rendered useless. This will also apply to any special plant intended for the manufacture of military material, except such as may be recognised as necessary for equipping the authorised strength of the German army.

The surrender in question will be effected at such points in German territory as may be selected by the said Governments.

Within the same period arms, munitions and war material, including anti-aircraft material, of origin other than German, in whatever state they may be, will be delivered to the said Governments, who will decide as to their disposal.

Arms and munitions which on account of the successive reductions in the strength of the German army become in excess of the amounts authorised by Tables II and III annexed to this Section must be handed over in the manner laid down above within such periods as may be decided by the Conferences referred to in Article 163.

Article 170. Importation into Germany of arms, munitions and war material of every kind shall be strictly prohibited.

The same applies to the manufacture for, and export to, foreign countries of arms, munitions and war material of every kind.

Article 171. The use of asphyxiating, poisonous or other gases and all analogous liquids, materials or devices being prohibited, their manufacture and importation are strictly forbidden in Germany.

The same applies to materials specially intended for the manufacture, storage and use of the said products or devices.

The manufacture and the importation into Germany of armoured cars, tanks and all similar constructions suitable for use in war are also prohibited.

Article 172. Within a period of three months from the coming into force of the present Treaty, the German Government will disclose to the Governments of the Principal Allied and Associated Powers the nature and mode of manufacture of all explosives, toxic substances or other like chemical preparations used by them in the war or prepared by them for the purpose of being so used.

CHAPTER III: RECRUITING AND MILITARY TRAINING

Article 173. Universal compulsory military service shall be abolished in Germany.

The German Army may only be constituted and recruited by means of voluntary enlistment.

Article 174. The period of enlistment for non-commissioned officers and privates must be twelve consecutive years.

The number of men discharged for any reason before the expiration of their term of enlistment must not exceed in any year five per cent. of the total effectives fixed by the second subparagraph of paragraph (1) of Article 160 of the present Treaty.

Article 175. The officers who are retained in the Army must undertake the obligation to serve in it up to the age of forty-five years at least.

Officers newly appointed must undertake to serve on the active list for twenty-five consecutive years at least.

Officers who have previously belonged to any formations whatever of the Army, and who are not retained in the units allowed to be maintained, must not take part in any military exercise whether theoretical or practical, and will not be under any military obligations whatever.

The number of officers discharged for any reason before the expiration of their term of service must not exceed in any year five per cent. of the total effectives of officers provided for in the third subparagraph (1) of Article 160 of the present Treaty.

Article 176. On the expiration of two months from the coming into force of the present Treaty there must only exist in Germany the number of military schools which is absolutely indispensable for the recruitment of the officers of the units allowed. These schools will be exclusively intended for the recruitment of officers of each arm, in the proportion of one school per arm.

The number of students admitted to attend the courses of the said schools will be strictly in proportion to the vacancies to be filled in the cadres of officers. The students and the cadres will be reckoned in the effectives fixed by the second and third subparagraphs of paragraph (1) of Article 160 of the present Treaty.

Consequently, and during the period fixed above, all military academies or similar institutions in Germany, as well as the different military schools for officers, student officers (*Aspiranten*), cadets, non-commissioned officers or student non-commissioned officers (*Aspiranten*), other than the schools above provided for, will be abolished.

Article 177. Educational establishments, the universities, societies of discharged soldiers, shooting or touring clubs and, generally speaking, associations of every description, whatever be the age of their members, must not occupy themselves with any military matters.

In particular they will be forbidden to instruct or exercise their members or to allow them to be instructed or exercised, in the profession or use of arms.

These societies, associations, educational establishments and universities must have no connection with the Ministries of War or any other military authority.

Article 178. All measures of mobilisation or appertaining to mobilisation are forbidden.

In no case must formations, administrative services or General Staffs include supplementary cadres.

Article 179. Germany agrees, from the coming into force of the present Treaty, not to accredit nor to send to any foreign country any military, naval or air mission, nor to allow any such mission to leave her territory, and Germany further agrees to take appropriate measures to prevent German nationals from leaving her territory to become enrolled in the Army, Navy or Air service of any foreign Power, or to be attached to such Army, Navy or Air Service for the purpose of assisting in the military, naval or air training thereof, or otherwise for the purpose of giving military, naval or air instruction in any foreign country.

The Allied and Associated Powers agree, so far as they are concerned, from the coming into force of the present Treaty, not to enrol in nor to attach to their armies or naval or air forces any German national for the purpose of assisting in the military training of such armies or naval or air forces, or otherwise to employ any such German national as military, naval or aeronautic instructor.

The present provision does not, however, affect the right of France to recruit for the Foreign Legion in accordance with French military laws and regulations.

CHAPTER IV: FORTIFICATIONS

Article 180. All fortified works, fortresses and field works situated in German territory to the west of a line drawn fifty kilometres to the east of the Rhine shall be disarmed and dismantled.

Within a period of two months from the coming into force of the present Treaty such of the above fortified works, fortresses and field works as are situated in territory not occupied by Allied and Associated troops shall be disarmed, and within a further period of four months they shall be dismantled. Those which are situated in territory occupied by Allied and Associated troops shall be disarmed and dismantled within such periods as may be fixed by the Allied High Command.

The construction of any new fortification, whatever its nature and importance, is forbidden in the zone referred to in the first paragraph above.

The system of fortified works of the southern and eastern frontiers of Germany shall be maintained in its existing state.

SECTION II: NAVAL CLAUSES

Article 181. After the expiration of a period of two months from the coming into force of the present Treaty the German naval forces in commission must not exceed:

6 battleships of the *Deutschland or Lothringen* type,
6 light cruisers,
12 destroyers,
12 torpedo boats,

or an equal number of ships constructed to replace them as provided in Article 190.

No submarines are to be included.

All other warships, except where there is provision to the contrary in the present Treaty, must be placed in reserve or devoted to commercial purposes.

Article 182. Until the completion of the minesweeping prescribed by Article 193 Germany will keep in commission such number of minesweeping vessels as may be fixed by the Governments of the Principal Allied and Associated Powers.

Article 183. After the expiration of a period of two months from the coming into force of the pres-

TABLE I   STATE AND ESTABLISHMENT OF ARMY CORPS HEADQUARTERS STAFFS AND OF INFANTRY AND CAVALRY DIVISIONS

These tabular statements do not form a fixed establishment to be imposed on Germany, but the figures contained in them (number of units and strengths) represent maximum figures, which should not in any case be exceeded.

I. Army Corps Headquarters Staffs.

Unit	Maximum Number Authorised	Maximum Strength of each Unit	
		Officers	N.C.O.s and Men
Army Corps Headquarters Staff	2	30	150
Total for Headquarters Staff		60	300

II. Establishment of an Infantry Division.

Unit	Maximum Number Authorised	Officers	N.C.O.s and Men
Headquarters of an infantry division	1	25	70
Headquarters of divisional infantry	1	4	30
Headquarters of divisional artillery	1	4	30
Regiment of infantry (Each regiment comprises 3 battalions of infantry. Each battalion comprises 3 companies of infantry and 1 machine-gun company.)	3	70	2,300
Trench mortar company	3	6	150
Divisional squadron	1	6	150
Field artillery regiment (Each regiment comprises 3 groups of artillery. Each group comprises 3 batteries.)	1	85	1,300
Pioneer battalion (This battalion comprises 2 companies of pioneers, 1 pontoon detachment, 1 searchlight section.)	1	12	400
Signal detachment (This detachment comprises 1 telephone detachment, 1 listening section, 1 carrier-pigeon section.)	1	12	300
Divisional medical service	1	20	400
Parks and convoys		14	800
Total for infantry division		410	10,830

III. Establishment of a Cavalry Division.

Unit	Maximum Number Authorised	Officers	N.C.O.s and Men
Headquarters of a cavalry division	1	15	50
Cavalry regiment (Each regiment comprises 4 squadrons.)	6	40	800
Horse artillery group (3 batteries)	1	20	400
Total for cavalry division		275	5,250

ent Treaty, the total personnel of the German Navy, including the manning of the fleet, coast defences, signal stations, administration and other land services, must not exceed fifteen thousand, including officers and men of all grades and corps.

The total strength of officers and warrant officers must not exceed fifteen hundred.

Within two months from the coming into force of the present Treaty the personnel in excess of the above strength shall be demobilised.

TABLE II   TABULAR STATEMENT OF ARMAMENT ESTABLISHMENT FOR A MAXIMUM OF 7 INFANTRY DIVISIONS, 3 CAVALRY DIVISIONS, AND 2 ARMY CORPS HEADQUARTERS STAFFS

Material	Infantry Division (1)	For 7 Infantry Divisions (2)	Cavalry Division (3)	For 3 Cavalry Divisions (4)	For 2 Army Corps Headquarters Staffs (5)	Total of Columns 2, 4 and 5 (6)
Rifles	12,000	84,000			This establish-	84,000
Carbines			6,000	18,000	ment must be	18,000
Heavy machine-guns	108	756	12	36	drawn from	792
Light machine-guns	162	1,134			the increased	1,134
Medium trench mortars	9	63			armaments of	63
Light trench mortars	27	189			the divisional	189
7.7 cm. guns	24	168	12	36	infantry.	204
10.5 cm. howitzers	12	84				84

TABLE III   MAXIMUM STOCKS AUTHORISED

Material	Maximum number of arms authorised	Establishment per unit	Maximum totals
		Rounds	*Rounds*
Rifles	84,000		
Carbines	18,000	400	40,800,000
Heavy machine-guns	792		
Light machine-guns	1,134	8,000	15,408,000
Medium trench mortars	63	400	25,200
Light trench mortars	189	800	151,200
Field Artillery:			
7.7 cm. guns	204	1,000	204,000
10.5 cm. howitzers	84	800	67,200

No naval or military corps or reserve force in connection with the Navy may be organised in Germany without being included in the above strength.

Article 184. From the date of the coming into force of the present Treaty all the German surface warships which are not in German ports cease to belong to Germany, who renounces all rights over them. Vessels which, in compliance with the Armistice of November 11, 1918, are now interned in the ports of the Allied and Associated powers are declared to be finally surrendered.

Vessels which are now interned in neutral ports will be there surrendered to the Governments of the Principal Allied and Associated Powers. The German Government must address a notification to that effect to the neutral Powers on the coming into force of the present Treaty.

Article 185. Within a period of two months from the coming into force of the present Treaty the Ger-

man surface warships enumerated below will be surrendered to the Governments of the Principal Allied and Associated Powers in such Allied ports as the said powers may direct.

These warships will have been disarmed as provided in Article XXIII of the Armistice of November 11, 1918. Nevertheless they must have all their guns on board.

Battleships

Oldenburg	*Posen*
Thuringen	*Westfalen*
Ostfriesland	*Rheinland*
Helgoland	*Nassau*

Light Cruisers

Stettin	*Stralsund*
Danzig	*Augsburg*
München	*Kolberg*
Lübeck	*Stuttgart*

And, in addition, forty-two modern destroyers and fifty modern torpedo boats, as chosen by the Governments of the Principal Allied and Associated Powers.

Article 186. On the coming into force of the present Treaty the German Government must undertake, under the supervision of the Governments of the Principal Allied and Associated Powers, the breaking up of all the German surface warships now under construction.

Article 187. The German auxiliary cruisers and fleet auxiliaries enumerated below will be disarmed and treated as merchant ships.

Interned in Neutral Countries:

Berlin	*Seydlitz*
Santa Fé	*Yorck*

In Germany:

Ammon	*Fürst Bülow*
Answald	*Gertrud*
Bosnia	*Kigoma*
Cordoba	*Rugia*
Cassel	*Santa Elena*
Dania	*Schleswig*
Rio Negro	*Möwe*
Rio Pardo	*Sierra Ventana*
Santa Cruz	*Chemnitz*
Schwaben	*Emil Georg von Strauss*
Solingen	*Habsburg*
Steigerwald	*Meteor*
Franken	*Waltraute*
Gundomar	*Scharnhorst*

Article 188. On the expiration of one month from the coming into force of the present Treaty all German submarines, submarine salvage vessels and docks for submarines, including the tubular dock, must have been handed over to the Governments of the Principal Allied and Associated Powers.

Such of these submarines, vessels and docks as are considered by the said Governments to be fit to proceed under their own power or to be towed shall be taken by the German Government into such Allied ports as have been indicated.

The remainder, and also those in course of construction, shall be broken up entirely by the German Government under the supervision of the said Governments. The breaking-up must be completed within three months at the most after the coming into force of the present Treaty.

Article 189. Articles, machinery and material arising from the breaking-up of German warships of all kinds, whether surface vessels or submarines, may not be used except for purely industrial or commercial purposes.

They may not be sold or disposed of to foreign countries.

Article 190. Germany is forbidden to construct or acquire any warships other than those intended to replace the units in commission provided for in Article 181 of the present Treaty.

The warships intended for replacement purposes as above shall not exceed the following displacement:

Armoured ships	10,000	tons,
Light cruisers	6,000	tons,
Destroyers	800	tons,
Torpedo boats	200	tons.

Except where a ship has been lost, units of the different classes shall only be replaced at the end of a period of twenty years in the case of battleships and cruisers, and fifteen years in the case of destroyers and torpedo boats, counting from the launching of the ship.

Article 191. The construction or acquisition of any submarine, even for commercial purposes, shall be forbidden in Germany.

Article 192. The warships in commission of the German fleet must have on board or in reserve only the allowance of arms, munitions and war material fixed by the Principal Allied and Associated Powers.

Within a month from the fixing of the quantities as above, arms, munitions and war material of all kinds, including mines and torpedoes, now in the hands of the German Government and in excess of the said quantities, shall be surrendered to the Governments of the said Powers at places to be indicated by them. Such arms, munitions and war material will be destroyed or rendered useless.

All other stocks, depots or reserves of arms, munitions or naval war material of all kinds are forbidden.

The manufacture of these articles in German territory for, and their export to, foreign countries shall be forbidden.

Article 193. On the coming into force of the present Treaty Germany will forthwith sweep up the mines in the following areas in the North Sea to the eastward of longitude 4° 00′ E. of Greenwich: (1)

Between parallels of latitude 53° 00′ N. and 59° 00′ N.; (2) To the northward of latitude 60° 30′ N.

Germany must keep these areas free from mines.

Germany must also sweep and keep free from mines such areas in the Baltic as may ultimately be notified by the Governments of the Principal Allied and Associated Powers.

Article 194. The personnel of the German Navy shall be recruited entirely by voluntary engagements entered into for a minimum period of twenty-five consecutive years for officers and warrant officers; twelve consecutive years for petty officers and men.

The number engaged to replace those discharged for any reason before the expiration of their term of service must not exceed five per cent. per annum of the totals laid down in this Section (Article 183).

The personnel discharged from the Navy must not receive any kind of naval or military training or undertake any further service in the Navy or Army.

Officers belonging to the Germany Navy and not demobilised must engage to serve till the age of forty-five, unless discharged for sufficient reasons.

No officer or man of the German mercantile marine shall receive any training in the Navy.

[Articles 195–197 appear in the demilitarization section of this volume.]

SECTION III: AIR CLAUSES

Article 198. The armed forces of Germany must not include any military or naval air forces.

Germany may, during a period not extending beyond October 1, 1919, maintain a maximum number of one hundred seaplanes or flying boats, which shall be exclusively employed in searching for submarine mines, shall be furnished with the necessary equipment for this purpose, and shall in no case carry arms, munitions or bombs of any nature whatever.

In addition to the engines installed in the seaplanes or flying boats above mentioned, one spare engine may be provided for each engine of each of these craft.

No dirigible shall be kept.

Article 199. Within two months from the coming into force of the present Treaty the personnel of air forces on the rolls of the German land and sea forces shall be demobilised. Up to October 1, 1919, however, Germany may keep and maintain a total number of one thousand men, including officers, for the whole of the cadres and personnel, flying and non-flying, of all formations and establishments.

Article 200. Until the complete evacuation of German territory by the Allied and Associated troops, the aircraft of the Allied and Associated Powers shall enjoy in Germany freedom of passage through the air, freedom of transit and of landing.

Article 201. During the six months following the coming into force of the present Treaty, the manufacture and importation of aircraft, parts of aircraft, engines for aircraft, and parts of engines for aircraft, shall be forbidden in all German territory.

Article 202. On the coming into force of the present Treaty, all military and naval aeronautical material, except the machines mentioned in the second and third paragraphs of Article 198, must be delivered to the Governments of the Principal Allied and Associated Powers.

Delivery must be effected at such places as the said Governments may select, and must be completed within three months.

In particular, this material will include all items under the following heads which are or have been in use or were designed for warlike purposes:

- Complete aeroplanes and seaplanes, as well as those being manufactured, repaired or assembled.
- Dirigibles able to take the air, being manufactured, repaired or assembled.
- Plant for the manufacture of hydrogen.
- Dirigible sheds and shelters of every kind for aircraft.
- Pending their delivery, dirigibles will, at the expense of Germany, be maintained inflated with hydrogen; the plant for the manufacture of hydrogen, as well as the sheds for dirigibles, may, at the discretion of the said Powers, be left to Germany until the time when the dirigibles are handed over.
- Engines for aircraft.
- Nacelles and fuselages.
- Armament (guns, machine guns, light machine guns, bomb-dropping apparatus, torpedo-dropping apparatus, synchronisation apparatus, aiming apparatus).
- Munitions (cartridges, shells, bombs loaded or unloaded, stocks of explosives or of material for their manufacture).

- Instruments for use on aircraft.
- Wireless apparatus and photographic or cinematograph apparatus for use on aircraft.
- Component parts of any of the items under the preceding heads.

The material referred to above shall not be removed without special permission from the said Governments.

SECTION IV: INTER-ALLIED COMMISSIONS OF CONTROL

Article 203. All the military, naval and air clauses contained in the present Treaty, for the execution of which a time-limit is prescribed, shall be executed by Germany under the control of Inter-Allied Commissions specially appointed for this purpose by the Principal Allied and Associated Powers.

Article 204. The Inter-Allied Commissions of Control will be specially charged with the duty of seeing to the complete execution of the delivery, destruction, demolition and rendering things useless to be carried out at the expense of the German Government in accordance with the present Treaty.

They will communicate to the German authorities the decisions which the Principal Allied and Associated Powers have reserved the right to take, or which the execution of the military, naval and air clauses may necessitate.

Article 205. The Inter-Allied Commissions of Control may establish their organisations at the seat of the central German Government.

They shall be entitled as often as they think desirable to proceed to any point whatever in German territory, or to send subcommissions, or to authorise one or more of their members to go, to any such point.

Article 206. The German Government must give all necessary facilities for the accomplishment of their missions to the Inter-Allied Commissions of Control and to their members.

It shall attach a qualified representative to each Inter-Allied Commission of Control for the purpose of receiving the communications which the Commission may have to address to the German Government and of supplying or procuring for the Commission all information or documents which may be required.

The German Government must in all cases furnish at its own cost all labour and material required to effect the deliveries and the works of destruc-tion, dismantling, demolition, and of rendering things useless, provided for in the present Treaty.

Article 207. The upkeep and cost of the Commissions of Control and the expenses involved by their work shall be borne by Germany.

Article 208. The Military Inter-Allied Commission of Control will represent the Governments of the Principal Allied and Associated Powers in dealing with the German Government in all matters concerning the execution of the military clauses. In particular it will be its duty to receive from the German Government the notifications relating to the location of the stocks and depots of munitions, the armament of the fortified works, fortresses and forts which Germany is allowed to retain, and the location of the works or factories for the production of arms, munitions and war material and their operations.

It will take delivery of the arms, munitions and war material, will select the points where such delivery is to be effected, and will supervise the works of destruction, demolition, and of rendering things useless, which are to be carried out in accordance with the present Treaty.

The German Government must furnish to the Military Inter-Allied Commission of Control all such information and documents as the latter may deem necessary to ensure the complete execution of the military clauses, and in particular all legislative and administrative documents and regulations.

Article 209. The Naval Inter-Allied Commission of Control will represent the Governments of the Principal Allied and Associated Powers in dealing with the German Government in all matters concerning the execution of the naval clauses.

In particular it will be its duty to proceed to the building yards and to supervise the breaking-up of the ships which are under construction there, to take delivery of all surface ships or submarines, salvage ships, docks and the tubular docks, and to supervise the destruction and breaking-up provided for.

The German Government must furnish to the Naval Inter-Allied Commission of Control all such information and documents as the Commission may deem necessary to ensure the complete execution of the naval clauses, in particular the designs of the warships, the composition of their armaments, the details and models of the guns, munitions, torpedoes, mines, explosives, wireless telegraphic apparatus and, in general, everything relating to naval war material, as well as all legislative or administrative documents or regulations.

Article 210. The Aeronautical Inter-Allied Commission of Control will represent the Governments of the Principal Allied and Associated Powers in dealing with the German Government in all matters concerning the execution of the air clauses.

In particular it will be its duty to make an inventory of the aeronautical material existing in German territory, to inspect aeroplane, balloon and motor manufactories, and factories producing arms, munitions and explosives capable of being used by aircraft, to visit all aerodromes, sheds, landing grounds, parks and depots, to authorise, where necessary, a removal of material and to take delivery of such material.

The German Government must furnish to the Aeronautical Inter-Allied Commission of Control all such information and legislative, administrative or other documents which the Commission may consider necessary to ensure the complete execution of the air clauses, and in particular a list of the personnel belonging to all the German Air Services, and of the existing material, as well as of that in process of manufacture or on order, and a list of all establishments working for aviation, of their positions, and of all sheds and landing grounds.

[Fred L. Israel, ed., *Major Peace Treaties of Modern History, 1648–1967* (New York: Chelsea House, 1967), vol. 2, pp. 1363–1383]

The League of Nations and Disarmament

League Covenant, Article 8 (1919)

The Covenant of the League of Nations, 28 June 1919, speaks to the issue of disarmament.

Article 8

1. The Members of the League recognize that the maintenance of peace requires the reduction of national armaments to the lowest point consistent with national safety and the enforcement by common action of international obligations.

2. The Council, taking account of the geographical situation and circumstances of each State, shall formulate plans for such reduction for the consideration and action of the several Governments.

3. Such plans shall be subject to reconsideration and revision at least every ten years.

4. After these plans shall have been adopted by the several Governments, the limits of armaments therein fixed shall not be exceeded without the concurrence of the Council.

5. The Members of the League agree that the manufacture by private enterprise of munitions and implements of war is open to grave objections. The Council shall advise how the evil effects attendant upon such manufacture can be prevented, due regard being had to the necessities of those Members of the League which are not able to manufacture the munitions and implements of war necessary for their safety.

6. The Members of the League undertake to interchange full and frank information as to the scale of their armaments, their military, naval and air programmes and the condition of such of their industries as are adaptable to warlike purposes.

[U.S. Library of Congress, Legislative Reference Service, *Disarmament and Security: A Collection of Documents, 1919–55* (Washington, D.C., 1956), p. 90]

Preparatory Commission's Draft (1930)

Following is the text of the Commission's Draft Convention, 9 December 1930, which subsequently was presented to the "World" or General Disarmament Conference that met in 1932.[1,2,3]

Article 1.[4] The High Contracting Parties agree to limit and, so far as possible, to reduce their respective armaments as provided in the present Convention.

PART I. PERSONNEL[5]

Chapter A. Effectives

Article 2. The average daily effectives in the land, sea, and air armed forces and formations organized on a military basis of each of the High Contracting Parties shall not exceed, in each of the categories of effectives defined in the tables annexed to this chapter, the figure laid down for such party in the corresponding column of the said tables.

Article 3. The average daily effectives are reckoned by dividing the total number of days' duty performed in each year by the number of days in such year.

Article 4. By formations organized on a military basis shall be understood police forces of all kinds, gendarmerie, customs officials, forest guards, which, whatever their legal purpose, are, in time of peace, by reason of their staff of officers, establishment, training, armament, equipment, capable of being employed for military purposes without measures of mobilization, as well as any other organization complying with the above condition.

By mobilization, within the meaning of the present article, shall be understood all the measures for the purpose of providing the whole or part of the various corps, services and units with the personnel and material required to pass from a peace-time footing to a war-time footing.

The Tables annexed to Chapter A of Part I are:[6]

1. Average daily effectives not to be exceeded in Land Armed Forces.
   Table I. Maximum Land Armed Forces in Home Country.
   Table II. (optional) Maximum Land Armed Forces Overseas.
   Table III. Maximum of Total Land Armed Forces.
   Table IV. Maximum Formations organized on a Military Basis stationed in Home Country.

Table V. Maximum Formations organized on a Military Basis stationed Overseas.

These five Tables each contain the following categories:
   (a) Total Effectives (including *(b)* and *(c)*).
   (b) Officers.
   (c) Other Effectives who have completed at least *x* months of service.
x (This figure to be determined by the duration of the longest period of service which is in force in the conscript land army of any High Contracting Party at the time of the signature of the Convention.)

2. Average daily effectives not to be exceeded in Sea Armed Forces.
   Table VI. Maximum Sea Armed Forces.
   Table VII. Maximum Sea Formations organized on a Military Basis.
   In these two Tables:
   Total Effectives (officers, petty officers, and men) are given in one column.

3. Average daily effectives not to be exceeded in the Air Armed Forces.
   Table VIII. (optional) Maximum Air Armed Forces stationed in Home Country.
   Table IX. (optional) Maximum Air Armed Forces stationed Overseas.
   Table X. Maximum of the Total Air Armed Forces.

These three Tables each contain the following categories:
   (a) Total effectives (including column *(b)*).
   (b) Effectives who have completed at least *z* months of service (Officers, N.C.O.'s and Men).
z (This figure to be determined by the duration of the longest period of service which is in force in the conscript air army of any High Contracting Party at the time of the signature of the Convention.)

Chapter B. Period of Service

Article 5. The provisions of this chapter apply only to effectives recruited by conscription.

Article 6. For each of the High Contracting Parties concerned, the maximum total periods of service to which the effectives recruited by conscription are liable in the land, sea or air armed forces or formations organized on a military basis respectively, shall not exceed the figures laid down for such party in the table annexed to this chapter.

Article 7. For each man, the total period of service is the total number of days comprised in the different periods of service which he is liable under the national law to perform.

Article 8. As an exception, each of the High Contracting Parties concerned may exceed the limits which he has accepted by the table annexed to this chapter in so far as, owing to a falling-off in the number of births, such an increase may be necessary to enable the maximum total number of effectives fixed in his case by the tables annexed to Chapter A of this part to be attained.

It is understood that any High Contracting Party which avails itself of this option will immediately notify the measures taken and the reasons justifying them to the other High Contracting Parties and to the Permanent Disarmament Commission referred to in Part VI of the present Convention.

Article 9. In any case, the total period of service shall not exceed . . . months.

Table annexed to Chapter B of Part I[7]

Maximum total period of service to which the effectives recruited by conscription are liable in the armed forces or formations organized on a military basis of each High Contracting Party, with separate columns for Land, Sea and Air.

PART II. MATERIAL

Chapter A. Land Armaments[8]

Article 10[9] (Provisional text subject to the drafting of the Annex.) The annual expenditure of each High Contracting Party on the upkeep, purchase and manufacture of war material for land armaments shall be limited to the figures laid down for such Party, and in accordance with the conditions prescribed in the Annex . . . to this Article.

Chapter B. Naval Armaments[10,11]

Article 11.[12,13] Throughout the duration of the present Convention, the global tonnage of the vessels of war of each of the High Contracting Parties, other than the vessels exempt from limitation under Annex I to this Chapter and the special vessels enumerated in Annex II, shall not exceed the figure laid down for such Party in Table I annexed to this Chapter.

Article 12.[13] Table II annexed to this Chapter shows, by tonnage per category, the way in which each High Contracting Party intends to distribute during the period of application of the present Convention the global tonnage which is limited in the case of such Party to the figure laid down in Table I.

Article 13. Within the limits of the global tonnage fixed for such Party in Table I, and failing any stricter conditions resulting from special conventions to which it is or may become a party, each of the High Contracting Parties may modify the distribution shown for it in Table II, subject to the following conditions:

(1) The tonnage by category shown for each High Contracting Party in Table II shall in no case be the object of increase beyond the figures shown for it in Table III annexed to this Chapter.

(2) Before the laying-down of the ship or ships for the construction of which the transferred tonnage has been assigned, due notice must be given to all the other High Contracting Parties and the Secretary-General and the Permanent Disarmament Commission, of the amount of tonnage transferred, the length of such notice being that laid down for each of the High Contracting Parties in Table III.

Article 14.[14] No capital ship shall exceed 35,000 tons (35,560 metric tons) standard displacement or carry a gun exceeding 16 inches (406 mm.) in calibre.

Article 15.[15] No aircraft carrier shall exceed 27,000 tons (27,432 metric tons) standard displacement or carry a gun with a calibre in excess of 8 inches (203 mm.)

No aircraft carrier of 10,000 tons (10,160 metric tons) or less standard displacement shall carry a gun exceeding 6.1 inches (155 mm.) in calibre.

If the armament carried includes guns exceeding 6.1 inches (155 mm.) in calibre, the total number of guns carried, except anti-aircraft guns and guns not exceeding 5.1 inches (130 mm.), shall not exceed ten. If, alternatively, the armament contains no guns exceeding 6.1 inches (155 mm.) in calibre, the number of guns is not limited. In either case, the number of anti-aircraft guns and of guns not exceeding 5.1 inches (130 mm.) in calibre, is not limited.

Article 16. No submarine shall exceed 2,000 tons (2,032 metric tons) standard displacement or carry a gun exceeding 5.1 inches (130 mm.) in calibre.

Article 17. No vessel of war exceeding the limitations as to displacement or armament prescribed by the present Convention shall be acquired by, or constructed by, for or within the jurisdiction of any of the High Contracting Parties.

Article 18. In regard to the replacement of the vessels of war limited by the present Convention, the High Contracting Parties will comply with the rules set out in Annex IV to this Chapter.

Article 19.[16] No preparation shall be made in merchant ships in time of peace for the installation of warlike armaments for the purpose of converting such ships into vessels of war, other than the necessary stiffening of decks for the mounting of guns not exceeding 6.1 inches (155 mm.) in calibre.

Article 20. In the event of a High Contracting Party's being engaged in war, such Party shall not use as a vessel of war any vessel of war which may be under construction within its jurisdiction for any other Power, or which may have been constructed within its jurisdiction for another Power and not delivered.

Article 21. Each of the High Contracting Parties undertakes not to dispose, by gift, sale, or any mode of transfer, of any vessel of war in such a manner that such vessel may become a vessel of war in the navy of any foreign Power.

Article 22. Any vessels of war which have to be disposed of as being surplus to the tonnage figures allowed by the present Convention shall be disposed of in accordance with the rules set out in Annex V to this chapter.

Article 23. Existing ships of various types, which, prior to April 1, 1930, have been used as stationary training establishments or hulks, may be retained in a non-seagoing condition.

Article 24.[17,18] (Provisional text, subject to the drafting of the Annex.)

The annual expenditure of each High Contracting Party on the upkeep, purchase and manufacture of war material for naval armaments shall be limited to the figures laid down for such Party, and in accordance with the conditions prescribed, in Annex . . .

Note: The two following articles appear in Part III of the London Naval Treaty, and are quoted as examples of supplementary restrictions which certain High Contracting Parties may be prepared to accept:[19]

'Article . . .

'Not more than 25 per cent. of the allowed total tonnage in the cruiser category may be fitted with a landing-on platform or deck for aircraft.'

'Article . . .

'In the destroyer category, not more than 16 per cent. of the allowed total tonnage shall be employed in vessels of over 1,500 tons (1,524 metric tons) standard displacement.'

Tables annexed to Chapter B of Part II

Table I. The Total Global Tonnage not to be exceeded by each High Contracting Party.

Table II. The Distribution of Tonnage between five categories of war vessels. i.e.

(a) Capital ships (with a subsection for States which do not possess any capital ship of a standard displacement exceeding 8,000 tons)[20];

(b) Aircraft carriers;

(c) Cruisers (i) with guns exceeding 6.1 in., (ii) with guns of 6.1 in. or less;

(d) Destroyers (these two categories classified as (c.d.) light surface vessels);

(e) Submarines.

Table III. Rules for Transfer.

The figures to be entered in this table will be calculated on the following principles:

1. Account must be taken of the special circumstances of each Power, and of the classes of ships involved in the transfer.

2. Powers whose total tonnage does not exceed 100,000 tons[21] will have full freedom of transfer as regards surface ships.

3. As regards the other Powers, the amount of the transfer should vary in inverse ratio to the amount of the total (global) tonnage of each of them.

(Annexes contain definitions and lists of exempt vessels; definitions of capital ships, aircraft carriers, cruisers, destroyers (and light surface vessels), and standard displacement; rules for replacement; rules for disposal either by scrapping or conversion. These definitions and rules are the same as those adopted at the London Naval Conference.)

Chapter C. Air Armaments

Article 25.[22,23] The number and total horsepower of the aeroplanes, capable of use in war, in commission and in immediate reserve in the land, sea and air armed forces of each of the High Contracting Parties shall not exceed the figures laid down for such Party in the corresponding columns of Table I annexed to this Chapter.

The number and total horse-power of the aeroplanes, capable of use in war, in commission and in immediate reserve in the land, sea and air formations organized on a military basis of each of the High Contracting Parties shall not exceed the figures laid down for such Party in the corresponding columns of Table II annexed to this Chapter.

Article 26.[22, 23] The number, total horse-power, and total volume of dirigibles, capable of use in war, in commission in the land, sea and air armed forces of each of the High Contracting Parties shall not exceed the figures laid down for such Party in the corresponding columns of Table III annexed to this Chapter.

The number, total horse-power and total volume of dirigibles capable of use in war, in commission in the land, sea and air formations organized on a military basis of each of the High Contracting Parties shall not exceed the figures laid down for such Party in the corresponding columns of Table IV annexed to this Chapter.

Article 27. Horse-power shall be measured according to the following rules . . .

The volume of dirigibles shall be expressed in cubic metres.

Article 28

1. The High Contracting Parties shall refrain from prescribing the embodiment of military features in the construction of civil aviation material, so that this material may be constructed for purely civil purposes, more particularly with a view to providing the greatest possible measure of security and the most economic return. No preparations shall be made in civil aircraft in time of peace for the installation of warlike armaments for the purpose of converting such aircraft into military aircraft.

2. The High Contracting Parties undertake not to require civil aviation enterprises to employ personnel specially trained for military purposes. They undertake to authorize only as a provisional and temporary measure the seconding of personnel to, and the employment of military aviation material in, civil aviation undertakings. Any such personnel or military material which may thus be employed in civil aviation of whatever nature shall be included in the limitation applicable to the High Contracting Party concerned in virtue of Part I, or Articles 25 and 26, of the present Convention, as the case may be.[24]

3. The High Contracting Parties undertake not to subsidize, directly or indirectly, air lines principally established for military purposes instead of being established for economic, administrative or social purposes.

4. The High Contracting Parties undertake to encourage as far as possible the conclusion of economic agreements between civil aviation undertakings in the different countries and to confer together to this end.

The following Tables are annexed to Part II, Chapter C:

Table I. Aeroplanes of the Land, Sea and Air Armed Forces.

Table II. Aeroplanes of the Land, Sea and Air Formations organized on a Military Basis.

Table III. Dirigibles of the Land, Sea and Air Forces.

Table IV. Dirigibles of the Land, Sea and Air Formations organized on a Military Basis.

These four Tables contain the following categories:[25]

(a) Total Aeroplanes/Dirigibles of the Armed Forces.

(b) (optional) Aeroplanes/Dirigibles stationed in the Home Country.

(c) (optional) Aeroplanes/Dirigibles stationed Overseas.

(d) (optional) (only in Tables I and III) Aeroplanes/Dirigibles in aircraft carriers. (Columns indicating number and total horse-power—and volume for dirigibles).

PART III. BUDGETARY EXPENDITURE[26]

Article 29.[27] (Provisional text subject to the drafting of the Annex.)

The total annual expenditure of each of the High Contracting Parties on his land, sea and air forces and formations organized on a military basis shall be limited to the figure laid down for such Party and in accordance with the conditions prescribed in the Annex. . . .

PART IV. EXCHANGE OF INFORMATION

Article 30. For each category of effectives defined in the model tables annexed to this Article, the exchange of information each year shall apply to the average daily number of effectives reached during the preceding year in the land, sea and air armed forces and formations organized on a military basis of each of the High Contracting Parties.

For this purpose, each of the High Contracting Parties will forward to the Secretary-General of the

League of Nations, within . . . months after the end of each year, the necessary information to enable the said tables to be drawn up in the case of such Party. Each Party shall attach to this statement an explanatory note showing the elements on which the figures supplied are based, and stating, in particular, for each sort of effectives (recruits, militiamen, reservists, territorials, &c.), the number of these effectives and the number of days' service they have performed.

The said tables shall be drawn up and published with the explanatory note referred to above by the Secretary-General not later than . . . in each year.

The annexed Tables are as follows:[28]

Table I. Land Armed Forces in Home Country.

Table II. Land Armed Forces Overseas.

Table III. Total Land Armed Forces.

Table IV. Land Formations organized on a Military Basis.

Table V. Land Formations organized on a Military Basis—Overseas.

These five Tables contain the following categories:

(a) Total Effectives (including those specified separately in each column).

(b) Officers.

(c) Other Effectives who have completed at least x^{29} months of service.

(d) Soldiers whose period of service has exceeded the legal period of service but is less than x^{29} months. (Information to be supplied only for effectives recruited by conscription.)

(e) (optional) Recruits not trained as defined in national legislation.

Table VI. Naval Forces.

Table VII. Sea Formations Organized on a Military Basis.

These two Tables contain the following categories:

(a) Total Effectives (including those specified separately in each column).

(b) Officers.

(c) Other Effectives who have completed at least y^{29} months of service.

(d) (optional) Recruits not trained as defined in national legislation.

Table VIII. Air Armed Forces in Home Country.

Table IX. Air Armed Forces Overseas.

Table X. Total Air Armed Forces.

Table XI. Air Formations on a Military Basis—Home Country.

Table XII. Air Formations on a Military Basis—Overseas.

These five Tables contain the following categories:

(a) Total Effectives (including those specified separately in each column).

(b) Effectives who have completed at least z^{29} months of service (Officers, N.C.O.'s and Men.)

(c) (optional) Recruits not trained as defined in national legislation.

Article 31.[30] If any youths have compulsorily received, during any year, preparatory military training within the jurisdiction of any High Contracting Party, such Party shall communicate to the Secretary-General of the League of Nations, within x months after the end of each year, the number of youths who have received such instruction.

The above information shall be published by the Secretary-General not later than . . . in each year.

Article 32. The High Contracting Parties concerned shall forward to the Secretary-General of the League of Nations at the end of each year the following information as to the provisions of their law relating to the effectives recruited by conscription in their land, sea and air forces and formations organized on a military basis respectively: (1) The total number of days comprised in the first period of service; (2) The total duration in days of the ensuing periods.

The above information shall be published by the Secretary-General not later than . . . in each year.

Article 33.[31, 32] Each of the High Contracting Parties shall, within . . . months from the end of each budgetary year, communicate to the Secretary-General of the League of Nations a statement, drawn up in accordance with a standard model, showing by categories of materials the total actual expenditure in the course of the said year on the upkeep, purchase and manufacture of war materials of the land and sea armed forces and formations organized on a military basis of such Party.

The information contained in this statement shall be published by the Secretary-General not later than . . . in each year.

Article 34. Within one month after the date of laying down and the date of completion respectively of each vessel of war, other than the vessels exempt from limitation under Annex I to Chapter B of Part II, laid down or completed by or for them or within their jurisdiction after the coming into force of the present Convention, the High Contracting Parties shall communicate to the Secretary-General of the League of Nations the information detailed below:

(a) The date of laying down the keel and the following particulars: Classification of the vessel and

for whom built (if not for the High Contracting Party); Standard displacement in tons and metric tons; Principal dimensions—namely, length of water-line, extreme beam at or below water-line;

Mean draught at standard displacement;

Calibre of the largest gun.

(b) The date of completion, together with the foregoing particulars relating to the vessel at that date.

The above information shall be immediately communicated by the Secretary-General to all the High Contracting Parties and shall be published by the Secretary-General not later than ... in each year.

Article 35. Each of the High Contracting Parties shall communicate to the Secretariat of the League of Nations the name and the tonnage of any vessel constructed in accordance with Article 19 (Chapter II). With regard to existing vessels of this type, this communication shall be made within two months after ratification of the present Convention. With regard to vessels to be constructed, the communication shall be made on the date of completion.

Article 36.[33] For each of the categories of aircraft defined in the model tables annexed to this Article, the exchange of information shall apply to the maximum figures attained in each year in respect of the number and total horse-power, and for dirigibles the total volume, by the aircraft referred to in Articles 25 and 26 of the present Convention.

For this purpose each of the High Contracting Parties will forward to the Secretary-General of the League of Nations within ... months after the end of each year the necessary information to enable the said tables to be drawn up in the case of such Party.

The tables referred to in the preceding paragraph shall be drawn up and published by the Secretary-General not later than ... in each year.

Annexed to this Article are the following Tables:[34]

Table I. Aeroplanes of the Land, Sea and Air Armed Forces.

Table II. Aeroplanes of the Land, Sea and Air Formations organized on a Military Basis.

Table III. Dirigibles of the Land, Sea and Air Forces.

Table IV. Dirigibles of the Land, Sea and Air Formations organized on a Military Basis.

These four Tables contain the following categories, each category containing columns for number and total horse-power, also total volume for dirigibles:

(a) Total Aeroplanes of the Armed Forces.

(b) (optional) Aeroplanes stationed in the Home Country.

(c) (optional) Aeroplanes stationed Overseas.

(d) (optional) Aeroplanes in Aircraft Carriers (only in Tables I and IV).

Article 37.[35] In order to ensure publicity as regards civil aviation, each of the High Contracting Parties shall indicate within x months after the end of each year to the Secretary-General of the League of Nations the number and total horse-power of civil aeroplanes and dirigibles registered within the jurisdiction of such Party. Each Party shall also indicate the amounts expended on civil aviation by the Government and by local authorities.

The above information shall be published by the Secretary-General not later than ... in each year.

Article 38.[36] Each of the High Contracting Parties shall communicate to the Secretary-General of the League of Nations within ... months of the end of each budgetary year a statement drawn up in accordance with the standard model annexed to this Article[37] showing the total amounts actually expended in the course of the said year on the land, sea and air armaments of such Party.

The information supplied in this statement shall be published by the Secretary-General not later than ... in each year.

PART V. CHEMICAL ARMS[38]

Article 39. The High Contracting Parties undertake, subject to reciprocity, to abstain from the use in war of asphyxiating, poisonous or similar gases, and of all analogous liquids, substances or processes.

They undertake unreservedly to abstain from the use of all bacteriological methods of warfare.

PART VI. MISCELLANEOUS PROVISIONS

Chapter A. Permanent Disarmament Commission

Article 40.[39] There shall be set up at the seat of the League of Nations a Permanent Disarmament Commission with the duty of following the execution of the present Convention. It shall consist of x (figure to be fixed by the Conference) members appointed respectively by the Governments of ... (list to be drawn up by the Conference).

Members of the Commission shall not represent their Governments. They shall be appointed for x years, but shall be re-eligible. During their term of office, they may be replaced only on death or in the case of voluntary resignation or serious and permanent illness.

They may be assisted by technical experts.

Article 41. The Commission shall meet for the first time, on being summoned by the Secretary-General of the League of Nations, within three months from the entry into force of the present Convention, to elect a provisional President and Vice-President and to draw up its Rules of Procedure.

Thereafter it shall meet annually in ordinary session on the date fixed in its Rules of Procedure.

It may also, if summoned by its President, meet in extraordinary session in the cases provided for in the present Convention and whenever an application to that effect is made by a High Contracting Party.

Article 42. The Commission shall have full power to lay down its own Rules of Procedure on the basis of the provisions of the present Convention.

Article 43. The Commission may only transact business if at least two-thirds of its members are present.

Article 44. Any High Contracting Party not having a member of its nationality on the Commission shall be entitled to send a member appointed for the purpose to sit at any meetings of the Commission during which a question specially affecting the interests of that Party is considered.

Article 45. Each member of the Commission shall have only one vote.

All decisions of the Commission shall be taken by a majority of the votes of the members present at the meeting.

In the cases provided for in Articles 50 and 52 the votes of members appointed by the Parties concerned in the discussion shall not be counted in determining the majority.

A minority report may be drawn up.

Article 46. Each member of the Commission shall be entitled on his own responsibility to have any person heard or consulted who is in a position to throw any light on the question which is being examined by the Commission.

Article 47. Each member of the Commission shall be entitled to require that, in any report by the Commission, account shall be taken of the opinions or suggestions put forward by him, if necessary in the form of a separate report.

Article 48. All reports by the Commission shall, under conditions specified in each case in the present Convention, or in the Rules of Procedure of the Commission, be communicated to all the High Contracting Parties and to the Council of the League of Nations, and shall be published.

Article 49. The Permanent Disarmament Commission shall receive all the information supplied by the High Contracting Parties to the Secretary-General of the League in pursuance of their international obligations in this regard.

Each year, the Commission shall make at least one report on the information submitted to it and on any other information that may reach it from a responsible source and that it may consider worth attention, showing the situation as regards the fulfillment of the present Convention.

This report shall be communicated forthwith to all the High Contracting Parties and to the Council of the League and shall be published on the date fixed in the Rules of Procedure of the Commission.

Chapter B. Derogations

Article 50. If, during the term of the present Convention, a change of circumstances constitutes, in the opinion of any High Contracting Party, a menace to its national security, such High Contracting Party may suspend temporarily, in so far as concerns itself, any provision or provisions of the present Convention, other than those expressly designed to apply in the event of war, provided:

(a) That such Contracting Party shall immediately notify the other Contracting Parties and at the same time the Permanent Disarmament Commission, through the Secretary-General of the League of Nations, of such temporary suspension, and of the extent thereof.

(b) That simultaneously with the said notification, the Contracting Party shall communicate to the other Contracting Parties, and at the same time, to the Permanent Disarmament Commission through the Secretary-General, a full explanation of the change of circumstances referred to above.

Thereupon the other High Contracting Parties shall promptly advise as to the situation thus presented.

When the reasons for such temporary suspension have ceased to exist, the said High Contracting Party shall reduce its armaments to the level agreed upon in the Convention, and shall make immediate notification to the other Contracting Parties.

Chapter C. Procedure Regarding Complaints

Article 51. The High Contracting Parties recognize that any violation of the provisions of the present Convention is a matter of concern to all the Parties.

Article 52. If, during the term of the present Convention, a High Contracting Party is of opinion that another Party to the Convention is maintaining armaments in excess of the figures agreed upon or is in any way violating or endeavouring to violate the provisions of the present Convention, such Party may lay the matter, through the Secretary-General of the League of Nations, before the Permanent Disarmament Commission.

The Commission, after hearing a representative of the High Contracting Party whose action is questioned, should such Party so desire, and the representative of any other Party which may be specially concerned in the matter and which asks to be heard, shall, as soon as possible, present a report thereon to the High Contracting Parties and to the Council of the League. The report and any proceedings thereon shall be published as soon as possible.

The High Contracting Parties shall promptly advise as to the conclusions of the report.

If the High Contracting Parties directly concerned are Members of the League of Nations, the Council shall exercise the rights devolving upon it in such circumstances in virtue of the Covenant with a view to ensuring the observance of the present Convention and to safeguarding the peace of nations.

Chapter D. Final Provisions

Article 53.[40] The present Convention shall not affect the provisions of previous treaties under which certain of the High Contracting Parties have agreed to limit their land, sea or air armaments, and have thus fixed in relation to one another their respective rights and obligations in this connexion.

The following High Contracting Parties . . . signatory to the said Treaties declare that the limits fixed for their armaments under the present Convention are accepted by them in relation to the obligations referred to in the preceding paragraph, the maintenance of such provisions being for them an essential condition for the observance of the present Convention.

Article 54. If a dispute arises between two or more of the High Contracting Parties concerning the interpretation or application of the provisions of the present Convention, and cannot be settled either directly between the parties or by some other method of friendly settlement, the parties will, at the request of any one of them, submit such dispute to the decision of the Permanent Court of International Justice or to an arbitral tribunal chosen by them.

[Subsequent articles deal with ratification and termination procedures.]

Notes

1. John W. Wheeler-Bennett, *Documents on International Affairs,* 1931 (London: Humphrey Milford, 1932), pp. 18–39. All footnotes are Wheeler-Bennett's.

2. *British Blue Book,* Cmd. 3757 (in which is also included the Report of the Preparatory Disarmament Commission), also League Documents C.P.D. 292 (2) and C.P.D. 295 (1).

3. A number of general reservations were made to the Convention as a whole. The Soviet Delegation declared its inability to accept the draft Convention or the Commission's Report. The German Delegation, while accepting the Report because it contained all its reservations, rejected the draft Convention. The German, Soviet, Turkish, and Chinese Delegations reserved the right to submit their proposals to the Disarmament Conference. (The Norwegian and Irish Free State Delegations reserved the attitude of their Governments as they had not taken part in the earlier work of the Commission.)

4. A number of Governments, while accepting Article 1 in principle, stated that reduction of all or some categories of armaments was not possible, their present armaments being far from sufficient to guarantee national safety.

5. The German Delegation made a reservation to *the whole of Part I,* regarding trained reserves:

The stipulations do not provide—either directly or by a reduction in the numbers of the annual contingent, or by a strict determination of the period of active service— for a reduction or limitation of trained reserves who, after having completed their service with the colours, continue to be registered and liable by law for military service, notwithstanding the fact that these reserves, though they do not exist in professional armies in the strict sense of the term, constitute the main body of the personnel in countries possessing conscript armies.

Moreover, the stipulations do not provide for any method whereby the effectives of conscript armies serving with the colours and in reserve, and professional effectives, whose military value is naturally not capable of comparison, could be reduced to comparable units of calculation.

6. The German and Italian Delegations made the following reservations regarding the distinction between the effectives and armaments of the home country and those stationed overseas:

for the purposes of the reduction and limitation of armaments, the importance of the forces and materials which one contracting party assigns to its overseas territories may vary, in relation to another contracting party, by reason of the geographical situation of its territory in relation to the home territories of the two contracting parties. Consequently, one contracting party will have every reason to regard the overseas forces of another contracting party as forming part of the latter's home forces, if the proximity of the overseas territories in relation to the home territories of the two parties justifies such an assumption (e.g., the North African possessions of France).

The Italian Delegation thought that no distinction should be made between armed air forces stationed in the home country and overseas, and the Turkish Delegation made reservations regarding the optional indication of land and air forces stationed overseas and the non-indication of the maximum forces stationed in each of the overseas territories. (The Soviet Delegation also proposed the indication of the apportionment of forces in the various parts of a State's territory.)

The French Delegation could not accept specific limitation of professional soldiers in land or air forces unless there was similar limitation in sea forces.

7. The German Delegation considered that the numbers of annual contingents should also be limited. (It drew attention to the reservation entered to the whole of Part I.)

8. The United States' Delegation was unable to accept the principle of budgetary limitation in any form. It was, however, prepared to withdraw its objections and to accept and apply direct limitation in the case of the U.S.A., if other States agreed upon a practical and sufficiently detailed method of budgetary limitation.

The Turkish Delegation accepted budgetary limitation on condition that account should be taken—as also with any other method of limitation—of the special position of countries in which industry was not adequately developed.

The German Delegation reserved its opinion about the method of budgetary limitation until it had studied the Report of the Committee of Experts. It also made a general reservation to the effect that 'notwithstanding its extraordinary importance, the material in service and in reserve of land armed forces and of land formations organized on a military basis only covered—contrary to the method applied to air armaments and to naval floating material—by limitation of expenditure, and not by a reduction and limitation of specific articles and numbers.'

9. *Note:* In pronouncing on this article, the Governments will take into account at the Conference the report requested from the Committee of Budgetary Experts, which will have been forwarded to them in order to permit of the drawing up of the annex to this Article. League Document, 1931, ix, 3.

The Preparatory Commission, by sixteen votes to three and six abstentions, adopted the principle of limitation by expenditure. It also discussed the following resolution:

The Preparatory Commission is of opinion that the principle of direct limitation should be applied to land war material.

When this resolution was put to the vote, there were nine votes in favour, nine against and seven abstentions.

Lastly, it examined the principle of a combination of the two methods. Nine members of the Commission voted in favour of this principle; eleven voted against and five abstained.

10. *Note:* Such figures and dates as appear in this Chapter are only given as an illustration; most of them correspond to the figures and dates laid down in the Treaties of Washington and London.

11. The Italian Delegation made a general reservation to the effect that its Government could not finally agree to any specific method of limitation before all the Naval Powers had agreed on the proportions and levels of maximum tonnage.

The German Delegation made a reservation in view of the great value of non-floating material, on the ground that the latter—unlike floating material—would not be subject to any direct limitation by specific articles and by numbers, and would only be affected indirectly by limitation by expenditure.

12. The Yugoslav Delegation (and the Finnish Delegation) reserved the right to ask at the Conference that recently created countries, whose expenditure was distributed over several years, should have the right to mention separately what proportion of their programme would be carried out during the period of the Convention.

The Chinese, Spanish, Persian, Roumanian, and Yugoslav Delegations stated that after the expiration of the Convention the particulars of total tonnage would not in any way be binding on their countries.

13. The Italian Delegation proposed the omission of Table I and the substitution for Articles II and 12 of a single Article to read:

The limitation of naval armaments, accepted by each of the High Contracting Parties, is indicated in the following table.... (in the form of Table II).

14. The Soviet Delegation suggested that capital ships should be limited to 10,000 tons and their guns to 12 in. calibre. It also emphasized the importance of providing against preparations in merchant ships with a view to conversion into fighting vessels in war time.

15. The Spanish Delegation made a reservation regarding the limitation of gun calibre in aircraft carriers of a displacement not exceeding 10,000 tons to 6.1 in., the calibre for larger aircraft carriers being 8.1 in.

16. The Japanese Delegation reserved the right to raise later the question of the limitation of aircraft equip-

ment on merchant vessels, to prevent their conversion into aircraft carriers.

17.   In pronouncing on this article, the Governments will take into account at the Conference the report requested from the Committee of Budgetary Experts, which will have been forwarded to them in order to permit of the drawing up of the Annex to this Article. League Document, 1931, ix, 3.

18.   Certain delegations objected to the introduction (Article 24) of indirect limitation of naval material in addition to its direct limitation as provided for in other articles of this Chapter. The United States and German Delegations repeated their reservations about budgetary limitation.

The French and Japanese Delegations opposed the special limitation of expenditure on non-floating material. This was limited, they pointed out, by the direct limitation of floating material and the limitation of the aggregate expenditure on armaments.

The British and Italian Delegations made their acceptance of the principle conditional upon the acceptance of other naval Powers.

19.   The Greek and Spanish Delegations made a formal reservation in regard to the possibility of these supplementary restrictions being applied.

20.   For Parties who do not possess any capital ship of a standard displacement exceeding 8,000 tons (8,128 metric tons).

21.   This figure is given as an indication.

22, 23.   The German and Turkish Delegations made reservations urging the extension of direct limitation to air armaments in reserve. The German reservation was to the effect that 'reduction and limitation do not apply to the aggregate of war material, including material in reserve, and that in its view the countries are left free to increase their stocks of aircraft not yet put together, and to arrange their air armaments as they please, without exceeding the limits fixed by the Convention.'

The German, Italian, and Turkish Delegations repeated the reservations, already made to the Tables annexed to Chapter A of Part 1, regarding the distinction between home and overseas forces.

(The British Delegation wished to limit annual expenditure on material for air armaments.)

24.   The Canadian Delegation submitted a reservation in regard to the 'temporary and provisional' character of the seconding of personnel to, and the employment of military aviation in, civil aviation undertakings in view of its special needs and in order to develop its country of vast distances.

25.   The German, Italian and Turkish Delegations repeated the reservations made to the Tables annexed to Chapter A of Part I.

26.   The German Delegation made a reservation pending the presentation of the report of the Committee of Budgetary Experts.

The United States Delegation repeated the general reservation already made with regard to this method.

27.   *Note:* In pronouncing on this article, and in particular as regards the possibility of a distinct limitation of the expenditure on land, sea and air forces, the Governments will take into account at the Conference the report requested from the Committee of Budgetary Experts, which will have been forwarded to them in order to permit of the drawing up of the Annex to this Article. League Document, 1931, ix, 3.

28.   The German Delegation made a reservation on the ground that the tables do not provide publicity regarding trained reserves and the figure of the annual contingent, and also regarding the option allowed to States to show in a special column the number of recruits not trained as defined in national legislation. This option should not be allowed unless publicity regarding the numbers of their trained reserves were included in the same tables.

The Turkish Delegation repeated its reservation regarding the distinction between forces stationed at home and overseas forces.

The French, British, and Japanese Delegations made reservations as to the desirability of separate publication of the average daily effectives in each oversea territory, on the grounds that detailed publicity was materially impossible owing to constant transfers.

29.   See previous notes for explanation of this figure.

30.   German and Italian Delegations considered that particulars should be given of all who have received preparatory military training, whether compulsorily or voluntarily.

31.   The German Delegation considered that publicity, in order to be effective, should be given to the total of land and air material and of naval non-floating material, such information to be published by categories and numbers. It reserved its opinion regarding publicity in respect of expenditure.

32.   *Note:* In giving an opinion on this article, the Governments will take into account the report requested from the Committee of Budgetary Experts regarding the number and nature of the categories to be laid down and the methods of publicity thus adopted in connexion with the provisions of the annex regarding limitation referred to in Article 29 of the present Convention.

33.   The German Delegation considered that publicity should apply to the total air material including material in reserve.

34.   The German and Turkish Delegations repeated the reservations made to the Tables annexed to Chapter A of Part I and Chapter C of Part II.

35. The German Delegation considered that rules concerning publicity in regard to peace time means of communication could not properly be included in a purely military convention, and for this reason they should be dealt with in a special convention.

36. The German Delegation reserved its opinion regarding the publication of expenditure pending the presentation of the report of the Budgetary Experts. Such information should not be used for purposes of comparison and limitation.

37. *Note:* In drawing up this annex, the Conference will have before it the standard model statement which will be submitted to it by the Committee of Budgetary Experts. League Document, 1931, ix, 3.

38. The German Delegation considered that the effect of the prohibition of the use of chemical weapons would be incomplete unless it referred also to preparations for the use of those weapons (instruction of troops, &c.). It considered that a scheme for disarmament should include the prohibition of essentially offensive weapons, such as bombs from the air, large calibre guns, and tanks of every kind, which menaced not only armies but also civilian populations with their destructive powers.

39. The French Delegation favoured the inclusion of a clause providing that members of the Commission must themselves be technical experts giving purely technical opinions and not prejudging any political conclusions that the Governments might draw from those opinions.

40. The German Delegation made the following reservation to Article 53:

In so far as it does not refer to the Washington and London Treaties, the German Delegation would vote against the draft Convention as a whole. The draft, as drawn up by the majority of the Preparatory Commission, excludes essential elements from the limitation and reduction of land armaments. Instead of leading to real disarmament, this draft would serve only to conceal the real state of world armaments or would even allow armaments to be increased. To accept it would at the same time be tantamount to a renewal of the German signature to the disarmament clauses of the Treaty of Versailles.
[John W. Wheeler-Bennett, *Documents on International Affairs, 1931* (London, 1932), pp. 18–39. All footnotes are Wheeler-Bennett's.]

League's One-Year Armament Truce (1931)

Resolution Proposing One-Year Armament Truce, Adopted by the Twelfth Assembly of the League of Nations, 29 September 1931.

Convinced that the crisis which at the present time is creating such profound disturbance among the nations of the world is due to a number of economic and political causes originating principally in the lack of mutual confidence between the nations, and

Convinced that a renewal of the competition in armaments would necessarily lead to an international and social catastrophe:

The Assembly addresses a solemn appeal to all those who are desirous that practical effect should be given to the principles of peace and justice upon which the Covenant is based and urges them to devote all their efforts towards creating a world opinion strong enough to enable the General Disarmament Conference to achieve positive results, including, in particular, a gradual reduction of armaments to be continued until such time as the object laid down in Article 8 of the Covenant is attained.

In view of the fact that an undertaking on the part of all States not to increase their armaments would help to create an atmosphere of confidence, to prevent competition in armaments, and to prepare the ground for the success of the forthcoming Conference:

The Assembly,

Requests the Governments invited to the Disarmament Conference to prepare for this event by means of an armaments truce, and, accordingly,

Requests the Council to urge the Governments convened to the said Conference to give proof of their earnest desire for the successful issue of the efforts to ensure and organize peace and, without prejudging the decisions of the conference or the programmes or proposals submitted to it by each Government, to refrain from any measure involving an increase in their armaments;

Likewise requests the Council to ask the Governments to state, before November 1, 1931, whether they are prepared for a period of one year as from that date to accept this truce in armaments.
[John W. Wheeler-Bennett, ed., *Documents on International Affairs, 1931* (London: Humphrey Milford, 1932), pp. 40–41]

Washington Naval Limitation System

The "Washington naval limitation system" began with the Washington treaty of 1922 and concluded with the London treaty of 1936, along with the 1937 protocols to the latter. The 1922 treaty established many of the basic premises to be subsequently modified and employed.

Washington Naval Treaty (1922)

A Treaty Between the United States of America, the British Empire, France, Italy, and Japan, Limiting Naval Armament, 6 February 1922

CHAPTER I: GENERAL PROVISIONS RELATING TO THE LIMITATION OF NAVAL ARMAMENT

Article I. The Contracting Powers agree to limit their respective naval armament as provided in the present Treaty.

Article II. The Contracting Powers may retain respectively the capital ships which are specified in Chapter II, Part 1. On the coming into force of the present Treaty, but subject to the following provisions of this Article, all other capital ships, built or building, of the United States, the British Empire and Japan shall be disposed of as prescribed in Chapter II, Part 2.

In addition to the capital ships specified in Chapter II, Part 1, the United States may complete and retain two ships of the *West Virginia* class now under construction. On the completion of these two ships the *North Dakota* and *Delaware* shall be disposed of as prescribed in Chapter II, Part 2.

The British Empire may, in accordance with the replacement table in Chapter II, Part 3, construct two new capital ships not exceeding 35,000 tons (35,560 metric tons) standard displacement each. On the completion of the said two ships the *Thunderer, King George V, Ajax* and *Centurion* shall be disposed of as prescribed in Chapter II, Part 2.

Article III. Subject to the provisions of Article II, the Contracting Powers shall abandon their respective capital ship building programs, and no new capital ships shall be constructed or acquired by any of the Contracting Powers except replacement tonnage which may be constructed or acquired as specified in Chapter II, Part 3.

Ships which are replaced in accordance with Chapter II, Part 3, shall be disposed of as prescribed in Part 2 of that Chapter.

Article IV. The total capital ship replacement tonnage of each of the Contracting Powers shall not exceed in standard displacement, for the United States 525,000 tons (533,400 metric tons); for the British Empire 525,000 tons (533,400 metric tons); for France 175,000 tons (177,800 metric tons); for Italy 175,000 tons (177,800 metric tons); for Japan 315,000 tons (320,040 metric tons).

Article V. No capital ship exceeding 35,000 tons (35,560 metric tons) standard displacement shall be acquired by, or constructed by, for, or within the jurisdiction of, any of the Contracting Powers.

Article VI. No capital ship of any of the Contracting Powers shall carry a gun with a calibre in excess of 16 inches (406 millimetres).

Article VII. The total tonnage for aircraft carriers of each of the Contracting Powers shall not exceed in standard displacement, for the United States 135,000 tons (137,160 metric tons); for the British Empire 135,000 tons (137,160 metric tons); for France 60,000 tons (60,960 metric tons); for Italy 60,000 tons (60,960 metric tons); for Japan 81,000 tons (82,296 metric tons).

Article VIII. The replacement of aircraft carriers shall be effected only as prescribed in Chapter II, Part 3, provided, however, that all aircraft carrier tonnage in existence or building on November 12,

1921, shall be considered experimental, and may be replaced, within the total tonnage limit prescribed in Article VII, without regard to its age.

Article IX. No aircraft carrier exceeding 27,000 tons (27,432 metric tons) standard displacement shall be acquired by, or constructed by, for or within the jurisdiction of, any of the Contracting Powers.

However, any of the Contracting Powers may, provided that its total tonnage allowance of aircraft carriers is not thereby exceeded, build not more than two aircraft carriers, each of a tonnage of not more than 33,000 tons (33,528 metric tons) standard displacement, and in order to effect economy any of the Contracting Powers may use for this purpose any two of their ships, whether constructed or in course of construction, which would otherwise be scrapped under the provisions of Article II. The armament of any aircraft carriers exceeding 27,000 tons (27,432 metric tons) standard displacement shall be in accordance with the requirements of Article X, except that the total number of guns to be carried in case any of such guns be of a calibre exceeding 6 inches (152 millimetres), except anti-aircraft guns and guns not exceeding 5 inches (127 millimetres), shall not exceed eight.

Article X. No aircraft carrier of any of the Contracting Powers shall carry a gun with a calibre in excess of 8 inches (203 millimetres). Without prejudice to the provisions of Article IX, if the armament carried includes guns exceeding 6 inches (152 millimetres) in calibre the total number of guns carried, except anti-aircraft guns and guns not exceeding 5 inches (127 millimetres), shall not exceed ten. If alternatively the armament contains no guns exceeding 6 inches (152 millimetres) in calibre, the number of guns is not limited. In either case the number of anti-aircraft guns and of guns not exceeding 5 inches (127 millimetres) is not limited.

Article XI. No vessel of war exceeding 10,000 tons (10,160 metric tons) standard displacement, other than a capital ship or aircraft carrier, shall be acquired by, or constructed by, for, or within the jurisdiction of, any of the Contracting Powers. Vessels not specifically built as fighting ships nor taken in time of peace under government control for fighting purposes, which are employed on fleet duties or as troop transports or in some other way for the purpose of assisting in the prosecution of hostilities otherwise than as fighting ships, shall not be within the limitations of this Article.

Article XII. No vessel of war of any of the Contracting Powers, hereafter laid down, other than a capital ship, shall carry a gun with a calibre in excess of 8 inches (203 millimetres).

Article XIII. Except as provided in Article IX, no ship designated in the present Treaty to be scrapped may be reconverted into a vessel of war.

Article XIV. No preparations shall be made in merchant ships in time of peace for the installation of warlike armaments for the purpose of converting such ships into vessels of war, other than the necessary stiffening of decks for the mounting of guns not exceeding 6 inch (152 millimetres) calibre.

Article XV. No vessel of war constructed within the jurisdiction of any of the Contracting Powers for a non-Contracting Power shall exceed the limitations as to displacement and armament prescribed by the present Treaty for vessels of a similar type which may be constructed by or for any of the Contracting Powers; provided, however, that the displacement for aircraft carriers constructed for a non-Contracting Power shall in no case exceed 27,000 tons (27,432 metric tons) standard displacement.

Article XVI. If the construction of any vessel of war for a non-Contracting Power is undertaken within the jurisdiction of any of the Contracting Powers, such Power shall promptly inform the other Contracting Powers of the date of the signing of the contract and the date on which the keel of the ship is laid; and shall also communicate to them the particulars relating to the ship prescribed in Chapter II, Part 3, Section I (b), (4) and (5).

Article XVII. In the event of a Contracting Power being engaged in war, such Power shall not use as a vessel of war any vessel of war which may be under construction within its jurisdiction for any other Power, or which may have been constructed within its jurisdiction for another Power and not delivered.

Article XVIII. Each of the Contracting Powers undertakes not to dispose by gift, sale or any mode of transfer of any vessel of war in such a manner that such vessel may become a vessel of war in the Navy of any foreign Power.

[Article XIX dealing with nonfortification of Pacific Islands is included in the demilitarization section of this volume.]

Article XX. The rules for determining tonnage displacement prescribed in Chapter II, Part 4, shall apply to the ships of each of the Contracting Powers.

CHAPTER II: RULES RELATING TO THE EXECUTION OF THE TREATY-DEFINITION OF TERMS

Part 1: Capital Ships Which May Be Retained By The Contracting Powers

In accordance with Article II ships may be retained by each of the Contracting Powers as specified in this Part.

Part 2: Rules for Scrapping Vessels of War

The following rules shall be observed for the scrapping of vessels of war which are to be disposed of in accordance with Articles II and III.

I. A vessel to be scrapped must be placed in such condition that it cannot be put to combatant use.

II. This result must be finally effected in any one of the following ways:

(a) Permanent sinking of the vessel;

(b) Breaking the vessel up. This shall always involve the destruction or removal of all machinery, boilers and armour, and all deck, side and bottom plating;

(c) Converting the vessel to target use exclusively. In such case all the provisions of paragraph

Ships which may be retained by the United States

Name	Tonnage
Maryland	32,600
California	32,300
Tennessee	32,300
Idaho	32,000
New Mexico	32,000
Mississippi	32,000
Arizona	31,400
Pennsylvania	31,400
Oklahoma	27,500
Nevada	27,500
New York	27,000
Texas	27,000
Arkansas	26,000
Wyoming	26,000
Florida	21,825
Utah	21,825
North Dakota	20,000
Delaware	20,000
Total tonnage	500,650

On the completion of the two ships of the *West Virginia* class and the scrapping of the *North Dakota* and *Delaware,* as provided in Article II, the total tonnage to be retained by the United States will be 525,850 tons.

Ships which may be retained by the British Empire

Name	Tonnage
Royal Sovereign	25,750
Royal Oak	25,750
Revenge	25,750
Resolution	25,750
Ramillies	25,750
Malaya	27,500
Valiant	27,500
Barham	27,500
Queen Elizabeth	27,500
Warspite	27,500
Benbow	25,000
Emperor of India	25,000
Iron Duke	25,000
Marlborough	25,000
Hood	41,200
Renown	26,500
Repulse	26,500
Tiger	28,500
Thunderer	22,500
King George V	23,000
Ajax	23,000
Centurion	23,000
Total tonnage	580,450

On the completion of the two new ships to be constructed and the scrapping of the *Thunderer, King George V, Ajax* and *Centurion,* as provided in Article II, the total tonnage to be retained by the British Empire will be 558,950 tons.

Ships which may be retained by France

Name	Tonnage (metric tons)
Bretagne	23,500
Lorraine	23,500
Provence	23,500
Paris	23,500
France	23,500
Jean Bart	23,500
Courbet	23,500
Condorcet	18,890
Diderot	18,890
Voltaire	18,890
Total tonnage	221,170

France may lay down new tonnage in the years 1927, 1929, and 1931, as provided in Part 3, Section 11.

Ships which may be retained by Italy

Name	Tonnage (metric tons)
Andrea Doria	22,700
Caio Duilio	22,700
Conte Di Cavour	22,500
Giulio Cesare	22,500
Leonardo da Vinci	22,500
Dante Alighieri	19,500
Roma	12,600
Napoli	12,600
Vittorio Emanuele	12,600
Regina Elena	12,600
Total tonnage	182,800

Italy may lay down new tonnage in the years 1927, 1929, and 1931, as provided in Part 3, Section II.

Ships which may be retained by Japan

Name	Tonnage
Mutsu	33,800
Nagato	33,800
Hiuga	31,260
Ise	31,260
Yamashiro	30,600
Fu-So	30,600
Kirishima	27,500
Haruna	27,500
Hiyei	27,500
Kongo	27,500
Total tonnage	301,320

III of this Part, except sub-paragraph (6), in so far as may be necessary to enable the ship to be used as a mobile target, and except sub-paragraph (7), must be previously complied with. Not more than one capital ship may be retained for this purpose at one time by any of the Contracting Powers.

(d) Of the capital ships which would otherwise be scrapped under the present Treaty in or after the year 1931, France and Italy may each retain two seagoing vessels for training purposes exclusively, that is, as gunnery or torpedo schools. The two vessels retained by France shall be of the *Jean Bart* class, and of those retained by Italy one shall be the *Dante Alighieri,* the other of the *Giulio Cesare* class. On retaining these ships for the purpose above stated, France and Italy respectively undertake to remove and destroy their conning-towers, and not to use the said ships as vessels of war.

III. (a) Subject to the special exceptions contained in Article IX, when a vessel is due for scrapping, the first stage of scrapping, which consists in rendering a ship incapable of further warlike service, shall be immediately undertaken.

(b) A vessel shall be considered incapable of further warlike service when there shall have been removed and landed, or else destroyed in the ship: (1) All guns and essential portions of guns, fire-control tops and revolving parts of all barbettes and turrets; (2) All machinery for working hydraulic or electric mountings; (3) All fire-control instruments and range-finders; (4) All ammunition, explosives and mines; (5) All torpedoes, war-heads and torpedo tubes; (6) All wireless telegraphy installations; (7) The conning tower and all side armour, or alternatively all main propelling machinery; and (8) All landing and flying-off platforms and all other aviation accessories.

IV. The periods in which scrapping of vessels is to be effected are as follows:

(a) In the case of vessels to be scrapped under the first paragraph of Article II, the work of rendering the vessels incapable of further warlike service, in accordance with paragraph III of this Part, shall be completed within six months from the coming into force of the present Treaty, and the scrapping shall be finally effected within eighteen months from such coming into force.

(b) In the case of vessels to be scrapped under the second and third paragraphs of Article II, or under Article III, the work of rendering the vessel incapable of further warlike service in accordance with paragraph III of this Part shall be commenced not later than the date of completion of its successor, and shall be finished within six months from the date of such completion. The vessel shall be finally scrapped, in accordance with paragraph II of this Part, within eighteen months from the date of completion of its successor. If, however, the completion of the new vessel be delayed, then the work of rendering the old vessel incapable of further warlike service in accordance with paragraph III of this Part shall be commenced within four years from the laying of the keel of the new vessel, and shall be finished within six months from the date on which such work was commenced, and the old vessel shall be finally scrapped in accordance with paragraph II of this Part within eighteen months from the date when the work of rendering it incapable of further warlike service was commenced.

Part 3: Replacement

The replacement of capital ships and aircraft carriers shall take place according to the rules in Section I and the tables in Section II of this Part.

Section I: *Rules for Replacement*

(a) Capital ships and aircraft carriers twenty years after the date of their completion may, except as otherwise provided in Article VIII and in the tables in Section II of this Part, be replaced by new construction, but within the limits prescribed in Article IV and Article VII. The keels of such new construction may, except as otherwise provided in Article VIII and in the tables in Section II of this Part, be laid down not earlier than seventeen years from the date of completion of the tonnage to be replaced, provided, however, that no capital ship tonnage, with the exception of the ships referred to in the third paragraph of Article II, and the replacement tonnage specifically mentioned in Section II of this Part, shall be laid down until ten years from November 12, 1921.

(b) Each of the Contracting Powers shall communicate promptly to each of the other Contracting Powers the following information:

(1) The names of the capital ships and aircraft carriers to be replaced by new construction;

(2) The date of governmental authorization of replacement tonnage;

(3) The date of laying the keels of replacement tonnage.

(4) The standard displacement in tons and metric tons of each new ship to be laid down, and the principal dimensions, namely, length at waterline, extreme beam at or below waterline, mean draft at standard displacement;

(5) The date of completion of each new ship and its standard displacement in tons and metric tons, and the principal dimensions, namely, length at waterline, extreme beam at or below waterline, mean draft at standard displacement, at time of completion.

(c) In case of loss or accidental destruction of capital ships or aircraft carriers, they may immediately be replaced by new construction subject to the tonnage limits prescribed in Articles IV and VII and in conformity with the other provisions of the present Treaty, the regular replacement program being deemed to be advanced to that extent.

(d) No retained capital ships or aircraft carriers shall be reconstructed except for the purpose of providing means of defense against air and submarine attack, and subject to the following rules:

The Contracting Powers may, for that purpose, equip existing tonnage with bulge or blister or anti-air attack deck protection, providing the increase of displacement thus effected does not exceed 3,000 tons (3,048 metric tons) displacement for each ship. No alterations in side armor, in calibre, number of general type of mounting of main armament shall be permitted except:

(1) in the case of France and Italy, which countries within the limits allowed for bulge may increase their armor protection and the calibre of the guns now carried on their existing capital ships so as not to exceed 16 inches (406 millimeters); and

(2) the British Empire shall be permitted to complete, in the case of the *Renown*, the alterations to armor that have already been commenced but temporarily suspended.

Section II: *Replacement and Scrapping of Capital Ships* [See the tables on following pages.]

Part 4: Definitions

For the purposes of the present Treaty, the following expressions are to be understood in the sense defined in this Part.

Capital Ship. A capital ship, in the case of ships hereafter built, is defined as a vessel of war, not an aircraft carrier, whose displacement exceeds 10,000 tons (10,160 metric tons) standard displacement, or which carries a gun with a calibre exceeding 8 inches (203 millimetres).

Aircraft Carrier. An aircraft carrier is defined as a vessel of war with a displacement in excess of 10,000 tons (10,160 metric tons) standard displacement designed for the specific and exclusive purpose of carrying aircraft. It must be so constructed that aircraft can be launched therefrom and landed thereon, and not designed and constructed for carrying a more powerful armament than that allowed to it under Article IX or Article X as the case may be.

Standard Displacement. The standard displacement of a ship is the displacement of the ship complete, fully manned, engined, and equipped ready for sea, including all armament and ammunition, equipment, outfit, provisions and fresh water for crew, miscellaneous stores and implements of every description that are intended to be carried in war, but without fuel or reserve feed water on board.

The word "ton" in the present Treaty, except in the expression "metric tons", shall be understood to mean the ton of 2240 pounds (1016 kilos).

Replacement and scrapping of capital ships

UNITED STATES

Year	Ships laid down	Ships completed	Ships scrapped (age in parentheses)	Ships retained Summary	
				Pre-Jutland	Post-Jutland
			Maine (20), Missouri (20), Virginia (17), Nebraska (17), Georgia (17), New Jersey (17), Rhode Island (17), Connecticut (17), Louisiana (17), Vermont (16), Kansas (16), Minnesota (16), New Hampshire (15), South Carolina (13), Michigan (13), Washington (0), South Dakota (0), Indiana (0), Montana (0), North Carolina (0), Iowa (0), Massachusetts (0), Lexington (0), Constitution (0), Constellation (0), Saratoga (0), Ranger (0), United States (0).*	17	1
1922		A, B, #	Delaware (12), North Dakota (12)	15	3
1923				15	3
1924				15	3
1925				15	3
1926				15	3
1927				15	3
1928				15	3
1929				15	3
1930				15	3
1931	C, D			15	3
1932	E, F			15	3
1933	G			15	3
1934	H, I	C, D	Florida (23), Utah (23), Wyoming (22)	12	5
1935	J	E, F	Arkansas (23), Texas (21), New York (21)	9	7
1936	K, L	G	Nevada (20), Oklahoma (20)	7	8
1937	M	H, I	Arizona (21), Pennsylvania (21)	5	10
1938	N, O	J	Mississippi (21)	4	11
1939	P, Q	K, L	New Mexico (21), Idaho (20)	2	13
1940		M	Tennessee (20)	1	14
1941		N, O	California (20), Maryland (20)	0	15
1942		P, Q	2 ships West Virginia class	0	15

*The United States may retain the *Oregon* and *Illinois*, for noncombatant purposes, after complying with the provisions of Part 2, III, (b).

#Two West Virginia class.

NOTE: A, B, C, D, etc., represent individual capital ships of 35,000 tons standard displacement, laid down and completed in the years specified.

Vessels now completed shall retain their present ratings of displacement tonnage in accordance with their national system of measurement. However, a Power expressing displacement in metric tons shall be considered for the application of the present Treaty as owning only the equivalent displacement in tons of 2240 pounds.

A vessel completed hereafter shall be rated at its displacement tonnage when in the standard condition defined herein.

Replacement and scrapping of capital ships

BRITISH EMPIRE

Year	Ships laid down	Ships completed	Ships scrapped (age in parentheses)	Ships retained Summary	
				Pre-Jutland	Post-Jutland
			Commonwealth (16), Agamemnon (13), Dreadnought (15), Bellerophon (12), St. Vincent (11), Inflexible (13), Superb (12), Neptune (10), Hercules (10), Indomitable (13), Temeraire (12), New Zealand (9), Lion (9), Princess Royal (9), Conqueror (9), Monarch (9), Orion (9), Australia (8), Agincourt (7), Erin (7), 4 building or projected.*	21	1
1922	A, B,#			21	1
1923				21	1
1924				21	1
1925		A, B	King George V (13), Ajax (12), Centurion (12), Thunderer (13)	17	3
1926				17	3
1927				17	3
1928				17	3
1929				17	3
1930				17	3
1931	C, D			17	3
1932	E, F			17	3
1933	G			17	3
1934	H, I	C, D	Iron Duke (20), Marlborough (20), Emperor of India (20), Benbow (20)	13	5
1935	J	E, F	Tiger (21), Queen Elizabeth (20), Warspite (20), Barham (20)	9	7
1936	K, L	G	Malaya (20), Royal Sovereign (20)	7	8
1937	M	H, I	Revenge (21), Resolution (21)	5	10
1938	N, O	J	Royal Oak (22)	4	11
1939	P, Q	K, L	Valiant (23), Repulse (23)	2	13
1940		M	Renown (24)	1	14
1941		N, O	Ramillies (24), Hood (21)	0	15
1942		P, Q	A (17), B (17)	0	15

*The British Empire may retain the *Colossus* and *Collingwood* for noncombatant purposes, after complying with the provisions of Part 2, III, (b).

#Two 35,000-ton ships, standard displacement.

NOTE: A, B, C, D, etc., represent individual capital ships of 35,000 tons standard displacement laid down and completed in the years specified.

Replacement and scrapping of capital ships

ITALY

Year	Ships laid down	Ships completed	Ships scrapped (age in parentheses)	Ships retained Summary Pre-Jutland	Ships retained Summary Post-Jutland
1922				6	0
1923				6	0
1924				6	0
1925				6	0
1926				6	0
1927	35,000 tons			6	0
1928				6	0
1929	35,000 tons			6	0
1930				6	0
1931	35,000 tons	35,000 tons	Dante Alighieri (19)	5	(*)
1932	45,000 tons			5	(*)
1933	25,000 tons	35,000 tons	Leonardo da Vinci (19)	4	(*)
1934				4	(*)
1935		35,000 tons	Giulio Cesare (21)	3	(*)
1936		45,000 tons	Conte di Cavour (21), Duilio (21)	1	(*)
1937		25,000 tons	Andrea Doria (21)	0	(*)

*Within tonnage limitations; number not fixed.

NOTE: Italy expressly reserves the right of employing the capital ship tonnage allotment as she may consider advisable, subject solely to the limitations that the displacement of individual ships should not surpass 35,000 tons, and the total capital ship tonnage should keep within the limits imposed by the present Treaty.

CHAPTER III: MISCELLANEOUS PROVISIONS

Article XXI. If during the term of the present Treaty the requirements of the national security of any Contracting Power in respect of naval defence are, in the opinion of that Power, materially affected by any change of circumstances, the Contracting Powers will, at the request of such Power, meet in conference with a view to the reconsideration of the provisions of the Treaty and its amendment by mutual agreement.

In view of possible technical and scientific developments, the United States, after consultation with the other Contracting Powers, shall arrange for a conference of all the Contracting Powers which shall convene as soon as possible after the expiration of eight years from the coming into force of the present Treaty to consider what changes, if any, in the Treaty may be necessary to meet such developments.

Article XXII. Whenever any Contracting Power shall become engaged in a war which in its opinion affects the naval defence of its national security, such Power may after notice to the other Contracting Powers suspend for the period of hostilities its obligations under the present Treaty other than those under Articles XIII and XVII, provided that such Power shall notify the other Contracting Powers that the emergency is of such a character as to require such suspension.

The remaining Contracting Powers shall in such case consult together with a view to agreement as to what temporary modifications if any should be made in the Treaty as between themselves. Should such consultation not produce agreement, duly made in accordance with the constitutional methods of the respective Powers, any one of said Contracting Powers may, by giving notice to the other Contracting Powers, suspend for the period of hostilities its obligations under the present Treaty, other than those under Articles XIII and XVII.

On the cessation of hostilities the Contracting Powers will meet in conference to consider what modifications, if any, should be made in the provisions of the present Treaty.

Replacement and scrapping of capital ships

FRANCE

Year	Ships laid down	Ships completed	Ships scrapped (age in parentheses)	Ships retained Summary	
				Pre-Jutland	Post-Jutland
1922				7	0
1923				7	0
1924				7	0
1925				7	0
1926				7	0
1927	35,000 tons			7	0
1928				7	0
1929	35,000 tons			7	0
1930		35,000 tons	Jean Bart (17), Courbet (17)	5	(*)
1931	35,000 tons			5	(*)
1932	35,000 tons	35,000 tons	France (18)	4	(*)
1933	35,000 tons			4	(*)
1934		35,000 tons	Paris (20), Bretagne (20)	2	(*)
1935		35,000 tons	Provence (20)	1	(*)
1936		35,000 tons	Lorraine (20)	0	(*)
1937				0	(*)
1938				0	(*)
1939				0	(*)
1940				0	(*)
1941				0	(*)
1942				0	(*)

*Within tonnage limitations; number not fixed.

NOTE: France expressly reserves the right of employing the capital ship tonnage allotment as she may consider advisable, subject solely to the limitations that the displacement of individual ships should not surpass 35,000 tons, and that the total capital ship tonnage should keep within the limits imposed by the present Treaty.

Article XXIII. The present Treaty shall remain in force until December 31st, 1936, and in case none of the Contracting Powers shall have given notice two years before that date of its intention to terminate the Treaty, it shall continue in force until the expiration of two years from the date on which notice of termination shall be given by one of the Contracting Powers, whereupon the Treaty shall terminate as regards all the Contracting Powers. Such notice shall be communicated in writing to the Government of the United States, which shall immediately transmit a certified copy of the notification to the other Powers and inform them of the date on which it was received. The notice shall be deemed to have been given and shall take effect on that date. In the event of notice of termination being given by the Government of the United States, such notice shall be given to the diplomatic representatives at Washington of the other Contracting Powers, and the notice shall be deemed to have been given and shall take effect on the date of the communication made to the said diplomatic representatives.

Within one year of the date on which a notice of termination by any Power has taken effect, all the Contracting Powers shall meet in conference.

[Ratification]

[U.S. Senate, 67th Cong., 2d Sess., *Armament Conference Treaties: Treaties and Resolutions Approved and Adopted by the Conference on the Limitation of Armament* (Washington, D.C.: G.P.O., 1922), Doc. 124]

Replacement and scrapping of capital ships

JAPAN

Year	Ships laid down	Ships completed	Ships scrapped (age in parentheses)	Ships retained Summary	
				Pre-Jutland	Post-Jutland
			Hizen (20), Mikasa (20), Kashima (16), Katori (16), Satsuma (12), Aki (11), Setsu (10), Ikoma (14), Ibuki (12), Kurama (11), Amagi (0), Akagi (0), Kaga (0), Tosa (0), Takao (0), Atago (0). Projected program 8 ships not laid down.*	8	2
1922				8	2
1923				8	2
1924				8	2
1925				8	2
1926				8	2
1927				8	2
1928				8	2
1929				8	2
1930				8	2
1931	A			8	2
1932	B			8	2
1933	C			8	2
1934	D	A	Kongo (21)	7	3
1935	E	B	Hiyei (21), Haruna (20)	5	4
1936	F	C	Kirishima (21)	4	5
1937	G	D	Fuso (22)	3	6
1938	H	E	Yamashiro (21)	2	7
1939	I	F	Ise (22)	1	8
1940		G	Hiuga (22)	0	9
1941		H	Nagato (21)	0	9
1942		I	Mutsu (21)	0	9

*Japan may retain the *Skikishima* and *Asahi* for noncombatant purposes, after complying with the provisions of Part 2, III, (b).

NOTE: A, B, C, D, etc., represent individual capital ships of 35,000 tons standard displacement, laid down and completed in the years specified. Note applicable to all the tables in Section II.

Note Applicable to All the Tables in Section II: The order above prescribed in which ships are to be scrapped is in accordance with their age. It is understood that when replacement begins according to the above tables the order of scrapping in the case of the ships of each of the Contracting Powers may be varied at its option; provided, however, that such Power shall scrap in each year the number of ships above stated.

London Naval Treaty (1930)

Treaty on Limitation and Reduction of Naval Armament, London, 22 April 1930

PART I

Article 1. The High Contracting Parties agree not to exercise their rights to lay down the keels of capital ship replacement tonnage during the years 1931–1936 inclusive as provided in Chapter II, Part 3 of the Treaty for the Limitation of Naval Armament signed between them at Washington on the 6th February, 1922, and referred to in the present Treaty as the Washington Treaty.

This provision is without prejudice to the disposition relating to the replacement of ships accidentally lost or destroyed contained in Chapter II, Part 3, Section 1, paragraph (*c*) of the said Treaty.

France and Italy may, however, build the replacement tonnage which they were entitled to lay down in 1927 and 1929 in accordance with the provisions of the said Treaty.

Article 2

1. The United States, the United Kingdom of Great Britain and Northern Ireland and Japan shall dispose of the following capital ships as provided in this Article:

United States:
"Florida" and "Utah"
"Arkansas" or "Wyoming"
United Kingdom:
"Benbow", "Iron Duke" and "Marlborough"
"Emperor of India" and "Tiger"
Japan:
"Hiyei"

(a) Subject to the provisions of sub-paragraph *(b)*, the above ships, unless converted to target use exclusively in accordance with Chapter II, Part 2, paragraph II *(c)* of the Washington Treaty, shall be scrapped in the following manner:

One of the ships to be scrapped by the United States, and two of those to be scrapped by the United Kingdom shall be rendered unfit for warlike service, in accordance with Chapter II, Part 2, paragraph III *(b)* of the Washington Treaty, within twelve months from the coming into force of the present Treaty. These ships shall be finally scrapped, in accordance with paragraph II *(a)* or *(b)* of the said Part 2, within twenty-four months from the said

coming into force. In the case of the second of the ships to be scrapped by the United States, and of the third and fourth of the ships to be scrapped by the United Kingdom, the said periods shall be eighteen and thirty months respectively from the coming into force of the present Treaty.

(b) Of the ships to be disposed of under this Article, the following may be retained for training purposes:

by the United States: "Arkansas" or "Wyoming";
by the United Kingdom: "Iron Duke";
by Japan: "Hiyei".

These ships shall be reduced to the condition prescribed in Section V of Annex II to Part II of the present Treaty. The work of reducing these vessels to the required condition shall begin, in the case of the United States and the United Kingdom, within twelve months, and in the case of Japan within eighteen months from the coming into force of the present Treaty; the work shall be completed within six months of the expiration of the above-mentioned periods.

Any of these ships which are not retained for training purposes shall be rendered unfit for warlike service within eighteen months and finally scrapped within thirty months, of the coming into force of the present Treaty.

2. Subject to any disposal of capital ships which might be necessitated, in accordance with the Washington Treaty, by the building by France or Italy of the replacement tonnage referred to in Article I of the present Treaty, all existing capital ships mentioned in Chapter II, Part 3, Section II of the Washington Treaty and not designated above to be disposed of may be retained during the term of the present Treaty.

3. The right of replacement is not lost by delay in laying down replacement tonnage, and the old vessel may be retained until replaced even though due for scrapping under Chapter II, Part 3, Section II, of the Washington Treaty.

Article 3

1. For the purposes of the Washington Treaty, the definition of an aircraft carrier given in Chapter II, Part 4 of the said Treaty is hereby replaced by the following definition:

The expression "aircraft carrier" includes any surface vessel of war, whatever its displacement, designed for the specific and exclusive purpose of carrying aircraft and so constructed that aircraft can be launched therefrom and landed thereon.

2. The fitting of a landing-on or flying-off platform or deck on a capital ship, cruiser or destroyer, provided such vessel was not designed or adapted exclusively as an aircraft carrier, shall not cause any vessel so fitted to be charged against or classified in the category of aircraft carriers.

3. No capital ship in existence on the 1st April, 1930, shall be fitted with a landing-on platform or deck.

Article 4

1. No aircraft carrier of 10,000 tons (10,160 metric tons) or less standard displacement mounting a gun above 6.1-inch (155 mm.) calibre shall be acquired by or constructed by or for any of the High Contracting Parties.

2. As from the coming into force of the present Treaty in respect of all the High Contracting Parties, no aircraft carrier of 10,000 tons (10,160 metric tons) or less standard displacement mounting a gun above 6.1-inch (155 mm.) calibre shall be constructed within the jurisdiction of any of the High Contracting Parties.

Article 5. An aircraft carrier must not be designed and constructed for carrying a more powerful armament than that authorized by Article IX or X of the Washington Treaty, or by Article 4 of the present Treaty, as the case may be.

Wherever in the said Articles IX and X the calibre of 6 inches (152 mm.) is mentioned, the calibre of 6.1 inches (155 mm.) is substituted therefor.

PART II

Article 6

1. The rules for determining standard displacement prescribed in Chapter II, Part 4 of the Washington Treaty shall apply to all surface vessels of war of each of the High Contracting Parties.

2. The standard displacement of a submarine is the surface displacement of the vessel complete (exclusive of the water in non-watertight structure) fully manned, engined, and equipped ready for sea, including all armament and ammunition, equipment, outfit, provisions for crew, miscellaneous stores, and implements of every description that are intended to be carried in war, but without fuel, lubricating oil, fresh water or ballast water of any kind on board.

3. Each naval combatant vessel shall be rated at its displacement tonnage when in the standard condition. The word "ton", except in the expression "metric tons", shall be understood to be the ton of 2,240 pounds (1,016 kilos.).

Article 7

1. No submarine the standard displacement of which exceeds 2,000 tons (2,032 metric tons) or with a gun above 5.1-inch (130 mm.) calibre shall be acquired by or constructed by or for any of the High Contracting Parties.

2. Each of the High Contracting Parties may, however, retain, build or acquire a maximum number of three submarines of a standard displacement not exceeding 2,800 tons (2,845 tons); these submarines may carry guns not above 6.1-inch (155 mm.) calibre. Within this number, France may retain one unit, already launched, of 2,880 tons (2,926 metric tons), with guns the calibre of which is 8 inches (203 mm.).

3. The High Contracting Parties may retain the submarines which they possessed on the 1st April, 1930, having a standard displacement not in excess of 2,000 tons (2,032 metric tons) and armed with guns above 5.1-inch (130 mm.) calibre.

4. As from the coming into force of the present Treaty in respect of all the High Contracting Parties, no submarine the standard displacement of which exceeds 2,000 tons (2,032 metric tons) or with a gun above 5.1-inch (130 mm.) calibre shall be constructed within the jurisdiction of any of the High contracting Parties, except as provided in paragraph 2 of this Article.

Article 8. Subject to any special agreements which may submit them to limitation, the following vessels are exempt from limitation:

(a) naval surface combatant vessels of 600 tons (610 metric tons) standard displacement and under;

(b) naval surface combatant vessels exceeding 600 tons (610 metric tons), but not exceeding 2,000 tons (2,032 metric tons) standard displacement, provided they have none of the following characteristics: (1) mount a gun above 6.1-inch (155 mm.) calibre; (2) mount more than four guns above 3-inch (76 mm.) calibre; (3) are designed or fitted to launch torpedoes; (4) are designed for a speed greater than twenty knots.

(c) naval surface vessels not specifically built as fighting ships which are employed on fleet duties or as troop transports or in some other way than as fighting ships, provided they have none of the following characteristics: (1) mount a gun above 6.1-inch (155 mm.) calibre; (2) mount more than four guns above 3-inch (76 mm.) calibre; (3) are designed or fitted to launch torpedoes; (4) are de-

signed for a speed greater than twenty knots; (5) are protected by armour plate; (6) are designed or fitted to launch mines; (7) are fitted to receive aircraft on board from the air; (8) mount more than one aircraft-launching apparatus on the centre line; or two, one on each broadside; (9) if fitted with any means of launching aircraft into the air, are designed or adapted to operate at sea more than three aircraft.

Article 9. The rules as to replacement contained in Annex I to this Part II are applicable to vessels of war not exceeding 10,000 tons (10,160 metric tons) standard displacement, with the exception of aircraft carriers, whose replacement is governed by the provisions of the Washington Treaty.

Article 10. Within one month after the date of laying down and the date of completion respectively of each vessel of war, other than capital ships, aircraft carriers and the vessels exempt from limitation under Article 8, laid down or completed by or for them after the coming into force of the present Treaty, the High Contracting Parties shall communicate to each of the other High Contracting Parties the information detailed below:

(a) the date of laying the keel and the following particulars: the classification of the vessel; standard displacement in tons and metric tons; principal dimensions, namely: length at water-line, extreme beam at or below water-line; mean draft at standard displacement; calibre of the largest gun.

(b) the date of completion together with the foregoing particulars relating to the vessel at that date.

The information to be given in the case of capital ships and aircraft carriers is governed by the Washington Treaty.

Article 11. Subject to the provisions of Article 2 of the present Treaty, the rules for disposal contained in Annex II to this Part II shall be applied to all vessels of war to be disposed of under the said Treaty, and to aircraft carriers as defined in Article 3.

Article 12

1. Subject to any supplementary agreements which may modify, as between the High Contracting Parties concerned, the lists in Annex III to this Part II, the special vessels shown therein may be retained and their tonnage shall not be included in the tonnage subject to limitation.

2. Any other vessel constructed, adapted or acquired to serve the purposes for which these special vessels are retained shall be charged against the tonnage of the appropriate combatant category, ac-

cording to the characteristics of the vessel, unless such vessel conforms to the characteristics of vessels exempt from limitation under Article 8.

3. Japan may, however, replace the minelayers "Aso" and "Tokiwa" by two new minelayers before the 31st December, 1936. The standard displacement of each of the new vessels shall not exceed 5,000 tons (5,080 metric tons); their speed shall not exceed twenty knots, and their other characteristics shall conform to the provisions of paragraph *(b)* of Article 8. The new vessels shall be regarded as special vessels and their tonnage shall not be chargeable to the tonnage of any combatant category. The "Aso" and "Tokiwa" shall be disposed of in accordance with Section I or II or Annex II to this Part II, on completion of the replacement vessels.

4. The "Asama", "Yakumo", "Izumo", "Iwate" and "Kasuga" shall be disposed of in accordance with Section I or II of Annex II to this Part II when the first three vessels of the "Kuma" class have been replaced by new vessels. These three vessels of the "Kuma" class shall be reduced to the condition prescribed in Section V, sub-paragraph *(b)* 2 of Annex II to this Part II, and are to be used for training ships, and their tonnage shall not thereafter be included in the tonnage subject to limitation.

Article 13. Existing ships of various types, which, prior to the 1st April, 1930, have been used as stationary training establishments or hulks, may be retained in a nonseagoing condition.

ANNEX I: *Rules for Replacement*

Section I. Except as provided in Section III of this Annex and Part III of the present Treaty, a vessel shall not be replaced before it becomes "over-age". A vessel shall be deemed to be "over-age" when the following number of years have elapsed since the date of its completion:

(a) For a surface vessel exceeding 3,000 tons (3,048 metric tons) but not exceeding 10,000 tons (10,160 metric tons) standard displacement: (i) if laid down before the 1st January, 1920: 16 years; (ii) if laid down after the 31st December, 1919: 20 years.

(b) For a surface vessel not exceeding 3,000 tons (3,048 metric tons) standard displacement: (i) if laid down before the 1st January, 1921: 12 years; (ii) if laid down after the 31st December, 1920: 16 years.

(c) For a submarine: 13 years.

The keels of replacement tonnage shall not be laid down more than three years before the year in which the vessel to be replaced becomes "over-age"; but this period is reduced to two years in the case of any replacement surface vessel not exceeding 3,000 tons (3,048 metric tons) standard displacement.

The right of replacement is not lost by delay in laying down replacement tonnage.

Section II. Except as otherwise provided in the present Treaty the vessel or vessels, whose retention would cause the maximum tonnage permitted in the category to be exceeded, shall, on the completion or acquisition of replacement tonnage, be disposed of in accordance with Annex II to this Part II.

Section III. In the event of loss or accidental destruction a vessel may be immediately replaced.

ANNEX II: *Rules for Disposal of Vessels of War*

The present Treaty provides for the disposal of vessels of war in the following ways: (i) by scrapping (sinking or breaking up); (ii) by converting the vessel to a hulk; (iii) by converting the vessel to target use exclusively; (iv) by retaining the vessel exclusively for experimental purposes; (v) by retaining the vessel exclusively for training purposes.

Any vessel of war to be disposed of, other than a capital ship, may either be scrapped or converted to a hulk at the option of the High Contracting Party concerned.

Vessels, other than capital ships, which have been retained for target, experimental or training purposes, shall finally be scrapped or converted to hulks.

Section I. Vessels to Be Scrapped

(a) A vessel to be disposed of by scrapping, by reason of its replacement, must be rendered incapable of warlike service within six months of the date of the completion of its successor, or of the first of its successors if there are more than one. If, however, the completion of the new vessel or vessels be delayed, the work of rendering the old vessel incapable of warlike service shall, nevertheless, be completed within four and a half years from the date of laying the keel of the new vessel, or of the first of the new vessels; but should the new vessel, or any of the new vessels, be a surface vessel not exceeding 3,000 tons (3,048 metric tons) standard displacement, this period is reduced to three and a half years.

(b) A vessel to be scrapped shall be considered incapable of warlike service when there shall have been removed and landed or else destroyed in the ship: (1) all guns and essential parts of guns, fire control tops and revolving parts of all barbettes and turrets; (2) all hydraulic or electric machinery for operating turrets; (3) all fire control instruments and rangefinders; (4) all ammunition, explosives, mines and mine rails; (5) all torpedoes, war heads, torpedo tubes and training racks; (6) all wireless telegraphy installations; (7) all main propelling machinery, or alternatively the armoured conning tower and all side armour plate; (8) all aircraft cranes, derricks, lifts and launching apparatus. All landing-on or flying-off platforms and decks, or alternatively all main propelling machinery; (9) in addition, in the case of submarines, all main storage batteries, air compressor plants and ballast pumps.

(c) Scrapping shall be finally effected in either of the following ways within twelve months of the date on which the work of rendering the vessel incapable of warlike service is due for completion: (1) permanent sinking of the vessel; (2) breaking the vessel up; this shall always include the destruction or removal of all machinery, boilers and armour, and all deck side and bottom plating.

Section II. Vessels to Be Converted to Hulks

A vessel to be disposed of by conversion to a hulk shall be considered finally disposed of when the conditions prescribed in Section 1, paragraph (b), have been complied with, omitting subparagraphs (6), (7) and (8), and when the following have been effected: (1) mutilation beyond repair of all propeller shafts, thrust blocks, turbine gearing or main propelling motors, and turbines or cylinders or main engines; (2) removal of propeller brackets; (3) removal and breaking up of all aircraft lifts, and the removal of all aircraft cranes, derricks and launching apparatus.

The vessel must be put in the above condition within the same limits of time as provided in Section I for rendering a vessel incapable of warlike service.

Section III. Vessels to Be Converted to Target Use

(a) A vessel to be disposed of by conversion to target use exclusively shall be considered incapable of warlike service when there have been removed and landed, or rendered unserviceable on board, the following: (1) all guns; (2) all fire control tops and instruments and main fire control communi-

cation wiring; (3) all machinery for operating gun mountings or turrets; (4) all ammunition, explosives, mines, torpedoes and torpedo tubes; (5) all aviation facilities and accessories.

The vessel must be put into the above condition within the same limits of time as provided in Section I for rendering a vessel incapable of warlike service.

(b) In addition to the rights already possessed by each High Contracting Party under the Washington Treaty, each High Contracting Party is permitted to retain, for target use exclusively, at any one time: (1) not more than three vessels (cruisers or destroyers), but of these three vessels only one may exceed 3,000 tons (3,048 metric tons) standard displacement; (2) one submarine.

(c) On retaining a vessel for target use, the High Contracting Party concerned undertakes not to recondition it for warlike service.

Section IV. Vessels Retained for Experimental Purposes

(a) A vessel to be disposed of by conversion to experimental purposes exclusively shall be dealt with in accordance with the provisions of Section III (a) of this Annex.

(b) Without prejudice to the general rules, and provided that due notice be given to the other High Contracting Parties, reasonable variation from the conditions prescribed in Section III (a) of this Annex, in so far as may be necessary for the purposes of a special experiment, may be permitted as a temporary measure.

Any High Contracting Party taking advantage of this provision is required to furnish full details of any such variations and the period for which they will be required.

(c) Each High Contracting Party is permitted to retain for experimental purposes exclusively at any one time: (1) not more than two vessels (cruisers or destroyers), but of these two vessels only one may exceed 3,000 tons (3,048 metric tons) standard displacement; (2) one submarine.

(d) The United Kingdom is allowed to retain, in their present conditions, the monitor "Roberts", the main armament guns and mountings of which have been mutilated, and the seaplane carrier "Ark Royal", until no longer required for experimental purposes. The retention of these two vessels is without prejudice to the retention of vessels permitted under (c) above.

(e) On retaining a vessel for experimental purposes the High Contracting Party concerned undertakes not to recondition it for warlike service.

Section V. Vessels Retained for Training Purposes

(a) In addition to the rights already possessed by any High Contracting Party, under the Washington Treaty, each High Contracting Party is permitted to retain for training purposes exclusively the following vessels:

United States: 1 capital ship ("Arkansas" or "Wyoming");

France: 2 surface vessels, one of which may exceed 3,000 tons (3,048 metric tons) standard displacement;

United Kingdom: 1 capital ship ("Iron Duke");

Italy: 2 surface vessels, one of which may exceed 3,000 tons (3,048 metric tons) standard displacement;

Japan: 1 capital ship ("Hiyei"), 3 cruisers ("Kuma" class).

(b) Vessels retained for training purposes under the provisions of paragraph (a) shall, within six months of the date on which they are required to be disposed of, be dealt with as follows:

1. *Capital Ships.* The following is to be carried out: (1) removal of main armament guns, revolving parts of all barbettes and turrets; machinery for operating turrets; but three turrets with their armament may be retained in each ship; (2) removal of all ammunition and explosives in excess of the quantity required for target practice training for the guns remaining on board; (3) removal of conning tower and the side armour belt between the foremost and aftermost barbettes; (4) removal or mutilation of all torpedo tubes; (5) removal or mutilation on board of all boilers in excess of the number required for a maximum speed of eighteen knots.

2. *Other surface vessels retained by France, Italy and Japan.* The following is to be carried out: (1) removal of one half of the guns, but four guns of main calibre may be retained on each vessel; (2) removal of all torpedo tubes; (3) removal of all aviation facilities and accessories; (4) removal of one half of the boilers.

(c) The High Contracting Party concerned undertakes that vessels retained in accordance with the provisions of this Section shall not be used for any combatant purpose.

[Annex III omitted.]

PART III

The President of the United States of America, His Majesty the King of Great Britain, Ireland and the British Dominions beyond the Seas, Emperor of India, and His Majesty the Emperor of Japan, have agreed as between themselves to the provisions of this Part III:

Article 14. The naval combatant vessels of the United States, the British Commonwealth of Nations and Japan, other than capital ships, aircraft carriers and all vessels exempt from limitation under Article 8, shall be limited during the term of the present Treaty as provided in this Part III, and, in the case of special vessels, as provided in Article 12.

Article 15. For the purpose of this Part III the definition of the cruiser and destroyer categories shall be as follows:

Cruisers. Surface vessels of war, other than capital ships or aircraft carriers, the standard displacement of which exceeds 1,850 tons (1,880 metric tons), or with a gun above 5.1-inch (130 mm.) calibre. The cruiser category is divided into two sub-categories, as follows:

(a) cruisers carrying a gun above 6.1-inch (155 mm.) calibre;

(b) cruisers carrying a gun not above 6.1-inch (155 mm.) calibre.

Destroyers. Surface vessels of war the standard displacement of which does not exceed 1,850 tons (1,880 metric tons), and with a gun not above 5.1-inch (130 mm.) calibre.

Article 16

1. The completed tonnage in the cruiser, destroyer and submarine categories which is not to be exceeded on the 31st December, 1936, is given in the following table:

2. Vessels which cause the total tonnage in any category to exceed the figures given in the foregoing table shall be disposed of gradually during the period ending on the 31st December, 1936.

3. The maximum number of cruisers of sub-category (a) shall be as follows: for the United States, eighteen; for the British Commonwealth of Nations, fifteen; for Japan, twelve.

4. In the destroyer category not more than sixteen per cent. of the allowed total tonnage shall be employed in vessels of over 1,500 tons (1,524 metric tons) standard displacement. Destroyers completed or under construction on the 1st April, 1930, in excess of this percentage may be retained, but no other destroyers exceeding 1,500 tons (1,524 metric tons) standard displacement shall be constructed or acquired until a reduction to such sixteen per cent. has been effected.

5. Not more than twenty-five per cent. of the allowed total tonnage in the cruiser category may be fitted with a landing-on platform or deck for aircraft.

6. It is understood that the submarines referred to in paragraphs 2 and 3 of Article 7 will be counted as part of the total submarine tonnage of the High Contracting Party concerned.

7. The tonnage of any vessels retained under Article 13 or disposed of in accordance with Annex II to Part II of the present Treaty shall not be included in the tonnage subject to limitation.

Article 17. A transfer not exceeding ten per cent. of the allowed total tonnage of the category or sub-category into which the transfer is to be made shall be permitted between cruisers of sub-category (b) and destroyers.

Categories	United States	British Commonwealth of Nations	Japan
Cruisers:			
(a) with guns of more than 6.1-inch (155 mm.) calibre.	180,000 tons (182,880 metric tons)	146,800 tons (149,149 metric tons)	108,400 tons (110,134 metric tons)
(b) with guns of 6.1-inch (155 mm.) calibre or less.	143,500 tons (145,796 metric tons)	192,200 tons (195,275 metric tons)	100,450 tons (102,057 metric tons)
Destroyers	150,000 tons (152,400 metric tons)	150,000 tons (152,400 metric tons)	105,500 tons (107,188 metric tons)
Submarines	52,700 tons (53,543 metric tons)	52,700 tons (53,543 metric tons)	52,700 tons (53,543 metric tons)

Article 18. The United States contemplates the completion by 1935 of fifteen cruisers of sub-category (a) of an aggregate tonnage of 150,000 tons (152,400 metric tons). For each of the three remaining cruisers of sub-category (a) which it is entitled to construct the United States may elect to substitute 15,166 tons (15,409 metric tons) of cruisers of sub-category (b). In case the United States shall construct one or more of such three remaining cruisers of sub-category (a), the sixteenth unit will not be laid down before 1933 and will not be completed before 1936; the seventeenth will not be laid down before 1934 and will not be completed before 1937; the eighteenth will not be laid down before 1935 and will not be completed before 1938.

Article 19. Except as provided in Article 20, the tonnage laid down in any category subject to limitation in accordance with Article 16 shall not exceed the amount necessary to reach the maximum allowed tonnage of the category, or to replace vessels that become "overage" before the 31st December, 1936. Nevertheless, replacement tonnage may be laid down for cruisers and submarines that become "overage" in 1937, 1938 and 1939, and for destroyers that become "overage" in 1937 and 1938.

Article 20. Notwithstanding the rules for replacement contained in Annex I to Part II:

(a) The "Frobisher" and "Effingham" (United Kingdom) may be disposed of during the year 1936. Apart from the cruisers under construction on the 1st April, 1930, the total replacement tonnage of cruisers to be completed, in the case of the British Commonwealth of Nations, prior to the 31st December, 1936, shall not exceed 91,000 tons (92,456 metric tons).

(b) Japan may replace the "Tama" by new construction to be completed during the year 1936.

(c) In addition to replacing destroyers becoming "overage" before the 31st December, 1936, Japan may lay down, in each of the years 1935 and 1936, not more than 5,200 tons (5,283 metric tons) to replace part of the vessels that become "overage" in 1938 and 1939.

(d) Japan may anticipate replacement during the term of the present Treaty by laying down not more than 19,200 tons (19,507 metric tons) of submarine tonnage, of which not more than 12,000 tons (12,192 metric tons) shall be completed by the 31st December, 1936.

Article 21. If, during the term of the present Treaty, the requirements of the national security of any High Contracting Party in respect of vessels of war limited by Part III of the present Treaty are in the opinion of that Party materially affected by new construction of any Power other than those who have joined in Part III of this Treaty, that High Contracting Party will notify the other Parties to Part III as to the increase required to be made in its own tonnages within one or more of the categories of such vessels of war, specifying particularly the proposed increases and the reasons therefor, and shall be entitled to make such increase. Thereupon the other Parties to Part III of this Treaty shall be entitled to make a proportionate increase in the category or categories specified; and the said other Parties shall promptly advise with each other through diplomatic channels as to the situation [thus] presented.

PART IV

Article 22. The following are accepted as established rules of International Law:

1. In their action with regard to merchant ships, submarines must conform to the rules of International Law to which surface vessels are subject.

2. In particular, except in the case of persistent refusal to stop on being duly summoned, or of active resistance to visit or search, a warship, whether surface vessel or submarine, may not sink or render incapable of navigation a merchant vessel without having first placed passengers, crew and ship's papers in a place of safety. For this purpose the ship's boats are not regarded as a place of safety unless the safety of the passengers and crew is assured, in the existing sea and weather conditions, by the proximity of land, or the presence of another vessel which is in a position to take them on board.

The High Contracting Parties invite all other Powers to express their assent to the above rules.

PART V

Article 23. The present Treaty shall remain in force until the 31st December, 1936, subject to the following exceptions:

1. Part IV shall remain in force without limit of time;

2. the provisions of Articles 3, 4 and 5, and of Article 11 and Annex II to Part II so far as they relate to aircraft carriers, shall remain in force for the same period as the Washington Treaty.

Unless the High Contracting Parties should agree otherwise by reason of a more general agreement limiting naval armaments, to which they all become parties, they shall meet in conference in 1935 to frame a new treaty to replace and to carry out the purposes of the present Treaty, it being understood that none of the provisions of the present Treaty shall prejudice the attitude of any of the High Contracting Parties at the conference agreed to.

[Ratification]
[Signatures]
[U.S. Library of Congress, Legislative Reference Service, *Disarmament and Security: A Collection of Documents, 1919–55* (Washington, D.C., 1956), Doc. 6]

Anglo-German Naval Agreement (1935)

Following is the exchange of notes between the United Kingdom and Germany regarding the Limitation of Naval Armaments, London, 18 June 1935.

No. 1. *His Majesty's Principal Secretary of State for Foreign Affairs to the German Ambassador in London*

Foreign Office, June 18, 1935
Your Excellency,

During the last few days the representatives of the German Government and His Majesty's Government in the United Kingdom have been engaged in conversations, the primary purpose of which has been to prepare the way for the holding of a general conference on the subject of the limitation of naval armaments. I have now much pleasure in notifying your Excellency of the formal acceptance by His Majesty's Government in the United Kingdom of the proposal of the German Government discussed at those conversations that the future strength of the German navy in relation to the aggregate naval strength of the members of the British Commonwealth of Nations should be in the proportion of 35:100. His Majesty's Government in the United Kingdom regard this proposal as a contribution of the greatest importance to the cause of future naval limitation. They further believe that the agreement which they have now reached with the German Government, and which they regard as a permanent and definite agreement as from today between the two Governments, will facilitate the conclusion of a general agreement on the subject of naval limitation between all the naval Powers of the world.

2. His Majesty's Government in the United Kingdom also agree with the explanations which were furnished by the German representatives in the course of the recent discussions in London as to the method of application of this principle. These explanations may be summarised as follows:

(a) The ratio of 35:100 is to be a permanent relationship, i.e., the total tonnage of the German fleet shall never exceed a percentage of 35 of the aggregate tonnage of the naval forces, as defined by treaty, of the members of the British Commonwealth of Nations, or, if there should in future be no treaty limitations of this tonnage, a percentage of 35 of the aggregate of the actual tonnages of the members of the British Commonwealth of Nations.

(b) If any future general treaty of naval limitation should not adopt the method of limitation by agreed ratios between the fleets of different Powers, the German Government will not insist on the incorporation of the ratio mentioned in the preceding sub-paragraph in such future general treaty, provided that the method therein adopted for the future limitation of naval armaments is such as to give Germany full guarantees that this ratio can be maintained.

(c) Germany will adhere to the ratio 35:100 in all circumstances, e.g., the ratio will not be affected by the construction of other Powers. If the general equilibrium of naval armaments, as normally maintained in the past, should be violently upset by any abnormal and exceptional construction by other Powers, the German Government reserve the right to invite His Majesty's Government in the United Kingdom to examine the new situation thus created.

(d) The German Government favour, in the matter of limitation of naval armaments, that system which divides naval vessels into categories, fixing the maximum tonnage and/or armament for vessels

in each category, and allocates the tonnage to be allowed to each Power by categories of vessels. Consequently, in principle, and subject to (f) below, the German Government are prepared to apply the 35 per cent. ratio to the tonnage of each category of vessel to be maintained, and to make any variation of this ratio in a particular category or categories dependent on the arrangements to this end that may be arrived at in a future general treaty on naval limitation, such arrangements being based on the principle that any increase in one category would be compensated for by a corresponding reduction in others. If no general treaty on naval limitation should be concluded, or if the future general treaty should not contain provision creating limitation by categories, the manner and degree in which the German Government will have the right to vary the 35 per cent. ratio in one or more categories will be a matter for settlement by agreement between the German Government and His Majesty's Government in the United Kingdom, in the light of the naval situation then existing.

(e) If, and for so long as, other important naval Powers retain a single category for cruisers and destroyers, Germany shall enjoy the right to have a single category for these two classes of vessels, although she would prefer to see these classes in two categories.

(f) In the matter of submarines, however, Germany, while not exceeding the ratio of 35:100 in respect of total tonnage, shall have the right to possess a submarine tonnage equal to the total submarine tonnage possessed by the members of the British Commonwealth of Nations. The German Government, however, undertake that, except in the circumstances indicated in the immediately following sentence, Germany's submarine tonnage shall not exceed 45 per cent. of the total of that possessed by the members of the British Commonwealth of Nations. The German Government reserve the right, in the event of a situation arising which in their opinion makes it necessary for Germany to avail herself of her right to a percentage of submarine tonnage exceeding the 45 per cent. above mentioned, to give notice to this effect to His Majesty's Government in the United Kingdom, and agree that the matter shall be the subject of friendly discussion before the German Government exercise that right.

(g) Since it is highly improbable that the calculation of the 35 per cent. ratio should give for each category of vessels tonnage figures exactly divisible by the maximum individual tonnage permitted for ships in that category, it may be necessary that adjustments should be made in order that Germany shall not be debarred from utilising her tonnage to the full. It has consequently been agreed that the German Government and His Majesty's Government in the United Kingdom will settle by common accord what adjustments are necessary for this purpose, and it is understood that this procedure shall not result in any substantial or permanent departure from the ratio 35:100 in respect of total strengths.

3. With reference to sub-paragraph (c) of the explanations set out above, I have the honour to inform you that His Majesty's Government in the United Kingdom have taken note of the reservation and recognise the right therein set out, on the understanding that the 35:100 ratio will be maintained in default of agreement to the contrary between the two Governments.

4. I have the honour to request your Excellency to inform me that the German Government agree that the proposal of the German Government has been correctly set out in the preceding paragraphs of this note.

Samuel Hoare

No. 2. *The German Ambassador in London to His Majesty's Principal Secretary of State for Foreign Affairs.* [*Translation*]

London, June 18, 1935
Your Excellency,

I have the honour to acknowledge the receipt of your Excellency's note of today's date, in which you were so good as to communicate to me on behalf of His Majesty's Government in the United Kingdom the following:

[*A German translation of paragraphs 1 to 3 of No. 1, not repeated.*]

I have the honour to confirm to your Excellency that the proposal of the German Government is correctly set forth in the foregoing note, and I note with pleasure that His Majesty's Government in the United Kingdom accept this proposal.

The German Government, for their part, are also of the opinion that the agreement at which they have now arrived with His Majesty's Government in the United Kingdom, and which they regard as a permanent and definite agreement with effect from today between the two Governments, will facilitate the conclusion of a general agreement on this question between all the naval Powers of the world.

Joachim von Ribbentrop

[*British and Foreign State Papers,* vol. 139 (1935) (London: H.M.S.O., 1941–1948), pp. 182–185. *Treaty Series* No. 22 (1935) (Cmd. 4953)]

London Naval Treaty (1936)

The British government subsequently, in 1937, negotiated bilateral treaties "Extending the Principles of the London (1936) Treaty" with Germany and the Soviet Union.

Treaty on Limitation and Reduction of Naval Armament, London, 25 March 1936

PART I. Definitions

Article I. For the purposes of the present Treaty, the following expressions are to be understood in the sense hereinafter defined.

A. Standard Displacement

1. The standard displacement of a surface vessel is the displacement of the vessel, complete, fully manned, engined, and equipped ready for sea, including all armament and ammunition, equipment, outfit, provisions and fresh water for crew, miscellaneous stores and implements of every description that are intended to be carried in war, but without fuel or reserve feed water on board.

2. The standard displacement of a submarine is the surface displacement of the vessel complete (exclusive of the water in nonwatertight structure), fully manned, engined and equipped ready for sea, including all armament and ammunition, equipment, outfit, provisions for crew, miscellaneous stores and implements of every description that are intended to be carried in war, but without fuel, lubricating oil, fresh water or ballast water of any kind on board.

3. The word "ton" except in the expression "metric tons" denotes the ton of 2,240 lb. (1,016 kilos).

B. Categories

1. *Capital Ships* are surface vessels of war belonging to one of the two following sub-categories: (a) surface vessels of war, other than aircraft carriers, auxiliary vessels, or capital ships of sub-category (b), the standard displacement of which exceeds 10,000 tons (10,160 metric tons) or which carry a gun with a calibre exceeding 8 in. (203 mm.); (b) surface vessels of war, other than aircraft-carriers, the standard displacement of which does not exceed 8,000 tons (8,128 metric tons) and which carry a gun with a calibre exceeding 8 in. (203 mm.).

2. *Aircraft Carriers* are surface vessels of war, whatever their displacement, designed or adapted primarily for the purpose of carrying and operating aircraft at sea. The fitting of a landing-on or flying-off deck on any vessel of war, provided such vessel has not been designed or adapted primarily for the purpose of carrying and operating aircraft at sea, shall not cause any vessel so fitted to be classified in the category of aircraft carriers.

The category of aircraft carriers is divided into two sub-categories as follows: (a) vessels fitted with a flight deck, from which aircraft can take off, or on which aircraft can land from the air; (b) vessels not fitted with a flight deck as described in (a) above.

3. *Light Surface Vessels* are surface vessels of war other than aircraft carriers, minor war vessels or auxiliary vessels, the standard displacement of which exceeds 100 tons (102 metric tons) and does not exceed 10,000 tons (10,160 metric tons), and which do not carry a gun with a calibre exceeding 8 in. (203 mm.).

The category of light surface vessels is divided into three sub-categories as follows: (a) vessels which carry a gun with a calibre exceeding 6.1 in. (155 mm.); (b) vessels which do not carry a gun with a calibre exceeding 6.1 in. (155 mm.) and the standard displacement of which exceeds 3,000 tons (3,048 metric tons); (c) vessels which do not carry a gun with a calibre exceeding 6.1 in. (155 mm.) and the standard displacement of which does not exceed 3,000 tons (3,048 metric tons).

4. *Submarines* are all vessels designed to operate below the surface of the sea.

5. *Minor War Vessels* are surface vessels of war, other than auxiliary vessels, the standard displacement of which exceeds 100 tons (102 metric tons) and does not exceed 2,000 tons (2,032 metric tons), provided they have none of the following characteristics: (a) mount a gun with a calibre exceeding 6.1 in. (155 mm.); (b) are designed or fitted to launch torpedoes; (c) are designed for a speed greater than twenty knots.

6. *Auxiliary Vessels* are naval surface vessels the standard displacement of which exceeds 100 tons (102 metric tons), which are normally employed on fleet duties or as troop transports, or in some other way than as fighting ships, and which are not specifically built as fighting ships, provided they have none of the following characteristics: (a) mount a gun with a calibre exceeding 6.1 in. (155 mm.); (b) mount more than eight guns with a calibre exceeding 3 in. (76 mm.); (c) are designed or fitted to launch torpedoes; (d) are designed for protection by armour plate; (e) are designed for a speed greater than twenty-eight knots; (f) are designed or adapted primarily for operating aircraft at sea; (g) mount more than two aircraft-launching apparatus.

7. *Small Craft* are naval surface vessels the standard displacement of which does not exceed 100 tons (102 metric tons).

C. Over Age

Vessels of the following categories and sub-categories shall be deemed to be "over-age" when the undermentioned number of years have elapsed since completion:

(a) Capital ships—26 years.

(b) Aircraft carriers—20 years.

(c) Light surface vessels, sub-categories (a) and (b): (i) if laid down before 1st January, 1920—16 years; (ii) if laid down after 31st December, 1919—20 years.

(d) Light surface vessels, sub-category (c)—16 years.

(e) Submarines—13 years.

D. Month

The word "month" in the present Treaty with reference to a period of time denotes the month of thirty days.

PART II. Limitation

Article 2. After the date of the coming into force of the present Treaty, no vessel exceeding the limitations as to displacement or armament prescribed by this Part of the present Treaty shall be acquired by any High Contracting Party or constructed by, for or within the jurisdiction of any High Contracting Party.

Article 3. No vessel which at the date of the coming into force of the present Treaty carries guns with a calibre exceeding the limits prescribed by this Part of the present Treaty shall, if reconstructed or modernised, be rearmed with guns of a greater calibre than those previously carried by her.

Article 4

1. No capital ship shall exceed 35,000 tons (35,560 metric tons) standard displacement.

2. No capital ship shall carry a gun with a calibre exceeding 14 in. (356 mm.); provided however that if any of the Parties to the Treaty for the Limitation of Naval Armament signed at Washington on the 6th February, 1922, should fail to enter into an agreement to conform to this provision prior to the date of the coming into force of the present Treaty, but in any case not later than the 1st April, 1937, the maximum calibre of gun carried by capital ships shall be 16 in. (406 mm.).

3. No capital ship of sub-category (a), the standard displacement of which is less than 17,500 tons (17,780 metric tons), shall be laid down or acquired prior to the 1st January, 1943.

4. No capital ship, the main armament of which consists of guns of less than 10 in. (254 mm.) calibre, shall be laid down or acquired prior to the 1st January, 1943.

Article 5

1. No aircraft carrier shall exceed 23,000 tons (23,368 metric tons) standard displacement or carry a gun with a calibre exceeding 6.1 in. (155 mm.).

2. If the armament of any aircraft carrier includes guns exceeding 5.25 in. (134 mm.) in calibre, the total number of guns carried which exceed that calibre shall not be more than ten.

Article 6

1. No light surface vessel of sub-category (b) exceeding 8,000 tons (8,128 metric tons) standard displacement, and no light surface vessel of sub-category (a) shall be laid down or acquired prior to the 1st January, 1943.

2. Notwithstanding the provisions of paragraph (1) above, if the requirements of the national security of any High Contracting Party are, in His opinion, materially affected by the actual or authorised amount of construction by any Power of light

surface vessels of sub-category (b), or of light sur-face vessels not conforming to the restrictions of paragraph (1) above, such High Contracting Party shall, upon notifying the other High Contracting Parties of His intentions and the reasons therefor, have the right to lay down or acquire light surface vessels of sub-categories (a) and (b) of any standard displacement up to 10,000 tons (10,160 metric tons) subject to the observance of the provisions of Part III of the present Treaty. Each of the other High Contracting Parties shall thereupon be entitled to exercise the same right.

3. It is understood that the provisions of para-graph (1) above constitute no undertaking ex-pressed or implied to continue the restrictions therein prescribed after the year 1942.

Article 7. No submarine shall exceed 2,000 tons (2,032 metric tons) standard displacement or carry a gun exceeding 5.1 in. (130 mm.) in calibre.

Article 8. Every vessel shall be rated at its stan-dard displacement, as defined in Article 1A of the present Treaty.

Article 9. No preparations shall be made in mer-chant ships in time of peace for the installation of warlike armaments for the purpose of converting such ships into vessels of war, other than the nec-essary stiffening of decks for the mounting of guns not exceeding 6.1 in. (155 mm.) in calibre.

Article 10. Vessels which were laid down before the date of the coming into force of the present Treaty, the standard displacement or armament of which exceeds the limitations or restrictions pre-scribed in this Part of the present Treaty for their category or sub-category, or vessels which before that date were converted to target use exclusively or retained exclusively for experimental or training purposes under the provision of previous treaties, shall retain the category or designation which ap-plied to them before the said date.

PART III: Advance Notification and Exchange of Information

Article 11

1. Each of the High Contracting Parties shall communicate every year to each of the other High Contracting Parties information, as hereinafter pro-vided, regarding His annual programme for the construction and acquisition of all vessels of the cat-egories and sub-categories mentioned in Article 12 (a), whether or not the vessels concerned are con-structed within His own jurisdiction, and periodical information giving details of such vessels and of any alterations to vessels of the said categories or sub-categories already completed.

2. For the purposes of this and the succeeding Parts of the present Treaty, information shall be deemed to have reached a High Contracting Party on the date upon which such information is com-municated to His Diplomatic Representatives ac-credited to the High Contracting Party by whom the information is given.

3. This information shall be treated as confiden-tial until published by the High Contracting Party supplying it.

Article 12. The information to be furnished un-der the preceding Article in respect of vessels con-structed by or for a High Contracting Party shall be given as follows; and so as to reach all the other High Contracting Parties within the periods or at the times mentioned:

(a) Within the first four months of each calen-dar year, the Annual Programme of construction of all vessels of the following categories and sub-categories, stating the number of vessels of each category or sub-category and, for each vessel, the calibre of the largest gun. The categories and sub-categories in question are: Capital Ships sub-category (a) and (b); Aircraft-Carriers sub-category (a) and (b); Light Surface Vessels sub-category (a), (b) and (c); Submarines.

(b) Not less than four months before the date of the laying of the keel, the following particulars in respect of each such vessel:

- Name or designation;
- Category and sub-category;
- Standard displacement in tons and metric tons;
- Length at waterline at standard displacement;
- Extreme beam at or below waterline at standard displacement;
- Mean draught at standard displacement;
- Designed horse-power;
- Designed speed;
- Type of machinery;
- Type of fuel;
- Number and calibre of all guns of 3 in. (76 mm.) calibre and above;
- Approximate number of guns of less than 3 in. (76 mm.) calibre;
- Number of torpedo tubes;
- Whether designed to lay mines;
- Approximate number of aircraft for which provi-sion is to be made.

(c) As soon as possible after the laying-down of the keel of each such vessel, the date on which it was laid.

(d) Within one month after the date of completion of each such vessel, the date of completion together with all the particulars specified in paragraph (b) above relating to the vessel on completion.

(e) Annually during the month of January, in respect of vessels belonging to the categories and sub-categories mentioned in paragraph (a) above: (i) Information as to any important alterations which it may have proved necessary to make during the preceding year in vessels under construction, in so far as these alterations affect the particulars mentioned in paragraph (b) above. (ii) Information as to any important alterations made during the preceding year in vessels previously completed, in so far as these alterations affect the particulars mentioned in paragraph (b) above. (iii) Information concerning vessels which may have been scrapped or otherwise disposed of during the preceding year. If such vessels are not scrapped, sufficient information shall be given to enable their new status and condition to be determined.

(f) Not less than four months before undertaking such alterations as would cause a completed vessel to come within one of the categories or sub-categories mentioned in paragraph (a) above, or such alterations as would cause a vessel to change from one to another of the said categories or sub-categories: information as to her intended characteristics as specified in paragraph (b) above.

Article 13. No vessel coming within the categories or sub-categories mentioned in Article 12 (a) shall be laid down by any High Contracting Party until after the expiration of a period of four months both from the date on which the Annual Programme in which the vessel is included, and from the date on which the particulars in respect of that vessel prescribed by Article 12 (b), have reached all the other High Contracting Parties.

Article 14. If a High Contracting Party intends to acquire a completed or partially completed vessel coming within the categories or sub-categories mentioned in Article 12 (a), that vessel shall be declared at the same time and in the same manner as the vessels included in the Annual Programme prescribed in the said Article. No such vessel shall be acquired until after the expiration of a period of four months from the date on which such declaration has reached all the other High Contracting Parties. The particulars mentioned in Article 12 (b), together with the date on which the keel was laid, shall be furnished in respect of such vessel so as to reach all the other High Contracting Parties within one month after the date on which the contract for the acquisition of the vessel was signed. The particulars mentioned in Article 12 (d), (e) and (f) shall be given as therein prescribed.

Article 15. At the time of communicating the Annual Programme prescribed by Article 12 (a), each High Contracting Party shall inform all the other High Contracting Parties of all vessels included in His previous Annual Programmes and declarations that have not yet been laid down or acquired, but which it is the intention to lay down or acquire during the period covered by the first mentioned Annual Programme.

Article 16. If, before the keel of any vessel coming within the categories or sub-categories mentioned in Article 12 (a) is laid, any important modification is made in the particulars regarding her which have been communicated under Article 12 (b), information concerning this modification shall be given, and the laying of the keel shall be deferred until at least four months after this information has reached all the other High Contracting Parties.

Article 17. No High Contracting Party shall lay down or acquire any vessel of the categories or sub-categories mentioned in Article 12 *(a),* which has not previously been included in His Annual Programme of construction or declaration of acquisition for the current year or in any earlier Annual Programme or declaration.

Article 18. If the construction, modernisation or reconstruction of any vessel coming within the categories or sub-categories mentioned in Article 12 (a), which is for the order of a Power not a party to the present Treaty, is undertaken within the jurisdiction of any High Contracting Party, He shall promptly inform all the other High Contracting Parties of the date of the signing of the contract and shall also give as soon as possible in respect of the vessel all the information mentioned in Article 12 (b), (c) and (d).

Article 19. Each High Contracting Party shall give lists of all His minor war vessels and auxiliary vessels with their characteristics, as enumerated in Article 12 (b), and information as to the particular service for which they are intended, so as to reach all the other High Contracting Parties within one month after the date of the coming into force of the present Treaty; and, so as to reach all the other High Contracting Parties within the month of January in each subsequent year, any amendments in the lists and changes in the information.

Article 20. Each of the High Contracting Parties shall communicate to each of the other High Contracting Parties, so as to reach the latter within one month after the date of the coming into force of the present Treaty, particulars, as mentioned in Article 12 (b), of all vessels of the categories or sub-categories mentioned in Article 12 (a), which are then under construction for Him, whether or not such vessels are being constructed within His own jurisdiction, together with similar particulars relating to any such vessels then under construction within His own jurisdiction for a Power not a party to the present Treaty.

Article 21

1. At the time of communicating His initial Annual Programme of construction and declaration of acquisition, each High Contracting Party shall inform each of the other High Contracting Parties of any vessels of the categories or sub-categories mentioned in Article 12 (a), which have been previously authorised and which it is the intention to lay down or acquire during the period covered by the said Programme.

2. Nothing in this Part of the present Treaty shall prevent any High Contracting Party from laying down or acquiring, at any time during the four months following the date of the coming into force of the Treaty, any vessel included, or to be included, in His initial Annual Programme of construction or declaration of acquisition, or previously authorised, provided that the information prescribed by Article 12 (b) concerning each vessel shall be communicated so as to reach all the other High Contracting Parties within one month after the date of the coming into force of the present Treaty.

3. If the present Treaty should not come into force before the 1st May, 1937, the initial Annual Programme of construction and declaration of acquisition, to be communicated under Articles 12 (a) and 14 shall reach all the other High Contracting Parties within one month after the date of the coming into force of the present Treaty.

PART IV: General and Safeguarding Clauses

Article 22. No High Contracting Party shall, by gift, sale or any mode of transfer, dispose of any of His surface vessels of war or submarines in such a manner that such vessel may become a surface vessel of war or a submarine in any foreign navy. This provision shall not apply to auxiliary vessels.

Article 23

1. Nothing in the present Treaty shall prejudice the right of any High Contracting Party, in the event of loss or accidental destruction of a vessel, before the vessel in question has become over-age, to replace such vessel by a vessel of the same category or sub-category as soon as the particulars of the new vessel mentioned in Article 12 (b) shall have reached all the other High Contracting Parties.

2. The provisions of the preceding paragraph shall also govern the immediate replacement, in such circumstances, of a light surface vessel of the sub-category (b) exceeding 8,000 tons (8,128 metric tons) standard displacement, or of a light surface vessel of sub-category (a), before the vessel in question has become over-age, by a light surface vessel of the same sub-category of any standard displacement up to 10,000 tons (10,160 metric tons).

Article 24

1. If any High Contracting Party should become engaged in war, such High Contracting Party may, if He considers the naval requirements of His defence are materially affected, suspend, in so far as He is concerned, any or all of the obligations of the present Treaty, provided that He shall promptly notify the other High Contracting Parties that the circumstances require such suspension, and shall specify the obligations it is considered necessary to suspend.

2. The other High Contracting Parties shall in such case promptly consult together, and shall examine the situation thus presented with a view to agreeing as to the obligations of the present Treaty, if any, which each of the said High Contracting Parties may suspend. Should such consultation not produce agreement, any of the said High Contracting Parties may suspend, in so far as He is concerned, any or all of the obligations of the present Treaty, provided that He shall promptly give notice to the other High Contracting Parties of the obligations which it is considered necessary to suspend.

3. On the cessation of hostilities, the High Contracting Parties shall consult together with a view to fixing a date upon which the obligations of the Treaty which have been suspended shall again become operative, and to agreeing upon any amendments in the present Treaty which may be considered necessary.

Article 25

1. In the event of any vessel not in conformity with the limitations and restrictions as to standard displacement and armament prescribed by Articles 4, 5 and 7 of the present Treaty being authorised, constructed or acquired by a Power not a party to the present Treaty, each High Contracting Party reserves the right to depart if, and to the extent to which, He considers such departures necessary in order to meet the requirements of His national security; (a) during the remaining period of the Treaty, from the limitations and restrictions of Articles 3, 4, 5, 6 (1) and 7, and (b) during the current year, from His Annual Programmes of construction and declarations of acquisition. This right shall be exercised in accordance with the following provisions:

2. Any High Contracting Party who considers it necessary that such right should be exercised, shall notify the other High Contracting Parties to that effect, stating precisely the nature and extent of the proposed departures and the reason therefor.

3. The High Contracting Parties shall thereupon consult together and endeavour to reach an agreement with a view to reducing to a minimum the extent of the departures which may be made.

4. On the expiration of a period of three months from the date of the first of any notifications which may have been given under paragraph (2) above, each of the High Contracting Parties shall, subject to any agreement which may have been reached to the contrary, be entitled to depart during the remaining period of the present Treaty from the limitations and restrictions prescribed in Articles 3, 4, 5, 6 (1) and 7 thereof.

5. On the expiration of the period mentioned in the preceding paragraph, any High Contracting Party shall be at liberty, subject to any agreement which may have been reached during the consultations provided for in paragraph (3) above, and on informing all the other High Contracting Parties, to depart from His Annual Programmes of construction and declarations of acquisition and to alter the characteristics of any vessels building or which have already appeared in His Programmes or declarations.

6. In such event, no delay in the acquisition, the laying of the keel, or the altering of any vessel shall be necessary by reason of any of the provisions of Part III of the present Treaty. The particulars mentioned in Article 12 (b) shall, however, be communicated to all the other High Contracting Parties before the keels of any vessels are laid. In the case of acquisition, information relating to the vessel shall be given under the provisions of Article 14.

Article 26

1. If the requirements of the national security of any High Contracting Party should, in His opinion, be materially affected by any change of circumstances, other than those provided for in Articles 6 (2), 24 and 25 of the present Treaty, such High Contracting Party shall have the right to depart for the current year from His Annual Programmes of construction and declarations of acquisition. The amount of construction by any Party to the Treaty, within the limitations and restrictions thereof shall not, however, constitute a change of circumstances for the purposes of the present Article. The above mentioned right shall be exercised in accordance with the following provisions:

2. Such High Contracting Party shall, if He desires to exercise the above mentioned right, notify all the other High Contracting Parties to that effect, stating in what respects He proposes to depart from His Annual Programmes of construction and declarations of acquisition, giving reasons for the proposed departure.

3. The High Contracting Parties will thereupon consult together with a view to agreement as to whether any departures are necessary in order to meet the situation.

4. On the expiration of a period of three months from the date of the first of any notifications which may have been given under paragraph (2) above, each of the High Contracting Parties shall, subject to any agreement which may have been reached to the contrary, be entitled to depart from His Annual Programmes of construction and declarations of acquisition, provided notice is promptly given to the other High Contracting Parties stating precisely in what respects He proposes so to depart.

5. In such event, no delay in the acquisition, the laying of the keel, or the altering of any vessel shall be necessary by reason of any of the provisions of Part III of the present Treaty. The particulars mentioned in Article 12 (b) shall, however, be communicated to all the other High Contracting Parties before the keels of any vessels are laid. In the case of acquisition, information relating to the vessel shall be given under the provisions of Article 14.

PART V: Final Clauses

Article 27. The present Treaty shall remain in Force until the 31st December, 1942.

Article 28

1. His Majesty's Government in the United Kingdom of Great Britain and Northern Ireland will, during the last quarter of 1940, initiate through the diplomatic channel a consultation between the Governments of the Parties to the present Treaty with a view to holding a conference in order to frame a new treaty for the reduction and limitation of naval armament. This conference shall take place in 1941 unless the preliminary consultations should have shown that the holding of such a conference at that time would not be desirable or practicable.

2. In the course of the consultation referred to in the preceding paragraph, views shall be exchanged in order to determine whether, in the light of the circumstances then prevailing and the experience gained in the interval in the design and construction of capital ships, it may be possible to agree upon a reduction in the standard displacement or calibre of guns of capital ships to be constructed under future annual programmes and thus, if possible, to bring about a reduction in the cost of capital ships.

Article 29. None of the provisions of the present Treaty shall constitute a precedent for any future treaty.

Article 30

1. The present Treaty shall be ratified by the Signatory Powers in accordance with their respective constitutional methods, and the instruments of ratification shall be deposited as soon as possible with His Majesty's Government in the United Kingdom, which will transmit certified copies of all the *procès-verbaux* of the deposits of ratifications to the Governments of the said Powers and of any country on behalf of which accession has been made in accordance with the provisions of Article 31.

2. The Treaty shall come into force on the 1st January, 1937, provided that by that date the instruments of ratification of all the said Powers shall have been deposited. If all the above-mentioned instruments of ratification have not been deposited by the 1st January, 1937, the Treaty shall come into force so soon thereafter as these are all received.

[Provisions for the accession of other parties]
[Signatures]

[U.S. Department of State, *The London Naval Conference, 1935* (Washington, D.C.: G.P.O., 1936), pp. 28ff]

Other Interwar Treaties

Central American Arms Limitation Treaty (1923)

This convention went into force on 24 November 1924.

Convention on the Limitation of Armaments of Central American States, Washington, D.C., 7 February 1923

The Governments of the Republics of Guatemala, El Salvador, Honduras, Nicaragua, and Costa Rica having signed on this date a General Treaty of Peace and Amity. . . .

Article 1. The Contracting Parties having taken into consideration their relative population, area, extent of frontiers and various other factors of military importance, agree that for a period of five years from the date of the coming into force of the present Convention, they shall not maintain a standing Army and National Guard in excess of the number of men hereinafter provided, except in case of civil war, or impending invasion by another State.

Guatemala	5,200
El Salvador	4,200
Honduras	2,500
Nicaragua	2,500
Costa Rica	2,000

General officers and officers of a lower rank of the standing Army, who are necessary in accordance with the military regulations of each country, are not included in the provisions of this Article, nor are those of the National Guard. The Police Force is also not included.

Article 2. As the first duty of armed forces of the Central American Governments is to preserve public order, each of the Contracting Parties obligates itself to establish a National Guard to cooperate with the existing Armies in the preservation of order in the various districts of the country and on the frontiers, and shall immediately consider the best means for establishing it. With this end in view the Governments of the Central American States shall give consideration to the employment of suitable instructors, in order to take advantage, in this manner, of experience acquired in other countries in organizing such corps.

In no case shall the total combined force of the Army and of the National Guard exceed the maximum limit fixed in the preceeding Article, except in the cases therein provided.

Article 3. The Contracting Parties undertake not to export or permit the exportation of arms or munitions or any other kind of military stores from one Central American country to another.

Article 4. None of the Contracting Parties shall have the right to possess more than ten war aircraft. Neither may any of them acquire war vessels; but armed coast guard boats shall not be considered as war vessels.

The following cases shall be considered as exceptions to this Article: civil war or threatened attack by a foreign state; in such cases the right of defence shall have no other limitations than those established by existing Treaties.

Article 5. The Contracting Parties consider that the use in warfare of asphyxiating gases, poisons, or similar substances as well as analogous liquids, materials or devices, is contrary to humanitarian principles and to international law, and obligate themselves by the present Convention not to use said substances in time of war.

Article 6. Six months after the coming into force of the present Convention each of the Contracting Governments shall submit to the other Central American Governments a complete report on the measures adopted by said Government for the execution of this Convention. Similar reports shall be submitted semiannually, during the aforesaid period of the five years. The reports shall include the units of the army, if any, and of the National Guard; and any other information which the Parties shall sanction.

Article 7. The present Convention shall take effect with respect to the Parties that have ratified it, from the date of its ratification by at least four of the signatory States.

Article 8. The present Convention shall remain in force until the first of January, one thousand nine hundred and twenty-nine, notwithstanding any prior denunciation, or any other cause. After the first of January, one thousand nine hundred and twenty-nine, it shall continue in force until one year after the date on which one of the Parties bound thereby notifies the others of its intention to denounce it. The denunciation of this Convention by any of said Parties shall leave it in force for those Parties which have ratified it and have not denounced it, provided that these be not less than four in number. Any of the Republics of Central America which should fail to ratify this Convention, shall have the right to adhere to it while it is in force.

[Ratification]

[Signatures]

[U.S. Library of Congress, Legislative Reference Service, *Disarmament and Security: A Collection of Documents, 1919–55,* Washington, D.C., 1956), Doc. 5]

Turko-Greek Naval Protocol (1930)

This agreement was part of a general settlement that sought to improve relations between the two nations—relations that had been badly strained during World War I and in its aftermath.

Protocol to Treaty Between Greece and Turkey, Signed at Ankara, 30 October 1930

The two High Contracting Parties, inspired by the principles which have led them to sign the Convention of Friendship and Arbitration of to-day's date, and desirous of preventing any unnecessary increase in their expenditure on naval armaments and of keeping peace with one another in the limitation of their respective forces, with due regard to the conditions particular to each of the said States, undertake to effect no order, acquisition or construction of war units or armaments, without having notified the other Party six months previously, so that both Governments may thus be enabled if necessary to prevent any competition in the sphere of naval armaments by means of a friendly exchange of views and of explanations on either side in a spirit of perfect sincerity.

[League of Nations, *Treaty Series*, vol. 125 (1931–1932), p. 21]

Turko-Soviet Naval Protocol (1931)

Protocol Supplementing Article II of the Protocol of 17 December 1929, with Protocol of Signature, 7 March 1931

The two High Contracting Parties, basing their action on the essential principles contained in the Treaty of December 17, 1925, and in the Protocol of December 17, 1929, being desirous of strengthening the peaceful and friendly relations between them, being firmly convinced that the only reliable guarantee of permanent peace is the effective reduction of all kinds of existing armaments and manifesting their inflexible desire to pursue in the future also their efforts to bring about a universal reduction of armaments, have considered it desirable, in order to give a fresh proof of the mutual confidence so happily established between the two countries, to supplement Article II of the Protocol of December 17, 1929 by the following reciprocal undertaking:

Neither of the High Contracting Parties shall proceed to lay down any naval fighting unit whatsoever for the purpose of strengthening its fleet in the Black Sea or in neighboring seas, or to place orders for any such unit in foreign shipyards, or to take any other measure the effect of which would be to increase the present strength of its war fleet in the above-mentioned seas, without having notified the second Contracting Party six months previously.

The present Supplementary Protocol shall be ratified and shall become from this moment an integral part of the Protocol of December 17, 1929.
[Leonard Shapiro, ed., *Soviet Treaty Series,* vol. 2, 1929–1939 (Washington, D.C.: Georgetown University Press, 1955), Doc. No. 347]

German Disarmament and Rearmament (1945–1954)

The Berlin (Potsdam) Protocol (1 August 1945)

One of the results of the "Big Three" meeting—Great Britain, the United States, and the Soviet Union—at Potsdam from 17 July to 2 August 1945 was an outline for the disarming of Germany.

II. THE PRINCIPLES TO GOVERN THE TREATMENT OF GERMANY IN THE INITIAL CONTROL PERIOD

A. POLITICAL PRINCIPLES

1. In accordance with the Agreement on Control Machinery in Germany, supreme authority in Germany is exercised, on instructions from their respective Governments, by the Commanders-in-Chief of the armed forces of the United States of America, the United Kingdom, the Union of Soviet Socialist Republics, and the French Republic, each in his own zone of occupation, and also jointly, in matters affecting Germany as a whole, in their capacity as members of the Control Council.

2. So far as is practicable, there shall be uniformity of treatment of the German population throughout Germany.

3. The purposes of the occupation of Germany by which the Control Council shall be guided are:

(i) The complete disarmament and demilitarization of Germany and the elimination or control of all German industry that could be used for military production. To these ends:

(a) All German land, naval and air forces, The S.S., S.A., S.D., and Gestapo, with all their organizations, staffs, and institutions, including the General Staff, the Officers' Corps, Reserve Corps, military schools, war veterans' organizations and all other military or semi-military organizations together with all clubs and associations which serve to keep alive the military tradition in Germany, shall be completely and finally abolished in such manner as permanently to prevent the revival or reorganization of German militarism and Nazism;

(b) All arms, ammunition and implements of war and all specialized facilities for their production shall be held at the disposal of the Allies or destroyed. The maintenance and production of all aircraft and all arms, ammunition and implements of war shall be prevented.

(ii) To convince the German people that they have suffered a total military defeat and that they cannot escape responsibility for what they have brought upon themselves, since their own ruthless warfare and the fanatical Nazi resistance have destroyed German economy and made chaos and suffering inevitable.

(iii) To destroy the National Socialist Party and its affiliated and supervised organizations, to dissolve all Nazi institutions, to ensure that they are not revived in any form, and to prevent all Nazi and militarist activity or propaganda.

[U.S. Department of State Press Release No. 238, 24 March 1947]

Declaration Regarding the Defeat of Germany and the Assumption of Supreme Authority with Respect to Germany (5 June 1945)

The German armed forces on land, at sea and in the air have been completely defeated and have surrendered unconditionally and Germany, which bears the responsibility for the war, is no longer capable of resisting the will of the victorious Powers. The unconditional surrender of Germany has thereby been effected, and Germany has become subject to such requirements as may now or hereafter be imposed upon her.

There is no central Government or authority in Germany capable of accepting responsibility for the maintenance of order, the administration of the country and compliance with the requirements of the victorious Powers.

It is in these circumstances necessary, without prejudice to any subsequent decisions that may be taken respecting Germany, to make provision for the cessation of any further hostilities on the part of the German armed forces, for the maintenance of order in Germany and for the administration of the country, and to announce the immediate requirements with which Germany must comply....

In virtue of the supreme authority and powers thus assumed by the four Governments, the Allied Representatives announce the following requirements arising from the complete defeat and unconditional surrender of Germany with which Germany must comply:

Article 1. Germany and all German military, naval and air authorities and all forces under German control shall immediately cease hostilities in all theatres of war against the forces of the United Nations on land, at sea and in the air.

Article 2

(a) All armed forces of Germany or under German control, wherever they may be situated, including land, air, anti-aircraft and naval forces, the SS, SA and Gestapo, and all other forces or auxiliary organisations equipped with weapons, shall be completely disarmed, handing over their weapons and equipment to local Allied Commanders or to officers designated by the Allied Representatives.

(b) The personnel of the formations and units of all the forces referred to in paragraph (a) above shall, at the discretion of the Commander-in-Chief of the Armed Forces of the Allied State concerned, be declared to be prisoners of war, pending further decisions, and shall be subject to such conditions and directions as may be prescribed by the respective Allied Representatives.

(c) All forces referred to in paragraph (a) above, wherever they may be, will remain in their present positions pending instruction from the Allied Representatives.

(d) Evacuation by the said forces of all territories outside the frontiers of Germany as they existed on the 31st December, 1937, will proceed according to instructions to be given by the Allied Representatives.

(e) Detachments of civil police to be armed with small arms only, for the maintenance of order and for guard duties, will be designated by the Allied Representatives.

Article 3

(a) All aircraft of any kind or nationality in Germany or German-occupied or controlled territories or waters, military, naval or civil, other than aircraft in the service of the Allies, will remain on the ground, on the water or aboard ships pending further instructions.

(b) All German or German-controlled aircraft in or over territories or waters not occupied or controlled by Germany will proceed to Germany or to such place or places as may be specified by the Allied Representatives.

Article 4

(a) All German or German-controlled naval vessels, surface and submarine, auxiliary naval craft, and merchant and other shipping, wherever such vessels may be at the time of this Declaration, and all other merchant ships of whatever nationality in German ports, will remain in or proceed immediately to ports and bases as specified by the Allied Representatives. The crews of such vessels will remain on board pending further instructions.

(b) All ships and vessels of the United Nations, whether or not title has been transferred as the result of prize court or other proceedings, which are at the disposal of Germany or under German control at the time of this Declaration, will proceed at the dates and to the ports or bases specified by the Allied Representatives.

Article 5

(a) All or any of the following articles in the possession of the German armed forces or under German control or at German disposal will be held intact and in good condition at the disposal of the Allied Representatives, for such purposes and at such times and places as they may prescribe:

(i) all arms, ammunition, explosives, military equipment, stores and supplies and other implements of war of all kinds and all other war material;

(ii) all naval vessels of all classes, both surface and submarine, auxiliary naval craft and all merchant shipping, whether afloat, under repair or construction, built or building;

(iii) all aircraft of all kinds, aviation and anti-aircraft equipment devices;

(iv) all transportation and communications facilities and equipment by land, water or air;

(v) all military installations and establishments, including airfields, seaplane bases, ports and naval bases, storage depots, permanent and temporary land and coast fortifications, fortresses and other fortified areas, together with plans and drawings of all such fortifications, installations and establishments;

(vi) all factories, plants, shops, research institutions, laboratories, testing stations, technical data, patents, plans, drawings and inventions, designed or intended to produce or to facilitate the production or use of the articles, materials and facilities referred to in sub-paragraphs (i), (ii), (iii), (iv) and (v) above or otherwise to further the conduct of war.

(b) At the demand of the Allied Representatives the following will be furnished: (i) the labour, services and plant required for the maintenance or operation of any of the six categories mentioned in paragraph (a) above; and (ii) any information or records that may be required by the Allied Representatives in connection with the same.

(c) At the demand of the Allied Representatives all facilities will be provided for the movement of Allied troops and agencies, their equipment and supplies, on the railways, roads and other land communications or by sea, river or air. All means of transportation will be maintained in good order and repair, and the labour, services and plant necessary therefor will be furnished.

Article 6

(a) The German authorities will release to the Allied Representatives, in accordance with the procedure to be laid down by them, all prisoners of war at present in their power, belonging to the forces of the United Nations, and will furnish full lists of these persons, indicating the places of their detention in Germany or territory occupied by Germany. Pending the release of such prisoners of war, the German authorities and people will protect them in their persons and property and provide them with adequate food, clothing, shelter, medical attention and money in accordance with their rank or official position.

(b) The German authorities and people will in like manner provide for and release all other nationals of the United Nations who are confined, interned or otherwise under restraint, and all other persons who may be confined, interned or otherwise under restraint for political reasons or as a result of any Nazi action, law or regulation which discriminates on the ground of race, colour, creed or political belief.

(c) The German authorities will, at the demand of the Allied Representatives, hand over control of places of detention to such officers as may be designated for the purpose by the Allied Representatives.

Article 7. The German authorities concerned will furnish to the Allied Representatives:

(a) full information regarding the forces referred to in Article 2 (a), and, in particular, will furnish forthwith all information which the Allied Representatives may require concerning the numbers, locations and dispositions of such forces, whether located inside or outside Germany;

(b) complete and detailed information concerning mines, minefields and other obstacles to movement by land, sea or air, and the safety lanes in connection therewith. All such safety lanes will be kept open and clearly marked; all mines, minefields and other dangerous obstacles will as far as possible be rendered safe, and all aids to navigation will be reinstated. Unarmed German military and civilian personnel with the necessary equipment will be made available and utilised for the above purposes and for the removal of mines, minefields and other obstacles as directed by the Allied Representatives.

Article 8. There shall be no destruction, removal, concealment, transfer or scuttling of, or damage to, any military, naval, air, shipping, port, industrial and other like property and facilities and all records and archives, wherever they may be situated, except as may be directed by the Allied Representatives.

Article 9. Pending the institution of control by the Allied Representatives over all means of communication, all radio and telecommunication installations and other forms of wire or wireless communications, whether ashore or afloat, under German control, will cease transmission except as directed by the Allied Representatives.

Article 10. The forces, ships, aircraft, military equipment, and other property in Germany or in German control or service or at German disposal, of any other country at war with any of the Allies, will be subject to the provisions of this Declaration and of any proclamations, orders, ordinances or instructions issued thereunder.

Article 11

(a) The principal Nazi leaders as specified by the Allied Representatives, and all persons from time to time named or designated by rank, office or employment by the Allied Representatives as being suspected of having committed, ordered or abetted war crimes or analogous offences, will be apprehended and surrendered to the Allied Representatives.

(b) The same will apply in the case of any national of any of the United Nations who is alleged to have committed an offence against his national law, and who may at any time be named or designated by rank, office or employment by the Allied Representatives.

(c) The German authorities and people will comply with any instructions given by the Allied Representatives for the apprehension and surrender of such persons.

Article 12. The Allied Representatives will station forces and civil agencies in any or all parts of Germany as they may determine.

Article 13

(a) In the exercise of the supreme authority with respect to Germany assumed by the Governments of the United Kingdom, the United States of America and the Union of Soviet Socialist Republics, and the Provisional Government of the French Republic, the four Allied governments will take such steps, including the complete disarmament an demilitarisation of Germany, as they deem requisite for future peace and security.

(b) The Allied Representatives will impose on Germany additional political, administrative, economic, financial, military and other requirements arising from the complete defeat of Germany. The Allied Representatives, or persons or agencies duly designated to act on their authority, will issue proclamations, orders, ordinances and instructions for the purpose of laying down such additional requirements, and of giving effect to the other provisions of this Declaration. All German authorities and the German people shall carry out unconditionally the requirements of the Allied Representatives, and shall fully comply with all such proclamations, orders, ordinances and instructions.

Article 14. This Declaration enters into force and effect at the date and hour set forth below. In the event of failure on the part of the German authorities or people promptly and completely to fulfil their obligations hereby or hereafter imposed, the Allied Representatives will take whatever action may be deemed by them to be appropriate under the circumstances.

[Signatures]

[Beate Ruhm von Oppen, ed., *Documents on Germany Under Occupation, 1945–1954* (Oxford, 1955), pp. 29–34]

Communiqué Issued at the London Six Power Conference on German Problems (7 June 1948)

V. SECURITY

This problem was considered in three aspects: (A) General Provisions. (B) Measures during the period in which the occupying powers retain supreme authority in Germany. (C) Measures after the period in which the occupying powers retain supreme authority in Germany.

GENERAL PROVISIONS

The United States, United Kingdom and French Delegates reiterated the firm views of their governments that there could not be any general withdrawal of their forces from Germany until the peace of Europe is secured and without prior consultation. During this period there should be no general withdrawal of the forces of occupation of the United States, France or the United Kingdom without prior consultation. It was further recommended that the governments concerned should consult if any of them should consider that there was a danger of resurgence of German military power or of the adoption by Germany of a policy of aggression.

MEASURES DURING THE PERIOD IN WHICH
THE OCCUPYING POWERS RETAIN SUPREME
AUTHORITY IN GERMANY

The prohibitions on the German armed forces and the German General Staff as contained in 4-power agreements were reaffirmed, as well as the exercise of controls by the military governors with respect to disarmament and demilitarization, level of industry and certain aspects of scientific research. To ensure the maintenance of disarmament and demilitarization in the interests of security, the three military governors should set up a military security board in the western zones of Germany to carry out the proper inspections and make the necessary recommendations to the military governors, who decide the action to be taken.

MEASURES AFTER THE PERIOD IN WHICH
THE OCCUPYING POWERS RETAIN SUPREME
AUTHORITY IN GERMANY

It was affirmed that Germany must not again be permitted to become an aggressive power and that prior to the general withdrawal of the forces of occupation agreement will be reached among the governments concerned with respect to necessary measures of demilitarization, disarmament and control of industry and with respect to occupation of key areas. Also there should be a system of inspection to ensure the maintenance of the agreed provisions of German disarmament and demilitarization.

The present recommendations, which in no way preclude and on the contrary should facilitate eventual 4-power agreement on the German problem are designed to solve the urgent political and economic problems arising out of the present situation in Germany. Because of the previous failure to reach comprehensive 4-power decisions on Germany, the measures recommended mark a step forward in the policy which the powers represented at these talks are determined to follow with respect to the economic reconstruction of western Europe, including Germany, and with respect to the establishment of a basis for the participation of a democratic Germany in the community of free peoples. [U.S. Department of State Bulletin, vol. 18, p. 807]

Directive on the Organization of the Military Security Board for the Western Zones of Germany (17 January 1949)

PART I. TERMS OF REFERENCE

1. In accordance with the terms of the London Agreement, a Military Security Board for the Western Zones of Germany will be set up by the Military Governors in order to ensure the maintenance of disarmament and demilitarization in the interests of security.

2. The Board's responsibilities will cover the whole field of disarmament and demilitarization, taking into consideration the laws and directives which have been agreed already on a quadripartite basis. In particular the Board will advise the Military Governors on the maintenance and enforcement of disarmament and demilitarization restrictions. It will carry out the appropriate inspections and will

recommend to the Military Governors measures necessary to:

(a) prevent the revival of military or para-military organizations of the militaristic spirit;

(b) ensure that there shall be no manufacture or import of any arms, war materials or any other materials or equipment which are or may be prohibited:

(c) prevent the infringement by Germans of restrictions in respect of certain industries;

(d) ensure that any military buildings, structures, laboratories, and all shipyards, or factories capable of producing armaments which may be retained are used for peaceful purposes only;

(e) ensure that scientific research is not directed to warlike ends;

(f) ensure that in connection with the construction and operation of merchant shipping and the operation of civil airlines, no war potential is created.

3. In carrying out its task, the Board will:

(a) Study the existing laws and directives, both quadripartite and zonal, and make recommendations if they require additions or amendments, and where advisable produce uniformity throughout the three zones;

(b) Recommend to the Military Governors any laws or regulations to be enacted which may be necessary for the completion of disarmament, or for the prohibition or limitation of specified military, industrial, scientific research or other activities;

(c) Ensure the implementation of the regulations by inspection and ensure that the statistics necessary for the Board are maintained by Germans. The reports of inspections will be presented to the Military Governors, together with the observations of the Board;

(d) Advise the Military Governors on revisions, which may be necessary from time to time, of the prohibitions of and limitations on capacity or production imposed upon German industry;

(e) Collect, centralize and keep up to date full documentation on the elements which might reconstitute a war potential in the military, industrial and scientific fields.

PART II. CONSTITUTION AND FUNCTIONING

4. *The Military Security Board will be made up of the following elements:*

(a) A Commission

(b) A Committee of Deputies

(c) A Secretariat

(d) Three Divisions: Military, Industrial and Scientific Research

(e) Inspection Groups.

5. *Security in the Ruhr.* The Board will establish such machinery and liaison for co-operation with the International Authority for the Ruhr as may be found necessary....

10. *Inspection Groups.*

(a) The Divisions will organize, instruct and dispatch inspectors and/or integrated tripartite inspection groups formed from personnel assigned or attached to the Board as often as necessary in order to verify in the three Zones the conditions of execution of the measures ordered by the Military Governors. The Commission may order any special inspections it deems necessary.

(b) Administrative arrangements for these inspections will be made by the Secretariat.

(c) Inspection groups shall have free access at any time to inspect without prior notice for the purposes set forth in paragraph 2 hereof, any place, installation or activity, except that the local Military Government shall be given reasonable advance notice of such intended visits.

[U.S. Department of State Bulletin, vol. 20, p. 195]

Agreement Between the Governments of the United States, France, and the United Kingdom on Prohibited and Limited Industries in the Western Zones of Germany (13 April 1949)

Pursuant to instructions received from their respective governments to conclude the agreement hereinafter set forth, concerning prohibited and limited industries in the United States, United Kingdom and French Occupied Areas of Germany (hereinafter referred to for the purposes of this Agreement as Germany), the United States, United Kingdom and French Military Governors and Commanders-in-Chief hereby promulgate the following agreement, effective forthwith:

Article I. The prohibitions laid down in this Agreement shall remain in force until the peace settlement.

The limitations laid down in this Agreement shall remain in force until 1st January, 1953, or until the peace settlement, whichever is the earlier, and thereafter as may be agreed.

Should no peace settlement have been concluded by 30th June, 1952, the Military Governors shall forthwith review these limitations in the light of the conditions then prevailing, taking into account the requirements of security of the Allied Powers, the state and effectiveness of the arrangements made to preserve security, and the requirements of European Recovery. Should the Military Governors be unable within 90 days from 30th June, 1952, to reach agreement on the limitations which in the absence of an earlier peace settlement shall be considered after 1st January 1953, the matter shall be considered forthwith by the three Governments.

ANNEX A
SCHEDULE A TO CONTROL
COUNCIL LAW NO. 43

Group I
(a) All weapons including atomic means of warfare or apparatus of all callibres and natures capable of projecting lethal or destructive projectiles, liquids, gasses, or toxic substances, their carriages and mountings.

(b) All projectiles for the above and their means of projection or propulsion. Examples of means of propulsion are cartridges, charges etc.

(c) All military means of destruction such as grenades, bombs, torpedoes, mines, depth mines, depth and demolition charges and self-propelled charges.

(d) All military cutting or piercing weapons (in French: white arms) (in Russian: cold arms), such as bayonets, swords, daggers, and lances.

Group II
(a) All vehicles specially equipped or designed for military purposes such as tanks, armoured cars, tank-carrying trailers, armoured railway rolling stock, etc.

(b) Armour of all types for military purposes.

(c) Harness specially designed for military purposes.

Group III
(a) (i) Range-finding apparatus of all kinds for military purposes; (ii) Aiming, guiding, and computing devices for fire control; (iii) Locating devices of all kinds (particularly all devices for radio direction finding and all devices for radio detention); (iv) Instruments for assisting observations of fire or for the remote control of all moving objects.

(b) All signalling and inter-communication equipment and installations specially designed for war purposes; all apparatus for radio interference.

(c) Searchlights with mirror diameter of more than 45 cms.

(d) Optical instruments of all kinds specially designed or intended for war purposes.

(e) Survey and cartographic equipment and instruments of all kinds specially designed for war purposes. Military maps and equipment for using them.

(f) Military engineering tools, machinery and equipment such as special bridging materials.

(g) Personal military equipment and uniforms, and military insignia and decorations.

(h) Cryptographic machines and devices used for cipher purposes.

(i) All camouflage and dazzle devices. Any of the materials listed in Group III, except for electronic devices such as radar, radiogoniometric and similar equipment, that have a normal peacetime use and are not specially designed for military use, are excluded from the provisions of paragraph 1, Article I of the Law.

Group IV

(a) Warships of all classes. All ships and floating equipment specially designed for servicing warships. All ships with characteristics exceeding those required for normal peacetime uses, or designed or constructed for conversion into warships or for military use.

(b) Special machinery, equipment and installations which in time of peace are normally used solely in warships.

(c) Submersible craft of all kinds; submersible devices of all kinds, designed for military purposes. Special equipment pertaining to these craft and devices.

(d) All military and landing devices.

(e) Material, equipment and installations for the military defense of coasts, harbours, etc.

Group V

(a) Aircraft of all types, heavier or lighter than air; with or without means of propulsion, including kites, captive balloons, gliders and model aircraft, and all auxiliary equipment, including aircraft engines and component parts accessories, and spare parts specifically designed for aircraft use.

(b) Ground equipment for servicing, testing or aiding the operation of aircraft, such as catapults, winches and beacons; material for the rapid preparation of airfields such as landing mats; special equipment used in conjunction with air photography; excluding however, from the provisions of paragraph 1, Article I of this Law any such equipment and materials for landing fields and air beacons that have a normal peacetime use and are not specifically designed for military use as listed in Schedule B.

Group VI. All drawings, specifications, designs, models and reproductions directly relating to the development, manufacture, testing, or inspection of the war material, or to experiments or research in connection with war material.

Group VII. Machinery and other manufacturing equipment and tooling used for the development, manufacture, testing or inspection of the war material defined in this Schedule, and not capable of conversion to peacetime production.

Group VIII

(a) The following War Chemicals:

- High explosives with the exception of those listed in Schedule B, Group VIIa. (NOTE: By "high explosives" is meant organic explosives used as fillings for shells, bombs, etc.)
- Double-base propellants (i.e. Nitrocellulose propellants containing nitroglycerine, diethyleneglycol dinitrate or analogous substance).
- Single-base propellants for any weapons except sporting weapons.
- Nitroguanidine Poison war gasses (including liquids and solids customarily included in this term) with the exception of those listed in Group IIb of Schedule B.
- Rocket fuels: hydrogen peroxide of above 37% concentration; hydrazine hydrate; methyl nitrate.
- Highly toxic products from bacteriological or plant sources (with the exception of those bacteriological and plant products which are used for therapeutic purposes).

(b) All special means for individual and collective defense used in peace exclusively by the armed forces, such as protective masks against toxic or lethal devices used for war, detection apparatus etc.

Group IX. All apparatus, devices, and material specially designed for training and instructing personnel in the use, and handling, manufacture or maintenance of war material.

[U.S. Library of Congress, Legislative Reference Service, *Disarmament and Security: A Collection of Documents, 1919–55* (Washington, D.C., 1956), Doc. 117]

Protocols to the Brussels Treaty (23 October 1954)

Protocol No. 1 Modifying and Completing the Brussels Treaty

Article I. The Federal Republic of Germany and the Italian Republic hereby accede to the Treaty as modified and completed by the present Protocol.

The High Contracting Parties to the present Protocol consider the Protocol on Forces of Western European Union (hereinafter referred to as Protocol No. II), the Protocol on the Control of Armaments and its Annexes (hereinafter referred to as Protocol No. III), and the Protocol on the Agency of Western European Union for the Control of Armaments (hereinafter referred to as Protocol No. IV) to be an integral part of the present Protocol.

Article II. The sub-paragraph of the Preamble to the Treaty: "to take such steps as may be held necessary in the event of renewal by Germany of a policy of aggression" shall be modified to read: "To promote the unity and to encourage the progressive integration of Europe."

The opening words of the 2nd paragraph of Article I shall read: "The co-operation provided for in the preceding paragraph, which will be effected through the Council referred to in Article VII."

Article III. The following new Article shall be inserted in the Treaty as Article IV:

In the execution of the Treaty the High Contracting Parties and any organs established by Them under the Treaty shall work in close co-operation with the North Atlantic Treaty Organization.

Recognizing the undesirability of duplicating the Military Staffs of NATO, the Council and its agency will rely on the appropriate Military Authorities of NATO for information and advice on military matters.

Articles IV, V, VI and VII of the Treaty will become respectively Articles V, VI, VII and VIII.

ANNEX I

The Federal Chancellor declares:

that the Federal Republic undertakes not to manufacture in its territory any atomic weapons, chemical weapons or biological weapons, as detailed in paragraphs I, II, and III of the attached list [reproduced in Annex II];

that it undertakes further not to manufacture in its territory such weapons as those detailed in paragraphs IV, V, and VI of the attached list [reproduced in Annex III]. Any amendment to or cancellation of the substance of paragraphs IV, V and VI can, on the request of the Federal Republic, be carried out by a two-thirds majority, if in accordance with the needs of the armed forces a request is made by the competent Supreme Commander of the North Atlantic Treaty Organization;

that the Federal Republic agrees to supervision by the competent authority of the Brussels Treaty Organization to ensure that these undertakings are observed.

ANNEX II

This list comprises the weapons defined in paragraphs I to III and the factories earmarked solely for their production. All apparatus, parts, equipment, installations, substances and organisms, which are used for civilian purposes or for scientific, medical and industrial research in the fields of pure and applied science shall be excluded from this definition.

I. Atomic Weapons

(a) An atomic weapon is defined as any weapon which contains, or is designed to contain or utilize, nuclear fuel or radioactive isotopes and which, by explosion or other uncontrolled nuclear transformation of the nuclear fuel, or by radioactivity of the nuclear fuel or radioactive isotopes, is capable of mass destruction, mass injury or mass poisoning.

(b) Furthermore, any part, device, assembly or material especially designed for, or primarily useful in, any weapon as set forth under paragraph (a), shall be deemed to be an atomic weapon.

(c) Nuclear fuel as used in the preceding definition includes plutonium, Uranium 233, Uranium 235 (including Uranium 235 contained in Uranium enriched to over 2.1 per cent. by weight of Uranium 235) and any other material capable of releasing substantial quantities of atomic energy through nuclear fission or fusion or other nuclear reaction of the material. The foregoing materials shall be considered to be nuclear fuel regardless of the chemical or physical form in which they exist.

II. Chemical Weapons

(a) A chemical weapon is defined as any equipment or apparatus expressly designed to use, for military purposes, the asphyxiating, toxic, irritant paralysant, growth-regulating, anti-lubricating or catalysing properties of any chemical substance.

(b) Subject to the provisions of paragraph (c), chemical substances, having such properties and capable of being used in the equipment or apparatus referred to in paragraph (a), shall be deemed to be included in this definition.

(c) Such apparatus and such quantities of the chemical substances as are referred to in paragraphs (a) and (b) which do not exceed peaceful civilian requirements shall be deemed to be excluded from this definition.

III. Biological Weapons

(a) A biological weapon is defined as any equipment or apparatus expressly designed to use, for military purposes, harmful insects or other living or dead organisms, or their toxic products.

(b) Subject to the provisions of paragraph (c), insects, organisms and their toxic products of such nature and in such amounts as to make them capable of being used in the equipment or apparatus referred to in (a) shall be deemed to be included in this definition.

(c) Such equipment or apparatus and such quantities of the insects, organisms and their toxic products as are referred to in paragraphs (a) and (b) which do not exceed peaceful civilian requirements shall be deemed to be excluded from the definition of biological weapons.

ANNEX III

This list comprises the weapons defined in paragraphs IV to VI and the factories earmarked solely for their production. All apparatus, parts, equipment, installations, substances and organisms, which are used for civilian purposes or for scientific, medical and industrial research in the fields of pure and applied science shall be excluded from this definition.

[U.S. Library of Congress, Legislative Reference Service, *Disarmament and Security: A Collection of Documents, 1919–55* (Washington, D.C., 1956), Doc. 121]

Joint Declaration of the Federal Republic of Germany and of the German Democratic Republic on Non-Proliferation of Nuclear, Chemical and Biological Weapons (22 August 1990)

This declaration was delivered at the Fourth Non-Proliferation Treaty Review Conference, 22 August 1990.

The Governments of the Federal Republic of Germany and the German Democratic Republic reaffirm their contractual and unilateral undertaking not to manufacture, possess or have control over nuclear, biological and chemical weapons. They declare that the united Germany, too, will abide by its obligations.

Rights and obligations under the instruments of the Treaty of 1 July 1968 on the Non-Proliferation of Nuclear Weapons will continue to apply to the united Germany. The united Germany will seek the continued validity of the Non-Proliferation Treaty beyond 1995 and supports the strengthening of the non-proliferation régime.

At the Geneva Conference on Disarmament, the united Germany will strive for a comprehensive, worldwide and verifiable ban on chemical weapons at the earliest possible date and intends to be one of the original signatories of the convention.

[United Nations, *Disarmament* 14:1 (1991):219]

World War II Treaties and Arms Limitations

Italian Peace Treaty (1947)

Treaty texts for other defeated Axis nations are similar, for example the Bulgarian Peace Treaty (1947), Finnish Peace Treaty (1947), Hungarian Peace Treaty (1947), and Romanian Peace Treaty (1947), all of which are reprinted in Disarmament and Security: A Collection of Documents, 1919–55 (Washington, D.C., 1956).

Treaty of Peace with Italy, 10 February 1947

PART IV. NAVAL, MILITARY, AND AIR CLAUSES

SECTION I. DURATION OF APPLICATION

Article 46. Each of the military, naval and air clauses of the present Treaty shall remain in force until modified in whole or in part by agreement between the Allied and Associated Powers and Italy or, after Italy becomes a member of the United Nations, by agreement between the Security Council and Italy.

SECTION II. GENERAL LIMITATIONS

Article 47

1. (a) The system of permanent Italian fortifications and military installations along the Franco-Italian frontier, and their armaments, shall be destroyed or removed.

(b) This system is deemed to comprise only artillery and infantry fortifications whether in groups or separated, pillboxes of any type, protected accommodation for personnel, stores and ammunition, observation posts and military cableways, whatever may be their importance and actual condition of maintenance or state of construction, which are constructed of metal, masonry or concrete or excavated in the rock.

2. The destruction or removal, mentioned in paragraph 1 above, is limited to a distance of 20 kilometers from any point on the frontier as defined by the present Treaty, and shall be completed within one year from the coming into force of the Treaty.

3. Any reconstruction of the above-mentioned fortifications and installations is prohibited.

4. (a) The following construction to the east of the Franco-Italian frontier is prohibited: permanent fortifications where weapons capable of firing into French territory or territorial waters can be emplaced; permanent military installations capable of being used to conduct or direct fire into French territory or territorial waters; and permanent supply and storage facilities emplaced solely for the use of the above-mentioned fortifications and installations.

(b) This prohibition does not include other types of non-permanent fortifications or surface accommodations and installations which are designed to meet only requirements of an internal character and of local defence of the frontiers.

5. In a coastal area 15 kilometers deep, stretching from the Franco-Italian frontier to the meridian of 9°30′ E., Italy shall not establish any new, nor expand any existing, naval bases or permanent naval installations. This does not prohibit minor alterations to, nor the maintenance in good repair of, existing naval installations provided that their overall capacity will not thereby be increased.

Article 48

1. (a) Any permanent Italian fortifications and military installations along the Italo-Yugoslav frontier, and their armaments, shall be destroyed or removed.

(b) These fortifications and installations are deemed to comprise only artillery and infantry fortifications whether in groups or separated, pillboxes of any type, protected accommodation for personnel, stores and ammunition, observation posts and military cableways, whatever may be their importance and actual condition of maintenance or state of construction, which are constructed of metal, masonry or concrete or excavated in the rock.

2. The destruction or removal, mentioned in paragraph 1 above, is limited to a distance of 20 kilometers from any point on the frontier, as defined by the present Treaty, and shall be completed within one year from the coming into force of the Treaty.

3. Any reconstruction of the above-mentioned fortifications and installations is prohibited.

4. (a) The following construction to the west of the Italo-Yugoslav frontier is prohibited: permanent fortifications where weapons capable of firing into Yugoslav territory or territorial waters can be emplaced; permanent military installations capable of being used to conduct or direct fire into Yugoslav territory or territorial waters; and permanent supply and storage facilities emplaced solely for the use of the above-mentioned fortifications and installations.

(b) This prohibition does not include other types of non-permanent fortifications or surface accommodations and installations which are designed to meet only requirements of an internal character and of local defence of the frontiers.

5. In a coastal area 15 kilometers deep, stretching from the frontier between Italy and Yugoslavia and between Italy and the Free Territory of Trieste to the latitude of 44° 50′ N. and in the islands adjacent to this coast, Italy shall not establish any new, nor expand any existing, naval bases or permanent naval installations. This does not prohibit minor alterations to, nor the maintenance in good repair of, existing naval installations and bases provided that their overall capacity will not thereby be increased.

In the Apulian Peninsula east of longitude 17° 45′ E., Italy shall not construct any new permanent military, naval or military air installations nor expand existing installations. This does not prohibit minor alterations to, nor the maintenance in good repair of, existing installations provided that their overall capacity will not thereby be increased. Accommodation for such security forces as may be required

for tasks of an internal character and local defence of frontiers will, however, be permitted.

Article 49

1. Pantellaria, the Pelagian Islands (Lampedusa, Lampione and Linosa) and Pianosa (in the Adriatic) shall be and shall remain demilitarised.

2. Such demilitarisation shall be completed within one year from the coming into force of the present Treaty.

Article 50

1. In Sardinia all permanent coast defence artillery emplacements and their armaments and all naval installations which are located within a distance of 30 kilometers from French territorial waters shall be removed to the mainland of Italy or demolished within one year from the coming into force of the present Treaty.

2. In Sicily and Sardinia all permanent installations and equipment for the maintenance and storage of torpedoes, sea mines and bombs shall be demolished or removed to the mainland of Italy within one year from the coming into force of the present Treaty.

3. No improvements to, reconstruction of, or extensions of existing installations or permanent fortifications in Sicily and Sardinia shall be permitted; however, with the exception of the northern Sardinia areas described in paragraph 1 above, normal maintenance of such installations or permanent fortifications and weapons already installed in them may take place.

4. In Sicily and Sardinia Italy shall be prohibited from constructing any naval, military and air force installations or fortifications except for such accommodation for security forces as may be required for tasks of an internal character.

Article 51. Italy shall not possess, construct or experiment with (i) any atomic weapon, (ii) any self-propelled or guided missiles or apparatus connected with their discharge (other than torpedoes and torpedo-launching gear comprising the normal armament of naval vessels permitted by the present Treaty), (iii) any guns with a range of over 30 kilometers, (iv) sea mines or torpedoes of non-contact types actuated by influence mechanisms, (v) any torpedoes capable of being manned.

Article 52. The acquisition of war material of German or Japanese origin or design, either from inside or outside Italy, or its manufacture, is prohibited to Italy.

Article 53. Italy shall not manufacture or possess, either publicly or privately, any war material different in type from, or exceeding in quantity, that required for the forces permitted in Sections III, IV and V below.

Article 54. The total number of heavy and medium tanks in the Italian armed forces shall not exceed 200.

Article 55. In no case shall any officer or non-commissioned officer of the former Fascist Militia or of the former Fascist Republican Army be permitted to hold officer's or non-commissioned officer's rank in the Italian Navy, Army, Air Force or Carabiniere, with the exception of such persons as shall have been exonerated by the appropriate body in accordance with Italian law.

SECTION III. LIMITATION OF THE ITALIAN NAVY

Article 56

1. The present Italian Fleet shall be reduced to the units listed in Annex XII A.

2. Additional units not listed in Annex XII and employed only for the specific purpose of mine-sweeping, may continue to be employed until the end of the mine clearance period as shall be determined by the International Central Board for Mine Clearance of European Waters.

3. Within two months from the end of the said period, such of these vessels as are on loan to the Italian Navy from other Powers shall be returned to those Powers, and all other additional units shall be disarmed and converted to civilian use.

Article 57

1. Italy shall effect the following disposal of the units of the Italian Navy specified in Annex XII B:

(a) The said units shall be placed at the disposal of the Governments of the Soviet Union, of the United Kingdom, of the United States of America, and of France;

(b) Naval vessels required to be transferred in compliance with subparagraph (a) above shall be fully equipped, in operational condition including a full outfit of armament stores, and complete with onboard spare parts and all necessary technical data;

(c) The transfer of the naval vessels mentioned above shall be effected within three months from the coming into force of the present Treaty, except that, in the case of naval vessels that cannot be refitted within three months, the time limit for the transfer may be extended by the Four Governments;

(d) Reserve allowance of spare parts and armament stores for the naval vessels mentioned above

shall, as far as possible, be supplied with the vessels.

The balance of reserve spare parts and armament stores shall be supplied to an extent and at dates to be decided by the Four Governments, in any case within a maximum of one year from the coming into force of the present Treaty.

2. Details relating to the above transfers will be arranged by a Four Power Commission to be established under a separate protocol.

3. In the event of loss or damage, from whatever cause, to any of the vessels in Annex XII B scheduled for transfer, and which cannot be made good by the agreed date for transfer of the vessel or vessels concerned, Italy undertakes to replace such vessel or vessels by equivalent tonnage from the list in Annex XII A, the actual vessel or vessels to be substituted being selected by the Ambassadors in Rome of the Soviet Union, of the United Kingdom, of the United States of America, and of France.

Article 58

1. Italy shall effect the following disposal of submarines and non-operational naval vessels. The time limits specified below shall be taken as commencing with the coming into force of the present Treaty.

(a) Surface naval vessels afloat not listed in Annex XII, including naval vessels under construction afloat, shall be destroyed or scrapped for metal within nine months.

(b) Naval vessels under construction on slips shall be destroyed or scrapped for metal within nine months.

(c) Submarines afloat and not listed in Annex XII B shall be sunk in the open sea in a depth of over 100 fathoms within three months.

(d) Naval vessels sunk in Italian harbours and approach channels, in obstruction of normal shipping, shall, within two years, either be destroyed on the spot or salvaged and subsequently destroyed or scrapped for metal.

(e) Naval vessels sunk in shallow Italian waters not in obstruction of normal shipping shall within one year be rendered incapable of salvage.

(f) Naval vessels capable of reconversion which do not come within the definition of war material, and which are not listed in Annex XII, may be reconverted to civilian uses or are to be demolished within two years.

2. Italy undertakes, prior to the sinking or destruction of naval vessels and submarines as provided for in the preceding paragraph, to salvage

such equipment and spare parts as may be useful in completing the on-board and reserve allowances of spare parts and equipment to be supplied, in accordance with Article 57, paragraph 1, for all ships specified in Annex XII B.

3. Under the supervision of the Ambassadors in Rome of the Soviet Union, of the United Kingdom, of the United States of America, and of France, Italy may also salvage such equipment and spare parts of a non-warlike character as are readily adaptable for use in Italian civil economy.

Article 59

1. No battleship shall be constructed, acquired or replaced by Italy.

2. No aircraft carrier, submarine or other submersible craft, motor torpedo boat or specialised types of assault craft shall be constructed, acquired, employed or experimented with by Italy.

3. The total standard displacement of the war vessels, other than battleships, of the Italian Navy, including vessels under construction after the date of launching, shall not exceed 67,500 tons.

4. Any replacement of war vessels by Italy shall be effected within the limit of tonnage given in paragraph 3. There shall be no restriction on the replacement of auxiliary vessels.

5. Italy undertakes not to acquire or lay down any war vessels before January 1, 1950, except as necessary to replace any vessel, other than a battleship, accidentally lost, in which case the displacement of the new vessel is not to exceed by more than ten percent the displacement of the vessel lost.

6. The terms used in this Article are, for the purposes of the present Treaty, defined in Annex XIII A.

Article 60

1. The total personnel of the Italian Navy, excluding any naval air personnel, shall not exceed 25,000 officers and men.

2. During the mine clearance period as determined by the International Central Board for Mine Clearance of European Waters, Italy shall be authorized to employ for this purpose an additional number of officers and men not to exceed 2,500.

3. Permanent naval personnel in excess of that permitted under paragraph 1 shall be progressively reduced as follows, time limits being taken as commencing with the coming into force of the present Treaty:

(a) To 30,000 within six months
(b) To 25,000 within nine months.

Two months after the completion of minesweeping by the Italian Navy, the excess personnel authorized by paragraph 2 is to be disbanded or absorbed within the above numbers.

4. Personnel, other than those authorized under paragraphs 1 and 2, and other than any naval air personnel authorized under Article 65, shall not receive any form of naval training as defined in Annex XIII B.

SECTION IV. LIMITATION OF THE ITALIAN ARMY

Article 61. The Italian Army, including the Frontier Guards, shall be limited to a force of 185,000 combat, service and overhead personnel and 65,000 Carabinieri, though either of the above elements may be varied by 10,000 as long as the total ceiling does not exceed 250,000. The organisation and armament of the Italian ground forces, as well as their deployment throughout Italy, shall be designed to meet only tasks of an internal character, local defence of Italian frontiers and anti-aircraft defence.

Article 62. The Italian Army, in excess of that permitted under Article 61 above, shall be disbanded within six months from the coming into force of the present Treaty.

Article 63. Personnel other than those forming part of the Italian Army or Carabinieri shall not receive any form of military training as defined in Annex XIII B.

SECTION V. LIMITATION OF THE ITALIAN AIR FORCE

Article 64

1. The Italian Air Force, including any naval air arm, shall be limited to a force of 200 fighter and reconnaissance aircraft and 150 transport, air-sea rescue, training (school type) and liaison aircraft. These totals include reserve aircraft. All aircraft except for fighter and reconnaissance aircraft shall be unarmed. The organisation and armament of the Italian Air Force as well as their deployment throughout Italy shall be designed to meet only tasks of an internal character, local defence of Italian frontiers and defence against air attack.

2. Italy shall not possess or acquire any aircraft designed primarily as bombers with internal bomb-carrying facilities.

Article 65

1. The personnel of the Italian Air Force, including any naval air personnel, shall be limited to a

total of 25,000 effectives, which shall include combat, service and overhead personnel.

2. Personnel other than those forming part of the Italian Air Force shall not receive any form of military air training as defined in Annex XIII B.

Article 66. The Italian Air Force, in excess of that permitted under Article 65 above, shall be disbanded within six months from the coming into force of the present Treaty.

SECTION VI. DISPOSAL OF WAR MATERIAL
(as defined in ANNEX XIII C)

Article 67

1. All Italian war material in excess of that permitted for the armed forces specified in Sections III, IV and V shall be placed at the disposal of the Governments of the Soviet Union, of the United Kingdom, of the United States of America, and of France, according to such instructions as they may give to Italy.

2. All Allied war material in excess of that permitted for the armed forces specified in Sections III, IV and V shall be placed at the disposal of the Allied or Associated Power concerned according to the instructions to be given to Italy by the Allied or Associated Power concerned.

3. All German and Japanese war material in excess of that permitted for the armed forces specified in Sections III, IV and V, and all German or Japanese drawings, including existing blueprints, prototypes, experimental models and plans, shall be placed at the disposal of the Four Governments in accordance with such instructions as they may give to Italy.

4. Italy shall renounce all rights to the abovementioned war material and shall comply with the provisions of this Article within one year from the coming into force of the present Treaty except as provided for in Articles 56 to 58 thereof.

5. Italy shall furnish to the Four Governments lists of all excess war material within six months from the coming into force of the present Treaty.
[U.S. Library of Congress, Legislative Reference Service, *Disarmament and Security: A Collection of Documents, 1919–55* (Washington, D.C., 1956), Doc. 107]

Japanese Constitution (1946)

The Japanese Constitution, drafted on 3 November 1946, was enacted by the Japanese parliament in 1947.

We, the Japanese people, acting through our duly elected representatives in the National Diet, determined that we shall secure for ourselves and our posterity the fruits of peaceful cooperation with all nations and the blessings of liberty throughout this land, and resolved that never again shall we be visited with the horrors of war through the action of government, do proclaim that sovereign power resides with the people and do firmly establish this Constitution. Government is a sacred trust of the people, the authority for which is derived from the people, the powers of which are exercised by the representatives of the people, and the benefits of which are enjoyed by the people. This is a universal principle of mankind upon which this Constitution is founded. We reject and revoke all constitutions, laws, ordinances and rescripts in conflict herewith.

We, the Japanese people, desire peace for all time and are deeply conscious of the high ideals controlling human relationship, and we have determined to preserve our security and existence, trusting in the justice and faith of the peace-loving peoples of the world. We desire to occupy an honoured place in an international society striving for the preservation of peace, and the banishment of tyranny and slavery, oppression and intolerance for all time from the earth. We recognize that all peoples of the world have the right to live in peace, free from fear and want.

We believe that no nation is responsible to itself alone, but that laws of political morality are universal; and that obedience to such laws is incumbent upon all nations who would sustain their own sovereignty and justify their sovereign relationship with other nations.

We, the Japanese people, pledge our national honor to accomplish these high ideals and purposes with all our resources. . . .

CHAPTER II: RENUNCIATION OF WAR

Article 9. Aspiring sincerely to an international peace based on justice and order, the Japanese people forever renounce war as a sovereign right of the nation and the threat or use of force as means of settling international disputes.

In order to accomplish the aim of the preceding paragraph, land, sea, and air forces, as well as other war potential, will never be maintained. The right of belligerency of the state will not be recognized. [Amos J. Peaslee, *Constitutions of Nations*, 3d rev. ed., vol. 2 (The Hague, 1966)]

Proposals for General and Complete Disarmament

The 1928 draft convention for general and complete disarmament was transmitted to the Secretary General of the League of Nations in a letter of February 15 from Deputy Foreign Commissar Litvinov. It was later discussed at the fifth session of the Preparatory Commission.

Soviet Draft Convention (1928)

Soviet Draft Convention for Immediate, Complete and General Disarmament, February 15, 1928

CHAPTER I. EFFECTIVES OF THE ARMED FORCES

Article 1. All military units and formations, as well as all the effectives of the land, naval and air forces, whether of the home country or of its oversea possessions, shall be disbanded within four years as from the entry into force of the present Convention, and shall not in future be allowed in any form, whether open or secret.

The disbandment of the effectives shall be carried out in four successive stages:

(a) in the first year, as from the entry into force of the effectives in service, whether officials, officers, or other ranks, shall be disbanded, and

(b) In the following years the remaining effectives in equal parts.

Remark: By *effectives of the armed forces* is meant effectives serving with the colours in the active army, as well as the trained military reserves in each of the Contracting States entered on the muster-rolls of the various military and public organisations.

Article 2. The Ministries of War, Marine and Aviation, as well as general staffs, all military schools and all kinds of military commands, institutions and establishments shall be abolished, except as provided for in Article 5 of the present Convention, within one year from the entry into force of the present Convention, and may not be reconstituted.

Article 3. Within a period of one year as from the entry into force of the present Convention, all returns and documents relating to military trained reserves, and kept by Government institutions and public organisations, shall be destroyed.

Within the same period, all laws concerning the organisation shall be repealed.

Article 4. Within one year from the entry into force of the present Convention, all documents relating to the mobilisation of armed forces shall be destroyed; all mobilisation measures shall be prohibited in future.

Article 5. For four years as from the entry into force of the present Convention, it shall be permissible, in accordance with a special convention, to maintain staffs, commands, institutions and establishments to the extent strictly necessary for the application of the technical measures required by the disbandment of the armed forces, and by the performance of the necessary administrative and economic work relating to disarmament.

Article 6. All the files concerning the disbandment of the armed forces shall be forwarded to the civilian Ministries within four years as from the entry into force of the present Convention.

All the files and archives of the Ministries of War, Marine and Aviation, of the Army units and of the staffs, commands, institutions and establishments, shall be destroyed within the same period.

Article 7. The personnel of the disbanded armed forces shall be provided with employment in other spheres of social and economic work.

Until they are provided with employment, they may be provisionally maintained at the expense of the general State budget.

When the aforesaid persons are awarded pensions based on the number of years of service, the years spent in military service shall be reckoned as spent in the service of the State.

Article 8. The credits assigned for the upkeep of the armed forces, either in the State budget or out of the funds of the various associations, must be confined to the sums strictly necessary for the upkeep of the armed forces remaining in actual military service in accordance with a special convention.

Within four years, the budget for the upkeep of the armed forces must be abolished, and may not figure under any heading in the State budget.

Article 9. Within a period of one year from the entry into force of the present Convention, all laws concerning military service, whether compulsory, voluntary or by recruiting, shall be abrogated.

The conditions of service in the armed forces until the completion of total disarmament shall be laid down in special regulations by each of the contracting States.

Article 10. Immediately after the entry into force of the present Convention the following shall be prohibited by law:

1. Special military publications: (a) Scientific research and theoretical treatises; (b) Works on military history; (c) Manuals of military training; (d) Military regulations; (e) Manuals of all kinds for the study of the technical implements of war.

2. The military training of the population, including the calling-up of trained reserves, and military propaganda among the population.

3. The military training of young people, either by the State or by public associations.

CHAPTER II. MATERIAL

Part 1. Land Armaments

Article 11. Within one year of the entry into force of the present Convention, the reserves of arms, ammunition and other instruments of armament and destruction enumerated below and at the disposal of the Ministry of War shall be destroyed.

Tanks, poisonous war materials and the appliances by which these materials are diffused (gas projectors, pulverisers, balloons and other apparatus), whether in service or in reserve, shall first be destroyed.

The arms strictly necessary for the effectives remaining with the colours may be retained by the armed forces of each of the contracting States. The proportion between the armed forces of each State and the quantity of technical implements of war enumerated in the list given below shall be determined in a special convention.

In the second, third and fourth years as from the entry into force of the present Convention, the destruction of all the types of armament shall be carried out by consecutive stages in proportion to the limitation of personnel.

After the completion of disarmament in each of the contracting States, the minimum quantity of arms and ammunition required for all kinds of police forces and for personal use may be retained in accordance with Article[s] 39, 43 and 44.

List of war material to be destroyed:

1. Automatic and magazine rifles.

2. All kinds of machine guns, including machine rifles and light and heavy machine-guns.

3. Mine throwers and grenade and bomb throwers.

4. Revolvers and automatic pistols issued to troops.

5. Rifle and hand grenades.

6. Rifle and military revolver ammunition.

7. Guns of all calibres and types, and ammunition for same, whether complete or in component parts.

8. Tanks.

9. Gunpowder and explosives employed for exclusively military purposes.

10. All poisonous materials for war, as well as the appliances by which they are diffused, such as gas projectors, pulverisers, balloons and other apparatus.

11. Flame throwers.

12. All technical military implements not enumerated above and intended for the wounding and destruction of man by man, as well as all parts of the articles enumerated above.

Article 12. All orders placed by the Ministries of War, Marine and Aviation for any of the armaments enumerated in the Annex to Article 11 of the present Convention shall be cancelled.

War material for the manufacture of which orders have been placed abroad shall be destroyed in the country in which it is manufactured.

Article 13. Compensation shall be paid for loss due to the cancelling of the orders mentioned in Article 12, and of the orders for the special naval and air force armaments enumerated in Articles 21 and 27, placed by the Ministries of War, Marine and Aviation. Such compensation shall be given either in conformity with the legislative practice of the several contracting States or in accordance with the terms of the contracts.

Article 14. Armoured cars and all other armoured means of transport, except tanks, must be disarmed, that is to say, stripped of their armour-plating and their weapons, which must be destroyed. This must be effected within one year of the coming into force of the present Convention.

Article 15. Revolvers and sporting guns (of a non-military pattern), intended respectively for personal defence and sport, may be left in the hands of private persons in virtue of special permits. The number of these revolvers and sporting guns which each of the contracting States may possess shall be fixed by a special convention in proportion to the number of the population.

Article 16. Explosives capable of being used for industrial, agricultural or other socially useful purposes shall not be liable to destruction, but shall be handed over by the Ministries of War, Marine and Aviation to the respective economic organisations within one year of the coming into force of the present Convention.

Part 2. Naval Armaments

Article 17. Within one year of the coming into force of the present Convention, all capital ships, cruisers, aircraft-carriers and submarines shall be withdrawn from the naval establishments.

Article 18. All other vessels and floating material constructed for the special purposes of war and enumerated in the annexed list, together with naval aircraft, shall be withdrawn from the naval establishments within four years, withdrawal proceeding in equal parts each year, in conformity with a special convention.

List of vessels to be disarmed:

1. Coast-defence battleships.
2. Torpedo craft of all types.
3. Monitors.
4. Gunboats of over 3,000 tons.
5. Floating batteries.
6. Hydroplanes of all types.

NOTE: Vessels and their armaments may be retained under the conditions laid down in Articles 43 and 44 of the present Convention for the establishment of a maritime police force and for the protection of frontiers.

Article 19. The personnel of vessels withdrawn from the naval establishments shall be immediately disbanded.

At the end of three months from the removal of the vessels from the naval lists, the ordnance of such vessels and their mines and torpedo appliances shall be rendered useless in accordance with special technical arrangements; the reserve naval ordnance intended for these vessels, and torpedos and mines, shall be destroyed.

During the nine following months the ordnance rendered useless and the mines and torpedo appliances shall be removed from the vessels and destroyed.

Article 20. Within three months of the removal from the naval establishment of vessels which cannot be employed for pacific purposes, all the machinery on board shall be rendered useless in accordance with special technical arrangements. During the following nine months, the machinery on board shall be removed, after which the vessels themselves shall be entirely dismantled.

Article 21. As from the entry into force of the present Convention, the existing naval programmes shall be cancelled; any new construction of warships shall be forbidden.

All warships under construction or undergoing repair on orders given either in the home country or abroad shall be disarmed in the same way as vessels of the service fleet of the contracting States.

Article 22. The armament of vessels belonging to the mercantile marine shall be destroyed in the same way as that of warships during the first year of the coming into force of the present Convention.

It shall be forbidden in future to adapt and arm vessels belonging to the mercantile marine for military purposes.

Part 3. Air Armaments

Article 23. During the first year of the coming into force of the present Convention, heavy bombing aircraft, torpedo-carriers and dirigibles shall be removed from the air force lists.

Article 24. All other military aircraft not mentioned in Article 23 above and which, by reason of their specifically military properties, cannot be used for social or economic purposes shall be destroyed within four years, destruction proceeding in equal parts each year, in conformity with special technical arrangements.

Article 25. Within one year of the coming into force of the present Convention, all stocks of aircraft bombs and other weapons intended to be discharged from aircraft shall be destroyed.

Article 26. The whole of the armament of military aircraft which are to be preserved for social or economic uses must be removed and destroyed at the end of three months from the time of their withdrawal from the air force effectives. Such aircraft shall then be handed over to the respective civil organisations.

Article 27. All the aircraft belonging to the active air force must be disarmed, as well as all aircraft which are in reserve or under construction on orders given in the home country or abroad.

Article 28. The arming of aircraft and all fittings for mounting weapons on aircraft shall be prohibited in future.

Aircraft intended for peaceful purposes may only be retained to an extent which is strictly in accordance with the real economic or social requirements of each country. The number to be allowed to each contracting State shall be determined by a special convention.

Part 4. Fortifications and Bases

Article 29. Within three years of the entry into force of the present Convention, the whole of the armament of fortresses and other fortified works and of naval and air force bases shall be rendered useless in conformity with a list contained in a special convention.

During the following year, the armament shall be removed and destroyed and the fortifications dismantled and demolished; it shall in future be forbidden to construct new fortified works of any kind.

Part 5. Armament Industries

Article 30. With the entry into force of the present Convention, all State and private undertakings shall cease to produce any of the armaments enumerated in the list annexed to Article 11 or any of those mentioned in Articles 19, 23, 24 and 25; preparations shall be made to convert these undertakings for purposes of peaceful manufacture.

Until these undertakings are re-equipped for peaceful purposes or until the workers in armament undertakings have found employment in other enterprises, these workers shall be supported by the State, which shall provide for their requirements out of the defence budget.

Article 31. During the first year following the entry into force of the present Convention, the plans, testing apparatus and models intended for armament industries shall be destroyed.

Article 32. Within two years of the coming into force of the present Convention, factories and enterprises engaged in the manufacture of war material and also arsenals shall cease to operate, except in the cases provided in Article 34 of the present Convention.

In State or private undertakings, all frames, machines, tools, and appliances intended exclusively for the manufacture of the war material enumerated in the Annex to Article II of the present Convention and in Articles 19, 23, 24, and 25 shall be destroyed.

Article 33. It shall be forbidden in future to restore any factories, enterprises and arsenals engaged in the manufacture of war material or to prepare any State or private productive undertakings for the manufacture of the war material enumerated in Articles 11, 19, 23, 24, and 25.

Article 34. In order to produce the minimum of arms and ammunition necessary for the police forces of all kinds provided for in Chapter III of the present Convention, and for the personal use of citizens for the purposes referred to in Article 15 of the present Convention, each contracting State shall be authorised to retain the necessary undertakings, of which the number, productive capacity and method of production, as well as the arrangements concerning the trade in arms, shall be laid down in a special convention.

Article 35. Industries shall be regulated by the several contracting States in strict conformity with economic requirements, and shall be subject to control in virtue of a special convention.

Article 36. It shall be forbidden by law to patent any form of armament or any means of destruction.

CHAPTER III. ORGANISATION OF PROTECTION

Part 1. Protection on Land

Article 37. The effectives of the Customs guards, local police and forest and other guards, in each of the contracting States, and the amount of their armament, shall not for a period of four years after the conclusion of the present Convention exceed the number and amount as at January 1st, 1928; these effectives shall not be organised in such a way that they can be utilised for war.

Article 38. On the expiry of the period of four years laid down in the present Convention for effecting complete and general disarmament, the maintenance of a protective and police service, the personnel of which shall be engaged by voluntary contracts of service, shall be authorised in the territory of each of the contracting States, for the purpose of Customs and revenue police supervision, internal police and the protection of State and private property; the amount of weapons and simple armament strictly necessary may also be retained.

The effectives of these categories of services shall be laid down in a special convention and shall be proportionate to the population of the several contracting States, the length of the means of communication, the existence of objects which are deemed by the State to require protection, the development of forestry, etc.

Article 39. Magazine rifles firing ten rounds and pistols of a calibre not exceeding 0.8 cm. may be retained for arming the police forces and guards.

Reserve ammunition may be stored in places laid down in a special convention, but must not exceed 1,000 pounds per rifle and 100 rounds per pistol.

The annual supply of munitions must not exceed the amount strictly required to replace worn-out armament and the actual consumption of ammunition.

Part 2. Protection at Sea

Article 40. On the expiry of the period of four years laid down in the present Convention for effecting complete and general disarmament, a maritime police service shall be organised which shall exercise its functions in conformity with a special convention and which is intended for the necessary protection of the natural products of the sea and of submarine cables, the suppression of piracy and of the slave trade, and other objects which may in future form the subject of international protection on the high seas.

Article 41. With a view to protection at sea, the waters of the globe shall be divided into sixteen zones, as enumerated below. [The sixteen zones, whose boundaries were given in small detail, have been omitted.]

Article 42. The safeguarding of the international interests mentioned in Article 40 shall be entrusted, in accordance with a special convention, to regional groups of States having access to the waters enumerated in the list annexed to Article 31 of the present Convention.

Article 43. Supervision shall be exercised by maritime police vessels with a tonnage not exceeding 3,000 tons and armed with not more than two guns the calibre of which shall not exceed 50 mm.

The crews of police vessels shall be recruited by voluntary enlistment.

A maximum of 20 rifles or pistols may be retained for the armament of the crew in conformity with Article 39 of the present Convention.

Article 44. Customs supervision in territorial waters shall be exercised by unarmed vessels of the maritime Customs police having a tonnage of not more than 100 tons.

The number of the above-mentioned vessels in the possession of each contracting State shall be determined by a special convention and shall be proportionate to the length of coastline.

The personnel of the maritime Customs police may be armed with rifles and pistols and shall serve on the terms laid down in Article 43 of the present Convention.

NOTE: The limits of territorial waters shall be fixed by a special agreement.

CHAPTER IV. CONTROL

Article 45. Within three months of the coming into force of the present Convention, there shall be organised a Permanent International Commission of Control, Commission of Control in each of the Contracting States, and local Commissions of Control.

Article 46. The Permanent International Commission of Control shall be entrusted with:

(a) The supervision and control of the normal and proportional progress of disarmament, with the general coordination of measures for carrying out the provisions of the present Convention, and with the notification to each State of offenses against its stipulations;

(b) The preparation of an agreement for bringing pressure by non-military measures upon any States which disturb the normal progress of disarmament as laid down by the present Convention and conventions supplementary thereto;

(c) The selection of localities, the procedure and the technical conditions for the destruction of material, and the preparation of all the necessary supplementary technical agreements;

(d) The selection of centres for the manufacture of arms, the volume of such manufacture and the regulation of the trade in arms;

(e) The publication of information concerning progress in the work of disarmament.

Article 47. The Permanent International Commission of Control shall consist of an equal number of representatives of the legislative bodies and of the trade unions and other workmen's organisations of all the States participating in the present Convention.

Later, the Permanent International Commission of Control may be supplemented by representatives of international associations whose aim it is to establish pacific relations between States and which have pursued this aim with success, provided that these organisations express a wish to participate in the work of the Permanent International Commission of Control.

The seat of the Permanent International Commission of Control shall be at . . .

Article 48. The Permanent International Commission of Control shall be assisted by a Permanent International Committee of Experts, consisting of an equal number of military, naval, air and other experts belonging to all the States acceding to the present Convention.

Article 49. The Permanent International Committee of Experts shall act under the orders of the Permanent International Commission of Control; it shall give opinions and shall deal with all especially technical questions referring to the execution of the present Convention.

Article 50. The Commission of Control in each of the States shall consist of representatives of the Permanent International Commission of Control appointed by the Commission, representatives of public associations, trade unions and workmen's organisations, and of representatives of the peas-

ants and of the rank and file of the armed forces of the State in question.

The appointment of members of the Commission of Control shall be confirmed by the Permanent International Commission of Control.

The seat of the Commission of Control shall be the capital of the State concerned.

Article 51. The Commission of Control in each State shall coordinate the disarmament work of the local Commissions of Control in absolute conformity with the present Convention and in accordance with the instructions of the Permanent International Commission of Control.

Article 52. The local Commissions of Control shall consist of representatives of municipal and public organisations, trade unions and workmen's associations, and of representatives of the peasants and of the rank and file of the army.

The number of local Commissions of Control, their headquarters and the radius of their activities shall be determined by the Commission of Control of the State in question. The latter Commission shall approve the composition of the local Commissions of Control.

Article 53. The local Commissions of Control shall proceed directly with the work of disarmament within the radius of their activities, in accordance with the instructions of the Commission of Control in their country.

Article 54. The following may not be members of central or local Commissions of Control:

(a) Professional ex-soldiers and officials of the Ministries of War, Marine and Military Aviation;

(b) Owners of and large shareholders in military industrial undertakings, owners of and large shareholders in banking and commercial enterprises with interests in military undertakings and the trade in arms, and higher employees in all these undertakings.

Article 55. All the contracting States shall seek to give the widest publicity to the progress of disarmament, and shall afford the organs of the Permanent International Commission of Control every facility for the full investigation of all activities of the State, of public associations and of private persons which are connected with the application of disarmament, or which, in the view of the Permanent International Commission of Control or its organs, give rise to doubts concerning the observance of the undertakings solemnly entered into with regard to disarmament and the discontinuance of all military preparations.

Article 56. The decision of the Permanent International Commission of Control shall be taken by a majority vote and shall be binding on all the contracting States.

Article 57. The costs of maintenance of the Permanent International Commission of Control and its organs, as well as the expenses relating to the work of control, shall be defrayed by all the contracting States in a proportion to be settled in a special convention.

The expenses of the national and local Commissions of Control shall be defrayed by each of the contracting States.

CHAPTER V. SUPPLEMENTARY AGREEMENTS; BREACHES OF THE CONVENTION; RATIFICATIONS

Article 58. Within one year of the entry into force of the present Convention, all the contracting States shall enact legislation providing that a breach of any of the stipulations of the Convention shall be regarded as a grave offence against the State.

At the same time, all acts of national or international importance which are contrary to the abovementioned clauses shall be repealed or amended.

Article 59. Within nine months of the entry into force of the present Convention, the following conventions shall be concluded:

(a) In conformity with Article 8 of the present Convention, a convention on the number of staffs, commands, establishments and institutions left to each of the contracting States until the completion of full and general disarmament.

(b) In conformity with Article 15 of the present Convention, a convention on the quantity of arms allowed for personal defence and sport.

(c) In conformity with Article 28 of the present Convention, a convention on the number of aircraft required for the social and economic needs of each of the contracting States.

(d) In conformity with Article 29 of the present Convention, a convention giving a list of the for-

tresses, fortifications and naval and air bases to be destroyed.

(e) In conformity with Articles 34, 35, and 39 of the present Convention, a convention concerning the storage and production of, and trade in, a minimum quantity of war material.

(f) In conformity with Articles 41, 42, 43, and 44 of the present Convention, a convention concerning protection at sea, the allocation of the areas of protection at sea and the number of vessels required for maritime police and Customs purposes.

(g) A convention laying down the constitution of the Permanent International Commission of Control and of its organs, as well as the allocation of the costs connected therewith.

(h) A convention regarding the measures of nonmilitary pressure to be taken against States disturbing the normal progress of disarmament as provided for in the present Convention and in the supplementary agreements thereto.

Note.-The International Commission of Control shall be responsible for arranging to summon the States participating in the present Convention to a Conference for the conclusion of all the supplementary conventions mentioned in the present article.

Article 60. In the case of a direct breach of the present Convention by one of the contracting States, an extraordinary assembly of the representatives of the contracting States participating in the present Convention shall be summoned as expeditiously as possible by the Permanent International Commission of Control to decide upon the steps to be taken.

The steps taken to exercise pressure must not be of a military character.

All disputes between States shall be settled by the Permanent International Commission of Control.

[Ratification]

[Robert W. Lambert, "Soviet Disarmament Policy," pp. 158–186. *Documents of the Preparatory Commission for the Disarmament* [*Conference*], series VI, pp. 324–337]

Soviet Proposal for General and Complete Disarmament (1962)

Soviet Proposal Submitted to the Eighteen Nation Disarmament Committee, 15 March 1962

PART II
FIRST STAGE OF GENERAL
AND COMPLETE DISARMAMENT

Article 4. First Stage Tasks. The States parties to the Treaty undertake, in the course of the first stage of general and complete disarmament, to effect the simultaneous elimination of all means of delivering nuclear weapons and of all foreign military bases on alien territories, to withdraw all foreign troops from these territories, and to reduce their armed forces, conventional armaments and their production, and military expenditures.

Chapter I. Elimination of the Means of Delivering Nuclear Weapons and Foreign Military Bases on Alien Territories, and Withdrawal of Foreign Troops from those Territories. Control over such Measures

A. Means of Delivery

Article 5. Elimination of Rockets Capable of Delivering Nuclear Weapons

1. All rockets capable of delivering nuclear weapons, of any calibre and range, whether strategic, operational or tactical (except for strictly limited numbers of rockets to be converted to peaceful uses), as well as pilotless aircraft of all types shall be eliminated from the armed forces, and destroyed. All launching pads, silos and platforms for the launching of rockets and pilotless aircraft, other than those pads that will be retained for peaceful launchings under the provisions of Article 15 of the present Treaty, shall be completely demolished. All instruments for the equipment, launching and guidance of the above mentioned rockets and pilotless aircraft shall be destroyed. All underground depots for such rockets, pilotless aircraft and auxiliary facilities shall be demolished.

2. The production of all kinds of rockets and pilotless aircraft, and of the materials and instruments for their equipment, launching and guidance referred to in Paragraph 1 of this Article shall be completely discontinued. All enterprises, or workshops thereof, engaged in their production shall be dis-

mantled; machine tools and equipment specially and exclusively designed for the production of such items shall be destroyed; the premises of such enterprises, as well as general purpose machine tools and equipment shall be converted to peaceful uses. All proving grounds for tests of such rockets and pilotless aircraft shall be demolished.

3. Inspectors of the International Disarmament Organization shall verify the implementation of the measures referred to above in Paragraphs 1 and 2.

4. For the peaceful exploration of space the production and testing of appropriate rockets shall be allowed, provided that the plants producing such rockets, as well as the rockets themselves, will be subject to supervision by the inspectors of the International Disarmament Organization.

Article 6. Elimination of Military Aircraft, Capable of Delivering Nuclear Weapons

1. All military aircraft capable of delivering nuclear weapons shall be eliminated from the armed forces and destroyed. Military airfields serving as bases for such aircraft, repair and maintenance facilities, and storage places at these airfields shall be rendered inoperative or converted to peaceful uses. Training establishments for crews of such aircraft shall be closed.

2. The production of all military aircraft referred to in Paragraph 1 of this Article shall be completely discontinued. Enterprises, or workshops thereof, designed for the production of such military aircraft shall be either dismantled or converted to the production of civil aircraft or other peaceful items.

3. Inspectors of the International Disarmament Organization shall verify the implementation of the measures referred to above in Paragraphs 1 and 2.

Article 7. Elimination of all Surface Warships, Capable of Being Used as Vehicles for Nuclear Weapons, and Submarines

1. All surface warships, capable of being used as vehicles for nuclear weapons, and submarines of any class or type shall be eliminated from the armed forces, and destroyed. Naval bases and other installations for the maintenance of the above warships and submarines shall be demolished or dismantled and handed over to the merchant marine for peaceful uses.

2. The building of warships and submarines referred to in Paragraph 1 of this Article shall be completely discontinued. Shipyards and plants, wholly or in part designed for the building of such warships and submarines, shall be dismantled or converted to peaceful production.

3. Inspectors of the International Disarmament Organization shall verify the implementation of the measures referred to above in Paragraphs 1 and 2.

Article 8. Elimination of All Artillery Systems, Capable of Serving as Means of Delivering Nuclear Weapons

1. All artillery systems, capable of serving as means of delivery for nuclear weapons shall be eliminated from the armed forces, and destroyed. All subsidiary instruments and technical facilities designed for controlling the fire of such artillery systems shall be destroyed. Surface storage places and transport facilities for such systems shall be destroyed or converted to peaceful uses. The entire non-nuclear stock of munitions for such artillery systems, whether at the gun site or in depots, shall be completely destroyed. Underground depots for such artillery systems, and for the non-nuclear munitions thereof, shall be destroyed.

2. The production of the artillery systems referred to above in Paragraph 1 of this Article shall be completely discontinued. To this end all plants, or workshops thereof, engaged in the production of such systems shall be closed or dismantled. All specialized equipment and machine tools at these plants and workshops shall be destroyed, the remainder being converted to peaceful uses. The production of non-nuclear munitions for these artillery systems shall be discontinued. Plants and workshops engaged in the production of such munitions shall be completely dismantled, and their specialized equipment destroyed.

3. Inspectors of the International Disarmament Organization shall verify the implementation of the measures referred to above in Paragraphs 1 and 2.

B. Foreign Military Bases and Troops in Alien Territories

Article 9. Dismantling of Foreign Military Bases

1. Simultaneously with the destruction of the means of delivering nuclear weapons under Articles 5-8 of the present Treaty, the States parties to the Treaty, which have army, air force or naval bases in foreign territories, shall dismantle all such bases, both the principal and the reserve bases, as well as all depot bases of any designation. All personnel of such bases shall be evacuated to their national territory. All installations and armaments existing at such bases and coming under Article 5-8 of the present Treaty, shall be destroyed on the spot. Other armaments shall be destroyed on the spot in accordance with Article 11 of the present Treaty or evacuated to the territory of the State which owned the base.

All installations of a military nature at such bases shall be destroyed. Living quarters and subsidiary installations of foreign bases shall be transferred for peaceful uses to the States on whose territory they are located.

2. The measures referred to in Paragraph 1 of this Article shall be fully applicable to those military bases that are used by foreign troops even though legally they may belong to the State on whose territory they are located. The said measures shall also be implemented in regard to those army, air force and naval bases that have been set up under military treaties and agreements for use by other States or groups of States, regardless of whether any foreign troops are present at these bases at the time of the conclusion of the present Treaty.

All previous treaty obligations, decisions of the organs of military blocs, and any rights or privileges pertaining to the establishment and use of military bases in foreign territories, shall become invalid and unrenewable. The granting henceforth of military bases for use by foreign troops, and the concluding to this end of any bilateral or multilateral treaties and agreements shall be prohibited.

3. The Legislatures and Governments of the States parties to the present Treaty, shall enact legislation and promulgate decrees to ensure that no military bases to be used by foreign troops are established in their territory. Inspectors of the International Disarmament Organization shall verify the implementation of the measures referred to in Paragraphs 1 and 2 of this Article.

Article 10. Withdrawal of Foreign Troops from Alien Territories

1. Simultaneously with the elimination of the means of delivering nuclear weapons under Articles 5–8 of the present Treaty, the States parties to the Treaty which have troops, or military personnel of any nature, in foreign territories, shall withdraw all such troops and personnel therefrom. All armaments, and all installations of a military nature, which are located at points where foreign troops are stationed, and which come under Articles 5–8 of the present Treaty, shall be destroyed on the spot.

Other armaments shall be destroyed on the spot under Article 11 of the present Treaty or evacuated to the territory of the State withdrawing its troops. Living quarters and subsidiary installations formerly held by such troops or personnel shall be transferred for peaceful uses to the States on whose territory such troops were stationed.

2. The measures set forth in Paragraph 1 of this Article shall be fully applicable to foreign civilians employed in the armed forces, or engaged in the production of armaments or any other activities serving military purposes on foreign territory.

The said persons shall be recalled to the territory of the State whose citizenship they hold, and all previous treaty obligations, decisions by the organs of military blocs, and any rights or privileges pertaining to their activities, shall be invalidated and unrenewable. The future dispatching of foreign troops, military personnel, or the said civilians, to foreign territories, shall be prohibited.

3. Inspectors of the International Disarmament Organization shall verify the withdrawal of troops, the destruction of installations, and the transfer of the premises referred to in Paragraph 1 of this Article. The International Disarmament Organization shall have the right to exercise control also over the recall of the civilians referred to in Paragraph 2 of this Article. The legislation and decrees referred to in Paragraph 3 of Article 9 of the present Treaty, shall include provisions prohibiting the citizens of States parties to the Treaty from serving in the armed forces or from engaging in any other activities for military purposes in foreign States.

Chapter II. Reduction of Armed Forces, Conventional Armaments and Military Expenditures. Control Over Such Measures

Article 11. Reduction of Armed Forces and Conventional Armaments

1. In the first stage of general and complete disarmament the armed forces of the States parties to the Treaty shall be reduced to the following levels:

The United States of America—1,700,000 enlisted men, officers and civilian employees;

The Union of Soviet Socialist Republics—1,700,000 enlisted men, officers and civilian employees ... (Agreed force levels for other States parties to the Treaty shall be included in this Article).

2. The reduction of the armed forces shall be carried out primarily through the demobilization of personnel released as a result of the elimination of the means of delivering nuclear weapons, the dismantling of foreign bases and the withdrawal of foreign troops from alien territories, as provided for in Articles 5–10 of the present Treaty, and chiefly by way of the complete disbandment of units and ships' crews, their officers and enlisted men being demobilized.

3. All released conventional armaments, military equipment and munitions of the disbanded units shall be destroyed, and the means of transportation and subsidiary equipment shall be either destroyed or converted to peaceful uses. Conventional armaments and equipment intended for reserve forces shall also be destroyed.

All living quarters, depots and special premises previously occupied by units being disbanded, as well as the territories of all proving grounds, firing ranges and drill grounds, shall be transferred for peaceful uses to the civilian authorities.

4. Inspectors of the International Disarmament Organization shall exercise control at places where troops are disbanded and released, conventional armaments and military equipment destroyed, and shall also verify the conversion to peaceful uses of means of transportation and other non-combat equipment, premises, proving grounds, etc.

Article 12. Reduction of Conventional Armaments Production

1. Proportionately to the reduction of armed forces, as provided for in Article 11 of the present Treaty, the production of conventional armaments and munitions not coming under Articles 5–8 of the present Treaty, shall be reduced. Such reduction shall be carried out primarily through the elimination of enterprises engaged exclusively in the production of such armaments and munitions. These enterprises shall be dismantled, their specialized machine tools and equipment shall be destroyed, and their premises, and general purpose machine tools and equipment shall be converted to peaceful uses.

2. Inspectors of the International Disarmament Organization shall exercise control over the measures referred to in Paragraph 1 of this Article.

Article 13. Reduction of Military Expenditures

1. The States parties to the present Treaty shall reduce their military budgets and appropriations for military purposes proportionately to the destruction of the means of delivering nuclear weapons and the discontinuance of their production, to the dismantling of foreign military bases and withdrawals of foreign troops from alien territories, as

well as to the reduction of armed forces and conventional armaments and to the reduction of the production of such armaments as provided for in Articles 5–12 of the present Treaty.

The funds released through the implementation of the first-stage measures shall be used for peaceful purposes, including the reduction of taxes on the population and the subsidizing of the national economy. At the same time a certain portion of the funds, thus released, shall be diverted to economic and technical assistance to underdeveloped countries. The size of this portion shall be subject to agreement between the parties to the Treaty.

2. The International Disarmament Organization shall verify the implementation of the measures, referred to in Paragraph 1 of this Article, through its financial inspectors, to whom the States parties to the Treaty undertake to grant unhindered access to the records of central financial offices concerning the reduction of the budgetary allocations of States in connexion with the elimination of the means of delivering nuclear weapons, the dismantling of foreign military bases and the reduction of armed forces and conventional armaments, including the relevant decisions of their legislative and executive bodies on this subject.

Chapter III. Measures to Safeguard the Security of States

Article 14. Restriction of Displacements of the Means of Delivering Nuclear Weapons

1. From the very beginning of the first-stage and until the final destruction of all means of delivering nuclear weapons under Article[s] 5–8 of the present Treaty, the placing into orbit or stationing in outer space of any special devices capable of delivering weapons of mass destruction, the leaving of their territorial waters by warships, and the flying beyond the limits of their national territory by military aircraft capable of carrying weapons of mass destruction, shall be prohibited.

2. The International Disarmament Organization shall exercise control over compliance by the States parties to the Treaty, with the provisions of Paragraph 1 of this Article. The States parties to the Treaty shall provide advance information to the International Disarmament Organization about all launchings of rockets for peaceful purposes, as provided for in Article 15 of the present Treaty, as well as about all flights of military aircraft within their national frontiers and movements of warships within their territorial waters.

Article 15. Control Over Launchings of Rockets for Peaceful Purposes

1. The launching of rockets and space devices shall be carried out exclusively for peaceful purposes.

2. The International Disarmament Organization shall exercise control over the implementation of the provisions of Paragraph 1 of this Article through the establishment of inspection teams at the sites for peaceful rocket launchings who shall be present at the launchings and shall thoroughly examine every rocket or satellite before their launching.

Article 16. Prevention of the Further Spread of Nuclear Weapons. The States parties to the Treaty, possessing nuclear weapons, undertake to refrain from transferring control over nuclear weapons and from transmitting information necessary for their production to States not possessing them.

The States parties to the Treaty not possessing nuclear weapons undertake to refrain from producing or otherwise obtaining nuclear weapons and shall refuse to admit the nuclear weapons of any other State into their territories.

Article 17. Prohibition of Nuclear Tests. The conducting of nuclear tests of any kind shall be prohibited. (If such prohibition is not implemented under other international agreements by the time this Treaty is signed.)

Article 18. Measures to Strengthen the Capacity of the United Nations to Ensure International Peace and Security

1. To ensure that the United Nations is capable of effectively protecting States against threats to or breaches of the peace, all States parties to the Treaty shall, between the signing of the Treaty and its entry into force, conclude agreements with the Security Council by which they undertake to make available to the latter armed forces, assistance and facilities, including rights of passage, as provided for in Article 43 of the United Nations Charter.

2. The armed forces provided under the said agreements shall form part of the national armed forces of the corresponding States and shall be stationed within their territories. They shall be kept up to full strength, equipped and prepared for combat. When used under Article 42 of the United Nations Charter, these forces, commanded by the military authorities of the corresponding States, shall be placed at the disposal of the Security Council.

Chapter IV. Time-limits for Measures of the First Stage Transition from First to Second Stage

Article 19. Time-limits for Measures of the First Stage

1. The first stage of general and complete disarmament shall be initiated six months after the Treaty comes into force (under Article 46 of the present Treaty), within which period the International Disarmament Organization shall be set up.

2. The duration of the first stage of general and complete disarmament shall be 15 months.

Article 20. Transition from First to Second Stage

In the course of the last 3 months of the first stage the International Disarmament Organization shall review the results of the implementation of the first-stage measures of general and complete disarmament with a view to reporting on them to the States parties to the Treaty, as well as to the Security Council and the General Assembly of the United Nations.

PART III. SECOND STAGE OF GENERAL AND COMPLETE DISARMAMENT

Article 21. Second Stage Tasks. The States parties to the Treaty undertake, in the course of the second stage of general and complete disarmament, to effect the complete elimination of nuclear and other weapons of mass destruction, as well as the further reduction of their armed forces, conventional armaments and their production, and military expenditures.

Chapter V. Elimination of Nuclear, Chemical, Biological and Radiological Weapons. Control over such Measures

Article 22. Elimination of Nuclear Weapons

1. (a) Nuclear weapons of all kinds, types and capacities shall be eliminated from the armed forces, and destroyed. Fissionable materials extracted from such weapons, whether directly attached to the troops or stored in various depots, shall be appropriately processed to render them unfit for the direct re-establishment of weapons and they shall form a special fund for peaceful uses, belonging to the State which previously owned the nuclear weapons. Non-nuclear components of such weapons shall be fully destroyed.

All depots and special storage spaces for nuclear weapons shall be demolished.

(b) All stockpiles of nuclear materials intended for the production of nuclear weapons shall be appropriately processed to render them unfit for direct use in nuclear weapons, and shall be transferred to the above-mentioned special funds.

(c) Inspectors of the International Disarmament Organization shall verify the implementation of the measures to eliminate nuclear weapons referred to above in Sub-paragraphs (a) and (b) of this Paragraph.

2. (a) The production of nuclear weapons, and of fissionable materials for weapons purposes shall be completely discontinued. All plants, installations and laboratories specially designed for the production of nuclear weapons or their components shall be eliminated or converted to production for peaceful purposes. All workshops, installations and laboratories for the production of the components of nuclear weapons at plants that are partially engaged in the production of such weapons, shall be destroyed or converted to production for peaceful purposes.

(b) The measures for the discontinuance of the production of nuclear weapons and of fissionable materials for weapons purposes referred to above in Sub-paragraph (a), shall be implemented under the control of inspectors of the International Disarmament Organization.

The International Disarmament Organization shall have the right to inspect all enterprises which extract raw materials for atomic production or which produce or use fissionable materials or atomic energy.

The States parties to the Treaty shall make available to the International Disarmament Organization documents pertaining to the extraction of nuclear raw materials, to their processing and to their utilization for military or peaceful purposes.

3. Each State party to the Treaty shall, in accordance with its constitutional procedure, enact legislation on the complete prohibition of nuclear weapons and on amenability under the criminal law for any attempt at its re-establishment by individuals or organizations.

Article 23. Elimination of Chemical, Biological and Radiological Weapons

1. All kinds of chemical, biological and radiological weapons, whether directly attached to the troops or stored in various depots and storage places shall be eliminated from the arsenals of States, and destroyed (neutralized). Simultaneously all instruments and facilities for the combat use of such weapons as well as all special devices and fa-

cilities for their storage and conservation shall be destroyed.

2. The production of all kinds of chemical, biological and radiological weapons and of all means and devices for their combat use, transportation and storage shall be completely discontinued. All plants, installations, and laboratories that are wholly or in part engaged in the production of such weapons, shall be destroyed or converted to production for peaceful purposes.

3. The measures referred to above in Paragraphs 1 and 2 shall be implemented under the control of inspectors of the International Disarmament Organization.

Chapter VI. Further Reduction of Armed Forces, Conventional Armaments and Military Expenditures. Control over such Measures

Article 24. Further Reduction of Armed Forces and Conventional Armaments

1. In the second stage of general and complete disarmament the armed forces of the States parties to the Treaty shall be further reduced to the following levels:

The United States of America One million enlisted men, officers and civilian employees;

The Union of Soviet Socialist Republics One million enlisted men, officers and civilian employees.

(Agreed force levels for other States parties to the Treaty shall be included in this Article).

The reduction of the armed forces shall be carried out primarily through the demobilization of personnel previously attached to the nuclear or other weapons subject to elimination under Articles 22 and 23 of the present Treaty, and chiefly by way of the complete disbandment of units and ships' crews, their officers and enlisted men being demobilized.

2. All released conventional armaments, military equipment and munitions of the units being disbanded shall be destroyed, and the means of transportation and subsidiary equipment shall be either destroyed or converted to peaceful uses.

All living quarters, depots and special premises previously occupied by units being disbanded, as well as the territories of all proving grounds, firing ranges and drill grounds, shall be transferred for peaceful uses to the civilian authorities.

3. As in the implementation of such measures in the first stage of general and complete disarmament, inspectors of the International Disarmament Organization shall exercise control at places where

troops are disbanded and released conventional armaments and military equipment destroyed, and shall also verify the conversion to peaceful uses of means of transportation and other non-combat equipment, premises, proving grounds, etc.

Article 25. Further Reduction of Conventional Armaments Production

1. Proportionately to the reduction of armed forces, as provided for in Article 24 of the present Treaty, the production of conventional armaments and munitions shall be reduced. Such reduction shall as in the first stage of general and complete disarmament, be carried out primarily through the elimination of enterprises engaged exclusively in the production of such armaments and munitions. These enterprises shall be dismantled, their specialized machine tools and equipment shall be destroyed, and their premises and general purpose machine tools and equipment shall be converted to peaceful uses.

2. The measures referred to in Paragraph 1 of this Article shall be carried out under the control of inspectors of the International Disarmament Organization.

Article 26. Further Reduction of Military Expenditures

1. The States parties to the Treaty shall further reduce their military budgets and appropriations for military purposes proportionately to the destruction of nuclear, chemical, biological and radiological weapons, and the discontinuance of their production, as well as to the further reduction of armed forces and conventional armaments and to the reduction of the production of such armaments as provided for in Articles 22 through 25 of the Treaty.

The funds released through the implementation of the second-stage measures shall be used for peaceful purposes, including the reduction of taxes on the population and the subsidizing of the national economy. At the same time a certain portion of the funds, thus released, shall be diverted to economic and technical assistance to underdeveloped countries. The size of this portion shall be subject to agreement between the parties to the Treaty.

2. Control over the measures referred to in Paragraph 1 of this Article shall be exercised in accordance with the provisions of Paragraph 2 of Article 13 of the Treaty. Financial inspectors of the International Disarmament Organization shall also be granted unhindered access to records concerning the reduction of the budgetary allocations of States

in connexion with the elimination of nuclear, chemical, biological and radiological weapons.

Chapter VII. Measures to Safeguard the Security of States

Article 27. Continued Strengthening of the Capacity of the United Nations to Ensure International Peace and Security. The States parties to the Treaty shall continue to implement the measures, referred to in Article 18 of the present Treaty, regarding the placing of armed forces at the disposal of the Security Council for use under Article 42 of the United Nations Charter.

Chapter VIII. Time-limits for Measures of the Second Stage. Transition from Second to Third Stage

Article 28. Time-limits for Measures of the Second Stage. The duration of the second stage of general and complete disarmament shall be 15 months.

Article 29. Transition from Second to Third Stage. In the course of the last three months of the second stage the International Disarmament Organization shall review the results of the implementation of this stage.

Measures pertaining to the transition from the second to the third stage of general and complete disarmament shall be similar to those for the first stage, as provided for in Article 20 of the present Treaty.

PART IV. THIRD STAGE OF GENERAL AND COMPLETE DISARMAMENT

Article 30. Third Stage Tasks. The States parties to the Treaty undertake, in the course of the third stage of general and complete disarmament, to fully disband all their armed forces and thereby to complete the elimination of the military machinery of States.

Chapter IX. Completion of the Elimination of the Military Machinery of States. Control over such Measures

Article 31. Completion of the Elimination of Armed Forces and Conventional Armaments

1. With a view to completing the process of the elimination of armed forces the States parties to the Treaty shall disband the entire personnel of the armed forces which remained at their disposal after the accomplishment of the first two stages of disarmament. The system of military reserves of each State party to the Treaty shall be completely abolished.

2. The States parties to the Treaty shall destroy all armaments, military equipment and munitions, whether held by the troops or in depots, that remained at their disposal after the accomplishment of the first two stages of the Treaty. All military equipment which cannot be converted to peaceful uses shall be destroyed.

3. Inspectors of the International Disarmament Organization shall exercise control over the disbanding of troops, and over the destruction of armaments and military equipment, and shall control the conversion of transport and other noncombat equipment, premises, proving grounds, etc. to peaceful uses.

The International Disarmament Organization shall have access to documents pertaining to the disbanding of all personnel of the armed forces of the States parties to the Treaty.

Article 32. Complete Cessation of Military Production

1. Military production at factories and plants shall be discontinued with the exception of the production of agreed types and quantities of light firearms for the purposes referred to in Paragraph 2 of Article 36 of the present Treaty. The factories and plants, subject to elimination, shall be dismantled, their specialized machine tools and equipment shall be destroyed, and the premises, general purpose machine tools and equipment shall be converted to peaceful uses. All scientific research in the military field at all scientific and research institutions and at designing offices shall be discontinued. All blueprints and other documents necessary for the production of the weapons and military equipment subject to elimination, shall be destroyed.

All orders placed by military departments for the production of armaments, military equipment, munitions and material with national or foreign Government-owned enterprises and private firms, shall be annulled.

2. Inspectors of the International Disarmament Organization shall exercise control over the measures referred to in Paragraph 1 of this Article.

Article 33. Abolition of Military Establishments

1. War ministries, general staffs, and all other military and paramilitary organizations and institutions designed to organize the military effort of States parties to the Treaty shall be abolished. The States parties to the Treaty shall:

(a) demobilize all personnel of these institutions and organizations;

(b) abrogate all legislative acts, rules and regulations governing the organization of the military effort, and the status, structure and activities of such institutions and organizations;

(c) destroy all documents pertaining to the planning of the mobilization and the operational deployment of the armed forces in time of war.

2. The entire process of the abolition of military and paramilitary institutions and organizations shall be carried out under the control of inspectors of the International Disarmament Organization.

Article 34. Abolition of Military Conscription and Military Training. In accordance with their respective constitutional procedures the States parties to the Treaty shall enact legislation prohibiting all military training, abolishing military conscription and all other forms of recruiting the armed forces, and discontinuing all military courses for reservists. Simultaneously all establishments and organizations dealing with military training shall be disbanded, as provided for in Article 33 of the present Treaty. The disbanding of all military training institutions and organizations shall be carried out under the control of inspectors of the International Disarmament Organization.

Article 35. Prohibition of the Appropriation of Funds for Military Purposes

1. The appropriation of funds for military purposes in any form, whether from government bodies or private individuals and public organizations, shall be discontinued.

The funds released through the implementation of general and complete disarmament shall be used for peaceful purposes, including the reduction or complete abolition of taxes on the population, and the subsidizing of the national economy. At the same time a certain portion of the funds, thus released, shall be diverted to economic and technical assistance to underdeveloped countries. The size of this portion shall be subject to agreement between the parties to the Treaty.

2. To organize control over the implementation of the provisions of this Article, the International Disarmament Organization shall have the right of access to legislative acts and budgetary documents of the States parties to the present Treaty.

Chapter X. Measures to Safeguard the Security of States and to Maintain International Peace

Article 36. Contingents of Police (Militia)

1. To maintain internal order, including the safeguarding of the frontiers and of the personal security of citizens, and to ensure compliance with their obligations in regard to the maintenance of international peace and security under the United Nations Charter, the States parties to the Treaty shall be entitled to have, after the complete abolition of armed forces, strictly limited contingents of police (militia), equipped with light firearms.

The strength of these contingents of police (militia) for each State party to the Treaty shall be, as follows: . . .

2. The States parties to the Treaty shall be allowed to manufacture strictly limited quantities of light firearms intended for such contingents of police (militia). The list of plants producing such arms, their quotas and types for each party to the Treaty shall be specified in a special agreement.

3. Inspectors of the International Disarmament Organization shall exercise control over compliance by the States parties to the Treaty with their obligations with regard to the restricted production of the said light firearms.

Article 37. Police (Militia) Units to be made Available to the Security Council

1. The States parties to the Treaty undertake to place at the disposal of the Security Council, on its request, units from the number of contingents of police (militia) retained by them, as well as to provide assistance and facilities, including rights of passage. The placing of such units at the disposal of the Security Council shall be carried out under the provisions of Article 43 of the United Nations Charter. To ensure that urgent military measures may be undertaken, the States parties to the Treaty shall maintain in a state of immediate readiness that part of the police (militia) contingents which is intended for joint international enforcement action. The size of the units which the States parties to the Treaty undertake to place at the disposal of the Security Council, as well as the areas where they are stationed, shall be specified in agreements to be concluded by the States parties to the Treaty with the Security Council.

2. The command of the units referred to in Paragraph 1 shall be made up of representatives of the three principal groups of States existing in the world on the basis of equal representation. The commanding body shall decide on all questions by agreement among its members representing the three groups of States.

Article 38. Control over the Prevention of the Reestablishment of Armed Forces

1. The police (militia) contingents retained by the States parties to the Treaty after the completion

of general and complete disarmament shall be under the control of the International Disarmament Organization which shall verify the reports by States concerning the areas where such contingents are stationed, their strength and armaments in every such area, and concerning all movements of substantial contingents of police (militia).

2. For purposes of control over the prevention of the re-establishment of armed forces and armaments, abolished as a result of general and complete disarmament, the International Disarmament Organization shall have the right of access at any time to any point within the territory of each State party to the Treaty.

3. The International Disarmament Organization shall have the right to institute a system of aerial inspection and aerial photography over the territories of the States parties to the Treaty.

Chapter XI. Time-limits for Measures of the Third Stage

Article 39. The third stage of general and complete disarmament shall be completed over a period of one year. During the last three months of this stage the International Disarmament Organization shall review the results of the implementation of the third-stage measures of general and complete disarmament, with a view to reporting on them to the States parties to the Treaty, as well as to the Security Council and the General Assembly of the United Nations.

[U.S. Department of State, *Documents on Disarmament, 1945–1959* (Washington, D.C., 1960), vol. 1, Doc. 16; U.N. doc. AEC/24, June 11, 1947]

U.S. Proposal for General and Complete Disarmament (1962)

United States Proposal Submitted to the Eighteen Nation Disarmament Committee: Outline of Basic Provisions of a Treaty on General and Complete Disarmament in a Peaceful World, 18 April 1962

In order to assist in the preparation of a treaty on general and complete disarmament in a peaceful world, the United States submits the following outline of basic provisions of such a treaty. The Preamble of such a treaty has already been the subject of negotiations and is therefore not submitted as part of this treaty outline.

A. Objectives

1. To ensure that (a) disarmament is general and complete and war is no longer an instrument for settling international problems, and (b) general and complete disarmament is accompanied by the establishment of reliable procedures for the settlement of disputes and by effective arrangements for the maintenance of peace in accordance with the principles of the Charter of the United Nations.

2. Taking into account paragraphs 3 and 4 below, to provide, with respect to the military establishment of every nation, for:

(a) Disbanding of armed forces, dismantling of military establishments, including bases, cessation of the production of armaments as well as their liquidation or conversion to peaceful uses;

(b) Elimination of all stockpiles of nuclear, chemical, biological and other weapons of mass destruction and cessation of the production of such weapons;

(c) Elimination of all means of delivery of weapons of mass destruction;

(d) Abolition of the organizations and institutions designed to organize the military efforts of states, cessation of military training, and closing of all military training institutions;

(e) Discontinuance of military expenditures.

3. To ensure that, at the completion of the program for general and complete disarmament, states would have at their disposal only those non-nuclear armaments, forces, facilities and establishments as are agreed to be necessary to maintain internal order and protect the personal security of citizens.

4. To ensure that during and after implementation of general and complete disarmament, states also would support and provide agreed manpower for a United Nations Peace Force to be equipped with agreed types of armaments necessary to en-

sure that the United Nations can effectively deter or suppress any threat or use of arms.

5. To establish and provide for the effective operation of an International Disarmament Organization within the framework of the United Nations for the purpose of ensuring that all obligations under the disarmament program would be honored and observed during and after implementation of general and complete disarmament; and to this end to ensure that the International Disarmament Organization and its inspectors would have unrestricted access without veto to all places as necessary for the purpose of effective verification.

B. Principles

The guiding principles during the achievement of these objectives are:

1. Disarmament would be implemented until it is completed by stages to be carried out within specified time limits.

2. Disarmament would be balanced so that at no stage of the implementation of the treaty could any state or group of states gain military advantage, and so that security would be ensured equally for all.

3. Compliance with all disarmament obligations would be effectively verified during and after their entry into force. Verification arrangements would be instituted progressively as necessary to ensure throughout the disarmament process that agreed levels of armaments and armed forces were not exceeded.

4. As national armaments are reduced, the United Nations would be progressively strengthened in order to improve its capacity to ensure international security and the peaceful settlement of differences as well as to facilitate the development of international cooperation in common tasks for the benefit of mankind.

5. Transition from one stage of disarmament to the next would take place upon decision that all measures in the preceding stage had been implemented and verified and that any additional arrangements required for measures in the next stage were ready to operate.

Introduction

The Treaty would contain three stages designed to achieve a permanent state of general and complete disarmament in a peaceful world. The Treaty would enter into force upon the signature and ratification of the United States of America, the Union of Soviet Socialist Republics and such other states

as might be agreed. Stage II would begin when all militarily significant states had become Parties to the Treaty and other transition requirements had been satisfied. Stage III would begin when all states possessing armed forces and armaments had become Parties to the Treaty and other transition requirements had been satisfied. Disarmament, verification, and measures for keeping the peace would proceed progressively and proportionately beginning with the entry into force of the Treaty.

STAGE I

Stage I would begin upon the entry into force of the Treaty and would be completed within three years from that date.

During Stage I the Parties to the Treaty would undertake:

1. To reduce their armaments and armed forces and to carry out other agreed measures in the manner outlined below;

2. To establish the International Disarmament Organization upon the entry into force of the Treaty in order to ensure the verification in the agreed manner of the obligations undertaken; and

3. To strengthen arrangements for keeping the peace through the measures outlined below.

A. Armaments

1. Reduction of Armaments

a. Specified Parties to the Treaty, as a first stage toward general and complete disarmament in a peaceful world, would reduce by thirty per cent the armaments in each category listed in subparagraph b, below. Except as adjustments for production would be permitted in Stage I in accordance with paragraph 3 below, each type of armament in the categories listed in subparagraph b. would be reduced by thirty per cent of the inventory existing at an agreed date.

b. All types of armaments within agreed categories would be subject to reduction in Stage I (the following list of categories, and of types within categories, is illustrative):

(1) Armed combat aircraft having an empty weight of 40,000 kilograms or greater; missiles having a range of 5,000 kilometres or greater, together with their related fixed launching pads-, and submarine-launched missiles and air-to-surface missiles having a range of 300 kilometres or greater.

(Within this category, the United States, for example, would declare as types of armaments: the B-52 aircraft; Atlas missiles together with their related fixed launching pads; Titan missiles together with their related fixed launching pads; Polaris missiles; Hound Dog missiles; and each new type of armament, such as Minuteman missiles, which came within the category description, together with, where applicable, their related fixed launching pads. The declared inventory of types within the category by other Parties to the Treaty would be similarly detailed.)

(2) Armed combat aircraft having an empty weight of between 15,000 kilograms and 40,000 kilograms and those missiles not included in category (1) having a range between 300 kilometres and 5,000 kilometres, together with any related fixed launching pads. (The Parties would declare their armaments by types within the category.)

(3) Armed combat aircraft having an empty weight of between 2,500 and 15,000 kilograms. (The Parties would declare their armaments by types within the category.)

(4) Surface-to-surface (including submarine-launched missiles) and air-to-surface aerodynamic and ballistic missiles and free rockets having a range of between 10 kilometres and 300 kilometres, together with any related fixed launching pads. (The Parties would declare their armaments by types within the category.)

(5) Anti-missile missile systems, together with related fixed launching pads. (The Parties would declare their armaments by types within the category.)

(6) Surface-to-air missiles other than anti-missile missile systems, together with any related fixed launching pads. (The Parties would declare their armaments by types within the category.)

(7) Tanks. (The Parties would declare their armaments by types within the category.)

(8) Armoured cars and armoured personnel carriers. (The Parties would declare their armaments by types within the category.)

(9) All artillery, and mortars and rocket launchers having a caliber of 100 mm. or greater. (The Parties would declare their armaments by types within the category.)

(10) Combatant ships with standard displacement of 400 tons or greater of the following classes: Aircraft carriers, battleships, cruisers, destroyer types and submarines. (The Parties would declare their armaments by types within the category.)

2. Method of Reduction

a. Those Parties to the Treaty which were subject to the reduction of armaments would submit to the International Disarmament Organization an appropriate declaration respecting inventories of their armaments existing at the agreed date.

b. The reduction would be accomplished in three steps, each consisting of one year. One-third of the reduction to be made during Stage I would be carried out during each step.

c. During the first part of each step, one-third of the armaments to be eliminated during Stage I would be placed in depots under supervision of the International Disarmament Organization. During the second part of each step, the deposited armaments would be destroyed, or, where appropriate, converted to peaceful uses. The number and location of such depots and arrangements respecting their establishment and operation would be set forth in an annex to the Treaty.

d. In accordance with arrangements which would be set forth in a Treaty annex on verification, the International Disarmament Organization would verify the foregoing reduction and would provide assurance that retained armaments did not exceed agreed levels.

3. Limitation on Production of Armaments and on Related Activities

a. Production of all armaments listed in subparagraph b. of paragraph 1. above would be limited to agreed allowances during Stage I and, by the beginning of Stage 11, would be halted except for production within agreed limits of parts for maintenance of the agreed retained armaments.

b. The allowances would permit limited production in each of the categories of armaments listed in subparagraph b. of paragraph 1. above. In all instances during the process of eliminating production of armaments:

(1) any armament produced within a category would be compensated for by an additional armament destroyed within that category to the end that the ten per cent reduction in numbers in each category in each step, and the resulting thirty per cent reduction in Stage I, would be achieved; and furthermore

(2) in the case of armed combat aircraft having an empty weight of 15,000 kilograms or greater and of missiles having a range of 300 kilometres or greater, the destructive capability of any such armaments produced within a category would be compensated for by the destruction of sufficient armaments within that category to the end that the ten per cent reduction in destructive capability as

well as numbers in each of these categories in each step, and the resulting thirty per cent reduction in Stage I, would be achieved.

c. Should a Party to the Treaty elect to reduce its production in any category at a more rapid rate than required by the allowances provided in subparagraph b. above, that Party would be entitled to retain existing armaments to the extent of the unused portion of its production allowance. In any such instance, any armament so retained would be compensated for in the manner set forth in subparagraph b.(1) and, where applicable, b.(2) above, to the end that the ten per cent reduction in numbers and, where applicable, destructive capability in each category in each step, and the resulting thirty per cent reduction in Stage I would be achieved.

d. The flight testing of missiles would be limited to agreed annual quotas.

e. In accordance with arrangements which would be set forth in the annex on verification, the International Disarmament Organization would verify the foregoing measures at declared locations and would provide assurance that activities subject to the foregoing measures were not conducted at undeclared locations.

4. Additional Measures

The Parties to the Treaty would agree to examine unresolved questions relating to means of accomplishing in Stages II and Ill the reduction and eventual elimination of production and stockpiles of chemical and biological weapons of mass destruction. In light of this examination, the Parties to the Treaty would agree to arrangements concerning chemical and biological weapons of mass destruction.

B. Armed Forces

1. Reduction of Armed Forces

Force levels for the United States of America and the Union of Soviet Socialist Republics would be reduced to 2.1 million each and for other specified Parties to the Treaty to agreed levels not exceeding 2.1 million each. All other Parties to the Treaty would, with agreed exceptions, reduce their force levels to 100,000 or one per cent of their population, whichever were higher, provided that in no case would the force levels of such other Parties to the Treaty exceed levels in existence upon the entry into force of the Treaty.

2. Armed Forces Subject to Reduction

Agreed force levels would include all full-time, uniformed personnel maintained by national governments in the following categories:

a. Career personnel of active armed forces and other personnel serving in the active armed forces on fixed engagements or contracts.

b. Conscripts performing their required period of full-time active duty as fixed by national law.

c. Personnel of militarily organized security forces and of other forces or organizations equipped and organized to perform a military mission.

3. Method of Reduction of Armed Forces

The reduction of force levels would be carried out in the following manner:

a. Those Parties to the Treaty which were subject to the foregoing reductions would submit to the International Disarmament Organization a declaration stating their force levels at the agreed date.

b. Force level reductions would be accomplished in three steps, each having a duration of one year. During each step force levels would be reduced by one-third of the difference between force levels existing at the agreed date and the levels to be reached at the end of Stage 1.

c. In accordance with arrangements that would be set forth in the annex on verification, the International Disarmament Organization would verify the reduction of force levels and provide assurance that retained forces did not exceed agreed levels.

4. Additional Measures

The Parties to the Treaty which were subject to the foregoing reductions would agree upon appropriate arrangements, including procedures for consultation, in order to ensure that civilian employment by military establishments would be in accordance with the objectives of the obligations respecting force levels.

C. Nuclear Weapons

1. Production of Fissionable Materials for Nuclear Weapons

a. The Parties to the Treaty would halt the production of fissionable materials for use in nuclear weapons.

b. This measure would be carried out in the following manner:

(1) The Parties to the Treaty would submit to the International Disarmament Organization a declara-

tion listing by name, location and production capacity every facility under their jurisdiction capable of producing and processing fissionable materials at the agreed date.

(2) Production of fissionable materials for purposes other than use in nuclear weapons would be limited to agreed levels. The Parties to the Treaty would submit to the International Disarmament Organization periodic declarations stating the amounts and types of fissionable materials which were still being produced at each facility.

(3) In accordance with arrangements which would be set forth in the annex on verification, the International Disarmament Organization would verify the foregoing measures at declared facilities and would provide assurance that activities subject to the foregoing limitations were not conducted at undeclared facilities.

2. Transfer of Fissionable Material to Purposes Other Than Use in Nuclear Weapons

a. Upon the cessation of production of fissionable materials for use in nuclear weapons, the United States of America and the Union of Soviet Socialist Republics would each transfer to purposes other than use in nuclear weapons an agreed quantity of weapons-grade U-235 from past production. The purposes for which such materials would be used would be determined by the state to which the material belonged, provided that such materials were not used in nuclear weapons.

b. To ensure that the transferred materials were not used in nuclear weapons, such materials would be placed under safeguards and inspection by the International Disarmament Organization either in stockpiles or at the facilities in which they would be utilized for purposes other than use in nuclear weapons.

Arrangements for such safeguards and inspection would be set forth in the annex on verification.

3. Transfer of Fissionable Materials Between States for Peaceful Uses of Nuclear Energy

a. Any transfer of fissionable materials between states would be for purposes other than for use in nuclear weapons and would be subject to a system of safeguards to ensure that such materials were not used in nuclear weapons.

b. The system of safeguards to be applied for this purpose would be developed in agreement with the International Atomic Energy Agency and would be set forth in an annex to the Treaty.

4. Non-Transfer of Nuclear Weapons

The Parties to the Treaty would agree to seek to prevent the creation of further national nuclear forces. To this end the Parties would agree that:

a. Any Party to the Treaty which had manufactured, or which at any time manufacturers, a nuclear weapon would:

(1) Not transfer control over any nuclear weapons to a state which had not manufactured a nuclear weapon before an agreed date;

(2) Not assist any such state in manufacturing any nuclear weapons.

b. Any Party to the Treaty which had not manufactured a nuclear weapon before the agreed date would:

(1) Not acquire, or attempt to acquire, control over any nuclear weapons;

(2) Not manufacture, or attempt to manufacture, any nuclear weapons.

5. Nuclear Weapons Test Explosions

a. If an agreement prohibiting nuclear weapons test explosions and providing for effective international control had come into force prior to the entry into force of the Treaty, such agreement would become an annex to the Treaty, and all the Parties to the Treaty would be bound by the obligations specified in the agreement.

b. If, however, no such agreement had come into force prior to the entry into force of the Treaty, all nuclear weapons test explosions would be prohibited, and the procedures for effective international control would be set forth in an annex to the Treaty.

6. Additional Measures

The Parties to the Treaty would agree to examine remaining unresolved questions relating to the means of accomplishing in Stages II and III the reduction and eventual elimination of nuclear weapons stockpiles. In the light of this examination, the Parties to the Treaty would agree to arrangements concerning nuclear weapons stockpiles.

D. Outer Space

1. Prohibition of Weapons of Mass Destruction in Orbit. The Parties to the Treaty would agree not to place in orbit weapons capable of producing mass destruction.

2. Peaceful Cooperation on Space. The Parties to the Treaty would agree to support increased international cooperation in peaceful uses of outer space in the United Nations or through other appropriate arrangements.

3. Notification and Pre-Launch Inspection. With respect to the launching of space vehicles and missiles:

a. Those Parties to the Treaty which conducted launchings of space vehicles or missiles would provide advance notification of such launchings to other Parties to the Treaty and to the International Disarmament Organization together with the track of the space vehicle or missile. Such advance notification would be provided on a timely basis to permit pre-launch inspection of the space vehicle or missile to be launched.

b. In accordance with arrangements which would be set forth in the annex on verification, the International Disarmament Organization would conduct pre-launch inspection of space vehicles and missiles and would establish and operate any arrangements necessary for detecting unreported launchings.

4. Limitations on Production and on Related Activities

The production, stockpiling and testing of boosters for space vehicles would be subject to agreed limitations. Such activities would be monitored by the International Disarmament Organization in accordance with arrangements which would be set forth in the annex on verification.

E. Military Expenditures

1. Report On Expenditures. The Parties to the Treaty would submit to the International Disarmament Organization at the end of each step of each stage a report on their military expenditures. Such reports would include an itemization of military expenditures.

2. Verifiable Reduction of Expenditures. The Parties to the Treaty would agree to examine questions related to the verifiable reduction of military expenditures. In the light of this examination, the Parties to the Treaty would consider appropriate arrangements respecting military expenditures.

F. Reduction of the Risk of War

In order to promote confidence and reduce the risk of war, the Parties to the Treaty would agree to the following measures:

1. Advance Notification of Military Movements and Manoeuvres. Specified Parties to the Treaty would give advance notification of major military movements and manoeuvres to other Parties to the Treaty and to the International Disarmament Organization. Specific arrangements relating to this commitment, including the scale of movements and manoeuvres to be reported and the information to be transmitted, would be agreed.

2. Observation Posts. Specified Parties to the Treaty would permit observation posts to be established at agreed locations, including major ports, railway centres, motor highways, river crossings, and air bases to report on concentrations and movements of military forces. The number of such posts could be progressively expanded in each successive step of Stage I. Specific arrangements relating to such observation posts, including the location and staffing of posts, the method of receiving and reporting information, and the schedule for installation of posts would be agreed.

3. Additional Observation Arrangements. The Parties to the Treaty would establish such additional observation arrangements as might be agreed. Such arrangements could be extended in an agreed manner during each step of Stage 1.

4. Exchange of Military Missions. Specified Parties to the Treaty would undertake the exchange of military missions between states or groups of states in order to improve communications and understanding between them. Specific arrangements respecting such exchanges would be agreed.

5. Communications between Heads of Government. Specified Parties to the Treaty would agree to the establishment of rapid and reliable communications among their heads of government and with the Secretary-General of the United Nations. Specific arrangements in this regard would be subject to agreement among the Parties concerned and between such Parties and the Secretary-General.

6. International Commission on Reduction of the Risk of War. The Parties to the Treaty would establish an International Commission on Reduction of the Risk of War as a subsidiary body of the International Disarmament Organization to examine and make recommendations regarding further measures that might be undertaken during Stage I or subsequent stages of disarmament to reduce the risk of war by accident, miscalculation, failure of communications, or surprise attack. Specific arrangements for such measures as might be agreed to by all or some of the Parties to the Treaty would be subject to agreement among the Parties concerned.

G. The International Disarmament Organization

1. Establishment of the International Disarmament Organization. The International Disarmament Organization would be established upon the entry into force of the Treaty and would function within the framework of the United Nations and in accordance with the terms and conditions of the Treaty.

2. Cooperation of the Parties to the Treaty. The Parties to the Treaty would agree to cooperate promptly and fully with the International Disarmament Organization and to assist the Disarmament Organization in the performance of its functions and in the execution of the decisions made by it in accordance with the provisions of the Treaty.

3. Verification Functions of the International Disarmament Organization. The International Disarmament Organization would verify disarmament measures in accordance with the following principles which would be implemented through specific arrangements set forth in the annex on verification:

a. Measures providing for reduction of armaments would be verified by the International Disarmament Organization at agreed depots and would include verification of the destruction of armaments and, where appropriate, verification of the conversion of armaments to peaceful uses. Measures providing for reduction of armed forces would be verified by the International Disarmament Organization either at the agreed depots or other agreed locations.

b. Measures halting or limiting production, testing, and other specified activities would be verified by the International Disarmament Organization. Parties to the Treaty would declare the nature and location of all production and testing facilities and other specified activities. The International Disarmament Organization would have access to relevant facilities and activities wherever located in the territory of such Parties.

c. Assurance that agreed levels of armaments and armed forces were not exceeded and that activities limited or prohibited by the Treaty were not being conducted clandestinely would be provided by the International Disarmament Organization through agreed arrangements which would have the effect of providing that the extent of inspection during any step or stage would be related to the amount of disarmament being undertaken and to the degree of risk to the Parties to the Treaty of possible violations. This might be accomplished, for example, by an arrangement embodying such features as the following:

(1) All parts of the territory of those Parties to the Treaty to which this form of verification was applicable would be subject to selection for inspection from the beginning of Stage I as provided below.

(2) Parties to the Treaty would divide their territory into an agreed number of appropriate zones and at the beginning of each step of disarmament would submit the International Disarmament Organization a declaration stating the total level of armaments, forces, and specified types of activities subject to verification within each zone. The exact location of armaments and forces within a zone would not be revealed prior to its selection for inspection.

(3) An agreed number of these zones would be progressively inspected by the International Disarmament Organization during Stage I according to an agreed time schedule. The zones to be inspected would be selected by procedures which would ensure their selection by Parties to the Treaty other than the Party whose territory was to be inspected or any Party associated with it. Upon selection of each zone, the Party to the Treaty whose territory was to be inspected would declare the exact location of armaments, forces and other agreed activities within the selected zone. During the verification process, arrangements would be made to provide assurance against undeclared movements of the objects of verification to or from the zone or zones being inspected. Both aerial and mobile ground inspection would be employed within the zone being inspected. In so far as agreed measures being verified were concerned access within the zone would be free and unimpeded, and verification would be carried out with the full cooperation of the state being inspected.

(4) Once a zone had been inspected it would remain open for further inspection while verification was being extended to additional zones.

(5) By the end of Stage III, when all disarmament measures had been completed, inspection would have been extended to all parts of the Territory of Parties to the Treaty.

4. Composition of the International Disarmament Organization

a. The International Disarmament Organization would have:

(1) A General Conference of all the Parties to the Treaty;

(2) A Control Council consisting of representatives of all the major signatory powers as permanent members and certain other Parties to the Treaty on a rotating basis; and

(3) An Administrator who would administer the International Disarmament Organization under the direction of the Control Council and who would have the authority, staff, and finances adequate to ensure effective and impartial implementation of the functions of the International Disarmament Organization.

b. The General Conference and the Control Council would have power to establish such subsidiary bodies, including expert study groups, as either of them might deem necessary.

5. *Functions of the General Conference.* The General Conference would have the following functions, among others which might be agreed:

a. Electing non-permanent members to the Control Council;

b. Approving certain accessions to the Treaty;

c. Appointing the Administrator upon recommendation of the Control Council;

d. Approving agreements between the International Disarmament Organization and the United Nations and other international organizations;

e. Approving the budget of the International Disarmament Organization;

f. Requesting and receiving reports from the Control Council and deciding upon matters referred to it by the Control Council;

g. Approving reports to be submitted to bodies of the United Nations;

h. Proposing matters for consideration by the Control Council;

i. Requesting the International Court of Justice to give advisory opinions on legal questions concerning the interpretation or application of the Treaty, subject to a general authorization of this power by the General Assembly of the United Nations;

j. Approving amendments to the Treaty for possible ratification by the Parties to the Treaty;

k. Considering matters of mutual interest pertaining to the Treaty or disarmament in general.

6. *Functions of the Control Council.* The Control Council would have the following functions, among others which might be agreed:

a. Recommending appointment of the Administrator;

b. Adopting rules for implementing the terms of the Treaty;

c. Establishing procedures and standards for the installation and operation of the verification arrangements, and maintaining supervision over such arrangements and the Administrator;

d. Establishing procedures for making available to the Parties to the Treaty data produced by verification arrangements;

e. Considering reports of the Administrator on the progress of disarmament measures and of their verification, and on the installation and operation of the verification arrangements;

f. Recommending to the Conference approval of the budget of the International Disarmament Organization;

g. Requesting the International Court of Justice to give advisory opinions on legal questions concerning the interpretation or application of the Treaty, subject to a general authorization of this power by the General Assembly of the United Nations;

h. Recommending to the Conference approval of certain accessions to the Treaty;

i. Considering matters of mutual interests pertaining to the Treaty or to disarmament in general.

7. *Functions of the Administrator.* The Administrator would have the following functions, among others which might be agreed:

a. Administering the installation and operation of the verification arrangements, and serving as Chief Executive Officer of the International Disarmament Organization;

b. Making available to the Parties to the Treaty data produced by the verification arrangements;

c. Preparing the budget of the International Disarmament Organization;

d. Making reports to the Control Council on the progress of disarmament measures and of their verification, and on the installation and operation of the verification arrangements.

8. *Privileges and Immunities.* The privileges and immunities which the Parties to the Treaty would grant to the International Disarmament Organization and its staff and to the representatives of the Parties to the International Disarmament Organization, and the legal capacity which the International Disarmament Organization should enjoy in the territory of each of the parties to the Treaty would be specified in an annex to the Treaty.

9. *Relations with the United Nations and Other International Organizations*

a. The International Disarmament Organization, being established within the framework of the

United Nations, would conduct its activities in accordance with the purposes and principles of the United Nations. It would maintain close working arrangements with the United Nations, and the Administrator of the International Disarmament Organization would consult with the Secretary General of the United Nations on matters of mutual interest.

b. The Control Council of the International Disarmament Organization would transmit to the United Nations annual and other reports on the activities of the International Disarmament Organization.

c. Principal organs of the United Nations could make recommendations to the International Disarmament Organization, which would consider them and report to the United Nations on action taken.

NOTE: The above outline does not cover all the possible details or aspects of relationships between the International Disarmament Organization and the United Nations.

H. Measures To Strengthen Arrangements for Keeping the Peace

1. Obligations Concerning Threat or Use of Force. The Parties to the Treaty would undertake obligations to refrain, in their international relations, from the threat or use of force of any type-including nuclear, conventional, chemical or biological means of warfare-contrary to the purposes and principles of the United Nations Charter.

2. Rules of International Conduct

a. The Parties to the Treaty would agree to support a study by a subsidiary body of the International Disarmament Organization of the codification and progressive development of rules of international conduct related to disarmament.

b. The Parties to the Treaty would refrain from indirect aggression and subversion. The subsidiary body provided for in subparagraph a would also study methods of assuring states against indirect aggression or subversion.

3. Peaceful Settlement of Disputes

a. The Parties to the Treaty would utilize all appropriate processes for the peaceful settlement of all disputes which might arise between them and any other state, whether or not a Party to the Treaty, including negotiation, inquiry, mediation, conciliation, arbitration, judicial settlement, resort to regional agencies or arrangements, submission to the Security Council or the General Assembly of the United Nations, or other peaceful means of their choice.

b. The Parties to the Treaty would agree that disputes concerning the interpretation or application of the Treaty which were not settled by negotiation or by the International Disarmament Organization would be subject to referral by any party to the dispute to the International Court of Justice, unless the parties concerned agreed on another mode of settlement.

c. The Parties to the Treaty would agree to support a study under the General Assembly of the United Nations of measures which should be undertaken to make existing arrangements for the peaceful settlement of international disputes, whether legal or political in nature, more effective; and to institute new procedures and arrangements where needed.

4. Maintenance of International Peace and Security. The Parties to the Treaty would agree to support measures strengthening the structure, authority, and operation of the United Nations so as to improve its capability to maintain international peace and security.

5. United Nations Peace Force. The Parties to the Treaty would undertake to develop arrangements during Stage I for the establishment in Stage II of a United Nations Peace Force. To this end, the Parties to the Treaty would agree on the following measures within the United Nations.

a. Examination of the experience of the United Nations leading to a further strengthening of United Nations forces for keeping the peace;

b. Examination of the feasibility of concluding promptly the agreements envisaged in Article 43 of the United Nations Charter;

c. Conclusion of an agreement for the establishment of a United Nations Peace Force in Stage II, including definitions of its purpose, mission, composition, and strength, disposition, command and control, training, logistical support, financing, equipment and armaments.

6. United Nations Peace Observation Corps. The Parties to the Treaty would agree to support the establishment within the United Nations of a Peace Observation Corps, staffed with a standing cadre of observers who could be despatched promptly to investigate any situation which might constitute a threat to or a breach of the peace. Elements of the Peace Observation Corps could also be stationed as appropriate in selected areas throughout the world.

I. Transition

1. Transition from Stage I to Stage II would take place at the end of Stage I, upon a determination that the following circumstances existed:

a. All undertakings to be carried out in Stage I had been carried out;

b. All preparations required for Stage II had been made; and

c. All militarily significant states had become Parties to the Treaty.

2. During the last three months of Stage I, the Control Council would review the situation respecting these circumstances with a view to determining whether these circumstances existed at the end of Stage I.

3. If, at the end of Stage 1, one or more permanent members of the Control Council should declare that the foregoing circumstances did not exist, the agreed period of Stage I would, upon the request of such permanent member or members, be extended by a period or periods totalling no more than three months for the purpose of bringing about the foregoing circumstances.

4. If, upon the expiration of such period or periods, one or more of the permanent members of the Control Council would declare that the foregoing circumstances still did not exist, the question would be placed before a special session of the Security Council; transition to Stage II would take place upon a determination by the Security Council that the foregoing circumstances did in fact exist.

STAGE II

Stage II would begin upon the transition from Stage I and would be completed within three years from that date.

During Stage II, the Parties to the Treaty would undertake:

1. To continue all obligations undertaken during Stage I;

2. To reduce further the armaments and armed forces reduced during Stage I and to carry out additional measures of disarmament in the manner outlined below;

3. To ensure that the International Disarmament Organization would have the capacity to verify in the agreed manner the obligations undertaken during Stage II; and

4. To strengthen further the arrangements for keeping the peace through the establishment of a United Nations Peace Force and through the additional measures outlined below.

A. Armaments

1. Reduction of Armaments

a. Those Parties to the Treaty which had during Stage I reduced their armaments in agreed categories by thirty per cent would during Stage II further reduce each type of armaments in the categories listed in Section A, subparagraph 1.b. of Stage I by fifty percent of the inventory existing at the end of Stage I.

b. Those Parties to the Treaty which had not been subject to measures for the reduction of armaments during Stage I would submit to the International Disarmament Organization an appropriate declaration respecting the inventories by types, within the categories listed in Stage I, of their armaments existing at the beginning of Stage II. Such Parties to the Treaty would during Stage II reduce the inventory of each type of such armaments by sixty-five per cent in order that such Parties would accomplish the same total percentage of reduction by the end of Stage II as would be accomplished by those Parties to the Treaty which had reduced their armaments by thirty per cent in Stage I.

2. Additional Armaments Subject to Reduction

a. The Parties to the Treaty would submit to the International Disarmament Organization a declaration respecting their inventories existing at the beginning of Stage II of the additional types of armaments in the categories listed in subparagraph b. below, and would during Stage II reduce the inventory of each type of such armaments by fifty per cent.

b. All types of armaments within further agreed categories would be subject to reduction in Stage II (the following list of categories is illustrative):

(1) Armed combat aircraft having an empty weight of up to 2,500 kilograms (declarations by types),

(2) Specified types of unarmed military aircraft (declarations by types).

(3) Missiles and free rockets having a range of less than 20 kilometers (declarations by types).

(4) Mortars and rocket launchers having a caliber of less than 100 mm. (declarations by types).

(5) Specified types of unarmoured personnel carriers and transport vehicles (declarations by types).

(6) Combatant ships with standard displacement of 400 tons or greater which had not been included among the armaments listed in Stage I, and combatant ships with standard displacement of less than 400 tons (declarations by types).

(7) Specified types of non-combatant naval vessels (declarations by types).

(8) Specified types of small arms (declarations by types).

c. Specified categories of ammunition for armaments listed in Stage I, Section A, subparagraph 1.b., and in subparagraph b. above would be reduced to levels consistent with the levels of armaments agreed for the end of Stage II.

3. Method of Reduction. The foregoing measures would be carried out and would be verified by the International Disarmament Organization in a manner corresponding to that provided for in Stage I, Section A, paragraph 2.

4. Limitation on Production of Armaments and on Related Activities

a. The Parties to the Treaty would halt the production of armaments in the specified categories except for production, within agreed limits, of parts required for maintenance of the agreed retained armaments.

b. The production of ammunition in specified categories would be reduced to agreed levels consistent with the levels of armaments agreed for the end of Stage II.

c. The Parties to the Treaty would halt development and testing of new types of armaments. The flight testing of existing types of missiles would be limited to agreed annual quotas.

d. In accordance with arrangements which would be set forth in the annex on verification, the International Disarmament Organization would verify the foregoing measures at the declared locations and would provide assurance that activities subject to the foregoing measures were not conducted at undeclared locations.

5. Additional Measures

a. In the light of their examination during Stage I of the means of accomplishing the reduction and eventual elimination of production and stockpiles of chemical and biological weapons of mass destruction, the Parties to the Treaty would undertake the following measures respecting such weapons;

(1) The cessation of all production and field testing of chemical and biological weapons of mass destruction.

(2) The reduction, by agreed categories, of stockpiles of chemical and biological weapons of mass destruction to levels fifty per cent below those existing at the beginning of Stage II.

(3) The dismantling or conversion to peaceful uses of all facilities engaged in the production or field testing of chemical and biological weapons of mass destruction.

b. The foregoing measures would be carried out in an agreed sequence and through arrangements which would be set forth in an annex to the Treaty.

c. In accordance with arrangements which would be set forth in the annex on verification the International Disarmament Organization would verify the foregoing measures and would provide assurance that retained levels of chemical and biological weapons did not exceed agreed levels and that activities subject to the foregoing limitations were not conducted at undeclared locations.

B. Armed Forces

1. Reduction of Armed Forces

a. Those Parties to the treaty which had been subject to measures providing for reduction of force levels during Stage I would further reduce their force levels on the following basis:

(1) Force levels of the United States of America and the Union of Soviet Socialist Republics would be reduced to levels fifty per cent below the levels agreed for the end of Stage I.

(2) Force levels of other Parties to the Treaty which had been subject to measures providing for the reduction of force levels during Stage I would be further reduced, on the basis of an agreed percentage, below the levels agreed for the end of Stage I to levels which would not in any case exceed the agreed level for the United States of America and the Union of Soviet Socialist Republics at the end of Stage II.

b. Those Parties to the Treaty which had not been subject to measures providing for the reduction of armed forces during Stage I would reduce their force levels to agreed levels consistent with those to be reached by other parties which had reduced their force levels during Stage I as well as Stage II. In no case would such agreed levels exceed the agreed level for the United States of America and the Union of Soviet Socialist Republics at the end of Stage II.

c. Agreed levels of armed forces would include all personnel in the categories set forth in Section B, paragraph 2 of Stage I.

2. Method of Reduction. The further reduction of force levels would be carried out and would be verified by the International Disarmament Organization in a manner corresponding to that provided for in Section B, paragraph 3 of Stage I.

3. Additional Measures. Agreed limitations consistent with retained force levels would be placed on compulsory military training, and on refresher training for reserve forces of the Parties to the Treaty.

C. Nuclear Weapons

1. Reduction of Nuclear Weapons. In the light of their examination during Stage I of the means of accomplishing the reduction and eventual elimination of nuclear weapons stockpiles, the Parties of the Treaty would undertake to reduce in the following manner remaining nuclear weapons and fissionable materials for use in nuclear weapons:

a. The Parties to the Treaty would submit to the International Disarmament Organization a declaration stating the amounts, types, and nature of utilization of all their fissionable materials.

b. The Parties to the Treaty would reduce the amounts and types of fissionable materials declared for use in nuclear weapons to minimum levels on the basis of agreed percentages. The foregoing reduction would be accomplished through the transfer of such materials to purposes other than use in nuclear weapons. The purposes for which such materials would be used would be determined by the state to which the materials belonged, provided that such materials were not used in nuclear weapons.

c. The Parties to the Treaty would destroy the non-nuclear components and assemblies of nuclear weapons from which fissionable materials had been removed to effect the foregoing reduction of fissionable materials for use in nuclear weapons.

d. Production or refabrication of nuclear weapons from any remaining fissionable materials would be subject to agreed limitations.

e. The foregoing measures would be carried out in an agreed sequence and through arrangements which would be set forth in an annex to the Treaty.

f. In accordance with arrangements that would be set forth in the verification annex to the Treaty, the International Disarmament Organization would verify the foregoing measures at declared locations and would provide assurance that activities subject to the foregoing limitations were not conducted at undeclared locations.

2. Registration of Nuclear Weapons for Verification Purposes. To facilitate verification during Stage Ill that no nuclear weapons remained at the disposal of the Parties to the Treaty, those Parties to the Treaty which possessed nuclear weapons would, during the last six months of Stage II, register and serialize their remaining nuclear weapons and would register fissionable materials for use in such weapons. Such registration and serialization would be carried out with the International Disarmament Organization in accordance with procedures which would be set forth in the annex on verification.

D. Military Bases and Facilities

1. Reduction of Military Bases and Facilities. The Parties to the Treaty would dismantle or convert to peaceful uses agreed military bases and facilities, wherever they might be located.

2. Method of Reduction

a. The list of military bases and facilities subject to the foregoing measures and the sequence and arrangements for dismantling or converting them to peaceful uses would be set forth in an annex to the Treaty.

b. In accordance with arrangements which would be set forth in the annex on verification, the International Disarmament Organization would verify the foregoing measures.

E. Reduction of the Risk of War

In the light of the examination by the International Commission on Reduction of the Risk of War during Stage I the Parties to the Treaty would undertake such additional arrangements as appeared desirable to promote confidence and reduce the risk of war. The Parties to the Treaty would also consider extending and improving the measures undertaken in Stage I for this purpose. The Commission would remain in existence to examine extensions, improvements or additional measures which might be undertaken during and after Stage II.

F. The International Disarmament Organization

The International Disarmament Organization would be strengthened in the manner necessary to ensure its capacity to verify the measures undertaken in Stage II through an extension of the arrangements based upon the principles set forth in Section G, paragraph 3 of Stage I.

G. Measures To Strengthen Arrangements
for Keeping the Peace

1. Peaceful Settlement of Disputes

a. In light of the study of peaceful settlement of disputes conducted during Stage I, the Parties to the Treaty would agree to such additional steps and arrangements as were necessary to assure the just and peaceful settlement of international disputes, whether legal or political in nature.

b. The Parties to the Treaty would undertake to accept without reservation, pursuant to Article 36, Paragraph (1) of the Statute of the International Court of Justice, the compulsory jurisdiction of that Court to decide international legal disputes.

2. Rules of International Conduct

a. The Parties to the Treaty would continue their support of the study by the subsidiary body of the International Disarmament Organization initiated in Stage I to study the codification and progressive development of rules of international conduct related to disarmament. The Parties to the Treaty would agree to the establishment of procedures whereby rules recommended by the subsidiary body and approved by the Control Council would be circulated to all Parties to the Treaty and would become effective three months thereafter unless a majority of the Parties to the Treaty signified their disapproval, and whereby the Parties to the Treaty would be bound by rules which had become effective in this way unless, within a period of one year from the effective date, they formally notified the International Disarmament Organization that they did not consider themselves so bound. Using such procedures, the Parties to the Treaty would adopt such rules of international conduct related to disarmament as might be necessary to begin Stage III.

b. In the light of the study of indirect aggression and subversion conducted in Stage I, the Parties to the Treaty would agreed to arrangements necessary to assure states against indirect aggression and subversion.

3. United Nations Peace Force. The United Nations Peace Force to be established as the result of the agreement reached during Stage I would come into being within the first year of Stage II and would be progressively strengthened during Stage II.

4. United Nations Peace Observation Corps. The Parties to the Treaty would conclude arrangement for the expansion of the activities of the United Nations Peace Observation Corps.

5. National Legislation. Those Parties to the Treaty which had not already done so would, in accordance with their constitutional processes, enact national legislation in support of the Treaty imposing legal obligations on individuals and organizations under their jurisdiction and providing appropriate penalties for noncompliance.

H. Transition

1. Transition from Stage II to Stage III would take place at the end of Stage II, upon a determination that the following circumstances existed:

a. All undertakings to be carried out in Stage II had been carried out;

b. All preparations required for Stage III had been made; and

c. All states possessing armed forces and armaments had become Parties to the Treaty.

2. During the last three months of Stage II, the Control Council would review the situation respecting these circumstances with a view to determining at the end of Stage II whether they existed.

3. If, at the end of Stage II, one or more permanent members of the Control Council should declare that the foregoing circumstances did not exist, the agreed period of Stage II would, upon the request of such permanent member or members, be extended by a period or periods totalling no more than three months for the purpose of bringing about the foregoing circumstances.

4. If, upon the expiration of such period or periods, one or more of the permanent members of the Control Council should declare that the foregoing circumstances still did not exist, the question would be placed before a special session of the Security Council; transition to Stage III would take place upon a determination by the Security Council that the foregoing circumstances did in fact exist.

STAGE III

Stage III would begin upon the transition from Stage II and would be completed within an agreed period of time as promptly as possible.

During Stage III, the Parties to the Treaty would undertake:

1. To continue all obligations undertaken during Stages I and II;

2. To complete the process of general and complete disarmament in the manner outlined below;

3. To ensure that the International Disarmament Organization would have the capacity to verify in

the agreed manner the obligations undertaken during Stage III and of continuing verification subsequent to the completion of Stage II; and

4. To strengthen further the arrangements for keeping the peace during and following the achievement of general and complete disarmament through the additional measures outlined below.

A. Armaments

1. Reduction of Armaments. Subject to agreed requirements for non-nuclear armaments of agreed types for national forces required to maintain internal order and protect the personal security of citizens, the Parties to the Treaty would eliminate all armaments remaining at their disposal at the end of Stage II.

2. Method of Reduction

a. The foregoing measure would be carried out in an agreed sequence and through arrangements that would be set forth in an annex to the Treaty.

b. In accordance with arrangements that would be set forth in the annex on verification, the International Disarmament Organization would verify the foregoing measures and would provide assurance that retained armaments were of the agreed types and did not exceed agreed levels.

3. Limitations on Production of Armaments and on Related Activities

a. Subject to agreed arrangements in support of national forces required to maintain internal order and protect the personal security of citizens and subject to agreed arrangements in support of the United Nations Peace Force, the Parties to the Treaty would halt all applied research, development, production, and testing of armaments and would cause to be dismantled or converted to peaceful uses all other facilities for such purposes.

b. The foregoing measures would be carried out in an agreed sequence and through arrangements which would be set forth in an annex to the Treaty.

c. In accordance with arrangements which would be set forth in the annex on verification, the International Disarmament Organization would verify the foregoing measures at declared locations and would provide assurance that activities subject to the foregoing measures were not conducted at undeclared locations.

B. Armed Forces

1. Reduction of Armed Forces. To the end that upon completion of Stage III they would have at their disposal only those forces and organizational arrangements necessary for agreed forces to maintain internal order and protect the personal security of citizens and that they would be capable of providing agreed manpower for the United Nations Peace Force, the Parties to the Treaty would complete the reduction of their force levels, disband systems of reserve forces, cause to be disbanded organizational arrangements comprising and supporting their national military establishment, and terminate the employment of civilian personnel associated with the foregoing.

2. Method of Reduction

a. The foregoing measures would be carried out in an agreed sequence through arrangements which would be set forth in an annex to the Treaty.

b. In accordance with arrangements which would be set forth in the annex on verification, the International Disarmament Organization would verify the foregoing measures and would provide assurance that the only forces and organizational arrangements retained or subsequently established were those necessary for agreed forces required to maintain internal order and to protect the personal security of citizens and those for providing agreed manpower for the United Nations Peace Force.

3. Other Limitations. The Parties to the Treaty would halt all military conscription and would undertake to annul legislation concerning national military establishments or military service inconsistent with the foregoing measures.

C. Nuclear Weapons

1. Reduction of Nuclear Weapons. In light of the steps taken in Stages I and II to halt the production of fissionable material for use in nuclear weapons and to reduce nuclear weapons stockpiles, the Parties to the Treaty would eliminate all nuclear weapons remaining at their disposal, would cause to be dismantled or converted to peaceful use all facilities for production of such weapons, and would transfer all materials remaining at their disposal for use in such weapons to purposes other than use in such weapons.

2. Method of Reduction

a. The foregoing measures would be carried out in an agreed sequence and through arrangements which would be set forth in an annex to the Treaty.

b. In accordance with arrangements which would be set forth in the annex on verification, the International Disarmament Organization would verify the foregoing measures and would provide assurance that no nuclear weapons or materials for use in such weapons remained at the disposal of the Parties to the Treaty and that no such weapons or materials were produced at undeclared facilities.

D. Military Bases and Facilities

1. Reduction of Military Bases and Facilities. The Parties to the Treaty would dismantle or convert to peaceful uses the military bases and facilities remaining at their disposal, wherever they might be located, in an agreed sequence except for such agreed bases or facilities within the territory of the Parties to the Treaty for agreed forces required to maintain internal order and protect the personal security of citizens.

2. Method of Reduction

a. The list of military bases and facilities subject to the foregoing measure and the sequence and arrangements for dismantling or converting them to peaceful uses during Stage III would be set forth in an annex to the Treaty.

b. In accordance with arrangements which would be set forth in the annex on verification, the International Disarmament Organization would verify the foregoing measure at declared locations and provide assurance that there were no undeclared military bases and facilities.

E. Research and Development of Military Significance

1. Reporting Requirement. The Parties to the Treaty would undertake the following measures respecting research and development of military significance subsequent to Stage III:

a. The Parties to the Treaty would report to the International Disarmament Organization any basic scientific discovery and any technological invention having potential military significance.

b. The Control Council would establish such expert study groups as might be required to examine the potential military significance of such discoveries and inventions and, if necessary, to recommend appropriate measures for their control. In the light of such expert study, the Parties to the Treaty would, where necessary, establish agreed arrangements providing for verification by the International Disarmament Organization that such discoveries and inventions were not utilized for military purposes. Such arrangements would become an annex to the Treaty.

c. The Parties to the Treaty would agree to appropriate arrangements for protection of the ownership rights of all discoveries and inventions reported to the International Disarmament Organization in accordance with subparagraph a. above.

2. International Cooperation. The Parties to the Treaty would agree to support full international cooperation in all fields of scientific research and development, and to engage in free exchange of scientific and technical information and free interchange of views among scientific and technical personnel.

F. Reduction of the Risk of War

1. Improved Measures. In the light of the Stage II examination by the International Commission on Reduction of the Risk of War, the Parties to the Treaty would undertake such extensions and improvements of existing arrangements and such additional arrangements as appeared desirable to promote confidence and reduce the risk of war. The Commission would remain in existence to examine extensions, improvements or additional measures which might be taken during and after Stage III.

2. Application of Measures to Continuing Forces. The Parties to the Treaty would apply to national forces required to maintain internal order and protect the personal security of citizens those applicable measures concerning the reduction of the risk of war that had been applied to national armed forces in Stages I and II.

G. International Disarmament Organization

The International Disarmament Organization would be strengthened in the manner necessary to ensure its capacity (1) to verify the measures undertaken in Stage III through an extension of arrangements based upon the principles set forth in Section G, paragraph 3 of Stage I so that by the end of Stage III, when all disarmament measures had been completed, inspection would have been extended to all parts of the territory of Parties to the Treaty; and (2) to provide continuing verification of disarmament after the completion of Stage III.

H. Measures to Strengthen Arrangements for Keeping the Peace

1. Peaceful Change and Settlement of Disputes. The Parties to the Treaty would undertake such additional steps and arrangements as were necessary to provide a basis for peaceful change in a disarmed world and to continue the just and peaceful settlement of all international disputes, whether legal or political in nature.

2. Rules of International Conduct. The Parties to the Treaty would continue the codification and progressive development of rules of international conduct related to disarmament in the manner provided in Stage II and by any other agreed procedure.

3. United Nations Peace Force. The Parties to the Treaty would progressively strengthen the United Nations Peace Force established in Stage II until it had sufficient armed forces and armaments so that no state could challenge it.

I. Completion of Stage III

1. At the end of the time period for Stage III, the Control Council would review the situation with a view to determining whether all undertakings to be carried out in Stage III had been carried out.

2. In the event that one or more of the permanent members of the Control Council should de-clare that such undertakings had not been carried out, the agreed period of Stage III would, upon the request of such permanent member or members, be extended for a period or periods totalling no more than three months for the purpose of completing any uncompleted undertakings. If, upon the expiration of such period or periods, one or more of the permanent members of the Control Council should declare that such undertakings still had not been carried out, the question would be placed before a special session of the Security Council, which would determine whether Stage III had been completed.

3. After the completion of Stage III, the obligations undertaken in Stages I, II and III would continue . . . .

[U.S. Department of State, *Documents on Disarmament, 1962,* vol. 1, pp. 351–380. ENDC/30, Apr. 18, and Corr. 1, Apr. 25, 1962. U.S. amendments, pp. 718, 728–730]

Nuclear Weapons Limitation Negotiations

Initial proposals to limit atomic weapons begin with the Baruch Plan of 1946 and with the Soviet Union's counterproposal of 1947.

Baruch Plan (1946)

Following is the text of the statement made by United States Representative Bernard Baruch to the United Nations Atomic Energy Commission on 14 June 1946.

My fellow members of the United Nations Atomic Energy Commission, and my fellow citizens of the world:

We are here to make a choice between the quick and the dead.

That is our business.

Behind the black portent of the new atomic age lies a hope which, seized upon with faith, can work our salvation. If we fail, then we have damned every man to be the slave of Fear. Let us not deceive ourselves: We must elect World Peace or World Destruction.

Science has torn from nature a secret so vast in its potentialities that our minds cower from the terror it creates. Yet terror is not enough to inhibit the use of the atomic bomb. The terror created by weapons has never stopped man from employing them. For each new weapon a defense has been produced, in time. But now we face a condition in which adequate defense does not exist.

Science, which gave us this dread power, shows that it *can* be made a giant help to humanity, but science does *not* show us how to prevent its baleful use. So we have been appointed to obviate that peril by finding a meeting of the minds and the hearts of our people. Only in the will of mankind lies the answer.

It is to express this will and make it effective that we have been assembled. We must provide the mechanism to assure that atomic energy is used for peaceful purposes and preclude its use in war. To that end, we must provide immediate, swift, and sure punishment of those who violate the agreements that are reached by the nations. Penalization is essential if peace is to be more than a feverish interlude between wars. And, too, the United Nations can prescribe individual responsibility and punishment on the principles applied at Nürnberg by the Union of Soviet Socialist Republics, the United Kingdom, France, and the United States—a formula certain to benefit the world's future.

In this crisis, we represent not only our governments but, in a larger way, we represent the peoples of the world. We must remember that the peoples do not belong to the governments but that the governments belong to the peoples. We must answer their demands; we must answer the world's longing for peace and security.

In that desire the United States shares ardently and hopefully. The search of science for the absolute weapon has reached fruition in this country. But she stands ready to proscribe and destroy this instrument-to lift its use from death to life-if the world will join in a pact to that end.

In our success lies the promise of a new life, freed from the heart-stopping fears that now beset the world. The beginning of victory for the great ideals for which millions have bled and died lies in building a workable plan. Now we approach fulfilment of the aspirations of mankind. At the end of the road lies the fairer, better, surer life we crave and mean to have.

Only by a lasting peace are liberties and democracies strengthened and deepened. War is their enemy. And it will not do to believe that any of us can escape war's devastation. Victor, vanquished, and neutrals alike are affected physically, economically, and morally.

Against the degradation of war we can erect a safeguard. That is the guerdon for which we reach. Within the scope of the formula we outline here there will be found, to those who seek it, the essential elements of our purpose. Others will see only emptiness. Each of us carries his own mirror in which is reflected hope — or determined desperation—courage or cowardice.

There is a famine throughout the world today. It starves men's bodies. But there is a greater famine — the hunger of men's spirit. That starvation can be cured by the conquest of fear, and the substitution of hope, from which springs faith — faith in each other, faith that we want to work together toward salvation, and determination that those who threaten the peace and safety shall be punished.

The peoples of these democracies gathered here have a particular concern with our answer, for their peoples hate war. They will have a heavy exaction to make of those who fail to provide an escape. They are not afraid of an internationalism that protects; they are unwilling to be fobbed off by mouthings about narrow sovereignty, which is today's phrase for yesterday's isolation.

The basis of a sound foreign policy, in this new age, for all the nations here gathered, is that anything that happens, no matter where or how, which menaces the peace of the world, or the economic stability, concerns each and all of us.

That, roughly, may be said to be the central theme of the United Nations. It is with that thought we begin consideration of the most important subject that can engage mankind — life itself.

Let there be no quibbling about the duty and the responsibility of this group and of the governments we represent. I was moved, in the afternoon of my life, to add my effort to gain the world's quest, by the broad mandate under which we were created. The resolution of the General Assembly, passed January 24, 1946 in London, reads:

Section V. Terms of Reference of the Commission

The Commission shall proceed with the utmost despatch and enquire into all phases of the problems, and make such recommendations from time to time with respect to them as it finds possible. In particular the Commission shall make specific proposals:

(a) For extending between all nations the exchange of basic scientific information for peaceful ends;

(b) For control of atomic energy to the extent necessary to ensure its use only for peaceful purposes;

(c) For the elimination from national armaments of atomic weapons and of all other major weapons adaptable to mass destruction;

(d) For effective safeguards by way of inspection and other means to protect complying States against the hazards of violations and evasions.

The work of the Commission should proceed by separate stages, the successful completion of each of which will develop the necessary confidence of the world before the next stage is undertaken....

Our mandate rests, in text and in spirit, upon the outcome of the Conference in Moscow of Messrs. Molotov of the Union of Soviet Socialist Republics, Bevin of the United Kingdom, and Byrnes of the United States of America. The three Foreign Ministers on December 27, 1945 proposed the establishment of this body.

Their action was animated by a preceding conference in Washington on November 15, 1945, when the President of the United States, associated with Mr. Attlee, Prime Minister of the United Kingdom, and Mr. Mackenzie King, Prime Minister of Canada, stated that international control of the whole field of atomic energy was immediately essential. They proposed the formation of this body. In examining that source, the Agreed Declaration, it will be found that the fathers of the concept recognized the final means of world salvation—the abolition of war. Solemnly they wrote:

We are aware that the only complete protection for the civilized world from the destructive use of scientific knowledge lies in the prevention of war. No system of safeguards that can be devised will of itself provide an effective guarantee against production of atomic weapons by a nation bent on aggression. Nor can we ignore the possibility of the development of other weapons, or of new methods of warfare, which may constitute as great a threat to civilization as the military use of atomic energy.

Through the historical approach I have outlined, we find ourselves here to test if man can produce, through his will and faith, the miracle of peace, just as he has, through science and skill, the miracle of the atom.

The United States proposes the creation of an International Atomic Development Authority, to which should be entrusted all phases of the development and use of atomic energy, starting with the raw material and including

1. Managerial control or ownership of all atomic energy activities potentially dangerous to world security.

2. Power to control, inspect, and license all other atomic activities.

3. The duty of fostering the beneficial uses of atomic energy.

4. Research and development responsibilities of an affirmative character intended to put the Authority in the forefront of atomic knowledge and thus to enable it to comprehend, and therefore to detect, misuse of atomic energy. To be effective, the Authority must itself be the world's leader in the field of atomic knowledge and development and thus supplement its legal authority with the great power inherent in possession of leadership in knowledge.

I offer this as a basis for beginning our discussion.

But I think the peoples we serve would not believe—and without faith nothing counts—that a treaty, merely outlawing possession or use of the atomic bomb, constitutes effective fulfilment of the instructions to this Commission. Previous failures have been recorded in trying the method of simple renunciation, unsupported by effective guaranties of security and armament limitation. No one would have faith in that approach alone.

Now, if ever, is the time to act for the common good. Public opinion supports a world movement toward security. If I read the signs aright, the peoples want a program not composed merely of pious thoughts but of enforceable sanctions—an international law with teeth in it.

We of this nation, desirous of helping to bring peace to the world and realizing the heavy obligations upon us arising from our possession of the means of producing the bomb and from the fact that it is part of our armament, are prepared to make our full contribution toward effective control of atomic energy.

When an adequate system for control of atomic energy, including the renunciation of the bomb as a weapon, has been agreed upon and put into effective operation and condign punishments set up

for violations of the rules of control which are to be stigmatized as international crimes, we propose that

1. Manufacture of atomic bombs shall stop;

2. Existing bombs shall be disposed of pursuant to the terms of the treaty; and

3. The Authority shall be in possession of full information as to the know-how for the production of atomic energy.

Let me repeat, so as to avoid misunderstanding: My country is ready to make its full contribution toward the end we seek, subject of course to our constitutional processes and to an adequate system of control becoming fully effective, as we finally work it out.

Now as to violations: In the agreement, penalties of as serious a nature as the nations may wish and as immediate and certain in their execution as possible should be fixed for

1. Illegal possession or use of an atomic bomb;

2. Illegal possession, or separation, of atomic material suitable for use in an atomic bomb;

3. Seizure of any plant or other property belonging to or licensed by the Authority;

4. Wilful interference with the activities of the Authority;

5. Creation or operation of dangerous projects in a manner contrary to, or in the absence of, a license granted by the international control body.

It would be a deception, to which I am unwilling to lend myself, were I not to say to you and to our peoples that the matter of punishment lies at the very heart of our present security system. It might as well be admitted, here and now, that the subject goes straight to the veto power contained in the Charter of the United Nations so far as it relates to the field of atomic energy. The Charter permits penalization only by concurrence of each of the five great powers—the Union of Soviet Socialist Republics, the United Kingdom, China, France, and the United States.

I want to make very plain that I am concerned here with the veto power only as it affects this particular problem. There must be no veto to protect those who violate their solemn agreements not to develop or use atomic energy for destructive purposes.

The bomb does not wait upon debate. To delay may be to die. The time between violation and preventive action or punishment would be all too short for extended discussion as to the course to be followed.

As matters now stand several years may be necessary for another country to produce a bomb, *de novo*. However, once the basic information is generally known, and the Authority has established producing plants for peaceful purposes in the several countries, an illegal seizure of such a plant might permit a malevolent nation to produce a bomb in 12 months, and if preceded by secret preparation and necessary facilities perhaps even in a much shorter time. The time required—the advance warning given of the possible use of a bomb—can only be generally estimated but obviously will depend upon many factors, including the success with which the Authority has been able to introduce elements of safety in the design of its plants and the degree to which illegal and secret preparation for the military use of atomic energy will have been eliminated. Presumably no nation would think of starting a war with only one bomb.

This shows how imperative speed is in detecting and penalizing violations.

The process of prevention and penalization—a problem of profound statecraft—is, as I read it, implicit in the Moscow statement, signed by the Union of Soviet Socialist Republics, the United States, and the United Kingdom a few months ago.

But before a country is ready to relinquish any winning weapons it must have more than words to reassure it. It must have a guarantee of safety, not only against the offenders in the atomic area but against the illegal users of other weapons—bacteriological, biological, gas—perhaps—why not?—against war itself.

In the elimination of war lies our solution, for only then will nations cease to compete with one another in the production and use of dread "secret" weapons which are evaluated solely by their capacity to kill. This devilish program takes us back not merely to the Dark Ages but from cosmos to chaos. If we succeed in finding a suitable way to control atomic weapons, it is reasonable to hope that we may also preclude the use of other weapons adaptable to mass destruction. When a man learns to say "A" he can, if he chooses, learn the rest of the alphabet too.

Let this be anchored in our minds:

Peace is never long preserved by weight of metal or by an armament race. Peace can be made tranquil and secure only by understanding and agreement fortified by sanctions. We must embrace international cooperation or international disintegration.

Science has taught us how to put the atom to work. But to make it work for good instead of for evil lies in the domain dealing with the principles of human duty. We are now facing a problem more of ethics than of physics.

The solution will require apparent sacrifice in pride and in position, but better pain as the price of peace than death as the price of war.

I now submit the following measures as representing the fundamental features of a plan which would give effect to certain of the conclusions which I have epitomized.

1. *General.* The Authority should set up a thorough plan for control of the field of atomic energy, through various forms of ownership, dominion, licenses, operation, inspection, research, and management by competent personnel. After this is provided for, there should be as little interference as may be with the economic plans and the present private, corporate, and state relationships in the several countries involved.

2. *Raw Materials.* The Authority should have as one of its earliest purposes to obtain and maintain complete and accurate information on world supplies of uranium and thorium and to bring them under its dominion. The precise pattern of control for various types of deposits of such materials will have to depend upon the geological, mining, refining, and economic facts involved in different situations.

The Authority should conduct continuous surveys so that it will have the most complete knowledge of the world geology of uranium and thorium. Only after all current information on world sources of uranium and thorium is known to us all can equitable plans be made for their production, refining, and distribution.

3. *Primary Production Plants.* The Authority should exercise complete managerial control of the production of fissionable materials. This means that it should control and operate all plants producing fissionable materials in dangerous quantities and must own and control the product of these plants.

4. *Atomic Explosives.* The Authority should be given sole and exclusive right to conduct research in the field of atomic explosives. Research activities

in the field of atomic explosives are essential in order that the Authority may keep in the forefront of knowledge in the field of atomic energy and fulfil the objective of preventing illicit manufacture of bombs. Only by maintaining its position as the best-informed agency will the Authority be able to determine the line between intrinsically dangerous and non-dangerous activities.

5. *Strategic Distribution of Activities and Materials.* The activities entrusted exclusively to the Authority because they are intrinsically dangerous to security should be distributed throughout the world. Similarly, stockpiles of raw materials and fissionable materials should not be centralized.

6. *Non-Dangerous Activities.* A function of the Authority should be promotion of the peacetime benefits of atomic energy.

Atomic research (except in explosives), the use of research reactors: the production of radioactive traces by means of non-dangerous reactors, the use of such tracers, and to some extent the production of power should be open to nations and their citizens under reasonable licensing arrangements from the Authority. Denatured materials, whose use we know also requires suitable safeguards, should be furnished for such purposes by the Authority under lease or other arrangement. Denaturing seems to have been overestimated by the public as a safety measure.

7. *Definition of Dangerous and Non-Dangerous Activities.* Although a reasonable dividing line can be drawn between dangerous and nondangerous activities, it is not hard and fast. Provision should, therefore, be made to assure constant reexamination of the questions and to permit revision of the dividing line as changing conditions and new discoveries may require.

8. *Operations of Dangerous Activities.* Any plant dealing with uranium or thorium after it once reaches the potential of dangerous use must be not only subject to the most rigorous and competent inspection by the Authority, but its actual operation shall be under the management, supervision, and control of the Authority.

9. *Inspection.* By assigning intrinsically dangerous activities exclusively to the Authority, the difficulties of inspection are reduced. If the Authority is the only agency which may lawfully conduct dangerous activities, then visible operation by others than the Authority will constitute an unambiguous danger signal. Inspection will also occur in connection with the licensing functions of the Authority.

10. *Freedom of Access.* Adequate ingress and egress for all qualified representatives of the Authority must be assured. Many of the inspection activities of the Authority should grow out of, and be incidental to, its other functions. Important measures of inspection will be associated with the tight control of raw materials, for this is a keystone of the plan. The continuing activities of prospecting, survey, and research in relation to raw materials will be designed not only to serve the affirmative development functions of the Authority but also to assure that no surreptitious operations are conducted in the raw-materials field by nations or their citizens.

11. *Personnel.* The personnel of the Authority should be recruited on a basis of proven competence but also so far as possible on an international basis.

12. *Progress by Stages.* A primary step in the creation of the system of control is the setting forth, in comprehensive terms, of the functions, responsibilities, powers, and limitations of the Authority. Once a charter for the Authority has been adopted, the Authority and the system of control for which it will be responsible will require time to become fully organized and effective. The plan of control will, therefore, have to come into effect in successive stages. These should be specifically fixed in the charter or means should be otherwise set forth in the charter for transitions from one stage to another, as contemplated in the resolution of the United Nations Assembly which created this Commission.

13. *Disclosures.* In the deliberations of the United Nations Commission on Atomic Energy, the United States is prepared to make available the information essential to a reasonable understanding of the proposals which it advocates. Further disclosures must be dependent, in the interests of all, upon the effective ratification of the treaty. When the Authority is actually created, the United States will join the other nations in making available the further information essential to that organization for the performance of its functions. As the successive stages of international control are reached, the United States will be prepared to yield, to the extent required by each stage, national control of activities in this field to the Authority.

14. *International Control.* There will be questions about the extent of control to be allowed to national bodies, when the Authority is established. Purely national authorities for control and devel-

opment of atomic energy should to the extent necessary for the effective operation of the Authority be subordinate to it. This is neither an endorsement nor a disapproval of the creation of national authorities. The Commission should evolve a clear demarcation of the scope of duties and responsibilities of such national authorities.

And now I end. I have submitted an outline for present discussion. Our consideration will be broadened by the criticism of the United States proposals and by the plans of the other nations, which, it is to be hoped, will be submitted at their early convenience. I and my associates of the United States Delegation will make available to each member of this body books and pamphlets, including the Acheson-Lilienthal report, recently made by the United States Department of State, and the McMahon Committee Monograph No. I entitled "Essential Information on Atomic Energy" relating to the McMahon bill recently passed by the United States Senate, which may prove of value in assessing the situation.

All of us are consecrated to making an end of gloom and hopelessness. It will not be an easy job. The way is long and thorny, but supremely worth traveling. All of us want to stand erect, with our faces to the sun, instead of being forced to burrow into the earth, like rats.

The pattern of salvation must be worked out by all for all.

The light at the end of the tunnel is dim, but our path seems to grow brighter as we actually begin our journey. We cannot yet light the way to the end. However, we hope the suggestions of my Government will be illuminating.

Let us keep in mind the exhortation of Abraham Lincoln, whose words, uttered at a moment of shattering national peril, form a complete text for our deliberation. I quote, paraphrasing slightly:

We cannot escape history. We of this meeting will be remembered in spite of ourselves. No personal significance or insignificance can spare one or another of us. The fiery trial through which we are passing will light us down in honor or dishonor to the latest generation.

We say we are for Peace. The world will not forget that we say this. We know how to save Peace. The world knows that we do. We, even we here, hold the power and have the responsibility.

We shall nobly save, or meanly lose, the last, best hope of earth. The way is plain, peaceful, generous, just—a way which, if followed, the world will forever applaud.

My thanks for your attention.

[U.S Department of State, *Documents on Disarmament, 1945–1959,* vol. 1, Doc. 4. *The United States and the United Nations: Report by the President to the Congress for the Year 1946.* Department of State publ. 2735 (1947), pp. 169–178]

Soviet Proposals for International Control of Atomic Energy (1947)

The following proposals were introduced to the United Nations Atomic Energy Commission on 11 June 1947.

The Soviet Government, in addition and in development of its proposal on the conclusion of an international convention on the prohibition of atomic and other major weapons of mass destruction, submitted for the consideration of the Atomic Energy Commission on 19 June 1946, presents for the consideration of the above-mentioned Commis-

sion the following basic provisions on which an international agreement or convention on atomic energy control should be based.

1. For ensuring the use of atomic energy only for peaceful purposes, in accordance with the international convention on the prohibition of atomic and other major weapons of mass destruction and also

with the purpose of preventing violations of the convention on the prohibition of atomic weapons and for the protection of complying States against hazards of violations and evasions, there shall be established strict international control simultaneously over all facilities engaged in mining of atomic raw materials and in production of atomic materials and atomic energy.

2. For carrying out measures of control of atomic energy facilities, there shall be established, within the framework of the Security Council, an international commission for atomic energy control to be called the International Control Commission.

3. The International Control Commission shall have its own inspectorial apparatus.

4. Terms and organizational principles of international control of atomic energy, and also composition, rights and obligations of the International Control Commission, as well as provisions on the basis of which it shall carry out its activities, shall be determined by a special international convention on atomic energy control, which is to be concluded in accordance with the convention on the prohibition of atomic weapons.

5. With the purpose of ensuring the effectiveness of international control of atomic energy, the convention on the control of atomic energy shall be based on the following fundamental provisions:

(a) The International Control Commission shall be composed of the Representatives of States Members of the Atomic Energy Commission established by the General Assembly decision of 24 January 1946, and may create such subsidiary organs which it finds necessary for the fulfilment of its functions.

(b) The International Control Commission shall establish its own rules of procedure.

(c) The personnel of the International Control Commission shall be selected on an international basis.

(d) The International Control Commission shall periodically carry out inspection of facilities for mining of atomic raw materials and for the production of atomic materials and atomic energy.

6. While carrying out inspection of atomic energy facilities, the International Control Commission shall undertake the following actions:

(a) Investigates the activities of facilities for mining atomic raw materials, for the production of atomic materials and atomic energy as well as verifies their accounting.

(b) Checks existing stocks of atomic raw materials, atomic materials, and unfinished products.

(c) Studies production operations to the extent necessary for the control of the use of atomic materials and atomic energy.

(d) Observes the fulfilment of the rules of technical exploitation of the facilities prescribed by the convention on control as well as works out and prescribes the rules of technological control of such facilities.

(e) Collects and analyses data on the mining of atomic raw materials and on the production of atomic materials and atomic energy.

(f) Carries on special investigations in cases when suspicion of violations of the convention on the prohibition of atomic weapons arises.

(g) Makes recommendations to Governments on the questions relating to production, stockpiling and use of atomic materials and atomic energy.

(h) Makes recommendations to the Security Council on measures for prevention and suppression in respect to violators of the conventions on the prohibition of atomic weapons and on the control of atomic energy.

7. For the fulfilment of the tasks of control and inspection entrusted to the International Control Commission, the latter shall have the right of:

(a) Access to any facilities for mining, production, and stockpiling of atomic raw materials and atomic materials, as well as to the facilities for the exploitation of atomic energy.

(b) Acquaintance with the production operations of the atomic energy facilities, to the extent necessary for the control of use of atomic materials and atomic energy.

(c) The carrying out of weighing, measurements, and various analyses of atomic raw materials, atomic materials, and unfinished products.

(d) Requesting from the Government of any nation, and checking of, various data and reports on the activities of atomic energy facilities.

(e) Requesting of various explanations on the questions relating to the activities of atomic energy facilities.

(f) Making recommendations and presentations to Governments on the matters of the production and use of atomic energy.

(g) Submitting recommendations for the consideration of the Security Council on measures in regard to violators of the conventions on the prohibition of atomic weapons and on the control of atomic energy.

8. In accordance with the tasks of international control of atomic energy, scientific research activi-

ties in the field of atomic energy shall be based on the following provisions:

(a) Scientific research activities in the field of atomic energy must comply with the necessity of carrying out the convention on the prohibition of atomic weapons and with the necessity of preventing its use for military purposes.

(b) Signatory States to the convention on the prohibition of atomic weapons must have a right to carry on unrestricted scientific research activities in the field of atomic energy, directed toward discovery of methods of its use for peaceful purposes.

(c) In the interests of an effective fulfilment of its control and inspectorial functions, the International Control Commission must have a possibility to carry out scientific research activities in the field of discovery of methods of the use of atomic energy for peaceful purposes. The carrying out of such activities will enable the Commission to keep itself informed on the latest achievements in this field

and to have its own skilled international personnel, which is required by the Commission for practical carrying out of the measures of control and inspection.

(d) In conducting scientific research in the field of atomic energy, one of the most important tasks of the International Control Commission should be to ensure a wide exchange of information among nations in this field and to render necessary assistance, through advice, to the countries parties to the convention, which may request such assistance.

(e) The International Control Commission must have at its disposal material facilities including research laboratories and experimental installations necessary for the proper organization of the research activities to be conducted by it.

[U.S. Department of State, *Documents on Disarmament, 1945–1959,* vol. 1, Doc. 16. U.N. doc. AEC/24, June 11, 1947]

SALT I **Treaty (1972)**

Interim Agreement Between the United States of America and the Union of Soviet Socialist Republics on Certain Measures With Respect to the Limitation of Strategic Offensive Arms, 26 May 1972

Article I. The Parties undertake not to start construction of additional fixed land-based intercontinental ballistic missile (ICBM) launchers after July 1, 1972.

Article II. The Parties undertake not to convert land-based launchers for light ICBMs, or for ICBMs of older types deployed prior to 1964, into land-based launchers for heavy ICBMs of types deployed after that time.

Article III. The Parties undertake to limit submarine-launched ballistic missile (SLBM) launchers and modern ballistic missile submarines to the numbers operational and under construction on the date of signature of this Interim Agreement, and in addition to launchers and submarines constructed under procedures established by the Parties as replacements for an equal number of ICBM launchers of older types deployed prior to 1964 or for launchers on older submarines.

Article IV. Subject to the provisions of this Interim Agreement, modernization and replacement of strategic offensive ballistic missiles and launchers covered by this Interim Agreement may be undertaken.

Article V

1. For the purpose of providing assurance of compliance with the provisions of this Interim Agreement, each Party shall use national technical means of verification at its disposal in a manner consistent with generally recognized principles of international law.

2. Each party undertakes not to interfere with the national technical means of verification of the other Party operating in accordance with paragraph 1 of this Article.

3. Each Party undertakes not to use deliberate concealment measures which impede verification by national technical means of compliance with the provisions of this Interim Agreement. This obligation shall not require changes in current construction, assembly, conversion, or overhaul practices.

Article VI. To promote the objectives and implementation of the provisions of this Interim Agreement, the Parties shall use the Standing Consultative Commission established under Article XIII of the Treaty on the Limitation of Anti-Ballistic Missile Systems in accordance with the provisions of that Article.

Article VII. The Parties undertake to continue active negotiations for limitations on strategic offensive arms. The obligations provided for in this Interim Agreement shall not prejudice the scope or terms of the limitations on strategic offensive arms which may be worked out in the course of further negotiations.

Article VIII

1. This Interim Agreement shall enter into force upon exchange of written notices of acceptance by each Party, which exchange shall take place simultaneously with the exchange of instruments of ratification of the Treaty on the Limitation of Anti-Ballistic Missile Systems.

2. This Interim Agreement shall remain in force for a period of five years unless replaced earlier by an agreement on more complete measures limiting strategic offensive arms. It is the objective of the parties to conduct active follow-on negotiations with the aim of concluding such an agreement as soon as possible.

3. Each Party shall, in exercising its national sovereignty, have the right to withdraw from this Interim Agreement if it decides that extraordinary events related to the subject matter of this Interim Agreement have jeopardized its supreme interests. It shall give notice of its decision to the other Party six months prior to withdrawal from this Interim Agreement. Such notice shall include a statement of the extraordinary events the notifying Party regards as having jeopardized its supreme interests.

[Signatures]

Protocol to the Interim Agreement Between the United States of America and the Union of Soviet Socialist Republics on Certain Measures With Respect to the Limitation of Strategic Offensive Arms

The United States of America and the Union of Soviet Socialist Republics, hereinafter referred to as the Parties, Having agreed on certain limitations relating to submarine-launched ballistic missile launchers and modern ballistic missile submarines, and to replacement procedures, in the Interim Agreement,

Have agreed as follows:

The Parties understand that, under Article III of the Interim Agreement, for the period during which that Agreement remains in force:

The U.S. may have no more than 710 ballistic missile launchers on submarines (SLBMS) and no more than 44 modern ballistic missile submarines. The Soviet Union may have no more than 950 ballistic missile launchers on submarines and no more than 62 modern ballistic missile submarines.

Additional ballistic missile launchers on submarines up to the above-mentioned levels, in the U.S.—over 656 ballistic missile launchers on nuclear-powered submarines, and in the U.S.S.R.—over 740 ballistic missile launchers on nuclear-powered submarines, operational and under construction, may become operational as replacements for equal numbers of ballistic missile launchers of older types deployed prior to 1964 or of ballistic missile launchers on older submarines.

The deployment of modern SLBMS on any submarine, regardless of type, will be counted against the total level of SLBMS permitted for the U.S. and the U.S.S.R.

This Protocol shall be considered an integral part of the Interim Agreement.

[Signatures]

Agreed Statements, Common Understandings, and Unilateral Statements Regarding the Interim Agreement Between the United States of America and the Union of Soviet Socialist Republics on Certain Measures With Respect to the Limitation of Strategic Offensive Arms

1. Agreed Statements

[*The document set forth below was agreed upon and initialed by the Heads of the Delegations on 26 May 1972.*]

AGREED STATEMENTS REGARDING THE INTERIM AGREEMENT BETWEEN THE UNITED STATES OF AMERICA AND THE UNION OF SOVIET SOCIALIST REPUBLICS ON CERTAIN MEASURES WITH RESPECT TO THE LIMITATION OF STRATEGIC OFFENSIVE ARMS

A. The Parties understand that land-based ICBM launchers referred to in the Interim Agreement are understood to be launchers for strategic ballistic missiles capable of ranges in excess of the shortest distance between the northeastern border of the continental U.S. and the northwestern border of the continental U.S.S.R.

B. The Parties understand that fixed land-based ICBM launchers under active construction as of the date of signature of the Interim Agreement may be completed.

C. The Parties understand that in the process of modernization and replacement the dimensions of land-based ICBM silo launchers will not be significantly increased.

D. The Parties understand that during the period of the Interim Agreement there shall be no significant increase in the number of ICBM or SLBM test and training launchers, or in the number of such launchers for modern land-based heavy ICBMS. The Parties further understand that construction or conversion of ICBM launchers at test ranges shall be undertaken only for purposes of testing and training.

E. The Parties understand that dismantling or destruction of ICBM launchers of older types deployed prior to 1964 and ballistic missile launchers on older submarines being replaced by new SLBM launchers on modern submarines will be initiated at the time of the beginning of sea trials of a replacement submarine, and will be completed in the shortest possible agreed period of time. Such dismantling or destruction, and timely notification thereof, will be accomplished under procedures to be agreed in the Standing Consultative Commission.

2. Common Understandings

Common understanding of the Parties on the following matters was reached during the negotiations:

A. *Increase in* ICBM *Silo Dimensions*

Ambassador Smith made the following statement on May 26, 1972:

The Parties agree that the term "significantly increased" means that an increase will not be greater than 10–15 percent of the present dimensions of land-based ICBM silo launchers.

Minister Semenov replied that this statement corresponded to the Soviet understanding.

B. *Standing Consultative Commission*

Ambassador Smith made the following statement on May 22, 1972:

The United States proposes that the sides agree that, with regard to initial implementation of the ABM Treaty's Article XIII on the Standing Consultative Commission (SCC) and of the consultation Articles to the Interim Agreement on offensive arms and the

Accidents Agreement, agreement establishing the SCC will be worked out early in the follow-on SALT negotiations; until that is completed, the following arrangements will prevail: when SALT is in session, any consultation desired by either side under these Articles can be carried out by the two SALT Delegations; when SALT is not in session, *ad hoc* arrangements for any desired consultations under these Articles may be made through diplomatic channels.

Minister Semenov replied that, on an *ad referendum* basis, he could agree that the U.S. statement corresponded to the Soviet understanding.

C. *Standstill*

On May 6, 1972, Minister Semenov made the following statement:

In an effort to accommodate the wishes of the U.S. side, the Soviet Delegation is prepared to proceed on the basis that the two sides will in fact observe the obligations of both the Interim Agreement and the ABM Treaty beginning from the date of signature of these two documents.

In reply, the U.S. Delegation made the following statement on May 20, 1972:

The U.S. agrees in principle with the Soviet statement made on May 6 concerning observance of obligations beginning from date of signature but we would like to make clear our understanding that this means that, pending ratification and acceptance, neither side would take any action prohibited by the agreements after they had entered into force. This understanding would continue to apply in the absence of notification by either signatory of its intention not to proceed with ratification or approval.

The Soviet Delegation indicated agreement with the U.S. statement.

3. Unilateral Statements

(a) The following noteworthy unilateral statements were made during the negotiations by the United States Delegation:

A. *Withdrawal from the* ABM *Treaty*

The U.S. Delegation has stressed the importance the U.S. Government attaches to achieving agreement on more complete limitations on strategic offensive arms, following agreement on an ABM Treaty and on an Interim Agreement on certain measures with respect to the limitation of strategic offensive arms. The U.S. Delegation believes that an objective of the follow-on negotiations should be to constrain and reduce on a long-term basis threats to the survivability of our respective strategic retaliatory forces. The U.S.S.R. Delegation has also indicated that the objectives of SALT would remain unfulfilled without the achievement of an agreement providing for more complete limitations on strategic offensive arms. Both sides recognize that the initial agreements would be steps toward the achievement of more complete limitations on strategic arms. If an agreement providing for more complete strategic offensive arms limitations were not achieved within five years, U.S. supreme interests could be jeopardized. Should that occur, it would constitute a basis for withdrawal from the ABM Treaty. The U.S. does not wish to see such a situation occur, nor do we believe that the U.S.S.R. does. It is because we wish to prevent such a situation that we emphasize the importance the U.S. Government attaches to achievement of more complete limitations on strategic offensive arms. The U.S. Executive will inform the Congress, in connection with Congressional consideration of the ABM Treaty and the Interim Agreement, of this statement of the U.S. position.

B. Land-Mobile ICBM Launchers

The U.S. Delegation made the following statement on May 20, 1972:

In connection with the important subject of land-mobile ICBM launchers, in the interest of concluding the Interim Agreement the U.S. Delegation now withdraws its proposal that Article I or an agreed statement explicitly prohibit the deployment of mobile land-based ICBM launchers. I have been instructed to inform you that, while agreeing to defer the question of limitation of operational land-mobile ICBM launchers to the subsequent negotiations on more complete limitations on strategic offensive arms, the U.S. would consider the deployment of operational land-mobile ICBM launchers during the period of the Interim Agreement as inconsistent with the objectives of that Agreement.

C. Covered Facilities

The U.S. Delegation made the following statement on May 20, 1972:

I wish to emphasize the importance that the United States attaches to the provisions of Article V, including in particular their application to fitting out or berthing submarines.

D. "Heavy" ICBMS

The U.S. Delegation made the following statement on May 26, 1972:

The U.S. Delegation regrets that the Soviet Delegation has not been willing to agree on a common definition of a heavy missile. Under these circumstances, the U.S. Delegation believes it necessary to state the following: The United States would consider any ICBM having a volume significantly greater than that of the largest light ICBM now operational on either side to be a heavy ICBM. The U.S. proceeds on the premise that the Soviet side will give due account to this consideration.

(b) The following noteworthy unilateral statement was made by the Delegation of the U.S.S.R. and is shown here with the U.S. reply:

On May 17, 1972, Minister Semenov made the following unilateral "Statement of the Soviet Side":

Taking into account that modern ballistic missile submarines are presently in the possession of not only the U.S., but also of its NATO allies, the Soviet Union agrees that for the period of effectiveness of the Interim 'Freeze' Agreement the U.S. and its NATO allies have up to 50 such submarines with a total of up to 800 ballistic missile launchers thereon (including 41 U.S. submarines with 656 ballistic missile launchers). However, if during the period of effectiveness of the Agreement U.S. allies in NATO should increase the number of their modern submarines to exceed the numbers of submarines they would have operational or under construction on the date of the signature of the Agreement, the Soviet Union will have the right to a corresponding increase in the number of its submarines. In the opinion of the Soviet side, the solution of the question of modern ballistic missile submarines provided for in the Interim Agreement only partially compensates for the strategic imbalance in the deployment of the nuclear-powered missile submarines of the USSR and the U.S. Therefore, the Soviet side believes that this whole question, and above all the question of liquidating the American missile submarine bases outside the U.S., will be appropriately resolved in the course of follow-on negotiations.

On May 24, Ambassador Smith made the following reply to Minister Semenov:

The United States side has studied the "statement made by the Soviet side" of May 17 concerning compensation for submarine basing and SLBM submarines belonging to third countries. The United States does not accept the validity of the considerations in that statement.

On May 26 Minister Semenov repeated the unilateral statement made on May 17. Ambassador Smith also repeated the U.S. rejection on May 26. [U.S. Arms Control and Disarmament Agency, *Arms Control and Disarmament Agreements,* 5th ed. (Washington, D.C., 1982), pp. 150–157]

ABM Treaty (1972)

Following is a chronology of the ratification procedure for the ABM Treaty:

- *Signed at Moscow 26 May 1972*
- *Ratification advised by U.S. Senate 3 August 1972*
- *Ratified by U.S. President 30 September 1972*
- *Proclaimed by U.S. President 3 October 1972*
- *Instruments of ratification exchanged 3 October 1972*
- *Entered into force 3 October 1972*

Treaty Between the United States of America and the Union of Soviet Socialist Republics on the Limitation of Anti-Ballistic Missile Systems

The United States of America and the Union of Soviet Socialist Republics, hereinafter referred to as the Parties,

Proceeding from the premise that nuclear war would have devastating consequences for all mankind,

Considering that effective measures to limit anti-ballistic missile systems would be a substantial factor in curbing the race in strategic offensive arms and would lead to a decrease in the risk of outbreak of war involving nuclear weapons,

Proceeding from the premise that the limitation of anti-ballistic missile systems, as well as certain agreed measures with respect to the limitation of strategic offensive arms, would contribute to the creation of more favorable conditions for further negotiations on limiting strategic arms,

Mindful of their obligations under Article VI of the Treaty on the Non-Proliferation of Nuclear Weapons,

Declaring their intention to achieve at the earliest possible date the cessation of the nuclear arms race and to take effective measures toward reductions in strategic arms, nuclear disarmament, and general and complete disarmament,

Desiring to contribute to the relaxation of international tension and the strengthening of trust between States,

Have agreed as follows:

Article I

1. Each party undertakes to limit anti-ballistic missile (ABM) systems and to adopt other measures in accordance with the provisions of this Treaty.

2. Each Party undertakes not to deploy ABM systems for a defense of the territory of its country and not to provide a base for such a defense, and not to deploy ABM systems for defense of an individual region except as provided for in Article III of this Treaty.

Article II

1. For the purpose of this Treaty an ABM system is a system to counter strategic ballistic missiles or their elements in flight trajectory, currently consisting of:

(a) ABM interceptor missiles, which are interceptor missiles constructed and deployed for an ABM role, or of a type tested in an ABM mode;

(b) ABM Launchers, which are launchers constructed and deployed for launching ABM interceptor missiles; and

(c) ABM radars, which are radars constructed and deployed for an ABM role, or of a type tested in an ABM mode.

2. The ABM system components listed in paragraph 1 of this Article include those which are: (a) operational; (b) under construction; (c) undergoing testing; (d) undergoing overhaul, repair or conversion; or (e) mothballed.

Article III. Each Party undertakes not to deploy ABM systems or their components except that:

(a) within one ABM system deployment area having a radius of one hundred and fifty kilometers and centered on the Party's national capital, a Party may deploy:

(1) no more than one hundred ABM launchers and no more than one hundred ABM interceptor missiles at launch sites, and

(2) ABM radars within no more than six ABM radar complexes, the area of each complex being circular and having a diameter of no more than three kilometers; and

(b) within one ABM system deployment area having a radius of one hundred and fifty kilometers and containing ICBM silo launchers, a Party may deploy:

(1) no more than one hundred ABM launchers and no more than one hundred ABM interceptor missiles at launch sites,

(2) two large phased-array ABM radars comparable in potential to corresponding ABM radars operational or under construction on the date of signature of the Treaty in an ABM system deployment area containing ICBM silo launchers, and

(3) no more than eighteen ABM radars each having a potential less than the potential of the smaller of the above-mentioned two large phased-array ABM radars.

Article IV. The limitations provided for in Article III shall not apply to ABM systems or their components used for development or testing, and located within current or additionally agreed test ranges. Each Party may have no more than a total of fifteen ABM launchers at test ranges.

Article V

1. Each Party undertakes not to develop, test, or deploy ABM systems or components which are sea-based, air-based, space-based, or mobile land-based.

2. Each Party undertakes not to develop, test, or deploy ABM launchers for launching more than one ABM interceptor missile at a time from each launcher, not to modify deployed launchers to provide them with such a capability, not to develop, test, or deploy automatic or semi-automatic or other similar systems for rapid reload of ABM launchers.

Article VI. To enhance assurance of the effectiveness of the limitations on ABM systems and their components provided by the Treaty, each Party undertakes:

(a) not to give missiles, launchers, or radars, other than ABM interceptor missiles, ABM launchers, or ABM radars, capabilities to counter strategic ballistic missiles or their elements in flight trajectory, and not to test them in an ABM mode; and

(b) not to deploy in the future radars for early warning of strategic ballistic missile attack except at locations along the periphery of its national territory and oriented outward.

Article VII. Subject to the provisions of this Treaty, modernization and replacement of ABM systems or their components may be carried out.

Article VIII. ABM systems or their components in excess of the numbers or outside the areas specified in this Treaty, as well as ABM systems or their components prohibited by this Treaty, shall be destroyed or dismantled under agreed procedures within the shortest possible agreed period of time.

Article IX. To assure the viability and effectiveness of this Treaty, each Party undertakes not to

transfer to other States, and not to deploy outside its national territory, ABM systems or their components limited by this Treaty.

Article X. Each Party undertakes not to assume any international obligations which would conflict with this Treaty.

Article XI. The Parties undertake to continue active negotiations for limitations on strategic offensive arms.

Article XII

1. For the purpose of providing assurance of compliance with the provisions of this Treaty, each Party shall use national technical means of verification at its disposal in a manner consistent with generally recognized principles of international law.

2. Each Party undertakes not to interfere with the national technical means of verification of the other Party operating in accordance with paragraph 1 of this Article.

3. Each Party undertakes not to use deliberate concealment measures which impede verification by national technical means of compliance with the provisions of this Treaty. This obligation shall not require changes in current construction, assembly, conversion, or overhaul practices.

Article XIII

1. To promote the objectives and implementation of the provisions of this Treaty, the Parties shall establish promptly a Standing Consultative Commission, within the framework of which they will:

(a) consider questions concerning compliance with the obligations assumed and related situations which may be considered ambiguous;

(b) provide on a voluntary basis such information as either Party considers necessary to assure confidence in compliance with the obligations assumed;

(c) consider questions involving unintended interference with national technical means of verification;

(d) consider possible changes in the strategic situation which have a bearing on the provisions of this Treaty;

(e) agree upon procedures and dates for destruction or dismantling of ABM systems or their components in cases provided for by the provisions of this Treaty;

(f) consider, as appropriate, possible proposals for further increasing the viability of this Treaty; including proposals for amendments in accordance with the provisions of this Treaty;

(g) consider, as appropriate, proposals for further measures aimed at limited strategic arms.

2. The Parties through consultation shall establish, and may amend as appropriate, Regulations for the Standing Consultative Commission governing procedures, composition and other relevant matters.

Article XIV

1. Each Party may propose amendments to this Treaty. Agreed amendments shall enter into force in accordance with the procedures governing the entry into force of this Treaty.

2. Five years after entry into force of this Treaty, and at five-year intervals thereafter, the Parties shall together conduct a review of this Treaty.

Article XV

1. This Treaty shall be of unlimited duration.

2. Each Party shall, in exercising its national sovereignty, have the right to withdraw from this Treaty if it decides that extraordinary events related to the subject matter of this Treaty have jeopardized its supreme interests. It shall give notice of its decision to the other Party six months prior to withdrawal from the Treaty. Such notice shall include a statement of the extraordinary events the notifying Party regards as having jeopardized its supreme interests.

Article XVI

1. This Treaty shall be subject to ratification in accordance with the constitutional procedures of each Party. The Treaty shall enter into force on the day of the exchange of instruments of ratification.

2. This Treaty shall be registered pursuant to Article 102 of the Charter of the United Nations.

DONE at Moscow on May 26, 1972, in two copies, each in the English and Russian languages, both texts being equally authentic.

[Signatures]

Agreed Statements, Common Understandings, and Unilateral Statements Regarding the Treaty Between the United States of America and the Union of Soviet Socialist Republics on the Limitation of Anti-Ballistic Missiles

1. Agreed Statements

[*The document below was initialed by the Heads of the Delegations on 26 May 1972.*]

AGREED STATEMENTS REGARDING THE TREATY BETWEEN THE UNITED STATES OF AMERICA AND THE UNION OF SO-

VIET SOCIALIST REPUBLICS ON THE LIMITATION OF ANTI-BALLISTIC MISSILE SYSTEMS

A. The Parties understand that, in addition to the ABM radars which may be deployed in accordance with subparagraph (a) of Article III of the Treaty, those non-phased-array ABM radars operational on the date of signature of the Treaty within the ABM system deployment area for defense of the national capital may be retained.

B. The Parties understand that the potential (the product of mean emitted power in watts and antenna area in square meters) of the smaller of the two large phased-array ABM radars referred to in subparagraph (b) of Article III of the Treaty is considered for purposes of the Treaty to be three million.

C. The Parties understand that the center of the ABM system deployment area centered on the national capital and the center of the ABM system deployment area containing ICBM silo launchers for each Party shall be separated by no less than thirteen hundred kilometers.

D. In order to insure fulfillment of the obligation not to deploy ABM systems and their components except as provided in Article III of the Treaty, the Parties agree that in the event ABM systems based on other physical principles and including components capable of substituting for ABM interceptor missiles, ABM launchers, or ABM radars are created in the future, specific limitations on such systems and their components would be subject to discussion in accordance with Article XIII and agreement in accordance with Article XIV of the Treaty.

E. The Parties understand that Article V of the Treaty includes obligations not to develop, test or deploy ABM interceptor missiles for the delivery by each ABM interceptor missile of more than one independently guided warhead.

F. The Parties agree not to deploy phased-array radars having a potential (the product of mean emitted power in watts and antenna area in square meters) exceeding three million, except as provided for in Articles III, IV and VI of the Treaty, or except for the purposes of tracking objects in outer space or for use as national technical means of verification.

G. The Parties understand that Article IX of the Treaty includes the obligation of the U.S. and the U.S.S.R. not to provide to other States technical descriptions or blue prints specially worked out for the construction of ABM systems and their components limited by the Treaty.

2. Common Understandings

Common understanding of the Parties on the following matters was reached during the negotiations.

A. Location of ICBM Defenses

The U.S. Delegation made the following statement on May 26, 1972:

Article III of the ABM Treaty provides for each side one ABM system deployment area centered on its national capital and one ABM system deployment area containing ICBM silo launchers. The two sides have registered agreement on the following statement: "The Parties understand that the center of the ABM system deployment area centered on the national capital and the center of the ABM system deployment area containing ICBM silo launchers for each Party shall be separated by no less than thirteen hundred kilometers." In this connection, the U.S. side notes that its ABM system deployment area for defense of ICBM silo launchers, located west of the Mississippi River, will be centered in the Grand Forks ICBM silo launcher deployment area. (See Agreed Statement [C].)

B. ABM Test Ranges

The U.S. Delegation made the following statement on April 26, 1972:

Article IV of the ABM Treaty provides that "the limitations provided for in Article III shall not apply to ABM systems or their components used for development or testing, and located within current or additionally agreed test ranges." We believe it would be useful to assure that there is no misunderstanding as to current ABM test ranges. It is our understanding that ABM test ranges encompass the area within which ABM components are located for test purposes. The current U.S. ABM test ranges are at White Sands, New Mexico, and at Kwajalein Atoll, and the current Soviet ABM test range is near Sary Shagan in Kazakhstan. We consider that non-phased array radars of types used for range safety or instrumentation purposes may be located outside of ABM test ranges. We interpret the reference in Article IV to "additionally agreed test ranges" to mean that ABM components will not be located at any other test ranges without prior agreement between our Governments that there will be such additional ABM test ranges.

On May 5, 1972, the Soviet Delegation stated that there was a common understanding on what ABM test ranges were, that the use of the types of non-ABM radars for range safety or instrumentation was not limited under the Treaty, that the reference in Article IV to "additionally agreed" test ranges was sufficiently clear, and that national means permitted identifying current test ranges.

C. Mobile ABM Systems

On January 29, 1972, the U.S. Delegation made the following statement:

Article V(I) of the Joint Draft Text of the ABM Treaty includes an undertaking not to develop, test, or deploy mobile land-based ABM systems and their components. On May 5, 1971, the U.S. side indicated that, in its view, a prohibition on deployment of mobile ABM systems and components would rule out the deployment of ABM launchers and radars which were not permanent fixed types. At that time, we asked for the Soviet view of this interpretation. Does the Soviet side agree with the U.S. side's interpretation put forward on May 5, 1971?

On April 13, 1972, the Soviet Delegation said there is a general common understanding on this matter.

D. Standing Consultative Commission

Ambassador Smith made the following statement on May 22, 1972:

The United States proposes that the sides agree that, with regard to initial implementation of the ABM Treaty's Article XIII on the Standing Consultative Commission (SCC) and of the consultation Articles to the Interim Agreement on offensive arms and the Accidents Agreement, agreement establishing the SCC will be worked out early in the follow-on SALT negotiations; until that is completed, the following arrangements will prevail: when SALT is in session, any consultation desired by either side under these Articles can be carried out by the two SALT Delegations; when SALT is not in session, *ad hoc* arrangements for any desired consultations under these Articles may be made through diplomatic channels.

Minister Semenov replied that, on an *ad referendum* basis, he could agree that the U.S. statement corresponded to the Soviet understanding.

E. Standstill

On May 6, 1972, Minister Semenov made the following statement:

In an effort to accommodate the wishes of the U.S. side, the Soviet Delegation is prepared to proceed on the basis that the two sides will in fact observe the obligations of both the Interim Agreement and the ABM Treaty beginning from the date of signature of these two documents.

In reply, the U.S. Delegation made the following statement on May 20, 1972:

The U.S. agrees in principle with the Soviet statement made on May 6 concerning observance of obligations beginning from date of signature but we would like to make clear our understanding that this means that, pending ratification and acceptance, neither side would take any action prohibited by the agreements after they had entered into force. This understanding would continue to apply in the absence of notification by either signatory of its intention not to proceed with ratification or approval.

The Soviet Delegation indicated agreement with the U.S. statement.

3. Unilateral Statements

The following noteworthy unilateral statements were made during the negotiations by the United States Delegation:

A. *Withdrawal from the* ABM *Treaty*

On May 9, 1972, Ambassador Smith made the following statement:

The U.S. Delegation has stressed the importance the U.S. Government attaches to achieving agreement on more complete limitations on strategic offensive arms, following agreement on an ABM Treaty and on an Interim Agreement on certain measures with respect to the limitation of strategic offensive arms. The U.S. Delegation believes that an objective of the follow-on negotiations should be to constrain and reduce on a long-term basis threats to the survivability of our respective strategic retaliatory forces. The U.S.S.R. Delegation has also indicated that the objectives of SALT would remain unfulfilled without the achievement of an agreement providing for more complete limitations on strategic offensive arms. Both sides recognize that the initial agreements would be steps toward the achievement of more complete limitations on strategic arms. If an agreement providing for more complete strategic offensive arms limitations were not achieved within five years, U.S. supreme interests could be jeopardized. Should that occur, it would constitute a basis for withdrawal from the ABM Treaty. The U.S. does not wish to see such a situation occur, nor do we believe that the U.S.S.R. does. It is because we wish to prevent such a situation that we emphasize the importance the U.S. Government attaches to achievement of more complete limitations on strategic offensive arms. The U.S. Executive will inform the Congress, in connection with Congressional consideration of the ABM Treaty

and the Interim Agreement, of this statement of the U.S. position.

B. *Tested in* ABM *Mode*

On April 7, 1972, the U.S. Delegation made the following statement:

Article II of the Joint Text Draft uses the term "tested in an ABM mode," in defining ABM components, and Article VI includes certain obligations concerning such testing. We believe that the sides should have a common understanding of this phrase. First, we would note that the testing provisions of the ABM Treaty are intended to apply to testing which occurs after the date of signature of the Treaty, and not to any testing which may have occurred in the past. Next, we would amplify the remarks we have made on this subject during the previous Helsinki phase by setting forth the objectives which govern the U.S. view on the subject, namely, while prohibiting testing of non-ABM components for ABM purposes: not to prevent testing of ABM components, and not to prevent testing of non-ABM components for non-ABM purposes. To clarify our interpretation of "tested in an ABM mode," we note that we would consider a launcher, missile or radar to be "tested in an ABM mode" if, for example, any of the following events occur: (1) a launcher is used to launch an ABM interceptor missile, (2) an interceptor missile is flight tested against a target vehicle which has a flight trajectory with characteristics of a strategic ballistic missile flight trajectory, or is flight tested in conjunction with the test of an ABM interceptor missile or an ABM radar at the same test range, or is flight tested to an altitude inconsistent with interception of targets against which air defenses are deployed, (3) a radar makes measurements on a cooperative target vehicle of the kind referred to in item (2) above during the reentry portion of its trajectory or makes measurements in conjunction with the test of an ABM interceptor missile or an ABM radar at the same test range. Radars used for purposes such as range safety or instrumentation would be exempt from application of these criteria.

C. *No-Transfer Article of* ABM *Treaty*

On April 18, 1972, the U.S. Delegation made the following statement:

In regard to this Article [IX], I have a brief and I believe self-explanatory statement to make. The U.S. side wishes to make clear that the provisions of this Article do not set a precedent for whatever provision may be considered for a Treaty on Limiting Strategic Offensive Arms. The question of transfer of strategic offensive arms is a far more complex issue, which may require a different solution.

D. No Increase in Defense of Early Warning Radars

On July 28, 1970, the U.S. Delegation made the following statement:

Since Hen House radars [Soviet ballistic missile early warning radars] can detect and track ballistic missile warheads at great distances, they have a significant ABM potential. Accordingly, the U.S. would regard any increase in the defenses of such radars by surface-to-air missiles as inconsistent with an agreement.

[U.S. Arms Control and Disarmament Agency, *Arms Control and Disarmament Agreements,* 5th ed. (Washington, D.C., 1982), pp. 139–147]

Protocol on ABM Treaty (1974)

Protocol to the Treaty Between the United States of America and the Union of Soviet Socialist Republics on the Limitation of Anti-Ballistic Missile Systems, 3 July 1974

Desiring to further the objectives of the Treaty between the United States of America and the Union of Soviet Socialist Republics on the Limitation of Anti-Ballistic Missile Systems signed on May 26, 1972, hereinafter referred to as the Treaty,

Reaffirming their conviction that the adoption of further measures for the limitation of strategic arms would contribute to strengthening international peace and security,

Proceeding from the premise that further limitation of anti-ballistic missile systems will create more favorable conditions for the completion of work on a permanent agreement on more complete measures for the limitation of strategic offensive arms,

Have agreed as follows:

Article I

1. Each Party shall be limited at any one time to a single area out of the two provided in Article II of the Treaty for deployment of anti-ballistic missile (ABM) systems or their components and accordingly shall not exercise its right to deploy an ABM system or its components in the second of the two ABM system deployment areas permitted by Article III of the Treaty, except as an exchange of one permitted area for the other in accordance with Article II of this Protocol.

2. Accordingly, except as permitted by Article II of this Protocol: the United States of America shall not deploy an ABM system or its components in the area centered on its capital, as permitted by Article III(a) of the Treaty, and the Soviet Union shall not deploy an ABM system or its components in the deployment area of intercontinental ballistic missile (ICBM) silo launchers as permitted by Article III(b) of the Treaty.

Article II

1. Each Party shall have the right to dismantle or destroy its ABM system and the components thereof in the area where they are presently deployed and to deploy an ABM system or its components in the alternative area permitted by Article III of the Treaty, provided that prior to initiation of construction, notification is given in accord with the procedure agreed to in the Standing Consultative Commission, during the year beginning October 3, 1977 and ending October 2, 1978, or during any year which commences at five year intervals thereafter, those being the years for periodic review of the Treaty, as provided in Article XIV of the Treaty. This right may be exercised only once.

2. Accordingly, in the event of such notice, the United States would have the right to dismantle or destroy the ABM system and its components in the deployment area of ICBM silo launchers and to deploy an ABM system or its components in an area centered on its capital, as permitted by Article III(a) of the Treaty, and the Soviet Union would have the right to dismantle or destroy the ABM system and its components in the area centered on its capital and to deploy an ABM system or its components in an area containing ICBM silo launchers, as permitted by Article III(b) of the Treaty.

3. Dismantling or destruction and deployment of ABM systems or their components and the notification thereof shall be carried out in accordance with Article VIII of the ABM Treaty and procedures agreed to in the Standing Consultative Commission.

Article III. The rights and obligations established by the Treaty remain in force and shall be complied with by the Parties except to the extent modified by this Protocol. In particular, the deployment of an ABM system or its components within the area selected shall remain limited by the levels and other requirements established by the Treaty.

Article IV. This Protocol shall be subject to ratification in accordance with the constitutional procedures of each Party. It shall enter into force on the day of the exchange of instruments of ratification and shall thereafter be considered an integral part of the Treaty.

[Signatures]

[U.S. Arms Control and Disarmament Agency, *Arms Control and Disarmament Agreements*, 5th ed. (Washington, D.C., 1982), pp. 162–163]

SALT II Treaty (1979)

The text of the SALT II Treaty and Protocol is accompanied by a set of Agreed Statements and Common Understandings, also signed by Presidents Carter and Brezhnev, which is prefaced with the following:

In connection with the Treaty Between the United States of America and the Union of Soviet Socialist Republics on the Limitation of Strategic Offensive Arms, the Parties have agreed on the following Agreed Statements and Common Understandings undertaken on behalf of the Government of the United States and the Government of the Union of Soviet Socialist Republics.

The texts of the Agreed Statements and Common Understandings are beneath the articles of the Treaty or Protocol to which they pertain.

Treaty Between the United States of America and the Union of Soviet Socialist Republics on the Limitation of Strategic Offensive Arms, 18 June 1979

The United States of America and the Union of the Soviet Socialist Republics, hereinafter referred to as the Parties,

Conscious that nuclear war would have devastating consequences for all mankind,

Proceeding from the Basic Principles of Relations Between the United States of America and the Union of Soviet Socialist Republics of May 29, 1972,

Attaching particular significance to the limitation of strategic arms and determined to continue their efforts begun with the Treaty on the Limitation of Anti-Ballistic Missile Systems and the Interim Agreement on Certain Measures with Respect to the Limitation of Strategic Offensive Arms, of May 26, 1972,

Convinced that the additional measures limiting strategic offensive arms provided for in this Treaty will contribute to the improvement of relations between the Parties, help to reduce the risk of outbreak of nuclear war and strengthen international peace and security,

Mindful of their obligations under Article VI of the Treaty on the Non-Proliferation of Nuclear Weapons,

Guided by the principle of equality and equal security,

Recognizing that the strengthening of strategic stability meets the interests of the Parties and the interests of international security,

Reaffirming their desire to take measures for the further limitation and for the further reduction of strategic arms, having in mind the goal of achieving general and complete disarmament,

Declaring their intention to undertake in the near future negotiations further to limit and further to reduce strategic offensive arms,

Have agreed as follows:

Article I. Each Party undertakes, in accordance with the provisions of this Treaty, to limit strategic offensive arms quantitatively and qualitatively, to exercise restraint in the development of new types of strategic offensive arms, and to adopt other measures provided for in this Treaty.

Article II. For the purposes of this Treaty:

1. Intercontinental ballistic missile (ICBM) launchers are land-based launchers of ballistic missiles capable of a range in excess of the shortest distance between the northeastern border of the continental part of the territory of the United States of America and the northwestern border of the continental part of the territory of the Union of Soviet Socialist Republics, that is, a range in excess of 5,500 kilometers.

First Agreed Statement. The term "intercontinental ballistic missile launchers," as defined in paragraph 1 of Article II of the Treaty, includes all launchers which have been developed and tested for launching ICBMS. If a launcher has been developed and tested for launching an ICBM, all launchers of that type shall be considered to have been developed and tested for launching ICBMS.

First Common Understanding. If a launcher contains or launches an ICBM, that launcher shall be considered to have been developed and tested for launching ICBMS.

Second Common Understanding. If a launcher has been developed and tested for launching an ICBM, all launchers of that type, except for ICBM test and training launchers, shall be included in the aggregate numbers of strategic offensive arms provided for in Article III of the Treaty, pursuant to the provisions of Article VI of the Treaty.

Third Common Understanding. The one hundred and seventy-seven former Atlas and Titan I ICBM launchers of the United States of America, which are no longer operational and are partially dismantled, shall not be considered as subject to the limitations provided for in the Treaty.

Second Agreed Statement. After the date on which the Protocol ceases to be in force, mobile ICBM launchers shall be subject to the relevant limitations provided for in the Treaty which are applicable to ICBM launchers, unless the Parties agree that mobile ICBM launchers shall not be deployed after that date.

2. Submarine-launched ballistic missile (SLBM) launchers are launchers of ballistic missiles installed on any nuclear-powered submarine or launchers of modern ballistic missiles installed on any submarine, regardless of its type.

Agreed Statement. Modern submarine-launched ballistic missiles are: for the United States of America, missiles installed in all nuclear-powered submarines; for the Union of Soviet Socialist Republics, missiles of the type installed in nuclear-powered submarines made operational since 1965; and for both Parties, submarine-launched ballistic missiles first flight-tested since 1965 and installed in any submarine, regardless of its type.

3. Heavy bombers are considered to be:

(a) currently, for the United States of America, bombers of the B-52 and B-1 types, and for the Union of Soviet Socialist Republics, bombers of the Tupolev-95 and Myasishchev types; (b) in the future, types of bombers which can carry out the mission of a heavy bomber in a manner similar or superior to that of bombers listed in subparagraph (a) above; (c) types of bombers equipped for cruise missiles capable of a range in excess of 600 kilometers; and (d) types of bombers equipped for ASBMS.

First Agreed Statement. The term "bombers," as used in paragraph 3 of Article II and other provisions of the Treaty, means airplanes of types initially constructed to be equipped for bombs or missiles.

Second Agreed Statement. The Parties shall notify each other on a case-by-case basis in the Standing Consultative Commission of inclusion of types of bombers as heavy bombers pursuant to the provisions of paragraph 3 of Article II of the Treaty; in this connection the Parties shall hold consultations, as appropriate, consistent with the provisions of paragraph 2 of Article XVII of the Treaty.

Third Agreed Statement. The criteria the Parties shall use to make case-by-case determinations of which types of bombers in the future can carry out the mission of a heavy bomber in a manner similar or superior to that of current heavy bombers, as referred to in subparagraph 3(b) of Article II of the Treaty, shall be agreed upon in the Standing Consultative Commission.

Fourth Agreed Statement. Having agreed that every bomber of a type included in paragraph 3 of Article II of the Treaty is to be considered a heavy bomber, the Parties further agree that:

(a) airplanes which otherwise would be bombers of a heavy bomber type shall not be considered to be bombers of a heavy bomber type if they have functionally related observable differences which indicate that they cannot perform the mission of a heavy bomber;

(b) airplanes which otherwise would be bombers of a type equipped for cruise missiles capable of a range in excess of 600 kilometers shall not be considered to be bombers of a type equipped for cruise missiles capable of a range in excess of 600 kilometers if they have functionally related observable differences which indicate that they cannot perform the mission of a bomber equipped for cruise missiles capable of a range in excess of 600 kilometers, except that heavy bombers of current types, as designated in subparagraph 3(a) of Article II of the Treaty, which otherwise would be of a type equipped for cruise missiles capable of a range in excess of 600 kilometers shall not be considered to be heavy bombers of a type equipped for cruise missiles capable of a range in excess of 600 kilometers if they are distinguishable on the basis of externally observable differences from heavy bombers of a type equipped for cruise missiles capable of a range in excess of 600 kilometers; and

(c) airplanes which otherwise would be bombers of a type equipped for ASBMS shall not be considered to be bombers of a type equipped for ASBMS if they have functionally related observable differences which indicate that they cannot perform the mission of a bomber equipped for ASBMS, except that heavy bombers of current types, as designated in subparagraph 3(a) of Article II of the Treaty, which otherwise would be of a type equipped for ASBMS shall not be considered to be heavy bombers of a type equipped for ASBMS if they are distinguishable on the basis of externally observable differences from heavy bombers of a type equipped for ASBMS.

First Common Understanding. Functionally related observable differences are differences in the observable features of airplanes which indicate whether or not these airplanes can perform the mission of a heavy bomber, or whether or not they can perform the mission of a bomber equipped for cruise missiles capable of a range in excess of 600 kilometers or whether or not they can perform the mission of a bomber equipped for ASBMS. Functionally related observable differences shall be verifiable by national technical means. To this end, the Parties may take, as appropriate, cooperative measures contributing to the effectiveness of verification by national technical means.

Fifth Agreed Statement. Tupolev-142 airplanes in their current configuration, that is, in the configuration for anti-submarine warfare, are considered to be airplanes of a type different from types of heavy bombers referred to in subparagraph 3(a) of Article II of the Treaty and not subject to the Fourth Agreed Statement to paragraph 3 of Article II of the Treaty. This Agreed Statement does not preclude improvement of Tupolev-142 airplanes as an anti-submarine system, and does not prejudice or set a

precedent for designation in the future of types of airplanes as heavy bombers pursuant to subparagraph 3(b) of Article II of the Treaty or for application of the Fourth Agreed Statement to paragraph 3 of Article II of the Treaty to such airplanes.

Second Common Understanding. Not later than six months after entry into force of the Treaty the Union of Soviet Socialist Republics will give its thirty-one Myasishchev airplanes used as tankers in existence as of the date of signature of the Treaty functionally related observable differences which indicate that they cannot perform the mission of a heavy bomber.

Third Common Understanding. The designations by the United States of America and by the Union of Soviet Socialist Republics for heavy bombers referred to in subparagraph 3(a) of Article II of the Treaty correspond in the following manner:

Heavy bombers of the types designated by the United States of America as the B-52 and the B-1 are known to the Union of Soviet Socialist Republics by the same designations;

Heavy bombers of the type designated by the Union of Socialist Republics as the Tupolev-95 are known to the United States of America as heavy bombers of the Bear type; and

Heavy bombers of the type designated by the Union of Soviet Socialist Republics as the Myasishchev are known to the United States of America as heavy bombers of the Bison type.

4. Air-to-surface ballistic missiles (ASBMS) are any such missiles capable of a range in excess of 600 kilometers and installed in an aircraft or on its external mountings.

5. Launchers of ICBMS and SLBMS equipped with multiple independently targetable reentry vehicles (MIRVS) are launchers of the types developed and tested for launching ICBMS or SLBMS equipped with MIRVS.

First Agreed Statement. If a launcher has been developed and tested for launching an ICBM or an SLBM equipped with MIRVS, all launchers of that type shall be considered to have been developed and tested for launching ICBMS or SLBMS equipped with MIRVS.

First Common Understanding. If a launcher contains or launches an ICBM or an SLBM equipped with MIRVS, that launcher shall be considered to have been developed and tested for launching ICBMS or SLBMS equipped with MIRVS.

Second Common Understanding. If a launcher has been developed and tested for launching an ICBM or an SLBM equipped with MIRVS, all launchers of that type, except for ICBM and SLBM test and training launchers, shall be included in the corresponding aggregate numbers provided for in Article V of the Treaty, pursuant to the provisions of Article VI of the Treaty.

Second Agreed Statement. ICBMS and SLBMS equipped with MIRVS are ICBMS and SLBMS of the types which have been flight-tested with two or more independently targetable reentry vehicles, regardless of whether or not they have also been flight-tested with a single reentry vehicle or with multiple reentry vehicles which are not independently targetable. As of the date of signature of the Treaty, such ICBMS and SLBMS are: for the United States of America, Minuteman III ICBMS, Poseidon C-3 SLBMS, and Trident C-4 SLBMS; and for the Union of Soviet Socialist Republics, RS-16, RS-18, RS-20 ICBMS and RSM-50 SLBMS.

Each Party will notify the other Party in the Standing Consultative Commission on a case-by-case basis of the designation of the one new type of light ICBM, if equipped with MIRVS, permitted pursuant to paragraph 9 of Article IV of the Treaty when first flight-tested; of designations of additional types of SLBMS equipped with MIRVS when first installed on a submarine; and of designations of types of ASBMS equipped with MIRVS when first flight-tested.

Third Common Understanding. The designations by the United States of America and by the Union of Soviet Socialist Republics for ICBMS and SLBMS equipped with MIRVS correspond in the following manner:

Missiles of the type designated by the United States of America as the Minuteman III and known to the Union of Soviet Socialist Republics by the same designation, a light ICBM that has been flight-tested with multiple independently targetable reentry vehicles;

Missiles of the type designated by the United States of America as the Poseidon C-3 and known to the Union of Soviet Socialist Republics by the same designation, an SLBM that was first flight-tested in 1968 and that has been flight-tested with multiple independently targetable reentry vehicles;

Missiles of the type designated by the United States of America as the Trident C-4 and known to the Union of Soviet Socialist Republics by the same designation, an SLBM that was first flight-tested in 1977 and that has been flight-tested with multiple independently targetable reentry vehicles;

Missiles of the type designated by the Union of Soviet Socialist Republics as the RS-16 and known

to the United States of America as the SS-17, a light ICBM that has been flight-tested with a single reentry vehicle and with multiple independently targetable reentry vehicles;

Missiles of the type designated by the Union of Soviet Socialist Republics as the RS-18 and known to the United States of America as the SS-19, the heaviest in terms of launch-weight and throw-weight of light ICBMS, which has been flight-tested with a single reentry vehicle and with multiple independently targetable reentry vehicles;

Missiles of the type designated by the Union of Soviet Socialist Republics as the RS-20 and known to the United States of America as the SS-18, the heaviest in terms of launch-weight and throw-weight of heavy ICBMS, which has been flight-tested with a single reentry vehicle and with multiple independently targetable reentry vehicles;

Missiles of the type designated by the Union of Soviet Socialist Republics as the RSM-50 and known to the United States of America as the SS-N-18, an SLBM that has been flight-tested with a single reentry vehicle and with multiple independently targetable reentry vehicles.

Third Agreed Statement. Reentry vehicles are independently targetable:

(a) if, after separation from the booster, maneuvering and targeting of the reentry vehicles to separate aim points along trajectories which are unrelated to each other are accomplished by means of devices which are installed in a self-contained dispensing mechanism or on the reentry vehicles, and which are based on the use of electronic or other computers in combination with devices using jet engines, including rocket engines, or aerodynamic systems;

(b) if maneuvering and targeting of the reentry vehicles to separate aim points along trajectories which are unrelated to each other are accomplished by means of other devices which may be developed in the future.

Fourth Common Understanding. For the purposes of this Treaty, all ICBM launchers in the Derazhnya and Pervomaysk areas in the Union of Soviet Socialist Republics are included in the aggregate numbers provided for in Article V of the Treaty.

Fifth Common Understanding. If ICBM or SLBM launchers are converted, constructed or undergo significant changes to their principal observable structural design features after entry into force of the Treaty, any such launchers which are launchers of missiles equipped with MIRVS shall be distinguishable from launchers of missiles not equipped with MIRVS, and any such launchers which are launchers of missiles not equipped with MIRVS shall be distinguishable from launchers of missiles equipped with MIRVS, on the basis of externally observable design features of the launchers. Submarines with launchers of SLBMS equipped with MIRVS shall be distinguishable from submarines with launchers of SLBMS not equipped with MIRVS on the basis of externally observable design features of the submarines.

This Common Understanding does not require changes to launcher conversion or construction programs, or to programs including significant changes to the principal observable structural design features of launchers, underway as of the date of signature of the Treaty.

6. ASBMS equipped with MIRVS are ASBMS of the types which have been flight-tested with MIRVS.

First Agreed Statement. ASBMS of the types which have been flight-tested with MIRVS are all ASBMS of the types which have been flight-tested with two or more independently targetable reentry vehicles, regardless of whether or not they have also been flight-tested with a single reentry vehicle or with multiple reentry vehicles which are not independently targetable.

Second Agreed Statement. Reentry vehicles are independently targetable:

(a) if, after separation from the booster, maneuvering and targeting of the reentry vehicles to separate aim points /along trajectories which are unrelated to each other are accomplished by means of devices which are installed in a self-contained dispensing mechanism or on the reentry vehicles, and which are based on the use of electronic or other computers in combination with devices using jet engines, including rocket engines, or aerodynamic systems;

(b) if maneuvering and targeting of the reentry vehicles to separate aim points along trajectories which are unrelated to each other are accomplished by means of other devices which may be developed in the future.

7. Heavy ICBMS are ICBMS which have a launch-weight greater or a throw-weight greater than that of the heaviest, in terms of either launch-weight or throw-weight, respectively, of the light ICBMS deployed by either Party as of the date of signature of this Treaty.

First Agreed Statement. The launch-weight of an ICBM is the weight of the fully loaded missile itself at the time of launch.

Second Agreed Statement. The throw-weight of an ICBM is the sum of the weight of:

(a) its reentry vehicle or reentry vehicles;

(b) any self-contained dispensing mechanisms or other appropriate devices for targeting one reentry vehicle, or for releasing or for dispensing and targeting two or more reentry vehicles; and

(c) its penetration aids, including devices for their release.

Common Understanding. The term "other appropriate devices," as used in the definition of the throw-weight of an ICBM in the Second Agreed Statement to paragraph 7 of Article II of the Treaty, means any devices for dispensing and targeting two or more reentry vehicles; and any devices for releasing two or more reentry vehicles or for targeting one reentry vehicle, which cannot provide their reentry vehicles or reentry vehicle with additional velocity of more than 1,000 meters per second.

8. Cruise missiles are unmanned, self-propelled, guided, weapon-delivery vehicles which sustain flight through the use of aerodynamic lift over most of their flight path and which are flight-tested from or deployed on aircraft, that is, air-launched cruise missiles, or such vehicles which are referred to as cruise missiles in subparagraph 1(b) of Article IX.

First Agreed Statement. If a cruise missiles is capable of a range in excess of 600 kilometers, all cruise missiles of that type shall be considered to be cruise missiles capable of a range in excess of 600 kilometers.

First Common Understanding. If a cruise missile has been flight-tested to a range in excess of 600 kilometers, it shall be considered to be a cruise missile capable of a range in excess of 600 kilometers.

Second Common Understanding. Cruise missile not capable of a range in excess of 600 kilometers shall not be considered to be of a type capable of a range in excess of 600 kilometers if they are distinguishable on the basis of externally observable design features from cruise missiles of types capable of a range in excess of 600 kilometers.

Second Agreed Statement. The range of which a cruise missile is capable is the maximum distance which can be covered by the missile in its standard design mode flying until fuel exhaustion, determined by projecting its flight path onto the Earth's sphere from the point of launch to the point of impact.

Third Agreed Statement. if an unmanned, self-propelled, guided vehicle which sustains flight through the use of aerodynamic lift over most of its flight path has been flight-tested or deployed for weapon delivery, all vehicles of that type shall be considered to be weapon-delivery vehicles.

Third Common Understanding. Unmanned, self-propelled, guided vehicles which sustain flight through the use of aerodynamic lift over most of their flight path and are not weapon-delivery vehicles, that is, unarmed, pilotless, guided vehicles, shall not be considered to be cruise missiles if such vehicles are distinguishable from cruise missiles on the basis of externally observable design features.

Fourth Common Understanding. Neither Party shall convert unarmed, pilotless, guided vehicles into cruise missiles capable of a range in excess of 600 kilometers, nor shall either Party convert cruise missiles capable of a range in excess of 600 kilometers into unarmed, pilotless, guided vehicles.

Fifth Common Understanding. Neither Party has plans during the term of the Treaty to flight-test from or deploy on aircraft unarmed, pilotless, guided vehicles which are capable of a range in excess of 600 kilometers. In the future, should a Party have such plans, that Party will provide notification thereof to the other Party well in advance of such flight-testing or deployment. This Common Understanding does not apply to target drones.

Article III

1. Upon entry into force of this Treaty, each Party undertakes to limit ICBM launchers, SLBM launchers, heavy bombers, and ASBMs to an aggregate number not to exceed 2,400.

2. Each Party undertakes to limit, from January 1, 1981, strategic offensive arms referred to in paragraph 1 of this Article to an aggregate number not to exceed 2,250, and to initiate reductions of those arms which as of that date would be in excess of this aggregate number.

3. Within the aggregate numbers provided for in paragraphs 1 and 2 of this Article and subject to the provisions of this Treaty, each Party has the right to determine the composition of these aggregates.

4. For each bomber of a type equipped for ASBMs, the aggregate numbers provided for in paragraphs 1 and 2 of this Article shall include the maximum number of such missiles for which a bomber of that type is equipped for one operational mission.

5. A heavy bomber equipped only for ASBMs shall not itself be included in the aggregate numbers provided for in paragraphs 1 and 2 of this Article.

6. Reductions of the numbers of strategic offensive arms required to comply with the provisions of paragraphs 1 and 2 of this Article shall be carried out as provided for in Article XI.

Article IV

1. Each Party undertakes not to start construction of additional fixed ICBM launchers.

2. Each Party undertakes not to relocate fixed ICBM launchers.

3. Each Party undertakes not to convert launchers of light ICBMs, or of ICBMs of older types deployed prior to 1964, into launchers of heavy ICBMs of types deployed after that time.

4. Each Party undertakes in the process of modernization and replacement of ICBM silo launchers not to increase the original internal volume of an ICBM silo launcher by more than thirty-two percent. Within this limit each Party has the right to determine whether such an increase will be made through an increase in the original diameter or in the original depth of an ICBM silo launcher, or in both of these dimensions.

Agreed Statement. The word "original" in paragraph 4 of Article IV of the Treaty refers to the internal dimensions of an ICBM silo launcher, including its internal volume, as of May 26, 1972, or as of the date on which such launcher becomes operational, whichever is later.

Common Understanding. The obligations provided for in paragraph 4 of Article IV of the Treaty and in the Agreed Statement thereto mean that the original diameter or the original depth of an ICBM silo launcher may not be increased by an amount greater than that which would result in an increase in the original internal volume of the ICBM silo launcher by thirty-two percent solely through an increase in one of these dimensions.

5. Each Party undertakes:

(a) not to supply ICBM launcher deployment areas with intercontinental ballistic missiles in excess of a number consistent with normal deployment, maintenance, training, and replacement requirements;

(b) not to provide storage facilities for or to store ICBMs in excess of normal deployment requirements at launch sites of ICBM launchers;

(c) not to develop, test, or deploy systems for rapid reload of ICBM launchers.

Agreed Statement. The term "normal deployment requirements," as used in paragraph 5 of Article IV of the Treaty, means the deployment of one missile at each ICBM launcher.

6. Subject to the provisions of this Treaty, each Party undertakes not to have under construction at any time strategic offensive arms referred to in paragraph 1 of Article III in excess of numbers consistent with a normal construction schedule.

Common Understanding. A normal construction schedule, in paragraph 6 of Article IV of the Treaty, is understood to be one consistent with the past or present construction practices of each Party.

7. Each Party undertakes not to develop, test, or deploy ICBMs which have a launch-weight greater or a throw-weight greater than that of the heaviest, in terms of either launch-weight or throw-weight, respectively, of the heavy ICBMs, deployed by either Party as of the date of signature of this Treaty.

First Agreed Statement. The launch-weight of an ICBM is the weight of the fully loaded missile itself at the time of launch.

Second Agreed Statement. The throw-weight of an ICBM is the sum of the weight of:

(a) its reentry vehicle or reentry vehicles;

(b) any self-contained dispensing mechanisms or other appropriate devices for targeting one reentry vehicle, or for releasing or for dispensing and targeting two or more reentry vehicles; and

(c) its penetration aids, including devices for their release.

Common Understanding. The term "other appropriate devices," as used in the definition of the throw-weight of an ICBM in the Second Agreed Statement to paragraph 7 of Article IV of the Treaty, means any devices for dispensing and targeting two or more reentry vehicles; and any devices for releasing two or more reentry vehicles or for targeting one reentry vehicle, which cannot provide their reentry vehicles or reentry vehicle with additional velocity of more than 1,000 meters per second.

8. Each Party undertakes not to convert land-based launchers of ballistic missiles which are not ICBMs into launchers for launching ICBMs, and not to test them for this purpose.

Common Understanding. During the term of the Treaty, the Union of Soviet Socialist Republics will not produce, test, or deploy ICBMs of the type designated by the Union of Soviet Socialist Republics as the RS-14 and known to the United States of America as the SS-16, a light ICBM first flight-tested after 1970 and flight-tested only with a single reentry vehicle; this Common Understanding also means that the Union of Soviet Socialist Republics will not produce the third stage of that missile, the reentry vehicle of that missile, or the appropriate device for targeting the reentry vehicle of that missile.

9. Each Party undertakes not to flight-test or deploy new types of ICBMs, that is, types of ICBMs not flight-tested as of May 1, 1979, except that each Party may flight-test and deploy one new type of light ICBM.

First Agreed Statement. The term "new types of ICBMs," as used in paragraph 9 of Article IV of the Treaty, refers to any ICBM which is different from those ICBMs flight-tested as of May 1, 1979 in any one or more of the following respects:

(a) the number of stages, the length, the largest diameter, the launch-weight, or the throw-weight, of the missile;

(b) the type of propellant (that is, liquid or solid) of any of its stages.

First Common Understanding. As used in the First Agreed Statement to paragraph 9 of Article IV of the Treaty, the term "different," referring to the length, the diameter, the launch-weight, and the throw-weight, of the missile, means a difference in excess of five percent.

Second Agreed Statement. Every ICBM of the one new type of light ICBM permitted to each Party pursuant to paragraph 9 of Article IV of the Treaty shall have the same number of stages and the same type of propellant (that is, liquid or solid) of each stage as the first ICBM of the one new type of light ICBM launched by that Party. In addition, after the twenty-fifth launch of an ICBM of that type, or after the last launch before deployment begins of ICBMs of that type, whichever occurs earlier, ICBMs of the one new type of light ICBM permitted to that Party shall not be different in any one or more of the following respects: the length, the largest diameter, the launch-weight, or the throw-weight, of the missile.

A Party which launches ICBMs of the one new type of light ICBM permitted pursuant to paragraph 9 of Article IV of the Treaty shall promptly notify the other Party of the date of the first launch and of the date of either the twenty-fifth or the last launch before deployment begins of ICBMs of that type, whichever occurs earlier.

Second Common Understanding. As used in the Second Agreed Statement to paragraph 9 of Article IV of the Treaty, the term "different," referring to the length, the diameter, the launch-weight, and the throw-weight, of the missile, means a difference in excess of five percent from the value established for each of the above parameters as of the twenty-fifth launch or as of the last launch before deployment begins, whichever occurs earlier. The values demonstrated in each of the above parameters during the last twelve of the twenty-five launches or during the last twelve launches before deployment begins, whichever twelve launches occur earlier, shall not vary by more than ten percent from any other of the corresponding values demonstrated during those twelve launches.

Third Common Understanding. The limitations with respect to launch-weight and throw-weight, provided for in the First Agreed Statement and the First Common Understanding to paragraph 9 of Article IV of the Treaty, do not preclude the flight-testing or the deployment of ICBMs with fewer reentry vehicles, or fewer penetration aids, or both, than the maximum number of reentry vehicles and the maximum number of penetration aids with which ICBMs of that type have been flight-tested as of May 1, 1979, even if this results in a decrease in launch-weight or in throw-weight in excess of five percent.

In addition to the aforementioned cases, those limitations do not preclude a decrease in launch-weight or in throw-weight in excess of five percent, in the case of the flight-testing or the deployment of ICBMs with a lesser quantity of propellant, including the propellant of a self-contained dispensing mechanism or other appropriate device, than the maximum quantity of propellant, including the propellant of a self-contained dispensing mechanism or other appropriate device, with which ICBMs of that type have been flight-tested as of May 1, 1979, provided that such an ICBM is at the same time flight-tested or deployed with fewer reentry vehicles, or fewer penetration aids, or both, than the maximum number of reentry vehicles and the maximum number of penetration aids with which ICBMs of that type have been flight-tested as of May 1, 1979, and the decrease in launch-weight and throw-weight in such cases results only from the reduction in the number of reentry vehicles, or penetration aids, or both, and the reduction in the quantity of propellant.

Fourth Common Understanding. The limitations with respect to launch-weight and throw-weight, provided for in the Second Agreed Statement and the Second Common Understanding to paragraph 9 of Article IV of the Treaty, do not preclude the flight-testing or the deployment of ICBMs of the one new type of light ICBM permitted to each Party pursuant to paragraph 9 of Article IV of the Treaty with fewer reentry vehicles, or fewer penetration aids, or both, than the maximum number of re-

entry vehicles and the maximum number of penetration aids with which ICBMs of that type have been flight-tested, even if this results in a decrease in launch-weight or in throw-weight in excess of five percent.

In addition to the aforementioned cases, those limitations do not preclude a decrease in launch-weight or in throw-weight in excess of five percent, in the case of the flight-testing or the deployment of ICBMs of that type with a lesser quantity of propellant, including the propellant of a self-contained dispensing mechanism or other appropriate device, than the maximum quantity of propellant, including the propellant of a self-contained dispensing mechanism or other appropriate device, with which ICBMs of that type have been flight-tested, provided that such an ICBM is at the same time flight-tested or deployed with fewer reentry vehicles, or fewer penetration aids, or both, than the maximum number of reentry vehicles and the maximum number of penetration aids with which ICBMs of that type have been flight-tested, and the decrease in launch-weight and throw-weight in such cases results only from the reduction in the number of reentry vehicles, or penetration aids, or both, and the reduction in the quantity of propellant.

10. Each Party undertakes not to flight-test or deploy ICBMs of a type flight-tested as of May 1, 1979 with a number of reentry vehicles greater than the maximum number of reentry vehicles with which an ICBM of that type has been flight-tested as of that date.

First Agreed Statement. The following types of ICBMs and SLBMs equipped with MIRVs have been flight-tested with the maximum number of reentry vehicles set forth below:

> *For the United States of America*
> ICBMs of the Minuteman III type-seven reentry vehicles;
> SLBMs of the Poseidon C-3 type-fourteen reentry vehicles;
> SLBMs of the Trident C-4 type-seven reentry vehicles.

> *For the Union of Soviet Socialist Republics*
> ICBMs of the RS-16 type-four reentry vehicles;
> ICBMs of the RS-18 type-six reentry vehicles;
> ICBMs of the RS-20 type-ten reentry vehicles;
> SLBMs of the RSM-50 type-seven reentry vehicles.

Common Understanding. Minuteman III ICBMs of the United States of America have been deployed with no more than three reentry vehicles. During the term of the Treaty, the United States of America has no plans to and will not flight-test or deploy missiles of this type with more than three reentry vehicles.

Second Agreed Statement. During the flight-testing of any ICBM, SLBM, or ASBM after May 1, 1979, the number of procedures for releasing or for dispensing may not exceed the maximum number of reentry vehicles established for missiles of corresponding types as provided for in paragraphs 10, 11, 12, and 13 of Article IV of the Treaty. In this Agreed Statement "procedures for releasing or for dispensing" are understood to mean maneuvers of a missile associated with targeting and releasing or dispensing its reentry vehicles to aim points, whether or not a reentry vehicle is actually released or dispensed. Procedures for releasing anti-missile defense penetration aids will not be considered to be procedures for releasing or for dispensing a reentry vehicle so long as the procedures for releasing anti-missile defense penetration aids differ from those for releasing or for dispensing reentry vehicles.

Third Agreed Statement. Each Party undertakes:

(a) not to flight-test or deploy ICBMs equipped with multiple reentry vehicles, of a type flight-tested as of May 1, 1979, with reentry vehicles the weight of any of which is less than the weight of the lightest of those reentry vehicles with which an ICBM of that type has been flight-tested as of that date,

(b) not to flight-test or deploy ICBMs equipped with a single reentry vehicle and without an appropriate device for targeting a reentry vehicle, of a type flight-tested as of May 1, 1979, with a reentry vehicle the weight of which is less than the weight of the lightest reentry vehicle on an ICBM of a type equipped with MIRVs and flight-tested by that Party as of May 1, 1979; and

(c) not to flight-test or deploy ICBMs equipped with a single reentry vehicle and with an appropriate device for targeting a reentry vehicle, of a type flight-tested as of May 1, 1979, with a reentry vehicle the weight of which is less than fifty percent of the throw-weight of that ICBM.

11. Each Party undertakes not to flight-test or deploy ICBMs of the one new type permitted pursuant to paragraph 9 of this Article with a number of reentry vehicles greater than the maximum number of reentry vehicles with which an ICBM of either Party has been flight-tested as of May 1, 1979, that is, ten.

First Agreed Statement. Each Party undertakes not to flight-test or deploy the one new type of light ICBM permitted to each Party pursuant to paragraph 9 of Article IV of the Treaty with a number of reentry vehicles greater than the maximum number of reentry vehicles with which an ICBM of that type has been flight-tested as of the twenty-fifth launch or the last launch before deployment begins of ICBMs of that type, whichever occurs earlier.

Second Agreed Statement. During the flight-testing of any ICBM, SLBM, or ASBM after May 1, 1979 the number of procedures for releasing or for dispensing may not exceed the maximum number of reentry vehicles established for missiles of corresponding types as provided for in paragraphs 10, 11, 12, and 13 of Article IV of the Treaty. In this Agreed Statement "procedures for releasing or for dispensing" are understood to mean maneuvers of a missile associated with targeting and releasing or dispensing its reentry vehicles to aim points, whether or not a reentry vehicle is actually released or dispensed. Procedures for releasing anti-missile defense penetration aids will not be considered to be procedures for releasing or for dispensing a reentry vehicle so long as the procedures for releasing anti-missile defense penetration aids differ from those for releasing or for dispensing reentry vehicles.

12. Each Party undertakes not to flight-test or deploy SLBMs with a number of reentry vehicles greater than the maximum number of reentry vehicles with which an SLBM of either Party has been flight-tested as of May 1, 1979, that is, fourteen.

First Agreed Statement. The following types of ICBMs and SLBMs equipped with MIRVs have been flight-tested with the maximum number of reentry vehicles set forth below:

For the United States of America
ICBMs of the Minuteman III type-seven reentry vehicles;
SLBMs of the Poseidon C-3 type-fourteen reentry vehicles;
SLBMs of the Trident C-4 type-seven reentry vehicles.

For the Union of Soviet Socialist Republics
ICBMs of the RS-16 type-four reentry vehicles;
ICBMs of the RS-18 type-six reentry vehicles;
ICBMs of the RS-20 type-ten reentry vehicles;
SLBMs of the RSM-50 type-seven reentry vehicles.

Second Agreed Statement. During the flight-testing of any ICBM, SLBM, or ASBM after May 1, 1979 the number of procedures for releasing or for dispensing may not exceed the maximum number of reentry vehicles established for missiles of corresponding types as provided for in paragraphs 10, 11, 12, and 13 of Article IV of the Treaty. In this Agreed Statement "procedures for releasing or dispensing" are understood to mean maneuvers of a missile associated with targeting and releasing or dispensing its reentry vehicles to aim points, whether or not a reentry vehicle is actually released or dispensed. Procedures for releasing anti-missile defense penetration aids will not be considered to be procedures for releasing or for dispensing a reentry vehicle so long as the procedures for releasing anti-missile defense penetration aids differ from those for releasing or for dispensing reentry vehicles.

13. Each Party undertakes not to flight-test or deploy ASBMS with a number of reentry vehicles greater than the maximum number of reentry vehicles with which an ICBM of either Party has been flight-tested as of May 1, 1979, that is, ten.

Agreed Statement. During the flight-testing of any ICBM, SLBM, or ASBM after May 1, 1979 the number of procedures for releasing or for dispensing may not exceed the maximum number of reentry vehicles established for missiles of corresponding types as provided for in paragraphs 10, 11, 12, and 13 of Article IV of the Treaty. In this Agreed Statement "procedures for releasing or for dispensing" are understood to mean maneuvers of a missile associated with targeting and releasing or dispensing its reentry vehicles to aim points, whether or not a reentry vehicle is actually released or dispensed. Procedures for releasing anti-missile defense penetration aids will not be considered to be procedures for releasing or for dispensing a reentry vehicle so long as the procedures for releasing anti-missile defense penetration aids differ from those for releasing or for dispensing reentry vehicles.

14. Each Party undertakes not to deploy at any one time on heavy bombers equipped for cruise missiles capable of a range in excess of 600 kilometers a number of such cruise missiles which exceeds the product of 28 and the number of such heavy bombers.

First Agreed Statement. For the purposes of the limitation provided for in paragraph 14 of Article IV of the Treaty, there shall be considered to be deployed on each heavy bomber of a type equipped for cruise missiles capable of a range in excess of 600 kilometers the maximum number of such missiles for which any bomber of that type is equipped for one operational mission.

Second Agreed Statement. During the term of the Treaty no bomber of the B-52 or B-1 types of the United States of America and no bomber of the Tupolev-95 or Myasishchev types of the Union of Soviet Socialist Republics will be equipped for more than twenty cruise missiles capable of a range in excess of 600 kilometers.

Article V

1. Within the aggregate numbers provided for in paragraphs 1 and 2 of Article III, each Party undertakes to limit launchers of ICBMS and SLBMS equipped with MIRVS, ASBMS equipped with MIRVS, and heavy bombers equipped for cruise missiles capable of a range in excess of 600 kilometers to an aggregate number not to exceed 1,320.

2. Within the aggregate number provided for in paragraph 1 of this Article, each Party undertakes to limit launchers of ICBMS and SLBMS equipped with MIRVS, and ASBMS equipped with MIRVS to an aggregate number not to exceed 1,200.

3. Within the aggregate number provided for in paragraph 2 of this Article, each Party undertakes to limit launchers of ICBMS equipped with MIRVS to an aggregate number not to exceed 820.

4. For each bomber of a type equipped for ASBMS equipped with MIRVS, the aggregate numbers provided for in paragraphs 1 and 2 of this Article shall include the maximum number of ASBMS for which a bomber of that type is equipped for one operational mission.

Agreed Statement. If a bomber is equipped for ASBMS equipped with MIRVS, all bombers of that type shall be considered to be equipped for ASBMS equipped with MIRVS.

5. Within the aggregate numbers provided for in paragraphs 1, 2, and 3 of this Article and subject to the provisions of this Treaty, each Party has the right to determine the composition of these aggregates.

Article VI

1. The limitations provided for in this Treaty shall apply to those arms which are: (a) operational; (b) in the final stage of construction; (c) in reserve, in storage, or mothballed; (d) undergoing overhaul, repair, modernization, or conversion.

2. Those arms in the final stage of construction are:

(a) SLBM launchers on submarines which have begun sea trials;

(b) ASBMS after a bomber of a type equipped for such missiles has been brought out of the shop, plant, or other facility where its final assembly or conversion for the purpose of equipping it for such missiles has been performed;

(c) other strategic offensive arms which are finally assembled in a shop, plant, or other facility after they have been brought out of the shop, plant, or other facility where their final assembly has been performed.

3. ICBM and SLBM launchers of a type not subject to the limitation provided for in Article V, which undergo conversion into launchers of a type subject to that limitation, shall become subject to that limitation as follows:

(a) fixed ICBM launchers when work on their conversion reaches the stage which first definitely indicates that they are being so converted;

(b) SLBM launchers on a submarine when that submarine first goes to sea after their conversion has been performed.

Agreed Statement. The procedures referred to in paragraph 7 of Article VI of the Treaty shall include procedures determining the manner in which mobile ICBM launchers of a type not subject to the limitation provided for in Article V of the Treaty, which undergo conversion into launchers of a type subject to that limitation, shall become subject to that limitation, unless the Parties agree that mobile ICBM launchers shall not be deployed after the date on which the Protocol ceases to be in force.

4. ASBMS on a bomber which undergoes conversion from a bomber of a type equipped for ASBMS which are not subject to the limitation provided for in Article V into a bomber of a type equipped for ASBMS which are subject to that limitation shall become subject to that limitation when the bomber is brought out of the shop, plant, or other facility where such conversion has been performed.

5. A heavy bomber of a type not subject to the limitation provided for in paragraph 1 of Article V shall become subject to that limitation when it is brought out of the shop, plant, or other facility where it has been converted into a heavy bomber of a type equipped for cruise missiles capable of a range in excess of 600 kilometers. A bomber of a type not subject to the limitation provided for in paragraph 1 or 2 of Article III shall become subject to that limitation and to the limitation provided for in paragraph 1 of Article V when it is brought out of the shop, plant, or other facility where it has been converted into a bomber of a type equipped for cruise missiles capable of a range in excess of 600 kilometers.

6. The arms subject to the limitations provided for in this Treaty shall continue to be subject to these limitations until they are dismantled, are destroyed, or otherwise cease to be subject to these limitations under procedures to be agreed upon.

Agreed Statement. The procedures for removal of strategic offensive arms from the aggregate numbers provided for in the Treaty, which are referred to in paragraph 6 of Article VI of the Treaty, and which are to be agreed upon in the Standing Consultative Commission, shall include:

(a) procedures for removal from the aggregate numbers, provided for in Article V of the Treaty, of ICBM and SLBM launchers which are being converted from launchers of a type subject to the limitation provided for in Article V of the Treaty, into launchers of a type not subject to that limitation;

(b) procedures for removal from the aggregate numbers, provided for in Articles III and V of the Treaty, of bombers which are being converted from bombers of a type subject to the limitations provided for in Article III of the Treaty or in Articles III and V of the Treaty into airplanes or bombers of a type not so subject.

Common Understanding. The procedures referred to in subparagraph (b) of the Agreed Statement to paragraph 6 of Article VI of the Treaty for removal of bombers from the aggregate numbers provided for in Articles III and V of the Treaty shall be based upon the existence of functionally related observable differences which indicate whether or not they can perform the mission of a heavy bomber, or whether or not they can perform the mission of a bomber equipped for cruise missiles capable of a range in excess of 600 kilometers.

7. In accordance with the provisions of Article XVII, the Parties will agree in the Standing Consultative Commission upon procedures to implement the provisions of this Article.

Article VII

1. The limitations provided for in Article III shall not apply to ICBM and SLBM test and training launchers or to space vehicle launchers for exploration and use of outer space. ICBM and SLBM test and training launchers are ICBM and SLBM launchers used only for testing or training.

Common Understanding. The term "testing," as used in Article VII of the Treaty, includes research and development.

2. The Parties agree that:

(a) there shall be no significant increase in the number of ICBM or SLBM test and training launchers or in the number of such launchers of heavy ICBMS;

(b) construction or conversion of ICBM launchers at test ranges shall be undertaken only for purposes of testing and training;

(c) there shall be no conversion of ICBM test and training launchers or of space vehicle launchers into ICBM launchers subject to the limitations provided for in Article III.

First Agreed Statement. The term "significant increase," as used in subparagraph 2(a) of Article VII of the Treaty, means an increase of fifteen percent or more. Any new ICBM test and training launchers which replace ICBM test and training launchers at test ranges will be located only at test ranges.

Second Agreed Statement. Current test ranges where ICBMS are tested are located: for the United States of America, near Santa Maria, California, and at Cape Canaveral, Florida; and for the Union of Soviet Socialist Republics, in the areas of Tyura-Tam and Plesetskaya. In the future, each Party shall provide notification in the Standing Consultative Commission of the location of any other test range used by that Party to test ICBMS.

First Common Understanding. At test ranges where ICBMS are tested, other arms, including those not limited by the Treaty, may also be tested.

Second Common Understanding. Of the eighteen launchers of fractional orbital missiles at the test range where ICBMS are tested in the area of Tyura-Tam, twelve launchers shall be dismantled or destroyed and six launchers may be converted to launchers for testing missiles undergoing modernization.

Dismantling or destruction of the twelve launchers shall begin upon entry into force of the Treaty and shall be completed within eight months, under procedures for dismantling or destruction of these launchers to be agreed upon in the Standing Consultative Commission. These twelve launchers shall not be replaced.

Conversion of the six launchers may be carried out after entry into force of the Treaty. After entry into force of the Treaty, fractional orbital missiles shall be removed and shall be destroyed pursuant to the provisions of subparagraph 1(c) of Article IX and of Article XI of the Treaty and shall not be replaced by other missiles, except in the case of conversion of these six launchers for testing missiles undergoing modernization. After removal of the fractional orbital missiles, and prior to such conversion, any activities associated with these launchers shall be limited to normal maintenance requirements for launchers in which missiles are not deployed. These six launchers shall be subject to the provisions of Article VII of the Treaty and, if converted, to the provisions of the Fifth Common Understanding to paragraph 5 of Article II of the Treaty.

Article VIII

1. Each Party undertakes not to flight-test cruise missiles capable of a range in excess of 600 kilometers or ASBMS from aircraft other than bombers or to convert such aircraft into aircraft equipped for such missiles.

Agreed Statement. For purposes of testing only, each Party has the right, through initial construction or, as an exception to the provisions of paragraph 1 of Article VIII of the Treaty, by conversion, to equip for cruise missiles capable of a range in excess of 600 kilometers or for ASBMS no more than sixteen airplanes, including airplanes which are prototypes of bombers equipped for such missiles. Each Party also has the right, as an exception to the provisions of paragraph 1 of Article VIII of the Treaty, to flight-test from such airplanes cruise missiles capable of a range in excess of 600 kilometers and, after the date on which the Protocol ceases to be in force, to flight-test ASBMS from such airplanes as well, unless the Parties agree that they will not flight-test ASBMS after that date. The limitations provided for in Article III of the Treaty shall not apply to such airplanes.

The aforementioned airplanes may include only:

(a) airplanes other than bombers which, as an exception to the provisions of paragraph 1 of Article VIII of the Treaty, have been converted into airplanes equipped for cruise missiles capable of a range in excess of 600 kilometers or for ASBMS;

(b) airplanes considered to be heavy bombers pursuant to subparagraph 3(c) or 3(d) of Article II of the Treaty; and

(c) airplanes other than heavy bombers which, prior to March 7, 1979, were used for testing cruise missiles capable of a range in excess of 600 kilometers.

The airplanes referred to in subparagraphs (a) and (b) of this Agreed Statement shall be distinguishable on the basis of functionally related observable differences from airplanes which otherwise would be of the same type but cannot perform the mission of a bomber equipped for cruise missiles capable of a range in excess of 600 kilometers or for ASBMS.

The airplanes referred to in subparagraph (c) of this Agreed Statement shall not be used for testing cruise missiles capable of a range in excess of 600 kilometers after the expiration of a six-month period from the date of entry into force of the Treaty, unless by the expiration of that period they are distinguishable on the basis of functionally related observable differences from airplanes which otherwise would be of the same type but cannot perform the mission of a bomber equipped for cruise missiles capable of a range in excess of 600 kilometers.

First Common Understanding. The term "testing," as used in the Agreed Statement to paragraph 1 of Article VIII of the Treaty, includes research and development.

Second Common Understanding. The Parties shall notify each other in the Standing Consultative Commission of the number of airplanes, according to type, used for testing pursuant to the Agreed Statement to paragraph 1 of Article VIII of the Treaty. Such notification shall be provided at the first regular session of the Standing Consultative Commission held after an airplane has been used for such testing.

Third Common Understanding. None of the sixteen airplanes referred to in the Agreed Statement to paragraph 1 of Article VIII of the Treaty may be replaced, except in the event of the involuntary destruction of any such airplane or in the case of the dismantling or destruction of any such airplane. The procedures for such replacement and for removal of any such airplane from that number, in case of its conversion, shall be agreed upon in the Standing Consultative Commission.

2. Each Party undertakes not to convert aircraft other than bombers into aircraft which can carry out the mission of a heavy bomber as referred to in subparagraph 3(b) of Article II.

Article IX

1. Each Party undertakes not to develop, test, or deploy:

(a) ballistic missiles capable of a range in excess of 600 kilometers for installation on waterborne vehicles other than submarines, or launchers of such missiles;

Common Understanding to subparagraph (a). The obligations provided for in subparagraph 1 (a) of Article IX of the Treaty do not affect current practices for transporting ballistic missiles.

(b) fixed ballistic or cruise missile launchers for emplacement on the ocean floor, on the seabed, or on the beds of internal waters and inland waters, or in the subsoil thereof, or mobile launchers of such missiles, which move only in contact with the ocean floor, the seabed, or the beds of internal waters and inland waters, or missiles for such launchers;

Agreed Statement to subparagraph (b). The obligations provided for in subparagraph 1 (b) of Article IX of the Treaty shall apply to all areas of the ocean floor and the seabed, including the seabed zone referred to in Articles I and II of the 1971 Treaty on the Prohibition of the Emplacement of Nuclear Weapons and Other Weapons of Mass Destruction on the Seabed and the Ocean Floor and in the Subsoil Thereof.

(c) systems for placing into Earth orbit nuclear weapons or any other kind of weapons of mass destruction, including fractional orbital missiles;

Common Understanding to subparagraph (c). The provisions of subparagraph 1 (c) of Article IX of the Treaty do not require the dismantling or destruction of any existing launchers of either Party.

(d) mobile launchers of heavy ICBMs;

(e) SLBMs which have a launch-weight greater or a throw-weight greater than that of the heaviest, in terms of either launch-weight or throw-weight, respectively, of the light ICBMs deployed by either Party as of the date of signature of this Treaty, or launchers of such SLBMs; or

(f) ASBMs which have a launch-weight greater or a throw-weight greater than that of the heaviest, in terms of either launch-weight or throw-weight, respectively, of the light ICBMs deployed by either Party as of the date of signature of this Treaty.

First Agreed Statement to subparagraphs (e) and (f). The launch-weight of an SLBM or of an ASBM is the weight of the fully loaded missile itself at the time of launch.

Second Agreed Statement to subparagraphs (e) and (f). The throw-weight of an SLBM or of an ASBM is the sum of the weight of:

(a) its reentry vehicle or reentry vehicles;

(b) any self-contained dispensing mechanisms or other appropriate devices for targeting one reentry vehicle, or for releasing or for dispensing and targeting two or more reentry vehicles; and

(c) its penetration aids, including devices for their release.

Common Understanding to subparagraphs (e) and (f). The term "other appropriate devices," as used in the definition of the throw-weight of an SLBM or of an ASBM in the Second Agreed Statement to subparagraphs 1 (e) and 1 (f) of Article IX of the Treaty, means any devices for dispensing and targeting two or more reentry vehicles; and any devices for releasing two or more reentry vehicles or for targeting one reentry vehicle, which cannot provide their reentry vehicles or reentry vehicle with additional velocity of more than 1,000 meters per second.

2. Each Party undertakes not to flight-test from aircraft cruise missiles capable of a range in excess of 600 kilometers which are equipped with multiple independently targetable warheads and not to deploy such cruise missiles on aircraft.

Agreed Statement. Warheads of a cruise missile are independently targetable if maneuvering or targeting of the warheads to separate aim points along ballistic trajectories or any other flight paths, which are unrelated to each other, is accomplished during a flight of a cruise missile.

Article X. Subject to the provisions of this Treaty, modernization and replacement of strategic offensive arms may be carried out.

Article XI

1. Strategic offensive arms which would be in excess of the aggregate numbers provided for in this Treaty as well as strategic offensive arms prohibited by this Treaty shall be dismantled or destroyed under procedures to be agreed upon in the Standing Consultative Commission.

2. Dismantling or destruction of strategic offensive arms which would be in excess of the aggregate number provided for in paragraph 1 of Article III shall begin on the date of the entry into force of this Treaty and shall be completed within the following periods from that date: four months for ICBM launchers; six months for SLBM launchers; and three months for heavy bombers.

3. Dismantling or destruction of strategic offensive arms which would be in excess of the aggregate number provided for in paragraph 2 of Article III shall be initiated no later than January 1, 1981, shall be carried out throughout the ensuing twelve-month period, and shall be completed no later than December 31, 1981.

4. Dismantling or destruction of strategic offensive arms prohibited by this Treaty shall be completed within the shortest possible agreed period of time, but not later than six months after the entry into force of this Treaty.

Article XII. In order to ensure the viability and effectiveness of this Treaty, each Party undertakes not to circumvent the provisions of this Treaty, through any other state or states, or in any other manner.

Article XIII. Each Party undertakes not to assume any international obligations which would conflict with this Treaty.

Article XIV. The Parties undertake to begin, promptly after the entry into force of this Treaty, active negotiations with the objective of achieving, as soon as possible, agreement on further measures for the limitation and reduction of strategic arms. It is also the objective of the Parties to conclude well in advance of 1985 an agreement limiting strategic offensive arms to replace this Treaty upon its expiration.

Article XV

1. For the purpose of providing assurance of compliance with the provisions of this Treaty, each Party shall use national technical means of verification at its disposal in a manner consistent with generally recognized principles of international law.

2. Each party undertakes not to interfere with the national technical means of verification of the other Party operating in accordance with paragraph 1 of this Article.

3. Each Party undertakes not to use deliberate concealment measures which impede verification by national technical means of compliance with the provisions of this Treaty. This obligation shall not require changes in current construction, assembly, conversion, or overhaul practices.

First Agreed Statement. Deliberate concealment measures, as referred to in paragraph 3 of Article XV of the Treaty, are measures carried out deliberately to hinder or deliberately to impede verification by national technical means of compliance with the provisions of the Treaty.

Second Agreed Statement. The obligation not to use deliberate concealment measures, provided for in paragraph 3 of Article XV of the Treaty, does not preclude the testing of anti-missile defense penetration aids.

First Common Understanding. The provisions of paragraph 3 of Article XV of the Treaty and the First Agreed Statement thereto apply to all provisions of the Treaty, including provisions associated with testing. In this connection, the obligation not to use deliberate concealment measures includes the obligation not to use deliberate concealment measures associated with testing, including those measures aimed at concealing the association between ICBMs and launchers during testing.

Second Common Understanding. Each Party is free to use various methods of transmitting telemetric information during testing, including its encryption, except that, in accordance with the provisions of paragraph 3 of Article XV of the Treaty, neither Party shall engage in deliberate denial of telemetric information, such as through the use of telemetry encryption, whenever such denial impedes verification of compliance with the provisions of the Treaty.

Third Common Understanding. In addition to the obligations provided for in paragraph 3 of Article XV of the Treaty, no shelters which impede verification by national technical means of compliance with the provisions of the Treaty shall be used over ICBM silo launchers.

Article XVI

1. Each Party undertakes, before conducting each planned ICBM launch, to notify the other Party well in advance on a case-by-case basis that such a launch will occur, except for single ICBM launches from test ranges or from ICBM launcher deployment areas, which are not planned to extend beyond its national territory.

First Common Understanding. ICBM launches to which the obligations provided for in Article XVI of the Treaty apply, include, among others, those ICBM launches for which advance notification is required pursuant to the provisions of the Agreement on Measures to Reduce the Risk of Outbreak of Nuclear War Between the United States of America and the Union of Soviet Socialist Republics, signed September 30, 1971, and the Agreement Between the Government of the United States of America and the Government of the Union of Soviet Socialists Republics on the Prevention of Incidents On and Over the High Seas, signed May 25, 1972. Nothing in Article XVI of the Treaty is intended to inhibit advance notification, on a voluntary basis, of any ICBM launches not subject to its provisions, the advance notification of which would enhance confidence between the Parties.

Second Common Understanding. A multiple ICBM launch conducted by a Party, as distinct from single ICBM launches referred to in Article XVI of the Treaty, is a launch which would result in two or more of its ICBMs being in flight at the same time.

Third Common Understanding. The test ranges referred to in Article XVI of the Treaty are those covered by the Second Agreed Statement to paragraph 2 of Article VII of the Treaty.

2. The Parties shall agree in the Standing Consultative Commission upon procedures to implement the provisions of this Article.

Article XVII

1. To promote the objectives and implementation of the provisions of this Treaty, the Parties shall use the Standing Consultative Commission established by the Memorandum of Understanding Between the Government of the United States of America and the Government of the Union of Soviet Socialist Republics Regarding the Establishment of a Standing Consultative Commission of December 21, 1972.

2. Within the framework of the Standing Consultative Commission, with respect to this Treaty, the Parties will:

(a) consider questions concerning compliance with the obligations assumed and related situations which may be considered ambiguous;

(b) provide on a voluntary basis such information as either Party considers necessary to assure confidence in compliance with the obligations assumed,

(c) consider questions involving unintended interference with national technical means of verification, and questions involving unintended impeding of verification by national technical means of compliance with the provisions of this Treaty;

(d) consider possible changes in the strategic situation which have a bearing on the provisions of this Treaty.

(e) agree upon procedures for replacement, conversion, and dismantling or destruction, of strategic offensive arms in cases provided for in the provisions of this Treaty and upon procedures for removal of such arms from the aggregate numbers when they otherwise cease to be subject to the limitations provided for in this Treaty, and at regular sessions of the Standing Consultative Commission, notify each other in accordance with the aforementioned procedures, at least twice annually, of actions completed and those in process;

(f) consider, as appropriate, possible proposals for further increasing the viability of this Treaty, including proposals for amendments in accordance with the provisions of this Treaty;

(g) consider, as appropriate, proposals for further measures limiting strategic offensive arms.

3. In the Standing Consultative Commission the Parties shall maintain by category the agreed data base on the numbers of strategic offensive arms es-

tablished by the Memorandum of Understanding Between the United States of America and the Union of Soviet Socialist Republics Regarding the Establishment of a Data Base on the Numbers of Strategic Offensive Arms of June 18, 1979.

Agreed Statement. In order to maintain the agreed data base on the numbers of strategic offensive arms subject to the limitations provided for in the Treaty in accordance with paragraph 3 of Article XVII of the Treaty, at each regular session of the Standing Consultative Commission the Parties will notify each other of and consider changes in those numbers in the following categories: launchers of ICBMS; fixed launchers of ICBMS, launchers of ICBMS equipped with MIRVS; launchers of SLBMS; launchers of SLBMS equipped with MIRVS; heavy bombers; heavy bombers equipped for cruise missiles capable of a range in excess of 600 kilometers; heavy bombers equipped only for ASBMS; ASBMS; and ASBMS equipped with MIRVS.

Article XVIII. Each Party may propose amendments to this Treaty. Agreed amendments shall enter into force in accordance with the procedures governing the entry into force of this Treaty.

Article XIX

1. This Treaty shall be subject to ratification in accordance with the constitutional procedures of each Party. This Treaty shall enter into force on the day of the exchange of instruments of ratification and shall remain in force through December 31, 1985, unless replaced earlier by an agreement further limiting strategic offensive arms.

2. This Treaty shall be registered pursuant to Article 102 of the Charter of the United Nations.

3. Each Party shall, in exercising its national sovereignty, have the right to withdraw from this Treaty if it decides that extraordinary events related to the subject matter of this Treaty have jeopardized its supreme interests. It shall give notice of its decision to the other Party six months prior to withdrawal from the Treaty. Such notice shall include a statement of the extraordinary events the notifying Party regards as having jeopardized its supreme interests.

[Signatures]

Protocol to the Treaty Between the United States of America and the Union of Soviet Socialist Republics on the Limitation of Strategic Offensive Arms

The United States of America and the Union of Soviet Socialist Republics, hereinafter referred to as the Parties,

Having agreed on limitations on strategic offensive arms in the Treaty,

Have agreed on additional limitations for the period during which this Protocol remains in force, as follows:

Article I. Each Party undertakes not to deploy mobile ICBM launchers or to flight-test ICBMS from such launchers.

Article II

1. Each Party undertakes not to deploy cruise missiles capable of a range in excess of 600 kilometers on sea-based launchers or on land-based launchers.

2. Each Party undertakes not to flight-test cruise missiles capable of a range in excess of 600 kilometers which are equipped with multiple independently targetable warheads from sea-based launchers or from land-based launchers.

Agreed Statement. Warheads of a cruise missile are independently targetable if maneuvering or targeting of the warheads to separate aim points along ballistic trajectories or any other flight paths, which are unrelated to each other, is accomplished during a flight of a cruise missile.

3. For the purposes of this Protocol, cruise missiles are unmanned, self-propelled, guided, weapon-delivery vehicles which sustain flight through the use of aerodynamic lift over most of their flight path and which are flight-tested from or deployed on sea-based or land-based launchers, that is, sea-launched cruise missiles and ground-launched cruise missiles, respectively.

First Agreed Statement. If a cruise missile is capable of a range in excess of 600 kilometers, all cruise missiles of that type shall be considered to be cruise missiles capable of a range in excess of 600 kilometers.

First Common Understanding. If a cruise missile has been flight-tested to a range in excess of 600 kilometers, it shall be considered to be a cruise missile capable of a range in excess of 600 kilometers.

Second Common Understanding. Cruise missiles not capable of a range in excess of 600 kilometers shall not be considered to be of a type capable of a range in excess of 600 kilometers if they are distinguishable on the basis of externally observable design features from cruise missiles of types capable of a range in excess of 600 kilometers.

Second Agreed Statement. The range of which a cruise missile is capable is the maximum distance which can be covered by the missile in its standard design mode flying until fuel exhaustion, determined by projecting its flight path onto the Earth's sphere from the point of launch to the point of impact.

Third Agreed Statement. If an unmanned, self-propelled, guided vehicle which sustains flight through the use of aerodynamic lift over most of its flight path has been flight-tested or deployed for weapon delivery, all vehicles of that type shall be considered to be weapon-delivery vehicles.

Third Common Understanding. Unmanned, self-propelled, guided vehicles which sustain flight through the use of aerodynamic lift over most of their flight path and are not weapon-delivery vehicles, that is, unarmed, pilotless, guided vehicles, shall not be considered to be cruise missiles if such vehicles are distinguishable from cruise missiles on the basis of externally observable design features.

Fourth Common Understanding. Neither Party shall convert unarmed, pilotless, guided vehicles into cruise missiles capable of a range in excess of 600 kilometers, nor shall either Party convert cruise missiles capable of a range in excess of 600 kilometers into unarmed, pilotless, guided vehicles.

Fifth Common Understanding. Neither Party has plans during the term of the Protocol to flight-test from or deploy on sea-based or land-based launchers unarmed, pilotless, guided vehicles which are capable of a range in excess of 600 kilometers. In the future, should a Party have such plans, that Party will provide notification thereof to the other Party well in advance of such flight-testing or deployment. This Common Understanding does not apply to target drones.

Article III. Each Party undertakes not to flight-test or deploy ASBMS.

Article IV. This Protocol shall be considered an integral part of the Treaty. It shall enter into force on the day of the entry into force of the Treaty and shall remain in force through December 31, 1981, unless replaced earlier by an agreement on further measures limiting strategic offensive arms.

DONE at Vienna on June 18, 1979, in two copies, each in the English and Russian languages, both texts being equally authentic.

[Signatures]

Memorandum of Understanding Between the United States of America and the Union of Soviet Socialist Republics Regarding the Establishment of a Data Base on the Numbers of Strategic Offensive Arms

For the purposes of the Treaty Between the United States of America and the Union of Soviet Socialist Republics on the Limitation of Strategic Offensive Arms, the Parties have considered data on numbers of strategic offensive arms and agree that as of November 1, 1978 there existed the following numbers of strategic offensive arms subject to the limitations provided for in the Treaty which is being signed today.

	U.S.A.	U.S.S.R.
Launchers of ICBMS	1,054	1,398
Fixed launchers of ICBMS	1,054	1,398
Launchers of ICBMS equipped with MIRVS	550	576
Launchers of SLBMS	656	950
Launchers of SLBMS equipped with MIRVS	496	128
Heavy bombers	574	156
Heavy bombers equipped for cruise missiles capable of a range in excess of 600 kilometers	0	0
Heavy bombers equipped only for ASBMS	0	0
ASBMS	0	0
ASBMS equipped with MIRVS	0	0

At the time of entry into force of the Treaty the Parties will update the above agreed data in the categories listed in this Memorandum.

DONE at Vienna on June 18, 1979, in two copies, each in the English and Russian languages, both texts being equally authentic.

[Signatures]

Statement of Data on the Numbers of Strategic Offensive Arms as of the Date of Signature of the Treaty

The United States of America declares that as of June 18, 1979 it possesses the following numbers of strategic offensive arms subject to the limitations provided for in the Treaty which is being signed today:

Launchers of ICBMS	1,054
Fixed launchers of ICBMS	1,054
Launchers of ICBMS equipped with MIRVS	550
Launchers of SLBMS	656
Launchers of SLBMS equipped with MIRVS	496
Heavy bombers	573

Heavy bombers equipped for cruise missiles capable of a range in excess of 600 kilometers	3
Heavy bombers equipped only for ASBMS	0
ASBMS	0
ASBMS equipped with MIRVS	0

Statement of Data on the Numbers of Strategic Offensive Arms as of the Date of Signature of the Treaty

The Union of Soviet Socialist Republics declares that as of June 18, 1979, it possesses the following numbers of strategic offensive arms subject to the limitations provided for in the Treaty which is being signed today:

Launchers of ICBMS	1,398
Fixed launchers of ICBMS	1,398
Launchers of ICBMS equipped with MIRVS	608
Launchers of SLBMS	950
Launchers of SLBMS equipped with MIRVS	144
Heavy bombers	156
Heavy bombers equipped for cruise missiles capable of a range in excess of 600 kilometers	0
Heavy bombers equipped only for ASBMS	0
ASBMS	0
ASBMS equipped with MIRVS	0

Joint Statement of Principles and Basic Guidelines for Subsequent Negotiations on the Limitation of Strategic Arms

The United States of America and the Union of Soviet Socialist Republics, hereinafter referred to as the Parties,

Having concluded the Treaty on the Limitation of Strategic Offensive Arms.

Reaffirming that the strengthening of strategic stability meets the interests of the Parties and the interests of international security.

Convinced that early agreement on the further limitation and further reduction of strategic arms would serve to strengthen international peace and security and to reduce the risk of outbreak of nuclear war,

Have agreed as follows:

First. The Parties will continue to pursue negotiations, in accordance with the principle of equality and equal security, on measures for the further lim-

itation and reduction in the numbers of strategic arms, as well as for their further qualitative limitation.

In furtherance of existing agreements between the Parties on the limitation and reduction of strategic arms, the Parties will continue, for the purposes of reducing and averting the risk of outbreak of nuclear war, to seek measures to strengthen strategic stability by, among other things, limitations on strategic offensive arms most destabilizing to the strategic balance and by measures to reduce and to avert the risk of surprise attack.

Second. Further limitations and reductions of strategic arms must be subject to adequate verification by national technical means, using additionally, as appropriate, cooperative measures contributing to the effectiveness of verification by national technical means. The Parties will seek to strengthen verification and to perfect the operation of the Standing Consultative Commission in order to promote assurance of compliance with the obligations assumed by the Parties.

Third. The Parties shall pursue in the course of these negotiations, taking into consideration factors that determine the strategic situation, the following objectives:

1. significant and substantial reductions in the numbers of strategic offensive arms;

2. qualitative limitations on strategic offensive arms, including restrictions on the development, testing, and deployment of new types of strategic offensive arms and on the modernization of existing strategic offensive arms;

3. resolution of the issues included in the Protocol to the Treaty Between the United States of America and the Union of Soviet Socialist Republics on the Limitation of Strategic Offensive Arms in the context of the negotiations relating to the implementation of the principles and objectives set out herein.

Fourth. The Parties will consider other steps to ensure and enhance strategic stability, to ensure the equality and equal security of the Parties, and to implement the above principles and objectives. Each Party will be free to raise any issue relative to the further limitation of strategic arms. The Parties will also consider further joint measures, as appropriate, to strengthen international peace and security and to reduce the risk of outbreak of nuclear war.

Vienna, June 18, 1979

[Signatures]

Soviet Backfire Statement

On June 16, 1979, President Brezhnev handed President Carter the following written statement [original Russian text was attached]:

The Soviet side informs the US side that the Soviet 'Tu-22M' airplane, called 'Backfire' in the USA, is a medium-range bomber, and that it does not intend to give this airplane the capability of operating at intercontinental distances. In this connection, the Soviet side states that it will not increase the radius of action of this airplane in such a way as to enable it to strike targets on the territory of the USA. Nor does it intend to give it such a capability in any other manner, including by in-flight refueling. At the same time, the Soviet side states that it will not increase the production rate of this airplane as compared to the present rate.

President Brezhnev confirmed that the Soviet Backfire production rate would not exceed 30 per year.

President Carter stated that the United States enters into the SALT II Agreement on the basis of the commitments contained in the Soviet statement and that it considers the carrying out of these commitments to be essential to the obligations assumed under the Treaty.

[U.S. Arms Control and Disarmament Agency, *Arms Control and Disarmament Agreements*, 5th ed. (Washington, D.C., 1982), pp. 246–277]

INF Treaty (1987)

The INF Treaty was signed at Washington, D.C., on 8 December 1987, and it entered into force on 1 June 1988.

Treaty Between the United States of America and the Union of Soviet Socialist Republics on the Elimination of Their Intermediate-Range and Shorter-Range Missiles.

The United States of America and the Union of Soviet Socialist Republics, hereinafter referred to as the Parties,

Conscious that nuclear war would have devastating consequences for all mankind,

Guided by the objective of strengthening strategic stability,

Convinced that the measures set forth in this Treaty will help to reduce the risk of outbreak of war and strengthen international peace and security, and

Mindful of their obligations under Article VI of the Treaty on the Non-Proliferation of Nuclear Weapons,

Have agreed as follows:

Article I. In accordance with the provisions of this Treaty which includes the Memorandum of Understanding and Protocols which form an integral part thereof, each Party shall eliminate its intermediate-range and shorter-range missiles, not have such systems thereafter, and carry out the other obligations set forth in this Treaty.

Article II. For the purposes of this Treaty:

1. The term "ballistic missile" means a missile that has a ballistic trajectory over most of its flight path. The term "ground-launched ballistic missile (GLBM)" means a ground-launched ballistic missile that is a weapon-delivery vehicle.

2. The term "cruise missile" means an unmanned, self-propelled vehicle that sustains flight through the use of aerodynamic lift over most of its flight path. The term "ground-launched cruise missile (GLCM)" means a ground-launched cruise missile that is a weapon-delivery vehicle.

3. The term "GLBM launcher" means a fixed launcher or a mobile land-based transporter-erector-launcher mechanism for launching a GLBM.

4. The term "GLCM launcher" means a fixed launcher or a mobile land-based transporter-erector-launcher mechanism for launching a GLCM.

5. The term "intermediate-range missile" means a GLBM or a GLCM having a range capability in excess of 1,000 kilometers but not in excess of 5,500 kilometers.

6. The term "shorter-range missile" means a GLBM or a GLCM having a range capability equal to or in excess of 500 kilometers but not in excess of 1,000 kilometers.

7. The term "deployment area" means a designated area within which intermediate range missiles and launchers of such missiles may operate and within which one or more missile operating bases are located.

8. The term "missile operating base" means:

(a) in the case of intermediate-range missiles, a complex of facilities, located within a deployment area, at which intermediate-range missiles and launchers of such missiles normally operate, in which support structures associated with such missiles and launchers are also located and in which support equipment associated with such missiles and launchers is normally located; and

(b) in the case of shorter-range missiles, a complex of facilities, located any place, at which shorter-range missiles and launchers of such missiles normally operate and in which support equipment associated with such missiles and launchers is normally located.

9. The term "missile support facility," as regards intermediate-range or shorter-range missiles and launchers of such missiles, means a missile production facility or a launcher production facility, a missile repair facility or a launcher repair facility, a training facility, a missile storage facility or a launcher storage facility, a test range, or an elimination facility as those terms are defined in the Memorandum of Understanding.

10. The term "transit" means movement, notified in accordance with paragraph 5(f) of Article IX of this Treaty, of an intermediate-range missile or a launcher of such a missile between missile support facilities, between such a facility and a deployment area or between deployment areas, or of a shorter-range missile or a launcher of such a missile from a missile support facility or a missile operating base to an elimination facility.

11. The term "deployed missile" means an intermediate-range missile located within a deployment area or a shorter-range missile located at a missile operating base.

12. The term "non-deployed missile" means an intermediate-range missile located outside a deployment area or a shorter-range missile located outside a missile operating base.

13. The term "deployed launcher" means a launcher of an intermediate-range missile located within a deployment area or a launcher of a shorter-range missile located at a missile operating base.

14. The term "non-deployed launcher" means a launcher of an intermediate-range missile located outside a deployment area or a launcher of a shorter-range missile located outside a missile operating base.

15. The term "basing country" means a country other than the United States of America or the Union of Soviet Socialist Republics on whose territory intermediate-range or shorter-range missiles of the Parties, launchers of such missiles or support structures associated with such missiles and launchers were located at any time after November 1, 1987. Missiles or launchers in transit are not considered to be "located."

Article III

1. For the purposes of this Treaty, existing types of intermediate-range missiles are:

(a) for the United States of America, missiles of the types designated by the United States of America as the Pershing II and the BGM-109G, which are known to the Union of Soviet Socialist Republics by the same designations; and

(b) for the Union of Soviet Socialist Republics, missiles of the types designated by the Union of Soviet Socialist Republics as the RSD-10, the R-12 and the R-14, which are known to the United States of America as the SS-20, the SS-4 and the SS-5, respectively.

2. For the purpose of this Treaty, existing types of shorter-range missiles are:

(a) for the United States of America, missiles of the type designated by the United States of America as the Pershing IA, which is known to the Union of Soviet Socialist Republics by the same designation; and

(b) for the Union of Soviet Socialist Republics, missiles of the types designated by the Union of Soviet Socialist Republics as the OTR-22 and the OTR-23, which are known to the United States of America as the SS-12 and the SS-23, respectively.

Article IV

1. Each Party shall eliminate all its intermediate-range missiles and launchers of such missiles, and all support structures and support equipment of the categories listed in the Memorandum of Understanding associated with such missiles and launchers, so that no later than three years after entry into force of this Treaty and thereafter no such missiles, launchers, support structures or support equipment shall be possessed by either Party.

2. To implement paragraph 1 of this Article, upon entry into force of this Treaty, both Parties shall begin and continue throughout the duration of each phase, the reduction of all types of their deployed

and non-deployed intermediate-range missiles and deployed and non-deployed launchers of such missiles and support structures and support equipment associated with such missiles and launchers in accordance with the provisions of this Treaty. These reductions shall be implemented in two phases so that:

(a) by the end of the first phase, that is, no later than 29 months after entry into force of this Treaty:

(i) the number of deployed launchers of intermediate-range missiles for each Party shall not exceed the number of launchers that are capable of carrying or containing at one time missiles considered by the Parties to carry 171 warheads;

(ii) the number of deployed intermediate-range missiles for each Party shall not exceed the number of such missiles considered by the Parties to carry 180 warheads;

(iii) the aggregate number of deployed and non-deployed launchers of intermediate-range missiles for each Party shall not exceed the number of launchers that are capable of carrying at one time missiles considered by the Parties to carry 200 warheads;

(iv) the aggregate number of deployed and non-deployed intermediate-range missiles for each Party shall not exceed the number of such missiles considered by the Parties to carry 200 warheads; and

(v) the ratio of the aggregate number of deployed and non-deployed intermediate-range GLBMS for existing types of each Party to the aggregate number of deployed and non-deployed intermediate-range missiles of existing types possessed by that Party shall not exceed the ratio of such intermediate-range GLBMS to such intermediate-range missiles for that Party as of November 1, 1987, as set forth in the Memorandum of Understanding; and

(b) by the end of the second phase, that is, no later than three years after entry into force of this Treaty, all intermediate-range missiles of each Party, launchers of such missiles and all support structures and support equipment of the categories listed in the Memorandum of Understanding associated with such missiles and launchers, shall be eliminated.

Article V

1. Each Party shall eliminate all its shorter-range missiles and launchers of such missiles, and all support equipment of the categories listed in the Memorandum of Understanding associated with such missiles and launchers, so that no later than 18 months after entry into force of this Treaty and

thereafter no such missiles, launchers or support equipment shall be possessed by either Party.

2. No later than 90 days after entry into force of this Treaty, each Party shall complete the removal of all its deployed shorter-range missiles and deployed and non-deployed launchers of such missiles to elimination facilities and shall retain them at those locations until they are eliminated in accordance with the procedures set forth in the Protocol on Elimination. No later than 12 months after entry into force of this Treaty, each Party shall complete the removal of all its non-deployed shorter-range missiles to elimination facilities and shall retain them at those locations until they are eliminated in accordance with the procedures set forth in the Protocol on Elimination.

3. Shorter-range missiles and launchers of such missiles shall not be located at the same elimination facility. Such facilities shall be separated by no less than 1,000 kilometers.

Article VI

1. Upon entry into force of this Treaty and thereafter, neither Party shall:

(a) produce or flight-test any intermediate-range missiles or produce any stages of such missiles or any launchers of such missiles; or

(b) produce, flight-test or launch any shorter-range missiles or produce any stages of such missiles or any launchers of such missiles.

2. Notwithstanding paragraph 1 of this Article, each Party shall have the right to produce a type of GLBM not limited by this Treaty that uses a stage that is outwardly similar to, but not interchangeable with, a stage of an existing type of intermediate-range GLBM having more than one stage, providing that that Party shall not produce any other stage that is outwardly similar to, but not interchangeable with, any other stage of an existing type of intermediate-range GLBM.

Article VII. For the purposes of this Treaty:

1. If a ballistic missile or a cruise missile has been flight-tested or deployed for weapon delivery, all missiles of that type shall be considered to be weapon-delivery vehicles.

2. If a GLBM or GLCM is an intermediate-range missile, all GLBMS or GLCMS of that type shall be considered to be intermediate-range missiles. If a GLBM or GLCM is a shorter-range missile, all GLBMS or GLCMS of that type shall be considered to be shorter-range missiles.

3. If a GLBM is of a type developed and tested solely to intercept and counter objects not located on the surface of the earth, it shall not be consid-

ered to be a missile to which the limitations of this Treaty apply.

4. The range capability of a GLBM not listed in Article III of this Treaty shall be considered to be the maximum range to which it has been tested. The range capability of a GLCM not listed in Article III of this Treaty shall be considered to be the maximum distance which can be covered by the missile in its standard design mode flying until fuel exhaustion, determined by projecting its flight path onto the earth's sphere from the point of launch to the point of impact. GLBMS or GLCMS that have a range capability equal to or in excess of 500 kilometers but not in excess of 1000 kilometers shall be considered to be shorter-range missiles. GLBMS or GLCMS that have a range capability in excess of 1000 kilometers but not in excess of 5500 kilometers shall be considered to be intermediate-range missiles.

5. The maximum number of warheads an existing type of intermediate-range missile or shorter-range missile carries shall be considered to be the number listed for missiles of that type in the Memorandum of Understanding.

6. Each GLBM or GLCM shall be considered to carry the maximum number of warheads listed for a GLBM or GLCM of the type in the Memorandum of Understanding.

7. If a launcher has been tested for launching a GLBM or a GLCM, all launchers of that type shall be considered to have been tested for launching GLBMS or GLCMS.

8. If a launcher has contained or launched a particular type of GLBM or GLCM, all launchers of that type shall be considered to be launchers of that type of GLBM or GLCM.

9. The number of missiles each launcher of an existing type of intermediate-range missile or shorter-range missile shall be considered to be capable of carrying or containing at one time is the number listed for launchers of missiles of that type in the Memorandum of Understanding.

10. Except in the case of elimination in accordance with the procedures set forth in the Protocol on Elimination, the following shall apply:

(a) for GLBMS which are stored or moved in separate stages, the longest stage of an intermediate-range or shorter-range GLBM shall be counted as a complete missile;

(b) for GLBMS which are not stored or moved in separate stages, a canister of the type used in the launch of an intermediate-range GLBM, unless a Party proves to the satisfaction of the other Party

that it does not contain such a missile, or an assembled intermediate-range or shorter-range GLBM, shall be counted as a complete missile; and

(c) for GLCMS, the airframe of an intermediate-range or shorter-range GLCM shall be counted as a complete missile.

11. A ballistic missile which is not a missile to be used in a ground-based mode shall not be considered to be a GLBM if it is test-launched at a test site from a fixed land-based launcher which is used solely for test purposes and which is distinguishable from GLBM launchers. A cruise missile which is not a missile to be used in a ground-based mode shall not be considered to be a GLCM if it is test-launched at a test site from a fixed land-based launcher which is used solely for test purposes and which is distinguishable from GLCM launchers.

12. Each Party shall have the right to produce and use for booster systems, which might otherwise be considered to be intermediate-range or shorter-range missiles, only existing types of booster stages for such booster systems. Launches of such booster systems shall not be considered to be flight-testing of intermediate-range or shorter-range missiles provided that:

(a) stages used in such booster systems are different from stages used in those missiles listed as existing types of intermediate-range or shorter-range missiles in Article III of this Treaty;

(b) such booster systems are used only for research and development purposes to test objects other than the booster systems themselves;

(c) the aggregate number of launchers for such booster systems shall not exceed 35 for each Party at any one time; and

(d) the launchers for such booster systems are fixed, emplaced above ground and located only at research and development launch sites which are specified in the Memorandum of Understanding.

Research and development launch sites shall not be subject to inspection pursuant to Article XI of this Treaty.

Article VIII

1. All intermediate-range missiles and launchers of such missiles shall be located in deployment areas, at missile support facilities or shall be in transit. Intermediate-range missiles or launchers of such missiles shall not be located elsewhere.

2. Stages of intermediate-range missiles shall be located in deployment areas, at missile support facilities or moving between deployment areas, between missile support facilities or between missile support facilities and deployment areas.

3. Until their removal to elimination facilities as required by paragraph 2 of Article V of this Treaty, all shorter-range missiles and launchers of such missiles shall be located at missile operating bases, at missile support facilities or shall be in transit. Shorter-range missiles or launchers of such missiles shall not be located elsewhere.

4. Transit of a missile or launcher subject to the provisions of this Treaty shall be completed within 25 days.

5. All deployment areas, missile operating bases and missile support facilities are specified in the Memorandum of Understanding or in subsequent updates of data pursuant to paragraphs 3, 5(a) or 5(b) of Article IX of this Treaty. Neither Party shall increase the number of, or change the location or boundaries of, deployment areas, missile operating bases or missile support facilities, except for elimination facilities, from those set forth in the Memorandum of Understanding. A missile support facility shall not be considered to be part of a deployment area even though it may be located within the geographic boundaries of a deployment area.

6. Beginning 30 days after entry into force of this Treaty, neither Party shall locate intermediate-range or shorter-range missiles, including stages of such missiles, or launchers of such missiles at missile production facilities, launcher production facilities or test ranges listed in the Memorandum of Understanding.

7. Neither Party shall locate any intermediate-range or shorter-range missiles at training facilities.

8. A non-deployed intermediate-range or shorter-range missile shall not be carried on or contained within a launcher of such a type of missile, except as required for maintenance conducted at repair facilities or for elimination by means of launching conducted at elimination facilities.

9. Training missiles and training launchers for intermediate-range or shorter-range missiles shall be subject to the same locational restrictions as are set forth for intermediate-range and shorter-range missiles and launchers of such missiles in paragraphs 1 and 3 of this Article.

Article IX

1. The Memorandum of Understanding contains categories of data relevant to obligations undertaken with regard to this Treaty and lists all intermediate-range and shorter-range missiles, launchers of such missiles, and support structures and support equipment associated with such missiles and launchers, possessed by the Parties as of November 1, 1987.

Updates of that data and notifications required by this Article shall be provided according to the categories of data contained in the Memorandum of Understanding.

2. The Parties shall update that data and provide the notifications required by this Treaty through the Nuclear Risk Reduction Centers, established pursuant to the Agreement Between the United States of America and the Union of Soviet Socialist Republics on the Establishment of Nuclear Risk Reduction Centers of September 15, 1987.

3. No later than 30 days after entry into force of this Treaty, each Party shall provide the other Party with updated data, as of the date of entry into force of this Treaty, for all categories of data contained in the Memorandum of Understanding.

4. No later than 30 days after the end of each six-month interval following the entry into force of this Treaty, each Party shall provide updated data for all categories of data contained in the Memorandum of Understanding by informing the other Party of all changes, completed and in process, in that data, which have occurred during the six-month interval since the preceding data exchange, and the net effect of those changes.

5. Upon entry into force of this Treaty and thereafter, each Party shall provide the following notifications to the other Party:

(a) notification, no less than 30 days in advance, of the scheduled date of the elimination of a specific deployment area, missile operating base or missile support facility;

(b) notification, no less than 30 days in advance, of changes in the number or location of elimination facilities, including the location and scheduled date of each change;

(c) notification, except with respect to launches of intermediate-range missiles for the purpose of their elimination, no less than 30 days in advance, of the scheduled date of the initiation of the elimination of intermediate-range and shorter-range missiles, and stages of such missiles, and launchers of such missiles and support structures and support equipment associated with such missiles and launchers, including:

(i) the number and type of items of missile systems to be eliminated;

(ii) the elimination site;

(iii) for intermediate-range missiles, the location from which such missiles, launchers of such missiles and support equipment associated with such missiles and launchers are moved to the elimination facility; and

(iv) except in the case of support structures, the point of entry to be used by an inspection team conducting an inspection pursuant to paragraph 7 of Article IX of this Treaty and the estimated time of departure of an inspection team from the point of entry to the elimination facility;

(d) notification, no less than ten days in advance, of the scheduled date of the launch, or the scheduled date of the initiation of a series of launches, of intermediate-range missiles for the purpose of their elimination, including:

(i) the type of missiles to be eliminated;

(ii) the location of the launch, or, if elimination is by a series of launches, the location of such launches and the number of launches in the series;

(iii) the point of entry to be used by an inspection team conducting an inspection pursuant to paragraph 7 of Article XI of this Treaty; and

(iv) the estimated time of departure of an inspection team from the point of entry to the elimination facility;

(e) notification, no later than 48 hours after they occur, of changes in the number of intermediate-range and shorter-range missiles, launchers of such missiles and support structures and support equipment associated with such missiles and launchers resulting from elimination as described in the Protocol on Elimination, including:

(i) the number and type of items of a missile system which were eliminated; and

(ii) the date and location of such elimination; and

(f) notification of transit of intermediate-range or shorter-range missiles or launchers of such missiles, or the movement of training missiles or training launchers for such intermediate-range and shorter-range missiles, no later than 48 hours after it has been completed, including:

(i) the number of missiles or launchers;

(ii) the points, dates, and times of departure and arrival;

(iii) the mode of transport; and

(iv) the location and time at that location at least once every four days during the period of transit.

6. Upon entry into force of this Treaty and thereafter, each Party shall notify the other Party, no less than ten days in advance, of the scheduled date and location of the launch of a research and development booster system as described in paragraph 12 of Article VII of this Treaty.

Article X

1. Each Party shall eliminate its intermediate-range and shorter-range missiles and launchers of such missiles and support structures and support equipment associated with such missiles and launchers in accordance with the procedures set forth in the Protocol on Elimination.

2. Verification by on-site inspection of the elimination of items of missile systems specified in the Protocol on Elimination shall be carried out in accordance with Article XI of this Treaty, the Protocol on Elimination and the Protocol on Inspection.

3. When a Party removes its intermediate-range missiles, launchers of such missiles and support equipment associated with such missiles and launchers from deployment areas to elimination facilities for the purpose of their elimination, it shall do so in complete deployed organizational units. For the United States of America, these units shall be Pershing II batteries and BGM-109G flights. For the Union of Soviet Socialist Republics, these units shall be SS-20 regiments composed of two or three battalions.

4. Elimination of intermediate-range and shorter-range missiles and launchers of such missiles and support equipment associated with such missiles and launchers shall be carried out at the facilities that are specified in the Memorandum of Understanding or notified in accordance with paragraph 5(b) of Article IX of this Treaty, unless eliminated in accordance with Sections IV or V of the Protocol on Elimination. Support structures, associated with the missiles and launchers subject to this Treaty, that are subject to elimination shall be eliminated *in situ*.

5. Each Party shall have the right, during the first six months after entry into force of this Treaty, to eliminate by means of launching no more than 100 of its intermediate-range missiles.

6. Intermediate-range and shorter-range missiles which have been tested prior to entry into force of this Treaty, but never deployed, and which are not existing types of intermediate-range or shorter-range missiles listed in Article III of this Treaty, and launchers of such missiles, shall be eliminated within six months after entry into force of this Treaty in accordance with the procedures set forth in the Protocol on Elimination. Such missiles are:

(a) for the United States of America, missiles of the type designated by the United States of America as the Pershing IB, which is known to the Union of Soviet Socialist Republics by the same designation; and

(b) for the Union of Soviet Socialist Republics, missiles of the type designated by the Union of Soviet Socialist Republics as the RK-55, which is known to the United States of America as the SSC-X-4.

7. Intermediate-range and shorter-range missiles and launchers of such missiles and support structures and support equipment associated with such missiles and launchers shall be considered to be eliminated after completion of the procedures set forth in the Protocol on Elimination and upon the notification provided for in paragraph 5(e) of Article IX of this Treaty.

8. Each Party shall eliminate its deployment areas, missile operating bases and missile support facilities. A Party shall notify the other Party pursuant to paragraph 5(a) of Article IX of this Treaty once the conditions set forth below are fulfilled:

(a) all intermediate-range and shorter-range missiles, launchers of such missiles and support equipment associated with such missiles and launchers located there have been removed;

(b) all support structures associated with such missiles and launchers located there have been eliminated; and

(c) all activity related to production, flight-testing, training, repair, storage or deployment of such missiles and launchers has ceased there.

Such deployment areas, missile operating bases and missile support facilities shall be considered to be eliminated either when they have been inspected pursuant to paragraph 4 of Article XI of this Treaty or when 60 days have elapsed since the date of the scheduled elimination which was notified pursuant to paragraph 5(a) of Article IX of this Treaty. A deployment area, missile operating base or missile support facility listed in the Memorandum of Understanding that met the above conditions prior to entry into force of this Treaty, and is not included in the initial data exchange pursuant to paragraph 3 of Article IX of this Treaty, shall be considered to be eliminated.

9. If a Party intends to convert a missile operating base listed in the Memorandum of Understanding for use as a base associated with GLBM or GLCM systems not subject to this Treaty, then that Party shall notify the other Party, no less than 30 days in advance of the scheduled date of the initiation of the conversion, of the scheduled date and the purpose for which the base will be converted.

Article XI

1. For the purpose of ensuring verification of compliance with the provisions of this Treaty, each Party shall have the right to conduct on-site inspections. The Parties shall implement on-site inspec-

tions in accordance with this Article, the Protocol on Inspection and the Protocol on Elimination.

2. Each Party shall have the right to conduct inspections provided for by this Article both within the territory of the other Party and within the territories of basing countries.

3. Beginning 30 days after entry into force of this Treaty, each Party shall have the right to conduct inspections at all missile operating bases and missile support facilities specified in the Memorandum of Understanding other than missile production facilities, and at all elimination facilities included in the initial data update required by paragraph 3 of Article IX of this Treaty. These inspections shall be completed no later than 90 days after entry into force of this Treaty. The purpose of these inspections shall be to verify the number of missiles, launchers, support structures and support equipment and other data, as of the date of entry into force of this Treaty, provided pursuant to paragraph 3 of Article IX of this Treaty.

4. Each Party shall have the right to conduct inspections to verify the elimination, notified pursuant to paragraph 5(a) of Article IX of this Treaty, of missile operating bases and missile support facilities other than missile production facilities, which are thus no longer subject to inspections pursuant to paragraph 5(a) of this Article. Such an inspection shall be carried out within 60 days after the scheduled date of the elimination of that facility. If a Party conducts an inspection at a particular facility pursuant to paragraph 3 of this Article after the scheduled date of the elimination of that facility, then no additional inspection of that facility pursuant to this paragraph shall be permitted.

5. Each Party shall have the right to conduct inspections pursuant to this paragraph for 13 years after entry into force of this Treaty. Each Party shall have the right to conduct 20 such inspections per calendar year during the first three years after entry into force of this Treaty, 15 such inspections per calendar year during the subsequent five years, and then such inspections per calendar year during the last five years. Neither Party shall use more than half of its total number of these inspections per calendar year within the territory of any one basing country. Each Party shall have the right to conduct:

(a) inspections, beginning 90 days after entry into force of this Treaty, of missile operating bases and missile support facilities other than elimination facilities and missile production facilities, to ascertain, according to the categories of data specified in the Memorandum of Understanding, the numbers of missiles, launchers, support structures and support equipment located at each missile operating base or missile support facility at the time of the inspection; and

(b) inspections of former missile operating bases and former missile support facilities eliminated pursuant to paragraph 8 of Article X of this Treaty other than former missile production facilities.

6. Beginning 30 days after entry into force of this Treaty, each Party shall have the right, for 13 years after entry into force of this Treaty, to inspect by means of continuous monitoring:

(a) the portals of any facility of the other Party at which the final assembly of a GLBM using stages, any of which is outwardly similar to a stage of a solid-propellant GLBM listed in Article III of this Treaty, is accomplished; or

(b) if a Party has no such facility, the portals of an agreed former missile production facility at which existing types of intermediate-range or shorter-range GLBMs were produced.

The Party whose facility is to be inspected pursuant to this paragraph shall ensure that the other Party is able to establish a permanent continuous monitoring system at that facility within six months after entry into force of this Treaty or within six months of initiation of the process of final assembly described in subparagraph (a). If, after the end of the second year after entry into force of this Treaty, neither Party conducts the process of final assembly described in subparagraph (a) for a period of 12 consecutive months, then neither Party shall have the right to inspect by means of continuous monitoring any missile production facility of the other Party unless the process of final assembly as described in subparagraph (a) is initiated again. Upon entry into force of this Treaty, the facilities to be inspected by continuous monitoring shall be: in accordance with subparagraph (b), for the United States of America, Hercules Plant Number 1, at Magna, Utah; in accordance with subparagraph (a), for the Union of Soviet Socialist Republics, the Votkinsk Machine Building Plant, Udmurt Autonomous Soviet Socialist Republic, Russian Soviet Federative Socialist Republic.

7. Each Party shall conduct inspections of the process of elimination, including elimination of intermediate-range missiles by means of launching, of intermediate-range and shorter-range missiles and launchers of such missiles and support equip-

ment associated with such missiles and launchers carried out at elimination facilities in accordance with Article X of this Treaty and the Protocol on Elimination. Inspectors conducting inspection provided for in this paragraph shall determine that the processes specified for the elimination of the missiles, launchers and support equipment have been completed.

8. Each Party shall have the right to conduct inspections to confirm the completion of the process of elimination of intermediate-range and shorter-range missiles and launchers of such missiles and support equipment associated with such missiles and launchers eliminated pursuant to Section V of the Protocol on Elimination, and of training missiles, training missile stages, training launch canisters and training launchers eliminated pursuant to Sections II, IV and V of the Protocol on Elimination.

Article XII

1. For the purpose of ensuring verification of compliance with the provisions of this Treaty, each party shall use national technical means of verification at its disposal in a manner consistent with generally recognized principles of international law.

2. Neither Party shall:

(a) interfere with national technical means of verification of the other Party operating in accordance with paragraph 1 of this Article; or

(b) use concealment measures which impede verification of compliance with the provisions of this Treaty by national technical means of verification carried out in accordance with paragraph 1 of this Article. This obligation does not apply to cover or concealment practices, within a deployment area, associated with normal training, maintenance and operations, including the use of environmental shelters to protect missiles and launchers.

3. To enhance observation by national technical means of verification, each Party shall have the right until a treaty between the Parties reducing and limiting strategic offensive arms enters into force, but in any event for no more than three years after entry into force of this Treaty, to request the implementation of cooperative measures at deployment bases for road-mobile GLBMs with a range capability in excess of 5500 kilometers, which are not former missile operating bases eliminated pursuant to paragraph 8 of Article X of this Treaty. The Party making such a request shall inform the other Party of the deployment base at which cooperative mea-

sures shall be implemented. The Party whose base is to be observed shall carry out the following co-operative measures:

(a) no later than six hours after such a request, the Party shall have opened the roofs of all fixed structures for launchers located at the base, removed completely all missiles on launchers from such fixed structures for launchers and displayed such missiles on launchers in the open without using concealment measures; and

(b) the Party shall leave the roofs open and the missiles on launchers in place until twelve hours have elapsed from the time of the receipt of a request for such an observation.

Each Party shall have the right to make six such requests per calendar year. Only one deployment base shall be subject to these cooperative measures at any one time.

Article XIII

1. To promote the objectives and implementation of the provisions of this Treaty, the Parties hereby establish the Special Verification Commission. The Parties agree that, if either Party so requests, they shall meet within the framework of the Special Verification Commission to:

(a) resolve questions relating to compliance with the obligations assumed; and (b) agree upon such measures as may be necessary to improve the viability and effectiveness of this Treaty.

2. The Parties shall use the Nuclear Risk Reduction Centers, which provide for continuous communication between the Parties, to:

(a) exchange data and provide notifications as required by paragraphs 3, 4, 5 and 6 of Article IX of this Treaty and the Protocol on Elimination;

(b) provide and receive the information required by paragraph 9 of Article X of this Treaty;

(c) provide and receive notifications of inspections as required by Article XI of this Treaty and the Protocol on Inspection; and

(d) provide and receive requests for cooperative measures as provided for in paragraph 3 of Article XII of this Treaty.

Article XIV. The Parties shall comply with this Treaty and shall not assume any international obligations or undertakings which would conflict with its provisions.

Article XV

1. This Treaty shall be of unlimited duration.

2. Each Party shall, in exercising its national sovereignty, have the right to withdraw from this Treaty if it decides that extraordinary events related to the subject matter of this Treaty have jeopardized its supreme interests. It shall give notice of its decision to withdraw to the other Party six months prior to withdrawal from this Treaty. Such notice shall include a statement of the extraordinary events the notifying Party regards as having jeopardized its supreme interests.

Article XVI. Each Party may propose amendments to this Treaty. Agreed amendments shall enter into force in accordance with the procedures set forth in Article XVII governing the entry into force of this Treaty.

Article XVII

1. This Treaty, including the Memorandum of Understanding and Protocols, which form an integral part thereof, shall be subject to ratification in accordance with the constitutional procedures of each Party. This Treaty shall enter into force on the date of the exchange of instruments of ratification.

2. This Treaty shall be registered pursuant to Article 102 of the Charter of the United Nations.

[Signatures]

Memorandum of Understanding Regarding the Establishment of the Data Base for the Treaty Between the Union of Soviet Socialist Republics and the United States of America on the Elimination of Their Intermediate-Range and Shorter-Range Missiles

Pursuant to and in implementation of the Treaty Between the Union of Soviet Socialist Republics and the United States of America on the Elimination of Their Intermediate-Range and Shorter-Range Missiles of December 8, 1987, hereinafter referred to as the Treaty, the Parties have exchanged data current as of November 1, 1987, on intermediate-range and shorter-range missiles and launchers of such missiles and support structures and support equipment associated with such missiles and launchers.

I. Definitions

For the purposes of this Memorandum of Understanding, the Treaty, the Protocol on Elimination, and the Protocol on Inspection:

1. The term "missile production facility" means a facility for the assembly or production of solid-propellant intermediate-range or shorter-range GLBMS, or existing types of GLCMS.

2. The term "missile repair facility" means a facility at which repair or maintenance of intermediate-range or shorter-range missiles takes place other than inspection and maintenance conducted at a missile operating base.

3. The term "launcher production facility" means a facility for final assembly of launchers of intermediate-range or shorter-range missiles.

4. The term "launcher repair facility" means a facility at which repair or maintenance of launchers of intermediate-range or shorter-range missiles takes place other than inspection and maintenance conducted at a missile operating base.

5. The term "test range" means an area at which flight-testing of intermediate-range or shorter-range missiles takes place.

6. The term "training facility" means a facility, not at a missile operating base, at which personnel are trained in the use of intermediate-range or shorter-range missiles or launchers of such missiles and at which launchers of such missiles are located.

7. The term "missile storage facility" means a facility, not at a missile operating base, at which intermediate-range or shorter-range missiles or stages of such missiles are stored.

8. The term "launcher storage facility" means a facility, not at a missile operating base, at which launchers of intermediate-range or shorter-range missiles are stored.

9. The term "elimination facility" means a facility at which intermediate-range or shorter-range missiles, missile stages and launchers of such missiles or support equipment associated with such missiles or launchers are eliminated.

10. The term "support equipment" means unique vehicles and mobile or transportable equipment that support a deployed intermediate-range or shorter-range missile or a launcher of such a missile. Support equipment shall include full-scale inert training missiles, full-scale inert training missile stages, full-scale inert training launch canisters, and training launchers not capable of launching a missile. A listing of such support equipment associated with each existing type of missile, and launchers of such missiles, except for training equipment, is contained in Section VI of this Memorandum of Understanding.

11. The term "support structure" means a unique fixed structure used to support deployed intermediate-range missiles or launchers of such missiles. A listing of such support structures associated with each existing type of missile, and launchers of such missiles, except for training equipment, is contained in Section VI of this Memorandum of Understanding.

12. The term "research and development launch site" means a facility at which research and development booster systems are launched.

II. Total Numbers of Intermediate-Range and Shorter-Range Missiles and Launchers of Such Missiles Subject to the Treaty

1. The numbers of intermediate-range missiles and launchers of such missiles for each Party are as follow:

	U.S.A.	U.S.S.R.
Deployed missiles	429	470
Non-deployed missiles	260	356
Aggregate number of deployed and non-deployed missiles	689	826
Aggregate number of second stages	236	650
Deployed launchers	214	484
Non-deployed launchers	68	124
Aggregate number of deployed and non-deployed launchers	282	608

2. The numbers of shorter-range missiles and launchers of such missiles for each Party are as follow:

	U.S.A.	U.S.S.R.
Deployed missiles	0	387
Non-deployed missiles	178	539
Aggregate number of deployed and non-deployed missiles	178	926
Aggregate number of second stages	182	726
Deployed launchers	0	197
Non-deployed launchers	1	40
Aggregate number of deployed and non-deployed launchers	1	237

[U.S. Arms Control and Disarmament Agency, *Arms Control and Disarmament Agreements: Texts and Histories of the Negotiations* (Washington, D.C., 1990), pp. 350–364]

START Treaty (1991)

Treaty Between the United States of America and the Union of Soviet Socialist Republics on the Reduction and Limitation of Strategic Offensive Arms

Article I. Each Party shall reduce and limit its strategic offensive arms in accordance with the provisions of this Treaty, and shall carry out the other obligations set forth in this Treaty and its Annexes, Protocols, and Memorandum of Understanding.

Article II

1. Each Party shall reduce and limit its ICBMs and ICBM launchers, SLBMS and SLBM launchers, heavy bombers, ICBM warheads, SLBM warheads, and heavy bomber armaments, so that seven years after entry into force of this Treaty and thereafter, the aggregate numbers, as counted in accordance with Article III of this Treaty, do not exceed:

(A) 1600, for deployed ICBMs and their associated launchers, deployed SLBMS and their associated launchers, and deployed heavy bombers, including 154 for deployed heavy ICBMs and their associated launchers;

(B) 6000, for warheads attributed to deployed ICBMs, deployed SLBMS, and deployed heavy bombers, including:

(i) 4900, for warheads attributed to deployed ICBMs and deployed SLBMS;

(ii) 1100, for warheads attributed to deployed ICBMs on mobile launchers of ICBMs;

(iii) 1540, for warheads attributed to deployed heavy ICBMs.

2. Each Party shall implement the reductions pursuant to paragraph 1 of this Article in three phases, so that its strategic offensive arms do not exceed:

(A) by the end of the first phase, that is, no later than 36 months after entry into force of this Treaty, and thereafter, the following aggregate numbers:

(i) 2100, for deployed ICBMs and their associated launchers, deployed SLBMS and their associated launchers, and deployed heavy bombers;

(ii) 9150, for warheads attributed to deployed ICBMs, deployed SLBMS, and deployed heavy bombers;

(iii) 8050, for warheads attributed to deployed ICBMs and deployed SLBMS;

(B) by the end of the second phase, that is, no later than 60 months after entry into force of this Treaty, and thereafter, the following aggregate numbers:

(i) 1900, for deployed ICBMs and their associated launchers, deployed SLBMS and their associated launchers, and deployed heavy bombers;

(ii) 7950, for warheads attributed to deployed ICBMs, deployed SLBMS, and deployed heavy bombers;

(iii) 6750, for warheads attributed to deployed ICBMs and deployed SLBMS;

(C) by the end of the third phase, that is, no later than 84 months after entry into force of this Treaty: the aggregate numbers provided for in paragraph 1 of this Article.

3. Each Party shall limit the aggregate throw-weight of its deployed ICBMs and deployed SLBMS so that seven years after entry into force of this Treaty and thereafter such aggregate throw-weight does not exceed 3600 metric tons.

Article III

1. For the purposes of counting toward the maximum aggregate limits provided for in subparagraphs 1(A), 2(A)(i), and 2(B)(i) of Article II of this Treaty:

(A) Each deployed ICBM and its associated launcher shall be counted as one unit; each deployed SLBM and its associated launcher shall be counted as one unit.

(B) Each deployed heavy bomber shall be counted as one unit.

2. For the purposes of counting deployed ICBMs and their associated launchers and deployed SLBMS and their associated launchers:

(A) Each deployed launcher of ICBMs and each deployed launcher of SLBMS shall be considered to contain one deployed ICBM or one deployed SLBM, respectively.

(B) If a deployed ICBM has been removed from its launcher and another missile has not been installed in that launcher, such an ICBM removed from its launcher and located at that ICBM base shall continue to be considered to be contained in that launcher.

(C) If a deployed SLBM has been removed from its launcher and another missile has not been installed in that launcher, such an SLBM removed from its launcher shall be considered to be contained in that launcher. Such an SLBM removed from its launcher shall be located only at a facility at which non-deployed SLBMS may be located pursuant to subparagraph 9(A) of Article IV of this Treaty or be in movement to such a facility.

3. For the purposes of this Treaty, including counting ICBMS and SLBMS:

(A) For ICBMS or SLBMS that are maintained, stored, and transported in stages, the first stage of an ICBM or SLBM of a particular type shall be considered to be an ICBM or SLBM of that type.

(B) For ICBMS or SLBMS that are maintained, stored, and transported as assembled missiles without launch canisters, an assembled missile of a particular type shall be considered to be an ICBM or SLBM of that type.

(C) For ICBMS that are maintained, stored, and transported as assembled missiles in launch canisters, an assembled missile of a particular type, in its launch canister, shall be considered to be an ICBM of that type.

(D) Each launch canister shall be considered to contain an ICBM from the time it first leaves a facility at which an ICBM is installed in it until an ICBM has been launched from it or until an ICBM has been removed from it for elimination. A launch canister shall not be considered to contain an ICBM if it contains a training model of a missile or has been placed on static display. Launch canisters for ICBMS of a particular type shall be distinguishable from launch canisters for ICBMS of a different type.

4. For the purposes of counting warheads:

(A) The number of warheads attributed to an ICBM or SLBM of each existing type shall be the number specified in the Memorandum of Understanding on the Establishment of the Data Base Relating to this Treaty, hereinafter referred to as the Memorandum of Understanding.

(B) The number of warheads that will be attributed to an ICBM or SLBM of a new type shall be the maximum number of reentry vehicles with which an ICBM or SLBM of that type has been flight-tested. The number of warheads that will be attributed to an ICBM or SLBM of a new type with a front section of an existing design with multiple reentry vehicles, or to an ICBM or SLBM of a new type with one reentry vehicle, shall be no less than the nearest integer that is smaller than the result of dividing 40 percent of the accountable throw-weight of the ICBM or SLBM by the weight of the lightest reentry vehicle flight-tested on an ICBM or SLBM of that type. In the case of an ICBM or SLBM of a new type with a front section of a fundamentally new design, the question of the applicability of the 40-percent rule to such an ICBM or SLBM shall be subject to agreement within the framework of the Joint Compliance and Inspection Commission. Until agreement has been reached regarding the rule that will apply to such an ICBM or SLBM, the number of warheads that will be attributed to such an ICBM or SLBM shall be the maximum number of reentry vehicles with which an ICBM or SLBM of that type has been flight-tested. The number of new types of ICBMS or SLBMS with a front section of a fundamentally new design shall not exceed two for each Party as long as this Treaty remains in force.

(C) The number of reentry vehicles with which an ICBM or SLBM has been flight-tested shall be considered to be the sum of the number of reentry vehicles actually released during the flight test, plus the number of procedures for dispensing reentry vehicles performed during that same flight test when no reentry vehicle was released. A procedure for dispensing penetration aids shall not be considered to be a procedure for dispensing reentry vehicles, provided that the procedure for dispensing penetration aids differs from a procedure for dispensing reentry vehicles.

(D) Each reentry vehicle of an ICBM or SLBM shall be considered to be one warhead.

(E) For the United States of America, each heavy bomber equipped for long-range nuclear ALCMS, up to a total of 150 such heavy bombers, shall be attributed with ten warheads. Each heavy bomber equipped for long-range nuclear ALCMS in excess of 150 such heavy bombers shall be attributed with a number of warheads equal to the number of long-range nuclear ALCMS for which it is actually equipped. The United States of America shall specify the heavy bombers equipped for long-range nuclear ALCMS that are in excess of 150 such heavy bombers by number, type, variant, and the air bases at which they are based. The number of long-range nuclear ALCMS for which each heavy bomber equipped for long-range nuclear ALCMS in excess of 150 such heavy bombers is considered to be actually equipped shall be the maximum number of long-range nuclear ALCMS for which a heavy bomber of the same type and variant is actually equipped.

(F) For the Union of Soviet Socialist Republics, each heavy bomber equipped for long-range nuclear ALCMS, up to a total of 180 such heavy bombers, shall be attributed with eight warheads. Each heavy bomber equipped for long-range nuclear ALCMS in excess of 180 such heavy bombers shall be attributed with a number of warheads equal to the number of long-range nuclear ALCMS for which it is actually equipped. The Union of Soviet Socialist Republics shall specify the heavy bombers equipped for long-range nuclear ALCMS that are in excess of 180 such heavy bombers by number, type, variant, and the air bases at which they are based. The number of long-range nuclear ALCMS for which each heavy bomber equipped for long-range nuclear ALCMS in excess of 180 such heavy bombers is considered to be actually equipped shall be the maximum number of long-range nuclear ALCMS for which a heavy bomber of the same type and variant is actually equipped.

(G) Each heavy bomber equipped for nuclear armaments other than long-range nuclear ALCMS shall be attributed with one warhead. All heavy bombers not equipped for long-range nuclear ALCMS shall be considered to be heavy bombers equipped for nuclear armaments other than long-range nuclear ALCMS, with the exception of heavy bombers equipped for non-nuclear armaments, test heavy bombers, and training heavy bombers.

5. Each Party shall have the right to reduce the number of warheads attributed to ICBMS and SLBMS only of existing types, up to an aggregate number of 1250 at any one time.

(A) Such aggregate number shall consist of the following:

(i) for the United States of America, the reduction in the number of warheads attributed to the type of ICBM designated by the United States of America as, and known to the Union of Soviet Socialist Republics as, Minuteman III, plus the reduction in the number of warheads attributed to ICBMS and SLBMS of no more than two other existing types;

(ii) for the Union of Soviet Socialist Republics, four multiplied by the number of deployed SLBMS designated by the Union of Soviet Socialist Republics as RSM-50, which is known to the United States of America as SS-N-18, plus the reduction in the number of warheads attributed to ICBMS and SLBMS of no more than two other existing types.

(B) Reductions in the number of warheads attributed to Minuteman III ICBMS shall be carried out subject to the following:

(i) Minuteman III ICBMS to which different numbers of warheads are attributed shall not be deployed at the same ICBM base.

(ii) Any such reductions shall be carried out no later than seven years after entry into force of this Treaty.

(iii) The reentry vehicle platform of each Minuteman III ICBM to which a reduced number of warheads is attributed shall be destroyed and replaced by a new reentry vehicle platform.

(C) Reductions in the number of warheads attributed to ICBMS and SLBMS of types other than Minuteman III shall be carried out subject to the following:

(i) Such reductions shall not exceed 500 warheads at any one time for each Party.

(ii) After a Party has reduced the number of warheads attributed to ICBMS or SLBMS of two existing types, that Party shall not have the right to reduce the number of warheads attributed to ICBMS or SLBMS of any additional type.

(iii) The number of warheads attributed to an ICBM or SLBM shall be reduced by no more than four below the number attributed as of the date of signature of this Treaty.

(iv) ICBMS of the same type, but to which different numbers of warheads are attributed, shall not be deployed at the same ICBM base.

(v) SLBMS of the same type, but to which different numbers of warheads are attributed, shall not be deployed on submarines based at submarine bases adjacent to the waters of the same ocean.

(vi) If the number of warheads attributed to an ICBM or SLBM of a particular type is reduced by more than two, the reentry vehicle platform of each ICBM or SLBM to which such a reduced number of warheads is attributed shall be destroyed and replaced by a new reentry vehicle platform.

(D) A Party shall not have the right to attribute to ICBMS of a new type a number of warheads greater than the smallest number of warheads attributed to any ICBM to which that Party has attributed a reduced number of warheads pursuant to subparagraph (C) of this paragraph. A Party shall not have the right to attribute to SLBMS of a new type a number of warheads greater than the smallest number of warheads attributed to any SLBM to which that Party has attributed a reduced number of warheads pursuant to subparagraph (C) of this paragraph.

6. Newly constructed strategic offensive arms shall begin to be subject to the limitations provided for in this Treaty as follows:

(A) an ICBM, when it first leaves a production facility;

(B) a mobile launcher of ICBMS, when it first leaves a production facility for mobile launchers of ICBMS;

(C) a silo launcher of ICBMS, when excavation for that launcher has been completed and the pouring of concrete for the silo has been completed, or 12 months after the excavation begins, whichever occurs earlier;

(D) for the purpose of counting a deployed ICBM and its associated launcher, a silo launcher of ICBM shall be considered to contain a deployed ICBM when excavation for that launcher has been completed and the pouring of concrete for the silo has been completed, or 12 months after the excavation begins, whichever occurs earlier, and a mobile launcher of ICBMS shall be considered to contain a deployed ICBM when it arrives at a maintenance facility, except for the non-deployed mobile launchers of ICBMS provided for in subparagraph 2(B) of Article IV of this Treaty, or when it leaves an ICBM loading facility;

(E) an SLBM, when it first leaves a production facility;

(F) an SLBM launcher, when the submarine on which that launcher is installed is first launched;

(G) for the purpose of counting a deployed SLBM and its associated launcher, an SLBM launcher shall be considered to contain a deployed SLBM when the submarine on which that launcher is installed is first launched;

(H) a heavy bomber or former heavy bomber, when its airframe is first brought out of the shop, plant, or building in which components of a heavy bomber or former heavy bomber are assembled to produce complete airframes; or when its airframe is first brought out of the shop, plant, or building in which existing bomber airframes are converted to heavy bomber or former heavy bomber airframes.

7. ICBM launchers and SLBM launchers that have been converted to launch an ICBM or SLBM, respectively, of a different type shall not be capable of launching an ICBM or SLBM of the previous type. Such converted launchers shall be considered to be launchers of ICBMS or SLBMS of that different type as follows:

(A) a silo launcher of ICBMS, when an ICBM of a different type or a training model of a missile of a different type is first installed in that launcher, or when the silo door is reinstalled, whichever occurs first;

(B) a mobile launcher of ICBMS, as agreed within the framework of the Joint Compliance and Inspection Commission;

(C) an SLBM launcher, when all launchers on the submarine on which that launcher is installed have been converted to launch an SLBM of that different type and that submarine begins sea trials, that is, when that submarine first operates under its own power away from the harbor or port in which the conversion of launchers was performed.

8. Heavy bombers that have been converted into heavy bombers of a different category or into former heavy bombers shall be considered to be heavy bombers of that different category or former heavy bombers as follows:

(A) a heavy bomber equipped for nuclear armaments other than long-range nuclear ALCMS converted into a heavy bomber equipped for long-range nuclear ALCMS, when it is first brought out of the shop, plant, or building where it was equipped for long-range nuclear ALCMS;

(B) a heavy bomber of one category converted into a heavy bomber of another category provided for in paragraph 9 of Section VI of the Protocol on Procedures Governing the Conversion or Elimination of the Items Subject to this Treaty, hereinafter referred to as the Conversion or Elimination Protocol, or into a former heavy bomber, when the inspection conducted pursuant to paragraph 13 of Section VI of the Conversion or Elimination Protocol is completed or, if such an inspection is not conducted, when the 20-day period provided for in paragraph 13 of Section VI of the Conversion or Elimination Protocol expires.

9. For the purposes of this Treaty:

(A) A ballistic missile of a type developed and tested solely to intercept and counter objects not located on the surface of the Earth shall not be considered to be a ballistic missile to which the limitations provided for in this Treaty apply.

(B) If a ballistic missile has been flight-tested or deployed for weapon delivery, all ballistic missiles of that type shall be considered to be weapon-delivery vehicles.

(C) If a cruise missile has been flight-tested or deployed for weapon delivery, all cruise missiles of that type shall be considered to be weapon-delivery vehicles.

(D) If a launcher, other than a soft-site launcher, has contained an ICBM or SLBM of a particular type, it shall be considered to be a launcher of ICBMS or

SLBMS of that type. If a launcher, other than a soft-site launcher, has been converted into a launcher of ICBMS or SLBMS of a different type, it shall be considered to be a launcher of ICBMS or SLBMS of the type for which it has been converted.

(E) If a heavy bomber is equipped for long-range nuclear ALCMS, all heavy bombers of that type shall be considered to be equipped for long-range nuclear ALCMS, except those that are not so equipped and are distinguishable from heavy bombers of the same type equipped for long-range nuclear ALCMS. If long-range nuclear ALCMS have not been flight-tested from any heavy bomber of a particular type, no heavy bomber of that type shall be considered to be equipped for long-range nuclear ALCMS. Within the same type, a heavy bomber equipped for long-range nuclear ALCMS, a heavy bomber equipped for nuclear armaments other than long-range nuclear ALCMS, a heavy bomber equipped for non-nuclear armaments, a training heavy bomber, and a former heavy bomber shall be distinguishable from one another.

(F) Any long-range ALCM of a type, any one of which has been initially flight-tested from a heavy bomber on or before December 31, 1988, shall be considered to be a long-range nuclear ALCM. Any long-range ALCM of a type, any one of which has been initially flight-tested from a heavy bomber after December 31, 1988, shall not be considered to be a long-range nuclear ALCM if it is a long-range non-nuclear ALCM and is distinguishable from long-range nuclear ALCMS. Long-range non-nuclear ALCMS not so distinguishable shall be considered to be long-range nuclear ALCMS.

(G) Mobile launchers of ICBMS of each new type of ICBM shall be distinguishable from mobile launchers of ICBMS of existing types of ICBMS and from mobile launchers of ICBMS of other new types of ICBMS. Such new launchers, with their associated missiles installed, shall be distinguishable from mobile launchers of ICBMS of existing types of ICBMS with their associated missiles installed, and from mobile launchers of ICBMS of other new types of ICBMS with their associated missiles installed.

(H) Mobile launchers of ICBMS converted into launchers of ICBMS of another type of ICBM shall be distinguishable from mobile launchers of ICBMS of the previous type of ICBM. Such converted launchers, with their associated missiles installed, shall be distinguishable from mobile launchers of ICBMS of the previous type of ICBM with their associated mis-

siles installed. Conversion of mobile launchers of ICBMS shall be carried out in accordance with procedures to be agreed within the framework of the Joint Compliance and Inspection Commission.

10. As of the date of signature of this Treaty:

(A) Existing types of ICBMS and SLBMS are:

(i) for the United States of America, the types of missiles designated by the United States of America as Minuteman II, Minuteman III, Peacekeeper, Poseidon, Trident I, and Trident II, which are known to the Union of Soviet Socialist Republics as Minuteman II, Minuteman III, MX, Poseidon, Trident I, and Trident II, respectively;

(ii) for the Union of Soviet Socialist Republics, the types of missiles designated by the Union of Soviet Socialist Republics as RS-10, RS-12, RS-16, RS-20, RS-18, RS-22, RS-12M, RSM-25, RSM-40, RSM-50, RSM-52, and RSM-54, which are known to the United States of America as SS-11, SS-13, SS-17, SS-18, SS-19, SS-24, SS 25, SS-N-6, SS-N-8, SS-N-18, SS-N-20, and SS-N-23, respectively.

(B) Existing types of ICBMS for mobile launchers of ICBMS are:

(i) for the United States of America, the type of missile designated by the United States of America as Peacekeeper, which is known to the Union of Soviet Socialist Republics as MX;

(ii) for the Union of Soviet Socialist Republics, the types of missiles designated by the Union of Soviet Socialist Republics as RS-22 and RS-12M, which are known to the United States of America as SS-24 and SS-25, respectively.

(C) Former types of ICBMS and SLBMS are the types of missiles designated by the United States of America as, and known to the Union of Soviet Socialist Republics as, Minuteman I and Polaris A-3.

(D) Existing types of heavy bombers are:

(i) for the United States of America, the types of bombers designated by the United States of America as, and known to the Union of Soviet Socialist Republics as, B-52, B-l, and B-2;

(ii) for the Union of Soviet Socialist Republics, the types of bombers designated by the Union of Soviet Socialist Republics as Tu-95 and Tu-160, which are known to the United States of America as Bear and Blackjack, respectively.

(E) Existing types of long-range nuclear ALCMS are:

(i) for the United States of America, the types of long-range nuclear ALCMS designated by the United States of America as, and known to the Union of

Soviet Socialist Republics as, AGM-86B and AGM-129;

(ii) for the Union of Soviet Socialist Republics, the types of long-range nuclear ALCMS designated by the Union of Soviet Socialist Republics as RKV-500A and RKV-500B, which are known to the United States of America as AS-15 A and AS-15 B, respectively.

Article IV

1. For ICBMS and SLBMS:

(A) Each Party shall limit the aggregate number of non-deployed ICBMS for mobile launchers of ICBMS to no more than 250. Within this limit, the number of non-deployed ICBMS for rail-mobile launchers of ICBMS shall not exceed 125.

(B) Each Party shall limit the number of non-deployed ICBMS at a maintenance facility of an ICBM base for mobile launchers of ICBMS to no more than two ICBMS of each type specified for that ICBM base. Non-deployed ICBMS for mobile launchers of ICBMS located at a maintenance facility shall be stored separately from non-deployed mobile launchers of ICBMS located at that maintenance facility.

(C) Each Party shall limit the number of non-deployed ICBMS and sets of ICBM emplacement equipment at an ICBM base for silo launchers of ICBMS to no more than:

(i) two ICBMS of each type specified for that ICBM base and six sets of ICBM emplacement equipment for each type of ICBM specified for that ICBM base; or

(ii) four ICBMS of each type specified for that ICBM base and two sets of ICBM emplacement equipment for each type of ICBM specified for that ICBM base.

(D) Each Party shall limit the aggregate number of ICBMS and SLBMS located at test ranges to no more than 35 during the seven-year period after entry into force of this Treaty. Thereafter, the aggregate number of ICBMS and SLBMS located at test ranges shall not exceed 25.

2. For ICBM launchers and SLBM launchers:

(A) Each Party shall limit the aggregate number of non-deployed mobile launchers of ICBMS to no more than 110. Within this limit, the number of non-deployed rail-mobile launchers of ICBMS shall not exceed 18.

(B) Each Party shall limit the number of non-deployed mobile launchers of ICBMS located at the maintenance facility of each ICBM base for mobile launchers of ICBMS to no more than two such ICBM launchers of each type of ICBM specified for that ICBM base.

(C) Each Party shall limit the number of non-deployed mobile launchers of ICBMS located at training facilities for ICBMS to no more than 40. Each such launcher may contain only a training model of a missile. Non-deployed mobile launchers of ICBMS that contain training models of missiles shall not be located outside a training facility.

(D) Each Party shall limit the aggregate number of test launchers to no more than 45 during the seven-year period after entry into force of this Treaty. Within this limit, the number of fixed test launchers shall not exceed 25, and the number of mobile test launchers shall not exceed 20. Thereafter, the aggregate number of test launchers shall not exceed 40. Within this limit, the number of fixed test launchers shall not exceed 20, and the number of mobile test launchers shall not exceed 20.

(E) Each Party shall limit the aggregate number of silo training launchers and mobile training launchers to no more than 60. ICBMS shall not be launched from training launchers. Each such launcher may contain only a training model of a missile. Mobile training launchers shall not be capable of launching ICBMS, and shall differ from mobile launchers of ICBMS and other road vehicles or railcars on the basis of differences that are observable by national technical means of verification.

3. For heavy bombers and former heavy bombers:

(A) Each Party shall limit the aggregate number of heavy bombers equipped for non-nuclear armaments, former heavy bombers, and training heavy bombers to no more than 75.

(B) Each Party shall limit the number of test heavy bombers to no more than 20.

4. For ICBMS and SLBMS used for delivering objects into the upper atmosphere or space:

(A) Each Party shall limit the number of space launch facilities to no more than five, unless otherwise agreed. Space launch facilities shall not overlap ICBM bases.

(B) Each Party shall limit the aggregate number of ICBM launchers and SLBM launchers located at space launch facilities to no more than 20, unless otherwise agreed. Within this limit, the aggregate number of silo launchers of ICBMS and mobile launchers of ICBMS located at space launch facilities shall not exceed ten, unless otherwise agreed.

(C) Each Party shall limit the aggregate number of ICBMS and SLBMS located at a space launch facility to no more than the number of ICBM launchers and SLBM launchers located at that facility.

5. Each Party shall limit the number of transporter-loaders for ICBMs for road-mobile launchers of ICBMs located at each deployment area or test range to no more than two for each type of ICBM for road-mobile launchers of ICBMs that is attributed with one warhead and that is specified for that deployment area or test range, and shall limit the number of such transporter-loaders located outside deployment areas and test ranges to no more than six. The aggregate number of transporter-loaders for ICBMs for road-mobile launchers of ICBMs shall not exceed 30.

6. Each Party shall limit the number of ballistic missile submarines in dry dock within five kilometers of the boundary of each submarine base to no more than two.

7. For static displays and ground trainers:

(A) Each Party shall limit the number of ICBM launchers and SLBM launchers placed on static display after signature of this Treaty to no more than 20, the number of ICBMs and SLBMs placed on static display after signature of this Treaty to no more than 20, the number of launch canisters placed on static display after signature of this Treaty to no more than 20, and the number of heavy bombers and former heavy bombers placed on static display after signature of this Treaty to no more than 20. Such items placed on static display prior to signature of this Treaty shall be specified in Annex I to the Memorandum of Understanding, but shall not be subject to the limitations provided for in this Treaty.

(B) Each Party shall limit the aggregate number of heavy bombers converted after signature of this Treaty for use as ground trainers and former heavy bombers converted after signature of this Treaty for use as ground trainers to no more than five. Such items converted prior to signature of this Treaty for use as ground trainers shall be specified in Annex I to the Memorandum of Understanding, but shall not be subject to the limitations provided for in this Treaty.

8. Each Party shall limit the aggregate number of storage facilities for ICBMs or SLBMs and repair facilities for ICBMs or SLBMs to no more than 50.

9. With respect to locational and related restrictions on strategic offensive arms:

(A) Each Party shall locate non-deployed ICBMs and non-deployed SLBMs only at maintenance facilities of ICBM bases; submarine bases; ICBM loading facilities; SLBM loading facilities; production facili-

ties for ICBMs or SLBMs; repair facilities for ICBMs or SLBMs; storage facilities for ICBMs or SLBMs; conversion or elimination facilities for ICBMs or SLBMs; test ranges; or space launch facilities. Prototype ICBMs and prototype SLBMs, however, shall not be located at maintenance facilities of ICBM bases or at submarine bases. Non-deployed ICBMs and non-deployed SLBMs may also be in transit. Non-deployed ICBMs for silo launchers of ICBMs may also be transferred within an ICBM base for silo launchers of ICBMs. Non-deployed SLBMs that are located on missile tenders and storage cranes shall be considered to be located at the submarine base at which such missile tenders and storage cranes are specified as based.

(B) Each Party shall locate non-deployed mobile launchers of ICBMs only at maintenance facilities of ICBM bases for mobile launchers of ICBMs, production facilities for mobile launchers of ICBMs, repair facilities for mobile launchers of ICBMs, storage facilities for mobile launchers of ICBMs, ICBM loading facilities, training facilities for ICBMs, conversion or elimination facilities for mobile launchers of ICBMs, test ranges, or space launch facilities. Mobile launchers of prototype ICBMs, however, shall not be located at maintenance facilities of ICBM bases for mobile launchers of ICBMs. Non-deployed mobile launchers of ICBMs may also be in transit.

(C) Each Party shall locate test launchers only at test ranges, except that rail-mobile test launchers may conduct movements for the purpose of testing outside a test range, provided that:

(i) each such movement is completed no later than 30 days after it begins;

(ii) each such movement begins and ends at the same test range and does not involve movement to any other facility;

(iii) movements of no more than six rail-mobile launchers of ICBMs are conducted in each calendar year; and

(iv) no more than one train containing no more than three rail-mobile test launchers is located outside test ranges at any one time.

(D) A deployed mobile launcher of ICBMs and its associated missile that relocates to a test range may, at the discretion of the testing Party, either continue to be counted toward the maximum aggregate limits provided for in Article II of this Treaty, or be counted as a mobile test launcher pursuant to paragraph 2(D) of this Article. If a deployed mobile launcher of ICBMs and its associated missile that relocates to a test range continues to be counted toward the maximum aggregate limits provided for in Article II of this Treaty, the period of time during which it continuously remains at a test range shall not exceed 45 days. The number of such deployed roadmobile launchers of ICBMs and their associated missiles located at a test range at any one time shall not exceed three, and the number of such deployed rail-mobile launchers of ICBMs and their associated missiles located at a test range at any one time shall not exceed three.

(E) Each Party shall locate silo training launchers only at ICBM bases for silo launchers of ICBMs and training facilities for ICBMs. The number of silo training launchers located at each ICBM base for silo launchers of ICBMs shall not exceed one for each type of ICBM specified for that ICBM base.

(F) Test heavy bombers shall be based only at heavy bomber flight test centers and at production facilities for heavy bombers. Training heavy bombers shall be based only at training facilities for heavy bombers.

10. Each Party shall locate solid rocket motors for first stages of ICBMs for mobile launchers of ICBMs only at locations where production and storage, or testing of such motors occurs and at production facilities for ICBMs for mobile launchers of ICBMs. Such solid rocket motors may also be moved between these locations. Solid rocket motors with nozzles attached for the first stages of ICBMs for mobile launchers of ICBMs shall only be located at production facilities for ICBMs for mobile launchers of ICBMs and at locations where testing of such solid rocket motors occurs. Locations where such solid rocket motors are permitted shall be specified in Annex I to the Memorandum of Understanding.

11. With respect to locational restrictions on facilities:

(A) Each Party shall locate production facilities for ICBMs of a particular type, repair facilities for ICBMs of a particular type, storage facilities for ICBMs of a particular type, ICBM loading facilities for ICBMs of a particular type, and conversion or elimination facilities for ICBMs of a particular type no less than 100 kilometers from any ICBM base for silo launchers of ICBMs of that type of ICBM, any ICBM base for rail-mobile launchers of ICBMs of that type of ICBM, any deployment area for road-mobile launchers of ICBMs of that type of ICBM, any test range from which ICBMs of that type are flight-tested, any production facility for mobile launchers of ICBMs of that type of ICBM, any repair facility for mobile launchers of ICBMs of that type of ICBM, any storage facility for mobile launchers of ICBMs of that type of ICBM, and any training facility for ICBMs at which non-deployed mobile launchers of ICBMs are located. New facilities at which non-deployed ICBMs for silo launchers of ICBMs of any type of ICBM may be located, and new storage facilities for ICBM emplacement equipment, shall be located no less than 100 kilometers from any ICBM base for silo launchers of ICBMs, except that existing storage facilities for intermediate-range missiles, located less than 100 kilometers from an ICBM base for silo launchers of ICBMs or from a test range, may be converted into storage facilities for ICBMs not specified for that ICBM base or that test range.

(B) Each Party shall locate production facilities for mobile launchers of ICBMs of a particular type of ICBM, repair facilities for mobile launchers of ICBMs of a particular type of ICBM, and storage facilities for mobile launchers of ICBMs of a particular type of ICBM no less than 100 kilometers from any ICBM base for mobile launchers of ICBMs of that type of ICBM and any test range from which ICBMs of that type are flight-tested.

(C) Each Party shall locate test ranges and space launch facilities no less than 100 kilometers from any ICBM base for silo launchers of ICBMs, any ICBM base for rail-mobile launchers of ICBMs, and any deployment area.

(D) Each Party shall locate training facilities for ICBMs no less than 100 kilometers from any test range.

(E) Each Party shall locate storage areas for heavy bomber nuclear armaments no less than 100 kilometers from any air base for heavy bombers equipped for non-nuclear armaments and any training facility for heavy bombers. Each Party shall locate storage areas for long-range nuclear ALCMs no less than 100 kilometers from any air base for heavy bombers equipped for nuclear armaments other than long-range nuclear ALCMs, any air base for heavy bombers equipped for non-nuclear armaments, and any training facility for heavy bombers.

12. Each Party shall limit the duration of each transit to no more than 30 days.

Article V

1. Except as prohibited by the provisions of this Treaty, modernization and replacement of strategic offensive arms may be carried out.

2. Each Party undertakes not to:

(A) produce, flight-test, or deploy heavy ICBMs of a new type, or increase the launch weight or throw-weight of heavy ICBMs of an existing type;

(B) produce, flight-test, or deploy heavy SLBMs;

(C) produce, test, or deploy mobile launchers of heavy ICBMs;

(D) produce, test, or deploy additional silo launchers of heavy ICBMs, except for silo launchers of heavy ICBMs that replace silo launchers of heavy ICBMs that have been eliminated in accordance with Section II of the Conversion or Elimination Protocol, provided that the limits provided for in Article II of this Treaty are not exceeded;

(E) convert launchers that are not launchers of heavy ICBMs into launchers of heavy ICBMs;

(F) produce, test, or deploy launchers of heavy SLBMs;

(G) reduce the number of warheads attributed to a heavy ICBM of an existing type.

3. Each Party undertakes not to deploy ICBMs other than in silo launchers of ICBMs, on road-mobile launchers of ICBMs, or on rail-mobile launchers of ICBMs. Each Party undertakes not to produce, test, or deploy ICBM launchers other than silo launchers of ICBMs, road-mobile launchers of ICBMs, or rail-mobile launchers of ICBMs.

4. Each Party undertakes not to deploy on a mobile launcher of ICBMs an ICBM of a type that was not specified as a type of ICBM for mobile launchers of ICBMs in accordance with paragraph 2 of Section VII of the Protocol on Notifications Relating to this Treaty, hereinafter referred to as the Notification Protocol, unless it is an ICBM to which no more than one warhead is attributed and the Parties have agreed within the framework of the Joint Compliance and Inspection Commission to permit deployment of such ICBMs on mobile launchers of ICBMs. A new type of ICBM for mobile launchers of ICBMs may cease to be considered to be a type of ICBM for mobile launchers of ICBMs if no ICBM of that type has been contained on, or flight-tested from, a mobile launcher of ICBMs.

5. Each Party undertakes not to deploy ICBM launchers of a new type of ICBM and not to deploy SLBM launchers of a new type of SLBM if such launchers are capable of launching ICBMs or SLBMs, respectively, of other types. ICBM launchers of existing types of ICBMs and SLBM launchers of existing types of SLBMs shall be incapable, without conversion, of launching ICBMs or SLBMs, respectively, of other types.

6. Each Party undertakes not to convert SLBMs into ICBMs for mobile launchers of ICBMs, or to load SLBMs on, or launch SLBMs from, mobile launchers of ICBMs.

7. Each Party undertakes not to produce, test, or deploy transporter-loaders other than transporter-loaders for ICBMs for road-mobile launchers of ICBMs attributed with one warhead.

8. Each Party undertakes not to locate deployed silo launchers of ICBMs outside ICBM bases for silo launchers of ICBMs.

9. Each Party undertakes not to locate soft-site launchers except at test ranges and space launch facilities. All existing soft-site launchers not at test ranges or space launch facilities shall be eliminated in accordance with the procedures provided for in the Conversion or Elimination Protocol no later than 60 days after entry into force of this Treaty.

10. Each Party undertakes not to:

(A) flight-test ICBMs or SLBMs of a retired or former type from other than test launchers specified for such use or launchers at space launch facilities. Except for soft-site launchers, test launchers specified for such use shall not be used to flight-test ICBMs or SLBMs of a type, any one of which is deployed;

(B) produce ICBMs for mobile launchers of ICBMs of a retired type.

11. Each Party undertakes not to convert silos used as launch control centers into silo launchers of ICBMs.

12. Each Party undertakes not to:

(A) produce, flight-test, or deploy an ICBM or SLBM with more than ten reentry vehicles;

(B) flight-test an ICBM or SLBM with a number of reentry vehicles greater than the number of warheads attributed to it, or, for an ICBM or SLBM of a retired type, with a number of reentry vehicles greater than the largest number of warheads that was attributed to any ICBM or SLBM of that type;

(C) deploy an ICBM or SLBM with a number of reentry vehicles greater than the number of warheads attributed to it;

(D) increase the number of warheads attributed to an ICBM or SLBM of an existing or new type.

13. Each Party undertakes not to flight-test or deploy an ICBM or SLBM with a number of reentry vehicles greater than the number of warheads attributed to it.

14. Each Party undertakes not to flight-test from space launch facilities ICBMs or SLBMs equipped with reentry vehicles.

15. Each Party undertakes not to use ICBMs or SLBMs for delivering objects into the upper atmosphere or space for purposes inconsistent with ex-

isting international obligations undertaken by the Parties.

16. Each Party undertakes not to produce, test, or deploy systems for rapid reload and not to conduct rapid reload.

17. Each Party undertakes not to install SLBM launchers on submarines that were not originally constructed as ballistic missile submarines.

18. Each Party undertakes not to produce, test, or deploy:

(A) ballistic missiles with a range in excess of 600 kilometers, or launchers of such missiles, for installation on waterborne vehicles, including free-floating launchers, other than submarines. This obligation shall not require changes in current ballistic missile storage, transport, loading, or unloading practices;

(B) launchers of ballistic or cruise missiles for emplacement on or for tethering to the ocean floor, the seabed, or the beds of internal waters and inland waters, or for emplacement in or for tethering to the subsoil thereof, or mobile launchers of such missiles that move only in contact with the ocean floor, the seabed, or the beds of internal waters and inland waters, or missiles for such launchers. This obligation shall apply to all areas of the ocean floor and the seabed, including the seabed zone referred to in Articles I and II of the Treaty on the Prohibition of the Emplacement of Nuclear Weapons and Other Weapons of Mass Destruction on the Seabed and the Ocean Floor and in the Subsoil Thereof of February 11, 1971;

(C) systems, including missiles, for placing nuclear weapons or any other kinds of weapons of mass destruction into Earth orbit or a fraction of an Earth orbit;

(D) air-to-surface ballistic missiles (ASBMS);

(E) long-range nuclear ALCMS armed with two or more nuclear weapons.

19. Each Party undertakes not to:

(A) flight-test with nuclear armaments an aircraft that is not an airplane, but that has a range of 8000 kilometers or more; equip such an aircraft for nuclear armaments; or deploy such an aircraft with nuclear armaments;

(B) flight-test with nuclear armaments an airplane that was not initially constructed as a bomber, but that has a range of 8000 kilometers or more, or an integrated platform area in excess of 310 square meters; equip such an airplane for nuclear armaments; or deploy such an airplane with nuclear armaments;

(C) flight-test with long-range nuclear ALCMS an aircraft that is not an airplane, or an airplane that was not initially constructed as a bomber; equip such an aircraft or such an airplane for long-range nuclear ALCMS; or deploy such an aircraft or such an airplane with long-range nuclear ALCMS.

20. The United States of America undertakes not to equip existing or future heavy bombers for more than 20 long-range nuclear ALCMS.

21. The Union of Soviet Socialist Republics undertakes not to equip existing or future heavy bombers for more than 16 long-range nuclear ALCMS.

22. Each Party undertakes not to locate long-range nuclear ALCMS at air bases for heavy bombers equipped for nuclear armaments other than long-range nuclear ALCMS, air bases for heavy bombers equipped for non-nuclear armaments, air bases for former heavy bombers, or training facilities for heavy bombers.

23. Each Party undertakes not to base heavy bombers equipped for long-range nuclear ALCMS, heavy bombers equipped for nuclear armaments other than long-range nuclear ALCMS, or heavy bombers equipped for non-nuclear armaments at air bases at which heavy bombers of either of the other two categories are based.

24. Each Party undertakes not to convert:

(A) heavy bombers equipped for nuclear armaments other than long-range nuclear ALCMS into heavy bombers equipped for long-range nuclear ALCMS, if such heavy bombers were previously equipped for long-range nuclear ALCMS;

(B) heavy bombers equipped for non-nuclear armaments into heavy bombers equipped for long-range nuclear ALCMS or into heavy bombers equipped for nuclear armaments other than long-range nuclear ALCMS;

(C) training heavy bombers into heavy bombers of another category;

(D) former heavy bombers into heavy bombers.

25. Each Party undertakes not to have underground facilities accessible to ballistic missile submarines.

26. Each Party undertakes not to locate railcars at the site of a rail garrison that has been eliminated in accordance with Section IX of the Conversion or Elimination Protocol, unless such railcars have differences, observable by national technical means of verification, in length, width, or height from rail-mobile launchers of ICBMS or launch-associated railcars.

27. Each Party undertakes not to engage in any activities associated with strategic offensive arms at eliminated facilities, notification of the elimination of which has been provided in accordance with paragraph 3 of Section I of the Notification Protocol, unless notification of a new facility at the same location has been provided in accordance with paragraph 3 of Section I of the Notification Protocol. Strategic offensive arms and support equipment shall not be located at eliminated facilities except during their movement through such facilities and during visits of heavy bombers or former heavy bombers at such facilities. Missile tenders may be located at eliminated facilities only for purposes not associated with strategic offensive arms.

28. Each Party undertakes not to base strategic offensive arms subject to the limitations of this Treaty outside its national territory.

29. Each Party undertakes not to use naval vessels that were formerly declared as missile tenders to transport, store, or load SLBMs. Such naval vessels shall not be tied to a ballistic missile submarine for the purpose of supporting such a submarine if such a submarine is located within five kilometers of a submarine base.

30. Each Party undertakes not to remove from production facilities for ICBMs for mobile launchers of ICBMs, solid rocket motors with attached nozzles for the first stages of ICBMs for mobile launchers of ICBMs, except for:

(A) the removal of such motors as part of assembled first stages of ICBMs for mobile launchers of ICBMs that are maintained, stored, and transported in stages;

(B) the removal of such motors as part of assembled ICBMs for mobile launchers of ICBMs that are maintained, stored, and transported as assembled missiles in launch canisters or without launch canisters; and

(C) the removal of such motors as part of assembled first stages of ICBMs for mobile launchers of ICBMs that are maintained, stored, and transported as assembled missiles in launch canisters or without launch canisters, for the purpose of technical characteristics exhibitions.

Article VI

1. Deployed road-mobile launchers of ICBMs and their associated missiles shall be based only in restricted areas. A restricted area shall not exceed five square kilometers in size and shall not overlap another restricted area. No more than ten deployed road-mobile launchers of ICBMs and their associated missiles may be based or located in a restricted area. A restricted area shall not contain deployed ICBMs for road-mobile launchers of ICBMs of more than one type of ICBM.

2. Each Party shall limit the number of fixed structures for road-mobile launchers of ICBMs within each restricted area so that these structures shall not be capable of containing more road-mobile launchers of ICBMs than the number of road-mobile launchers of ICBMs specified for that restricted area.

3. Each restricted area shall be located within a deployment area. A deployment area shall not exceed 125,000 square kilometers in size and shall not overlap another deployment area. A deployment area shall contain no more than one ICBM base for road-mobile launchers of ICBMs.

4. Deployed rail-mobile launchers of ICBMs and their associated missiles shall be based only in rail garrisons. Each Party shall have no more than seven rail garrisons. No point on a portion of track located inside a rail garrison shall be more than 20 kilometers from any entrance/exit for that rail garrison. This distance shall be measured along the tracks. A rail garrison shall not overlap another rail garrison.

5. Each rail garrison shall have no more than two rail entrances/exits. Each such entrance/exit shall have no more than two separate sets of tracks passing through it (a total of four rails).

6. Each Party shall limit the number of parking sites in each rail garrison to no more than the number of trains of standard configuration specified for that rail garrison. Each rail garrison shall have no more than five parking sites.

7. Each Party shall limit the number of fixed structures for rail-mobile launchers of ICBMs in each rail garrison to no more than the number of trains of standard configuration specified for that rail garrison. Each such structure shall contain no more than one train of standard configuration.

8. Each rail garrison shall contain no more than one maintenance facility.

9. Deployed mobile launchers of ICBMs and their associated missiles may leave restricted areas or rail garrisons only for routine movements, relocations, or dispersals. Deployed road-mobile launchers of ICBMs and their associated missiles may leave deployment areas only for relocations or operational dispersals.

10. Relocations shall be completed within 25 days. No more than 15 percent of the total number

of deployed road-mobile launchers of ICBMs and their associated missiles or five such launchers and their associated missiles, whichever is greater, may be outside restricted areas at any one time for the purpose of relocation. No more than 20 percent of the total number of deployed rail-mobile launchers of ICBMs and their associated missiles or five such launchers and their associated missiles, whichever is greater, may be outside rail garrisons at any one time for the purpose of relocation.

11. No more than 50 percent of the total number of deployed rail-mobile launchers of ICBMs and their associated missiles may be engaged in routine movements at any one time.

12. All trains with deployed rail-mobile launchers of ICBMs and their associated missiles of a particular type shall be of one standard configuration. All such trains shall conform to that standard configuration except those taking part in routine movements, relocations, or dispersals, and except that portion of a train remaining within a rail garrison after the other portion of such a train has departed for the maintenance facility associated with that rail garrison, has been relocated to another facility, or has departed the rail garrison for routine movement. Except for dispersals, notification of variations from standard configuration shall be provided in accordance with paragraphs 13, 14, and 15 of Section II of the Notification Protocol.

Article VII

1. Conversion and elimination of strategic offensive arms, fixed structures for mobile launchers of ICBMs, and facilities shall be carried out pursuant to this Article and in accordance with procedures provided for in the Conversion or Elimination Protocol. Conversion and elimination shall be verified by national technical means of verification and by inspection as provided for in Articles IX and XI of this Treaty; in the Conversion or Elimination Protocol; and in the Protocol on Inspections and Continuous Monitoring Activities Relating to this Treaty, hereinafter referred to as the Inspection Protocol.

2. ICBMs for mobile launchers of ICBMs, ICBM launchers, SLBM launchers, heavy bombers, former heavy bombers, and support equipment shall be subject to the limitations provided for in this Treaty until they have been eliminated, or otherwise cease to be subject to the limitations provided for in this Treaty, in accordance with procedures provided for in the Conversion or Elimination Protocol.

3. ICBMs for silo launchers of ICBMs and SLBMs shall be subject to the limitations provided for in this Treaty until they have been eliminated by rendering them inoperable, precluding their use for their original purpose, using procedures at the discretion of the Party possessing the ICBMs or SLBMs.

4. The elimination of ICBMs for mobile launchers of ICBMs, mobile launchers of ICBMs, SLBM launchers, heavy bombers, and former heavy bombers shall be carried out at conversion or elimination facilities, except as provided for in Sections VII and VIII of the Conversion or Elimination Protocol. Fixed launchers of ICBMs and fixed structures for mobile launchers of ICBMs subject to elimination shall be eliminated in situ. A launch canister remaining at a test range or ICBM base after the flight test of an ICBM for mobile launchers of ICBMs shall be eliminated in the open in situ, or at a conversion or elimination facility, in accordance with procedures provided for in the Conversion or Elimination Protocol.

Article VIII

1. A data base pertaining to the obligations under this Treaty is set forth in the Memorandum of Understanding, in which data with respect to items subject to the limitations provided for in this Treaty are listed according to categories of data.

2. In order to ensure the fulfillment of its obligations with respect to this Treaty, each Party shall notify the other Party of changes in data, as provided for in subparagraph 3(A) of this Article, and shall also provide other notifications required by paragraph 3 of this Article, in accordance with the procedures provided for in paragraphs 4, 5, and 6 of this Article, the Notification Protocol, and the Inspection Protocol.

3. Each Party shall provide to the other Party, in accordance with the Notification Protocol, and, for subparagraph (i) of this paragraph, in accordance with Section III of the Inspection Protocol:

(A) notifications concerning data with respect to items subject to the limitations provided for in this Treaty, according to categories of data contained in the Memorandum of Understanding and other agreed categories of data;

(B) notifications concerning movement of items subject to the limitations provided for in this Treaty;

(C) notifications concerning data on ICBM and SLBM throw-weight in connection with the Protocol on ICBM and SLBM Throw-weight Relating to this Treaty, hereinafter referred to as the Throw-weight Protocol;

(D) notifications concerning conversion or elimination of items subject to the limitations provided for in this Treaty or elimination of facilities subject to this Treaty;

(E) notifications concerning cooperative measures to enhance the effectiveness of national technical means of verification;

(F) notifications concerning flight tests of ICBMs or SLBMs and notifications concerning telemetric information;

(G) notifications concerning strategic offensive arms of new types and new kinds;

(H) notifications concerning changes in the content of information provided pursuant to this paragraph, including the rescheduling of activities;

(I) notifications concerning inspections and continuous monitoring activities; and

(J) notifications concerning operational dispersals.

4. Each Party shall use the Nuclear Risk Reduction Centers, which provide for continuous communication between the Parties, to provide and receive notifications in accordance with the Notification Protocol and the Inspection Protocol, unless otherwise provided for in this Treaty, and to acknowledge receipt of such notifications no later than one hour after receipt.

5. If a time is to be specified in a notification provided pursuant to this Article, that time shall be expressed in Greenwich Mean Time. If only a date is to be specified in a notification, that date shall be specified as the 24-hour period that corresponds to the date in local time, expressed in Greenwich Mean Time.

6. Except as otherwise provided in this Article, each Party shall have the right to release to the public all data current as of September 1, 1990, that are listed in the Memorandum of Understanding, as well as the photographs that are appended thereto. Geographic coordinates and site diagrams that are received pursuant to the Agreement Between the Government of the United States of America and the Government of the Union of Soviet Socialist Republics on Exchange of Geographic Coordinates and Site Diagrams Relating to the Treaty of July 31, 1991, shall not be released to the public unless otherwise agreed. The Parties shall hold consultations on releasing to the public data and other information provided pursuant to this Article or received otherwise in fulfilling the obligations provided for in this Treaty. The provisions of this Article shall not affect the rights and obligations of the Parties with respect to the communication of such data and

other information to those individuals who, because of their official responsibilities, require such data or other information to carry out activities related to the fulfillment of the obligations provided for in this Treaty.

Article IX

1. For the purpose of ensuring verification of compliance with the provisions of this Treaty, each Party shall use national technical means of verification at its disposal in a manner consistent with generally recognized principles of international law.

2. Each Party undertakes not to interfere with the national technical means of verification of the other Party operating in accordance with paragraph 1 of this Article.

3. Each Party undertakes not to use concealment measures that impede verification, by national technical means of verification, of compliance with the provisions of this Treaty. In this connection, the obligation not to use concealment measures includes the obligation not to use them at test ranges, including measures that result in the concealment of ICBMs, SLBMs, mobile launchers of ICBMs, or the association between ICBMs or SLBMs and their launchers during testing. The obligation not to use concealment measures shall not apply to cover or concealment practices at ICBM bases and deployment areas, or to the use of environmental shelters for strategic offensive arms.

4. To aid verification, each ICBM for mobile launchers of ICBMs shall have a unique identifier as provided for in the Inspection Protocol.

Article X

1. During each flight test of an ICBM or SLBM, the Party conducting the flight test shall make on-board technical measurements and shall broadcast all telemetric information obtained from such measurements. The Party conducting the flight test shall determine which technical parameters are to be measured during such flight test, as well as the methods of processing and transmitting telemetric information.

2. During each flight test of an ICBM or SLBM, the Party conducting the flight test undertakes not to engage in any activity that denies full access to telemetric information, including:

(A) the use of encryption;

(B) the use of jamming;

(C) broadcasting telemetric information from an ICBM or SLBM using narrow directional beaming; and

(D) encapsulation of telemetric information, including the use of ejectable capsules or recoverable reentry vehicles.

3. During each flight test of an ICBM or SLBM, the Party conducting the flight test undertakes not to broadcast from a reentry vehicle telemetric information that pertains to the functioning of the stages or the self-contained dispensing mechanism of the ICBM or SLBM.

4. After each flight test of an ICBM or SLBM, the Party conducting the flight test shall provide, in accordance with Section I of the Protocol on Telemetric Information Relating to the Treaty, hereinafter referred to as the Telemetry Protocol, tapes that contain a recording of all telemetric information that is broadcast during the flight test.

5. After each flight test of an ICBM or SLBM, the Party conducting the flight test shall provide, in accordance with Section II of the Telemetry Protocol, data associated with the analysis of the telemetric information.

6. Notwithstanding the provisions of paragraphs 1 and 2 of this Article, each Party shall have the right to encapsulate and encrypt on-board technical measurements during no more than a total of eleven flight tests of ICBMs or SLBMs each year. Of these eleven flight tests each year, no more than four shall be flight tests of ICBMs or SLBMs of each type, any missile of which has been flight-tested with a self-contained dispensing mechanism. Such encapsulation shall be carried out in accordance with Section I and paragraph 1 of Section III of the Telemetry Protocol, and such encryption shall be carried out in accordance with paragraph 2 of Section III of the Telemetry Protocol. Encapsulation and encryption that are carried out on the same flight test of an ICBM or SLBM shall count as two flight tests against the quotas specified in this paragraph.

Article XI

1. For the purpose of ensuring verification of compliance with the provisions of this Treaty, each Party shall have the right to conduct inspections and continuous monitoring activities and shall conduct exhibitions pursuant to this Article and the Inspection Protocol. Inspections, continuous monitoring activities, and exhibitions shall be conducted in accordance with the procedures provided for in the Inspection Protocol and the Conversion or Elimination Protocol.

2. Each Party shall have the right to conduct baseline data inspections at facilities to confirm the accuracy of data on the numbers and types of items specified for such facilities in the initial exchange of data provided in accordance with paragraph 1 of Section I of the Notification Protocol.

3. Each Party shall have the right to conduct data update inspections at facilities to confirm the accuracy of data on the numbers and types of items specified for such facilities in the notifications and regular exchanges of updated data provided in accordance with paragraphs 2 and 3 of Section I of the Notification Protocol.

4. Each Party shall have the right to conduct new facility inspections to confirm the accuracy of data on the numbers and types of items specified in the notifications of new facilities provided in accordance with paragraph 3 of Section I of the Notification Protocol.

5. Each Party shall have the right to conduct suspect-site inspections to confirm that covert assembly of ICBMs for mobile launchers of ICBMs or covert assembly of first stages of such ICBMs is not occurring.

6. Each Party shall have the right to conduct reentry vehicle inspections of deployed ICBMs and SLBMs to confirm that such ballistic missiles contain no more reentry vehicles than the number of warheads attributed to them.

7. Each Party shall have the right to conduct post-exercise dispersal inspections of deployed mobile launchers of ICBMs and their associated missiles to confirm that the number of mobile launchers of ICBMs and their associated missiles that are located at the inspected ICBM base and those that have not returned to it after completion of the dispersal does not exceed the number specified for that ICBM base.

8. Each Party shall conduct or shall have the right to conduct conversion or elimination inspections to confirm the conversion or elimination of strategic offensive arms.

9. Each Party shall have the right to conduct close-out inspections to confirm that the elimination of facilities has been completed.

10. Each Party shall have the right to conduct formerly declared facility inspections to confirm that facilities, notification of the elimination of which has been provided in accordance with paragraph 3 of Section I of the Notification Protocol, are not being used for purposes inconsistent with this Treaty.

11. Each Party shall conduct technical characteristics exhibitions, and shall have the right during such exhibitions by the other Party to conduct inspections of an ICBM and an SLBM of each type, and

each variant thereof, and of a mobile launcher of ICBMS and each version of such launcher for each type of ICBM for mobile launchers of ICBMS. The purpose of such exhibitions shall be to permit the inspecting Party to confirm that technical characteristics correspond to the data specified for these items.

12. Each Party shall conduct distinguishability exhibitions for heavy bombers, former heavy bombers, and long-range nuclear ALCMS, and shall have the right during such exhibitions by the other Party to conduct inspections, of:

(A) heavy bombers equipped for long-range nuclear ALCMS. The purpose of such exhibitions shall be to permit the inspecting Party to confirm that the technical characteristics of each type and each variant of such heavy bombers correspond to the data specified for these items in Annex G to the Memorandum of Understanding; to demonstrate the maximum number of long-range nuclear ALCMS for which a heavy bomber of each type and each variant is actually equipped; and to demonstrate that this number does not exceed the number provided for in paragraph 20 or 21 of Article V of this Treaty, as applicable;

(B) for each type of heavy bomber from any one of which a long-range nuclear ALCM has been flight-tested, heavy bombers equipped for nuclear armaments other than long-range nuclear ALCMS, heavy bombers equipped for non-nuclear armaments, training heavy bombers, and former heavy bombers. If, for such a type of heavy bomber, there are no heavy bombers equipped for long-range nuclear ALCMS, a test heavy bomber from which a long-range nuclear ALCM has been flight-tested shall be exhibited. The purpose of such exhibitions shall be to demonstrate to the inspecting Party that, for each exhibited type of heavy bomber, each variant of heavy bombers equipped for nuclear armaments other than long-range nuclear ALCMS, each variant of heavy bombers equipped for non-nuclear armaments, each variant of training heavy bombers, and a former heavy bomber are distinguishable from one another and from each variant of heavy bombers of the same type equipped for long-range nuclear ALCMS; and

(C) long-range nuclear ALCMS. The purpose of such exhibitions shall be to permit the inspecting Party to confirm that the technical characteristics of each type and each variant of such long-range ALCMS correspond to the data specified for these items in Annex H to the Memorandum of Understanding.

The further purpose of such exhibitions shall be to demonstrate differences, notification of which has been provided in accordance with paragraph 13, 14, or 15 of Section VII of the Notification Protocol, that make long-range non-nuclear ALCMS distinguishable from long-range nuclear ALCMS.

13. Each Party shall conduct baseline exhibitions, and shall have the right during such exhibitions by the other Party to conduct inspections, of all heavy bombers equipped for non-nuclear armaments, all training heavy bombers, and all former heavy bombers specified in the initial exchange of data provided in accordance with paragraph 1 of Section I of the Notification Protocol. The purpose of these exhibitions shall be to demonstrate to the inspecting Party that such airplanes satisfy the requirements for conversion in accordance with the Conversion or Elimination Protocol. After a long-range nuclear ALCM has been flight-tested from a heavy bomber of a type, from none of which a long-range nuclear ALCM had previously been flight-tested, the Party conducting the flight test shall conduct baseline exhibitions, and the other Party shall have the right during such exhibitions to conduct inspections, of 30 percent of the heavy bombers of such type equipped for nuclear armaments other than long-range nuclear ALCMS at each air base specified for such heavy bombers. The purpose of these exhibitions shall be to demonstrate to the inspecting Party the presence of specified features that make each exhibited heavy bomber distinguishable from heavy bombers of the same type equipped for long-range nuclear ALCMS.

14. Each Party shall have the right to conduct continuous monitoring activities at production facilities for ICBMS for mobile launchers of ICBMS to confirm the number of ICBMS for mobile launchers of ICBMS produced.

Article XII

1. To enhance the effectiveness of national technical means of verification, each Party shall, if the other Party makes a request in accordance with paragraph 1 of Section V of the Notification Protocol, carry out the following cooperative measures:

(A) a display in the open of the road-mobile launchers of ICBMS located within restricted areas specified by the requesting Party. The number of road-mobile launchers of ICBMS based at the restricted areas specified in each such request shall not exceed ten percent of the total number of deployed road-mobile launchers of ICBMS of the requested Party, and such launchers shall be contained within one ICBM base for road-mobile launchers of ICBMS. For each specified restricted area, the roofs of fixed structures for road-mobile launchers of ICBMS shall be open for the duration of a display. The road-mobile launchers of ICBMS located within the restricted area shall be displayed either located next to or moved halfway out of such fixed structures;

(B) a display in the open of the rail-mobile launchers of ICBMS located at parking sites specified by the requesting Party. Such launchers shall be displayed by removing the entire train from its fixed structure and locating the train within the rail garrison. The number of rail-mobile launchers of ICBMS subject to display pursuant to each such request shall include all such launchers located at no more than eight parking sites, provided that no more than two parking sites may be requested within any one rail garrison in any one request. Requests concerning specific parking sites shall include the designation for each parking site as provided for in Annex A to the Memorandum of Understanding; and

(C) a display in the open of all heavy bombers and former heavy bombers located within one air base specified by the requesting Party, except those heavy bombers and former heavy bombers that are not readily movable due to maintenance or operations. Such heavy bombers and former heavy bombers shall be displayed by removing the entire airplane from its fixed structure, if any, and locating the airplane within the air base. Those heavy bombers and former heavy bombers at the air base specified by the requesting Party that are not readily movable due to maintenance or operations shall be specified by the requested Party in a notification provided in accordance with paragraph 2 of Section V of the Notification Protocol. Such a notification shall be provided no later than 12 hours after the request for display has been made.

2. Road-mobile launchers of ICBMS, rail-mobile launchers of ICBMS, heavy bombers, and former heavy bombers subject to each request pursuant to paragraph 1 of this Article shall be displayed in open view without using concealment measures. Each Party shall have the right to make seven such requests each year, but shall not request a display at any particular ICBM base for road-mobile launchers of ICBMS, any particular parking site, or any particular air base more than two times each year. A Party shall have the right to request, in any single request, only a display of road-mobile launchers of

ICBMS, a display of rail-mobile launchers of ICBMS, or a display of heavy bombers and former heavy bombers. A display shall begin no later than 12 hours after the request is made and shall continue until 18 hours have elapsed from the time that the request was made. If the requested Party cannot conduct a display due to circumstances brought about by force majeure, it shall provide notification to the requesting Party in accordance with paragraph 3 of Section V of the Notification Protocol, and the display shall be cancelled. In such a case, the number of requests to which the requesting Party is entitled shall not be reduced.

3. A request for cooperative measures shall not be made for a facility that has been designated for inspection until such an inspection has been completed and the inspectors have departed the facility. A facility for which cooperative measures have been requested shall not be designated for inspection until the cooperative measures have been completed or until notification has been provided in accordance with paragraph 3 of Section V of the Notification Protocol.

Article XIII

1. Each Party shall have the right to conduct exercise dispersals of deployed mobile launchers of ICBMS and their associated missiles from restricted areas or rail garrisons. Such an exercise dispersal may involve either road-mobile launchers of ICBMS or rail-mobile launchers of ICBMS, or both road-mobile launchers of ICBMS and rail-mobile launchers of ICBMS. Exercise dispersals of deployed mobile launchers of ICBMS and their associated missiles shall be conducted as provided for below:

(A) An exercise dispersal shall be considered to have begun as of the date and time specified in the notification provided in accordance with paragraph 11 of Section II of the Notification Protocol.

(B) An exercise dispersal shall be considered to be completed as of the date and time specified in the notification provided in accordance with paragraph 12 of Section II of the Notification Protocol.

(C) Those ICBM bases for mobile launchers of ICBMS specified in the notification provided in accordance with paragraph 11 of Section II of the Notification Protocol shall be considered to be involved in an exercise dispersal.

(D) When an exercise dispersal begins, deployed mobile launchers of ICBMS and their associated missiles engaged in a routine movement from a restricted area or rail garrison of an ICBM base for mobile launchers of ICBMS that is involved in such a dispersal shall be considered to be part of the dispersal.

(E) When an exercise dispersal begins, deployed mobile launchers of ICBMs and their associated missiles engaged in a relocation from a restricted area or rail garrison of an ICBM base for mobile launchers of ICBMs that is involved in such a dispersal shall continue to be considered to be engaged in a relocation. Notification of the completion of the relocation shall be provided in accordance with paragraph 10 of Section II of the Notification Protocol, unless notification of the completion of the relocation was provided in accordance with paragraph 12 of Section II of the Notification Protocol.

(F) During an exercise dispersal, all deployed mobile launchers of ICBMs and their associated missiles that depart a restricted area or rail garrison of an ICBM base for mobile launchers of ICBMs involved in such a dispersal shall be considered to be part of the dispersal, except for such launchers and missiles that relocate to a facility outside their associated ICBM base during such a dispersal.

(G) An exercise dispersal shall be completed no later than 30 days after it begins.

(H) Exercise dispersals shall not be conducted:

(i) more than two times in any period of two calendar years;

(ii) during the entire period of time provided for baseline data inspections;

(iii) from a new ICBM base for mobile launchers of ICBMs until a new facility inspection has been conducted or until the period of time provided for such an inspection has expired; or

(iv) from an ICBM base for mobile launchers of ICBMs that has been designated for a data update inspection or reentry vehicle inspection, until completion of such an inspection.

(I) If a notification of an exercise dispersal has been provided in accordance with paragraph 11 of Section II of the Notification Protocol, the other Party shall not have the right to designate for data update inspection or reentry vehicle inspection an ICBM base for mobile launchers of ICBMs involved in such a dispersal, or to request cooperative measures for such an ICBM base, until the completion of such a dispersal.

(J) When an exercise dispersal is completed, deployed mobile launchers of ICBMs and their associated missiles involved in such a dispersal shall be located at their restricted areas or rail garrisons, except for those otherwise accounted for in accordance with paragraph 12 of Section II of the Notification Protocol.

2. A major strategic exercise involving heavy bombers, about which a notification has been provided pursuant to the Agreement Between the Government of the United States of America and the Government of the Union of Soviet Socialist Republics on Reciprocal Advance Notification of Major Strategic Exercises of September 23, 1989, shall be conducted as provided for below:

(A) Such exercise shall be considered to have begun as of the date and time specified in the notification provided in accordance with paragraph 16 of Section II of the Notification Protocol.

(B) Such exercise shall be considered to be completed as of the date and time specified in the notification provided in accordance with paragraph 17 of Section II of the Notification Protocol.

(C) The air bases for heavy bombers and air bases for former heavy bombers specified in the notification provided in accordance with paragraph 16 of Section II of the Notification Protocol shall be considered to be involved in such exercise.

(D) Such exercise shall begin no more than one time in any calendar year, and shall be completed no later than 30 days after it begins.

(E) Such exercise shall not be conducted during the entire period of time provided for baseline data inspections.

(F) During such exercise by a Party, the other Party shall not have the right to conduct inspections of the air bases for heavy bombers and air bases for former heavy bombers involved in the exercise. The right to conduct inspections of such air bases shall resume three days after notification of the completion of a major strategic exercise involving heavy bombers has been provided in accordance with paragraph 17 of Section II of the Notification Protocol.

(G) Within the 30-day period following the receipt of the notification of the completion of such exercise, the receiving Party may make a request for cooperative measures to be carried out in accordance with subparagraph 1(C) of Article XII of this Treaty at one of the air bases involved in the exercise. Such a request shall not be counted toward the quota provided for in paragraph 2 of Article XII of this Treaty.

Article XIV

1. Each Party shall have the right to conduct operational dispersals of deployed mobile launchers of ICBMs and their associated missiles, ballistic mis-

sile submarines, and heavy bombers. There shall be no limit on the number and duration of operational dispersals, and there shall be no limit on the number of deployed mobile launchers of ICBMs and their associated missiles, ballistic missile submarines, or heavy bombers involved in such dispersals. When an operational dispersal begins, all strategic offensive arms of a Party shall be considered to be part of the dispersal. Operational dispersals shall be conducted as provided for below:

(A) An operational dispersal shall be considered to have begun as of the date and time specified in the notification provided in accordance with paragraph 1 of Section X of the Notification Protocol.

(B) An operational dispersal shall be considered to be completed as of the date and time specified in the notification provided in accordance with paragraph 2 of Section X of the Notification Protocol.

2. During an operational dispersal each Party shall have the right to:

(A) suspend notifications that it would otherwise provide in accordance with the Notification Protocol except for notification of flight tests provided under the Agreement Between the United States of America and the Union of Soviet Socialist Republics on Notifications of Launches of Intercontinental Ballistic Missiles and Submarine-Launched Ballistic Missiles of May 31, 1988; provided that, if any conversion or elimination processes are not suspended pursuant to subparagraph (D) of this paragraph, the relevant notifications shall be provided in accordance with Section IV of the Notification Protocol;

(B) suspend the right of the other Party to conduct inspections;

(C) suspend the right of the other Party to request cooperative measures; and

(D) suspend conversion and elimination processes for its strategic offensive arms. In such case, the number of converted and eliminated items shall correspond to the number that has actually been converted and eliminated as of the date and time of the beginning of the operational dispersal specified in the notification provided in accordance with paragraph 1 of Section X of the Notification Protocol.

3. Notifications suspended pursuant to paragraph 2 of this Article shall resume no later than three days after notification of the completion of the operational dispersal has been provided in accordance with paragraph 2 of Section X of the Notification Protocol. The right to conduct inspections and

to request cooperative measures suspended pursuant to paragraph 2 of this Article shall resume four days after notification of the completion of the operational dispersal has been provided in accordance with paragraph 2 of Section X of the Notification Protocol. Inspections or cooperative measures being conducted at the time a Party provides notification that it suspends inspections or cooperative measures during an operational dispersal shall not count toward the appropriate annual quotas provided for by this Treaty.

4. When an operational dispersal is completed:

(A) All deployed road-mobile launchers of ICBMs and their associated missiles shall be located within their deployment areas or shall be engaged in relocations.

(B) All deployed rail-mobile launchers of ICBMs and their associated missiles shall be located within their rail garrisons or shall be engaged in routine movements or relocations.

(C) All heavy bombers shall be located within national territory and shall have resumed normal operations. If it is necessary for heavy bombers to be located outside national territory for purposes not inconsistent with this Treaty, the Parties will immediately engage in diplomatic consultations so that appropriate assurances can be provided.

5. Within the 30 day period after the completion of an operational dispersal, the Party not conducting the operational dispersal shall have the right to make no more than two requests for cooperative measures, subject to the provisions of Article XII of this Treaty, for ICBM bases for mobile launchers of ICBMs or air bases. Such requests shall not count toward the quota of requests provided for in paragraph 2 of Article XII of this Treaty.

Article XV. To promote the objectives and implementation of the provisions of this Treaty, the Parties hereby establish the Joint Compliance and Inspection Commission. The Parties agree that, if either Party so requests, they shall meet within the framework of the Joint Compliance and Inspection Commission to:

(A) resolve questions relating to compliance with the obligations assumed;

(B) agree upon such additional measures as may be necessary to improve the viability and effectiveness of this Treaty; and

(C) resolve questions related to the application of relevant provisions of this Treaty to a new kind of strategic offensive arm, after notification has been provided in accordance with paragraph 16 of Section VII of the Notification Protocol.

Article XVI. To ensure the viability and effectiveness of this Treaty, each Party shall not assume any international obligations or undertakings that would conflict with its provisions. The Parties shall hold consultations in accordance with Article XV of this Treaty in order to resolve any ambiguities that may arise in this regard. The Parties agree that this provision does not apply to any patterns of cooperation, including obligations, in the area of strategic offensive arms, existing at the time of signature of this Treaty, between a Party and a third State.

Article XVII

1. This Treaty, including its Annexes, Protocols, and Memorandum of Understanding, all of which form integral parts thereof, shall be subject to ratification in accordance with the constitutional procedures of each Party. This Treaty shall enter into force on the date of the exchange of instruments of ratification.

2. This Treaty shall remain in force for 15 years unless superseded earlier by a subsequent agreement on the reduction and limitation of strategic offensive arms. No later than one year before the expiration of the 15-year period, the Parties shall meet to consider whether this Treaty will be extended. If the Parties so decide, this Treaty will be extended for a period of five years unless it is superseded before the expiration of that period by a subsequent agreement on the reduction and limitation of strategic offensive arms. This Treaty shall be extended for successive five-year periods, if the Parties so decide, in accordance with the procedures governing the initial extension, and it shall remain in force for each agreed five-year period of extension unless it is superseded by a subsequent agreement on the reduction and limitation of strategic offensive arms.

3. Each Party shall, in exercising its national sovereignty, have the right to withdraw from this Treaty if it decides that extraordinary events related to the subject matter of this Treaty have jeopardized its supreme interests. It shall give notice of its decision to the other Party six months prior to withdrawal from this Treaty. Such notice shall include a statement of the extraordinary events the notifying Party regards as having jeopardized its supreme interests.

Selected Agreed Statements

First Agreed Statement. The Parties agree, in the interest of the viability and effectiveness of the Treaty, not to transfer strategic offensive arms subject to the limitations of the Treaty to third States.

The Parties further agree that this Agreed Statement and the provisions of Article XVI of the Treaty do not apply to any patterns of cooperation, including obligations, in the area of strategic offensive arms, existing at the time of signature of the Treaty, between a Party and a third State.

Second Agreed Statement. The Parties agree that, in the event of the emergence in the future of a new kind of arm that one Party considers could be a new kind of strategic offensive arm, that Party shall have the right to raise the question of such an arm for consideration by the Joint Compliance and Inspection Commission in accordance with subparagraph (C) of Article XV of the Treaty.

Fifth Agreed Statement. The Parties agree that the replacement of silo launchers of heavy ICBMS under the provisions of subparagraph 2(D) of Article V of the Treaty shall only take place in the case of silo launchers destroyed by accident or in the case of other exceptional circumstances that require the relocation of existing silo launchers of heavy ICBMS. If such relocation is required, the Party planning to construct the new silo launcher shall provide the other Party with the reasons and plans for such relocation in the Joint Compliance and Inspection Commission prior to carrying out such relocation.

Seventh Agreed Statement. The Parties agree that, with respect to the provisions of paragraph 1 of Article XIV of the Treaty authorizing operational dispersals, such dispersals shall be conducted only for national security purposes in time of crisis when a Party considers it necessary to act to ensure the survivability of its strategic forces. The Parties further agree that, while there are no limits on the number and frequency of such operational dispersals, in practice they will occur rarely.

Eighth Agreed Statement. The Parties agree that:

(A) With respect to paragraph 28 of Article V of the Treaty, the strategic offensive arms of each Party shall be based only within its national territory at permanent bases specified in the Treaty that are equipped to support the long-term operation of strategic offensive arms. The obligations of paragraph 28 of Article V of the Treaty shall not affect the Parties' rights under generally recognized principles and rules of international law relating to the passage of submarines or flights of aircraft, or relating to visits of submarines to ports of third States.

(B) With respect to heavy bombers, the provisions of paragraph 28 of Article V of the Treaty shall not preclude the temporary stationing of heavy bombers outside the territory of a Party for purposes not inconsistent with the Treaty. If a Party stations heavy bombers outside its national territory for a period in excess of 30 days at any one time, it shall so inform the other Party through diplomatic channels before the end of the 30-day period, except that, if a Party has stationed more than 30 heavy bombers outside its national territory at any one time, it shall so inform the other Party within 48 hours.

(C) The Parties have the obligation, if concerns arise under this Agreed Statement, to discuss any ambiguity and, if necessary, to provide each other with information to resolve concerns. Such discussions could occur through diplomatic channels, as well as in the Joint Compliance and Inspection Commission. The Parties do not rule out the possibility that clarifications provided in the Joint Compliance and Inspection Commission might, in certain cases, include inspections or visits. . . .

Thirty-fourth Agreed Statement. The Parties agree that, with respect to the criteria contained in subparagraph (F) of the definition of the term "new type" provided for in the Definitions Annex to the Treaty:

(A) The throw-weight of an ICBM or SLBM of a type declared to be a new type shall exceed the accountable throw-weight of an ICBM or SLBM of an existing type or of a previously declared new type by 21 percent or more. The change in the length of the first stage of an ICBM or SLBM of a type declared to be a new type shall be a change in relation to an ICBM or SLBM of the same existing type or the same previously declared new type by five percent or more.

(B) The change in the length of the first stage of an ICBM or SLBM of a type declared to be a new type in relation to an ICBM or SLBM of an existing type or previously declared new type shall be determined in accordance with paragraph 15 of Annex J to the Memorandum of Understanding.

(C) The throw-weight of an ICBM or SLBM of an existing type or previously declared new type shall be the accountable throw-weight of this existing type or previously declared new type, specified in the Memorandum of Understanding.

(D) The throw-weight of an ICBM or SLBM of a type declared to be a new type shall be the greatest throw-weight demonstrated in flight tests of an ICBM or SLBM of that type to a range of no less than 11,000 kilometers for an ICBM, or a range of no less than 9,500 kilometers for an SLBM. If an ICBM or SLBM of a type declared to be a new type is not capable of being flight-tested to such a range, it shall be flight-tested to a range of no less than 10,000 kilometers for an ICBM, or a range of no less than 8,500 kilometers for an SLBM.

(E) Should an ICBM of any type be declared to be a new type in relation to the SS-25 ICBM on the basis of an increase of 21 percent or more in throw-weight in conjunction with a change of five percent or more in the length of the first stage, the throw-weight of an ICBM of such a type declared to be a new type shall be the greatest throw-weight demonstrated in flight tests of an ICBM of that type to a range of no less than 11,000 kilometers.

Selected Definitions

For the purposes of the Treaty and its Annexes, Protocols, and Memorandum of Understanding:

The term "**heavy bomber**" means a bomber of a type, any one of which satisfies either of the following criteria:

(A) its range is greater than 8000 kilometers; or

(B) it is equipped for long-range nuclear ALCMS.

A bomber shall not be considered to be a heavy bomber if it meets neither criterion (A) nor criterion (B), or if otherwise agreed.

A bomber shall not be considered to be a heavy bomber if it is not equipped for long-range nuclear ALCMS, if it is not a model or modification of an accountable heavy bomber, and if it is tested, equipped, and configured exclusively for maritime operations. For the purposes of this definition, the term "modification of an accountable heavy bomber" is understood to mean an airplane having a design essentially identical to the design of an accountable heavy bomber.

A bomber of a type, any one of which has an integrated platform area in excess of 310 square meters, but that is not declared by a Party as a heavy bomber, shall be considered to be a heavy bomber unless the deploying Party provides the Joint Compliance and Inspection Commission with information demonstrating to the satisfaction of the other Party that this bomber does not meet the criterion provided for in subparagraph (A) and does not meet the criterion provided for in subparagraph (B).

Heavy bombers of the Parties of the types existing as of the date of signature of the Treaty are specified in Article III of the Treaty.

The term "**heavy ICBM**" means an ICBM of a type, any one of which has a launch weight greater than 106,000 kilograms or a throw-weight greater than 4350 kilograms.

The term "**long-range ALCM**" means an ALCM with a range in excess of 600 kilometers.

The term "**new type**" means, for ICBMS or SLBMS, a type of ICBM or SLBM, the technical characteristics of which differ from those of an ICBM or SLBM, respectively, of each type declared previously in at least one of the following respects:

(A) number of stages;

(B) type of propellant of any stage;

(C) launch weight, by ten percent or more;

(D) length of either the assembled missile without front section or length of the first stage, by ten percent or more;

(E) diameter of the first stage, by five percent or more; or

(F) throw-weight, by an increase of 21 percent or more, in conjunction with a change in the length of the first stage by five percent or more.

The term "**rapid reload**" means reloading a silo launcher of ICBMS in less than 12 hours or a mobile launcher of ICBMS in less than four hours after a missile has been launched or removed from such a launcher.

[*Arms Control Today* 21:9 (November 1991): Suppl. 7–20]

Conventional Arms Limitation in Europe

CFE Treaty (1990)

Treaty on Conventional Armed Forces in Europe

Article I

1. Each State Party shall carry out the obligations set forth in this Treaty in accordance with its provisions, including those obligations relating to the following five categories of conventional armed forces: battle tanks, armoured combat vehicles, artillery, combat aircraft and combat helicopters.

2. Each State Party also shall carry out the other measures set forth in this Treaty designed to ensure security and stability both during the period of reduction of conventional armed forces and after the completion of reductions.

3. This Treaty incorporates the Protocol on Existing Types of Conventional Armaments and Equipment, hereinafter referred to as the Protocol on Existing Types, with an Annex thereto; the Protocol on Procedures Governing the Reclassification of Specific Models or Versions of Combat-Capable Trainer Aircraft Into Unarmed Trainer Aircraft, hereinafter referred to as the Protocol on Aircraft Reclassification; the Protocol on Procedures Governing the Reduction of Conventional Armaments and Equipment Limited by the Treaty on Conventional Armed Forces in Europe, hereinafter referred to as the Protocol on Reduction; the Protocol on Procedures Governing the Categorisation of Combat Helicopters and the Recategorisation of Multi-Purpose Attack Helicopters, hereinafter referred to as the Protocol on Helicopter Recategorisation; the Protocol on Notification and Exchange of Information, hereinafter referred to as the Protocol on Information Exchange, with an Annex on the Format for the Exchange of Information, hereinafter referred to as the Annex on Format; the Protocol on Inspection; the Protocol on the Joint Consultative Group; and the Protocol on the Provisional Application of Certain Provisions of the Treaty on Conventional Armed Forces in Europe, hereinafter referred to as the Protocol on Provisional Application. Each of these documents constitutes an integral part of this Treaty.

Article II

1. For the purposes of this Treaty:

(A) The term "group of States Parties" means the group of States Parties that signed the Treaty of Warsaw of 1955 consisting of the Republic of Bulgaria, the Czech and Slovak Federal Republic, the Republic of Hungary, the Republic of Poland, Romania and the Union of Soviet Socialist Republics, or the group of States Parties that signed or acceded to the Treaty of Brussels of 1948 or the Treaty of Washington of 1949 consisting of the Kingdom of Belgium, Canada, the Kingdom of Denmark, the French Republic, the Federal Republic of Gemmany, the Hellenic Republic, the Republic of Iceland, the Italian Republic, the Grand Duchy of Luxembourg, the Kingdom of the Netherlands, the Kingdom of Norway, the Portuguese Republic, the Kingdom of Spain, the Republic of Turkey, the United Kingdom of Great Britain and Northern Ireland and the United States of America.

(B) The term "area of application" means the entire land territory of the States Parties in Europe from the Atlantic Ocean to the Ural Mountains, which includes all the European island territories of the States Parties, including the Faroe Islands of the Kingdom of Denmark, Svalbard including Bear Island of the Kingdom of Norway, the islands of Azores and Madeira of the Portuguese Republic, the Canary Islands of the Kingdom of Spain and Franz Josef Land and Novaya Zemlya of the Union of Soviet Socialist Republics. In the case of the Union of Soviet Socialist Republics, the area of application includes all territory lying west of the Ural River and the Caspian Sea. In the case of the Republic of Turkey, the area of application includes the territory of the Republic of Turkey north and west of a line extending from the point of intersection of the Turkish border with the 39th parallel to Muradiye, Patnos, Karayazi, Tekman, Kemaliye, Feke, Ceyhan, Dogankent, Gözne and thence to the sea.

(C) The term "battle tank" means a self-propelled armoured fighting vehicle, capable of heavy firepower, primarily of a high muzzle velocity direct fire main gun necessary to engage armoured and other targets, with high cross-country mobility, with a high level of self-protection, and which is not designed and equipped primarily to transport combat troops. Such armoured vehicles serve as the principal weapon system of ground-force tank and other armoured formations.

Battle tanks are tracked armoured fighting vehicles which weigh at least 16.5 metric tonnes unladen weight and which are armed with a 360-degree traverse gun of at least 75 millimetres calibre. In addition, any wheeled armoured fighting vehicles entering into service which meet all the other criteria stated above shall also be deemed battle tanks.

(D) The term "armoured combat vehicle" means a self-propelled vehicle with armoured protection and cross-country capability. Armoured combat vehicles include armoured personnel carriers, armoured infantry fighting vehicles and heavy armament combat vehicles.

The term "armoured personnel carrier" means an armoured combat vehicle which is designed and equipped to transport a combat infantry squad and which, as a rule, is armed with an integral or organic weapon of less than 20 millimetres calibre.

The term "armoured infantry fighting vehicle" means an armoured combat vehicle which is designed and equipped primarily to transport a combat infantry squad, which normally provides the capability for the troops to deliver fire from inside the vehicle under armoured protection, and which is armed with an integral or organic cannon of at least 20 millimetres calibre and sometimes an anti-tank missile launcher. Armoured infantry fighting vehicles serve as the principal weapon system of armoured infantry or mechanised infantry or motorised infantry formations and units of ground forces.

The term "heavy armament combat vehicle" means an armoured combat vehicle with an integral or organic direct fire gun of at least 75 millimetres calibre, weighing at least 6.0 metric tonnes unladen weight, which does not fall within the definitions of an armoured personnel carrier, or an armoured infantry fighting vehicle or a battle tank.

(E) The term "unladen weight" means the weight of a vehicle excluding the weight of ammunition; fuel, oil and lubricants; removable reactive armour; spare parts, tools and accessories; removable snorkelling equipment; and crew and their personal kit.

(F) The term "artillery" means large calibre systems capable of engaging ground targets by delivering primarily indirect fire. Such artillery systems provide the essential indirect fire support to combined arms formations.

Large calibre artillery systems are guns, howitzers, artillery pieces combining the characteristics of guns and howitzers, mortars and multiple launch rocket systems with a calibre of 100 millimetres and above. In addition, any future large calibre direct fire system which has a secondary effective indirect fire capability shall be counted against the artillery ceilings.

(G) The term "stationed conventional armed forces" means conventional armed forces of a State Party that are stationed within the area of application on the territory of another State Party.

(H) The term "designated permanent storage site" means a place with a clearly defined physical boundary containing conventional armaments and equipment limited by the Treaty, which are counted within overall ceilings but which are not subject to limitations on conventional armaments and equipment limited by the Treaty in active units.

(I) The term "armoured vehicle launched bridge" means a self-propelled armoured transporter-launcher vehicle capable of carrying and, through built-in mechanisms, of emplacing and retrieving a bridge structure. Such a vehicle with a bridge structure operates as an integrated system.

(J) The term "conventional armaments and equipment limited by the Treaty" means battle tanks, armoured combat vehicles, artillery, combat aircraft and attack helicopters subject to the numerical limitations set forth in Articles IV, V and VI.

(K) The term "combat aircraft" means a fixed-wing or variable-geometry wing aircraft armed and equipped to engage targets by employing guided missiles, unguided rockets, bombs, guns, cannons, or other weapons of destruction, as well as any model or version of such an aircraft which performs other military functions such as reconnaissance or electronic warfare. The term "combat aircraft" does not include primary trainer aircraft.

(L) The term "combat helicopter" means a rotary wing aircraft armed and equipped to engage targets or equipped to perform other military functions. The term "combat helicopter" comprises attack helicopters and combat support helicopters. The term "combat helicopter" does not include unarmed transport helicopters.

(M) The term "attack helicopter" means a combat helicopter equipped to employ anti-armour, air-to-ground, or air-to-air guided weapons and equipped with an integrated fire control and aiming system for these weapons. The term "attack helicopter" comprises specialised attack helicopters and multi-purpose attack helicopters.

(N) The term "specialised attack helicopter" means an attack helicopter that is designed primarily to employ guided weapons.

(O) The term "multi-purpose attack helicopter" means an attack helicopter designed to perform multiple military functions and equipped to employ guided weapons.

(P) The term "combat support helicopter" means a combat helicopter which does not fulfill the requirements to qualify as an attack helicopter and which may be equipped with a variety of self-defence and area suppression weapons, such as guns, cannons and unguided rockets, bombs or cluster bombs, or which may be equipped to perform other military functions.

(Q) The term "conventional armaments and equipment subject to the Treaty" means battle tanks, armoured combat vehicles, artillery, combat aircraft, primary trainer aircraft, unarmed trainer aircraft, combat helicopters, unarmed transport helicopters, armoured vehicle launched bridges, armoured personnel carrier look-alikes and armoured infantry fighting vehicle look-alikes subject to information exchange in accordance with the Protocol on Information Exchange.

(R) The term "in service," as it applies to conventional armed forces and conventional armaments and equipment, means battle tanks, armoured combat vehicles, artillery, combat aircraft, primary trainer aircraft, unarmed trainer aircraft, combat helicopters, unarmed transport helicopters, armoured vehicle launched bridges, armoured personnel carrier look-alikes and armoured infantry fighting vehicle look-alikes that are within the area of application, except for those that are held by organisations designed and structured to perform in peacetime internal security functions or that meet any of the exceptions set forth in Article III.

(S) The terms "armoured personnel carrier look-alike" and "armoured infantry fighting vehicle look-alike" mean an armoured vehicle based on the same chassis as, and externally similar to, an armoured personnel carrier or armoured infantry fighting vehicle, respectively, which does not have a cannon or gun of 20 millimetres calibre or greater and which has been constructed or modified in such a way as not to permit the transportation of a combat infantry squad. Taking into account the provisions of the Geneva Convention "For the Amelioration of the Conditions of the Wounded and Sick in Armed Forces in the Field" of 12 August 1949 that confer a special status on ambulances, armoured personnel carrier ambulances shall not be deemed armoured combat vehicles or armoured personnel carrier look-alikes.

(T) The term "reduction site" means a clearly designated location where the reduction of conventional armaments and equipment limited by the Treaty in accordance with Article VIII takes place.

(U) The term "reduction liability" means the number in each category of conventional armaments and equipment limited by the Treaty that a State Party commits itself to reduce during the period of 40 months following the entry into force of this Treaty in order to ensure compliance with Article VII.

2. Existing types of conventional armaments and equipment subject to the Treaty are listed in the Protocol on Existing Types. The lists of existing types shall be periodically updated in accordance with Article XVI, paragraph 2, subparagraph (D) and Section IV of the Protocol on Existing Types. Such updates to the existing types lists shall not be deemed amendments to this Treaty.

3. The existing types of combat helicopters listed in the Protocol on Existing Types shall be categorised in accordance with Section I of the Protocol on Helicopter Recategorisation.

Article III

1. For the purposes of this Treaty, the States Parties shall apply the following counting rules:

All battle tanks, armoured combat vehicles, artillery, combat aircraft and attack helicopters, as defined in Article II, within the area of application shall be subject to the numerical limitations and other provisions set forth in Articles IV, V and VI, with the exception of those which in a manner consistent with a State Party's normal practices:

(A) are in the process of manufacture, including manufacturing-related testing;

(B) are used exclusively for the purposes of research and development;

(C) belong to historical collections;

(D) are awaiting disposal, having been decommissioned from service in accordance with the provisions of Article IX;

(E) are awaiting, or are being refurbished for, export or re-export and are temporarily retained within the area of application. Such battle tanks, armoured combat vehicles, artillery, combat aircraft and attack helicopters shall be located elsewhere than at sites declared under the terms of Section V of the Protocol on Information Exchange or at no more than 10 such declared sites which shall have been notified in the previous year's annual information exchange. In the latter case, they shall be separately distinguishable from conventional armaments and equipment limited by the Treaty;

(F) are, in the case of armoured personnel carriers, armoured infantry fighting vehicles, heavy armament combat vehicles or multi-purpose attack helicopters, held by organisations designed and structured to perform in peacetime internal security functions; or

(G) are in transit through the area of application from a location outside the area of application to a final destination outside the area of application, and are in the area of application for no longer than a total of seven days.

2. If, in respect of any such battle tanks, armoured combat vehicles, artillery, combat aircraft attack helicopters, the notification of which is required under Section IV of the Protocol on Information Exchange, a State Party notifies an unusually high number in more than two successive annual information exchanges, it shall explain the reasons in the Joint Consultative Group, if so requested.

Article IV

1. Within the area of application, as defined in Article II, each State Party shall limit and, as necessary, reduce its battle tanks, armoured combat vehicles, artillery, combat aircraft and attack helicopters so that, 40 months after entry into force of this Treaty and thereafter, for the group of States Parties to which it belongs, as defined in Article II, the aggregate numbers do not exceed:

(A) 20,000 battle tanks, of which no more than 16,500 shall be in active units;

(B) 30,000 armoured combat vehicles, of which no more than 27,300 shall be in active units. Of the 30,000 armoured combat vehicles, no more than 18,000 shall be armoured infantry fighting vehicles and heavy armament combat vehicles; of armoured infantry fighting vehicles and heavy armament combat vehicles, no more than 1,500 shall be heavy armament combat vehicles;

(C) 20,000 pieces of artillery, of which no more than 17,000 shall be in active units;

(D) 6,800 combat aircraft; and

(E) 2,000 attack helicopters.

Battle tanks, armoured combat vehicles and artillery not in active units shall be placed in designated permanent storage sites, as defined in Article II, and shall be located only in the area described in paragraph 2 of this Article. Such designated permanent storage sites may also be located in that part of the territory of the Union of Soviet Socialist Republics comprising the Odessa Military District and the southern part of the Leningrad Military District. In the Odessa Military District, no more than 400 battle tanks and no more than 500 pieces of artillery may be thus stored. In the southern part of the Leningrad Military District, no more than 600 battle tanks, no more than 800 armoured combat vehicles, including no more than 300 armoured combat vehicles of any type with the remaining number consisting of armoured personnel carriers, and no more than 400 pieces of artillery may be thus stored. The southern part of the Leningrad Military District is understood to mean the territory within that military district south of the line East-West 60 degrees 15 minutes northern latitude.

2. Within the area consisting of the entire land territory in Europe, which includes all the European island territories, of the Kingdom of Belgium, the Czech and Slovak Federal Republic, the Kingdom of Denmark including the Faroe Islands, the French Republic, the Federal Republic of Germany, the Republic of Hungary, the Italian Republic, the Grand Duchy of Luxembourg, the Kingdom of the Netherlands, the Republic of Poland, the Portuguese Republic including the islands of Azores and Madeira, the Kingdom of Spain including the Canary Islands, the United Kingdom of Great Britain and Northern Ireland and that part of the territory of the Union of Soviet Socialist Republics west of the Ural Mountains comprising the Baltic, Byelorussian, Carpathian, Kiev, Moscow and Volga-Ural Military Districts, each State Party shall limit and, as necessary, reduce its battle tanks, armoured combat vehicles and artillery so that, 40 months after entry into force of this Treaty and thereafter, for the group of States Parties to which it belongs the aggregate numbers do not exceed:

(A) 15,300 battle tanks, of which no more than 11,800 shall be in active units;

(B) 24,100 armoured combat vehicles, of which no more than 21,400 shall be in active units;

(C) 14,000 pieces of artillery, of which no more than 11,000 shall be in active units.

3. Within the area consisting of the entire land territory in Europe, which includes all the European island territories, of the Kingdom of Belgium, the Czech and Slovak Federal Republic, the Kingdom of Denmark including the Faroe Islands, the French Republic, the Federal Republic of Germany, the Republic of Hungary, the Italian Republic, the Grand Duchy of Luxembourg, the Kingdom of the Netherlands, the Republic of Poland, the United Kingdom of Great Britain and Northern Ireland and that part of the territory of the Union of Soviet Socialist Republics comprising the Baltic, Byelorussian, Carpathian and Kiev Military Districts, each State Party shall limit and, as necessary, reduce its battle tanks, armoured combat vehicles and artillery so that, 40 months after entry into force of this Treaty and thereafter, for the group of States Parties to which it belongs the aggregate numbers in active units do not exceed:

(A) 10,300 battle tanks;

(B) 19,260 armoured combat vehicles; and

(C) 9,100 pieces of artillery; and

(D) in the Kiev Military District, the aggregate numbers in active units and designated permanent storage sites together shall not exceed:

(1) 2,250 battle tanks;

(2) 2,500 armoured combat vehicles; and

(3) 1,500 pieces of artillery.

4. Within the area consisting of the entire land territory in Europe, which includes all the European island territories, of the Kingdom of Belgium, the Czech and Slovak Federal Republic, the Federal Republic of Germany, the Republic of Hungary, the Grand Duchy of Luxembourg, the Kingdom of the Netherlands and the Republic of Poland, each State Party shall limit and, as necessary, reduce its battle tanks, armoured combat vehicles and artillery so that, 40 months after entry into force of this Treaty and thereafter, for the group of States Parties to which it belongs the aggregate numbers in active units do not exceed:

(A) 7,500 battle tanks;

(B) 11,250 armoured combat vehicles; and

(C) 5,000 pieces of artillery.

5. States Parties belonging to the same group of States Parties may locate battle tanks, armoured combat vehicles and artillery in active units in each of the areas described in this Article and Article V, paragraph 1, subparagraph (A) up to the numerical limitations applying in that area, consistent with the maximum levels for holdings notified pursuant to Article VII and provided that no State Party stations conventional armed forces on the territory of another State Party without the agreement of that State Party.

6. If a group of States Parties' aggregate numbers of battle tanks, armoured combat vehicles and artillery in active units within the area described in paragraph 4 of this Article are less than the numerical limitations set forth in paragraph 4 of this Article, and provided that no State Party is thereby prevented from reaching its maximum levels for holdings notified in accordance with Article VII, paragraphs 2, 3 and 5, then amounts equal to the difference between the aggregate numbers in each of the categories of battle tanks, armoured combat vehicles and artillery and the specified numerical limitations for that area may be located by States Parties belonging to that group of States Parties in the area described in paragraph 3 of this Article, consistent with the numerical limitations specified in paragraph 3 of this Article.

Article V

1. To ensure that the security of each State Party is not affected adversely at any stage:

(A) within the area consisting of the entire land territory in Europe, which includes all the European island territories, of the Republic of Bulgaria, the Hellenic Republic, the Republic of Iceland, the Kingdom of Norway, Romania, the part of the Republic of Turkey within the area of application and that part of the Union of Soviet Socialist Republics comprising the Leningrad, Odessa, Transcaucasus and North Caucasus Military Districts, each State Party shall limit and, as necessary, reduce its battle tanks, armoured combat vehicles and artillery so that, 40 months after entry into force of this Treaty and thereafter, for the group of States Parties to which it belongs the aggregate numbers in active units do not exceed the difference between the overall numerical limitations set forth in Article IV, paragraph 1 and those in Article IV, paragraph 2, that is:

(1) 4,700 battle tanks;

(2) 5,900 armoured combat vehicles; and

(3) 6,000 pieces of artillery;

(B) notwithstanding the numerical limitations set forth in subparagraph (A) of this paragraph, a State

Party or States Parties may on a temporary basis deploy into the territory belonging to the members of the same group of States Parties within the area described in subparagraph (A) of this paragraph additional aggregate numbers in active units for each group of States Parties not to exceed:

(1) 459 battle tanks;

(2) 723 armoured combat vehicles; and

(3) 420 pieces of artillery; and

(C) provided that for each group of States Parties no more than one-third of each of these additional aggregate numbers shall be deployed to any State Party with territory within the area described in subparagraph (A) of this paragraph, that is:

(1) 153 battle tanks;

(2) 241 armoured combat vehicles; and

(3) 140 pieces of artillery.

2. Notification shall be provided to all other States Parties no later than at the start of the deployment by the State Party or States Parties conducting the deployment and by the recipient State Party or States Parties, specifying the total number in each category of battle tanks, armoured combat vehicles and artillery deployed. Notification also shall be provided to all other States Parties by the State Party or States Parties conducting the deployment and by the recipient State Party or States Parties within 30 days of the withdrawal of those battle tanks, armoured combat vehicles and artillery that were temporarily deployed.

Article VI

With the objective of ensuring that no single State Party possesses more than approximately one-third of the conventional armaments and equipment limited by the Treaty within the area of application, each State Party shall limit and, as necessary, reduce its battle tanks, armoured combat vehicles, artillery, combat aircraft and attack helicopters so that, 40 months after entry into force of this Treaty and thereafter, the numbers within the area of application for that State Party do not exceed:

(A) 13,300 battle tanks;

(B) 20,000 armoured combat vehicles;

(C) 13,700 pieces of artillery;

(D) 5,150 combat aircraft; and

(E) 1,500 attack helicopters.

Article VIII

1. The numerical limitations set forth in Articles IV, V and VI shall be achieved only by means of reduction in accordance with the Protocol on Reduction, the Protocol on Helicopter Recategorisation,

the Protocol on Aircraft Reclassification, the Footnote to Section I, paragraph 2, subparagraph (A) of the Protocol on Existing Types and the Protocol on Inspection.

2. The categories of conventional armaments and equipment subject to reductions are battle tanks armoured combat vehicles, artillery, combat aircraft and attack helicopters. The specific types are listed in the Protocol on Existing Types.

(A) Battle tanks and armoured combat vehicles shall be reduced by destruction, conversion for non-military purposes, placement on static display, use as ground targets, or, in the case of armoured personnel carriers, modification in accordance with the Footnote to Section I, paragraph 2, subparagraph (A) of the Protocol on Existing Types.

(B) Artillery shall be reduced by destruction or placement on static display, or, in the case of self-propelled artillery, by use as ground targets.

(C) Combat aircraft shall be reduced by destruction, placement on static display, use for ground instructional purposes, or, in the case of specific models or versions of combat-capable trainer aircraft, reclassification into unarmed trainer aircraft.

(D) Specialised attack helicopters shall be reduced by destruction, placement on static display, or use for ground instructional purposes.

(E) Multi-purpose attack helicopters shall be reduced by destruction, placement on static display, use for ground instructional purposes, or recategorisation.

3. Conventional armaments and equipment limited by the Treaty shall be deemed to be reduced upon execution of the procedures set forth in the Protocols listed in paragraph 1 of this Article and upon notification as required by these Protocols. Armaments and equipment so reduced shall no longer be counted against the numerical limitations set forth in Articles IV, V and VI.

4. Reductions shall be effected in three phases and completed no later than 40 months after entry into force of this Treaty, so that:

(A) by the end of the first reduction phase, that is, no later than 16 months after entry into force of this Treaty, each State Party shall have ensured that at least 25 percent of its reduction liability in each of the categories of conventional armaments and equipment limited by the Treaty has been reduced;

(B) by the end of the second reduction phase, that is, no later than 28 months after entry into force of this Treaty, each State Party shall have ensured that at least 60 percent of its total reduction liability in each of the categories of conventional armaments and equipment limited by the Treaty has been reduced;

(C) by the end of the third reduction phase, that is, no later than 40 months after entry into force of this Treaty, each State Party shall have reduced its total reduction liability in each of the categories of conventional armaments and equipment limited by the Treaty. States Parties carrying out conversion for non-military purposes shall have ensured that the conversion of all battle tanks in accordance with Section VIII of the Protocol on Reduction shall have been completed by the end of the third reduction phase; and

(D) armoured combat vehicles deemed reduced by reason of having been partially destroyed in accordance with Section VIII, paragraph 6 of the Protocol on Reduction shall have been fully converted for non-military purposes, or destroyed in accordance with Section IV of the Protocol on Reduction, no later than 64 months after entry into force of this Treaty.

5. Conventional armaments and equipment limited by the Treaty to be reduced shall have been declared present within the area of application in the exchange of information at signature of this Treaty.

6. No later than 30 days after entry into force of this Treaty, each State Party shall provide notification to all other States Parties of its reduction liability.

7. Except as provided for in paragraph 8 of this Article, a State Party's reduction liability in each category shall be no less than the difference between its holdings notified, in accordance with the Protocol on Information Exchange, at signature or effective upon entry into force of this Treaty, whichever is the greater, and the maximum levels for holdings it notified pursuant to Article VII.

8. Any subsequent revision of a State Party's holdings notified pursuant to the Protocol on Information Exchange or of its maximum levels for holdings notified pursuant to Article VII shall be reflected by a notified adjustment to its reduction liability. Any notification of a decrease in a State Party's reduction liability shall be preceded or accompanied by either a notification of a corresponding increase in holdings not exceeding the maximum levels for holdings notified pursuant to Article VII by one or more States Parties belonging to the same group of States Parties, or a notification

of a corresponding increase in the reduction liability of one or more such States Parties.

9. Upon entry into force of this Treaty, each State Party shall notify all other States Parties, in accordance with the Protocol on Information Exchange, of the locations of its reduction sites, including those where the final conversion of battle tanks and armoured combat vehicles for non-military purposes will be carried out.

10. Each State Party shall have the right to designate as many reduction sites as it wishes, to revise without restriction its designation of such sites and to carry out reduction and final conversion simultaneously at a maximum of 20 sites. States Parties shall have the right to share or co-locate reduction sites by mutual agreement.

11. Notwithstanding paragraph 10 of this Article, during the baseline validation period, that is, the interval between entry into force of this Treaty and 120 days after entry into force of this Treaty, reduction shall be carried out simultaneously at no more than two reduction sites for each State Party.

12. Reduction of conventional armaments and equipment limited by the Treaty shall be carried out at reduction sites, unless otherwise specified in the Protocols listed in paragraph 1 of this Article, within the area of application.

13. The reduction process, including the results of the conversion of conventional armaments and equipment limited by the Treaty for non-military purposes both during the reduction period and in the 24 months following the reduction period, shall be subject to inspection, without right of refusal, in accordance with the Protocol on Inspection.

Article IX

1. Other than removal from service in accordance with the provisions of Article VIII, battle tanks, armoured combat vehicles, artillery, combat aircraft and attack helicopters within the area of application shall be removed from service only by decommissioning, provided that:

(A) such conventional armaments and equipment limited by the Treaty are decommissioned and awaiting disposal at no more than eight sites which shall be notified as declared sites in accordance with the Protocol on Information Exchange and shall be identified in such notifications as holding areas for decommissioned conventional armaments and equipment limited by the Treaty. If sites containing conventional armaments and equipment limited by the Treaty decommissioned from service also contain any other conventional armaments and equipment subject to the Treaty, the decommissioned conventional armaments and equipment limited by the Treaty shall be separately distinguishable; and

(B) the numbers of such decommissioned conventional armaments and equipment limited by the Treaty do not exceed, in the case of any individual State Party, one percent of its notified holdings of conventional armaments and equipment limited by the Treaty, or a total of 250, whichever is greater, of which no more than 200 shall be battle tanks, armoured combat vehicles and pieces of artillery, and no more than 50 shall be attack helicopters and combat aircraft.

2. Notification of decommissioning shall include the number and type of conventional armaments and equipment limited by the Treaty decommissioned and the location of decommissioning and shall be provided to all other States Parties in accordance with Section IX, paragraph 1, subparagraph (B) of the Protocol on Information Exchange.

Article X

1. Designated permanent storage sites shall be notified in accordance with the Protocol on Information Exchange to all other States Parties by the State Party to which the conventional armaments and equipment limited by the Treaty contained at designated permanent storage sites belong. The notification shall include the designation and location, including geographic coordinates, of designated permanent storage sites and the numbers by type of each category of its conventional armaments and equipment limited by the Treaty at each such storage site.

2. Designated permanent storage sites shall contain only facilities appropriate for the storage and maintenance of armaments and equipment (e.g., warehouses, garages, workshops and associated stores as well as other support accommodation). Designated permanent storage sites shall not contain firing ranges or training areas associated with conventional armaments and equipment limited by the Treaty. Designated permanent storage sites shall contain only armaments and equipment belonging to the conventional armed forces of a State Party.

3. Each designated permanent storage site shall have a clearly defined physical boundary that shall consist of a continuous perimeter fence at least 1.5 metres in height. The perimeter fence shall have no more than three gates providing the sole means of entrance and exit for armaments and equipment.

4. Conventional armaments and equipment limited by the Treaty located within designated permanent storage sites shall be counted as conventional armaments and equipment limited by the Treaty not in active units, including when they are temporarily removed in accordance with paragraphs 7, 8, 9 and 10 of this Article. Conventional armaments and equipment limited by the Treaty in storage other than in designated permanent storage sites shall be counted as conventional armaments and equipment limited by the Treaty in active units.

5. Active units or formations shall not be located within designated permanent storage sites, except as provided for in paragraph 6 of this Article.

6. Only personnel associated with the security or operation of designated permanent storage sites, or the maintenance of the armaments and equipment stored therein, shall be located within the designated permanent storage sites.

7. For the purpose of maintenance, repair or modification of conventional armaments and equipment limited by the Treaty located within designated permanent storage sites, each State Party shall have the right, without prior notification, to remove from and retain outside designated permanent storage sites simultaneously up to 10 percent, rounded up to the nearest even whole number, of the notified holdings of each category of conventional armaments and equipment limited by the Treaty in each designated permanent storage site, or 10 items of the conventional armaments and equipment limited by the Treaty in each category in each designated permanent storage site, whichever is less.

8. Except as provided for in paragraph 7 of this Article, no State Party shall remove conventional armaments and equipment limited by the Treaty from designated permanent storage sites unless notification has been provided to all other States Parties at least 42 days in advance of such removal. Notification shall be given by the State Party to which the conventional armaments and equipment limited by the Treaty belong. Such notification shall specify:

(A) the location of the designated permanent storage site from which conventional armaments and equipment limited by the Treaty are to be removed and the numbers by type of conventional armaments and equipment limited by the Treaty of each category to be removed;

(B) the dates of removal and return of conventional armaments and equipment limited by the Treaty; and

(C) the intended location and use of conventional armaments and equipment limited by the Treaty while outside the designated permanent storage site.

9. Except as provided for in paragraph 7 of this Article, the aggregate numbers of conventional armaments and equipment limited by the Treaty removed from and retained outside designated permanent storage sites by States Parties belonging to the same group of States Parties shall at no time exceed the following levels:

(A) 550 battle tanks;

(B) 1,000 armoured combat vehicles; and

(C) 300 pieces of artillery.

10. Conventional armaments and equipment limited by the Treaty removed from designated permanent storage sites pursuant to paragraphs 8 and 9 of this Article shall be returned to designated permanent storage sites no later than 42 days after their removal, except for those items of conventional armaments and equipment limited by the Treaty removed for industrial rebuild. Such items shall be returned to designated permanent storage sites immediately on completion of the rebuild.

11. Each State Party shall have the right to replace conventional armaments and equipment limited by the Treaty located in designated permanent storage sites. Each State Party shall notify all other States Parties, at the beginning of replacement, of the number, location, type and disposition of conventional armaments and equipment limited by the Treaty being replaced.

Article XI

1. Each State Party shall limit its armoured vehicle launched bridges so that, 40 months after entry into force of this Treaty and thereafter, for the group of States Parties to which it belongs the aggregate number of armoured vehicle launched bridges in active units within the area of application does not exceed 740.

2. All armoured vehicle launched bridges within the area of application in excess of the aggregate number specified in paragraph 1 of this Article for each group of States Parties shall be placed in designated permanent storage sites, as defined in Article II. When armoured vehicle launched bridges are placed in a designated permanent storage site, either on their own or together with conventional armaments and equipment limited by the Treaty, Article X, paragraphs 1 to 6 shall apply to armoured vehicle launched bridges as well as to conventional armaments and equipment limited by the Treaty.

Armoured vehicle launched bridges placed in designated permanent storage sites shall not be considered as being in active units.

3. Except as provided for in paragraph 6 of this Article, armoured vehicle launched bridges may be removed, subject to the provisions of paragraphs 4 and 5 of this Article, from designated permanent storage sites only after notification has been provided to all other States Parties at least 42 days prior to such removal. This notification shall specify:

(A) the locations of the designated permanent storage sites from which armoured vehicle launched bridges are to be removed and the numbers of armoured vehicle launched bridges to be removed from each such site;

(B) the dates of removal of armoured vehicle launched bridges from and return to designated permanent storage sites; and

(C) the intended use of armoured vehicle launched bridges during the period of their removal from designated permanent storage sites.

4. Except as provided for in paragraph 6 of this Article, armoured vehicle launched bridges removed from designated permanent storage sites shall be returned to them no later than 42 days after the actual date of removal.

5. The aggregate number of armoured vehicle launched bridges removed from and retained outside of designated permanent storage sites by each group of States Parties shall not exceed 50 at any one time.

6. States Parties shall have the right, for the purpose of maintenance or modification, to remove and have outside of designated permanent storage sites simultaneously up to 10 percent, rounded up to the nearest even whole number, of their notified holdings of armoured vehicle launched bridges in each designated permanent storage site, or 10 armoured vehicle launched bridges from each designated permanent storage site, whichever is less.

7. In the event of natural disasters involving flooding or damage to permanent bridges, States Parties shall have the right to withdraw armoured vehicle launched bridges from designated permanent storage sites. Notification to all other States Parties of such withdrawals shall be given at the time of withdrawal.

Article XII

1. Armoured infantry fighting vehicles held by organisations of a State Party designed and structured to perform in peacetime internal security functions, which are not structured and organised for ground

combat against an external enemy, are not limited by this Treaty. The foregoing notwithstanding, in order to enhance the implementation of this Treaty and to provide assurance that the number of such armaments held by such organisations shall not be used to circumvent the provisions of this Treaty, any such armaments in excess of 1,000 armoured infantry fighting vehicles assigned by a State Party to organisations designed and structured to perform in peacetime internal security functions shall constitute a portion of the permitted levels specified in Articles IV, V and VI. No more than 600 such armoured infantry fighting vehicles of a State Party, assigned to such organisations, may be located in that part of the area of application described in Article V, paragraph 1, subparagraph (A). Each State Party shall further ensure that such organisations refrain from the acquisition of combat capabilities in excess of those necessary for meeting internal security requirements.

2. A State Party that intends to reassign battle tanks, armoured infantry fighting vehicles, artillery, combat aircraft, attack helicopters and armoured vehicle launched bridges in service with its conventional armed forces to any organisation of that State Party not a part of its conventional armed forces shall notify all other States Parties no later than the date such reassignment takes effect. Such notification shall specify the effective date of the reassignment, the date such equipment is physically transferred, as well as the numbers, by type, of the conventional armaments and equipment limited by the Treaty being reassigned.

Article XIII

1. For the purpose of ensuring verification of compliance with the provisions of this Treaty, each State Party shall provide notifications and exchange information pertaining to its conventional armaments and equipment in accordance with the Protocol on Information Exchange.

2. Such notifications and exchange of information shall be provided in accordance with Article XVII.

3. Each State Party shall be responsible for its own information; receipt of such information and of notifications shall not imply validation or acceptance of the information provided.

Article XIV

1. For the purpose of ensuring verification of compliance with the provisions of this Treaty, each State Party shall have the right to conduct, and the obligation to accept, within the area of application,

inspections in accordance with the provisions of the Protocol on Inspection.

2. The purpose of such inspections shall be:

(A) to verify, on the basis of the information provided pursuant to the Protocol on Information Exchange, the compliance of States Parties with the numerical limitations set forth in Articles IV, V and VI;

(B) to monitor the process of reduction of battle tanks, armoured combat vehicles, artillery, combat aircraft and attack helicopters carried out at reduction sites in accordance with Article VIII and the Protocol on Reduction: and

(C) to monitor the certification of recategorised multi-purpose attack helicopters and reclassified combat-capable trainer aircraft carried out in accordance with the Protocol on Helicopter Recategorisation and the Protocol on Aircraft Reclassification, respectively

3. No State Party shall exercise the rights set forth in paragraphs 1 and 2 of this Article in respect of States Parties which belong to the group of States Parties to which it belongs in order to elude the objectives of the verification regime.

4. In the case of an inspection conducted jointly by more than one State Party, one of them shall be responsible for the execution of the provisions of this Treaty.

5. The number of inspections pursuant to Sections VII and VIII of the Protocol on Inspection which each State Party shall have the right to conduct and the obligation to accept during each specified time period shall be determined in accordance with the provisions of Section II of that Protocol.

6. Upon completion of the 120-day residual level validation period, each State Party shall have the right to conduct, and each State Party with territory within the area of application shall have the obligation to accept, an agreed number of aerial inspections within the area of application. Such agreed numbers and other applicable provisions shall be developed during negotiations referred to in Article XVIII.

Article XV

1. For the purpose of ensuring verification of compliance with the provisions of this Treaty, a State Party shall have the right to use, in addition to the procedures referred to in Article XIV, national or multinational technical means of verification at its disposal in a manner consistent with generally recognised principles of international law.

2. A State Party shall not interfere with national or multinational technical means of verification of another State Party operating in accordance with paragraph 1 of this Article.

3. A State Party shall not use concealment measures that impede verification of compliance with the provisions of this Treaty by national or multinational technical means of verification of another State Party operating in accordance with paragraph 1 of this Article. This obligation does not apply to cover or concealment practices associated with normal personnel training, maintenance or operations involving conventional armaments and equipment limited by the Treaty.

Article XVI

1. To promote the objectives and implementation of the provisions of this Treaty, the States Parties hereby establish a Joint Consultative Group.

2. Within the framework of the Joint Consultative Group, the States Parties shall:

(A) address questions relating to compliance with or possible circumvention of the provisions of this Treaty;

(B) seek to resolve ambiguities and differences of interpretation that may become apparent in the way this Treaty is implemented;

(C) consider and, if possible, agree on measures to enhance the viability and effectiveness of this Treaty;

(D) update the lists contained in the Protocol on Existing Types, as required by Article II, paragraph 2;

(E) resolve technical questions in order to seek common practices among the States Parties in the way this Treaty is implemented;

(F) work out or revise, as necessary, rules of procedure, working methods, the scale of distribution of expenses of the Joint Consultative Group and of conferences convened under this Treaty and the distribution of costs of inspections between or among States Parties;

(G) consider and work out appropriate measures to ensure that information obtained through exchanges of information among the States Parties or as a result of inspections pursuant to this Treaty is used solely for the purposes of this Treaty, taking into account the particular requirements of each State Party in respect of safeguarding information which that State Party specifies as being sensitive;

(H) consider, upon the request of any State Party, any matter that a State Party wishes to propose for examination by any conference to be convened in accordance with Article XXI; such consideration shall not prejudice the right of any State Party to resort to the procedures set forth in Article XXI; and

(I) consider matters of dispute arising out of the implementation of this Treaty.

3. Each State Party shall have the right to raise before the Joint Consultative Group, and have placed on its agenda, any issue relating to this Treaty.

4. The Joint Consultative Group shall take decisions or make recommendations by consensus. Consensus shall be understood to mean the absence of any objection by any representative of a State Party to the taking of a decision or the making of a recommendation.

5. The Joint Consultative Group may propose amendments to this Treaty for consideration and confirmation in accordance with Article XX. The Joint Consultative Group may also agree on improvements to the viability and effectiveness of this Treaty, consistent with its provisions. Unless such improvements relate only to minor matters of an administrative or technical nature, they shall be subject to consideration and confirmation in accordance with Article XX before they can take effect.

6. Nothing in this Article shall be deemed to prohibit or restrict any State Party from requesting information from or undertaking consultations with other States Parties on matters relating to this Treaty and its implementation in channels or fora other than the Joint Consultative Group.

7. The Joint Consultative Group shall follow the procedures set forth in the Protocol on the Joint Consultative Group.

Article XIX

1. This Treaty shall be of unlimited duration. It may be supplemented by a further treaty.

[Signatures]

[U.S. Arms Control and Disarmament Agency, *Treaty on Conventional Armed Forces in Europe, Paris, 19 November 1990* (Washington, D.C., 1991)]

Demilitarization, Denuclearization, and Neutralization

$\bigcirc$

See also Demilitarization and Neutralization Through World War II *and* Nuclear-Weapon-Free Zones. *Entries that are the subjects of essays in Volumes I and II are marked with asterisks.*

Demilitarization, or geographic disarmament, is perhaps the oldest of arms control techniques; certainly it has been the most widely practiced throughout history. In combination with denuclearization and neutralization, it has been employed for several purposes, among them: (1) to put "space" between armed forces, especially along a frontier, and thereby reduce the possibility of an accidental clash; (2) to remove fortifications from an area and thus reduce it as a threat to its neighbors; (3) to prohibit warships from a specific area and thus reduce any perception of a threat; and (4) to prohibit the introduction of nuclear weapons into a specific area.

Early Examples

Peace of Callias (ca. 448 B.C.)

The Peace of Callias was an agreement between Athens and Persia that demilitarized much of the Agean Sea. It was probably concluded in 448 B.C., apparently renewed in 424–423 B.C., and definitely repudiated in 412–411 B.C.

All the Greek cities of Asia are to live under laws of their own making; the satraps of the Persians are not to come nearer to the sea than a three days' journey and no Persian warship is to sail inside of Phaselis [a city of Lycia on the Pamphylian Gulf] or the Cyanean Rocks [at the entrance to the Black Sea at Byzantium]; and if these terms are observed by the king and his generals, the Athenians are not to send troops into the territory over which the king is ruler.

[*Diodorus of Sicily,* trans. by C.H. Oldfather, 12 vols. (Cambridge, Mass., 1946): IV: 383]

Peace of Westphalia (1688)

The Treaty of Münster, Peace of Westphalia, 24 October 1688, ended hostilities between France and the Holy Roman Empire. These articles relate to the defortification of specific areas along the Rhine.

Article LXXXIII. Immediately after the Restitution of Benfeld, the Fortifications of that Place shall be ras'd, and of the Fort Rhinau, which is hard by, as also of Tabern in Alsatia, of the Castle of Hohember and of Newburg on the Rhine: and there shall be in none of those Places any Soldiers or Garison.

Article LXXXIV. The Magistrates and the Inhabitants of the said City of Tabern shall keep an exact Neutrality, and the King's Troops shall freely pass thro' there as often as desir'd. No Forts shall be erected on the Banks of this side the Rhine, from Basle to Philipsburg; nor shall any Endeavours be made to divert the Course of the River, neither on the one side or the other.

Article CXVIII. Finally, that the Troops and Armys of all those who are making War in the Empire, shall be disbanded and discharg'd; only each Party shall send to and keep up as many Men in his own Dominion, as he shall judge necessary for his Security.

[Fred L. Israel, ed., *Major Peace Treaties of Modern Times, 1648–1947* (New York, 1967), vol. 1, pp. 33–34, 45.]

Defortification of Dunkirk (1713–1783)

Across the English Channel, the naval base at Dunkirk—which in wartime threatened vital British sea lanes and loomed as a potential base from which to launch an invasion of England—had been a matter of serious concern to the British since the Hundred Years' War, during which, in 1388, the British seized and burnt the city. In its subsequent checkered history, Dunkirk was occupied by the British, French, and Spanish: in the 16th Century, after occupying the city for many years, the English were expelled in 1558 by the French, who subsequently surrendered it to the Spaniards; in 1646 it was returned to the French who after a few years again returned it to the Spanish; in 1659 the British regained control of the naval base only to have Charles II sell the harbor facilities to the French for 2,500,000 livres in 1662. The harbor and its fortifications were expensive to maintain, requiring a 4,000-man garrison at the cost of nearly 100,000 pounds sterling a year.

Charles's action once again aroused the concern of many Englishmen. Consequently, when considerations of peace arose in 1709, both houses of Parliament asked Queen Anne to make one of the conditions of a peace treaty that of the razing of Dunkirk's fortifications. (The destruction of Dunkirk was stipulated in Article 17 of the preliminary articles agreed to before the ill-fated 1709 conference, and again as Article 4 of the preliminary articles of a general peace arrangement in 1712.) Under terms of the Treaty of Utrecht, signed 12 April 1713, the French agreed to British demands that the Dunkirk base be destroyed.

The Treaty of Utrecht

Article IX. The most *Christian King* [of France] shall take care that all the Fortifications of the City of *Dunkirk* be Razed, that the Harbour be filled up, and that the Sluices or Moles which serve to cleanse the Harbour be Levelled, and that at the said King's own Expence, within the space of Five Months after the Conditions of Peace are Concluded and Signed; that is to say, The Fortifications towards the Sea, within the Space of two Months, and those towards the Land, together with the said Banks, within three Months; on this express Condition also, That the said Fortifications, Harbour, Moles, or Sluices, be never repair'd again. All which shall not however be begun to be ruin'd, 'till after ev'ry Thing is put into his *Christian Majesty's* Hands, which is to giv'n him instead thereof, or as an Equivalent.

[*The Complete History of the Treaty of Utrecht As also that of Gertruydenberg Containing all the Acts, Memorials, Representations, Complaints, Demands, Letters, Speeches, Treaties and other Authentick pieces relating to the Negotiations there to which are added The Treaties of Radstate and Baden* (London: printed for A. Roper and S. Butler, next Bernard's Inn in Helborn, 1715), Pt. 1, II, 105]

His most Christian Majesty Louis XIV of France did not move with the speed required by the terms of the treaty to reduce the fortifications and to demolish the harbor facilities; indeed, he soon was charged with willful evasion of the Treaty of Utrecht. He ordered some 12,000 workmen to begin the "digging of another harbor at Mardyk, a village near Dunkirk, which was intended to be deeper than that which had been filled-up and which was connected by a canal of considerable length." Louis XIV's justification for this new project was that without the canal the surrounding farmland would be flooded.

In 1717, a new agreement—the Treaty of Triple Alliance, between Great Britain, France, and the States General [Netherlands]—clarified and stiffened the 1713 terms.

The Treaty of Triple Alliance

Article IV. The most Christain King, to shew his Inclination to execute what has been formerly agreed to, as well with Respect to *Dunkirk,* as all other Things, which appear'd necessary to the *King of Great Britain,* for the entire Destruction of the Harbour of *Dunkirk,* and to remove all Suspicion, that a new Harbour was design'd near the Canal of *Mardyke,* or to render that Place proper for other Uses, than letting out the Water, which otherwise would drown that Country, engages to execute every Thing which Monsieur *D'Iberville,* [A]mbassador of his most Christian Majesty, long since agreed to at Hampton Court, as it is express'd in the Memorial of the 19th of September 1716, sign'd by the Visount *Townshend* and Mr. *Methuen,* Secretaries of State of *Great Britain,* and by the said Monsieur *D'Iberville.*

[*The Historical Register Containing an Impartial Relation of all Transactions Foreign and Domestick For the Year 1717* (London: printed and sold by H. Meere in Black Fryers, 1718), II, 193]

During the years that followed, the threatening works were demolished, although France still endeavored to protect the countryside. Writing in the Cambridge Modern History, *volume five, a historian has observed that "the Dunkirk Clause, to the importance of which English public feeling had shown itself so alive, made its reappearance in a succession of treaties before the Peace of Versailles in 1783, when France at last obtained its abolition."*

Defortification of Liège (1715)

Following is an excerpt from the Treaty Between Spain, Great Britain, and the Netherlands, for a Barrier for the Netherlands, signed at Antwerp on 15 November 1715.

Article XXVII. The fortifications and all the works of the citadel of Liège, and also those of the chateau of Huy, including all forts and works, shall be razed and demolished, in such a way that they can never be rebuilt or restored. This demolition will of course be carried out at the expense of the state of Liège, which will retain possession of the materials and may sell them and transport them elsewhere. All work will be carried out at the orders and under the direction of the States General, which will send qualified persons to direct the demolitions. Work on the demolitions shall begin immediately after the signing of this treaty and shall be completed in three months, or sooner if possible. The garrisons of the States General shall not leave the places mentioned above until the demolitions have been completed.

Article XXVIII. And for the greater security and fulfillment of this treaty, His Britannic Majesty promises and undertakes to confirm and guarantee it in every particular and article, and hereby so confirms and guarantees it.

[Clive Parry, ed., *The Consolidated Treaty Series* (Dobbs Ferry, N.Y.: Oceana Publications, 1969), vol. 29, pp. 356–357. Trans. by Gay M. Hammerman]

Declaration of Swiss Neutrality (1815)

Act Signed by the Plenipotentiaries of Austria, France, Great Britain, Prussia, and Russia Conveying Recognition and Guarantee of the Perpetual Neutrality of Switzerland and of the Inviolability of its Territory, 20 November 1815.

Switzerland having acceded to the declaration issued on March 20, 1815, at Vienna by the signatory powers of the Treaty of Paris, by act of the Swiss Diet the following May 27, and this accession having been duly communicated to the ministers of the imperial and royal courts, there has since been no barrier to this act of recognition and guarantee of the perpetual neutrality of Switzerland within its new boundaries. The powers judged it proper, however, to delay until this day the signing of the act, because of the changes which the events of the war, and the arrangements that had to be made following it, might bring to the boundaries of Switzerland, and the modifications which also might result from these events and arrangements in the disposition of neighboring territory, to the benefit of Swiss neutrality.

These changes having been determined by the Treaty of Paris of this date, the signatory powers of the Declaration of Vienna of March 20 give, by the present act, a formal and authoritative recognition of the perpetual neutrality of Switzerland, and they guarantee the integrity and inviolability of its territory as defined by its new boundaries, both as they are established by the Congress of Vienna and by the Treaty of Paris of this date and as they shall be later; in accordance with the provisions of the protocol of November 3, an extract from which is attached below, which stipulates the annexation to Switzerland of new territory taken from Savoy, so as to round out the boundaries of Switzerland and make the canton of Geneva no longer an enclave in foreign territory.

The powers equally recognize and guarantee the neutrality of the parts of Savoy designated by the Act of the Congress of Vienna of May 20, 1815, and by the Treaty of Paris of this date, in exactly the terms in which the neutrality of Switzerland is herein guaranteed.

The signatory powers of the declaration of March 20 recognize authoritatively that the neutrality and inviolability of Switzerland, and its independence of all foreign influence, are in the true interest of all Europe.

They declare that no unfavorable conclusion as to the rights of Switzerland, relative to its neutrality and the inviolability of its territory, can or should be drawn from the events that brought about the passage of Allied troops across a portion of Swiss soil. This passage, freely consented to by the cantons in the Convention of May 20, was the necessary result of the adherence of Switzerland to the principles set forth by the signatory powers of the Treaty of Alliance of March 25.

The powers are pleased to recognize that the conduct of Switzerland under those difficult circumstances showed that it knows how to make great sacrifices for the common good and for the support of a cause that all the powers of Europe defended; and finally that Switzerland is worthy to obtain all advantages that are assured to it, whether by the arrangements of the Congress of Vienna, by the Treaty of Paris of this date, or by the present act, to which all the powers of Europe are invited to adhere.

[Great Britain, Foreign Office, *British and Foreign State Papers* (1815–1816), pp. 359–360. Trans. by Gay M. Hammerman]

Rush-Bagot Agreement (1817)

This agreement was effected by an Exchange of Notes Concerning Naval Force on the Great Lakes, 28–29 April 1817.

Washington, April 28, 1817

The Undersigned, His Britannick Majesty's Envoy Extraordinary and Minister Plenipotentiary, has the honour to acquaint Mr. Rush, that having laid before His Majesty's Government the correspondence which passed last year between the Secretary of the Department of State and the Undersigned upon the subject of a proposal to reduce the Naval Force of the respective Countries upon the American Lakes, he has received the commands of His Royal Highness The Prince Regent to acquaint the Government of the United States, that His Royal Highness is willing to accede to the proposition made to the Undersigned by the Secretary of the Department of State in his note of the 2d of August last.

His Royal Highness, acting in the name and on the behalf of His Majesty, agrees, that the Naval Force to be maintained upon the American Lakes by His Majesty and the Government of the United States shall henceforth be confined to the following Vessels on each side—that is

On Lake Ontario to one Vessel not exceeding one hundred Tons burthen and armed with one eighteen pound cannon.

On the Upper Lakes to two Vessels not exceeding like burthen each and armed with like force.

On the waters of Lake Champlain to one Vessel not exceeding like burthen and armed with like force.

And His Royal Highness agrees, that all other armed Vessels on these Lakes shall be forthwith dismantled, and that no other Vessels of War shall be there built or armed.

His Royal Highness further agrees, that if either Party should hereafter be desirous of annulling this Stipulation, and should give notice to that effect to the other Party, it shall cease to be binding after the expiration of six months from the date of such notice.

The Undersigned has it in command from His Royal Highness the Prince Regent to acquaint the American Government, that His Royal Highness has issued orders to His Majesty's Officers on the Lakes directing, that the Naval Force so to be limited shall be restricted to such services as will in no respect interfere with the proper duties of the armed vessels of the other Party.

The Undersigned has the honour to renew to Mr. Rush the assurances of his highest consideration.

CHARLES BAGOT

Department of State, April 29, 1817

The Undersigned, acting Secretary of State, has the honor to acknowledge the receipt of Mr. Bagot's note of the 28th of this month, informing him that having laid before the Government of His Britannick Majesty, the correspondence which passed last year between the Secretary of State and himself upon the subject of a proposal to reduce the naval force of the two countries upon the American Lakes, he had received the commands of His Royal Highness The Prince Regent to inform this Government that His Royal Highness was willing to accede to the proposition made by the Secretary of State in his note of the second of August last.

The Undersigned has the honor to express to Mr. Bagot the satisfaction which The President feels at His Royal Highness The Prince Regent's having acceded to the proposition of this Government as contained in the note alluded to. And in further answer to Mr. Bagot's note, the Undersigned, by direction of The President, has the honor to state, that this Government, cherishing the same sentiments expressed in the note of the second of August, agrees, that the naval force to be maintained upon the Lakes by the United States and Great Britain shall, henceforth, be confined to the following vessels on each side, that is:

On Lake Ontario to one vessel not exceeding One Hundred Tons burden, and armed with one eighteen-pound cannon.

On the Upper Lakes to two vessels not exceeding the like burden each, and armed with like force, and on the waters of Lake Champlain to one vessel not exceeding like burden and armed with like force.

And it agrees, that all other armed vessels on these Lakes shall be forthwith dismantled, and that no other vessels of war shall be there built or armed. And it further agrees, that if either party should hereafter be desirous of annulling this stipulation and should give notice to that effect to the other party, it shall cease to be binding after the expiration of six months from the date of such notice.

The Undersigned is also directed by The President to state, that proper orders will be forthwith issued by this Government to restrict the naval force thus limited to such services as will in no respect interfere with the proper duties of the armed vessels of the other party.

The Undersigned eagerly avails himself of this opportunity to tender to Mr. Bagot the assurances of his distinguished consideration and respect.

RICHARD RUSH

[William M. Malloy, ed., *Treaties, Conventions, International Acts, Protocols, and Agreements Between the United States of America and Other Powers, 1776–1909* (Washington, D.C., 1910), pp. 628–630]

Neutralization of Belgium (1831)

Treaty Between Great Britain, Austria, France, Prussia, and Russia, on the One Part, and the Netherlands, on the Other, 19 April 1839

Article I. His Majesty the King of the Netherlands, Grand Duke of Luxemburg, engages to cause to be immediately converted into a Treaty with His Majesty the King of the Belgians, the Articles annexed to the present Act, and agreed upon by common consent, under the auspices of the Courts of Great Britain, Austria, France, Prussia, and Russia.

Article II. Her Majesty the Queen of the United Kingdom of Great Britain and Ireland, His Majesty the Emperor of Austria, King of Hungary and Bohemia, His Majesty the King of the French, His Majesty the King of Prussia, and His Majesty the Emperor of All the Russias, declare that the Articles mentioned in the preceding Article, are considered as having the same force and validity as if they were textually inserted in the present Act, and that they are thus placed under the guarantee of their said Majesties.

Article III. The Union which has existed between Holland and Belgium, in virtue of the Treaty of Vienna of the 31st of May, 1815, is acknowledged by His Majesty the King of the Netherlands, Grand Duke of Luxemburg, to be dissolved.

[Signatures]

ANNEX

Article I. The Belgian Territory shall be composed of the Provinces of South Brabant; Liège; Namur; Hainault; West Flanders; East Flanders; Antwerp; and Limburg; such as they formed part of the United Kingdom of the Netherlands constituted in 1815, with the exception of those Districts of the Province of Limburg which are designated in Article IV.

The Belgian Territory shall, moreover, comprise that part of the Grand Duchy of Luxemburg which is specified in Article II.

[*Article II* designates in detail the part of the Grand Duchy of Luxembourg that is to be annexed to Belgium by the treaty.]

Article III. In return for the cessions made in the preceding Article, there shall be assigned to His Majesty the King of the Netherlands, Grand Duke of Luxemburg, a Territorial Indemnity in the Province of Limburg. . . .

Article V. His Majesty the King of the Netherlands, Grand Duke of Luxemburg, shall come to an Agreement with the Germanic Confederation, and with the Agnates of the House of Nassau, as to the application of the stipulations contained in Articles III and IV, as well as upon all the arrangements which the said Articles may render necessary, either with the above-mentioned Agnates of the House of Nassau, or with the Germanic Confederation.

Article VI. In consideration of the territorial arrangements above stated, each of the two Parties renounces reciprocally and for ever, all pretension to the Territories, Towns, Fortresses, and Places situated within the limits of the possessions of the other Party, such as those limits are described in Articles I, II, and IV.

The said limits shall be marked out in conformity with those Articles, by Belgian and Dutch Commissioners of Demarcation, who shall meet as soon as possible in the town of Maestricht.

Article VII. Belgium, within the limits specified in Articles I, II, and IV, shall form an Independent and perpetually Neutral State. It shall be bound to observe such Neutrality towards all other States.

[The remaining articles deal with drainage and navigation of rivers, and other matters not relevant to Belgian neutrality.]

[Sir Augustus Oakes and R. B. Mowat, eds., *The Great European Treaties of the Nineteenth Century* (Oxford, 1918), pp. 141–145]

Neutralization of Luxemburg (1867)

Treaty between Great Britain, Austria, Belgium, France, Italy, The Netherlands, Prussia, and Russia, relative to the Grand Duchy of Luxemburg, 11 May 1867

Article I. His Majesty the King of the Netherlands, Grand Duke of Luxemburg, maintains the ties which attach the said Grand Duchy to the House of Orange-Nassau, in virtue of the Treaties which placed that State under the Sovereignty of the King Grand Duke, his descendants and successors.

The Rights which the Agnates of the House of Nassau possess with regard to the Succession of the Grand Duchy, in virtue of the same Treaties, are maintained.

The High Contracting Parties accept the present Declaration, and place it upon record.

Article II. The Grand Duchy of Luxemburg, within the Limits determined by the Act annexed to the Treaties of the 19th April, 1839, under the Guarantee of the Courts of Great Britain, Austria, France, Prussia, and Russia, shall henceforth form a perpetually Neutral State. It shall be bound to observe the same Neutrality towards all other States.

The High Contracting Parties engage to respect the principle of Neutrality stipulated by the present Article.

That principle is and remains placed under the sanction of the collective Guarantee of the Powers signing Parties to the present Treaty, with the exception of Belgium, which is itself a Neutral State.

Article III. The Grand Duchy of Luxemburg being Neutralized, according to the terms of the preceding Article, the maintenance or establishment of Fortresses upon its Territory becomes without necessity as well as without object.

In consequence, it is agreed by common consent that the City of Luxemburg, considered in time past, in a military point of view, as a Federal Fortress, shall cease to be a fortified city.

His Majesty the King Grand Duke reserves to himself to maintain in that city the number of troops necesary to provide in it for the maintenance of good order.

Article IV. In conformity with the stipulations contained in Articles II and III, His Majesty the King of Prussia declares that his troops actually in garrison in the Fortress of Luxemburg shall receive orders to proceed to the Evacuation of that place immediately after the exchange of the Ratifications of the present Treaty. The withdrawal of the artillery, munitions, and every object which forms part of the equipment of the said Fortress shall commence simultaneously. During that operation there shall remain in it no more than the number of troops necessary to provide for the safety of the material of war, and to effect the dispatch thereof, which shall be completed within the shortest time possible.

Article V. His Majesty the King Grand Duke, in virtue of the rights of Sovereignty which he exercises over the City and Fortress of Luxemburg, engages, on his part, to take the necessary measures for converting the said Fortress into an open city by means of a demolition which His Majesty shall deem sufficient to fulfill the intentions of the High Contracting Parties expressed in Article III of the present Treaty. The works requisite for that purpose shall be commenced immediately after the withdrawal of the garrison. They shall be carried out with all the attention required for the interests of the inhabitants of the city.

His Majesty the King Grand Duke promises, moreover, that the Fortifications of the city of Luxemburg shall not be restored in future, and that no Military Establishment shall be there maintained or created.

Article VI. The Powers signing Parties to the present Treaty recognize that the Dissolution of the Germanic Confederation having equally produced the Dissolution of the ties which united the Duchy of Limburg, collectively with the Grand Duchy of Luxemburg, to the said Confederation, it results therefrom that the relations of which mention is made in Articles III, IV, and V of the Treaty of the 19th April 1839, between the Grand Duchy and certain Territories belonging to the Duchy of Limburg, have ceased to exist, the said Territories continuing to form an integral part of the Kingdom of the Netherlands.

[Sir Augustus Oakes and R. B. Mowat, eds., *The Great European Treaties of the Nineteenth Century* (Oxford, 1918), pp. 260–261]

Black Sea Convention (1856)

The Treaty of Paris, 30 March 1856

Article XI. The Black Sea is Neutralised; its Waters and its Ports, thrown open to the Mercantile Marine of every Nation, are formally and in perpetuity interdicted to the Flag of War, either of the Powers possessing its Coasts, or of any other Power, with the exceptions mentioned in Articles XIV and XIX of the present Treaty.

Article XII. Free from any impediment, the Commerce in the Ports and Waters of the Black Sea shall be subject only to Regulations of Health, Customs, and Police, framed in a spirit favourable to the development of Commercial transactions. In order to afford to the Commercial and Maritime interests of every Nation the security which is desired, Russia and the Sublime Porte will admit Consuls into their Ports situed upon the Coast of the Black Sea, in conformity with the principles of International Law.

Article XIII. The Black Sea being Neutralised according to the terms of Article XI, the maintenance or establishment upon its Coast of Military-Maritime Arsenals becomes alike unnecessary and purposeless; in consequence, His Majesty the Emperor of All the Russias, and His Imperial Majesty the Sultan, engage not to establish or to maintain upon that Coast any Military-Maritime Arsenal.

Article XIV. Their Majesties the Emperor of All the Russias and the Sultan having concluded a Convention for the purpose of settling the Force and the Number of Light Vessels, necessary for the service of their Coasts, which they reserve to themselves to maintain in the Black Sea, that Convention is annexed to the present Treaty, and shall have the same force and validity as if it formed an integral part thereof. It cannot be either annulled or modified without the assent of the Powers signing the present Treaty.

Article XV. The Act of the Congress of Vienna, having established the principles intended to regulate the Navigation of Rivers which separate or traverse different States, the Contracting Powers stipulate among themselves that those principles shall in future be equally applied to the Danube and its Mouths. They declare that its arrangement henceforth forms a part of the Public Law of Europe, and take it under their Guarantee.

The Navigation of the Danube cannot be subjected to any impediment or charge not expressly provided for by the Stipulations contained in the following Articles: in consequence, there shall not be levied any Toll founded solely upon the fact of the Navigation of the River, nor any Duty upon the Goods which may be on board of Vessels. The Regulations of Police and of Quarantine to be established for the safety of the States separated or traversed by that River, shall be so framed as to facilitate, as much as possible, the passage of Vessels. With the exception of such Regulations, no obstacle whatever shall be opposed to Free Navigation.

Article XVI. With a view to carry out the arrangements of the preceding Article, a Commission, in which Great Britain, Austria, France, Prussia, Russia, Sardinia, and Turkey, shall each be represented by one delegate, shall be charged to designate and to cause to be executed the Works necessary below

Isatcha, to clear the Mouths of the Danube, as well as the neighbouring parts of the Sea, from the sands and other impediments which obstruct them, in order to put that part of the River and the said parts of the Sea in the best possible state for Navigation.

In order to cover the Expenses of such Works, as well as of the establishments intended to secure and to facilitate the Navigation at the Mouths of the Danube, fixed Duties, of a suitable rate, settled by the Commission by a majority of votes, may be levied, on the express condition that, in this respect as in every other, the Flags of all Nations shall be treated on the footing of perfect equality.

Article XVII. A Commission shall be established, and shall be composed of delegates of Austria, Bavaria, the Sublime Porte, and Wurtemberg (one for each of those Powers), to whom shall be added Commissioners from the Three Danubian Principalities, whose nomination shall have been approved by the Porte. This Commission, which shall be permanent:

1. Shall prepare Regulations of Navigation and River Police;
2. Shall remove the impediments, of whatever nature they may be, which still prevent the application to the Danube of the Arrangements of the Treaty of Vienna;
3. Shall order and cause to be executed the necessary Works throughout the whole course of the River; and
4. Shall, after the dissolution of the European Commission, see to maintaining the Mouths of the Danube and the neighbouring parts of the Sea in a navigable state.

[Fred L. Israel, ed., *Major Peace Treaties of Modern Times, 1648–1967* (New York, 1967), vol. 2, pp. 949–951]

The Brussels Convention (1890)

The Brussels Convention was signed on 2 July 1890, and it was ratified by the United States on 19 January 1892.

General Act for the Repression of African Slave Trade

Article VIII. The experience of all nations that have intercourse with Africa having shown the pernicious and preponderating part played by fire-arms in operations connected with the slave-trade as well as internal wars between the native tribes; and this same experience having clearly proved that the preservation of the African population whose existence it is the express wish of the powers to protect, is a radical impossibility, if measures restricting the trade in fire-arms and ammunition are not adopted, the powers decide, so far as the present state of their frontiers permits, that the importation of fire-arms, and especially of rifles and improved weapons, as well as of powder, ball and cartridges, is except in the cases and under the conditions provided for in the following Article, prohibited in the territories comprised between the 20th parallel of North latitude and the 22d parallel of South latitude, and extending westward to the Atlantic Ocean and east ward to the Indian Ocean and its dependencies, including the islands adjacent to the coast within 100 nautical miles from the shore.

Article IX. The introduction of fire-arms and ammunition, when there shall be occasion to authorize it in the possessions of the signatory powers that exercise rights of sovereignty or of protectorate in Africa, shall be regulated, unless identical or stricter regulations have already been enforced, in the following manner in the zone defined in Article VIII:

All imported fire-arms shall be deposited, at the cost, risk and peril of the importers, in a public warehouse under the supervision of the State government. No withdrawal of fire-arms or imported ammunition shall take place from such warehouses without the previous authorization of the said government. This authorization shall, except in the cases hereinafter specified, be refused for the withdrawal of all arms for accurate firing, such as rifles, magazine guns, or breech-loaders, whether whole or in detached pieces, their cartridges, caps, or other ammunition intended for them.

In seaports and under conditions affording the needful guarantees, the respective governments may permit private warehouses, but only for ordinary powder and for flint-lock muskets, and to the exclusion of improved arms and ammunition therefor.

Independently of the measures directly taken by governments for the arming of the public force and the organization of their defence, individual exceptions may be allowed in the case of persons furnishing sufficient guarantees that the weapon and ammunition delivered to them shall not be given, assigned or sold to third parties, and for travelers provided with a declaration of their government stating that the weapon and ammunition are intended for their personal defence exclusively.

All arms, in the cases provided for in the preceding paragraph, shall be registered and marked by the supervising authorities, who shall deliver to the persons in question permits to bear arms, stating the name of the bearer and showing the stamp with which the weapon is marked. These permits shall be revocable in case proof is furnished that they have been improperly used, and shall be issued for five years only, but may be renewed.

The above rule as to warehousing shall also apply to gunpowder.

Only flint-lock guns, with unrifled barrels, and common gunpowder known as trade powder, may be withdrawn from the warehouses for sale. At each withdrawal of arms and ammunition of this kind for sale, the local authorities shall determine the regions in which such arms and ammunition may be sold. The regions in which the slave-trade is carried on shall always be excluded. Persons authorized to take arms or powder out of the public warehouses, shall present to the State government, every six months, detailed lists indicating the destinations of the arms and powder sold, as well as the quantities still remaining in the warehouses.

Article X. The Governments shall take all such measures as they may deem necessary to insure as complete a fulfillment as possible of the provisions respecting the importation, sale and transportation of fire-arms and ammunition, as well as to prevent either the entry or exit thereof via their inland frontiers, or the passage thereof to regions where the slave-trade is rife.

The Authorization of transit within the limits of the zone specified in Article VIII shall not be withheld when the arms and ammunition are to pass across the territory of the signatory or adherent power occupying the coast, towards inland territories under the sovereignty or protectorate of another signatory or adherent power, unless this latter power have direct access to the sea through its own territory. If this access be wholly interrupted, the authorization of transit can not be withheld. Any application for transit must be accompanied by a declaration emanating from the government of the power having the inland possessions, and certifying that the said arms and ammunition are not for sale, but are for the use of the authorities of such power, or of the military forces necessary for the protection of the missionary or commercial stations, or of persons mentioned by name in the declaration. Nevertheless, the territorial power of the coast retains the right to stop, exceptionally and provisionally, the transit of improved arms and ammunition across its territory, if, in consequence of inland disturbances or other serious danger, there is ground for fearing lest the dispatch of arms and ammunition may compromise its own safety.

Article XI. The powers shall communicate to one another information relating to the traffic in fire-arms and ammunition, the permits granted, and the measures of repression in force in their respective territories.

Article XII. The powers engage to adopt or to propose to their respective legislative bodies the measures necessary everywhere to secure the punishment of infringers of the prohibitions contained in Articles VIII and IX, and that of their accomplices, besides the seizure and confiscation of the prohibited arms and ammunition, either by fine or imprisonment, or by both of these penalties, in proportion to the importance of the infraction and in accordance with the gravity of each case.

Article XIII. The signatory powers that have possessions in Africa in contact with the zone specified in Article VIII, bind themselves to take the necessary measures for preventing the introduction of fire-arms and ammunition across their inland frontiers into the regions of said zone, at least that of improved arms and cartridges.

[William M. Malloy, ed., *Treaties, Conventions, International Acts, Protocols and Agreements Between the United States of America and Other Powers, 1776–1937,* 4 vols. (Washington, D.C., 1910–1938), vol. 2, pp. 1964–1973]

Straits and Canals

Clayton-Bulwer Treaty, or Panama Canal Treaty (1850)

This treaty was superseded by the Hay-Pauncefote Treaty, 18 November 1901, which gave the U.S. the right to fortify the Panama Canal.

The Convention as to Ship-Canal Connecting Atlantic and Pacific Oceans, 19 April 1850

Article I. The Governments of the United States and Great Britain hereby declare that neither the one nor the other will ever obtain or maintain for itself any exclusive control over the ship-canal; agreeing that neither will ever erect or maintain any fortifications commanding the same, or in the vicinity thereof, or occupy, or fortify, or colonize, or assume or exercise any dominion over Nicaragua, Costa Rica, the Mosquito coast, or any part of Central America; nor will either make use of any protection which either affords or may afford, or any alliance which either has or may have to or with any State or people for the purpose of erecting or maintaining any such fortifications, or of occupying, fortifying, or colonizing Nicaragua, Costa Rica, the Mosquito coast, or any part of Central America, or of assuming or exercising dominion over the same; nor will the United States or Great Britain take advantage of any intimacy, or use any alliance, connection, or influence that either may possess, with any State or Government through whose territory the said canal may pass, for the purpose of acquiring or holding, directly or indirectly, for the citizens or subjects of the one any rights or advantages in regard to commerce or navigation through the said canal which shall not be offered on the same terms to the citizens or subjects of the other.

Article II. Vessels of the United States or Great Britain traversing the said canal shall, in case of war between the contracting parties, be exempted from blockade, detention, or capture by either of the belligerents; and this provision shall extend to such a distance from the two ends of the said canal as may herafter be found expedient to establish. . . .

Article V. The contracting parties further engage that when the said canal shall have been completed they will protect it from interruption, seizure, or unjust confiscation, and that they will guarantee the neutrality thereof, so that the said canal may forever be open and free, and the capital invested therein secure. Nevertheless, the Governments of the United States and Great Britain, in according their protection to the construction of the said canal, and guaranteeing its neutrality and security when completed, always understand that this protection and guarantee are granted conditionally, and may be withdrawn by both Governments, or either Government. . . .

[Malloy, vol. 1, pt. 2, pp. 659–661]

Straits of Magellan Treaty (1881)

Following are excerpts from the treaty between the Argentine Republic and Chile, defining the boundaries between the two countries and establishing the neutrality of the Straits of Magellan. It was signed in Buenos Aires on 23 July 1881.

Article 5. The Straits of Magellan are neutralized, and free navigation thereon insured to the flags of all nations. With a view to guaranteeing this freedom and neutrality, no fortifications nor military defenses will be raised that may clash with that object.

[U.S. Department of State, *Papers Pertaining to the Foreign Relations of the United States, 1881* (Washington, D.C., 1881), p. 12]

The Treaty of Versailles (1919)

Baltic Channel

Article 195. In order to ensure free passage into the Baltic to all nations, Germany shall not erect any fortifications in the area comprised between latitudes 55° 27' N. and 54° 00' N. and longitudes 9° 00' E. and 16° 00' E. of the meridian of Greenwich, nor instal any guns commanding the maritime routes between the North Sea and the Baltic. The fortifications now existing in this area shall be demolished and the guns removed under the supervisions of the Allied Governments and in periods to be fixed by them.

Heligoland

Article 115. The fortifications, military establishments and harbours of the Islands of Heligoland and Dune shall be destroyed under the supervision of the Principal Allied Governments by German labour and at the expense of Germany within a period to be determined by the said Governments.

.　.　.　.　.

These fortifications, military establishments and harbours shall not be reconstructed, nor shall any similar works be constructed in future.

Article 196. All fortified works and fortifications, other than those mentioned in Section XIII (Heligoland) of Part III (Political Clauses for Europe) and in Article 195, now established within fifty kilometres of the German coast or on German islands off that coast shall be considered as of a defensive nature and may remain in their existing condition.

No new fortifications shall be constructed within these limits. The armament of these defences shall not exceed, as regards the number and calibre of guns, those in position at the date of the coming into force of the present Treaty. The German Government shall communicate forthwith particulars thereof to all the European Governments.

.　.　.　.　.

On the expiration of a period of two months from the coming into force of the present Treaty the stocks of ammunition for these guns shall be reduced to and maintained at a maximum figure of fifteen hundred rounds per piece for calibres of 4.1-inch and under, and five hundred rounds per piece for higher calibres.

Left Bank of the Rhine

Article 42. Germany is forbidden to maintain or construct any fortifications either on the left bank of the Rhine or on the right bank to the west of a line drawn 50 kilometres to the east of the Rhine.

Article 43. In the area defined above the maintenance and the assembly of armed forces, either permanently or temporarily, and military manoeuvres of any kind, as well as the upkeep of all permanent works for mobilisation, are in the same way forbidden.

Article 44. In case Germany fails in any manner whatever in the provisions of Articles 42 and 43, she shall be regarded as committing a hostile act against the Powers signatory of the present Treaty and as calculated to disturb the peace of the world.

[U.S. Library of Congress, Legislative Reference Service, *Disarmament and Security: A Collection of Documents, 1919–1955* (Washington, D.C., 1956), pp. 7–8]

Interwar Demilitarization Accords

Spitzbergen Convention (1920)

Treaty between Great Britain, Denmark, France, Italy, Japan, the Netherlands, Norway, Sweden, and the United States of America, relative to the Archipelago of Spitzbergen, 9 February 1920

Article I. The High Contracting Parties undertake to recognise, subject to the stipulations of the present Treaty, the full and absolute sovereignty of Norway over the Archipelago of Spitzbergen, comprising, with Bear Island or BeerenEiland, all the islands situated between 10° and 35° longitude East of Greenwich and between 74° and 81° latitude North, especially West Spitzbergen, North-East Land, Barents Island, Edge Island, Wiche Islands, Hope Island or Hopen-Eiland, and Prince Charles Foreland, together with all islands, great or small, and rocks appertaining thereto.

Article II. Ships and nations of all the High Contracting Parties shall enjoy equally the rights of fishing and hunting in the territories specified in Article I and in their territorial waters.

Norway shall be free to maintain, take or decree suitable measures to ensure the preservation and, if necessary, the reconstitution of the fauna and flora of the said regions, and their territorial waters; it being clearly understood that these measures shall always be applicable equally to the nations of all the High Contracting Parties without any exemption, privilege or favour whatsoever, direct or indirect, to the advantage of any one of them.

Occupiers of land whose rights have been recognised in accordance with the terms of Articles VI and VII will enjoy the exclusive right of hunting on their own land: (1) in the neighborhood of their habitations, houses, stores, factories and installations, constructed for the purpose of developing their property, under conditions laid down by the local police regulations; (2) within a radius of 10 kilometres round the headquarters of their place of business or works; and, in both cases, subject al-

ways to the observance of regulations made by the Norwegian Government in accordance with the conditions laid down in the present Article.

Article III. The nationals of all the High Contracting Parties shall have equal liberty of access and entry for any reason or object whatever to the waters, fjords and ports of the territories specified in Article 1; subject to the observance of local laws and regulations, they may carry on there without impediment all maritime, industrial, mining and commercial operations on a footing of absolute equality.

They shall be admitted under the same conditions of equality to the exercise and practice of all maritime, industrial, mining or commercial enterprises both on land and in the territorial waters, and no monopoly shall be established on any account or for any enterprise whatever.

Notwithstanding any rules relating to coasting trade which may be in force in Norway, ships of the High Contracting Parties going to or coming from the territories specified in Article I shall have the right to put into Norwegian ports on their outward or homeward voyage for the purpose of taking on board or disembarking passengers or cargo going to or coming from the said territories, or for any other purpose.

It is agreed that in every respect and especially with regard to exports, imports and transit traffic, the nations of all the High Contracting Parties, their ships and goods shall not be subject to any charges or restrictions whatever which are not borne by the nationals, ships or goods which enjoy in Norway the treatment of the most favoured nation; Norwegian nationals, ships or goods being for this purpose assimilated to those of the other High Contracting Parties, and not treated more favourably in any respect.

No charge or restriction shall be imposed on the exportation of any goods to the territories of any of the Contracting Powers other or more onerous than on the exportation of similar goods to the territory of any other Contracting Power (including Norway) or to any other destination.

Article IV. All public wireless telegraphy stations established or to be established by or with the authorisation of the Norwegian Government within the territories referred to in Article I shall always be open on a footing of absolute equality to communications from ships of all flags and from nationals of the High Contracting Parties, under the conditions laid down in the Wireless Telegraphy Convention of the 5th July, 1912 or in the subsequent International Convention which may be concluded to replace it.

Subject to international obligations arising out of state of war, owners of landed property shall always be at liberty to establish and use for their own purposes wireless telegraphy installations, which shall be free to communicate on private business with fixed or moving wireless stations, including those on board ships and aircraft.

Article V. The High Contracting Parties recognise the utility of establishing an international meteorological station in the territories specified in Article I, the organisation of which shall form the subject of a subsequent Convention.

Conventions shall also be concluded laying down the conditions under which scientific investigations may be conducted in the said territories.

Article VI. Subject to the provisions of the present Article, acquired rights of nationals of the High Contracting Parties shall be recognised.

Claims arising from taking possession or from occupation of land before the signature of the present Treaty shall be dealt with in accordance with the Annex hereto, which will have the same force and effect as the present Treaty.

Article VII. With regard to methods of acquisition, enjoyment and exercise of the right of ownership of property, including mineral rights, in the territories specified in Article I, Norway undertakes to grant to all nationals of the High Contracting Parties treatment based on complete equality and in conformity with the stipulations of the present Treaty.

Expropriation may be resorted to only on grounds of public utility and on payment of proper compensation.

Article VIII. Norway undertakes to provide for the territories specified in Article I mining regula-

tions which, especially from the point of view of imposts, taxes or charges of any kind, and of general or particular labour conditions, shall exclude all privileges, monopolies or favours for the benefit of the State or of the nationals of any one of the High Contracting Parties, including Norway, and shall guarantee to the paid staff of all categories the remuneration and protection necessary for their physical, moral and intellectual welfare.

Taxes, dues and duties levied shall be devoted exclusively to the said territories and shall not exceed what is required for the object in view.

So far, particularly, as the exportation of minerals is concerned, the Norwegian Government shall have the right to levy an export duty which shall not exceed 1 per cent. of the maximum value of the minerals exported up to 100,000 tons, and beyond that quantity the duty will be proportionately diminished. The value shall be fixed at the end of the navigation season by calculating the average free-on-board price obtained.

Three months before the date fixed for their coming into force, the draft mining regulations shall be communicated by the Norwegian Government to the other Contracting Powers. If during this period one or more of the said Powers propose to modify these regulations before they are applied, such proposals shall be communicated by the Norwegian Government to the other Contracting Powers in order that they may be submitted to examination and the decision of a Commission composed of one representative of each of the said Powers. This Commission shall meet at the invitation of the Norwegian Government and shall come to a decision within a period of three months from the date of its first meeting. Its decisions shall be taken by a majority.

Article IX. Subject to the rights and duties resulting from the admission of Norway to the League of Nations, Norway undertakes not to create nor to allow the establishment of any naval base in the territories specified in Article I and not to construct any fortification in the said territories, which may never be used for warlike purposes.

Article X. Until the recognition by the High Contracting Parties of a Russian Government shall permit Russia to adhere to the present Treaty, Russian nationals and companies shall enjoy the same rights as nationals of the High Contracting Parties.

Claims in the territories specified in Article I which they may have to put forward shall be presented under the conditions laid down in the present Treaty (Article VI and Annex) through the intermediary of the Danish Government, who declare their willingness to lend their good offices for this purpose.

[*British and Foreign State Papers,* vol. 131 (London, 1920), pp. 789–793]

Åland Islands Convention (1921)

The Åland [Aaland] Islands Convention was negotiated through the League of Nations and signed in Geneva on 20 October 1921.

Convention Respecting the Non-Fortification and Neutralization of the Aaland Islands

Article 1. Finland, confirming, to the extent requisite, in so far as she is concerned, the declaration made by Russia in the Convention of the 30th March, 1856, regarding the Aaland Islands, annexed to the Treaty of Paris of the same date, undertakes not to fortify the part of the Finnish archipelago called "the Aaland Islands."

. . . . .

Article 3. No military or naval establishment or base of operations, no military aeronautical establishment or base of operations, and no other installations utilized for war purposes shall be maintained or created in the zone. . . .

Article 4. Subject to the provisions of Article 7, no military, naval or air force of any Power shall enter or remain in the zone. . . ; the manufacture, import, transport and re-export of arms and war material therein are strictly prohibited.

The following provisions shall, however, be applied in time of peace:

(a) In addition to the regular police force necessary for the maintenance of order and public security in the zone, in conformity with the general provisions in force in the Finnish Republic, Finland may, if exceptional circumstances require, send into the zone and keep there temporarily such other armed forces as shall be strictly necessary for the maintenance of order.

(b) Finland also reserves the right for one or two of her light surface warships to visit the islands from time to time, which can, in this case, anchor temporarily in these waters. In addition to these ships, Finland may, if specially important circumstances require, send into the waters of the zone and keep there temporarily other surface vessels, which must in no case exceed a total displacement of 6,000 tons.

The right to enter the archipelago and to anchor there temporarily can be granted by the Finnish Government to only one warship of any other Power.

(c) Finland may fly her military or naval aircraft over the zone, but, except in cases of *force majeure,* landing there is prohibited.

Article 5. The prohibition to warships of entering and remaining in the zone . . . does not restrict the freedom of innocent passage through the territorial waters. Such passage shall remain subject to existing international rules and usages.

Article 6. In time of war, the zone . . . shall be considered as a neutral zone and shall not, directly or indirectly, be used for any purpose connected with military operations.

Nevertheless, in the event of a war effecting the Baltic Sea, it will be permissible for Finland, in order to assure respect for the neutrality of the zone, temporarily to lay mines in its territorial waters, and for this purpose to take such measures of a maritime nature as are strictly necessary.

. . . . .

[Signatures]
[*American Journal of International Law,* Supplement 17 (1923): 1–6]

Defortification of Pacific Islands (1922)

The following excerpt is from the Washington Five-Power Naval Treaty.

Article XIX. The United States, the British Empire and Japan agree that the status quo at the time of the signing of the present Treaty, with regard to fortifications and naval bases, shall be maintained in their respective territories and possessions specified hereunder:

(1) The insular possessions which the United States now holds or may hereafter acquire in the Pacific Ocean, except (a) those adjacent to the coast of the United States, Alaska and the Panama Canal Zone, not including the Aleutian Islands, and (b) the Hawaiian Islands;

(2) Hongkong and the insular possessions which the British Empire now holds or may hereafter acquire in the Pacific Ocean, east of the meridian of 110° east longitude, except (a) those adjacent to the coast of Canada, (b) the Commonwealth of Australia and its Territories, and (c) New Zealand;

(3) The following insular territories and possessions of Japan in the Pacific Ocean, to wit: the Kurile Islands, the Bonin Islands, Amami-Oshima, the Loochoo Islands, Formosa and the Pescadores, and any insular territories or possessions in the Pacific Ocean which Japan may hereafter acquire.

The maintenance of the status quo under the foregoing provisions implies that no new fortifications or naval bases shall be established in the territories and possessions specified; that no measures shall be taken to increase the existing naval facilities for the repair and maintenance of naval forces, and that no increase shall be made in the coast defences of the territories and possessions above specified. This restriction, however, does not preclude such repair and replacement of worn-out weapons and equipment as is customary in naval and military establishments in time of peace.

[U.S. Library of Congress, Legislative Reference Service, *Disarmament and Security: A Collection of Documents, 1919–1955* (Washington, D.C., 1956), p. 16]

Austrian Neutrality (1955)

Following is the official recognition of Austrian neutrality, the Austrian Note of 4 November 1955. This new law was required by the Austrian State Treaty signed 15 May 1955.

The Ambasssador of Austria presents his compliments to the Honorable the Acting Secretary of State and upon instructions of the Austrian Federal Government has the honor to convey the following:

On October 26th 1955 the Austrian Parliament has passed the constitutional law concerning the neutrality of Austria. This law has entered into force on November 5, 1955 and has the following wording:

Article I

(1) For the purpose of the lasting maintenance of her independence externally, and for the purpose of the inviolability of her territory, Austria declares of her own free will her perpetual neutrality. Austria will maintain and defend this with all means at her disposal.

(2) For the security of this purpose in all future times Austria will not join any military alliances and will not permit the establishment of any foreign military bases on her territory....

In bringing this constitutional law to the knowledge of the Government of the United States of America, the Austrian Federal Government has the honor to request that the Government of the United States of America recognize the perpetual neutrality of Austria as defined in the aforementioned law.

Recognition of Austrian Neutrality, U.S. Note of 6 December 1955

The Secretary of State presents his compliments to His Excellency the Ambassador of Austria and has the honor to acknowledge receipt of the note of the Embassy of Austria dated November 14, 1955, informing him that the Austrian Parliament approved on October 26, 1955, the federal constitutional law relative to the neutrality of Austria, which entered into force November 5, 1955.

The Secretary of State has the honor to inform the Austrian Ambassador, in compliance with the request expressed in the note under acknowledgement, that the Government of the United States has taken cognizance of this constitutional law and recognizes the perpetual neutrality of Austria as defined therein.

[U.S. Department of State *Bulletin* (19 December 1955): 1011–1012]

Antarctic Treaty (1959)

The Antarctic Treaty was signed in Washington, D.C., on 1 December 1959, and it entered into force on 23 June 1961.

The Governments of Argentina, Australia, Belgium, Chile, the French Republic, Japan, New Zealand, Norway, the Union of South Africa, the Union of Soviet Socialist Republics, the United Kingdom of Great Britain and Northern Ireland, and the United States of America,

Recognizing that it is in the interest of all mankind that Antarctica shall continue forever to be used exclusively for peaceful purposes and shall not become the scene or object of international discord;

Acknowledging the substantial contributions to scientific knowledge resulting from international cooperation in scientific investigation in Antarctica;

Convinced that the establishment of a firm foundation for the continuation and development of such cooperation on the basis of freedom of scientific investigation in Antarctica as applied during the International Geophysical Year accords with the interests of science and the progress of all mankind;

Convinced also that a treaty ensuring the use of Antarctica for peaceful purposes only and the continuance of international harmony in Antarctica will further the purposes and principles embodied in the Charter of the United Nations;

Have agreed as follows:

Article I

1. Antarctica shall be used for peaceful purposes only. There shall be prohibited, *inter alia,* any measures of a military nature, such as the establishment of military bases and fortifications, the carrying out of military maneuvers, as well as the testing of any type of weapons.

2. The present Treaty shall not prevent the use of military personnel or equipment for scientific research or for any other peaceful purposes.

Article II. Freedom of scientific investigation in Antarctica and cooperation toward that end, as applied during the International Geophysical Year, shall continue, subject to the provisions of the present Treaty.

Article III

1. In order to promote international cooperation in scientific investigation in Antarctica, as provided for in Article II of the present Treaty, the Contracting Parties agree that, to the greatest extent feasible and practicable:

(a) information regarding plans for scientific programs in Antarctica shall be exchanged to permit maximum economy and efficiency of operations;

(b) scientific personnel shall be exchanged in Antarctica between expeditions and stations;

(c) scientific observations and results from Antarctica shall be exchanged and made freely available.

2. In implementing this Article, every encouragement shall be given to the establishment of cooperative working relations with those Specialized Agencies of the United Nations and other international organizations having a scientific or technical interest in Antarctica.

Article IV

1. Nothing contained in the present Treaty shall be interpreted as:

(a) a renunciation by any Contracting Party of previously asserted rights of or claims to territorial sovereignty in Antarctica;

(b) a renunciation or diminution by any Contracting Party of any basis of claim to territorial sovereignty in Antarctica which it may have whether as a result of its activities or those of its nationals in Antarctica, or otherwise;

(c) prejudicing the position of any Contracting Party as regards its recognition or non-recognition of any other State's right of or claim or basis of claim to territorial sovereignty in Antarctica.

2. No acts or activities taking place while the present Treaty is in force shall constitute a basis for asserting, supporting or denying a claim to territorial sovereignty in Antarctica or create any rights of sovereignty in Antarctica. No new claim, or enlargement of an existing claim, to territorial sovereignty in Antarctica shall be asserted while the present Treaty is in force.

Article V

1. Any nuclear explosions in Antarctica and the disposal there of radioactive waste material shall be prohibited.

2. In the event of the conclusion of international agreements concerning the use of nuclear energy, including nuclear explosions and the disposal of radioactive waste material, to which all of the Contracting Parties whose representatives are entitled to participate in the meetings provided for under Article IX are parties, the rules established under such agreements shall apply in Antarctica.

Article VI. The provisions of the present Treaty shall apply to the area south of 60° South Latitude, including all ice shelves, but nothing in the present treaty shall prejudice or in any way affect the rights, or the exercise of the rights, of any State under international law with regard to the high seas within that area.

Article VII

1. In order to promote the objectives and ensure the observance of the provisions of the present Treaty, each Contracting Party whose representatives are entitled to participate in the meetings referred to in Article IX of the Treaty shall have the right to designate observers to carry out any inspection provided for by the present Article. Observers shall be nationals of the Contracting Parties which designate them. The names of observers shall be communicated to every other Contracting Party having the right to designate observers, and like notice shall be given of the termination of their appointment.

2. Each observer designated in accordance with the provisions of paragraph 1 of this Article shall have complete freedom of access at any time to any or all areas of Antarctica.

3. All areas of Antarctica, including all stations, installations and equipment within those areas, and all ships and aircraft at points of discharging or embarking cargoes or personnel in Antarctica, shall be open at all times to inspection by any observers designated in accordance with paragraph 1 of this Article.

4. Aerial observation may be carried out at any time over any or all areas of Antarctica by any of the Contracting Parties having the right to designate observers.

5. Each Contracting Party shall, at the time when the present Treaty enters into force for it, inform the other Contracting Parties, and thereafter shall give them notice in advance, of

(a) all expeditions to and within Antarctica, on the part of its ships or nationals, and all expeditions to Antarctica organized in or proceeding from its territory;

(b) all stations in Antarctica occupied by its nationals; and

(c) any military personnel or equipment intended to be introduced by it into Antarctica subject to the conditions prescribed in paragraph 2 of Article I of the present Treaty.

Article VIII

1. In order to facilitate the exercise of their functions under the present Treaty, and without prejudice to the respective positions of the Contracting Parties relating to jurisdiction over all other persons in Antarctica, observers designated under paragraph 1 of Article VII and scientific personnel exchanged under subparagraph 1 (b) of Article III of the Treaty, and members of the staffs accompanying any such persons, shall be subject only to the jurisdiction of the Contracting Party of which they are nationals in respect of all acts or omissions occurring while they are in Antarctica for the purpose of exercising their functions.

2. Without prejudice to the provisions of paragraph 1 of this Article, and pending the adoption of measures in pursuance of subparagraph 1 (e) of Article IX, the Contracting Parties concerned in any case of dispute with regard to the exercise of jurisdiction in Antarctica shall immediately consult together with a view to reaching a mutually acceptable solution.

Article IX

1. Representatives of the Contracting Parties named in the preamble to the present Treaty shall meet at the City of Canberra within two months after the date of entry into force of the Treaty, and thereafter at suitable intervals and places, for the purpose of exchanging information, consulting together on matters of common interest pertaining to Antarctica, and formulating and considering, and recommending to their Governments, measures in furtherance of the principles and objectives of the Treaty, including measures regarding:

(a) use of Antarctica for peaceful purposes only;

(b) facilitation of scientific research in Antarctica;

(c) facilitation of international scientific cooperation in Antarctica;

(d) facilitation of the exercise of the rights of inspection provided for in Article VII of the Treaty;

(e) questions relating to the exercise of jurisdiction in Antarctica;

(f) preservation and conservation of living resources in Antarctica.

2. Each Contracting Party which has become a party to the present Treaty by accession under Ar-

ticle XIII shall be entitled to appoint representatives to participate in the meetings referred to in paragraph 1 of the present Article, during such time as that Contracting Party demonstrates its interest in Antarctica by conducting substantial scientific research activity there, such as the establishment of a scientific station or the dispatch of a scientific expedition.

3. Reports from the observers referred to in Article VII of the present Treaty shall be transmitted to the representatives of the Contracting Parties participating in the meetings referred to in paragraph 1 of the present Article.

4. The measures referred to in paragraph 1 of this Article shall become effective when approved by all the Contracting Parties whose representatives were entitled to participate in the meetings held to consider those measures.

5. Any or all of the rights established in the present Treaty may be exercised as from the date of entry into force of the Treaty whether or not any measures facilitating the exercise of such rights have been proposed, considered or approved as provided in this Article.

Article X. Each of the Contracting Parties undertakes to exert appropriate efforts, consistent with the Charter of the United Nations, to the end that no one engages in any activity in Antarctica contrary to the principles or purposes of the present Treaty.

Article XI

1. If any dispute arises between two or more of the Contracting Parties concerning the interpretation or application of the present Treaty, those Contracting Parties shall consult among themselves with a view to having the dispute resolved by negotiation, inquiry, mediation, conciliation, arbitration, judicial settlement or other peaceful means of their own choice.

2. Any dispute of this character not so resolved shall, with the consent, in each case, of all parties to the dispute, be referred to the International Court of Justice for settlement; but failure to reach agreement on reference to the International Court shall not absolve parties to the dispute from the responsibility of continuing to seek to resolve it by any of the various peaceful means referred to in paragraph 1 of this Article.

Article XII

1. (a) The present Treaty may be modified or amended at any time by unanimous agreement of the Contracting Parties whose representatives are entitled to participate in the meetings provided for under Article IX. Any such modification or amendment shall enter into force when the depositary Government has received notice from all such Contracting Parties that they have ratified it.

(b) Such modification or amendment shall thereafter enter into force as to any other Contracting Party when notice of ratification by it has been received by the depositary Government. Any such Contracting Party from which no notice of ratification is received within a period of two years from the date of entry into force of the modification or amendment in accordance with the provisions of subparagraph 1 (a) of this Article shall be deemed to have withdrawn from the present Treaty on the date of the expiration of such period.

2. (a) If after the expiration of thirty years from the date of entry into force of the present Treaty, any of the Contracting Parties whose representatives are entitled to participate in the meetings provided for under Article IX so requests by a communication addressed to the depositary Government, a Conference of all the Contracting Parties shall be held as soon as practicable to review the operation of the Treaty.

(b) Any modification or amendment to the present Treaty which is approved at such a Conference by a majority of the Contracting Parties there represented, including a majority of those whose representatives are entitled to participate in the meetings provided for under Article IX, shall be communicated by the depositary Government to all the Contracting Parties immediately after the termination of the Conference and shall enter into force in accordance with the provisions of paragraph 1 of the present Article.

(c) If any such modification or amendment has not entered into force in accordance with the provisions of subparagraph 1 (a) of this Article within a period of two years after the date of its communication to all the Contracting Parties, any Contracting Party may at any time after the expiration of that period give notice to the depositary Government of its withdrawal from the present Treaty; and such withdrawal shall take effect two years after the receipt of the notice of the depositary Government.

[Ratification]

[Signatures]

[U.S. Department of State, *Documents on Disarmament, 1945–1959* (Washington, D.C., 1959), Doc. 398]

Rapacki Proposals [Europe] (1957, 1962)

The first proposal concerning the establishment of a denuclearized zone in Europe was submitted by the Government of the People's Republic of Poland to the United Nations General Assembly on 2 October 1957. (See U.S. Department of State, Documents on Disarmament, 1945–1959, vol. 2, Doc. 225.) This proposal provided for the establishment in central Europe of a zone without nuclear weapons comprising the territories of Poland, Czechoslovakia, the German Democratic Republic, and the Federal Republic of Germany.

Detailed explanations of the Polish proposal were contained in the Polish Memorandum of 14 February 1958 transmitted to the Governments concerned. (See Documents on Disarmament, 1945–1959, vol. 2, Doc. 244.)

On 4 November 1958, the Government of the People's Republic of Poland submitted an amended proposal for carrying out the plan for a denuclearized zone. At the fifteenth session of the United Nations General Assembly, Mr. Władysław Gomułka, the head of the Polish delegation, stated once again that Poland was willing to participate without delay in carrying out the plan for a denuclearized zone. (See Documents on Disarmament, 1960, pp. 254–260.)

During the few years that elapsed since Poland had proposed the establishment of a denuclearized zone in central Europe, world interest in the question of preventing the dissemination of nulcear weapons and in plans for the regional limitation of armaments considerably increased. This interest was manifested in the adoption by the United Nations General Assembly at its sixteenth session of a resolution recognizing Africa as a denuclearized zone. (See Documents on Disarmament, 1961, pp. 647–648.) As can be seen from the preliminary replies to the inquiry carried out under resolution No. 1664 (XVI) of the United Nations General Assembly, a number of European governments adopted a positive attitude to the idea of establishing regional denuclearized zones.

For the General Assembly resolution, see Documents on Disarmament, 1961, p. 693. The Swedish, U.K., Soviet, U.S., and French replies to the Secretary-General are printed on pp. 38–42, 82, 83–86, 87–90, and 166–167, respectively. For other replies, see Disarmament Commission Official Records: Supplement for January 1961 to December 1962, pp. 51–105.

In view of the fresh efforts being made to achieve general and complete disarmament, the idea of denuclearized zones in specific territories took on a new significance as a measure that could facilitate the achievement of this fundamental purpose of the nations of central Europe.

Taking the foregoing into consideration and acting in the spirit of the resolutions adopted by the United Nations General Assembly, the Polish delegation renewed the proposal to establish a denuclearized zone in Europe, linked with the elimination of rockets and the limitation of armed forces and conventional armaments and submitted it to the Eighteen Nation Committee on Disarmament.

News Conference Remarks by Polish Foreign Minister Rapacki Regarding an Atom-Free Zone in Central Europe, 4 November 1958

During the past months, we have repeatedly stressed that the Government of the Polish People's Republic does not consider the discussions on its proposal concerning the setting up in Central Europe of a denuclearized zone as terminated and that we are fully maintaining this proposal. This attitude of ours stems from the deep conviction toward the decreasing of tension and toward disarmament and the strengthening of security in Europe.

This necessity has been confirmed during the entire discussion on our initiative and in the positive attitude toward this initiative on the part of broad and varied circles of world public opinion, especially in Europe.

We have given repeated proof that we can take into consideration matter-of-fact arguments, even opinions differing from ours as well as the subjective difficulties of those or other interested circles.

I should like to recall here our memorandum of February 14, 1958, in which we have taken into account several such elements. In this memorandum, we have also developed the principles of a broad control system of the implementation of the obligations proposed by us.

Recently we have considered other arguments and misgivings voiced in the course of discussion. We are ready, in agreement with our allies, to make a new, in our opinion the maximum step possible toward taking into account the main comments and reservations put forward in connection with our proposal.

We are ready to consider the implementation of our plan in two stages: In the first stage a ban would be introduced on the production of nuclear weapons on the territories of Poland, Czechoslovakia, the German Democratic Republic and the German Federal Republic.

An obligation would also be undertaken within the proposed zone to renounce the equipping with nuclear weapons of the armies which do not yet possess them as well as the building of relevant installations for them. At the same time, appropriate measures of control would be introduced. This would amount therefore, one may say, to the freezing of nuclear armaments in the proposed zone.

The implementation of the second stage would be preceded by talks on the appropriate reduction of conventional forces. Such a reduction would be effected simultaneously with the complete denuclearization of the zone. Again it would be accompanied by the introduction of appropriate control measures. . . .

Such a modification, however, would meet the suggestions and conclusions resulting from the attitude of many Western politicians, who expressed their opinions in connection with our initiative. It should also eliminate major misgivings which have been voiced in the discussion and which were meant above all to serve as a justification for a negative attitude on the part of certain circles and governments toward the Polish proposal.

This concerns the fears, without considering here whether they are well founded or not, of "upsetting the existing military equilibrium" between the two groups in Europe, and weakening the defenses of the West, fears about the withdrawal of American forces from Europe, and so forth.

Attempts have been made to justify all these reservations with one key argument: "The implementation of the ban on the production and possession of nuclear weapons in Central Europe would deprive the NATO troops of the so-called shield in the face of the superiority of the Warsaw pact forces in the field of conventional arms."

We could not agree with such an argument, if only because of our basic attitude toward weapons of mass destruction. We were never against discussion on the reduction of conventional armament in Central Europe. On the contrary, we were always partisans of such discussion and of such a reduction. If, in the past year we have limited ourselves to an initiative of a narrower scope, to the proposal of the denuclearization of Central Europe, it was only because the discussion on the limitation of all arguments [*sic*] in this region ran into serious difficulties. Besides, we have considered the implementation of our proposal as a first step toward further disarmament measures in this zone.

Therefore, since many and serious voices have been raised asking for the linking of the denuclearization with reduction of other armaments in Central Europe, we are ready to consider such voices favorably, but under one condition: That the discussions on the two joint subjects will not be protracted endlessly while nuclear armaments come to be included in the arsenals of new armies.

These are the premises of such modifications in the ways of implementing the denuclearized zone, which we are ready to consider.

[U.S. Department of State, *Documents on Disarmament, 1945–1959*, vol. 2, Doc. 315]

Polish Memorandum Submitted to the Committee of the Whole of the Eighteen Nation Disarmament Committee: Rapacki Plan for Denuclearized and Limited Armaments Zone in Europe, March 28, 1962

Considering that simultaneously with the formulation of an agreement on general and complete disarmament the Eighteen Nation Committee on disarmament is to consider proposals for measures and arrangements designed to reduce international tension, to increase mutual trust between States and thus to facilitate the achievement of general and complete disarmament, and that one of the most important of such measures is the establishment of denuclearized and limited armaments zones.

The Delegation of the People's Republic of Poland, in agreement with the delegation of the Czechoslovak Socialist Republic submits for consideration by the Committee a proposal for the establishment of a denuclearized and limited armaments zone in Europe.

I. *Purpose.* The purpose of the Polish proposal is to eliminate nuclear weapons and the means of delivering them and to reduce armed forces and conventional armaments within a limited area in which these measures could help to reduce tension and substantially to limit the danger of conflict.

II. *Territory.* In principle, the zone should include the following States: the People's Republic of Poland, the Czechoslovak Socialist Republic, the German Democratic Republic and the Federal Republic of Germany.

The agreement concerning the zone will be open for accession by other European States.

III. *Rights and duties of States within the zone and of other States.* Rights and duties connected with establishment of the zone should be exercised and carried out in the following two stages:

Stage One

Freezing of nuclear weapons and rockets and prohibition of the establishment of new bases.

(a) *Rights and duties of States within the Zone*

1. The manufacture and preparations for the manufacture of any type of nuclear weapon or vehicle for the delivery of such a weapon in the territory of States within the zone shall be prohibited.

2. The introduction into their territory by States within the zone of any type of nuclear weapon or vehicle for the delivery of such a weapon shall be prohibited.

3. Authorization by States within the zone of the establishment of new bases or facilities for the stockpiling or use of nuclear weapons or of vehicles for their delivery shall be prohibited.

(b) *Rights and duties of other States*

1. All States possessing nuclear weapons and vehicles for their delivery shall be prohibited from transferring them to States within the zone.

2. All States possessing nuclear weapons and vehicles for their delivery shall be prohibited from introducing further quantities of such weapons or vehicles into the territory of the zone.

3. The establishment in the territory of the zone of new bases or facilities for the stockpiling or use of nuclear weapons or of vehicles for their delivery shall be prohibited.

Stage Two

Elimination of nuclear weapons and rockets and reduction of armed forces and conventional armaments.

(a) *Rights and duties of States within the zone*

1. Elimination of all nuclear weapon delivery vehicles from the armaments of States within the zone,

2. Reduction of the armed forces of States within the zone to an agreed level, linked with an appropriate reduction in conventional armaments.

(b) *Rights and obligations of other States*

1. Withdrawal from the territory of the zone of all types of nuclear weapons, all facilities for their stockpiling and use, all vehicles for the delivery of such weapons placed permanently or temporarily in that territory by other States, and all installations for the use of such vehicles.

2. Reduction to an agreed level of the armed forces of States outside the zone stationed in the territory of the zone, linked with an appropriate reduction in their conventional armaments.

IV. *Control*

1. In order to ensure the efficacy of the disarmament measures set out in section III of this memorandum, provision will be made for a system of strict international control and inspection on the ground and in the air, including the establishment of appropriate control posts.

2. A special control body will be set up to supervise the discharge of the duties proposed.

The composition, competence and working procedure of this body will be decided by agreement between the States concerned. The States signatories to the agreement on the establishment of a denuclearized zone will undertake to submit to control by this body and to grant it all the facilities and assistance it may need for the performance of its task.

3. The States signatories to the agreement on the establishment of a denuclearized zone will determine the extent of control and the measures for applying it in each of the two stages.

V. *Guarantee.* In order to guarantee the inviolability of the status of the denuclearized zone, the Powers possessing nuclear weapons will undertake:

(a) to abstain from any measures which might directly or indirectly impair the status of the zone;

(b) not to use nuclear weapons against the territory of the zone.

Taking the foregoing into consideration, the delegation of the People's Republic of Poland proposes that:

1. The Eighteen Nation Committee should request the States concerned to take immediate measures to give effect to the proposal concerning the establishment of a denuclearized and limited armaments zone.

2. The Committee should request ... to enter into appropriate negotiations with the States concerned in the establishment of the zone and to submit a report on those negotiations by 1962 at the latest.

3. The Committee should also request the General Assembly of the United Nations to adopt an appropriate resolution concerning the establishment of a denuclearized and limited armaments zone in Europe.

[U.S. Arms Control and Disarmament Agency, *Documents on Disarmament, 1962,* vol. 1, 201–205]

Outer Space Treaty (1967)

This treaty was signed on 27 January 1967, and it entered into force on 10 October 1967.

Treaty on Principles Governing the Activities of States in the Exploration and Use of Outer Space, Including the Moon and Other Celestial Bodies

The States Parties to this Treaty,

Inspired by the great prospects opening up before mankind as a result of man's entry into outer space,

Recognizing the common interest of all mankind in the progress of the exploration and use of outer space for peaceful purposes,

Believing that the exploration and use of outer space should be carried on for the benefit of all peoples irrespective of the degree of their economic or scientific development,

Desiring to contribute to broad international cooperation in the scientific as well as the legal aspects of the exploration and use of outer space for peaceful purposes,

Believing that such cooperation will contribute to the development of mutual understanding and to the strengthening of friendly relations between States and peoples,

Recalling resolution 1962 (XVIII), entitled "Declaration of Legal Principles Governing the Activities of States in the Exploration and Use of Outer Space," which was adopted unanimously by the United Nations General Assembly on 13 December 1963,

Recalling resolution 1884 (XVIII), calling upon States to refrain from placing in orbit around the Earth any objects carrying nuclear weapons or any other kinds of weapons of mass destruction or from installing such weapons on celestial bodies, which was adopted unanimously by the United Nations General Assembly on 17 October 1963,

Taking account of United Nations General Assembly resolution 110 (II) of 3 November 1947, which condemned propaganda designed or likely to provoke or encourage any threat to the peace, breach of the peace or act of aggression, and considering that the aforementioned resolution is applicable to outer space,

Convinced that a Treaty on Principles Governing the Activities of States in the Exploration and Use of Outer Space, including the Moon and Other Celestial Bodies, will further the Purposes and Principles of the Charter of the United Nations,

Have agreed on the following:

Article I. The exploration and use of outer space, including the moon and other celestial bodies, shall be carried out for the benefit and in the interests of all countries, irrespective of their degree of economic or scientific development, and shall be the province of all mankind.

Outer space, including the moon and other celestial bodies, shall be free for exploration and use by all States without discrimination of any kind, on a basis of equality and in accordance with international law, and there shall be free access to all areas of celestial bodies.

There shall be freedom of scientific investigation in outer space, including the moon and other celestial bodies, and States shall facilitate and encourage international cooperation in such investigation.

Article II. Outer space, including the moon and other celestial bodies, is not subject to national appropriation by claim of sovereignty, by means of use or occupation, or by any other means.

Article III. States Parties to the Treaty shall carry on activities in the exploration and use of outer space, including the moon and other celestial bodies, in accordance with international law, including the Charter of the United Nations, in the interest of maintaining international peace and security and promoting international cooperation and understanding.

Article IV. States Parties to the Treaty undertake not to place in orbit around the Earth any objects carrying nuclear weapons or any other kinds of weapons of mass destruction, install such weapons on celestial bodies, or station such weapons in outer space in any other manner.

The moon and other celestial bodies shall be used by all States Parties to the Treaty exclusively for peaceful purposes. The establishment of military bases, installations and fortifications, the testing of any type of weapons and the conduct of military maneuvers on celestial bodies shall be forbidden. The use of military personnel for scientific research or for any other peaceful purposes shall not be prohibited. The use of any equipment or facility necessary for peaceful exploration of the moon and other celestial bodies shall also not be prohibited.

Article V. States Parties to the Treaty shall regard astronauts as envoys of mankind in outer space and shall render to them all possible assistance in the event of accident, distress, or emergency landing on the territory of another State Party or on the high seas. When astronauts make such a landing, they shall be safely and promptly returned to the State of registry of their space vehicle.

In carrying on activities in outer space and on celestial bodies, the astronauts of one State Party shall render all possible assistance to the astronauts of other States Parties.

States Parties to the Treaty shall immediately inform the other States Parties to the Treaty or the Secretary-General of the United Nations of any phenomena they discover in outer space, including the moon and other celestial bodies, which could constitute a danger to the life or health of astronauts.

Article VI. States Parties to the Treaty shall bear international responsibility for national activities in outer space, including the moon and other celestial bodies, whether such activities are carried on by governmental agencies or by non-governmental entities, and for assuring that national activities are carried out in conformity with the provisions set forth in the present Treaty. The activities of non-governmental entities in outer space, including the moon and other celestial bodies, shall require authorization and continuing supervision by the appropriate State Party to the Treaty. When activities are carried on in outer space, including the moon and other celestial bodies, by an international organization, responsibility for compliance with this Treaty shall be borne both by the international organization and by the States Parties to the Treaty participating in such organization.

Article VII. Each State Party to the Treaty that launches or procures the launching of an object into outer space, including the moon and other celestial bodies, and each State Party from whose territory or facility an object is launched, is internationally liable for damage to another State Party to the Treaty or to its natural or juridical persons by such object or its component parts on the Earth, in air space or in outer space, including the moon and other celestial bodies.

Article VIII. A State Party to the Treaty on whose registry an object launched into outer space is carried shall retain jurisdiction and control over such object, and over any personnel thereof, while in outer space or on a celestial body. Ownership of objects launched into outer space, including objects landed or constructed on a celestial body, and of their component parts, is not affected by their presence in outer space or on a celestial body or by their return to the Earth. Such objects or component parts found beyond the limits of the State Party to the Treaty on whose registry they are carried shall be returned to that State Party, which shall, upon request, furnish identifying data prior to their return.

Article IX. In the exploration and use of outer space, including the moon and other celestial bodies, States Parties to the Treaty shall be guided by the principle of co-operation and mutual assistance and shall conduct all their activities in outer space, including the moon and other celestial bodies, with due regard to the corresponding interests of all other States Parties to the Treaty. States Parties to the Treaty shall pursue studies of outer space, including the moon and other celestial bodies, and conduct exploration of them so as to avoid their harmful contamination and also adverse changes in the environment of the Earth resulting from the introduction of extraterrestrial matter and, where necessary, shall adopt appropriate measures for this purpose. If a State Party to the Treaty has reason to believe that an activity or experiment planned by it or its nationals in outer space, including the moon and other celestial bodies, would cause potentially harmful interference with activities of other States Parties in the peaceful exploration and use of outer space, including the moon and other celestial bodies, it shall undertake appropriate international consultations before proceeding with any such activity or experiment. A State Party to the Treaty which has reason to believe that an activity or experiment planned by another State Party in outer space, including the moon and other celestial bodies, would cause potentially harmful interference with activities in the peaceful exploration and use of outer space, including the moon and other celestial bodies, may request consultation concerning the activity or experiment.

Article X. In order to promote international co-operation in the exploration and use of outer space, including the moon and other celestial bodies, in conformity with the purposes of this Treaty, the States Parties to the Treaty shall consider on a basis of equality any requests by other States Parties to the Treaty to be afforded an opportunity to observe the flight of space objects launched by those States.

The nature of such an opportunity for observation and the conditions under which it could be afforded shall be determined by agreement between the States concerned.

Article XI. In order to promote international co-operation in the peaceful exploration and use of outer space, States Parties to the Treaty conducting activities in outer space, including the moon and other celestial bodies, agree to inform the Secretary-General of the United Nations as well as the public and the international scientific community, to the greatest extent feasible and practicable, of the nature, conduct, locations and results of such activities. On receiving the said information, the Secretary-General of the United Nations should be prepared to disseminate it immediately and effectively.

Article XII. All stations, installations, equipment and space vehicles on the moon and other celestial bodies shall be open to representatives of other States Parties to the Treaty on a basis of reciprocity. Such representatives shall give reasonable advance notice of a projected visit, in order that appropriate consultations may be held and that maximum precautions may be taken to assure safety and to avoid interference with normal operations in the facility to be visited.

Article XIII. The provisions of this Treaty shall apply to the activities of States Parties to the Treaty in the exploration and use of outer space, including the moon and other celestial bodies, whether such activities are carried on by a single State Party to the Treaty or jointly with other States, including cases where they are carried on within the framework of international inter-governmental organizations.

Any practical questions arising in connection with activities carried on by international inter-governmental organizations in the exploration and use of outer space, including the moon and other celestial bodies, shall be resolved by the States Parties to the Treaty either with the appropriate international organization or with one or more States members of that international organization, which are Parties to this Treaty.

[Ratification]

[Signatures]

[U.S. Arms Control and Disarmament Agency, *Arms Control and Disarmament Agreements: Texts and Histories of the Negotiations,* 1982 ed. (Washington, D.C., 1982), pp. 51–55]

Latin American Denuclearization Treaty (1967)

The following treaty was signed in Mexico City on 14 February 1967, and it entered into force on 22 April 1968.

Treaty for the Prohibition of Nuclear Weapons in Latin America

Preamble

In the name of their peoples and faithfully interpreting their desires and aspirations, the Governments of the States which sign the Treaty for the Prohibition of Nuclear Weapons in Latin America,

Desiring to contribute, so far as lies in their power, towards ending the armaments race, especially in the field of nuclear weapons, and towards strengthening a world at peace, based on the sovereign equality of States, mutual respect and good neighbourliness,

Recalling that the United Nations General Assembly, in its Resolution 808 (IX), adopted unanimously as one of the three points of a coordinated programme of disarmament "the total prohibition of the use and manufacture of nuclear weapons and weapons of mass destruction of every type,"

Recalling that militarily denuclearized zones are not an end in themselves but rather a means for achieving general and complete disarmament at a later stage,

Recalling United Nations General Assembly Resolution 1911 (XVIII), which established that the measures that should be agreed upon for the denuclearization of Latin America should be taken "in the light of the principles of the Charter of the United Nations and of regional agreements,"

Recalling United Nations General Assembly Resolution 2028 (XX), which established the principle of an acceptable balance of mutual responsibilities and duties for the nuclear and non-nuclear powers, and

Recalling that the Charter of the Organization of American States proclaims that it is an essential purpose of the Organization to strengthen the peace and security of the hemisphere,

Convinced:

That the incalculable destructive power of nuclear weapons has made it imperative that the legal prohibition of war should be strictly observed in practice if the survival of civilization and of mankind itself is to be assured,

That nuclear weapons, whose terrible effects are suffered, indiscriminately and inexorably, by military forces and civilian population alike, constitute, through the persistence of the radioactivity they release, an attack on the integrity of the human species and ultimately may even render the whole earth uninhabitable,

That general and complete disarmament under effective international control is a vital matter which all the peoples of the world equally demand,

That the proliferation of nuclear weapons, which seems inevitable unless States, in the exercise of their sovereign rights, impose restrictions on themselves in order to prevent it, would make any agreement on disarmament enormously difficult and would increase the danger of the outbreak of a nuclear conflagration,

That the establishment of militarily denuclearized zones is closely linked with the maintenance of peace and security in the respective regions,

That the military denuclearization of vast geographical zones, adopted by the sovereign decision of the states comprised therein, will exercise a beneficial influence on other regions where similar conditions exist,

That the privileged situation of the signatory states, whose territories are wholly free from nuclear weapons, imposes upon them the inescapable duty of preserving that situation both in their own interests and for the good of mankind,

That the existence of nuclear weapons in any country of Latin America would make it a target for possible nuclear attacks and would inevitably set off, throughout the region, a ruinous race in nuclear weapons which would involve the unjustifiable diversion, for warlike purposes, of the limited resources required for economic and social development,

That the foregoing reasons, together with the traditional peace-loving outlook of Latin America, give rise to an inescapable necessity that nuclear energy should be used in that region exclusively for peaceful purposes, and that the Latin American countries should use their right to the greatest and most equitable possible access to this new source of energy in order to expedite the economic and social development of their peoples,

Convinced finally:

That the military denuclearization of Latin America—being understood to mean the undertaking entered into internationally in this Treaty to keep their territories forever free from nuclear weapons—will constitute a measure which will spare their peoples from the squandering of their limited resources on nuclear armaments and will protect them against possible nuclear attacks on their territories, and will also constitute a significant contribution towards preventing the proliferation of nuclear weapons and a powerful factor for general and complete disarmament, and

That Latin America, faithful to its tradition of universality, must not only endeavour to banish from its homelands the scourge of a nuclear war, but must also strive to promote the well-being and advancement of its peoples, at the same time cooperating in the fulfillment of the ideals of mankind, that is to say, in the consolidation of a permanent peace based on equal rights, economic fairness and social justice for all, in accordance with the principles and purposes set forth in the Charter of the United Nations and in the Charter of the Organization of American States,

Have agreed as follows:

Obligations

Article 1

1. The Contracting Parties hereby undertake to use exclusively for peaceful purposes the nuclear material and facilities which are under their jurisdiction, and to prohibit and prevent in their respective territories:

(a) The testing, use, manufacture, production or acquisition by any means whatsoever of any nuclear weapons, by the Parties themselves, directly or indirectly, on behalf of anyone else or in any other way, and

(b) The receipt, storage, installation, deployment and any form of possession of any nuclear weapons, directly or indirectly, by the Parties themselves, by anyone on their behalf or in any other way.

2. The Contracting Parties also undertake to refrain from engaging in, encouraging or authorizing, directly or indirectly, or in any way participating in the testing, use, manufacture, production, possession or control of any nuclear weapon.

Article 2. For the purposes of this Treaty, the Contracting Parties are those for whom the Treaty is in force.

Definition of Territory

Article 3. For the purposes of this Treaty, the term "territory" shall include the territorial sea, air space and any other space over which the State exercises sovereignty in accordance with its own legislation.

Zone of Application

Article 4

1. The zone of application of this Treaty is the whole of the territories for which the Treaty is in force.

2. Upon fulfillment of the requirements of article 28, paragraph 1, the zone of application of this Treaty shall also be that which is situated in the western hemisphere within the following limits (except the continental part of the territory of the United States of America and its territorial waters): starting at a point located at 35° north latitude, 75° west longitude; from this point directly southward to a point at 30° north latitude, 75° west longitude; from there, directly eastward to a point at 30° north latitude, 50° west longitude; from there, along a loxodromic line to a point at 5° north latitude, 20° west longitude; from there, directly southward to a point at 60° south latitude, 20° west longitude; from there, directly westward to a point at 60° south latitude, 115° west longitude; from there, directly northward to a point at 0° latitude, 115° west longitude; from there, along a loxodromic line to a point at 35° north latitude, 150° west longitude; from there, directly eastward to a point at 35° north latitude, 75° west longitude.

Definition of Nuclear Weapons

Article 5. For the purposes of this Treaty, a nuclear weapon is any device which is capable of releasing nuclear energy in an uncontrolled manner and which has a group of characteristics that are appropriate for use for warlike purposes. An instrument that may be used for the transport or propulsion of the device is not included in this definition if it is separable from the device and not an indivisible part thereof.

Meeting of Signatories

Article 6. At the request of any of the signatory States or if the Agency established by article 7 should so decide, a meeting of all the signatories may be convoked to consider in common questions which may affect the very essence of this instrument, including possible amendments to it. In either case, the meeting will be convoked by the General Secretary.

Article 7

1. In order to ensure compliance with the obligations of this Treaty, the Contracting Parties hereby establish an international organization to be known as the "Agency for the Prohibition of Nuclear Weapons in Latin America," hereinafter referred to as "the Agency." Only the Contracting Parties shall be affected by its decisions.

2. The Agency shall be responsible for the holding of periodic or extraordinary consultations among Member States on matters relating to the purposes, measures and procedures set forth in this Treaty and to the supervision of compliance with the obligations arising therefrom.

3. The Contracting Parties agree to extend to the Agency full and prompt cooperation in accordance with the provisions of this Treaty, of any agreements they may conclude with the Agency and of any agreements the Agency may conclude with any other international organization or body.

4. The headquarters of the Agency shall be in Mexico City.

Organs

Article 8

1. There are hereby established as principal organs of the Agency a General Conference, a Council and a Secretariat.

2. Such subsidiary organs as are considered necessary by the General Conference may be established within the purview of this Treaty.

The General Conference

Article 9

1. The General Conference, the supreme organ of the Agency, shall be composed of all the Contracting Parties; it shall hold regular sessions every two years, and may also hold special sessions whenever this Treaty so provides or, in the opinion of the Council, the circumstances so require.

2. The General Conference:

(a) May consider and decide on any matters or questions covered by this Treaty, within the limits thereof, including those referring to powers and functions of any organ provided for in this Treaty.

(b) Shall establish procedures for the control system to ensure observance of this Treaty in accordance with its provisions.

(c) Shall elect the Members of the Council and the General Secretary.

(d) May remove the General Secretary from office if the proper functioning of the Agency so requires.

(e) Shall receive and consider the biennial and special reports submitted by the Council and the General Secretary.

(f) Shall initiate and consider studies designed to facilitate the optimum fulfillment of the aims of this Treaty, without prejudice to the power of the General Secretary independently to carry out similar studies for submission to and consideration by the Conference.

(g) Shall be the organ competent to authorize the conclusion of agreements with Governments and other international organizations and bodies.

3. The General Conference shall adopt the Agency's budget and fix the scale of financial contributions to be paid by Member States, taking into account the systems and criteria used for the same purpose by the United Nations.

4. The General Conference shall elect its officers for each session and may establish such subsidiary organs as it deems necessary for the performance of its functions.

5. Each Member of the Agency shall have one vote. The decisions of the General Conference shall be taken by a two-thirds majority of the Members present and voting in the case of matters relating to the control system and measures referred to in article 20, the admission of new Members, the election or removal of the General Secretary, adoption of the budget and matters related thereto. Decisions on other matters, as well as procedural questions and also determination of which questions must be decided by a two-thirds majority, shall be taken by a simple majority of the Members present and voting.

6. The General Conference shall adopt its own rules of procedure.

The Council

Article 10

1. The Council shall be composed of five Members of the Agency elected by the General Conference from among the Contracting Parties, due

account being taken of equitable geographic distribution.

2. The Members of the Council shall be elected for a term of four years. However, in the first election three will be elected for two years. Outgoing Members may not be reelected for the following period unless the limited number of States for which the Treaty is in force so requires.

3. Each Member of the Council shall have one representative.

4. The Council shall be so organized as to be able to function continuously.

5. In addition to the functions conferred upon it by this Treaty and to those which may be assigned to it by the General Conference, the Council shall, through the General Secretary, ensure the proper operation of the control system in accordance with the provisions of this Treaty and with the decisions adopted by the General Conference.

6. The Council shall submit an annual report on its work to the General Conference as well as such special reports as it deems necessary or which the General Conference requests of it.

7. The Council shall elect its officers for each session.

8. The decisions of the Council shall be taken by a simple majority of its Members present and voting.

9. The Council shall adopt its own rules of procedure.

The Secretariat

Article 11

1. The Secretariat shall consist of a General Secretary, who shall be the chief administrative officer of the Agency, and of such staff as the Agency may require. The term of office of the General Secretary shall be four years and he may be re-elected for a single additional term. The General Secretary may not be a national of the country in which the Agency has its headquarters. In case the office of General Secretary becomes vacant, a new election shall be held to fill the office for the remainder of the term.

2. The staff of the Secretariat shall be appointed by the General Secretary, in accordance with rules laid down by the General Conference.

3. In addition to the functions conferred upon him by this Treaty and to those which may be assigned to him by the General Conference, the General Secretary shall ensure, as provided by article 10, paragraph 5, the proper operation of the control system established by this Treaty, in accordance with the provisions of the Treaty and the decisions taken by the General Conference.

4. The General Secretary shall act in that capacity in all meetings of the General Conference and of the Council and shall make an annual report to both bodies on the work of the Agency and any special reports requested by the General Conference or the Council or which the General Secretary may deem desirable.

5. The General Secretary shall establish the procedures for distributing to all Contracting Parties information received by the Agency from governmental sources and such information from nongovernmental sources as may be of interest to the Agency.

6. In the performance of their duties the General Secretary and the staff shall not seek or receive instructions from any Government or from any other authority external to the Agency and shall refrain from any action which might reflect on their position as international officials responsible only to the Agency; subject to their responsibility to the Agency, they shall not disclose any industrial secrets or other confidential information coming to their knowledge by reason of their official duties in the Agency.

7. Each of the Contracting Parties undertakes to respect the exclusively international character of the responsibilities of the General Secretary and the staff and not to seek to influence them in the discharge of their responsibilities.

Control System

Article 12

1. For the purpose of verifying compliance with the obligations entered into by the Contracting Parties in accordance with article 1, a control system shall be established which shall be put into effect in accordance with the provisions of articles 13–18 of this Treaty.

2. The control system shall be used in particular for the purpose of verifying:

(a) That devices, services and facilities intended for peaceful uses of nuclear energy are not used in the testing or manufacture of nuclear weapons,

(b) That none of the activities prohibited in article 1 of this Treaty are carried out in the territory of the Contracting Parties with nuclear materials or weapons introduced from abroad, and

(c) That explosions for peaceful purposes are compatible with article 18 of this Treaty.

IAEA Safeguards

Article 13. Each Contracting Party shall negotiate multilateral or bilateral agreements with the International Atomic Energy Agency for the application of its safeguards to its nuclear activities. Each Contracting Party shall initiate negotiations within a period of 180 days after the date of the deposit of its instrument of ratification of this Treaty. These agreements shall enter into force, for each Party, not later than eighteen months after the date of the initiation of such negotiations except in case of unforeseen circumstances or *force majeure.*

Reports of the Parties

Article 14

1. The Contracting Parties shall submit to the Agency and to the International Atomic Energy Agency, for their information, semi-annual reports stating that no activity prohibited under this Treaty has occurred in their respective territories.

2. The Contracting Parties shall simultaneously transmit to the Agency a copy of any report they may submit to the International Atomic Energy Agency which relates to matters that are the subject of this Treaty and to the application of safeguards.

3. The Contracting Parties shall also transmit to the Organization of American States, for its information, any reports that may be of interest to it, in accordance with the obligations established by the Inter-American System.

Special Reports Requested by the General Secretary

Article 15

1. With the authorization of the Council, the General Secretary may request any of the Contracting Parties to provide the Agency with complementary or supplementary information regarding any event or circumstance connected with compliance with this Treaty, explaining his reasons. The Contracting Parties undertake to cooperate promptly and fully with the General Secretary.

2. The General Secretary shall inform the Council and the Contracting Parties forthwith of such requests and of the respective replies.

Special Inspections

Article 16

1. The International Atomic Energy Agency and the Council established by this Treaty have the power of carrying out special inspections in the following cases:

(a) In the case of the International Atomic Energy Agency, in accordance with the agreements referred to in article 13 of this Treaty;

(b) In the case of the Council:

(i) When so requested, the reasons for the request being stated, by any Party which suspects that some activity prohibited by this Treaty has been carried out or is about to be carried out, either in the territory of any other Party or in any other place on such latter Party's behalf, the Council shall immediately arrange for such an inspection in accordance with article 10, paragraph 5.

(ii) When requested by any Party which has been suspected of or charged with having violated this Treaty, the Council shall immediately arrange for the special inspection requested in accordance with article 10, paragraph 5.

The above requests will be made to the Council through the General Secretary.

2. The costs and expenses of any special inspection carried out under paragraph 1, sub-paragraph (b), sections (i) and (ii) of this article shall be borne by the requesting Party or Parties, except where the Council concludes on the basis of the report on the special inspection that, in view of the circumstances existing in the case, such costs and expenses should be borne by the agency.

3. The General Conference shall formulate the procedures for the organization and execution of the special inspections carried out in accordance with paragraph 1, sub-paragraph (b), sections (i) and (ii) of this article.

4. The Contracting Parties undertake to grant the inspectors carrying out such special inspections full and free access to all places and all information which may be necessary for the performance of their duties and which are directly and intimately connected with the suspicion of violation of this Treaty. If so requested by the authorities of the Contracting Party in whose territory the inspection is carried out, the inspectors designated by the General Conference shall be accompanied by representatives of said authorities, provided that this does not in any way delay or hinder the work of the inspectors.

5. The Council shall immediately transmit to all the Parties, through the General Secretary, a copy of any report resulting from special inspections.

6. Similarly, the Council shall send through the General Secretary to the Secretary-General of the United Nations, for transmission to the United Nations Security Council and General Assembly, and to the Council of the Organization of American States, for its information, a copy of any report resulting from any special inspection carried out in accordance with paragraph 1, sub-paragraph (b), sections (i) and (ii) of this article.

7. The Council may decide, or any Contracting Party may request, the convening of a special session of the General Conference for the purpose of considering the reports resulting from any special inspection. In such a case, the General Secretary shall take immediate steps to convene the special session requested.

8. The General Conference, convened in special session under this article, may make recommendations to the Contracting Parties and submit reports to the Secretary-General of the United Nations to be transmitted to the United Nations Security Council and the General Assembly.

Use of Nuclear Energy for Peaceful Purposes

Article 17. Nothing in the provisions of this Treaty shall prejudice the rights of the Contracting Parties, in conformity with this Treaty, to use nuclear energy for peaceful purposes, in particular for their economic development and social progress.

Explosions for Peaceful Purposes

Article 18

1. The Contracting Parties may carry out explosions of nuclear devices for peaceful purposes—including explosions which involve devices similar to those used in nuclear weapons—or collaborate with third parties for the same purpose, provided that they do so in accordance with the provisions of this article and the other articles of the Treaty, particularly articles 1 and 5.

2. Contracting Parties intending to carry out, or to cooperate in carrying out, such an explosion shall notify the Agency and the International Atomic Energy Agency, as far in advance as the circumstances require, of the date of the explosion and shall at the same time provide the following information:

(a) The nature of the nuclear device and the source from which it was obtained,

(b) The place and purpose of the planned explosion,

(c) The procedures which will be followed in order to comply with paragraph 3 of this article.

(d) The expected force of the device, and

(e) The fullest possible information on any possible radioactive fall-out that may result from the explosion or explosions, and measures which will be taken to avoid danger to the population, flora, fauna and territories of any other Party or Parties.

3. The General Secretary and the technical personnel designated by the Council and the International Atomic Energy Agency may observe all the preparations, including the explosion of the device, and shall have unrestricted access to any area in the vicinity of the site of the explosion in order to ascertain whether the device and the procedures followed during the explosion are in conformity with the information supplied under paragraph 2 of this article and the other provisions of this Treaty.

4. The Contracting Parties may accept the collaboration of third parties for the purpose set forth in paragraph 1 of the present article, in accordance with paragraphs 2 and 3 thereof.

Relations with Other International Organizations

Article 19

1. The Agency may conclude such agreements with the International Atomic Energy Agency as are authorized by the General Conference and as it considers likely to facilitate the efficient operation of the control system established by this Treaty.

2. The Agency may also enter into relations with any international organization or body, especially any which may be established in the future to supervise disarmament or measures for the control of armaments in any part of the world.

3. The Contracting Parties may, if they see fit, request the advice of the Inter-American Nuclear Energy Commission on all technical matters connected with the application of this Treaty with which the Commission is competent to deal under its Statute.

Measures in the Event of Violation of the Treaty

Article 20

1. The General Conference shall take note of all cases in which, in its opinion, any Contracting Party is not complying fully with its obligations under

this Treaty and shall draw the matter to the attention of the Party concerned, making such recommendations as it deems appropriate.

2. If, in its opinion, such non-compliance constitutes a violation of this Treaty which might endanger peace and security, the General Conference shall report thereon simultaneously to the United Nations Security Council and the General Assembly through the Secretary-General of the United Nations, and to the Council of the Organization of American States. The General Conference shall likewise report to the International Atomic Energy Agency for such purposes as are relevant in accordance with its Statute.

United Nations and Organization of American States

Article 21. None of the provisions of this Treaty shall be construed as impairing the rights and obligations of the Parties under the Charter of the United Nations or, in the case of States Members of the Organization of American States, under existing regional treaties.

Privileges and Immunities

Article 22

1. The Agency shall enjoy in the territory of each of the Contracting Parties such legal capacity and such privileges and immunities as may be necessary for the exercise of its functions and the fulfillment of its purposes.

2. Representatives of the Contracting Parties accredited to the Agency and officials of the Agency shall similarly enjoy such privileges and immunities as are necessary for the performance of their functions.

3. The Agency may conclude agreements with the Contracting Parties with a view to determining the details of the application of paragraphs 1 and 2 of this article.

Notification of Other Agreements

Article 23. Once this Treaty has entered into force, the Secretariat shall be notified immediately of any international agreement concluded by any of the Contracting Parties on matters with which this Treaty is concerned; the Secretariat shall register it and notify the other Contracting Parties.

Settlement of Disputes

Article 24. Unless the Parties concerned agree on another mode of peaceful settlement, any question or dispute concerning the interpretation or application of this Treaty which is not settled shall be referred to the International Court of Justice with the prior consent of the Parties to the controversy.

[Ratification and deposit]

Amendments

Article 29

1. Any Contracting Party may propose amendments to this Treaty and shall submit its proposals to the Council through the General Secretary, who shall transmit them to all the other contracting Parties and, in addition, to all other signatories in accordance with article 6. The Council, through the General Secretary, shall immediately following the meeting of signatories convene a special session of the General Conference to examine the proposals made, for the adoption of which a two-thirds majority of the Contracting Parties present and voting shall be required.

2. Amendments adopted shall enter into force as soon as the requirements set forth in article 28 of this Treaty have been complied with.

Duration and Denunciation

Article 30

1. This Treaty shall be of a permanent nature and shall remain in force indefinitely, but any Party may denounce it by notifying the General Secretary of the Agency if, in the opinion of the denouncing State, there have arisen or may arise circumstances connected with the content of this Treaty or of the annexed Additional Protocols I and II which affect its supreme interests or the peace and security of one or more Contracting Parties.

2. The denunciation shall take effect three months after the delivery to the General Secretary of the Agency of the notification by the Government of the signatory State concerned. The General Secretary shall immediately communicate such notification to the other Contracting Parties and to the Secretary-General of the United Nations for the information of the United Nations Security Council and the General Assembly. He shall also communicate it to the Secretary-General of the Organization of American States.

Authentic Texts and Registration

Article 31. This Treaty, of which the Spanish, Chinese, English, French, Portuguese and Russian texts are equally authentic, shall be registered by the Depositary Government in accordance with article 102 of the United Nations Charter. The Depositary Government shall notify the Secretary-General of the United Nations of the signatures, ratifications and amendments relating to this Treaty and shall communicate them to the Secretary-General of the Organization of American States for its information.

Transitional Article

Denunciation of the declaration referred to in article 28, paragraph 2, shall be subject to the same procedures as the denunciation of this Treaty, except that it will take effect on the date of delivery of the respective notification.

[Signatures]

Additional Protocol I to the Treaty for the Prohibition of Nuclear Weapons in Latin America, signed by the United States at Washington, 26 May 1977

The undersigned Plenipotentiaries, furnished with full powers by their respective Governments,

Convinced that the Treaty for the Prohibition of Nuclear Weapons in Latin America, negotiated and signed in accordance with the recommendations of the General Assembly of the United Nations in Resolution 1911 (XVIII) of 27 November 1963, represents an important step towards ensuring the non-proliferation of nuclear weapons,

Aware that the non-proliferation of nuclear weapons is not an end in itself but, rather, a means of achieving general and complete disarmament at a later stage, and

Desiring to contribute, so far as lies in their power, towards ending the armaments race, especially in the field of nuclear weapons, and towards strengthening a world at peace, based on mutual respect and sovereign equality of States,

Have agreed as follows:

Article 1. To undertake to apply the statute of denuclearization in respect of warlike purposes as defined in articles 1, 3, 5 and 13 of the Treaty for the Prohibition of Nuclear Weapons in Latin America in territories for which, *de jure* or *de facto,* they are internationally responsible and which lie within the limits of the geographical zone established in that Treaty.

Article 2. The duration of this Protocol shall be the same as that of the Treaty for the Prohibition of Nuclear Weapons in Latin America of which this Protocol is an annex, and the provisions regarding ratification and denunciation contained in the Treaty shall be applicable to it.

Article 3. This Protocol shall enter into force, for the States which have ratified it, on the date of the deposit of their respective instruments of ratification.

[Signatures]

Additional Protocol II to the Treaty for the Prohibition of Nuclear Weapons in Latin America, signed by the United States at Mexico City, 1 April 1968

The Undersigned Plenipotentiaries, furnished with full powers by their respective Governments,

Convinced that the Treaty for the Prohibition of Nuclear Weapons in Latin America, negotiated and signed in accordance with the recommendations of the General Assembly of the United Nations in Resolution 1911 (XVIII) of 27 November 1963, represents an important step towards ensuring the non-proliferation of nuclear weapons,

Aware that the non-proliferation of nuclear weapons is not an end in itself but, rather, a means of achieving general and complete disarmament at a later stage, and

Desiring to contribute, so far as lies in their power, towards ending the armaments race, especially in the field of nuclear weapons, and towards promoting and strengthening a world at peace, based on mutual respect and sovereign equality of States,

Have agreed as follows:

Article 1. The statute of denuclearization of Latin America in respect of warlike purposes, as defined, delimited and set forth in the Treaty for the Prohibition of Nuclear Weapons in Latin America of which this instrument is an annex, shall be fully respected by the Parties to this Protocol in all its express aims and provisions.

Article 2. The Governments represented by the undersigned Plenipotentiaries undertake, therefore, not to contribute in any way to the performance of acts involving a violation of the obligations of article 1 of the Treaty in the territories to which the Treaty applies in accordance with article 4 thereof.

Article 3. The Governments represented by the undersigned Plenipotentiaries also undertake not to use or threaten to use nuclear weapons against the Contracting Parties of the Treaty for the Prohibition of Nuclear Weapons in Latin America.

Article 4. The duration of this Protocol shall be the same as that of the Treaty for the Prohibition of Nuclear Weapons in Latin America of which this Protocol is an annex, and the definitions of territory and nuclear weapons set forth in articles 3 and 5 of the Treaty shall be applicable to this Protocol, as well as the provisions regarding ratification, reservations, denunciation, authentic texts and registration contained in articles 26, 27, 30 and 31 of the Treaty.

Article 5. This Protocol shall enter into force, for the States which have ratified it, on the date of the deposit of their respective instruments of ratification.

[Signatures]

Proclamation by President Nixon on Ratification of Additional Protocol II to the Treaty for the Prohibition of Nuclear Weapons in Latin America

BY THE PRESIDENT OF THE UNITED STATES
OF AMERICA
A PROCLAMATION

Considering that:

Additional Protocol II to the Treaty for the Prohibition of Nuclear Weapons in Latin America, done at the City of Mexico on February 14, 1967, was signed on behalf of the United States of America on April 1, 1968, the text of which Protocol is word for word as follows:

[The text of the Protocol appears here.]

The Senate of the United States of America by its resolution of April 19, 1971, two-thirds of the Senators present concurring, gave its advice and consent to the ratification of Additional Protocol II, with the following understandings and declarations:

I. That the United States Government understands the reference in Article 3 of the treaty to "its own legislation" to relate only to such legislation as is compatible with the rules of international law and as involves an exercise of sovereignty consistent with those rules, and accordingly that ratification of Additional Protocol II by the United States

Government could not be regarded as implying recognition, for the purposes of this treaty and its protocols or for any other purpose, of any legislation which did not, in the view of the United States, comply with the relevant rules of international law.

That the United States Government takes note of the Preparatory Commission's interpretation of the treaty, as set forth in the Final Act, that, governed by the principles and rules of international law, each of the Contracting Parties retains exclusive power and legal competence, unaffected by the terms of the treaty, to grant or deny non-Contracting Parties transit and transport privileges.

That as regards the undertaking in Article 3 of Protocol II not to use or threaten to use nuclear weapons against the Contracting Parties, the United States Government would have to consider that an armed attack by a Contracting Party, in which it was assisted by a nuclear-weapon state, would be incompatible with the Contracting Party's corresponding obligations under Article 1 of the Treaty.

II. That the United States Government considers that the technology of making nuclear explosive devices for peaceful purposes is indistinguishable from the technology of making nuclear weapons, and that nuclear weapons and nuclear explosive devices for peaceful purposes are both capable of releasing nuclear energy in an uncontrolled manner and have the common group of characteristics of large amounts of energy generated instantaneously from a compact source. Therefore, the United States Government understands the definition contained in Article 5 of the treaty as necessarily encompassing all nuclear explosive devices. It is also understood that Articles 1 and 5 restrict accordingly the activities of the Contracting Parties under paragraph 1 of Article 18.

That the United States Government understands that paragraph 4 of Article 18 of the Treaty permits, and that United States adherence to Protocol II will not prevent, collaboration by the United States with Contracting Parties for the purpose of carrying out explosions of nuclear devices for peaceful purposes in a manner consistent with a policy of not contributing to the proliferation of nuclear weapons capabilities. In this connection, the United States Government notes Article V of the Treaty on the Non-Proliferation of Nuclear Weapons, under which it joined in an undertaking to take appropriate measures to ensure that potential benefits of peaceful applications of nuclear explosions would be made available to non-nuclear-weapon states party to that treaty, and reaffirms its willingness to extend such undertaking, on the same basis, to states precluded by the present treaty from manufacturing or acquiring any nuclear explosive device.

III. That the United States Government also declares that, although not required by Protocol II, it will act with respect to such territories of Protocol I adherents as are within the geographical area defined in paragraph 2 of Article 4 of the Treaty in the same manner as Protocol II requires it to act with respect to the territories of Contracting Parties.

The President ratified Additional Protocol II on May 8, 1971, with the above-recited understandings and declarations, in pursuance of the advice and consent of the Senate.

It is provided in Article 5 of Additional Protocol II that the Protocol shall enter into force, for the States which have ratified it, on the date of the deposit of their respective instruments of ratification.

The instrument of ratification of the United Kingdom of Great Britain and Northern Ireland was deposited on December 11, 1969 with understandings and a declaration, and the instrument of ratification of the United States of America was deposited on May 12, 1971 with the above-recited understandings and declarations.

In accordance with Article 5 of Additional Protocol II, the Protocol entered into force for the United States of America on May 12, 1971, subject to the above recited understandings and declarations.

[Signature]

[U.S. Arms Control and Disarmament Agency, *Arms Control and Disarmament Agreements: Texts and Histories of the Negotiations,* 1982 ed. (Washington, D.C., 1982), pp. 64–79]

Seabed Treaty (1971)

The following treaty was signed at Washington, London, and Moscow on 11 February 1971, and it entered into force on 18 May 1972.

Treaty on the Prohibition of the Emplacement of Nuclear Weapons and Other Weapons of Mass Destruction on the Seabed and the Ocean Floor and in the Subsoil Thereof

The States Parties to this Treaty,

Recognizing the common interest of mankind in the progress of the exploration and use of the seabed and the ocean floor for peaceful purposes,

Considering that the prevention of a nuclear arms race on the seabed and the ocean floor serves the interests of maintaining world peace, reduces international tensions and strengthens friendly relations among States,

Convinced that this Treaty constitutes a step towards the exclusion of the seabed, the ocean floor and the subsoil thereof from the arms race,

Convinced that this Treaty constitutes a step towards a treaty on general and complete disarmament under strict and effective international control, and determined to continue negotiations to this end,

Convinced that this Treaty will further the purposes and principles of the Charter of the United Nations, in a manner consistent with the principles of international law and without infringing the freedoms of the high seas,

Have agreed as follows:

Article I

1. The States Parties to this Treaty undertake not to emplant or emplace on the seabed and the ocean floor and in the subsoil thereof beyond the outer limit of a seabed zone, as defined in article II, any nuclear weapons or any other types of weapons of mass destruction as well as structures, launching installations or any other facilities specifically designed for storing, testing or using such weapons.

2. The undertakings of paragraph 1 of this article shall also apply to the seabed zone referred to in the same paragraph, except that within such seabed zone, they shall not apply either to the coastal State or to the seabed beneath its territorial waters.

3. The States Parties to this Treaty undertake not to assist, encourage or induce any State to carry out activities referred to in paragraph 1 of this article and not to participate in any other way in such actions.

Article II. For the purpose of this Treaty, the outer limit of the seabed zone referred to in article I shall be coterminous with the twelve-mile outer limit of the zone referred to in part II of the Convention on the Territorial Sea and the Contiguous Zone, signed at Geneva on April 29, 1958, and shall be measured in accordance with the provisions of part 1, section II, of that Convention and in accordance with international law.

Article III

1. In order to promote the objectives of and insure compliance with the provisions of this Treaty, each State Party to the Treaty shall have the right to verify through observations the activities of other States Parties to the Treaty on the seabed and the ocean floor and in the subsoil thereof beyond the zone referred to in article I, provided that observation does not interfere with such activities.

2. If after such observation reasonable doubts remain concerning the fulfillment of the obligations assumed under the Treaty, the State Party having such doubts and the State Party that is responsible for the activities giving rise to the doubts shall consult with a view to removing the doubts. If the doubts persist, the State Party having such doubts shall notify the other States Parties, and the Parties concerned shall cooperate on such further procedures for verification as may be agreed, including appropriate inspection of objects, structures, installations or other facilities that reasonably may be expected to be of a kind described in article I. The Parties in the region of the activities, including any coastal State, and any other Party so requesting, shall be entitled to participate in such consultation and cooperation. After completion of the further procedures for verification, an appropriate report shall be circulated to other Parties by the Party that initiated such procedures.

3. If the State responsible for the activities giving rise to the reasonable doubts is not identifiable by observation of the object, structure, installation or other facility, the State Party having such doubts shall notify and make appropriate inquiries of States Parties in the region of the activities and of any other State Party. If it is ascertained through these inquiries that a particular state Party is responsible for the activities, that State Party shall consult and cooperate with other Parties as provided in paragraph 2 of this article. If the identity of the State responsible for the activities cannot be ascertained through these inquiries, then further

verification procedures, including inspection, may be undertaken by the inquiring State Party, which shall invite the participation of the Parties in the region of the activities, including any coastal State, and of any other Party desiring to cooperate.

4. If consultation and cooperation pursuant to paragraphs 2 and 3 of this article have not removed the doubts concerning the activities and there remains a serious question concerning fulfillment of the obligations assumed under this Treaty, a State Party may, in accordance with the provisions of the Charter of the United Nations, refer the matter to the Security Council, which may take action in accordance with the Charter.

5. Verification pursuant to this article may be undertaken by any State Party using its own means, or with the full or partial assistance of any other State Party, or through appropriate international procedures within the framework of the United Nations and in accordance with its Charter.

6. Verification activities pursuant to this Treaty shall not interfere with activities of other States Parties and shall be conducted with due regard for rights recognized under international law, including the freedoms of the high seas and the rights of coastal States with respect to the exploration and exploitation of their continental shelves.

Article IV. Nothing in this Treaty shall be interpreted as supporting or prejudicing the position of any State Party with respect to existing international conventions, including the 1958 Convention on the Territorial Sea and the Contiguous Zone, or with respect to rights or claims which such State Party may assert, or with respect to recognition or nonrecognition of rights or claims asserted by any other State, related to waters off its coasts, including, *inter alia,* territorial seas and contiguous zones, or to the seabed and the ocean floor, including continental shelves.

Article V. The Parties to this Treaty undertake to continue negotiations in good faith concerning further measures in the field of disarmament for the prevention of an arms race on the seabed, the ocean floor and the subsoil thereof.

Article VI. Any State Party may propose amendments to this Treaty. Amendments shall enter into force for each State Party accepting the amendments upon their acceptance by a majority of the States Parties to the Treaty and, thereafter, for each remaining State Party on the date of acceptance by it.

Article VII. Five years after the entry into force of this Treaty, a conference of Parties to the Treaty shall be held at Geneva, Switzerland, in order to review the operation of this Treaty with a view to assuring that the purposes of the preamble and the provisions of the Treaty are being realized. Such review shall take into account any relevant technological developments. The review conference shall determine, in accordance with the views of a majority of those Parties attending, whether and when an additional review conference shall be convened.

[Ratification and Deposit]

[Signatures]

[U.S. Arms Control and Disarmament Agency, *Arms Control and Disarmament Agreements: Texts and Histories of the Negotiations,* 1982 ed. (Washington, D.C., 1982), pp. 102–104]

South Pacific Nuclear-Free-Zone Treaty (1985)

The following treaty was signed at Rarotonga on 6 August 1985, and it entered into force on 11 December 1986.

The Parties to this Treaty,

United in their commitment to a world at peace;

Gravely concerned that the continuing nuclear arms race presents the risk of nuclear war which would have devastating consequences for all people;

Convinced that all countries have an obligation to make every effort to achieve the goal of eliminating nuclear weapons, the terror which they hold for humankind and the threat which they pose to life on earth;

Believing that regional arms control measures can contribute to global efforts to reverse the nuclear arms race and promote the national security of each country in the region and the common security of all;

Determined to ensure, so far as lies within their power, that the bounty and beauty of the land and sea in their region shall remain the heritage of their peoples and their descendants in perpetuity to be enjoyed by all in peace;

Reaffirming the importance of the Treaty on the Non-Proliferation of Nuclear Weapons (NPT) in preventing the proliferation of nuclear weapons and in contributing to world security;

Noting, in particular, that Article VII of the NPT recognizes the right of any group of States to conclude regional treaties in order to assure the total absence of nuclear weapons in their respective territories;

Noting that the prohibitions of emplantation and emplacement of nuclear weapons on the seabed and the ocean floor and in the subsoil thereof contained in the Treaty on the Prohibition of Emplacement of Nuclear Weapons and Other Weapons of Mass Destruction on the Seabed and the Ocean Floor and in the Subsoil Thereof apply in the South Pacific;

Noting also that the prohibition of testing of nuclear weapons in the atmosphere or under water, including territorial waters or high seas, contained in the Treaty Banning Nuclear Weapon Tests in the Atmosphere, in Outer Space and Under Water applies in the South Pacific;

Determined to keep the region free of environmental pollution by radioactive wastes and other radioactive matter;

Guided by the decision of the Fifteenth South Pacific Forum at Tuvalu that a nuclear free zone should be established in the region at the earliest possible opportunity in accordance with the principles set out in the communiqué of that meeting;

Have agreed as follows:

Article I. Usage of Terms

For the purposes of this Treaty and its Protocols:

(a) "South Pacific Nuclear Free Zone" means the areas described in Annex 1 as illustrated by the map attached to that Annex;

(b) "territory" means internal waters, territorial sea and archipelagic waters, the seabed and subsoil beneath, the land territory and the airspace above them;

(c) "nuclear explosive device" means any nuclear weapon or other explosive device capable of releasing nuclear energy, irrespective of the purpose for which it could be used. The term includes such a weapon or device in unassembled and partly assembled forms, but does not include the means of transport or delivery of such a weapon or device if separable from and not an indivisible part of it;

(d) "stationing" means emplantation, emplacement, transportation on land or inland waters, stockpiling, storage, installation and deployment.

Article 2. Application of the Treaty

1. Except where otherwise specified, this Treaty and its Protocols shall apply to territory within the South Pacific Nuclear Free Zone.

2. Nothing in this Treaty shall prejudice or in any way affect the rights, or the exercise of the rights, of any State under international law with regard to freedom of the seas.

Article 3. Renunciation of Nuclear Explosive Devices

Each Party undertakes:

(a) not to manufacture or otherwise acquire, possess or have control over any nuclear explosive device by any means anywhere inside or outside the South Pacific Nuclear Free Zone;

(b) not to seek or receive any assistance in the manufacture or acquisition of any nuclear explosive device;

(c) not to take any action to assist or encourage the manufacture or acquisition of any nuclear explosive device by any State.

Article 4. Peaceful Nuclear Activities

Each Party undertakes:

(a) not to provide source or special fissionable material, or equipment or material especially designed or prepared for the processing, use or production of special fissionable material for peaceful purposes to:

(i) any non-nuclear-weapon State unless subject to the safeguards required by Article III.1 of the NPT, or

(ii) any nuclear-weapon State unless subject to applicable safeguards agreements with the International Atomic Energy Agency (IAEA).

Any such provisions shall be in accordance with strict non-proliferation measures to provide assurance of exclusively peaceful non-explosive use;

(b) to support the continued effectiveness of the international nonproliferation system based on the NPT and the IAEA safeguards system.

Article 5. Prevention of Stationing of Nuclear Explosive Devices

1. Each Party undertakes to prevent in its territory the stationing of any nuclear explosive device.

2. Each Party in the exercise of its sovereign rights remains free to decide for itself whether to allow visits by foreign ships and aircraft to its ports and airfields, transit of its airspace by foreign aircraft, and navigation by foreign ships in its territorial sea or archipelagic waters in a manner not covered by the rights of innocent passage, archipelagic sea lane passage or transit passage of straits.

Article 6. Prevention of Testing of Nuclear Explosive Devices

Each Party undertakes:

(a) to prevent in its territory the testing of any nuclear explosive device;

(b) not to take any action to assist or encourage the testing of any nuclear explosive device by any State.

Article 7. Prevention of Dumping

1. Each Party undertakes:

(a) not to dump radioactive wastes and other radioactive matter at sea anywhere within the South Pacific Nuclear Free Zone;

(b) to prevent the dumping of radioactive wastes and other radioactive matter by anyone in its territorial sea;

(c) not to take any action to assist or encourage the dumping by anyone of radioactive wastes and other radioactive matter at sea anywhere within the South Pacific Nuclear Free Zone;

(d) to support the conclusion as soon as possible of the proposed Convention relating to the protection of the natural resources and environment of the South Pacific region and its Protocol for the prevention of pollution of the South Pacific region by dumping, with the aim of precluding dumping at sea of radioactive wastes and other radioactive matter by anyone anywhere in the region.

2. Paragraphs 1 (a) and 1 (b) of this Article shall not apply to areas of the South Pacific Nuclear Free Zone in respect of which such a Convention and Protocol have entered into force.

Article 8. Control System

1. The Parties hereby establish a control system for the purpose of verifying compliance with their obligations under this Treaty.

2. The control system shall comprise:

(a) reports and exchange of information as provided for in Article 9;

(b) consultations as provided for in Article 10 and Annex 4 (1);

(c) the application to peaceful nuclear activities of safeguards by the IAEA as provided for in Annex 2;

(d) a complaints procedure as provided for in Annex 4.

Article 9. Reports and Exchanges of Information

1. Each Party shall report to the Director of the South Pacific Bureau for Economic Cooperation (the Director) as soon as possible any significant event within its jurisdiction affecting the implementation of this Treaty. The Director shall circulate such reports promptly to all Parties.

2. The Parties shall endeavour to keep each other informed on matters arising under or in relation to this Treaty. They may exchange information by communicating it to the Director, who shall circulate it to all Parties.

3. The Director shall report annually to the South Pacific Forum on the status of this Treaty and matters arising under or in relation to it, incorporating reports and communications made under paragraphs 1 and 2 of this Article and matters arising under Articles 8(2)(d) and 10 and Annex 2(4).

Article 10. Consultations and Review

Without prejudice to the conduct of consultations among Parties by other means, the Director, at the request of any Party, shall convene a meeting of the Consultative Committee established by Annex 3 for consultation and cooperation on any matter arising in relation to this Treaty or for reviewing its operation.

Article 11. Amendment

The Consultative Committee shall consider proposals for amendment of the provisions of this Treaty proposed by any Party and circulated by the Director to all Parties not less than three months prior to the convening of the Consultative Committee for this purpose. Any proposal agreed upon by consensus by the Consultative Committee shall be communicated to the Director who shall circulate it for acceptance to all Parties. An amendment shall enter into force thirty days after receipt by the depositary of acceptances from all Parties.

[Signature and ratification]

ANNEX 2. IAEA Safeguards

1. The safeguards referred to in Article 8 shall in respect of each Party be applied by the IAEA as set forth in an agreement negotiated and concluded with the IAEA on all source or special fissionable material in all peaceful nuclear activities within the territory of the Party, under its jurisdiction or carried out under its control anywhere.

2. The agreement referred to in paragraph 1 shall be, or shall be equivalent in its scope and effect to, an agreement required in connection with the NPT on the basis of the material reproduced in document INFCIRC/153 (Corrected) of the IAEA. Each Party shall take all appropriate steps to ensure that such an agreement is in force for it not later than 18 months after the date of entry into force for that party of this Treaty.

3. For the purposes of this Treaty, the safeguards referred to in paragraph 1 shall have as their purpose the verification of the non-diversion of nuclear material from peaceful nuclear activities to nuclear explosive devices.

4. Each Party agrees upon the request of any other Party to transmit to that party and to the Director for the information of all Parties a copy of the overall conclusions of the most recent report by the IAEA on its inspection activities in the territory of the Party concerned, and to advise the Director promptly of any subsequent findings of the Board of Governors of the IAEA in relation to those conclusions for the information of all Parties.

ANNEX 3. Consultative Committee

1. There is hereby established a Consultative Committee which shall be convened by the Director from time to time pursuant to Articles 10 and 11 and Annex 4 (2). The Consultative Committee shall be constituted of representatives of the Parties, each Party being entitled to appoint one representative who may be accompanied by advisers. Unless otherwise agreed, the Consultative Committee shall be chaired at any given meeting by the representative of the Party which last hosted the meeting of Heads of Government of Members of the South Pacific Forum. A quorum shall be constituted by representatives of half the Parties. Subject to the provisions of Article 11, decisions of the Consultative Committee shall be taken by consensus or, failing consensus, by a two-thirds majority of those present and voting. The Consultative Committee shall adopt such other rules of procedure as it sees fit.

2. The costs of the Consultative Committee, including the costs of special inspections pursuant to Annex 4, shall be borne by the South Pacific Bureau for Economic Cooperation. It may seek special funding should this be required.

ANNEX 4. Complaints Procedure

1. A Party which considers that there are grounds for a complaint that another Party is in breach of its obligations under this Treaty shall, before bringing such a complaint to the Director, bring the subject matter of the complaint to the attention of the Party complained of and shall allow the latter reasonable opportunity to provide it with an explanation and to resolve the matter.

2. If the matter is not so resolved, the complainant Party may bring the complaint to the Director with a request that the Consultative Committee be convened to consider it. Complaints shall be supported by an account of evidence of breach of obligations known to the complainant Party. Upon receipt of a complaint the Director shall convene the Consultative Committee as quickly as possible to consider it.

3. The Consultative Committee, taking account of efforts made under paragraph 1, shall afford the Party complained of a reasonable opportunity to provide it with an explanation of the matter.

4. If, after considering any explanation given to it by the representatives of the Party complained of, the Consultative Committee decides that there is sufficient substance in the complaint to warrant a special inspection in the territory of that Party or elsewhere, the Consultative Committee shall direct that such special inspection be made as quickly as possible by a special inspection team of three suitably qualified special inspectors appointed by the Consultative Committee in consultation with the complained of and complainant Parties, provided that no national of either Party shall serve on the special inspection team. If so requested by the Party complained of, the special inspection team shall be accompanied by representative of that Party. Neither the right of consultation on the appointment of special inspectors, nor the right to accompany special inspectors, shall delay the work of the special inspection team.

5. In making a special inspection, special inspectors shall be subject to the direction only of the Consultative Committee and shall comply with such directives concerning tasks, objectives, confidentiality and procedures as may be decided upon by it. Directives shall take account of the legitimate interests of the Party complained of in complying with its other international obligations and commitments and shall not duplicate safeguards procedures to be undertaken by the IAEA pursuant to agreements referred to in Annex 2 (1). The special inspectors shall discharge their duties with due respect for the laws of the Party complained of.

6. Each Party shall give to special inspectors full and free access to all information and places within its territory which may be relevant to enable the special inspectors to implement the directives given to them by the Consultative Committee.

7. The Party complained of shall take all appropriate steps to facilitate the special inspection, and shall grant to special inspectors privileges and immunities necessary for the performance of their functions, including inviolability for all papers and documents and immunity from arrest, detention and legal process for acts done and words spoken and written, for the purpose of the special inspection.

8. The special inspectors shall report in writing as quickly as possible to the Consultative Committee, outlining their activities, setting out relevant facts and information as ascertained by them, with supporting evidence and documentation as appropriate, and stating their conclusions. The Consultative Committee shall report fully to all Members of the South Pacific Forum, giving its decision as to whether the Party complained of is in breach of its obligations under this Treaty.

9. If the Consultative Committee has decided that the Party complained of is in breach of its obligations under this Treaty, or that the above provisions have not been complied with, or at any time at the request of either the complainant or complained of Party, the Parties shall meet promptly at a meeting of the South Pacific Forum.

Protocol 1

The Parties to this Protocol

Noting the South Pacific Nuclear Free Zone Treaty (the Treaty)

Have agreed as follows:

Article 1. Each Party undertakes to apply, in respect of the territories for which it is internationally responsible situated within the South Pacific Nuclear Free Zone, the prohibitions contained in Articles 3, 5 and 6, in so far as they relate to the manufacture, stationing and testing of any nuclear explosive device within those territories, and the safeguards specified in Article 8(2)(c) and Annex 2 of the Treaty.

Article 2. Each Party may, by written notification to the depositary, indicate its acceptance from the date of such notification of any alteration to its obligation under this Protocol brought about by the entry into force of an amendment to the Treaty pursuant to Article 11 of the Treaty.

Article 3. This Protocol shall be open for signature by the French Republic, the United Kingdom of Great Britain and Northern Ireland and the United States of America.

Article 4. This Protocol shall be subject to ratification.

Article 5. This Protocol is of a permanent nature and shall remain in force indefinitely, provided that each Party shall, in exercising its national sovereignty, have the right to withdraw from this Protocol if it decides that extraordinary events, related to the subject matter of this Protocol, have jeopardized its supreme interests. It shall give notice of such withdrawal to the depositary three months in advance. Such notice shall include a statement of the extraordinary events it regards as having jeopardized its supreme interests.

[Signatures]

Protocol 2

The Parties to this Protocol

Noting the South Pacific Nuclear Free Zone Treaty (the Treaty)

Have agreed as follows:

Article 1. Each Party undertakes not to use or threaten to use any nuclear explosive device against:

(a) Parties to the Treaty; or

(b) any territory within the South Pacific Nuclear Free Zone for which a State that has become a Party to Protocol 1 is internationally responsible.

Article 2. Each Party undertakes not to contribute to any act of a Party to the Treaty which constitutes a violation of the Treaty, or to any act of another Party to a Protocol which constitutes a violation of a Protocol.

Article 3. Each Party may, by written notification to the depositary, indicate its acceptance from the date of such notification of any alteration to its obligation under this Protocol brought about by the entry into force of an amendment to the Treaty pursuant to Article 11 of the Treaty or by the extension of the South Pacific Nuclear Free Zone pursuant to Article 12(3) of the Treaty.

Article 4. This Protocol shall be open for signature by the French Republic, the People's Republic of China, the Union of Soviet Socialist Republics, the United Kingdom of Great Britain and Northern Ireland and the United States of America.

Article 5. This Protocol shall be subject to ratification.

Article 6. This Protocol is of a permanent nature and shall remain in force indefinitely, provided that each Party shall, in exercising its national sovereignty, have the right to withdraw from this Protocol if it decides that extraordinary events, related to the subject matter of this Protocol, have jeopardized its supreme interests. It shall give notice of such withdrawal to the depositary three months in advance. Such notice shall include a statement of the extraordinary events it regards as having jeopardized its supreme interests,

Article 7. This Protocol shall enter into force for each State on the date of its deposit with the depositary of its instrument of ratification.

[Signatures]

Protocol 3

The Parties to this Protocol

Noting the South Pacific Nuclear Free Zone Treaty (the Treaty)

Have agreed as follows:

Article 1. Each Party undertakes not to test any nuclear explosive device anywhere within the South Pacific Nuclear Free Zone.

Article 2. Each Party may, by written notification to the depositary, indicate its acceptance from the date of such notification of any alteration to its obligation under this Protocol brought about by the entry into force of an amendment to the Treaty pursuant to Article 11 of the Treaty or by the extension of the South Pacific Nuclear Free Zone pursuant to Article 12(3) of the Treaty.

Article 3. This Protocol shall be open for signature by the French Republic, the People's Republic of China, the Union of Soviet Socialist Republics, the United Kingdom of Great Britain and Northern Ireland and the United States of America.

Article 4. This Protocol shall be subject to ratification.

Article 5. This Protocol is of a permanent nature and shall remain in force indefinitely, provided that each Party shall, in exercising its national sovereignty, have the right to withdraw from this Protocol if it decides that extraordinary events, related to the subject matter of this Protocol, have jeopardized its supreme interests. It shall give notice of such withdrawal to the depositary three months in advance. Such notice shall include a statement of the extraordinary events it regards as having jeopardized its supreme interests.

Article 6. This Protocol shall enter into force for each State on the date of its deposit with the depositary of its instrument of ratification.

[Text submitted to the Conference on Disarmament and reproduced in its report. *Official Records of the General Assembly, Fortieth Session, Supplement No. 27* (A/40/27 and Corr. 1), appendix II (CD/642), vol. 4, document CD/633 and Corr. 1. The text of Protocols 1, 2, and 3 is reproduced from document CD/633/annex 4/Rev. 1.]

Regulating and Outlawing Weapons and War

○

Entries that are the subjects of essays in Volumes I an II are marked with asterisks.

From the beginning of organized fighting or "warfare" there have evolved a series of prohibitions—some temporary, some more lasting—against the possession or employment of certain weapons or "military" practices. A sampling of these prohibitions are listed here, while others may be found in Neta Crawford's essay, "Restraining Violence in Early Societies."

The Outlawing of "Missile Weapons"

Polybius, a historian of ancient Rome, has chronicled some of these prohibitions. He lamented the treacherous practices of his own day—such as ambushes, employment of barbarous tactics, double-dealing with allies and enemies alike, and violating pledges. For his part, Polybius expressed admiration for earlier societies and leaders who demonstrated more honorable behavior and a sense of abhorrence for "secret" missiles launched from a distance—presumably such weapons as spears, arrows and stones from slings. He wrote:

The ancients, as we know, were far removed from such malpractices. For so far were they from plotting mischief against their friends with the purpose of aggrandizing their own power, that they would not even consent to get the better of their enemies by fraud, regarding no success as brilliant or secure unless they crushed the spirit of their adversaries in open battle.

For this reason they entered into a convention among themselves to use against each other neither secret missiles nor those discharged from a distance, and considered that it was only a hand-to-hand battle at close quarters which was truly decisive.

Hence they preceded war by a declaration, and when they intended to do battle gave notice of the fact and of the spot to which they would proceed and array their army.

[*Polybius: The Histories.* 6 vols. Trans. by W. R. Paton (New York: G. P. Putnam's Sons, 1927): Book 13, 3.2–4.3 (vol. 2, p. 415)]

Outlawing Crossbows (1139)

Medieval church leaders, apparently under the prodding of the nobles, barred the use of crossbows in wars against Christians, although their use may have been acceptable in wars against infidels and heretics. The crossbows—used by relatively untrained lower-class soldiers, often mercenaries—were likely the most lethal weapons of the twelfth century, in that their arrows could puncture armor, be aimed with accuracy, and were often laced with poison; noblemen of the time thus felt the use of crossbows was "unfair."

Although the Second Lateran Council did issue a decree that has been interpreted as a prohibition against the use of the crossbow, it did not prevent the use of the weapon.

Second Lateran Council Decrees, Canon 29 (1139)

We forbid under penalty of anathema that that deadly and God-detested art of slingers and archers be in the future exercised against Christians and Catholics.

[Latin text from Centro di Documentazione, Instituto per le Scienze Religiose, Bologna, *Consiliorum Oecumenicorum Decreta* (Basle, Barcelona, Freiburg, Rome, Vienna: Herder, 1962), p. 179; English text from H. J. Schroeder, ed., *Disciplinary Decrees of the General Councils,* (St. Louis, 1937), p. 213]

Limiting Use of War Elephants (202/188 B.C.)

Roman military leaders feared their opponents employing elephants in combat, because the sight of these huge beasts could, and did, cause panic among their troops. Consequently, when they had the opportunity to strip their enemies unilaterally of such "weapons," they did so in a manner similiar to twentieth century efforts of prohibiting former enemies from possessing chemical/biological and nuclear weapons.

Carthage-Rome Treaty of Peace (202 B.C.)

This treaty, popularly known as the "Treaty of Zama," ended the Second Punic War between the two warring Mediterranean commercial powers. Hannibal's defeat at the Battle of Zama forced Carthage to sue for peace. Roman leaders imposed harsh unilateral military terms on the vanquished, including the outlawing of Carthage's training and possession of trained war elephants.

Terms of peace were put to them [the envoys of Carthage]: . . . all the trained elephants in their possession were to be handed over and no more to be trained.
[Livy, *The War With Hannibal,* book 30. Trans. by Aubrey de Sélincourt. Baltimore, Md.: Penguin Books, 1965, pp. 36–37.]

Peace of Apamea (188 B.C.)

Polybius has described the treaty in some detail, including stripping King Antiochus of his war elephants:

He [King Antiochus] shall surrender all the elephants now in Apamea and not keep any in [the] future.
[*Polybius: The Histories.* 6 vols. Trans. by W. R. Paton (New York: G. P. Putnam's Sons, 1927): Book 13, 42.3–13 (vol. 2, p. 335)]

Prohibition of Poisoned Weapons

In accounts dealing with warfare and politics from the earliest societies to the nineteenth century there are several references to the use of "poisons." It was usually suggested that their use was uncivilized, and a prohibition of such use was advocated. The examples below reveal the evolution of this prohibition:

Ancient Greek Criticism

One of the first objections to the use of poison appears in an early literary classic, The Odyssey of Homer.

Odysseus, you see, had gone there also in his swift
   ship
in search of a poison to kill men, so he might have
   it
to smear on his bronze-headed arrows, but Ilos
   would not
give him any, since he feared the gods who endure
   forever.

[*The Odyssey of Homer.* Trans. by Richmond Lattimore (New York: Harper & Row). Copyright 1965, 1967 by Richmond Lattimore]

Treaty of Strassbury (1675)

Signed by the French and Germans, this treaty appears to be the first international agreement concerning poisoned weapons.

Article 57
[Virtually the same language as found in the "Lieber Code," see below.]

The "Lieber Code" (1863)

German-born Francis Lieber had served in the Prussian army and was seriously wounded in battles against Napoleon's forces. He received a doctorate in law from the University of Jena and migrated to the United States. There he was named a professor at Columbia College's new law school in 1858. When the Civil War broke out, he was asked by General Henry W. Halleck, the first "chief-of-staff," to prepare a set of rules to govern Union forces. The result appeared in the U.S. War Department General Order 100, issued 24 April 1863.

Article LXX. The use of poison in any manner, be it to poison wells, or food, or arms, is wholly excluded from modern warfare. He that uses it puts himself out of the pale of the law and usages of war. [Leon Friedman, ed., *The Law of War: A Documentary History,* 2 vols. (New York: Random House, 1972): vol. 1, p. 171]

The Declaration of Brussels (1874)

Representatives from fourteen European nations, convening at the request of Russia, reviewed several limitations on the conduct of warfare, including prohibiting the use of poison. The Conference of Brussels, on 27 August 1874, adopted the "International Declaration Concerning the Laws and Customs of War." The Declaration was never ratified due to British opposition; nevertheless, its provisions greatly influenced succeeding military operations.

Article XII. The laws of war do not allow to belligerents an unlimited power as to the choice of means of injuring the enemy.

Article XIII. According to this principle are strictly forbidden:

(a) The use of poison or poisoned weapons. . . .
[Leon Friedman, ed., *The Law of War: A Documentary History,* 2 vols. (New York: Random House, 1972), vol. 1, p. 196]

Restricting Submarine Warfare

Versailles Treaty Submarine Prohibition (1919)

A defeated Germany was prohibited from having submarines by the Treaty of Versailles, 1919.

Article 191. The construction or acquisition of any submarine, even for commercial purposes, shall be forbidden in Germany.

Washington Treaty on Use of Submarines and Gases in Wartime (1922)

Article I. The Signatory Powers declare that among the rules adopted by civilized nations for the protection of the lives of neutrals and noncombatants at sea in time of war, the following are to be deemed an established part of international law;

(1) A merchant vessel must be ordered to submit to visit and search to determine its character before it can be seized.

A merchant vessel must not be attacked unless it refuse to submit to visit and search after warning, or to proceed as directed after seizure.

A merchant vessel must not be destroyed unless the crew and passengers have been first placed in safety.

(2) Belligerent submarines are not under any circumstances exempt from the universal rules above stated; and if a submarine can not capture a merchant vessel in conformity with these rules the existing law of nations requires it to desist from attack and from seizure and to permit the merchant vessel to proceed unmolested.

Article II. The Signatory Powers invite all other civilized Powers to express their assent to the foregoing statement of established law so that there may be a clear public understanding throughout the world of the standards of conduct by which the public opinion of the world is to pass judgment upon future belligerents.

Article III. The Signatory Powers, desiring to insure the enforcement of the humane rules of existing law declared by them with respect to attacks upon and the seizure and destruction of merchant ships, further declare that any person in the service of any Power who shall violate any of those rules, whether or not such person is under orders of a governmental superior, shall be deemed to have violated the laws of war and shall be liable to trial and punishment as if for an act of piracy and may be brought to trial before the civil or military authorities of any Power within the jurisdiction of which he may be found.

Article IV. The Signatory Powers recognize the practical impossibility of using submarines as commerce destroyers without violating, as they were violated in the recent war of 1914–1918, the requirements universally accepted by civilized nations for the protection of the lives of neutrals and noncombatants, and to the end that the prohibition of the use of submarines as commerce destroyers shall be universally accepted as a part of the law of nations they now accept that prohibition as henceforth binding as between themselves and they invite all other nations to adhere thereto.

Article V. The use in war of asphyxiating, poisonous or other gases, and all analogous liquids, materials or devices, having been justly condemned by the general opinion of the civilized world and a prohibition of such use having been declared in treaties to which a majority of the civilized Powers are parties,

The Signatory Powers, to the end that this prohibition shall be universally accepted as a part of international law binding alike the conscience and practice of nations, declare their assent to such prohibition, agree to be bound thereby as between themselves and invite all other civilized nations to adhere thereto.

[Signatures]

[U.S. Senate, 67th Cong., 2nd Sess., Doc. 124, *Armament Conference Treaties: Treaties and Resolutions Approved and Adopted by the Conference on the Limitation of Armament* (Washington, D.C.: G.P.O., 1922)]

London Submarine Restrictions (1930)

The following article is repeated from the London Naval Limitation Treaty of 1930, which is reprinted in full in the first section of this volume, Limitation of Weapons and Personnel.

PART IV

Article 22. The following are accepted as established rules of International Law:

(1) In their action with regard to merchant ships, submarines must conform to the rules of International Law to which surface vessels are subject.

(2) In particular, except in the case of persistent refusal to stop on being duly summoned, or of active resistance to visit or search, a warship, whether surface vessel or submarine, may not sink or render incapable of navigation a merchant vessel without having first placed passengers, crew and ship's papers in a place of safety. For this purpose the ship's boats are not regarded as a place of safety unless the safety of the passengers and crew is assured, in the existing sea and weather conditions, by the proximity of land, or the presence of another vessel which is in a position to take them on board.

The High Contracting Parties invite all other Powers to express their assent to the above rules.

Submarine Protocol (1936)

This procès-verbal *comprised a verbatim incorporation of Article 22 that appeared in the 1930 London Naval Limitation Treaty—see above.*

Restricting Aerial Bombardment

The Hague Declaration Prohibiting Aerial Bombing (1907)

Declaration Prohibiting the Discharge of Projectiles and Explosives from Balloons, October 18, 1907

The Undersigned, Plenipotentiaries of the Powers invited to the Second International Peace Conference at The Hague, duly authorized to that effect by their Governments, inspired by the sentiments which found expression in the Declaration of St. Petersburg of the 29th November (11th December), 1868, and being desirous of renewing the declaration of The Hague of the 29th July, 1899, which has now expired,

Declare:

The Contracting Powers agree to prohibit, for a period extending to the close of the Third Peace Conference, the discharge of projectiles and explosives from balloons or by other new methods of a similar nature.

The present Declaration is only binding on the Contracting Powers in case of war between two or more of them.

It shall cease to be binding from the time when, in a war between the Contracting Powers, one of the belligerents is joined by a non-Contracting Power.

The present Declaration shall be ratified as soon as possible.

The ratifications shall be deposited at The Hague.

A *procès-verbal* shall be drawn up recording the receipt of the ratifications, of which a duly certified copy shall be sent, through the diplomatic channel, to all the Contracting Powers.

Non-Signatory Powers may adhere to the present Declaration. To do so, they must make known their adhesion to the Contracting Powers by means of a written notification, addressed to the Netherland Government, and communicated by it to all the other Contracting Powers.

In the event of one of the High Contracting Parties denouncing the present Declaration, such denunciation shall not take effect until a year after the notification made in writing to the Netherland Government, and forthwith communicated by it to all the other Contracting Powers.

This denunciation shall only have affect in regard to the notifying Power.

In faith whereof the Plenipotentiaries have appended their signatures to the present Declaration.

Done at The Hague, the 18th October, 1907, in a single copy, which shall remain deposited in the archives of the Netherland Government, and duly certified copies of which shall be sent, through the diplomatic channel, to the Contracting Powers.

[W. M. Malloy, *Treaties, Conventions, International Acts, Protocols, and Agreements Between the United States and Other Powers, 1776–1937*, 4 vols. (Washington, D.C., G.P.O., 1910–1938), pp. 2366–2367]

Hague Commission of Jurists: Rules of Air War (1923)

The following Rules of Air Warfare were drafted by a commission of jurists at The Hague, December 1922–February 1923. The rules were never ratified.

Article 1. The rules of aerial warfare apply to all aircraft, whether lighter or heavier than air, irrespective of whether they are, or are not, capable of floating on the water.

Article 2. The following shall be deemed to be public aircraft:

(a) Military aircraft.

(b) Non-military aircraft exclusively employed in the public service.

All other aircraft shall be deemed to be private aircraft.

Article 3. A military aircraft shall bear an external mark indicating its nationality and military character.

Article 4. A public non-military aircraft employed for customs or police purposes shall carry papers evidencing the fact that it is exclusively employed in the public service. Such an aircraft shall bear an external mark indicating its nationality and its public non-military character.

Article 5. Public non-military aircraft other than those employed for customs or police purposes shall in time of war bear the same external marks, and for the purposes of these rules shall be treated on the same footing, as private aircraft.

Article 6. Aircraft not comprised in articles 3 and 4 and deemed to be private aircraft shall carry such papers and bear such external marks as are required by the rules in force in their own country. These marks must indicate their nationality and character.

Article 7. The external marks required by the above articles shall be so affixed that they cannot be altered in flight. They shall be as large as is practicable and shall be visible from above, from below, and from each side.

Article 8. The external marks, prescribed by the rules in force in each State, shall be notified promptly to all other Powers.

Modifications adopted in time of peace of the rules prescribing external marks shall be notified to all other Powers before they are brought into force.

Modifications of such rules adopted at the outbreak of war or during hostilities shall be notified by each Power as soon as possible to all other Powers and at latest when they are communicated to its own fighting forces.

Article 9. A belligerent non-military aircraft, whether public or private, may be converted into a military aircraft, provided that the conversion is effected within the jurisdiction of the belligerent State to which the aircraft belongs and not on the high seas.

Article 10. No aircraft may possess more than one nationality.

Article 11. Outside the jurisdiction of any State, belligerent or neutral, all aircraft shall have full freedom of passage through the air and of alighting.

Article 12. In time of war any State, whether belligerent or neutral, may forbid or regulate the entrance, movement or sojourn of aircraft within its jurisdiction.

Article 13. Military aircraft are alone entitled to exercise belligerent rights.

Article 14. A military aircraft shall be under the command of a person duly commissioned or enlisted in the military service of the State; the crew must be exclusively military.

Article 15. Members of the crew of a military aircraft shall wear a fixed distinctive emblem of such character as to be recognisable at a distance in case they become separated from their aircraft.

Article 16. No aircraft other than a belligerent military aircraft shall engage in hostilities in any form.

The term "hostilities" includes the transmission during flight of military intelligence for the immediate use of a belligerent.

No private aircraft, when outside the jurisdiction of its own country, shall be armed in time of war.

Article 17. The principles laid down in the Geneva Convention, 1906, and the Convention for the adaptation of the said Convention to Maritime War (No. X of 1907) shall apply to aerial warfare and to flying ambulances, as well as to the control over flying ambulances exercised by a belligerent commanding officer.

In order to enjoy the protection and privileges allowed to mobile medical units by the Geneva Convention, 1906, flying ambulances must bear the distinctive emblem of the Red Cross in addition to the usual distinguishing marks.

Article 18. The use of tracer, incendiary or explosive projectiles by or against aircraft is not prohibited.

This provision applies equally to States which are parties to the Declaration of St. Petersburg, 1868, and to those which are not.

Article 19. The use of false external marks is forbidden.

Article 20. When an aircraft has been disabled, the occupants, when endeavouring to escape by means of a parachute, must not be attacked in the course of their descent.

Article 21. The use of aircraft for the purpose of disseminating propaganda shall not be treated as an illegitimate means of warfare.

Members of the crews of such aircraft must not be deprived of their rights as prisoners of war on the charge that they have committed such an act.

Article 22. Aerial bombardment for the purpose of terrorising the civilian population, of destroying or damaging private property not of military character, or of injuring non-combatants, is prohibited.

Article 23. Aerial bombardment for the purpose of enforcing compliance with requisitions in kind or payment of contributions in money is prohibited.

Article 24

1. Aerial bombardment is legitimate only when directed at a military objective, that is to say, an object of which the destruction or injury would constitute a distinct military advantage to the belligerent.

2. Such bombardment is legitimate only when directed exclusively at the following objectives: military forces; military works; military establishments or depots; factories constituting important and well-known centres engaged in the manufacture of arms, ammunition or distinctively military supplies; lines of communication or transportation used for military purposes.

3. The bombardment of cities, towns, villages, dwellings or buildings not in the immediate neighbourhood of the operations of land forces is pro-

hibited. In cases where the objectives specified in paragraph 2 are so situated that they cannot be bombarded without the indiscriminate bombardment of the civilian population, the aircraft must abstain from bombardment.

4. In the immediate neighbourhood of the operations of land forces, the bombardment of cities, towns, villages, dwellings or buildings is legitimate provided that there exists a reasonable presumption that the military concentration is sufficiently important to justify such bombardment, having regard to the danger thus caused to the civilian population.

5. A belligerent State is liable to pay compensation for injuries to person or to property caused by the violation by any of its officers or forces of the provisions of this article.

Article 25. In bombardment by aircraft, all necessary steps must be taken by the commander to spare as far as possible buildings dedicated to public worship, art, science, or charitable purposes, historic monuments, hospital ships, hospitals and other places where the sick and wounded are collected, provided such buildings, objects or places are not at the time used for military purposes. Such buildings, objects and places must by day be indicated by marks visible to aircraft. The use of marks to indicate other buildings, objects or places than those specified above is to be deemed an act of perfidy. The marks used as aforesaid shall be in the case of buildings protected under the Geneva Convention the red cross on a white ground, and in the case of other protected buildings a large rectangular panel divided diagonally into two pointed triangular portions, one black and the other white.

A belligerent who desires to secure by night the protection for the hospitals and other privileged buildings above mentioned must take the necessary measures to render the special signs referred to sufficiently visible.

Article 26. The following special rules are adopted for the purpose of enabling States to obtain more efficient protection for important historic monuments situated within their territory, provided that they are willing to refrain from the use of such monuments and a surrounding zone for military purposes, and to accept a special regime for their inspection:—

1. A State shall be entitled, if it sees fit, to establish a zone of protection round such monuments

situated in its territory. Such zones shall in time of war enjoy immunity from bombardment.

2. The monuments round which a zone is to be established shall be notified to other Powers in peace time through the diplomatic channel; the notification shall also indicate the limits of the zones. The notification may not be withdrawn in time of war.

3. The zone of protection may include, in addition to the area actually occupied by the monument or group of monuments, an outer zone, not exceeding 500 metres in width, measured from the circumference of the said area.

4. Marks clearly visible from aircraft either by day or by night will be employed for the purpose of ensuring the identification by belligerent airmen of the limits of the zones.

5. The marks on the monuments themselves will be those defined in article 25. The marks employed for indicating the surrounding zones will be fixed by each State adopting the provisions of this article, and will be notified to other Powers at the same time as the monuments and zones are notified.

6. Any abusive use of the marks indicating the zones referred to in paragraph 5 will be regarded as an act of perfidy.

7. A State adopting the provisions of this article must abstain from using the monument and the surrounding zone for military purposes, or for the benefit in any way whatever of its military organisation, or from committing within such monument or zone any act with a military purpose in view.

8. An inspection committee consisting of three neutral representatives accredited to the State adopting the provisions of this article, or their delegates, shall be appointed for the purpose of ensuring that no violation is committed of the provisions of paragraph 7. One of the members of the committee of inspection shall be the representative (or his delegate) of the State to which has been entrusted the interests of the opposing belligerent.

Article 27. Any person on board a belligerent or neutral aircraft is to be deemed a spy only if acting clandestinely or on false pretenses he obtains or seeks to obtain, while in the air, information within belligerent jurisdiction or in the zone of operations of a belligerent with the intention of communicating it to the hostile party.

Article 28. Acts of espionage committed after leaving the aircraft by members of the crew of an aircraft or by passengers transported by it are sub-

ject to the provisions of the Land Warfare Regulations.

Article 29. Punishment of the acts of espionage referred to in articles 27 and 28 is subject to articles 30 and 31 of the Land Warfare Regulations.

Article 30. In case a belligerent commanding officer considers that the presence of aircraft is likely to prejudice the success of the operations in which he is engaged at the moment, he may prohibit the passing of neutral aircraft in the immediate vicinity of his forces or may oblige them to follow a particular route. A neutral aircraft which does not conform to such directions, of which it has had notice issued by the belligerent commanding officer, may be fired upon.

Article 31. In accordance with the principles of article 53 of the Land Warfare Regulations, neutral private aircraft found upon entry in the enemy's jurisdiction by a belligerent occupying force may be requisitioned, subject to the payment of full compensation.

Article 32. Enemy public aircraft, other than those treated on the same footing as private aircraft, shall be subject to confiscation without prize proceedings.

Article 33. Belligerent non-military aircraft, whether public or private, flying within the jurisdiction of their own State, are liable to be fired upon unless they make the nearest available landing on the approach of enemy military aircraft.

Article 34. Belligerent non-military aircraft, whether public or private, are liable to be fired upon, if they fly (1) within the jurisdiction of the enemy, or (2) in the immediate vicinity thereof and outside the jurisdiction of their own State, or (3) in the immediate vicinity of the military operations of the enemy by land or sea.

Article 35. Neutral aircraft flying within the jurisdiction of a belligerent, and warned of the approach of military aircraft of the opposing belligerent, must make the nearest available landing. Failure to do so exposes them to the risk of being fired upon.

Article 36

When an enemy military aircraft falls into the hands of a belligerent, the members of the crew and the passengers, if any, may be made prisoners of war

The same rule applies to the members of the crew, and the passengers, if any, of an enemy public non-military aircraft, except that in the case of public non-military aircraft devoted exclusively to the transport of passengers, the passengers will be entitled to be released unless they are in the service of the enemy, or are enemy nationals fit for military service.

If an enemy private aircraft falls into the hand of a belligerent, members of the crew who are enemy nationals or who are neutral nationals in the service of the enemy, may be made prisoners of war. Neutral members of the crew, who are not in the service of the enemy, are entitled to be released if they sign a written undertaking not to serve in any enemy aircraft while hostilities last. Passengers are entitled to be released unless they are in the service of the enemy or are enemy nationals fit for military service, in which cases they may be made prisoners of war.

Release may in any case be delayed if the military interests of the belligerent so require.

The belligerent may hold as prisoners of war any member of the crew or any passenger whose service in a flight at the close of which he has been captured has been of special and active assistance to the enemy.

The names of individuals released after giving a written undertaking in accordance with the third paragraph of this article will be notified to the opposing belligerent, who must not knowingly employ them in violation of their undertaking.

Article 37. Members of the crew of a neutral aircraft which has been detained by a belligerent shall be released unconditionally, if they are neutral nationals and not in the service of the enemy. If they are enemy nationals or in the service of the enemy, they may be made prisoners of war.

Passengers are entitled to be released unless they are in the service of the enemy or are enemy nationals fit for military service, in which cases they may be made prisoners of war.

Release may in any case be delayed if the military interests of the belligerent so require.

The belligerent may hold as prisoners of war any member of the crew or any passenger whose service in a flight at the close of which he has been captured has been of special and active assistance to the enemy.

Article 38. Where under the provisions of articles 36 and 37 it is provided that members of the crew or passengers may be made prisoners of war, it is to be understood that, if they are not members of

the armed forces, they shall be entitled to treatment not less favourable than that accorded to prisoners of war.

Article 39. Belligerent aircraft are bound to respect the rights of neutral Powers and to abstain within the jurisdiction of a neutral State from the commission of any act which it is the duty of that State to prevent.

Article 40. Belligerent military aircraft are forbidden to enter the jurisdiction of a neutral State.

Article 41. Aircraft on board vessels of war, including aircraft-carriers, shall be regarded as part of such vessels.

Article 42. A neutral Government must use the means at its disposal to prevent the entry within its jurisdiction of belligerent military aircraft and to compel them to alight if they have entered such jurisdiction.

A neutral Government shall use the means at its disposal to intern any belligerent military aircraft which is within its jurisdiction after having alighted for any reason whatsoever, together with its crew and the passengers, if any.

Article 43. The personnel of a disabled belligerent military aircraft rescued outside neutral waters and brought into the jurisdiction of a neutral State by a neutral military aircraft and there landed shall be interned.

Article 44. The supply in any manner, directly or indirectly, by a neutral Government to a belligerent Power of aircraft, parts of aircraft, or material, supplies or munitions required for aircraft, is forbidden.

Article 45. Subject to the provisions of article 46, a neutral Power is not bound to prevent the export or transit on behalf of a belligerent of aircraft, parts of aircraft, or material, supplies or munitions for aircraft.

Article 46. A neutral Government is bound to use the means at its disposal:

1. To prevent the departure from its jurisdiction of an aircraft in a condition to make a hostile attack against a belligerent Power, or carrying or accompanied by appliances or materials the mounting or utilisation of which would enable it to make a hostile attack, if there is reason to believe that such aircraft is destined for use against a belligerent Power.

2. To prevent the departure of an aircraft the crew of which includes any member of the combatant forces of a belligerent Power.

3. To prevent work upon an aircraft designed to prepare it to depart in contravention of the purposes of this article.

On the departure by air of any aircraft dispatched by persons or companies in neutral jurisdiction to the order of a belligerent Power, the neutral Government must prescribe for such aircraft a route avoiding the neighbourhood of the military operations of the opposing belligerent, and must exact whatever guarantees may be required to ensure that the aircraft follows the route prescribed.

Article 47. A neutral State is bound to take such steps as the means at its disposal permit to prevent within its jurisdiction aerial observation of the movements, operations or defences of one belligerent, with the intention of informing the other belligerent.

This provision applies equally to a belligerent military aircraft on board a vessel of war.

Article 48. The action of a neutral Power in using force or other means at its disposal in the exercise of its rights or duties under these rules cannot be regarded as a hostile act.

Article 49. Private aircraft are liable to visit and search and to capture by belligerent military aircraft.

Article 50. Belligerent military aircraft have the right to order public non-military and private aircraft to alight in or proceed for visit and search to a suitable locality reasonably accessible

Refusal, after warning, to obey such orders to alight or to proceed to such a locality for examination exposes an aircraft to the risk of being fired upon.

Article 51. Neutral public non-military aircraft, other than those which are to be treated as private aircraft, are subject only to visit for the purpose of the verification of their papers.

Article 52. Enemy private aircraft are liable to capture in all circumstances.

Article 53. A neutral private aircraft is liable to capture if it

(a) Resists the legitimate exercise of belligerent rights.

(b) Violates a prohibition of which it has had notice issued by a belligerent commanding officer under article 30.

(c) Is engaged in unneutral service.

(d) Is armed in time of war when outside the jurisdiction of its own country.

(e) Has no external marks or uses false marks.

(f) Has no papers or insufficient or irregular papers.

(g) Is manifestly out of the line between the point of departure and the point of destination indicated in its papers and after such enquiries as the belligerent may deem necessary, no good cause is shown for the deviation. The aircraft, together with its crew and passengers, if any, may be detained by the belligerent, pending such enquiries.

(h) Carries, or itself constitutes, contraband of war.

(i) Is engaged in breach of a blockade duly established and effectively maintained.

(k) Has been transferred from belligerent to neutral nationality at a date and in circumstances indicating an intention of evading the consequences to which an enemy aircraft, as such, is exposed.

Provided that in each case (except (k)) the ground for capture shall be an act carried out in the flight in which the neutral aircraft came into belligerent hands, i.e., since it left its point of departure and before it reached its point of destination.

Article 54. The papers of a private aircraft will be regarded as insufficient or irregular if they do not establish the nationality of the aircraft and indicate the names and nationality of the crew and passengers, the points of departure and destination of the flight, together with particulars of the cargo and the conditions under which it is transported. The logs must also be included.

Article 55. Capture of an aircraft or of goods on board an aircraft shall be made the subject of prize proceedings, in order that any neutral claim may be duly heard and determined.

Article 56. A private aircraft captured upon the ground that it has no external marks or is using false marks, or that it is armed in time of war outside the jurisdiction of its own country, is liable to condemnation.

A neutral private aircraft captured upon the ground that it has disregarded the direction of a belligerent commanding officer under article 30 is liable to condemnation, unless it can justify its presence within the prohibited zone.

In all other cases, the prize court in adjudicating upon any case of capture of an aircraft or its cargo, or of postal correspondence on board an aircraft, shall apply the same rules as would be applied to a merchant vessel or its cargo or to postal correspondence on board a merchant vessel.

Article 57. Private aircraft which are found upon visit and search to be enemy aircraft may be destroyed if the belligerent commanding officer finds it necessary to do so, provided that all persons on board have first been placed in safety and all the papers of the aircraft have been preserved.

Article 58. Private aircraft which are found upon visit and search to be neutral aircraft liable to condemnation upon the ground of unneutral service, or upon the ground that they have no external marks or are bearing false marks, may be destroyed, if sending them in for adjudication would be impossible or would imperil the safety of the belligerent aircraft or the success of the operations in which it is engaged. Apart from the cases mentioned above, a neutral private aircraft must not be destroyed except in the gravest military emergency, which would not justify the officer in command in releasing it or sending it in for adjudication.

Article 59. Before a neutral private aircraft is destroyed, all persons on board must be placed in safety, and all the papers of the aircraft must be preserved.

A captor who has destroyed a neutral private aircraft must bring the capture before the prize court and must first establish that he was justified in destroying it under article 58. If he fails to do this, parties interested in the aircraft or its cargo are entitled to compensation. If the capture is held to be invalid, though the act of destruction is held to have been justifiable, compensation must be paid to the parties interested in place of the restitution to which they would have been entitled.

Article 60. Where a neutral private aircraft is captured on the ground that it is carrying contraband, the captor may demand the surrender of any absolute contraband on board, or may proceed to the destruction of such absolute contraband, if sending in the aircraft for adjudication is impossible or would imperil the safety of the belligerent aircraft or the success of the operations in which it is engaged. After entering in the log book of the aircraft the delivery or destruction of the goods, and securing, in original or copy, the relevant papers of the aircraft, the captor must allow the neutral aircraft to continue its flight.

The provisions of the second paragraph of Article 59 will apply where absolute contraband on board a neutral private aircraft is handed over or destroyed.

Article 61. The term "military" throughout these rules is to be read as referring to all branches of the forces, i.e., the land forces, the naval forces and the air forces.

Article 62. Except so far as special rules are here laid down and except also so far as the provisions of Chapter VII of these Rules or international conventions indicate that maritime law and procedure are applicable, aircraft personnel engaged in hostilities come under the laws of war and neutrality applicable to land troops in virtue of the custom and practice of international law and of the various declarations and conventions to which the States concerned are parties.

[J. M. Spraight, *Air Power and War Rights* (London, 1924), pp. 498–508]

Report of Air Commission, World Disarmament Conference (1932)

Report to the General Commission by the Air Commission of the Conference for the Reduction and Limitation of Armaments, 8 June 1932

The questions put to the Air Commission by the General Commission's resolution of April 22nd, 1932, were the following:

What are the air armaments:

(a) Whose character is the most specifically offensive;

(b) Which are the most efficacious against national defence;

(c) Which are the most threatening to civilians?

Although it was made clear in the discussions in the Air Commission that the offensiveness of the air armaments, their efficacy against national defence, and the threat that they represent to civilians vary considerably on account of the wide differences in the geographical position of different countries, the location of their vital centres, and the state of their anti-aircraft defences, and that any qualitative question in connection with air armaments is closely bound up with quantitative considerations, the Commission found it possible to set down certain general conclusions, which form Part I of this report. The Commission also undertook a technical study of the efficacy and the use of air armaments. The results of this study form Part II of the present report. Part III contains several comments in regard to Parts I and II, and Part IV contains statements by various delegations, with an introduction.

PART I

These conclusions are as follows:

1(a) All air armaments can be used to some extent for offensive purposes, without prejudice to the question of their defensive uses.

If used in time of peace for a sudden and unprovoked attack, air armaments assume a particularly offensive character. In effect, before the State victim of the aggression can take the defensive measures demanded by the situation, or before the League of Nations or States not involved in the conflict could undertake preventive or mediatory action, the aggressor State might in certain cases be able rapidly to obtain military or psychological results, such as would render difficult either the cessation of hostilities or the re-establishment of peace.

(b) Civil aircraft, to the extent that they might be incorporated into the armed forces of a State, could in varying degrees subserve military ends.

(c) Independently of the offensive character which air armaments may derive from their use, their capacity for offensive action depends on certain of their constructional characteristics.

(d) The possibilities of offensive action of aeroplanes carried by aircraft-carriers or warships equipped with landing-platforms (or landing-decks) must be regarded as being increased by the mobility of the vessels which carry them.

(e) The capacity for offensive action of air armaments resulting from such constructional characteristics should first be considered from the point of view of the efficacy of such armaments against national defence, and secondly from the point of view of the threat offered thereby to the civilian population.

Efficacy against National Defence

II (a) The aircraft forming a part of the air armaments of a country that may be regarded as most efficacious against national defence are those which are capable of the most effective direct action by the dropping or launching of means of warfare of any kind.

(b) The efficacy against national defence of an aircraft forming part of such armaments, and considered individually, depends upon its useful load and its capability of arriving at its objective.

(c) The efficacy against national defence of means of warfare of every kind launched from the air depends upon the material effect which they are capable of producing.

Threat to Civil Population

III (a) The aircraft forming part of the air armaments of a country which can be regarded as the most threatening to the civil population are those which are capable of the most effective direct action by the dropping or launching of means of warfare of any kind; this efficacy depends primarily upon the nature of the means of warfare employed and the manner in which they are employed.

(b) The degree of threat to the civil population represented by an aircraft forming part of those armaments, and considered individually, is in proportion to its useful load and its capability of arriving at its objective.

(c) The means of warfare, intended to be dropped from the air, which are the most threatening to the civil population are those which, considered individually, produce the most extended action, the greatest moral or material effect; that is to say, those which are the most capable of killing, wounding and immobilising the inhabitants of centres of civil population or of demoralising them, so far as concerns immediate consequences, and so far as concerns future consequences, of impairing the vitality of human beings. Among these means the Commission specially mentions poisonous gases, bacteria and incendiary and explosive appliances.

IV. The useful load of aircraft and their capability of arriving at their objective are determined by a large number of variable factors. Where useful load is concerned, the Air Commission has noted among these variable factors, for purposes of examination, the unladen weight, the horse-power and the wing area for aeroplanes, the volume and the horse-power for dirigibles.

PART II

The offensive character of air armaments cannot be determined arbitrarily and must depend on the examination of the conditions they must fulfil in order to be effective against whatever objectives may be assigned to them, and on the defence requirements which they meet.

Moreover, the General Commission will not be in a position to take decisions relating to the qualitative limitation of air armaments until the technical factors which are indispensable to enable it to form a reasoned opinion have been brought to its notice.

The Air Commission accordingly submits the following considerations which seem to it to meet the intentions of the General Commission. It would, however, emphasise that the figures given in Section III below are purely for purposes of indication; they are not absolute, and in no way bind the delegations in the matter of any proposals for qualitative limitation which they may submit elsewhere.

I. *General Considerations*

1. While the efficacy of air armaments against the different objectives which may be assigned to them depends on the vulnerability of those objectives and the useful load[2] which the aircraft can carry, on the other hand, the radius of action needed for such direct intervention and for scouting operations, particularly at sea, and communications with and between overseas territories depends essentially on the geographical situation and the special conditions of each country.

In particular, the effects of using air armaments cannot be the same for all countries; for examples, those with a small area, with their vulnerable points near the frontiers of other States, and those surrounded by a wide expanse of water.

2. The efficacy of air armaments against national defence depends on the possibility, in the event of an act of aggression, and independently of aerial means of defence, of their destroying the obstacles to the advance of the aggressor, attacking lines of communication, centres of military production and supply depots, air and naval bases, etc.

It is also necessary to examine the conditions governing the use of air armaments against mobile forces and other objectives of the land and naval battlefield in order to decide whether their offensive possibilities are greater than the requirements of defence.

3. The discussions of the Air Commission revealed the fact that for many countries the effectiveness of air armaments against national defence was due principally to the circumstance that aircraft could attack the vital centres of a State (towns, centres of population, etc.) and weaken the internal resistance. Leaving aside considerations regarding international engagements, it was thought desirable to examine the conditions governing their effectiveness.

II. *Special Points*

For information purposes it should be noted that the useful load of the heaviest aircraft at the present time is about 27,000 kg. for civil aircraft and 15,000 kg. for military aircraft.

Observations Relating to the General Conditions of Use

1. At present, military aircraft must have a crew varying from 1 to 5, together with the arms and ammunition necessary for their own defence. Nevertheless, only aircraft seating more than one and with a crew of at least three men to ensure their defence and an adequate radius of action are capable of flying long distances over other countries and may, in certain cases, offer a more offensive character than others.

2. The radius of action that is to say, the total distance which can be flown should take into account not only the absolute distance of the objective but also the additional distance which may have to be covered for tactical reasons or owing to atmospheric conditions.

In general, the radius of action necessary for air armaments depends on the special situation of the countries concerned.

In particular, against countries of small area and great density of population, or against countries whose vulnerable points are situated near their frontiers, air armaments might be effective with a small radius of action, especially if they were employed against the vital centres of these countries.

3. Under the normal conditions of inaccuracy of aerial aim at an objective of small dimensions, results cannot be obtained by the launching of a single projectile, however powerful.

A single aircraft cannot hope to obtain appreciable results from its action except by launching a salvo containing enough bombs to obtain at least one impact capable of causing serious damage. The dimensions, the nature and resistance of the objective, the altitude of the aircraft, the nature of the defence and the atmospheric conditions influence the precision of the bombardment and determine the characteristics and number of the bombs which must be carried in one and the same load.

If, however, the objective attacked is very extensive—in particular, when air armaments take the centres of population of a country as their objective precision of aim becomes less necessary, and even aircraft of low power but in large numbers may prove very effective owing to the moral, if not the material, results which they can obtain.

4. The effectiveness of attack by air against an objective increases with the number of aircraft employed, provided that these aircraft taken individually are effective against that objective.

III. *Effectiveness against National Defence*

A. *Action against Permanent Fortifications.* As the greater part of air armaments are at present ineffective against permanent fortifications, it would be unreasonable to use a single military aeroplane in an attempt to destroy such objectives.

It is pointed out, however:

(1) That aircraft capable of carrying a useful load of 5,000–6,000 kg. would be capable of producing serious results against permanent fortifications.

(2) That aircraft capable of transporting a useful load of from 3,000–5,000 kg. would be capable of producing appreciable results, in particular against dug-outs, but without decisive consequences.

B. *Action against Vital Centres.* If, regardless of international engagements, air armaments are employed against vital centres of population of a country, they may, both by the moral and material effects which they are capable of producing, exercise very important indirect action against its national defence.

In general, this action may be all the greater, the smaller the country attacked and the denser its population, or if the vital centres are situated near the frontier. It may even be of capital importance if it is directed against the works which, in certain cases, assure the life and existence of a country against a permanent natural menace.

As, however, the centres of population form extensive objectives, particularly vulnerable to the action of gas and especially incendiary bombs, and as the latter may cause very great damage even with a small tonnage, all aircraft having a sufficient radius of action and capable of transporting any useful load in addition to its pilot may, if such projectiles are employed, be effective against the vital centres of a country.

C. *Action against Lines of Communication.* In addition to direct action against convoys and troops upon the battlefield, which will be examined below, aircraft may also be used against troops in centres of mobilisation and against railway junctions and bridges. Where such objectives are in centres of population, aircraft attacking them constitute a menace to the civilian population in the immediate vicinity.

To be effective against troops in centres of mobilisation, aircraft must have a tonnage at least as great as those which can be used against columns on the march, and must be equipped with bombs each weighing from 50 to 100 kg.

To be effective against railway junctions and bridges, aircraft must carry the greatest possible number of bombs of from 100 to 500 kg. each.

D. *Action against Munition Factories and Supply Depots.* Munition factories and supply depots which would become important objectives in the case of prolonged warfare are not likely to be attacked by aircraft at the beginning of hostilities. At that stage of the war the principal military objectives of the aggressor are the destruction of the defence forces and the occupation of centres or lines of communication and of territory.

The aircraft best adapted for bombarding munition factories, etc., are similar to those required for attacking lines of communication.

E. *Action against Air and Naval Bases.* To be effective against military air bases, aircraft must be able to carry from 20 to 40 bombs of from 50 to 100 kg. Consequently, since the distance of one belligerent's air base from that of another belligerent will make it necessary for them to have a radius of action of from 1,200 to 1,500 km., they must carry a useful load of at least three tons.

To be effective against naval bases, aircraft must be able to carry from three to ten bombs of about 450 kg. each. Their radius of action depends essentially on the geographical situation of each country.

F. *Use in Battle.* The use of aircraft in battle does not give them a specifically offensive character. They are useful to the aggressor both to prepare his attack and to facilitate its development; but they are indispensable to the defence, whether for the purpose of obtaining information as to the dispositions of attack, in regard to which the assailant has the initiative, or for rapid intervention by direct action to delay the progress of attacking columns advancing on open ground or to prevent the offensive action of fleets.

1. *Direct Action*

(a) Aircraft which can be effectively employed against objectives of the land battlefield that are unprotected or only slightly protected, particularly against columns of troops in the open or against convoys and means of transport and food-supply, must be capable of carrying 40 to 50 bombs of 10 kg. or 20 to 30 bombs of 50 kg., and must have a radius of action of at least 500 km. Their useful load must amount to between 1,200 and 3,000 kg. according to circumstances.

(b) To be effective against naval forces, aircraft must carry either a torpedo of 800–1,000 kg. or a load of bombs of at least 1,250 kg. for attacking surface vessels (i.e., 3 bombs of 450 kg. for attacking capital ships, or 5 bombs of 250 kg. for attacking light vessels), and 600 kg. (4 bombs of 150 kg.) for attacking submarines.

Their radius of action depends essentially on the geographical situation of each country. The minimum radius of action enabling aircraft of coast or land bases to take part in defensive operations of the fleet against coastal attack may be taken as about 1,500 km.

Such aircraft, with their crew of five, maritime equipment and military defence armament (machine-guns), have a useful load of at least 4,500 to 5,000 kg.

2. *Scouting Operations.* Certain aircraft used for scouting purposes must be capable of carrying a crew of at least five persons and their own defensive armament, and should have a radius of action enabling them to travel at least 500 km. from their bases over the land and at least 1,000 km. over the sea—that is to say, taking the wind into account, a radius of action of 1,200 to 2,500 km.; the useful load which such aircraft must be able to carry is 3,000 to 6,500 kg.

G. *Action of Pursuit (Chaser) Aeroplanes.* Pursuit (chaser) aeroplanes possess an offensive character when used to facilitate aggression by bombing aeroplanes, but both meet defence requirements when used against an aggressor.

H. *Miscellaneous Uses.* Certain aircraft needed for communication with and between overseas territories must have a radius of action of at least 2,000 km. and must carry a crew of not less than 5, which, with the reserves necessary for the safety of the machine and the crew, means a useful load of about four or five tons.

Aircraft for the transport of troops, which are particularly useful for the maintenance of order in peace-time in overseas territories, must also have a useful load of three to six tons.

IV. *Menace of Air Armaments to Civilians*

All aircraft, without alterations of any kind and whatever their tonnage, may constitute a danger to civilians, whether used directly to attack civilians or against military objectives situated in densely-populated areas.

This threat is due chiefly to the fact that aircraft can make their action felt in the interior of a country in zones beyond the radius of action of land and naval armaments. They can act against a much larger part of the population; but, on the other hand, there is no doubt that the material effects they are capable of producing in the zone of the battlefield are far less than those caused by land or naval armaments.

Actually, the extent of the danger depends essentially on the nature of the projectiles used. Projectiles containing harmful gases or bacteria, and incendiary projectiles, though of small tonnage, may be highly efficient and produce a considerable moral effect. Explosive projectiles may produce a more or less considerable moral effect, but they are not capable of causing serious material damage unless used in large quantities.

PART III

The conclusions in Part I of this report give rise to the following comments:

In the first place, the German delegation submitted an amendment referring to all the foregoing conclusions, as follows: "All military aviation, and especially the dropping of means of warfare of every kind from the air, come into the three categories."

In order to specify the material of air armaments for this purpose, the German delegation, on the basis of the arguments advanced during the discussion, desired to supplement the above amendment as follows:

By military aircraft are to be understood all aircraft (e.g., aeroplanes, dirigibles, free and captive balloons):

(1) Which are identified by identity-marks as military aircraft, or

(2) Which have military specifications: that is to say, installations to receive means of warfare of every kind such as guns, machine-guns, torpedoes, bombs, or instruments for aiming or launching such means of warfare, or

(3) Which are manufactured for the armed forces of a country, or

(4) Which are manned by a military pilot or a military crew having orders to that effect, or

(5) Which form part of the equipment of an armed force or are requisitioned by such force.

The primary reasons given by the German delegation for this amendment was that for a country which has no means of anti-aircraft defence, either in the air or on the ground, all air armaments without any distinction must be regarded as answering to the three questions put by the General Commission's resolution.

A number of delegations which opposed the German proposal pointed out that only certain air armaments could be regarded as answering to these questions, while other delegations, which also could not see their way to accept the German proposal, expressed the view that in any case different forms of air armaments answered to these characteristics in different degrees.

The German amendment was rejected by 22 votes to 7—those of Austria, Bulgaria, China, Germany, Hungary, Turkey and the Union of Soviet Socialist Republics. In consequence of this vote, the Austrian and German delegations, though taking part in the discussion, abstained from voting on points I(a), (b), (c), (d), (e), II(a), (b) and (c), and III(a), (b) and (c).

In connection with the conclusion numbered I (a), first paragraph, the Italian delegation proposed the omission of the words: "without prejudice to the question of their defensive uses." As, however, this amendment was rejected by 18 votes to 12, the Italian, Turkish and Soviet delegations made an explicit reservation against the retention of these words, on the ground that the question of the use of air armaments for defensive purposes was outside the terms of the General Commission's resolution.

After a discussion in some detail, the Commission, not wishing to go at present into the question of the internationalisation or control of civil aviation, adopted conclusion I(b), with the two abstentions already mentioned. The Hungarian delegation made a declaration maintaining that the civil aircraft of a country which has no military aircraft cannot be incorporated in its armed forces. The Soviet delegation made a declaration to the effect that it held that all military aircraft were specifically offensive in character, whether they were built specially for military purposes or were subsequently converted to such purposes; and that it saw no need to mention civil aircraft in the report, as they could not be regarded as a weapon.

Conclusion I(d) was adopted by 16 votes to 2 (United States of America and Portugal). In consequence of this vote, the United States delegation made the following declaration:

The delegation of the United States considers that the statement in Paragraph I(d) as to the increased possibility of offensive action of ship-based aircraft is inappropriate for inclusion in a report which deals with aircraft generally and which does not otherwise discuss specific types of aircraft or the influence of the base of action upon their offensive capabilities.

One of the tests already contained in the report is that of capability of arriving at an objective. Thus the mobility feature of ship-based aircraft is already taken into account and any further reference in the report which might give the impression that individual ship-based aircraft are more specifically offensive than individual aircraft taking off from bases close to land frontiers is misleading.

The Portuguese delegation associated itself with this declaration, and the United Kingdom delegation stated that it shared the views therein expressed.

As regards the *efficacy of air armaments against national defence,* the following delegations: South Africa, Argentine Republic, Australia, Bolivia, Brazil, United Kingdom, Canada, Chile, Czechoslovakia, France, Greece, India, Japan, New Zealand, Poland, Portugal, Roumania, United States of America and Yugoslavia, voted for the inclusion in the text of the following statement: "The air armaments most efficacious against national defence may also in certain circumstances be the most efficacious for their own national defence."

Twenty-two other delegations—Afghanistan, Austria, Belgium, Bulgaria, China, Denmark, Estonia, Finland, Germany, Hungary, Italy, Latvia, Lithuania, Mexico, the Netherlands, Norway, Persia, Siam, Spain, Sweden, Turkey and the Union of Soviet Socialist Republics—though they did not deny the truth of this statement, considered that it was unnecessary to insert it in the reply to the General Commission.

In its consideration of the question of the *threat to civilians* constituted by air armaments, the Commission constantly bore in mind the existence of certain international undertakings for the protection of civilians in time of war. It considered, however, that its reply to the questions asked by the General Commission must be prepared solely from the point of view of technical possibilities, and apart from any legal or political considerations.

During the discussion on the question as to *which criterion or criteria* should be adopted among those considered by the Commission and set out under IV of Part 1—namely, unladen weight, horse-power and wing area for aeroplanes, volume and horse-power for dirigibles—a profound difference of opinion was manifested in the Commission. It was generally felt that there were great difficulties in the way of establishing formulae which, in view of the constant progress made in technique, were subject to modification. It was nevertheless agreed that unladen weight was an essential criterion for aeroplanes and volume for dirigibles and must be adopted.

A provisional definition of unladen weight was unanimously accepted by the Commission, and figures as Annex I to the present report.

Eighteen delegations—South Africa, Australia, United Kingdom, Canada, Czechoslovakia, Estonia, France, India, Japan, Latvia, Lithuania, the Netherlands, Poland, Portugal, Roumania, Siam, the United States of America, Yugoslavia—considered that for purposes of practical comparison unladen weight alone was an adequate criterion. They held that the addition of two other criteria for aeroplanes would considerably complicate the question owing to the facility with which wing area and especially horse-power could be modified. They added that they thought it impossible to obtain a satisfactory definition of horse-power and to form a practical estimate of its value and of the value of wing area, and, further, that the adoption of these two criteria might hinder the sound development of technique.

Twenty-one delegations—Afghanistan, Argentine, Austria, Belgium, Bolivia, Brazil, Bulgaria, Chile, China, Denmark, Finland, Germany, Greece, Hungary, Italy, Mexico, Spain, Sweden, Switzerland, Turkey and the Union of Soviet Socialist Republics—held that unladen weight alone was inadequate, and that horse-power and wing area should also be adopted. Certain of the delegations mentioned above considered that in dividing aeroplanes into categories it was necessary to take into consideration, not only the unladen weight, but also the horse-power and the ratio between horse-power and wing area, as criteria of equal value. They pointed out that unladen weight as the sole criterion could not give satisfactory results, since, even were the unladen weight constant, the useful load could vary considerably if there were a more powerful engine or a different wing area.

As regards the definitions or horse-power and the wing area, the Commission's discussions have shown that sufficient light has not yet been thrown on the technical aspect of these questions to enable a number of the delegations in favour of the three criteria to express an opinion on the definitions to be established for the two criteria mentioned above.

As regards horse-power, certain of those delegations referred to the conclusions of the report of the Committee of Experts to fix rules for the adoption of a standard horse-power measurement for aeroplane and dirigible engines (document C.259.M.115.1931), while the Italian delegation submitted a slightly different definition, which is annexed (Annex III) to the present report.

As regards wing area, proposed definitions have been furnished by the Spanish and Italian delegations and figure as Annexes II and III to the present report.

Certain delegations who declared themselves in favour of the three criteria added that they considered that both horse-power and wing area could be computed with sufficient accuracy (though less accurately than unladen weight) to enable them to be effectively used in the comparative measurement of the useful load of aircraft, and that three criteria, however, imperfect, would be more reliable than one.

Other delegations among the group favouring the three criteria considered that the question whether a single criterion should be adopted or whether the two others should be added as auxiliary criteria could not be finally settled until the Commission had come to a definite decision as to the figures to which those criteria would apply.

The technical study of which Part II consists was undertaken as the outcome of a questionnaire and draft reply thereto submitted by the French delegation.

The result of this study was not included in the report until a vote had been taken by the Air Commission, 23 delegations (South Africa, the Argentine, Australia, Belgium, Brazil, United Kingdom,

Czechoslovakia, Estonia, Finland, France, India, Japan, Latvia, Netherlands, Norway, Poland, Portugal, Roumania, Siam, Spain, Sweden, United States of America, Yugoslavia) voting in favour of its inclusion and 12 against (Afghanistan, Austria, Bolivia, Bulgaria, China, Germany, Hungary, Italy, Lithuania, Mexico, Turkey, Union of Soviet Socialist Republics). The reasons which led the minority to vote against it are clearly shown by the general reservations of the Austrian, Bulgarian, German, Hungarian, Italian and Soviet delegations.

Among the delegations which voted in favour of the inclusion of the study in question in the report or who abstained, the delegations of Belgium, Brazil, Denmark, Estonia, Mexico, Netherlands, Norway, Portugal, Spain, Sweden and Switzerland made reservations in regard to the figures given in this part of the report, and also stated that they entirely reserved their opinions as to the conclusions to be drawn from the findings contained therein.

Although certain delegations maintained that in view of the General Commission's three questions it was impossible to draw a distinction between the different kinds of air armaments,[3] it will nevertheless be seen from its deliberations that the Commission was unanimously of opinion that air bombardment is a grave threat to civilians.

In this connection, certain delegations which were in favour of the absolute prohibition of air bombardment contemplated the possibility of designating bombing aeroplanes as the most specifically offensive air arms, the most efficacious against national defence, and the most threatening to civilians. The Commission was unable to accept this solution, however, for the following reasons: The technical explanations given in different quarters have shown that bombing aeroplanes cannot simply be designated by name, as the same aeroplanes may be used for entirely different purposes. Thus, in several important countries, exactly the same aeroplanes form part of bombing and scouting units.

After considering the aeroplanes at present in service in the air armaments of different countries, however, certain delegations thought it would be possible to fix a limit based on technical data, above which the majority of aeroplanes were, in the opinion of these delegations, specially suitable for air bombardment.[4]

It should be noted that one delegation put forward definite proposals suggesting a very low limit, based on technical data, above which it considered

that all military aviation answered to the General Commission's three criteria.[5] Finally, it should be noted that one delegation proposed to classify among arms which are the most offensive, the most efficacious against national defence, and the most threatening to civilians, all kinds of air bombs and all appliances for the aiming and launching of such bombs.

DECLARATION BY THE GERMAN DELEGATION

I. *Reservation Relating to the Findings Contained in Part I of the Report.* The German delegation was not in a position to accept the "findings" of the Air Commission's report. The Air Commission, in accordance with the General Commission's decisions, should have considered what are the arms which, in view of their specific character, are most likely to lead rapidly to success, assuming that a State adopts a policy of armed aggression.

The German delegation considers that military aviation as a whole should be regarded as aggressive from this point of view. This consideration applies in particular to a country which possesses no military air force, or which has already abolished it by disarmament, and which has also no means of defence against aircraft either in the air or on the ground. In view of the situation of such a country, the German delegation considers that it is not possible to draw a distinction between the different categories of air arms according to their more or less offensive character, or their greater or lesser efficacy against national defence, or their greater or lesser threat to civilians. In the case of such a country, the air arm as a whole, without any distinction, comes, for purely technical reasons, under the three heads into which the question raised by the General Commission is divided. Germany, who was disarmed under the Treaty of Versailles, also bases her conception on the technical disarmament clauses which form part of that treaty.

The German delegation also wishes to point out that, in compiling its report, the majority of the Air Commission considered that the offensive character of air arms could only be determined after an examination of the degree of their efficacy against national defence and the extent of the threat constituted by them to civilians. However, after carrying out this examination, the Air Commission failed to reply to the first and most important of the questions asked by the General Commission, and did not reach any definite decision as to the arms which have a specifically offensive character.

Lastly, the German delegation considers that means of warfare of every kind capable of being launched from the air should be regarded in general as specifically offensive, particularly efficacious against national defence, and specially threatening to civilians. This applies *a fortiori* to a country without any anti-aircraft defence.

II. *Reservations Concerning Part II of the Report.* With reference to the foregoing reservation, the German delegation states that:

At the plenary meeting of the Air Commission the German delegation stated that it was opposed to the proposal to submit the General Commission's three questions to a thorough examination by a discussion of the French questionnaire—a procedure which would take a good deal of time in view of the necessity of clearing up these problems from the point of view of the science of warfare. It considered that this study was unnecessary in order to give a clear and adequate reply to the questions put by the General Commission. However, the Air Commission having decided that the French questionaire should be discussed by a sub-committee, and the French delegation having itself submitted a draft reply to that questionnaire, the German delegation endeavoured, with a view to cooperating in this examination, to amend the draft reply in order to take into account the position of countries which do not possess any military air force, and have no means of defence against aircraft.

Since the second point of this report as it results from the somewhat brief discussions in the Sub-Committee does not take into account the position of those countries, the German delegation does not consider it possible to accept this point.

DECLARATION BY THE AUSTRIAN DELEGATION

In the course of the discussion in the Air Commission, the Austrian delegation demonstrated that in certain conditions the capacity of an aircraft to attain its objective is decisively increased. In Austria's case, this increased capacity results from the present geographical and military circumstances of the country. These circumstances confer an offensive character even on aircraft which would be completely unfitted to act against the national defence or the civil population of another country.

Consequently it is impossible to make a *general* classification of aircraft corresponding to the three questions put by the General Commission.

The Austrian delegation urges that it is absolutely essential to take into account the present circum-

stances of each individual country, if any accurate definition of the offensiveness of aircraft is to be arrived at.

The Austrian delegation therefore associates itself with the reservation made by the German delegation.

DECLARATION BY THE BULGARIAN DELEGATION

The Bulgarian delegation considers that the answers to the three questions put by the General Commission present a different aspect in the case of countries which have no military air force and no anti-aircraft defence, thus:

1. For countries which have no anti-aircraft defence, all military aircraft are covered by the three criteria laid down by the General Commission.

2. For countries which have no military air force, it is very difficult, if not impossible, to make use of civil aircraft, owing to the absence of personnel trained for the purpose.

DECLARATION BY THE HUNGARIAN DELEGATION

From the beginning of the proceedings in the Air Commission, the Hungarian delegation has felt that the Commission was working on lines that could not lead to a satisfactory result. Instead of enquiring into the fighting force represented by the air arm as a whole and the destruction which, as a whole, it is capable of causing, the Commission has devoted chief attention to highly complicated details which have, no doubt, great scientific value, but whose relation to the problem set is exceedingly vague.

The essential object of the Disarmament Conference should be to bring under international regulation all such arms as are calculated to favour sudden and unexpected attacks. Now it is not unreasonable to ask whether there is any arm possessing more properties calculated to favour such attacks than the air arm as a whole. Convinced that this was so, the Hungarian delegation associated itself with the German proposal, and deeply regrets that that proposal was not accepted by the majority of the Commission.

The Hungarian delegation has continued none the less to take part in the proceedings of the Air Commission, in the hope that its collaboration might induce the Commission to decide upon an acceptable text.

Unhappily, the proposals that the Hungarian delegation had the honour to put forward during the discussion were not accepted by the Commission.

The latter decided to submit to the General Commission a reply which, in the Hungarian delegation's view, cannot result in a radical reduction of air armaments. The Hungarian delegation therefore sincerely regrets that it was unable to accept the texts established by the Commission and was forced to vote both against the conclusions in Part I of the report and against the inclusion of Part II in the report.

The Hungarian delegation must therefore again state that:

For Hungary, who is disarmed in the air and excessively vulnerable to air attacks, aircraft as a whole constitute:

The most offensive of all weapons;

A weapon that could easily crush her too feeble national defence, and that would expose:

(a) Her civil population, deprived of anti-aircraft defence, to certain death;

(b) Her capital and her industrial areas, situated only a few kilometres from the frontier, to complete destruction; and

(c) All movement on her system of communications to an abrupt stoppage.

DECLARATION BY THE DELEGATIONS OF BELGIUM, MEXICO, THE NETHERLANDS, PORTUGAL, SPAIN, SWEDEN AND SWITZERLAND

The delegations of Belgium, Mexico, the Netherlands, Portugal, Spain,[6] Sweden,[6] and Switzerland:[7]

Having examined a large number of aeroplanes at present in use in various countries with a view to finding numerical criteria to determine what aeroplanes come under the three categories indicated by the General Commission—namely:

The most specifically offensive,

The most efficacious against national defence,

The most threatening to civilians,

have come to the following conclusions:

(1) There is a limit, based on technical data, above which almost all aeroplanes possess the three characteristics mentioned above;

(2) There is a limit below which no aeroplane can be deemed to possess these three characteristics;

(3) For aeroplanes the characteristics of which lie between the two limits, it is impossible to lay down a simple rule enabling those possessing the three above-mentioned characteristics to be distinguished with certainty.

The limit under (1) might be fixed at an unladen weight of 1,500 to 1,600 kg. (with the addition of 300 to 400 kg. for seaplanes.)

The limit under (2) might be fixed, in general, at an unladen weight of 600 kg., a horse-power of 200, and a wing area of 25 sq. m., on the understanding that any aeroplane exceeding any one of these three limits would come under the category of (3) above.

RESERVATION BY THE ITALIAN DELEGATION

The Italian delegation took no part in the discussion and drafting of the second part of the report.

It considers that the statements and figures given in this part do not correspond to the present situation of mobilisable military aviation, and that, by leading the General Commission astray, they render more difficult the decisions which it will be called upon to take.

The Italian delegation considers that, among the means of aerial warfare at the disposal of military aviation, the following should be regarded as being the most specifically offensive, the most efficacious against national defence, and the most threatening to civilians:

(1) Dirigibles of any volume whatsoever,

(2) Aeroplanes seating two persons and over; always excepting two-seater aeroplanes used in schools, provided that their unladen weight does not exceed 400 kg. and the horse-power 100, and that the ratio between horse-power and wing area is not less than 4 to the square metre.

(3) Seaplanes seating two persons and over, always excepting two-seater seaplanes used in schools, provided that their unladen weight does not exceed 450 kg. and their horse-power 100, and that the ratio between horse-power and wing area is not less than 4 to the square metre.

(4) Aeroplanes which, although single-seaters, are of over 650 kg. unladen weight, over 200 h.p. and with a ratio between horse-power and wing area of less than 16 to the square metre.

(5) Single-seater aeroplanes of unladen weight less than 650 kg., which, although of horse-power between 200 and 100, have a ratio between horse-power and wing area less than that obtained by linear interpolation:

Between 16 and 12 h.p. to the square metre for machines of horse-power between 200 and 150.

Between 12 and 5 h.p. to the square metre for machines of horse-power between 150 and 100.

(6) Seaplanes which, although single-seaters, are of over 700 kg. unladen weight, over 200 h.p. and with ratio between horse-power and wing area less than 16 to the square metre.

(7) Single-seater seaplanes of unladen weight less than 700 kg., which, although of horse-power between 200 and 100, have a ratio between horse-power and wing area less than that laid down in paragraph 5.

DECLARATION BY THE BOLIVIAN DELEGATION.

In accordance with the declaration made by the Bolivian delegation at a plenary session of the Air Commission, it makes a reservation regarding the whole idea of figures; this reservation is due to Boliva's special geographical situation, and in particular to its altitude (averaging 4,000 metres). The delegation would merely point out that the fixing of figures would have a negative value where aircraft beginning to operate at that altitude were concerned.

DECLARATION BY THE CHINESE DELEGATION

The Chinese delegation, in view of the fact that the Air Commission is to submit its report to the General Commission without achieving a unanimous decision, wishes to place on record the following declaration:

The Chinese delegation maintains its original standpoint that all military aircraft are by nature offensive armaments, while bombing aeroplanes are armaments whose character is most specifically offensive, most efficacious against national defence, and most threatening to civilians, thus combining all the three characteristics mentioned in the General Commission's resolution of April 22nd, 1932.

The Chinese delegation considers that the proposal of the Belgian, Mexican, Netherlands, Portuguese, Spanish, Swedish and Swiss delegations (see above), which provides for the division of all military aeroplanes into three categories, is acceptable. It is, however, of the opinion that the limit fixed in the said proposal is somewhat high. The Chinese delegation is, in this connection, inclined to support the suggestion of the Swiss delegation that the limit set for unladen weight should be 1,200 kg. instead of 1,500 to 1,600 kg., in the interest of those countries whose air defence is still inadequate and whose undefended towns and cities are in consequence exposed to the dangers of aerial bombardment.

The Chinese delegation would further reiterate its proposal that all aerial bombardment as a means of carrying on civilised warfare should be abolished (see document Conf.D.88).

DECLARATION BY THE FRENCH DELEGATION

The French delegation considers that the statements of fact contained in the second part of the Commission's report show how impossible it is from the technical point of view to draw a clear dividing line between defensive aircraft and those more specifically offensive in character. Even if it is possible to fix a limit above which aircraft cannot be considered purely defensive, there is on the other hand a whole zone covering both specifically machines threatening to the civil population, and machines indispensable for national defence.

The French delegation would state that these were the considerations which led it to submit its proposals of February 5th last, and to fix for the capacity of aircraft two series of limits which it has reserved the right to define later: the first—the higher—above which no machine may be retained in a national air force; the second—the lower—(below which the use of military aircraft shall be subject only to those restrictions arising out of the quantitative limitation provided for in the convention to be drawn up and already laid down in the Preparatory Commission's draft.

All the aircraft included between these two limits, whether their predominant character be offensive or defensive, may only be retained by national air forces subject to a preliminary undertaking to place such machines at the disposal of the League of Nations in the event of the application of Article 1[6] of the Covenant.

DECLARATION BY THE NETHERLANDS DELEGATION

On Part I. The Netherlands delegation considers that bombing aircraft, all types of aerial bombs, and all instruments for aiming or launching such bombs, should be designated as weapons most specifically offensive, most efficacious against national defence, and most threatening to civilians.

On Part II. The Netherlands delegation states that the division of the load of bombs required for effective action against a certain objective among as large a number of aeroplanes as possible would result in lower tonnage figures for aircraft than those given in the report. These figures would be still further decreased if the radius of action of aircraft were reduced.

DECLARATION BY THE PERSIAN DELEGATION

Since the Persian delegation has, since the outset of the Commission's work, made it clear that it is in favour of the abolition of military aviation provided civil aviation be regulated by international statute, it is impossible for it to express an opinion on the aggressive character of military aviation alone, since the General Commission has as yet taken no decision regarding civil aviation. For this reason, the Persian delegation abstained from voting on Part II of the report.

DECLARATION OF THE DELEGATION OF THE UNION OF SOVIET SOCIALIST REPUBLICS

As the moment has come to draw conclusions from the Air Commission's work carried out in response to the three questions asked by the General Commission, the Soviet delegation feels bound to make the following declaration:

(1) The Air Commission has not found it possible to recognise the soundness of the statements of certain delegations—among them the Soviet—that all military aviation comes under the head of the General Commission's questionnaire. Nevertheless, the Air Commission has not indicated the limits above which military aeroplanes acquire the properties which bring them into the category of armaments envisaged in the General Commission's questionnaire.

(2) The drafting of certain articles, as well as certain statements in the report, which, moreover, exactly correspond to the declarations made by the different delegations, show that the majority of the Commission considers that air armaments are only offensive and threatening to national defence and the civil population when used for purposes of aggression or attack on specified localities. The Soviet delegation is firmly opposed to this point of view, considering that it is the technical characteristics of aircraft which determine the offensive properties of military aviation, and that the very existence of military aircraft, as well as of aerial bombs and other means of warfare intended to be dropped or launched from the air, are a danger to national defence and constitute a threat to the civil population,

(3) For the above reasons the Soviet delegation is unable to support the view that the offensive character of military aviation can only be determined after a review of the possibilities of its employment for defensive purposes. The Soviet delegation feels that it is the Air Commission's duty to determine the aggressive characteristics of air armaments, and not to defend such armaments by mere reference to the various possibilities of their defensive use.

(4) The references to be found in the report to the necessity for taking into account the geographical situation and special circumstances of each country, as well as atmospheric conditions and other factors, seem to the Soviet delegation to be an attempt to divert the questions asked by the General Commission into a discussion very far removed from the concrete task assigned to the Air Commission.

(5) Without raising any objection to the view of the majority of the Commission that aeroplanes become more aggressive and dangerous to national defence and the civil population with any increase in their useful load (provided they be considered singly), the Soviet delegation, basing its view on a technical study of the properties of military aircraft, once more declares that all military aircraft clearly come within the three categories referred to by the General Commission. The Soviet delegation is thus the less able to support the view that only large bombing aircraft should be considered offensive, even if the figures contained in the report are only given for purposes of indication. It feels that such a classification is far removed from reality, and can but prejudice qualitative disarmament.

In view of the foregoing, the Soviet delegation desires to state that the Air Commission, in confining itself to general statements, has failed to reply to the three questions asked by the General Commission. The Soviet delegation is therefore obliged to continue, in the General Commission, to defend its view as expressed in the present declaration as well as in earlier discussions.

The footnotes are from the document:

2. By "useful load" is meant all that an aircraft can carry in addition to its "unladen weight," as defined in Annex I of this report [not included here].

3. Declaration by the delegations of Austria, Bulgaria, Germany, Hungary, and Persia [all attached].

4. Declaration of Belgium, Mexico, Netherlands, Portugal, Spain, Sweden and Switzerland [attached].

5. Italian declaration [attached].

6. The Spanish and Swedish delegations state that their participation in the attempts to find as precise as possible a technical reply to the questions asked by the General Commission does not prejudice their attitude regarding the total abolition of military aviation, accompanied by the internationalism or strict control of civil aviation.

7. The Swiss delegation had in mind a lower figure for the limit proposed under (1)—namely, 1,200 kg.

[League of Nations, *Conference for the Reduction and Limitation of Armaments,* Geneva, 1932, Air Commission. (M. Boheman, Sweden, Rapporteur)]

Outlawing Chemical, Bacteriological, and Biological Weapons

The Hague Declaration (1899)

The following declaration was signed at The Hague on 29 July 1899.

Declaration concerning Asphyxiating Gases

The undersigned, plenipotentiaries of the Powers represented at the International Peace Conference at The Hague, duly authorized to that effect by their Governments, inspired by the sentiments which found expression in the Declaration of St. Petersburg of the 29th November (11th December), 1868,

Declare as follows:

The contracting Powers agree to abstain from the use of projectiles the sole object of which is the diffusion of asphyxiating or deleterious gases.

The present Declaration is only binding on the contracting Powers in the case of a war between two or more of them.

It shall cease to be binding from the time when, in a war between the contracting Powers, one of the belligerents shall be joined by a non-contracting Power.

The present Declaration shall be ratified as soon as possible.

The ratifications shall be deposited at The Hague.

A *procès-verbal* shall be drawn up on the receipt of each ratification, a copy of which, duly certified, shall be sent through the diplomatic channel to all the contracting Powers.

The non-signatory Powers can adhere to the present Declaration. For this purpose they must make their adhesion known to the contracting Powers by means of a written notification addressed to the Netherland Government, and by it communicated to all the other contracting Powers.

In the event of one of the high contracting Parties denouncing the present Declaration, such denunciation shall not take effect until a year after the notification made in writing to the Government of the Netherlands, and forthwith communicated by it to all the other contracting Powers.

This denunciation shall only affect the notifying Power.

In faith of which the plenipotentiaries have signed the present Declaration, and affixed their seals thereto.

Done at The Hague, the 29th July, 1899, in a single copy, which shall be kept in the archives of the Netherland Government, and copies of which, duly certified, shall be sent by the diplomatic channel to the contracting Powers.

[Signatures]

[James Brown Scott, *The Hague Conventions and Declarations of 1899 and 1907,* 3d ed. (New York, 1918), pp. 225–226]

Versailles Treaty "Poison Gas" Prohibitions (1919)

A defeated Germany was prohibited from having asphyxiating, poisonous or other gases by the Treaty of Versailles, 1919.

Article 171. The use of asphyxiating, poisonous or other gases and all analogous liquids, materials or devices being prohibited, their manufacture and importation are strictly forbidden in Germany. The same applies to materials specially intended for the manufacture, storage and use of the said products or devices.

The manufacture and the importation into Germany of armoured cars, tanks and all similar constructions suitable for use in war are also prohibited.

[Fred L. Israel, ed., *Major Peace Treaties of Modern History, 1648–1967* (New York, 1967), vol. 2, pp. 1363–1383]

Washington Treaty on Use of Gases in Wartime (1922)

This treaty repeated the Washington Treaty on Use of Submarines and Gases in Wartime, 1922, which is reprinted in full above.

Article V. The use in war of asphyxiating, poisonous or other gases, and all analogous liquids, materials or devices, having been justly condemned by the general opinion of the civilized world and a prohibition of such use having been declared in treaties to which a majority of the civilized Powers are parties,

The Signatory Powers, to the end that this prohibition shall be universally accepted as a part of international law binding alike the conscience and

practice of nations, declare their assent to such prohibition, agree to be bound thereby as between themselves and invite all other civilized nations to adhere thereto.

[U.S. Senate, 67th Congress, 2d Session, Doc. 124, *Armament Conference Treaties: Treaties and Resolutions Approved and Adopted by the Conference on the Limitation of Armament* ... (Washington, 1922)]

Geneva Protocol on Poisonous Gases (1925)

The following agreement was signed at Geneva on 17 June 1925. It entered into force on 8 February 1928 and was ratified by the United States on 22 January 1975.

Protocol for the Prohibition of the Use in War of Asphyxiating, Poisonous or Other Gases, and of Bacteriological Methods of Warfare

The undersigned plenipotentiaries, in the name of their respective Governments:

Whereas the use in war of asphyxiating, poisonous or other gases, and of all analogous liquids, ma-

terials or devices, has been justly condemned by the general opinion of the civilized world; and

Whereas the prohibition of such use has been declared in Treaties to which the majority of Powers of the World are Parties; and

To the end that this prohibition shall be universally accepted as a part of International Law, binding alike the conscience and the practice of nations;

Declare:

That the High Contracting Parties, so far as they are not already Parties to Treaties prohibiting such use, accept this prohibition, agree to extend this prohibition to the use of bacteriological methods of warfare and agree to be bound as between themselves according to the terms of this declaration.

The High Contracting Parties will exert every effort to induce other States to accede to the present Protocol. Such accession will be notified to the Government of the French Republic, and by the latter to all signatory and acceding Powers, and will take effect on the date of the notification by the Government of the French Republic.

The present Protocol, of which the French and English texts are both authentic, shall be ratified as soon as possible. It shall bear today's date.

The ratifications of the present Protocol shall be addressed to the Government of the French Republic, which will at once notify the deposit of such ratification to each of the signatory and acceding Powers.

The instruments of ratification of and accession to the present Protocol will remain deposited in the archives of the Government of the French Republic.

The present Protocol will come into force for each signatory Power as from the date of deposit of its ratification, and, from that moment, each Power will be bound as regards other powers which have already deposited their ratifications.

[Signatures]

[U.S. Library of Congress, Legislative Reference Service, *Disarmament and Security: A Collection of Documents, 1919–1955* (Washington, D.C., 1956), Doc. 29]

U.N. Resolution on Chemical and Bacteriological (Biological) Weapons (1969)

The following United Nations resolution was adopted on 16 December 1969. Part A was adopted by a vote of 80 to 3, with 36 abstentions, and Part B was approved 120 to 0, with one abstention.

General Assembly Resolution 2603 (XXIV): Question of Chemical and Bacteriological (Biological) Weapons, 16 December 1969

A

The General Assembly,

Considering that chemical and biological methods of warfare have always been viewed with horror and been justly condemned by the international community,

Considering that these methods of warfare are inherently reprehensible because their effects are often uncontrollable and unpredictable and may be injurious without distinction to combatants and non-combatants, and because any use would entail a serious risk of escalation,

Recalling that successive international instruments have prohibited or sought to prevent the use of such methods of warfare,

Noting specifically in this regard that:

(a) The majority of States then in existence adhered to the Protocol for the Prohibition of the Use in War of Asphyxiating, Poisonous or Other Gases, and of Bacteriological Methods of Warfare signed at Geneva on 17 June 1925,

(b) Since then, further States have become Parties to that Protocol,

(c) Still other States have declared that they will abide by its principles and objectives.

(d) These principles and objectives have commanded broad respect in the practice of States,

(e) The General Assembly, without any dissenting vote, has called for the strict observance by all States of the principles and objectives of the Geneva Protocol,

Recognizing therefore, in the light of all the above circumstances, that the Geneva Protocol embodies the generally recognized rules of international law prohibiting the use in international armed conflicts of all biological and chemical methods of warfare, regardless of any technical developments,

Mindful of the report of the Secretary-General, prepared with the assistance of the Group of Consultant Experts, appointed by him under General Assembly resolution 2454 A (XXIII) of 20 December 1968, and entitled *Chemical and Bacteriological (Biological) Weapons and the Effects of Their Possible Use,*

Considering that this report and the foreword to it by the Secretary-General add further urgency for an affirmation of these rules and for dispelling, for the future, any uncertainty as to their scope and, by such affirmation, to assure the effectiveness of the rules and to enable all States to demonstrate their determination to comply with them,

Declares as contrary to the generally recognized rules of international law, as embodied in the Protocol for the Prohibition of the Use in War of Asphyxiating, Poisonous or Other Gases, and of Bacteriological Methods of Warfare, signed at Geneva on 17 June 1925, the use in international armed conflict of:

(a) Any chemical agents of warfare—chemical substances, whether gaseous, liquid or solid—which might be employed because of their direct toxic effects on man, animals or plants;

(b) Any biological agents of warfare—living organisms, whatever their nature, or infective material dervied from them—which are intended to cause disease or death in man, animals or plants, and which depend for their effects on their ability to multiply in the person, animal or plant attacked.

B

The General Assembly,

Recalling its resolution 2454 A (XXIII) of 20 December 1968,

Having considered the report of the Secretary-General, entitled *Chemical and Bacteriological (Biological) Weapons and the Effects of Their Possible Use,*

Noting the conclusions of the report of the Secretary-General and the recommendations contained in the foreword to the report,

Noting also the discussion of the report of the Secretary-General at the Conference of the Committee on Disarmament and during the twenty-fourth session of the General Assembly,

Mindful of the conclusion of the report that the prospects for general and complete disarmament under effective international control and hence for peace throughout the world would brighten significantly if the development, production and stockpiling of chemical and bacteriological (biological) agents intended for purposes of war were to end and if they were eliminated from all military arsenals,

Recognizing the importance of the Protocol for the Prohibition of the Use in War of Asphyxiating, Poisonous or Other Gases, and of Bacteriological Methods of Warfare, signed at Geneva on 17 June 1925,

Conscious of the need to maintain inviolate the Geneva Protocol and to ensure its universal applicability,

Emphasizing the urgency of the need for achieving the earliest elimination of chemical and bacteriological (biological) weapons,

1. *Reaffirms* its resolution 2162 B (XXI) of 5 December 1966 and calls anew for strict observance by all States of the principles and objectives of the Protocol for the Prohibition of the Use in War of Asphyxiating, Poisonous or Other Gases, and of Bacteriological Methods of Warfare, signed at Geneva on 17 June 1925;

2. *Invites* all States which have not yet done so to accede to or ratify the Geneva Protocol in the course of 1970 in commemoration of the forty-fifth anniversary of its signing and the twenty-fifth anniversary of the United Nations;

II

1. *Welcomes* the report of the Secretary-General as an authoritative statement on chemical and bacteriological (biological) weapons and the effects of their possible use, and expresses its appreciation to the Secretary-General and to the consultant experts who assisted him;

2. *Requests* the Secretary-General to publicize the report in as many languages as is considered desirable and practicable, making use of the facilities of the United Nations Office of Public Information;

3. *Recommends* to all Governments the wide distribution of the report so as to acquaint public opinion with its contents, and invites the specialized agencies, intergovernmental organizations and national and international nongovernmental organizations to use their facilities to make the report widely known;

4. *Recommends* the report of the Secretary-General to the Conference of the Committee on Disarmament as a basis for its further consideration of the elimination of chemical and bacteriological (biological) weapons;

III

1. *Takes note* of the draft Convention on the Prohibition of the Development, Production and Stockpiling of Chemical and Bacteriological (Biological) Weapons and on the Destruction of such Weapons submitted to the General Assembly by the delegations of Bulgaria, the Byelorussian Soviet Socialist Republic, Czechoslovakia, Hungary, Mongolia, Poland, Romania, the Ukrainian Soviet Socialist Republic and the Union of Soviet Socialist Republics and of the draft Convention for the Prohibition of Biological Methods of Warfare submitted to the Conference of the Committee on Disarmament by the United Kingdom of Great Britain and Northern Ireland, as well as other proposals;

2. *Requests* the Conference of the Committee on Disarmament to give urgent consideration to reaching agreement on the prohibitions and other measures referred to in the draft conventions mentioned in paragraph 1 above and other relevant proposals;

3. *Requests* the Conference of the Committee on Disarmament to submit a report on progress on all aspects of the problem of the elimination of chemical and bacteriological (biological) weapons to the General Assembly at its twenty-fifth session;

4. *Requests* the Secretary-General to transmit to the Conference of the Committee on Disarmament all documents and records of the First Committee relating to questions connected with the problem of chemical and bacteriological (biological) weapons. [U.S. Arms Control and Disarmament Agency, *Documents on Disarmament,* 1969, pp. 716–718]

U.S. Unilateral Ban on Biological Weapons (1969)

Following is the text of the Statement by President Richard Nixon on Chemical and Biological Weapons, 25 November 1969.

Soon after taking office I directed a comprehensive study of our chemical arid biological defense policies and programs. There had been no such review in over 15 years. As a result, objectives and policies in this field were unclear and programs lacked definition and direction.

Under the auspices of the National Security Council, the Departments of State and Defense, the Arms Control and Disarmament Agency, the Office of Science and Technology, the intelligence community, and other agencies worked closely together on this study for over 6 months. These Government efforts were aided by contributions from the scientific community through the President's Science Advisory Committee.

This study has now been completed and its findings carefully considered by the National Security Council. I am now reporting the decisions taken on the basis of this review.

Chemical Warfare Program

As to our chemical warfare programs, the United States:

Reaffirms its oft-repeated renunciation of the first use of lethal chemical weapons.

Extends this renunciation to the first use of incapacitating chemicals.

Consonant with these decisions, the administration will submit to the Senate, for its advice and consent to ratification, the Geneva Protocol of 1925 which prohibits the first use of "Asphyxiating, Poisonous or other Gases and of Bacteriological Methods of Warfare." The United States has long supported the principles and objectives of this Protocol. We take this step toward formal ratification to reinforce our continuing advocacy of international constraints on the use of these weapons.

Biological Research Program

Biological weapons have massive, unpredictable and potentially uncontrollable consequences. They may produce global epidemics and impair the health of future generations. I have therefore decided that:

- The United States shall renounce the use of lethal biological agents and weapons, and all other methods of biological warfare.
- The United States will confine its biological research to defensive measures such as immunization and safety measures.
- The Department of Defense has been asked to make recommendations as to the disposal of existing stocks of bacteriological weapons.

In the spirit of these decisions, the United States associates itself with the principles and objectives of the United Kingdom Draft Convention which would ban the use of biological methods of warfare. We will seek, however, to clarify specific provisions of the draft to assure that necessary safeguards are included.

Neither our association with the Convention nor the limiting of our program to research will leave us vulnerable to surprise by an enemy who does not observe these rational restraints. Our intelligence community will continue to watch carefully the nature and extent of the biological programs of others.

These important decisions, which have been announced today, have been taken as an initiative toward peace. Mankind already carries in its own hands too many of the seeds of its own destruction. By the examples we set today, we hope to contribute to an atmosphere of peace and understanding between nations and among men.

[U.S. Arms Control and Disarmament Agency, *Documents on Disarmament,* 1969, pp. 592–593]

Biological Weapons Convention (1972)

The Biological Weapons Convention was signed at Washington, London, and Moscow on 10 April 1972, and it entered into force on 26 March 1975.

Convention on the Prohibition of the Development, Production and Stockpiling of Bacteriological (Biological) and Toxin Weapons and on Their Destruction.

The States Parties to this Convention,

Determined to act with a view to achieving effective progress towards general and complete disarmament, including the prohibition and elimination of all types of weapons of mass destruction, and convinced that the prohibition of the development, production and stockpiling of chemical and bacteriological (biological) weapons and their elimination, through effective measures, will facilitate the achievement of general and complete disarmament under strict and effective international control,

Recognizing the important significance of the Protocol for the Prohibition of the Use in War of Asphyxiating, Poisonous or Other Gases, and of Bacteriological Methods of Warfare, signed at Geneva on June 17, 1925, and conscious also of the contribution which the said Protocol has already made, and continues to make, to mitigating the horrors of war,

Reaffirming their adherence to the principles and objectives of that Protocol and calling upon all States to comply strictly with them,

Recalling that the General Assembly of the United Nations has repeatedly condemned all actions contrary to the principles and objectives of the Geneva Protocol of June 17, 1925,

Desiring to contribute to the strengthening of confidence between peoples and the general improvement of the international atmosphere,

Desiring also to contribute to the realization of the purposes and principles of the Charter of the United Nations,

Convinced of the importance and urgency of eliminating from the arsenals of States, through effective measures, such dangerous weapons of mass destruction as those using chemical or bacteriological (biological) agents,

Recognizing that an agreement on the prohibition of bacteriological (biological) and toxin weapons represents a first possible step towards the achievement of agreement on effective measures also for the prohibition of the development, production and stockpiling of chemical weapons, and determined to continue negotiations to that end,

Determined, for the sake of all mankind, to exclude completely the possibility of bacteriological (biological) agents and toxins being used as weapons,

Convinced that such use would be repugnant to the conscience of mankind and that no effort should be spared to minimize this risk, Have agreed as follows:

Article I. Each State Party to this Convention undertakes never in any circumstances to develop, produce, stockpile or otherwise acquire or retain:

(1) Microbial or other biological agents, or toxins whatever their origin or method of production, of types and in quantities that have no justification for prophylactic, protective or other peaceful purposes;

(2) Weapons, equipment or means of delivery designed to use such agents or toxins for hostile purposes or in armed conflict.

Article II. Each State Party to this Convention undertakes to destroy, or to divert to peaceful purposes, as soon as possible but not later than nine months after the entry into force of the Convention, all agents, toxins, weapons, equipment and means of delivery specified in article I of the Convention, which are in its possession or under its jurisdiction or control. In implementing the provisions of this article all necessary safety precautions shall be observed to protect populations and the environment.

Article III. Each State Party to this Convention undertakes not to transfer to any recipient whatsoever, directly or indirectly, and not in any way to assist, encourage, or induce any State, group of States or international organizations to manufacture or otherwise acquire any of the agents, toxins, weapons, equipment or means of delivery specified in article I of the Convention.

Article IV. Each State Party to this Convention shall, in accordance with its constitutional processes, take any necessary measures to prohibit and prevent the development, production, stockpiling, acquisition, or retention of the agents, toxins, weapons, equipment and means of delivery specified in article I of the Convention, within the territory of such State, under its jurisdiction or under its control anywhere.

Article V. The States Parties to this Convention undertake to consult one another and to cooperate in solving any problems which may arise in relation to the objective of, or in the application of the provisions of, the Convention. Consultation and cooperation pursuant to this article may also be undertaken through appropriate international procedures within the framework of the United Nations and in accordance with its Charter.

Article VI

(1) Any State Party to this Convention which finds that any other State Party is acting in breach of obligations deriving from the provisions of the Convention may lodge a complaint with the Security Council of the United Nations. Such a complaint should include all possible evidence confirming its validity, as well as a request for its consideration by the Security Council.

(2) Each State Party to this Convention undertakes to cooperate in carrying out any investigation which the Security Council may initiate, in accordance with the provisions of the Charter of the United Nations, on the basis of the complaint received by the Council. The Security Council shall inform the States Parties to the Convention of the results of the investigation.

Article VII. Each State Party to this Convention undertakes to provide or support assistance, in accordance with the United Nations Charter, to any Party to the Convention which so requests, if the Security Council decides that such Party has been exposed to danger as a result of violation of the Convention.

Article VIII. Nothing in this Convention shall be interpreted as in any way limiting or detracting from the obligations assumed by any State under the Protocol for the Prohibition of the Use in War of Asphyxiating, Poisonous or Other Gases, and of Bacteriological Methods of Warfare, signed at Geneva on June 17, 1925.

Article IX. Each State Party to this Convention affirms the recognized objective of effective prohibition of chemical weapons and, to this end, undertakes to continue negotiations in good faith with a view to reaching early agreement on effective measures for the prohibition of their development, production and stockpiling and for their destruction, and on appropriate measures concerning equipment and means of delivery specifically designed for the production or use of chemical agents for weapons purposes.

Article X

(1) The States Parties to this Convention undertake to facilitate, and have the right to participate in, the fullest possible exchange of equipment, materials and scientific and technological information for the use of bacteriological (biological) agents and toxins for peaceful purposes. Parties to the Convention in a position to do so shall also cooperate in contributing individually or together with other States or international organizations to the further development and application of scientific discoveries in the field of bacteriology (biology) for prevention of disease, or for other peaceful purposes.

(2) This Convention shall be implemented in a manner designed to avoid hampering the economic or technological development of States Parties to the Convention or international cooperation in the field of peaceful bacteriological (biological) activities, including the international exchange of bacteriological (biological) agents and toxins and equipment for the processing, use or production of bacteriological (biological) agents and toxins for peaceful purposes in accordance with the provisions of the Convention.

Article XI. Any State Party may propose amendments to this Convention. Amendments shall enter into force for each State Party accepting the amendments upon their acceptance by a majority of the States Parties to the Convention and thereafter for each remaining State Party on the date of acceptance by it.

Article XII. Five years after the entry into force of this Convention, or earlier if it is requested by a majority of Parties to the Convention by submitting a proposal to this effect to the Depositary Governments, a conference of States Parties to the Convention shall be held at Geneva, Switzerland, to review the operation of the Convention, with a view to assuring that the purposes of the preamble and the provisions of the Convention, including the provisions concerning negotiations on chemical weapons, are being realized. Such review shall take into account any new scientific and technological developments relevant to the Convention.

Article XIII

(1) This Convention shall be of unlimited duration.

(2) Each State Party to this Convention shall in exercising its national sovereignty have the right to withdraw from the Convention if it decides that extraordinary events, related to the subject matter of the Convention, have jeopardized the supreme interests of its country. It shall give notice of such withdrawal to all other States Parties to the Convention and to the United Nations Security Council three months in advance. Such notice shall include a statement of the extraordinary events it regards as having jeopardized its supreme interests.

Article XIV

(1) This Convention shall be open to all States for signature. Any State which does not sign the Convention before its entry into force in accordance with paragraph (3) of this Article may accede to it at any time.

(2) This Convention shall be subject to ratification by signatory States. Instruments of ratification and instruments of accession shall be deposited with the Governments of the United States of America, the United Kingdom of Great Britain and Northern Ireland and the Union of Soviet Socialist Republics, which are hereby designated the Depositary Governments.

(3) This Convention shall enter into force after the deposit of instruments of ratification by twenty-two Governments, including the Governments designated as Depositaries of the Convention.

(4) For States whose instruments of ratification or accession are deposited subsequent to the entry into force of this Convention, it shall enter into force on the date of the deposit of their instruments of ratification or accession.

(5) The Depositary Governments shall promptly inform all signatory and acceding States of the date of each signature, the date of deposit of each instrument of ratification or of accession and the date of the entry into force of this Convention, and of the receipt of other notices.

(6) This Convention shall be registered by the Depositary Governments pursuant to Article 102 of the Charter of the United Nations.

Article XV. This Convention, the English, Russian, French, Spanish and Chinese texts of which are equally authentic, shall be deposited in the archives of the Depositary Governments. Duly certified copies of the Convention shall be transmitted by the

Depositary Governments to the Governments of the signatory and acceding states.

IN WITNESS WHEREOF the undersigned, duly authorized, have signed this Convention.

DONE in triplicate, at the cities of Washington, London and Moscow, this tenth day of April, one thousand nine hundred and seventy-two.

[Signatures]

[U.S. Arms Control and Disarmament Agency, *Arms Control and Disarmament Agreements: Texts and Histories of the Negotiations,* 1982 ed. (Washington, 1982), pp. 124–127]

Outlawing War

Kellogg-Briand Pact (1928)

Kellogg-Briand Pact for the Renunciation of War, 27 August 1928

The President of the German Reich, the President of the United States of America, His Majesty the King of the Belgians, the President of the French Republic, His Majesty the King of Great Britain, Ireland and the British Dominions beyond the Seas, Emperor of India, His Majesty the King of Italy, His Majesty the Emperor of Japan, the President of the Republic of Poland, the President of the Czechoslovak Republic,

Deeply sensible of their solemn duty to promote the welfare of mankind;

Persuaded that the time has come when a frank renunciation of war as an instrument of national policy should be made to the end that the peaceful and friendly relations now existing between their peoples may be perpetuated;

Convinced that all changes in their relations with one another should be sought only by pacific means and be the result of a peaceful and orderly process, and that any signatory Power which shall hereafter seek to promote its national interests by resort to war should be denied the benefits furnished by this Treaty;

Hopeful that, encouraged by their example, all the other nations of the world will join in this humane endeavor and by adhering to the present Treaty as soon as it comes into force bring their peoples within the scope of its beneficent provisions, thus uniting the civilized nations of the world in a common renunciation of war as an instrument of their national policy;

Have decided to conclude a Treaty and for that purpose have appointed as their respective Plenipotentiaries:

[list of delegates] who, having communicated to one another their full powers found in good and due form have agreed upon the following articles:

Article I. The High Contracting Parties solemnly declare in the names of their respective peoples that they condemn recourse to war for the solution of international controversies, and renounce it as an instrument of national policy in their relations with one another.

Article II. The High Contracting Parties agree that the settlement or solution of all disputes or conflicts of whatever nature or of whatever origin they may be, which may arise among them, shall never be sought except by pacific means.

[Ratification]
[Signatures]
[U.S. Library of Congress, Legislative Reference Service, *Disarmament and Security: A Collection of Documents, 1919–55* (Washington, D.C., 1956), Doc. 12]

Argentina Antiwar Treaty (1933)

The Argentina Antiwar Treaty was signed at Rio de Janiero on 10 October 1933, and it entered into force on 13 November 1935. A U.S. reservation appended to the treaty reads as follows: "In adhering to this Treaty the United States does not thereby waive any rights it may have under other treaties or conventions or under international law."

Antiwar Treaty of Nonaggression and Conciliation (Saavedra Lamas Treaty)

The states designated below, in the desire to contribute to the consolidation of peace, and to express their adherence to the efforts made by all civilized nations to promote the spirit of universal harmony;

To the end of condemning wars of aggression and territorial acquisitions that may be obtained by armed conquest, making them impossible and establishing their invalidity through the positive provisions of this treaty, and in order to replace them with pacific solutions based on lofty concepts of justice and equity;

Convinced that one of the most effective means of assuring the moral and material benefits which peace offers to the world, is the organization of a permanent system of conciliation for international disputes, to be applied immediately on the violation of the principles mentioned:

Have decided to put these aims of nonaggression and concord in conventional form by concluding the present treaty, to which end they have appointed the undersigned plenipotentiaries, who, having exhibited their respective full powers, found to be in good and due form, have agreed upon the following:

Article I. The high contracting parties solemnly declare that they condemn wars of aggression in their mutual relations on in those with other states, and that the settlement of disputes or controversies of any kind that may arise among them shall be effected only by the pacific means which have the sanction of international law.

Article II. They declare that as between the high contracting parties territorial questions must not be settled by violence, and that they will not recognize any territorial arrangement which is not obtained by pacific means, nor the validity of the occupation or acquisition of territories that may be brought about by force of arms.

Article III. In case of noncompliance, by any state engaged in a dispute, with the obligations contained in the foregoing articles, the contracting states undertake to make every effort for the maintenance of peace. To that end they will adopt in their character as neutrals a common and solidary attitude; they will exercise the political, juridical, or economic means authorized by international law; they will bring the influence of public opinion to bear, but will in no case resort to intervention, either diplomatic or armed; subject to the attitude that may be incumbent on them by virtue of other collective treaties to which such states are signatories.

Article IV. The high contracting parties obligate themselves to submit to the conciliation procedure established by this treaty the disputes specially mentioned and any others that may arise in their reciprocal relations, without further limitations than those enumerated in the following article, in all controversies which it has not been possible to settle by diplomatic means within a reasonable period of time.

Article V. The high contracting parties and the states which may in the future adhere to this treaty may not formulate, at the time of signature, ratification, or adherence, other limitations to the conciliation procedure than those which are indicated below:

(a) Differences for the solution of which treaties, conventions, pacts, or pacific agreements of any kind whatever may have been concluded, which in no case shall be considered as annulled by this agreement, but supplemented thereby insofar as they tend to assure peace; as well as the questions or matters settled by previous treaties;

(b) Disputes which the parties prefer to solve by direct settlement or submit by common agreement to an arbitral of judicial solution;

(c) Questions which international law leaves to the exclusive competence of each state, under its constitutional system, for which reason the parties may object to their being submitted to the conciliation procedure before the national or local jurisdiction has decided definitively; except in the case of manifest denial or delay of justice, in which case the conciliation procedure shall be initiated within a year at the latest;

(d) Matters which affect constitutional precepts of the parties to the controversy. In case of doubt, each party shall obtain the reasoned opinion of its respective tribunal or supreme court of justice, if the latter should be invested with such powers.

The high contracting parties may communicate, at any time, and in the manner provided for by article XV, an instrument stating that they have abandoned wholly or in part the limitations established by them in the conciliation procedure.

The effect of the limitations formulated by one of the contracting parties shall be that the other parties shall not consider themselves obligated in regard to that party save in the measure of the exceptions established.

Article VI. In the absence of a permanent conciliation commission or of some other international organization charged with this mission by virtue of previous treaties in effect, the high contracting parties undertake to submit their differences to the examination and investigation of a conciliation commission which shall be formed as follows, unless there is an agreement to the contrary of the parties in each case:

The conciliation commission shall consist of five members. Each party to the controversy shall designate a member, who may be chosen by it from among its own nationals. The three remaining members shall be designated by common agreement by the parties from among the nationals of third powers, who must be of different nationalities, must not have their customary residence in the territory of the interested parties, nor be in the service of any of them. The parties shall choose the president of the conciliation commission from among the said three members.

If they cannot arrive at an agreement with regard to such designations, they may entrust the selection thereof to a third power or to some other existing international organism. If the candidates so designated are rejected by the parties or by any one of them, each party shall present a list of candidates equal in number to that of the members to be selected, and the names of those to sit on the conciliation commission shall be determined by lot.

Article VII. The tribunals or supreme courts of justice which, in accordance with the domestic legislation of each state, may be competent to interpret, in the last or the sole instance and in matters under their respective jurisdiction, the constitution, treaties, or the general principles of the law of nations, may be designated preferentially by the high contracting parties to discharge the duties entrusted by the present treaty to the conciliation commission. In this case the tribunal or court may function as a whole or may designate some of its members to proceed alone or by forming a mixed commission with members of other courts or tribunals, as may be agreed upon by common accord between the parties to the dispute.

Article VIII. The conciliation commission shall establish its own rules of procedure, which shall provide in all cases for hearing both sides.

The parties to the controversy may furnish, and the commission may require from them, all the antecedents and information necessary. The parties may have themselves represented by delegates and assisted by advisers or experts and also present evidence of all kinds.

Article IX. The labors and deliberations of the conciliation commission shall not be made public except by a decision of its own to that effect, with the assent of the parties.

In the absence of stipulation to the contrary, the decisions of the commission shall be made by a majority vote, but the commission may not pronounce judgment on the substance of the case except in the presence of all its members.

Article X. It is the duty of the commission to secure the conciliatory settlement of the disputes submitted to its consideration.

After an impartial study of the questions in dispute, it shall set forth in a report the outcome of its work and shall propose to the parties bases of settlement by means of a just and equitable solution.

The report of the commission shall in no case have the character of a final decision or arbitral award either with respect to the exposition of interpretation of the facts, or with regard to the considerations or conclusions of law.

Article XI. The conciliation commission must present its report within 1 year, counting from its first meeting, unless the parties should decide by common agreement to shorten or extend this period.

The conciliation procedure, having been once begun, may be interrupted only by a direct settlement between the parties or by their subsequent decision to submit the dispute by common accord to arbitration or to international justice.

Article XII. In communicating its report to the parties, the conciliation commission shall fix for them a period, which shall not exceed 6 months, within which they must decide as to the bases of the settlement it has proposed. On the expiration of this term, the commission shall record in a final act the decision of the parties.

This period having expired without acceptance of the settlement by the parties, or the adoption by common accord of another friendly solution, the parties to the dispute shall regain their freedom of action to proceed as they may see fit within the limitations flowing from articles I and II of this treaty.

Article XIII. From the initiation of the conciliatory procedure until the expiration of the period fixed by the commission for the parties to make a decision, they must abstain from any measure prejudicial to the execution of the agreement that may be proposed by the commission and, in general, from any act capable of aggravating or prolonging the controversy.

Article XIV. During the conciliation procedure the members of the commission shall receive honoraria the amount of which shall be established by common agreement by the parties to the controversy. Each of them shall bear its own expenses and a moiety of the joint expenses or honoraria.

Article XV. The present treaty shall be ratified by the high contracting parties as soon as possible, in accordance with their respective constitutional procedures.

The original treaty and the instruments of ratification shall be deposited in the Ministry of Foreign Relations and Worship of the Argentine Republic, which shall go into effect between the high contracting parties 30 days after the deposit of the respective ratifications, and in the order in which they are effected.

Article XVI. This treaty shall remain open to the adherence of all states.

Adherence shall be effected by the deposit of the respective instrument in the Ministry of Foreign Relations and Worship of the Argentine Republic, which shall give notice thereof to the other interested states.

Article XVII. The present treaty is concluded for an indefinite time, but may be denounced by 1 year's notice, on the expiration of which the effects thereof shall cease for the denouncing state, and remain in force for the other states which are parties thereto, by signature or adherence.

The denunciation shall be addressed to the Ministry of Foreign Relations and Worship of the Argentine Republic, which shall transmit it to the other interested states.

In witness whereof, the respective plenipotentiaries sign the present treaty in one copy, in the Spanish and Portuguese languages, and affix their seals thereto, at Rio de Janeiro, D.F., on the tenth day of October nineteen hundred and thirty-three.

[Signatures]

[Charles I. Bevans, *Treaties and Other International Agreements of the United States of America, 1776–1949: Multilateral* (Washington, D.C.: G.P.O., 1969), vol. 3, pp. 135–140]

Unilateral Cold War Prohibitions

Treaty of Peace with Italy (10 February 1947)

Article 51

Italy shall not possess, construct or experiment with (i) any atomic weapon, (ii) any self-propelled or guided missiles or apparatus connected with their discharge (other than torpedoes and torpedo-launching gear comprising the normal armament of naval vessels permitted by the present Treaty), (iii) any guns with a range of over 30 kilometers, (iv) sea mines or torpedoes of non-contact types actuated by influence mechanisms, (v) any torpedoes capable of being manned.

[See the first section of this volume, Limitation of Weapons and Personnel, for the text of the entire treaty.]

[U.S. Library of Congress, Legislative Reference Service, *Disarmament and Security: A Collection of Documents, 1919–55* (Washington, D.C., 1956), Doc. 107]

Protocol to the Brussels Treaty (1954)

This pact contains the West German pledge not to possess weapons of mass destruction. It was signed at Paris on 23 October 1954.

ANNEX I

The Federal Chancellor declares:

that the Federal Republic undertakes not to manufacture in its territory any atomic weapons, chemical weapons or biological weapons, . . . [and] that it undertakes further not to manufacture in its territory such weapons. . . .

[U.S. Library of Congress, Legislative Reference Service, *Disarmament and Security: A Collection of Documents, 1919–55* (Washington, D.C., 1956), Doc. 121]

Austrian State Treaty (1955)

State Treaty for the Reestablishment of an Independent and Democratic Austria, 15 May 1955

Article 13. Prohibition of Special Weapons

1. Austria shall not possess, construct, or experiment with-(a) Any atomic weapons, (b) any other major weapon adaptable now or in the future to mass destruction and defined as such by the appropriate organ of the United Nations, (c) any self-propelled or guided missile or torpedoes, or apparatus connected with their discharge of control, (d) sea mines, (e) torpedoes capable of being manned, (f) submarines or other submersible craft, (g) motor torpedo boats, (h) specialized types of assault craft, (i) guns with a range of more than 30 kilometers, (j) asphyxiating, vesicant or poisonous materials or biological substances in quantities greater than, or of types other than, are required for legitimate civil

purposes, or any apparatus designed to produce, project or spread any such materials or substances for war purposes.

2. The Allied and Associated Powers reserve the right to add to this Article prohibitions of any weapons which may be evolved as a result of scientific development.

[U.S. Library of Congress, Legislative Reference Service, *Disarmament and Security: A Collection of Documents, 1919–55* (Washington, D.C., 1956), Doc. 126]

U.N. Resolution Prohibiting Iraqi Possession of Weapons of Mass Destruction (1991)

Following is the text of U.N. Resolution 687, which was adopted on 3 April 1991.

The Security Council,

Affirming the commitment of all Member States to the sovereignty, territorial integrity and political independence of Kuwait and Iraq, and noting the intention expressed by the Member States cooperating with Kuwait under paragraph 2 of resolution 678 (1990) to bring their military presence in Iraq to an end as soon as possible consistent with paragraph 8 of resolution 686 (1991),

Reaffirming the need to be assured of Iraq's peaceful intentions in light of its unlawful invasion and occupation of Kuwait,

. . . . .

Conscious also of the statements by Iraq threatening to use weapons in violation of its obligations under the Geneva Protocol for the Prohibition of the Use in War of Asphyxiating, poisonous or Other Gases, and of Bacteriological Methods of Warfare, signed at Geneva on 17 June 1925, and of its prior use of chemical weapons and affirming that grave consequences would follow any further use by Iraq of such weapons,

Recalling that Iraq has subscribed to the Declaration adopted by all States participating in the Conference of States Parties to the 1925 Geneva Protocol and Other Interested States, held at Paris from 7 to 11 January 1989, establishing the objective of universal elimination of chemical and biological weapons,

Recalling further that Iraq has signed the Convention on the Prohibition of the Development, Production and Stockpiling of Bacteriological (Biological) and Toxin Weapons and on Their Destruction, of 10 April 1972,

Noting the importance of Iraq ratifying this Convention,

Noting moreover the importance of all States adhering to this Convention and encouraging its forthcoming Review Conference to reinforce the authority, efficiency and universal scope of the Convention,

Stressing the importance of an early conclusion by the Conference on Disarmament of its work on a Convention on the Universal Prohibition of Chemical Weapons and of universal adherence thereof,

Aware of the use by Iraq of ballistic missiles in unprovoked attacks and therefore of the need to take specific measures in regard to such missiles located in Iraq,

Concerned by the reports in the hands of Member States that Iraq has attempted to acquire materials for a nuclear-weapons programme contrary to its obligations under the Treaty on the Non-Proliferation of Nuclear Weapons of 1 July 1968,

Recalling the objective of the establishment of a nuclear-weapon-free zone in the region of the Middle East,

Conscious of the threat which all weapons of mass destruction pose to peace and security in the area and of the need to work towards the establishment in the Middle East of a zone free of such weapons,

Conscious also of the objective of achieving balanced and comprehensive control of armaments in the region,

. . . . .

5. *Requests* the Secretary-General, after consulting with Iraq and Kuwait, to submit within three days to the Security Council for its approval a plan for the immediate deployment of a United nations observer unit to monitor the Khor Abdullah and a demilitarized zone, which is hereby established, extending 10 kilometres into Iraq and 5 kilometres into Kuwait from the boundary referred to in the "Agreed Minutes Between the State of Kuwait and the Republic of Iraq Regarding the Restoration of Friendly Relations, Recognition and Related Matters" of 4 October 1963; to deter violations of the boundary through its presence in and surveillance of the demilitarized zone; to observe any hostile or potentially hostile action mounted from the territory of one State to the other; and for the Secretary-General to report regularly to the Council on the operations of the unit, and immediately if there are serious violations of the zone or potential threats to peace;

6. *Notes* that as soon as the Secretary-General notifies the Council of the completion of the deployment of the United Nations observer unit, the conditions will be established for the Member States cooperating with Kuwait in accordance with resolution 678 (1990) to bring their military presence in Iraq to an end consistent with resolution 686 (1991);

7. *Invites* Iraq to reaffirm unconditionally its obligations under the Geneva Protocol for the Prohibition of the Use in War of Asphyxiating, Poisonous or Other Gases, and of Bacteriological Methods of Warfare, signed at Geneva on 17 June 1925, and to ratify the Convention on the Prohibition of the Development, Production and Stockpiling of Bacteriological (Biological) and Toxin Weapons and on Their Destruction, of 10 April 1972;

8. *Decides* that Iraq shall unconditionally accept the destruction, removal, or rendering harmless, under international supervision, of:

a) all chemical and biological weapons and all stocks of agents and all related subsystems and components and all research, development, support and manufacturing facilities;

b) all ballistic missiles with a range greater than 150 kilometres and related major parts, and repair and production facilities;

9. *Decides,* for the implementation of paragraph 8 above, the following:

a) Iraq shall submit to the Secretary-General, within fifteen days of the adoption of this resolution, a declaration of the locations, amounts and

types of all items specified in paragraph 8 and agree to urgent, on-site inspection as specified below;

b) the Secretary-General, in consultation with the appropriate Governments and, where appropriate, with the Director-General of the World Health Organization (WHO), within 45 days of the passage of this resolution, shall develop, and submit to the Council for approval, a plan calling for the completion of the following acts within 45 days of such approval:

(i) the forming of a Special Commission, which shall carry out immediate on-site inspection of Iraq's biological, chemical and missile capabilities, based on Iraq's declarations and the designation of any additional locations by the Special Commission itself;

(ii) the yielding by Iraq of possession to the Special Commission for destruction, removal or rendering harmless, taking into account the requirements of public safety, of all items specified under paragraph 8 (a) above including items at the additional locations designated by the Special Commission under paragraph 9 (b) (i) above and the destruction by Iraq, under the supervision of the Special Commission, of all its missile capabilities including launchers as specified under paragraph 8 (b) above:

(iii) the provision by the Special Commission of the assistance and cooperation to the Director-General of the International Atomic Energy Agency (IAEA) required in paragraphs 12 and 13 below;

10. *Decides* that Iraq shall unconditionally undertake not to use, develop, construct or acquire any of the items specified in paragraphs 8 and 9 above and requests the Secretary-General, in consultation with the Special Commission, to develop a plan for the future ongoing monitoring and verification of Iraq's compliance with this paragraph, to be submitted to the Council for approval within 120 days of the passage of this resolution;

11. *Invites* Iraq to reaffirm unconditionally its obligations under the Treaty on the Non-Proliferation of Nuclear Weapons, of 1 July 1968;

12. *Decides* that Iraq shall conditionally agree not to acquire or develop nuclear weapons or nuclear-weapons-usable material or any subsystems or components or any research, development, support or manufacturing facilities related to the above; to submit to the Secretary-General and the Director-General of the International Atomic Energy Agency (IAEA) within 15 days of the adoption of this resolution a declaration of the locations, amounts, and

types of all items specified above; to place all of its nuclear-weapons-usable materials under the exclusive control, for custody and removal, of the IAEA, with the assistance and cooperation of the Special Commission as provided for in the plan of the Secretary-General discussed in paragraph 9 (b) above; to accept, in accordance with the arrangements provided for in paragraph 13 below, urgent on-site inspection and the destruction, removal, or rendering harmless as appropriate of all items specified above; and to accept the plan discussed in paragraph 13 below for the future ongoing monitoring and verification of its compliance with these undertakings;

13. *Requests* the Director-General of the International Atomic Energy Agency (IAEA) through the Secretary-General, with the assistance and cooperation of the Special Commission as provided for in the plan of the Secretary-General in paragraph 9 (b) above, to carry out immediate on-site inspection of Iraq's nuclear capabilities based on Iraq's declarations and the designation of any additional locations by the Special Commission; to develop a plan for submission to the Security Council within 45 days calling for the destruction, removal, or rendering harmless as appropriate of all items listed in paragraph 12 above; to carry out the plan within 45 days following approval by the Security Council; and to develop a plan, taking into account the rights and obligations of Iraq under the Treaty on the Non-Proliferation of Nuclear Weapons, of 1 July 1968, for the future ongoing monitoring and verification of Iraq's compliance with paragraph 12 above, including an inventory of all nuclear material in Iraq subject to the Agency's verification and inspections to confirm that IAEA safeguards cover all relevant nuclear activities in Iraq, to be submitted to the Council for approval within 120 days of the passage of this resolution;

14. *Takes note* that the actions to be taken by Iraq in paragraphs 8, 9, 10, 11, 12, and 13 of this resolution represent steps towards the goal of establishing in the Middle East a zone free from weapons of mass destruction and all missiles for their delivery and the objective of a global ban on chemical weapons;

. . . . .

21. *Decides* that the Council shall review the provisions of paragraph 20 above every sixty days in light of the policies and practices of the Government in Iraq, including the implementation of all relevant resolutions of the Security Council, for the purpose of determining whether to reduce or lift the prohibitions referred to therein;

22. *Decides* that upon the approval by the Council of the programme called for in paragraph 19 above and upon Council agreement that Iraq has completed all actions contemplated in paragraphs 8, 9, 10, 11, 12, and 13 above, the prohibitions against the import of commodities and products originating in Iraq and the prohibitions against financial transactions related thereto contained in resolution 661 (1990) shall have no further force or effect;

23. *Decides* that, pending action by the Council under paragraph 22 above, the Committee established under resolution 661 (1990) shall be empowered to approve, when required to assure adequate financial resources on the part of Iraq to carry out the activities under paragraph 20 above, exceptions to the prohibition against the import of commodities and products originating in Iraq;

24. *Decides* that, in accordance with resolution 661 (1990) and subsequent related resolutions and until a further decision is taken by the Council, all States shall continue to prevent the sale or supply, or promotion or facilitation of such sale or supply, to Iraq by their nationals, or from their territories or using their flag vessels or aircraft, of:

a) arms and related *materiel* of all types, specifically including the sale or transfer through other means of all forms of conventional military equipment, including for paramilitary forces, and spare parts and components and their means of production, for such equipment;

b) items specified and defined in paragraph 8 and 12 above not otherwise covered above;

c) technology under licensing or other transfer arrangements used in the production, utilization or stockpiling of items specified in subparagraphs (a) and (b) above;

d) personnel or materials for training or technical support services relating to the design, development, manufacture, use, maintenance or support of items specified in subparagraphs (a) and (b) above;

25. *Calls upon* all States and international organizations to act strictly in accordance with paragraph 24 above, notwithstanding the existence of any contracts, agreements, licences, or any other arrangements;

26. *Requests* the Secretary-General, in consultation with appropriate Governments, to develop within 60 days, for approval of the Council, guide-

lines to facilitate full international implementation of paragraphs 24 and 25 above and paragraph 27 below, and to make them available to all States and to establish a procedure for updating these guidelines periodically;

27. *Calls upon* all States to maintain such national controls and procedures and to take such other actions consistent with the guidelines to be established by the Security Council under paragraph 26 above as may be necessary to ensure compliance with the terms of paragraph 24 above, and calls upon international organizations to take all appropriate steps to assist in ensuring such full compliance; [and]

28. *Agrees* to review its decisions in paragraphs 22, 23, 24, and 25 above, except for the items specified and defined in paragraphs 8 and 12 above, on a regular basis and in any case 120 days following passage of this resolution, taking into account Iraq's compliance with this resolution and general progress towards the control of armaments in the region.

[United Nations, Department of Public Information, *United Nations Security Council Resolutions Relating to the Situation Between Iraq and Kuwait,* DP/1104/Rev. 3—41183 (December 1991), pp. 20–25]

Controlling Arms Manufacture and Traffic

○

See also Controlling the Arms Trade Since 1945 *and* Regulating Arms Sales Through World War II. *Entries that are the subjects of essays in Volumes I and II are marked with asterisks.*

Early Examples of Controlling Weapons Manufacture and Trade

Controlling Israel's "Blacksmiths" (ca. 1100 B.C.)

The Israelites and the Philistines were frequent opponents, with the latter gaining a technological advantage in weapons by having utilized iron before the Israelites. After having defeated Israel in their initial conflicts, the Philistines apparently sought to maintain their technological superiority by denying the Israelites access to iron-edged weapons. This imposed disarmament centered on Philistine control of the blacksmiths' forges. The following excerpts are from two of several versions of the Old Testament's first book of Samuel.

At this time, there were no workers in metal left in the whole of Israel; the Philistines had taken good care that the Hebrews should not be able to make sword or spear. When a man would sharpen share or spade, axe, or hoe, in whatever part of the country he lived, he must go down into the Philistine lands to do it.

In times of battle Saul and his son Jonathan were the only men in the army that carried sword or lance.

[*R.A. Knox,* The Old Testament in English. *vol. 1 (New York: Sheed & Ward, 1947), p. 393, sec. 19, 20*]

19. Now there was no smith found throughout all the land of Israel: for the Philistines said, Lest the Hebrews make them swords or spears:

20. But all the Israelites went down to the Philistines, to sharpen every man his share, and his coulter, and his axe, and his mattock.

. . . . .

22. So it came to pass in the day of battle, that there was neither sword or spear found in the hand of any of the people that were with Saul and Jonathan:

[*Holy Bible,* I Samuel 13:19–22, King James Version]

Early Church prohibitions, royal proclamations, and early (as well as recent) commercial treaties have been concerned with restricting the movements of munitions and weapons. The obvious purpose was to prevent these supplies from reaching the hands of their enemies.

During the protracted crusades, and their frequent military operations, the Christian leaders often found their Saracen enemies equipped with arms obtained from Western merchants. Thus the Church introduced prohibitions that sought to restrain this trade.

Canon 24 from the Third Lateran Council, or Eleventh Ecumenical Council (1179)

Greed so filled their souls that although they were Christians they nevertheless provided to the Saracens arms, iron and wood for their ships, and helped them become superior in evil from the provision of arms and necessities to fight the Christians. And there were also those who through their greed served as sailors and helmsmen in the Saracen galleys and piratical ships. These we condemn to be cut off from the communion of the Church and subject to excommunication for their iniquity and condemned to the loss of their goods, to be confiscated by the Catholic princes and consuls of cities. If they are captured they are to be enslaved by their captors. We order that this solemn decree of excommunication be published through the churches of maritime cities. We also put under pain of excommunication those who attempt to either capture or steal the goods of Romans or other Christians who are navigating on business or any other cause, or who have suffered shipwreck. Those who, instead of offering help according to the rule of faith attempt through damnable greed to rob them of their goods, unless they return them, are also subject to excommunication.

Canon 71 [Excerpt] from the Fourth Lateran Council, or Twelfth Ecumenical Council (1215)

This decree of the Pope concerned a new crusade and was approved by the Council as its final document. The text of Canon 17 of the Council of Lyon, or Thirteenth Ecumenical Council (1245) is virtually the same.

We excommunicate and anathematize those false and impious Christians who against Christ himself and the Christian people, furnish arms, iron and wood for ships to the Saracens, those who sell them ships, and also those who serve in the piratical ships of the Saracens or give them aid and counsel in any of their enterprises. We also authorize confiscation of their goods and their enslavement by those who capture them. This decree is to be published on Sundays and feast days in all seaports, and the Church is not to be opened to these people unless all they have gained from their damned commerce, and the same amount from their own goods, they pay over in aid of the Holy Land, so that by a just judgement they will suffer punishment in the same manner as their crimes. If they cannot give satisfaction in this manner, they must be punished in some other fashion, which will serve as an example to others.

[Charles-Joseph Hefele, *Histoire des Conciles, tome V, deuxieme partie (Paris: Letouzey et Ané, editeurs, 1913): 1104–1105; 1394]

Confirmatio Tractatus Flandriae (1370)

From the literally hundreds of similiar articles that have appeared in commercial conventions and treaties, the following examples have been selected. The first selection is an excerpt from a treaty between Edward III and the Count of Flanders and the three towns of Ghent, Bruges, and Ypres. The bulk of it concerns regulations for licensing the trade from the Low Countries with other parties and restrictions on trading any goods that could aid enemies of England.

Edward, by the grace of God, King of France and England, and Lord of Ireland, salutes all those who will see or have this present letter. Know that we have well examined the treaty recently made between us and our council on the one side, and our dear and well-loved cousin, the Count of Flanders and the three good towns, Ghent, Bruges and Ypres on the other side, which contains the following items.

. . . .

Item: it is agreed that none of the subjects of the Count of Flanders will bring, or will have brought, by sea, any arms, artillery or supplies for the aid and comfort of the enemies of the King of England. Excepted from this are the arms, artillery and suppliers necessary for the guard and defence of their own bodies of the masters, merchants, sailors and shipboard servants on board the boats and vessels of the Count.

Further, if other arms are found, or any other things are done contrary to the above points, by any of the countries of Flanders or other subjects of the said Count, the punishment of their bodies and goods will fall in the jurisdiction of the Count of Flanders.

The forfeit of goods, merchandise, supplies, arms and artillery of enemies, or otherwise shipped to enemies, of which the Count of Flanders will have knowledge, will fall under the jurisdiction of the King of England. These furnishings will be delivered to a person deputized by the King with the power to receive them, and to maintain his right and profit therein.

. . . .

Signed, by the witness of our Grand Seal, at our Royal House in Clarendon, the fourth day of the month of August, the year of the Lord one thousand, three hundred and seventy, in the thirty-first year of our reign in France and the forty-fourth year of our reign in England.

[Thomas Rymer, *Foedera, Conventiones, Literae, et Cujuscunque Generis Acta Publica Inter Reges Angliae et Alios Quosvis Imperatores, Reges, Pontifices, Principles vel Communitates,* tomus VI (London: J. Tonson, 1727): 659–661]

Treaty between Great Britain and Spain (28 August 1814)

The British government was concerned about the arms and munitions that were being supplied by British merchants to the rebels in Spain's American colonies.

III. His Britannic Majesty being anxious that the troubles and disturbances which unfortunately prevail in the Dominions of His Catholic Majesty in America should entirely cease, and the Subjects of those Provinces should return to their obedience to their lawful Sovereign, engages to take the most effectual measures for preventing his Subjects from furnishing Arms, Ammunition, or any other warlike article to the revolted in America.

[Reprinted in Clive Parry, *Consolidated Treaty Series,* vol. 63 *(Dobbs Ferry, N.Y.: Oceana Publications, 1969)*]

Convention as to the Pacific Ocean and Northwest Coast of America (1824)

Concluded between Russia and the United States, this agreement was to regulate commerce and fishing, and the parties were to concur in a mutual limited occupation of the northwest coast.

Article V. All Spirituous liquors, fire-arms, other arms, powder, and munitions of war of every kind, are always excepted from this same commerce permitted [with the "natives of the country"]; and the two Powers engage, reciprocally, neither to sell, nor suffer them to be sold, to the natives by their respective citizens and subjects, nor by an person who may be under their authority. . . .
[W. M. Malloy, *Treaties, Conventions, International Acts, Protocols, and Agreements Between the United States of America and Other Powers, 1776–1937,* 4 vols. (Washington, D.C.: G.P.O., 1910–1938), vol. 2, p. 1513]

Convention of Amity and Commerce (1833)

The United States–Siamese Treaty opened Siam's ports to U.S. ships.

Article II
. . . . Nothing contained in this article shall be understood as granting permission to import and sell munitions of war to any person excepting to the King, who, if he does not require, will not be bound to purchase them; neither is permission granted to import opium, which is contraband. . . .
[Malloy, vol. 3, p. 1627]

Treaty of Amity and Commerce (1833)

The United States–Muscat (Zanzibar) treaty opened trade with this Indian Ocean sultanate.

Article II
. . . . It is understood and agreed, however, that the articles of muskets, powder, and ball can only be sold to the Government in the island of Zanzibar; but, in all the other ports of the Sultan, the said munitions of war may be freely sold, without any restrictions whatever, to the highest bidder.
[Malloy, vol. 1, pp. 1228–1229]

Agreements, Conventions, and Treaties, 1919–1950

Restraining Sale of Armaments in China (1919)

Agreement by Which the Governments of Great Britain, Spain, Portugal, the United States, Russia, Brazil, France and Japan Restrain Trade in Arms and Munitions of War with China

[The Dean of the Diplomatic Corps at Peking to the Wei Chino Pu.]

May 5, 1919

SIR:

The Diplomatic Body in considering the present state of disunion between North and South in China have been impressed by the fact that the continued possibility of importing military arms and ammunition into the country from abroad could not but exercise a disturbing influence, and as the friendly Powers here represented are firmly determined to discountenance any condition or action which might favour the reversion to hostilities, I am desired by my Colleagues to make the following communication to the Chinese Government.

The Governments of Great Britain, Spain, Portugal, the United States, Russia, Brazil, France and Japan have agreed effectively to restrain their subjects and citizens from exporting to or importing into China, arms and munitions of war and material destined exclusively for their manufacture until the establishment of a government whose authority is recognized throughout the whole country and also to prohibit during the above period the delivery of arms and munitions for which contracts have already been made but not executed.

The Representatives of the Netherlands, Denmark, Belgium and Italy are also in full accord with the above policy but await the instructions of their respective Governments before announcing the adhesion of the latter.

The Foreign Representatives desire to express the earnest hope that the Chinese Government in keeping with this policy will on their part agree to suspend the issue of permits to import military arms, ammunition and munitions of war and will direct the Customs that the introduction of such articles is absolutely prohibited.

I avail etc.

(Signed)   J. N. JORDAN

[Malloy, vol. 3, p. 3821]

Convention for the Control of the Trade in Arms and Ammunition (10 September 1919)

This convention was signed at Saint-Germain-en-Laye and Paris on 10 September 1919.

The United States of America, Belgium, Bolivia, the British Empire, China, Cuba, Ecuador, France, Greece, Guatemala, Haiti, the Hedjaz, Italy, Japan, Nicaragua, Panama, Peru, Poland, Portugal, Roumania, the Serb-Croat-Slovene State, Siam and Czecho-Slovakia;

Whereas the long war now ended, in which most nations have successively become involved, has led to the accumulation in various parts of the world of considerable quantities of arms and munitions of war, the dispersal of which would constitute a danger to peace and public order;

Whereas in certain parts of the world it is necessary to exercise special supervision over the trade in, and the possession of, arms and ammunition;

Whereas the existing treaties and conventions, and particularly the Brussels Act of July 2, 1890, regulating the traffic in arms and ammunition in certain regions, no longer meet present conditions, which require more elaborate provisions applicable to a wider area in Africa and the establishment of a corresponding regime in certain territories in Asia;

Whereas a special supervision of the maritime zone adjacent to certain countries is necessary to ensure the efficacy of the measures adopted by the various Governments both as regards the importation of arms and ammunition into those countries and the export of such arms and ammunition from their own territory;

And with the reservation that, after a period of seven years, the present Convention shall be subject to revision in the light of the experience gained, if the Council of the League of Nations, acting if need be by a majority, so recommends;

Have appointed as their Plenipotentiaries: (here follow names)

Who, having communicated their full powers found in good and due form, have agreed as follows:

Chapter I. Export of Arms and Ammunition

Article 1. The High Contracting Parties undertake to prohibit the export of the following arms of war: artillery of all kinds, apparatus for the discharge of all kinds of projectiles explosive or gas-diffusing, flame-throwers, bombs, grenades, machine-guns and rifled small-bore breech-loading weapons of all kinds, as well as the exportation of the ammunition for use with such arms. The prohibition of exportation shall apply to all such arms and ammunition, whether complete or in parts.

Nevertheless, notwithstanding this prohibition, the High Contracting Parties reserve the right to grant, in respect of arms whose use is not prohibited by International Law, export licences to meet the requirements of their Governments or those of the Government of any of the High Contracting Parties, but for no other purpose.

In the case of firearms and ammunition adapted both to warlike and also to other purposes, the High Contracting Parties reserve to themselves the right to determine from the size, destination, and other circumstances of each shipment for what uses it is intended and to decide in each case whether the provisions of this Article are applicable to it.

Article 2. The High Contracting Parties undertake to prohibit the export of firearms and ammunition, whether complete or in parts, other than arms and munitions of war, to the areas and zone specified in Article 6.

Nevertheless, notwithstanding this prohibition, the High Contracting Parties reserve the right to grant export licences on the understanding that such licences shall be issued only by their own authorities. Such authorities must satisfy themselves in advance that the arms or ammunition for which an export licence is requested are not intended for export to any destination, or for disposal in any way, contrary to the provisions of this Convention.

Article 3. Shipments to be effected under contracts entered into before the coming into force of the present Convention shall be governed by its provisions.

Article 4. The High Contracting Parties undertake to grant no export licences to any country which refuses to accept the tutelage under which it has been placed, or which, after having been placed under the tutelage of any Power, may endeavour to obtain from any other Power any of the arms and ammunition specified in Articles 1 and 2.

Article 5. A Central International Office, placed under the control of the League of Nations, shall be established for the purpose of collecting and preserving documents of all kinds exchanged by the High Contracting Parties with regard to the trade in, and distribution of, the arms and ammunition specified in the present Convention.

Each of the High Contracting Parties shall publish an annual report showing the export licences which it may have granted, together with the quantities and destination of the arms and ammunition to which the export licences referred. A copy of this report shall be sent to the Central International Office and to the Secretary-General of the League of Nations.

Further, the High Contracting Parties agree to send to the Central International Office and to the

Secretary-General of the League of Nations full statistical information as to the quantities and destination of all arms and ammunition exported without licence.

Chapter II. Import of Arms and Ammunitions, Prohibited Areas and Zone of Maritime Supervision

Article 6. The High Contracting Parties undertake, each as far as the territory under its jurisdiction is concerned, to prohibit the importation of the arms and ammunition specified in Articles 1 and 2 into the following territorial areas, and also to prevent their importation and transportation in the maritime zone defined below:

1. The whole of the Continent of Africa with the exception of Algeria, Libya and the Union of South Africa.

Within this area are included all islands situated within a hundred nautical miles of the coast, together with Prince's Island, St. Thomas Island and the Islands of Annobon and Socotra.

2. Transcaucasia, Persia, Gwadar, the Arabian Peninsula and such continental parts of Asia as were included in the Turkish Empire on August 4, 1914.

3. A maritime zone, including the Red Sea, the Gulf of Aden, the Persian Gulf and the Sea of Oman, and bounded by a line drawn from Cape Guardafui, following the latitude of that cape to its intersection with the longitude 57° east of Greenwich, and proceeding thence direct to the eastern frontier of Persia in the Gulf of Oman.

Special licences for the import of arms or ammunition into the areas defined above may be issued. In the African area they shall be subject to the regulations specified in Articles 7 and 8 or to any local regulations of a stricter nature which may be in force. In the other areas specified in the present Article, these licences shall be subject to similar regulations put into effect by the Governments exercising authority there.

Chapter III. Supervision on Land

Article 7. Arms and ammunition imported under special licence into the prohibited areas shall be admitted only at ports designated for this purpose by the Authorities of the State, Colony, Protectorate or territory under mandate concerned.

Such arms and ammunition must be deposited by the importer at his own risk and expense in a public warehouse under the exclusive custody and permanent control of the Authority and of its agents, of whom one at least must be a civil official or a military officer. No arms or ammunition shall be deposited or withdrawn without the previous authorisation of the administration of the State, Colony, Protectorate or territory under mandate, unless the arms and ammunition to be deposited or withdrawn are intended for the forces of the Government or the defence of the national territory.

The withdrawal of arms or ammunition deposited in these warehouses shall be authorised only in the following cases:

1. For despatch to places designated by the Government where the inhabitants are allowed to possess arms, under the control and responsibility of the local Authorities, for the purpose of defence against robbers or rebels.

2. For despatch to places designated by the Government as warehouses and placed under the supervision and responsibility of the local Authorities.

3. For individuals who can show that they require them for their legitimate personal use.

Article 8. In the prohibited areas specified in Article 6, trade in arms and ammunition shall be placed under the control of officials of the Government and shall be subject to the following regulations:

1. No person may keep a warehouse for arms or ammunition without a licence.

2. Any person licenced to keep a warehouse for arms or ammunition must reserve for that special purpose enclosed premises having only one entry, provided with two locks, one of which can be opened only by the officers of the Government.

The person in charge of a warehouse shall be responsible for all arms or ammunition deposited therein and must account for them on demand. For this purpose all deposits or withdrawals shall be entered in a special register, numbered and initialed. Each entry shall be supported by references to the official documents authorising such deposits or withdrawals.

3. No transport of arms or ammunition shall take place without a special licence.

4. No withdrawal from a private warehouse shall take place except under licence issued by the local Authority on an application stating the purpose for which the arms or ammunition are required, and supported by a licence to carry arms or by a special permit for the purchase of ammunition. Every arm shall be registered and stamped; the Authority in

charge of the control shall enter on the licence to carry arms the mark stamped on the weapon.

5. No one shall without authority transfer to another person either by gift or for any consideration any weapon or ammunition which he is licenced to possess.

Article 9. In the prohibited areas and zone specified in Article 6 the manufacture and assembling of arms, or ammunition shall be prohibited, except at arsenals established by the local Government or, in the case of countries placed under tutelage, at arsenals established by the local Government, under the control of the mandatory Power, for the defence of its territory or for the maintenance of public order.

No arms shall be repaired except at arsenals or establishments licenced by the local Government for this purpose. No such licence shall be granted without guarantees for the observance of the rules of the present Convention.

Article 10. Within the prohibited areas specified in Article 6, a State which is compelled to utilize the territory of a contiguous State for the importation of arms or ammunition, whether complete or in parts, or of material or of articles intended for armament, shall be authorised on request to have them transported across the territory of such State.

It shall, however, when making any such request, furnish guarantees that the said articles are required for the needs of its own Government, and will at no time be sold, transferred or delivered for private use nor used in any way contrary to the interests of the High Contracting Parties.

Any violation of these conditions shall be formally established in the following manner:

(a) If the importing State is a sovereign independent Power, the proof of the violation shall be advanced by one or more of the Representatives accredited to it of contiguous States among the High Contracting Parties. After the Representatives of the other contiguous States have, if necessary, been informed, a joint enquiry into the facts by all these Representatives will be opened, and if need be, the importing State will be called upon to furnish explanations. If the gravity of the case should so require, and if the explanations of the importing State are considered unsatisfactory, the Representatives will jointly notify the importing State that all transit licences in its favor are suspended and that all future requests will be refused until it shall have furnished new and satisfactory guarantees.

The forms and conditions of the guarantees provided by the present Article shall be agreed upon previously by the Representatives of the contiguous States among the High Contracting Parties. These Representatives shall communicate to each other, as and when issued, the transit licences granted by the competent authorities.

(b) If the importing State has been placed under the mandatory system established by the League of Nations, the proof of the violation shall be furnished by one of the High Contracting Parties or on its own initiative by the Mandatory Power. The latter shall then notify or demand, as the case may be, the suspension and future refusal of all transit licences.

In cases where a violation has been duly proved, no further transit licence shall be granted to the offending State without the previous consent of the Council of the League of Nations.

If any proceedings on the part of the importing State or its disturbed condition should threaten the public order of one of the contiguous States signatories of the present Convention, the importation in transit of arms, ammunition, material and articles intended for armament shall be refused to the importing State by all the contiguous States until order has been restored.

Chapter IV. Maritime Supervision

Article 11. Subject to any contrary provisions in existing special agreements, or in future agreements, provided that in all cases such agreements comply with the provisions of the present Convention, the sovereign State or Mandatory Power shall carry out all supervision and police measures within territorial waters in the prohibited areas and zone specified in Article 6.

Article 12. Within the prohibited areas and maritime zone specified in Article 6, no native vessel of less than 500 tons burden shall be allowed to ship, discharge, or tranship arms or ammunition.

For this purpose, a vessel shall be considered as a native vessel if she is either owned by a native, or fitted out or commanded by a native, or if more than half of the crew are natives of the countries bordering on the Indian Ocean, the Red Sea, the Persian Gulf, or the Gulf of Oman.

This provision does not apply to lighters or barges, nor to vessels which, without going more than five miles from the shore, are engaged exclusively in the coasting trade between different ports of the same State, Colony, Protectorate or territory under mandate, where warehouses are situated.

No cargoes of arms or ammunition shall be shipped on the vessels specified in the preceding paragraph without a special licence from the territorial authority, and all arms or ammunition so shipped shall be subject to the provisions of the present Convention.

This licence shall contain all details necessary to establish the nature and quantity of the items of the shipment, the vessel on which the shipment is to be loaded, the name of the ultimate consignee, and the ports of loading and discharge. It shall also be specified thereon that the licence has been issued in conformity with the regulations of the present Convention.

The above regulations do not apply:

1. To arms or ammunition conveyed on behalf of the Government, provided that they are accompanied by a duly qualified official.

2. To arms or ammunition in the possession of persons provided with a licence to carry arms, provided such arms are for the personal use of the bearer and are accurately described on his licence.

Article 13. To prevent all illicit conveyancy of arms or ammunition within the zone of maritime supervision specified in Article 6 (3), native vessels of less than 500 tons burden not exclusively engaged in the coasting trade between different ports of the same State, Colony, Protectorate or territory under mandate, not going more than five miles from the shore, and proceeding to or from any point within the said zone, must carry a manifest of their cargo or similar document specifying the quantities and nature of the goods on board, their origin and destination. This document shall remain covered by the secrecy to which it is entitled by the law of the State to which the vessel belongs, and must not be examined during the proceedings for the verification of the flag unless the interested party consents thereto.

The provisions as to the above-mentioned documents shall not apply to vessels only partially decked, having a maximum crew of ten men, and exclusively employed in fishing within territorial waters.

Article 14. Authority to fly the flag of one of the High Contracting Parties within the zone of maritime supervision specified in Article 6 (3) shall be granted only to such native vessels as satisfy all the three following conditions:

1. The owners must be nationals of the Power whose flag they claim to fly.

2. They must furnish proof that they possess real estate in the district of the authority to which their application is addressed, or must supply a solvent security as a guarantee for any fines to which they may become liable.

3. Such owners, as well as the captain of the vessels, must furnish proof that they enjoy a good reputation, and especially that they have never been convicted of illicit conveyance of the articles referred to in the present Convention.

The authorisation must be renewed every year. It shall contain the indications necessary to identify the vessel, the name, tonnage, type of rigging, principal dimensions, registered number, and signal letters. It shall bear the date on which it was granted and the status of the official who granted it.

The name of the native vessel and the amount of her tonnage shall be incised and painted in Latin characters on the stern, and the initial letters of the name of the port of registry, as well as the registration number in the series of the numbers of that port, shall be painted in black on the sails.

Article 15. Native vessels to which, under the provisions of the last paragraph of Article 13, the regulations relating to the manifest of the cargo are not applicable, shall receive from the territorial or consular authorities, as the case may be, a special licence, renewable annually and revocable under the conditions provided for in Article 19.

This special licence shall show the name of the vessel, her description, nationality, port of registry, name of captain, name of owner and the waters in which she is allowed to sail.

Article 16. The High Contracting Parties agree to apply the following rules in the maritime zone specified in Article 6 (3):

1. When a warship belonging to one of the High Contracting Parties encounters outside territorial waters a native vessel of less than 500 tons burden flying the flag of one of the High Contracting Parties, and the commander of the warship has a good reason to believe that the native vessel is flying this flag without being entitled to do so, for the purpose of the illicit conveyance of arms or ammunition, he may proceed to verify the nationality of the vessel by examining the document authorising the flying of the flag, but no other papers.

2. With this object, a boat commanded by a commissioned officer in uniform may be sent to visit

the suspected vessel after she has been hailed to give notice of such intention. The officer sent on board the vessel shall act with all possible consideration and moderation; before leaving the vessel the officer shall draw up a *procès-verbal* in the form and language in use in his own country. This *procès-verbal* shall state the facts of the case and shall be dated and signed by the officer.

Should there be on board the warship no commissioned officer other than the commanding officer, the above-prescribed operations may be carried out by the warrant, petty, or non-commissioned officer highest in rank.

The captain or master of the vessel visited, as well as the witnesses, shall be invited to sign the *procès-verbal,* and shall have the right to add to it any explanation which they may consider expedient.

3. If the authorisation to fly the flag cannot be produced, or if this document is not in proper order, the vessel shall be conducted to the nearest port in the zone where there is a competent authority of the Power whose flag has been flown and shall be handed over to such authority.

Should the nearest competent authority representing the Power whose flag the vessel has flown be at some port at such a distance from the point of arrest that the warship would have to leave her station or patrol to escort the captured vessel to that port, the foregoing regulation need not be carried out. In such a case, the vessel may be taken to the nearest port where there is a competent authority of one of the High Contracting Parties of nationality other than that of the warship, and steps shall at once be taken to notify the capture to the competent authority representing the Power concerned.

No proceedings shall be taken against the vessel or her crew until the arrival of the representative of the Power whose flag the vessel was flying or without instructions from him.

4. The procedure laid down in paragraph 3 may be followed if, after the verification of the flag and in spite of the production of the manifest, the commander of the warship continues to suspect the native vessel of engaging in the illicit conveyance of arms or ammunition.

The High Contracting Parties concerned shall appoint in the zone territorial or consular authorities or special representatives competent to act in the foregoing cases, and shall notify their appointment to the Central Office and to the other Contracting Parties.

The suspected vessel may also be handed over to a warship of the nation whose flag she has flown, if the latter consents to take charge of her.

Article 17. The High Contracting Parties agree to communicate to the Central Office specimen forms of the documents mentioned in Articles 12, 13, 14 and 15, as well as a detailed list of the licences granted in accordance with the provisions of this Chapter whenever such licences are granted.

Article 18. The authority before whom the suspected vessel has been brought shall institute a full enquiry in accordance with the laws and rules of his country in the presence of an officer of the capturing warship.

If it is proved at this enquiry that the flag has been illegally flown, the detained vessel shall remain at the disposal of the captor, and those responsible shall be brought before the courts of his country.

If it should be established that the use of the flag by the detained vessel was correct, but that the vessel was engaged in the illicit conveyance of arms or ammunition, those responsible shall be brought before the courts of the State under whose flag the vessel sailed. The vessel herself and her cargo shall remain in charge of the authority directing the enquiry.

Article 19. Any illicit conveyance or attempted conveyance legally established against the captain or owner of a vessel authorised to fly the flag of one of the Signatory Powers or holding the licence provided for in Article 15 shall entail the immediate withdrawal of the said authorisation or licence.

The High Contracting Parties will take the necessary measures to ensure that their territorial authorities or their consuls shall send to the Central Office certified copies of all authorisations to fly their flag, as soon as such authorisations shall have been granted as well as notice of withdrawal of any such authorisation. They also undertake to communicate to the said Office copies of the licences provided for under Article 15.

Article 20. The commanding officer of a warship who may have detained a vessel flying a foreign flag shall in all cases make a report thereon to his Government, stating the grounds on which he acted.

An extract from this report, together with a copy of the *procès-verbal* drawn up by the officer, warrant officer, petty or non-commissioned officer sent on board the vessel detained shall be sent as soon as possible to the Central Office and at the same time to the Government whose flag the detained vessel was flying.

Article 21. If the authority entrusted with the enquiry decides that the detention and diversion of the vessel or the measures imposed upon her were irregular, he shall fix the amount of the compensation due. If the capturing officer, or the authorities to whom he is subject, do not accept the decision or contest the amount of the compensation awarded, the dispute shall be submitted to a court of arbitration consisting of one arbitrator appointed by the Government whose flag the vessel was flying, one appointed by the Government of the capturing officer, and an umpire chosen by the two arbitrators thus appointed. The two arbitrators shall be chosen, as far as possible, from among the diplomatic, consular or judicial officers of the High Contracting Parties. These appointments must be made with the least possible delay, and natives in the pay of the High Contracting Parties shall in no case be appointed. Any compensation awarded shall be paid to the person concerned within six months at most from the date of the award.

The decision shall be communicated to the Central Office and to the Secretary-General of the League of Nations.

Chapter V. General Provisions

Article 22. The High Contracting Parties who exercise authority over territories within the prohibited areas and zone specified in Article 6 agree to take, so far as each may be concerned, the measures required for the enforcement of the present Convention, and in particular for the prosecution and repression of offences against the provisions contained therein.

They shall communicate these measures to the Central Office and to the Secretary-General of the League of Nations, and shall inform them of the competent authorities referred to in the preceding Articles.

Article 23. The High Contracting Parties will use their best endeavours to secure the accession to the present Convention of the other States Members of the League of Nations.

This accession shall be notified through the diplomatic channel to the Government of the French Republic, and by it to all the signatory or adhering States. The accession will come into force from the date of such notification to the French Government.

Article 24. The High Contracting Parties agree that if any dispute whatever should arise between them relating to the application of the present Convention which cannot be settled by negotiation, this dispute shall be submitted to an arbitral tribunal in conformity with the provisions of the Covenant of the League of Nations.

Article 25. All the provisions of former general international Conventions, relating to the matters dealt with in the present Convention, shall be considered as abrogated in so far as they are binding between the Powers which are Parties to the present Convention.

[Article 26 deals with ratification and similar matters.]

[*International Conciliation: Documents for the Year, 1929* (Carnegie Endowment for International Peace, 1929), pp. 300–310]

Convention for the Supervision of the International Trade in Arms and Ammunition and in Implements of War (17 June 1925)

This Convention was not ratified and did not come into force.

Whereas the international trade in arms and ammunition and in implements of war should be subjected to a general and effective system of supervision and publicity;

Whereas such a system is not provided by existing Treaties and Conventions;

Whereas in relation to certain areas of the world a special supervision of this trade is necessary in order to render more effective the measures adopted by the various Governments as regards both the import of such arms and ammunition and implements of war into these areas and their export therefrom; and

Whereas the export or import of arms, ammunition or implements, the use of which in war is prohibited by International Law, must not be permitted for such purpose;

Have decided to conclude a Convention and have accordingly appointed as their Plenipotentiaries:

Who, having communicated their full powers, found in good and due form, HAVE AGREED AS FOLLOWS:

CHAPTER I. CATEGORIES

Article 1. For the purposes of the present Convention, five Categories of arms, ammunition and implements are established:

Category I. *Arms, Ammunition and Implements of War Exclusively Designed and Intended for Land, Sea or Aerial Warfare*

A. Arms, ammunition and implements exclusively designed and intended for land, sea or aerial warfare, which are or shall be comprised in the armaments of the armed forces of any State, or which, if they have been but are no longer comprised in such armament, are capable of military to the exclusion of any other use, except such arms, ammunition and implements which, though included in the above definition, are covered by other Categories.

Such arms, ammunition and implements are comprised in the following twelve headings:

1. Rifles, muskets, carbines.

2. (a) Machine-guns, automatic rifles and machine-pistols of all calibres;

(b) Mountings for machine-guns;

(c) Interrupter gears.

3. Projectiles and ammunition for the arms enumerated in Nos. 1 and 2 above.

4. Gun-sighting apparatus including aerial gun-sights and bombsights, and fire-control apparatus.

5. (a) Cannon, long or short, and howitzers, of a calibre less than 5.9 inches (15 cm.);

(b) Cannon, long or short, and howitzers, of a calibre of 5.9 inches (15 cm.) or above;

(c) Mortars of all kinds;

(d) Gun carriages, mountings, recuperators, accessories for mountings.

6. Projectiles and ammunition for the arms enumerated in No. 5 above.

7. Apparatus for the discharge of bombs, torpedoes, depth charges and other kinds of projectiles.

8. (a) Grenades;

(b) Bombs;

(c) Land mines, submarine mines, fixed or floating, depth charges;

(d) Torpedoes.

9. Appliances for use with the above arms and apparatus.

10. Bayonets.

11. Tanks and armoured cars.

12. Arms and ammunition not specified in the above enumeration.

B. Component parts, completely finished, of the articles covered by A above, if capable of being utilised only in the assembly or repair of the said articles, or as spare parts.

Category II. *Arms and Ammunition Capable of Use Both for Military and Other Purposes*

A. 1. Pistols and revolvers, automatic or self-loading, and developments of the same, designed for single-handed use or fired from the shoulder, of a calibre greater than 6.5 mm. and length of barrel greater than 10 cm.

2. Fire-arms designed, intended or adapted for non-military purposes, such as sport or personal defence, that will fire cartridges that can be fired from fire-arms in Category I; other rifled fire-arms firing from the shoulder, of a calibre of 6 mm. or above, not included in Category I, with the exception of rifled fire-arms with a "break-down" action.

3. Ammunition for the arms enumerated in the above two headings, with the exception of ammunition covered by Category I.

4. Swords and lances.

B. Component parts, completely finished, of the articles covered by A above, if capable of being utilised only in the assembly or repair of the said articles, or as spare parts.

Category III. *Vessels of War and Their Armament*

1. Vessels of war of all kinds.

2. Arms, ammunition and implements of war mounted on board vessels of war and forming part of their normal armament.

Category IV

1. Aircraft, assembled or dismantled.
2. Aircraft engines.

Category V

1. Gunpowder and explosives, except common black gunpowder.
2. Arms and ammunition other than those covered by Categories I and II, such as pistols and revolvers of all models, rifled weapons with a "break-down" action, other rifled fire-arms of a calibre of less than 6 mm. designed for firing from the shoulder, smooth-bore shot-guns, guns with more than one barrel of which at least one barrel is smooth-bore, fire-arms firing rimfire ammunition, muzzle-loading fire-arms.

CHAPTER II. SUPERVISION AND PUBLICITY

Article 2. The High Contracting Parties undertake not to export or permit the export of articles covered by Category I, except in accordance with the following conditions:

1. The export shall be for a direct supply to the Government of the importing State, or with the consent of such Government, to a public authority subordinate to it;
2. An order in writing, which shall be signed or endorsed by a representative of the importing Government duly authorised so to act, shall have been presented to the competent authorities of the exporting country. This order shall state that the articles to be exported are required for delivery to the importing Government or public authority as provided in paragraph I.

Article 3. Nevertheless, export for supply to private persons may be permitted in the following cases:

1. Articles covered by Category I exported direct to a manufacturer of war material for use by him for the requirements of his industry, provided their import has been duly authorised by the Government of the importing country.
2. Rifles, muskets and carbines and their ammunition exported for supply to rifle associations formed for the encouragement of individual sport and duly authorised by their own Government to use them, the import of which is not contrary to any other provisions of the present Convention. Such arms and ammunition shall be sent direct to the Government of the importing country for transmission by such Government to the associations for which they are supplied.

3. Samples of articles covered by Category I exported for demonstration purposes direct to a trade representative of the exporting manufacturer, such representative being duly authorised by the Government of the importing country to receive them.

In the above-mentioned cases, an order in writing, endorsed by the Government of the importing country or by its representative duly authorised so to act, must have been presented to the authorities of the exporting country. It shall contain all the information necessary to show that the order is properly made under this Article.

Article 4. Permission to export under Articles 2 and 3 shall be signified by a licence. An export declaration, if filed with and approved by the competent authorities of the exporting country, may take the place of a licence.

Such licence or declaration must contain:

(a) A description sufficient for the identification of the articles to which it relates, and giving their designation according to the headings in Category I, and their number or weight;

(b) The name and address of the exporter;

(c) The name and address of the importing consignee;

(d) The name of the Government which has authorised the import.

Each separate consignment which crosses the frontier of the exporting country, whether by land, water or air, shall be accompanied by a document containing the particulars indicated above. This document may be either the licence or export declaration or a certified copy thereof or a certificate issued by the customs authorities of the exporting country stating that the consignment is exported under licence or export declaration in accordance with the provisions of the present Convention.

Article 5. The articles covered by Category II shall only be exported under cover of an export document, which may be either a licence issued by the competent authorities of the exporting country or an export declaration endorsed by or filed with them. If the legislation of the importing country requires the endorsement of a duly authorised representative of its Government, and if this fact has been notified by the said Government to the Government of the exporting country, then such an endorsement must have been obtained and submitted to the competent authorities of the exporting country before the export may take place.

Neither the licence nor the export declaration shall entail any responsibility upon the Government of the exporting country as to the destination or ultimate use of any consignment.

Nevertheless, if the High Contracting Parties consider, on account of the size, destination or other circumstances of a consignment, that the arms and ammunition consigned are intended for war purposes, they undertake to apply to such consignment the provisions of Articles 2, 3 and 4.

Article 6. As a preliminary to a general system of publicity for armaments irrespective of their origin, the High Contracting Parties undertake to publish within two months of the close of each quarter, a statistical return of their foreign trade during this quarter in the articles covered by Categories I and II. This return shall be drawn up in accordance with the specimen forms contained in Annex I to the present Convention and shall show under each heading appearing in Categories I and II in Article 1 the value and the weight or number of the articles exported or imported under a licence or export declaration, allocated according to country of origin or destination.

In all cases where the consignment comes from, or is sent to, a territory possessing an autonomous Customs system, such territory shall be shown as the country of origin or destination.

The High Contracting Parties further undertake, so far as each may be concerned, to publish within the same time-limits a return containing the same information in respect of the consignments of articles covered by Categories I and II to other territories placed under their sovereignty, jurisdiction, protection or tutelage, or under the same sovereignty, jurisdiction, protection or tutelage.

The first statistical return to be published by each of the High Contracting Parties shall be for the quarter beginning on the first day of January, April, July or October, subsequent to the date on which the present Convention comes into force with regard to the High Contracting Party concerned.

The High Contracting Parties undertake to publish as an annex to the above-mentioned return the text of the provisions of all statutes, orders or regulations in force within their territory dealing with the export and import of articles covered by Article 1, and to include therein all provisions enacted for the purpose of carrying out the present Convention. Amendments and additions to these provisions shall be likewise published in annexes to subsequent quarterly returns.

Article 7. The High Contracting Parties, in all cases covered by Category III, undertake to publish within two months of the close of each quarter a return for that quarter, giving the information detailed below for each vessel of war constructed, in course of construction or to be constructed within their territorial jurisdiction on behalf of the Government of another state:

(a) The date of the signing of the contract for the construction of the vessel, the name of the Government for which the vessel is ordered, together with the following data:

Standard displacement in tons and metric tons;

The principal dimensions, namely: length at water-line, extreme beam at or below water-line, mean draft at standard displacement;

(b) The date of laying the keel, the name of the Government for which the vessel is being constructed, together with the following data:

Standard displacement in tons and metric tons;

The principal dimensions, namely: length at water-line, extreme beam at or below water-line, mean draft at standard displacement;

(c) The date of delivery, the name of the Government to which the vessel is delivered together with the following data with respect to the vessel at that date:

Standard displacement in tons and metric tons;

The principal dimensions, namely: length at water-line, extreme beam at or below water-line, mean draft at standard displacement;

As well as the following information regarding the armament installed on board the vessel at the date of delivery and forming part of the vessel's normal armament:

Number and calibre of guns;

Number and calibre of torpedo-tubes;

Number of bomb-throwers;

Number of machine-guns.

The above information concerning the armament of the vessel shall be furnished by means of a statement signed by the shipbuilder and countersigned by the commanding officer or such other representative fully authorised for the purpose by the Government of the State to whom the vessel is delivered. Such statement shall be transmitted to the competent authority of the Government of the constructing country.

Whenever a vessel of war belonging to one of the High Contracting Parties is transferred, whether by gift, sale or other mode of transfer, to the Government of another State, the transferor undertakes to publish within two months of the close of the quarter within which the transfer is effected the following information:

The date of transfer, the name of the Government to whom the vessel has been transferred and the data and information referred to in paragraph (c) above.

By the standard displacement in the present Article is to be understood the displacement of the vessel complete, fully manned, engined and equipped ready for sea, including all armament and ammunition, equipment, outfit, provisions and fresh water for crew, miscellaneous stores and implements of every description that are intended to be carried in war, but without fuel or reserve feedwater on board.

Article 8. Without prejudice to the provisions of Article 7, if the transport of any vessel of war is carried out otherwise than by such vessel's own motive power or towage, the vessel, whether assembled or in component parts, and the armament thereof will become subject also to the provisions of this Convention as if they were included in Category I.

Article 9. The High Contracting Parties undertake to publish, within six months of the close of each quarter, a return for that quarter of the export of aircraft and aircraft engines, giving quantities exported and the allocation according to country of destination.

Article 10. Subject to the provisions of Chapter III, the articles covered by Categories IV and V may be exported without formalities or restrictions.

Article 11. The High Contracting Parties undertake not to apply a more favourable regime to imports of articles referred to in Article 1 coming from territories of non-contracting States, than that which they will apply to such imports coming from territories of contracting States, and to subject these imports, of whatever origin, to the same conditions of authorisation and, so far as possible, of publicity.

CHAPTER III. SPECIAL ZONES

Article 12. The High Contracting Parties agree that the provisions of this Chapter apply to the territorial and maritime zones hereinafter defined and referred to in the present Convention as the "special zones."

1. *Land zone*

(a) The whole of the continent of Africa, with the exception of Egypt, Lybia, Tunisia, Algeria, the Spanish possessions in North Africa, Abyssinia, and of the Union of South Africa together with the territory under its mandate, and of Southern Rhodesia.

This zone also includes the adjacent islands which are situated within 100 marine miles from the coast thereof and also Prince's Island (Principe) in the Bight of Biafra, St. Thomas (São Thomé), Annobon and Socotra, but does not include the Spanish islands situated to the north of the parallel of 26° North latitude.

(b) The Arabian peninsula, Gwadar, Syria and Lebanon, Palestine and Transjordan, and Iraq.

2. *Maritime zone.* A maritime zone, which includes the Red Sea, the Gulf of Aden, the Persian Gulf and the Gulf of Oman and is bounded by a line drawn from and following the latitude of Cape Guardafui to the point of intersection with longitude 57° East of Greenwich and proceeding thence direct to the point at which the eastern frontier of Gwadar meets the sea.

Article 13. The High Contracting Parties undertake not to export or to permit articles covered by Categories I, II, IV and V to be exported to places within the special zones, unless a licence has been issued in conformity with the conditions defined in Article 14.

An export declaration, if filed with and approved by the competent authorities of the exporting country, may take the place of a licence.

The High Contracting Parties also undertake, each in respect of any territory under its sovereignty, jurisdiction, protection or tutelage situated within the special zones, not to permit articles covered by the Categories above mentioned to be imported into such territory unless their import has been authorised by the authorities of the territory concerned. Such articles shall only be admitted into territory within the special zones at such ports or other places as the authorities of the State, colony, protectorate or mandated territory concerned shall designate for this purpose.

Article 14. The High Contracting Parties undertake not to issue the export licences nor to approve the export declarations required under Article 13 unless they are satisfied that the conditions stated in paragraph (a) or (b) hereof are fulfilled also, as regards articles covered by Categories I and II, the conditions laid down in Articles 2, 3, 4 and 5.

(a) That, if an export is being made to territory under the sovereignty, jurisdiction, protection or tutelage of a High Contracting Party, articles covered by Categories I, II and IV to which the licence or export declaration applies are required for lawful purposes and that the authorities of the territory to which they are consigned are willing to admit them; and that, in the case of articles covered by Category V, a copy of the licence or export declaration has been sent to the authorities aforesaid before the export takes place.

(b) That, if an export is being made to territory which is not under the sovereignty, jurisdiction, protection or tutelage of a High Contracting Party, articles covered by Categories I, II, IV and V are required for lawful purposes.

Article 15. The High Contracting Parties undertake to publish, in addition to the returns provided for in Article 6 and Article 9 in respect of articles covered by Categories I, II and IV, a return of articles covered by Category V exported to territory situated within the special zones. This return shall be published within the same time-limits and at the same intervals as those provided in the first paragraph of Article 6, and shall contain, as far as possible, the same particulars.

Article 16. The trade in articles covered by Categories I, II, IV and V within the special zones shall be placed under the supervision of officials of the authorities of the State, colony, protectorate or mandated territory concerned.

The admission and transit of and trade in such articles within the said zones shall also be subject to the provisions of Section I, § § 1 and 2, of Annex II of the present Convention, to which provisions the High Contracting Parties undertake to conform.

An authorisation must be given by a duly authorised representative of the authorities aforesaid in each case before any such articles may be reconsigned to any place outside the territory to which they have been admitted.

Article 17. The manufacture, assembly and repair within the special zones of articles covered by Categories I, II, IV and V shall be subject to the provisions of Section I, § 3, of Annex II of the present Convention, to which provisions the High Contracting Parties undertake to conform.

Article 18. The High Contracting Parties undertake, each in respect of any territory under its sovereignty, jurisdiction, protection or tutelage, situated within the special zones, not to permit the transit by land across such territory of articles covered by Categories I, II, IV and V when their destination is another territory also situated in the special zones, unless their transport to their destination is assured and the authorities of the latter territory have authorised their import.

The prohibition referred to in the above paragraph shall not apply to the transit of such articles through a territory situated in the special zones when their destination is territory of one of the High Contracting Parties not included in the said zones, provided that their transport to their destination is assured.

If, for the purposes of transport to a territory situated within the special zones, it is necessary to pass through a contiguous territory likewise situated within the said zones, the transit shall be permitted, subject always to the conditions laid down in the first paragraph hereof, at the request of the authorities of the importing territory, provided that such authorities guarantee that the articles in respect of which the request is made shall not at any time be sold, or otherwise transferred, contrary to the provisions of the present Convention. Nevertheless, if the attitude or the disturbed condition of the importing State constitutes a threat to peace or public order, permission for transit shall be refused to such State by the authorities of all such contiguous territories until this threat has ceased to exist.

Article 19. Subject to any contrary provisions in existing special agreements or in any future agreements, provided that in all cases such agreements otherwise comply with the provisions of the present Convention, the High Contracting Parties agree that in the special zones the authorities of the State, colony, protectorate or mandated territory concerned shall carry out within their territorial waters the supervision and police measures necessary for the application of the present Convention.

Article 20. The High Contracting Parties agree that within the special zones no native vessel, as hereinafter defined, of less than 500 tons (net tonnage) shall be allowed to ship, discharge or transship articles covered by Categories I, II, IV and V.

A vessel shall be deemed to be a native vessel, if she is either owned, fitted out or commanded by a native of any country bordering on the Indian Ocean west of the meridian of 95° East of Greenwich and north of the parallel of 11° South latitude, the Red Sea, the Persian Gulf, or the Gulf of Oman, or if at least one half of the crew are natives of such countries.

The provisions of paragraph 1 hereof do not apply to lighters or barges or to vessels engaged exclusively in the coasting trade between different ports of the same State, colony, protectorate or mandated territory where warehouses are situated. The conditions under which articles covered by Categories I, II, IV and V may be carried by such vessels are laid down in § 1 of Section II of Annex II of the present Convention, to which the High Contracting Parties undertake to conform.

The provisions of this Article and of Section II, § 1, of Annex II do not apply:

(a) To arms, ammunition or implements carried on behalf of a Government either under an authorisation or accompanied by a duly authorised official of such Government; or

(b) To arms and ammunition in the possession of persons provided with a licence to carry arms on the condition that such arms are for the personal use of the bearer and are accurately described in such licence.

Article 21. The High Contracting Parties agree that, with the object of preventing all illicit conveyance within the special zones of articles covered by Categories I, II, IV and V, all native vessels within the meaning of Article 20 must carry a manifest of their cargo or a similar document specifying the quantities and nature of the goods on board, their origin and destination. This manifest shall remain covered by the secrecy to which it is entitled by the law of the State to which the vessel belongs, and must not be examined during proceedings for the verification of the flag, unless the interested party consents thereto.

The provisions of this Article shall not apply to:

(a) Vessels exclusively engaged in the coasting trade between different ports of the same State, colony, protectorate or mandated territory; or

(b) Vessels engaged in carrying arms, ammunition and implements on behalf of a Government under the conditions defined in Article 20 (a) and proceeding to or from any point within the said zones; or

(c) Vessels only partially decked, having a maximum crew of ten men, and exclusively employed in fishing within territorial waters.

Article 22. The High Contracting Parties agree that no authorisation to fly the flag of any of such High Contracting Parties shall be granted to native vessels of less than 500 tons (net tonnage) as defined in Article 20, except in accordance with the conditions prescribed in Section II, § 3 and 4, or Annex II of the present Convention. Such authorisation, which shall be in writing, shall be renewed every year and shall contain the particulars necessary to identify the vessel, the name, tonnage, type of rigging, principal dimensions, registered number and signal letters if any. It shall bear the date on which it was granted and the status of the official who granted it.

Article 23. The High Contracting Parties agree to communicate to any other High Contracting Party who so requests the forms of the documents to be issued by them under Articles 20 (a), 21 and 22 and Section II, § 1 of Annex II of the present Convention.

The High Contracting Parties further agree to take all necessary measures to ensure that the following documents shall be supplied as soon as possible to any other High Contracting Party who has requested the same:

(a) Certified copies of all authorisations to fly the flag granted under the provisions of Article 22;

(b) Notice of the withdrawal of such authorisations;

(c) Copies of authorisations issued under Section II, § 1, of Annex II.

Article 24. The High Contracting Parties agree to apply in the maritime zone the regulations laid down in Annex II, Section II, § 5, of the present Convention.

Article 25. The High Contracting Parties agree that any illicit conveyance or attempted conveyance legally established against the captain or owner of a vessel authorised to fly the flag of one of the High Contracting Parties, or holding the licence provided for in Section II, § 1, of Annex II, of the present Convention, shall entail the immediate withdrawal of the said authorisation or licence.

Article 26. The High Contracting Parties who have under their sovereignty, jurisdiction, protection or tutelage territory situated within the special zones, undertake so far as each is concerned, to take the necessary measures to ensure the application of the present Convention and, in particular, the prosecution and punishment of offences against the provisions thereof, and to appoint the territorial and consular officers or competent special representatives for the purpose.

They will communicate these measures to such High Contracting Parties as shall have expressed the desire to be informed thereof.

Article 27. The High Contracting Parties agree that the provisions of Articles 16 to 26 inclusive and of Annex II of the present Convention establishing a certain regime of supervision in the special zones shall not be interpreted, as regards such High Contracting Parties as have no territory under their sovereignty, jurisdiction, protection or tutelage within or immediately adjacent to the said special zones, either as constituting an obligation to apply the regime defined in the above-mentioned provisions or as involving their responsibility with respect to the application of this regime.

However, the said High Contracting Parties shall conform to the provisions of Articles 22, 23 and 25, which relate to the conditions under which native vessels under 500 tons (net tonnage) may be authorised to fly the flag of such High Contracting Parties.

CHAPTER IV. SPECIAL PROVISIONS

Article 28. Abyssinia, desirous of rendering as effective as possible the supervision of the trade in arms and ammunition and in implements of war, which is the subject of the present Convention, hereby undertakes, in the free exercise of her sovereign rights, to put into force, so far as concerns her own territory, all regulations which may be necessary to fulfill the provisions of Articles 12 and 18 inclusive of the said Convention relating to exports, imports and the transport of arms, ammunition and implements of war.

The High Contracting Parties take note of the above undertaking, and, being in full sympathy with the desire of Abyssinia to render as effective as possible the supervision of the trade in arms and ammunition and in implements of war, hereby undertake to conform to the provisions of the above-mentioned Articles so far as concerns Abyssinian territory, and to respect the regulations put into force, in accordance with the said undertaking, by Abyssinia as a sovereign State.

If a State, at present included in the special zones, should at the moment of its accession to the present Convention assume with respect to its own territory the same undertakings as those set forth in the first paragraph of this Article, and also, when such State possesses a seacoast, those contained in Articles 19 to 26 inclusive in so far as the same are applicable,

the High Contracting Parties hereby declare that they will consider such State as excluded from the said zones from the date that its accession becomes effective as specified in Article 41 and that they will accept as regards such State the obligations set forth in the second paragraph of the present Article, and also, when the State excluded possesses a seacoast, the obligations of Articles 19 to 27 inclusive in so far as they are applicable.

Article 29. The High Contracting Parties agree to accept reservations which may be made by Esthonia, Finland, Latvia, Poland and Roumania at the moment of their signature of the present Convention and which shall suspend in respect of these States, until the accession of Russia to the present Convention, the application of Articles 6 and 9, as regards both export to and import into these countries by the High Contracting Parties. These reservations shall not be interpreted as preventing the publication of statistics in accordance with the laws and regulations in effect within the territory of any High Contracting Party.

Article 30. High Contracting Parties who possess extraterritorial jurisdiction in the territory of another State party to the present Convention undertake in cases where the rules of this Convention cannot be enforced by the local courts as regards their nationals in such territory to prohibit all action by such nationals contrary to the provisions of the present Convention.

CHAPTER V. GENERAL PROVISIONS

Article 31. The provisions of the present Convention are completed by those of Annexes I and II, which have the same value and shall enter into force at the same time as the Convention itself.

Article 32. The High Contracting Parties agree that the provisions of the present Convention do not apply:

(a) To arms or ammunition or to implements of war forwarded from territory under the sovereignty, jurisdiction, protection or tutelage of a High Contracting Party for the use of the armed forces of such High Contracting Party, wherever situated, nor

(b) To arms or ammunition carried by individual members of such forces or by other persons in the service of a High Contracting Party and required by them by reason of their calling, nor

(c) To rifles, muskets, carbines and the necessary ammunition therefor, carried by members of rifle clubs for the sole purpose of individual use in international competitions in marksmanship.

Article 33. In time of war, and without prejudice to the rules of neutrality, the provisions of Chapter II shall be suspended from operation until the restoration of peace so far as concerns any consignment of arms or ammunition or of implements of war to or on behalf of a belligerent.

Article 34. All the provisions of general international Conventions anterior to the date of the present Convention, such as the Convention for the Control of the Trade in Arms and Ammunition and the Protocol signed at St. Germain-en-Laye on September 10th, 1919, shall be considered as abrogated in so far as they relate to the matters dealt with in the present Convention and are binding between the Powers which are Parties to the present Convention.

The present Convention shall not be deemed to affect any rights and obligations which may arise out of the provisions either of the Covenant of the League of Nations of the Treaties of Peace signed in 1919 and 1920 at Versailles, Neuilly, St. Germain and Trianon, or of the Treaty Limiting Naval Armaments signed at Washington on February 6th, 1922, or of any other treaty, convention, agreement or engagement concerning prohibition of import, export or transit of arms or ammunition or of implements of war; nor, without prejudice to the provisions of the present Convention itself, shall it affect any other treaty, convention, agreement or engagement other than those referred to in paragraph 1 of the present Article having as its object the supervision of import, export or transit of arms or ammunition or of implements of war.

Article 35. The High Contracting Parties agree that disputes arising between them relating to the interpretation or application of this Convention shall, if they cannot be settled by direct negotiation, be referred for decision to the Permanent Court of International Justice. In case either or both of the States to such a dispute should not be parties to the Protocol of December 16th, 1920, relating to the Permanent Court of International Justice, the dispute shall be referred, at the choice of the Parties and in accordance with the constitutional procedure of each State, either to the Permanent Court of International Justice or to a court of arbitration constituted in accordance with the Hague Convention of October 18th, 1907, or to some other court of arbitration.

Article 36. Any High Contracting Party may declare that its signature or ratification or accession does not, as regards the application of the provisions of Chapter II and of Articles 13, 14 and 15 of the present Convention, bind either all or any one of the territories subject to its sovereignty, jurisdiction or protection, provided that such territories are not situated in the special zones as defined in Article 12.

Any High Contracting Party which has made such a declaration may, subsequently, and in conformity with the provisions of Article 37, adhere entirely to the present Convention for any territories so excluded. Such High Contracting Party will use its best endeavours to ensure as soon as possible the accession of any territories so excluded.

Any High Contracting Party may also, as regards the application of the provisions of Chapter II and of Articles 13, 14 and 15 of the present Convention, and in conformity with the procedure laid down in Article 38, denounce the present Convention separately in respect of any territory referred to above.

Any High Contracting Party which shall have availed itself of the option of exclusion or of denunciation provided for in the preceding paragraphs undertakes to apply the provisions of Chapter II to consignments destined for territories in respect of which the option has been exercised.

Article 37. The High Contracting Parties will use their best endeavours to secure the accession to the present Convention of other States.

Each accession will be notified to the Government of the French Republic and by the latter to all the signatory or acceding States.

The instruments of accession shall remain deposited in the archives of the Government of the French Republic.

Article 38. The present Convention may be denounced by any High Contracting Party thereto after the expiration of four years from the date when it came into force in respect of that Party. Denunciation shall be effected by notification in writing addressed to the Government of the French Republic, which will forthwith transmit copies of such notification to the other Contracting Parties, informing them of the date on which it was received.

A denunciation shall take effect one year after the date of the receipt of the notification thereof by the Government of the French Republic and shall operate only in respect of the notifying State.

In case a denunciation has the effect of reducing the number of States parties to the Convention below fourteen, any of the remaining High Contracting Parties may also, within a period of one year from the date of such denunciation, denounce the Convention without waiting for the expiration of the period of four years mentioned above and may require that its denunciation shall take effect at the same date as the first-mentioned denunciation.

Article 39. The High Contracting Parties agree that, at the conclusion of a period of three years from the coming into force of the present Convention under the terms of Article 41, this Convention shall be subject to revision upon the request of one-third of the said High Contracting Parties addressed to the Government of the French Republic.

Article 40. [Ratification]

Article 41. [Deposit of Ratification]

Done at Geneva, in a single copy, this seventeenth day of June, One Thousand Nine Hundred and Twenty-Five.

[Carnegie Endowment for International Peace, *International Conciliation* 1929, pp. 312–328]

Draft Convention with Regard to the Supervision of the Private Manufacture and Publicity of the Manufacture of Arms and Ammunition and of Implements of War (1929)

This draft grew out of the early League discussions and those of the Preparatory Conference. It was submitted to the General Disarmament Conference that met in 1932.

CATEGORIES

Article 1. For the purposes of the present Convention, five categories of arms, ammunition and implements are established:

CATEGORY I. ARMS, AMMUNITION AND IMPLEMENTS OF WAR EXCLUSIVELY DESIGNED AND INTENDED FOR LAND, SEA OR AERIAL WARFARE

A. Arms, ammunition and implements exclusively designed and intended for land, sea or aerial warfare, both those which are or shall be comprised in the armament of the armed forces of a State, and those which have been comprised in such armament, except such arms, ammunition and implements which, though included in the above definition, are covered by other categories.

Such arms, ammunition and implements are comprised in the following twelve headings:

1. Rifles, muskets, carbines.

2. (a) Machine guns, automatic rifles and machine-pistols of all calibres;

(b) Mountings for machine-guns;

(c) Interrupter gears.

3. Projectiles and ammunition for the arms enumerated in Nos. 1 and 2 above.

4. Gun-sighting apparatus, including aerial gun-sights and bomb-sights, and fire-control apparatus.

5. (a) Cannon, long or short, and howitzers, of a calibre less than 5.9 inches (15 cm.);

(b) Cannon, long or short, and howitzers, of a calibre of 5.9 inches (15 cm.) or above;

(c) Mortars of all kinds;

(d) Gun carriages, mountings, recuperators, accessories for mountings.

6. Projectiles and ammunition for the arms enumerated in No. 5 above.

7. Apparatus for the discharge of bombs, torpedoes, depth charges and other kinds of projectiles.

8. (a) Grenades;

(b) Bombs;

(c) Land mines, submarine mines, fixed or floating, depth charges;

(d) Torpedoes.

9. Appliances for use with the above arms and apparatus.

10. Bayonets.

11. Tanks and armoured cars.

12. Arms and ammunition not specified in the above enumeration.

B. Essential and easily recognisable component parts, completely finished, of the articles covered by A above if capable of being utilised only in the assembly or repair of the said articles, or as spare parts.

CATEGORY II. ARMS AND AMMUNITION CAPABLE OF USE BOTH FOR MILITARY AND OTHER PURPOSES.

A. 1. Revolvers, and self-loading or automatic pistols, and developments of the same, designed for single-handed use or fired from the shoulder, of a calibre greater than 6.5 mm. and length of barrel greater than 10 cm.

2. Fire-arms designed, intended or adapted for non-military purposes, such as a sport or personal defence, that will fire cartridges that can be fired from fire-arms in Category I; other rifled fire-arms firing from the shoulder, of a calibre of 6 mm. or above, not included in Category I, with the exception of rifled fire-arms with a "break-down" action.

3. Ammunition for the arms enumerated in the above two headings, with the exception of ammunition covered by Category I.

4. Swords and lances.

B. Essential and easily recognisable component parts, completely finished, of the articles covered by A above, if capable of being utilised only in the assembly or repair of the said articles, or as spare parts.

CATEGORY III. VESSELS OF WAR AND THEIR ARMAMENT.

1. Vessels of war of all kinds.

2. Arms, ammunition and implements of war mounted on board vessels of war and forming part of their normal armament.

CATEGORY IV

1. Aircraft, assembled or dismantled.

2. Aircraft engines.

CATEGORY V

1. Gunpowder and explosives, except common black gunpowder.

2. Arms and ammunition other than those covered by Categories I and II, such as pistols and revolvers of all models, rifled weapons with a "breakdown" action, other rifled fire-arms of a calibre of less than 6 mm. designed for firing from the shoulder, smooth-bore shot-guns, guns with more than one barrel of which at least one barrel is smoothbore, fire-arms firing rimfire ammunition, muzzle-loading fire-arms.

Remarks

The delegation of the United States of America reserved the right to propose for incorporation in the final text of the Convention a statement limiting the material of Category IV of Article 1 to aircraft and aircraft engines manufactured under military specifications within their territory or jurisdiction, either on their own behalf or on behalf of the Government of another State.

The term "manufactured under military specifications" means both material manufactured for purely military purposes and material manufactured for commercial purposes, but on specifications designed to make it capable of military use.

The delegations of Germany and the Netherlands associated themselves with this reservation.

SUPERVISION AND PUBLICITY

Article 2. For the purposes of the present Convention, private manufacture shall be considered to mean manufacture of articles defined in Article 1 taking place in establishments of which the State is not the sole proprietor, and which are mainly or to a large extent engaged in the manufacture of the articles covered by Categories I, II, III, and IV of Article 1, excluding manufacture on the order and behalf of the State.

Article 3. The High Contracting Parties undertake not to permit, in the territory under their jurisdiction, the private manufacture as defined in Article 2 of the articles included in Categories I, II, III and IV, unless the manufacturers thereof are licensed by the Government to manufacture the articles referred to in this article.

This licence shall be valid for a period to be determined individually by each High Contracting Party, and shall be renewable for a further period at the discretion of the Government.

Remarks

The delegation of the United States of America recalled its declaration of principle made previously to the effect that its Government is powerless to prescribe or enforce a prohibition or a system of licences upon private manufacture, which takes place under the jurisdiction of the States which form the United States of America.

Article 4. The High Contracting Parties undertake to forward to the Secretary-General of the League of Nations, or to publish within two months after the close of each quarter beginning on the first day of January, April, July and October, a list of the licences granted or renewed during that quarter, together with:

(a) A description of the war material for which the licence is granted:

(b) The name and address of the registered or head office of the licensees and the period for which the licence has been granted.

Article 5. The High Contracting Parties further undertake to forward to the Secretary-General of the League of Nations, or to publish annually, a return showing the total production, in value, number and weight, of the private manufactures licensed in accordance with the provisions of Article 3, in respect of each of the twelve headings of Category I (A and B), of the four headings of Category II (A and B), and of the two headings of Category IV, set out in Article 1 of the present Convention.

The provisions of the foregoing paragraph shall also apply to the production of the material manufactured for it in establishments of which the State is the sole proprietor, or in any other establishment on behalf of the State.

The High Contracting Parties undertake to forward to the Secretary-General of the League of Nations, or to publish, the text of the provisions of all statutes, orders or regulations in force within their territory dealing with articles covered by Categories I, II and IV. All provisions enacted for the purpose of carrying out the present Convention and all amendments and additions to such statutes, orders, regulations and provisions shall also be published, or forwarded to the Secretary-General of the League of Nations.

Remarks

1. The Japanese delegation considered that publicity of the manufactures should in all cases be given in terms of value only.

2. The Czechoslovak, French, Italian, Polish and Roumanian delegations could not accept the second paragraph. They considered, together with the Belgian delegation, that publicity in regard to State manufacture could only be determined in connection with the decisions to be taken by the Preparatory Commission for the Disarmament Conference concerning publicity of material, in pursuance of its resolution of May 4th, 1929.

Article 6. The High Contracting Parties, in all cases covered by Category III, undertake to publish as soon as possible, and in any case not later than within two months after the close of each quarter beginning on January 1st, April 1st, July 1st and October 1st, the return for that quarter, giving the information detailed below for each vessel of war constructed, or in the course of construction, within their territorial jurisdiction.

(a) The date of laying the keel, and the following data:

Standard displacement in tons and metric tons; the principle dimensions, namely, length at water-line, extreme beam at or below water-line and mean draft at standard displacement;

(b) Date of delivery or date of completion, together with the following data with respect to the vessel at that date:

Standard displacement in tons and metric tons; the principal dimensions, namely, length at water-line, extreme beam at or below water-line, mean draft at standard displacement, as well as the following information regarding the armament installed on board the vessel at the date of delivery and forming part of the vessel's normal armament:

Number and calibre of guns;

Number and calibre of torpedo-tubes;

Number of bomb-throwers;

Number of machine-guns.

By standard displacement in the present article is to be understood the displacement of the vessel complete, fully manned, engined, and equipped ready for sea, including all armament and ammunition, equipment, outfit, provisions and fresh water for crew, miscellaneous stores and implements of every description that are intended to be carried in war, but without fuel or reserve feed water on board.

The standard displacement of a submarine is the surface displacement of a vessel complete (exclusive of the water in non-watertight structure), fully manned, engined and equipped ready for sea, including all armament and ammunition, equipment, outfit, provisions for crew, miscellaneous stores and implements of every description that are intended to be carried in war, but without fuel, lubricating oil, fresh water or ballast of any kind on board.

Article 7. The articles covered by Category V shall only be subject to such publicity as may be prescribed by the national legislation.

GENERAL PROVISIONS

Article 8. In time of war, the application of the present Convention shall be suspended as regards belligerents until the restoration of peace.

> *Remarks*
>
> The delegations of Finland, Germany, the Netherlands, Persia, Poland and Roumania have expressed the opinion that the following words should be added: "... and also as regards non-belligerents threatened by the war. Neutral High Contracting Parties who avail themselves of this right shall duly notify the other High Contracting Parties".

Article 9. The present Convention shall not be deemed to affect any rights and obligations which may arise out of the provisions of the Covenant of the League of Nations, or of the Treaties of Peace signed in 1919 and 1920 at Versailles, Neuilly, St. Germain and Trianon, or of the Treaty limiting Naval Armaments signed at Washington on February 6th, 1922, or of any other treaty, convention, agreement or engagement concerning the manufacture of arms and ammunition and of implements of war.

Article 10. The High Contracting Parties will use their best endeavours to secure the accession to the present Convention of other States.

Each accession will be notified to the Secretary-General of the League of Nations, and by the latter to all the signatory or acceding States.

The instruments of accession shall remain deposited in the archives of the Secretariat of the League of Nations.

Article 11. The present Convention may be denounced by any High Contracting Party thereto after the expiration of four years from the date when it came into force in respect of that Party. Denunciation shall be effected by notification in writing addressed to the Secretary-General of the League of Nations, who will forthwith communicate such notification to the other Contracting Parties, informing them of the date on which it was received.

A denunciation shall take effect one year after the date of the receipt of the notification thereof by the Secretary-General of the League of Nations, and shall operate only in respect of the notifying States.

Should the Convention be denounced by one of the Powers whose ratification is a condition of its entry into force, any other High Contracting Party may also, within a period of one year from the date of such denunciation, denounce the Convention without waiting for the expiration of the period of four years mentioned above, and may require that its denunciation shall take effect at the same date as the first-mentioned denunciation.

Article 12. Any State signing or acceding to the present Convention may declare, at the moment of its signature, ratification or accession, that its acceptance of the present Convention does not apply to any or all of the overseas territories under its sovereignty, authority or jurisdiction, and may accede subsequently, in accordance with the provisions of Article 10, on behalf of any territory so excluded. Denunciation may also be effected separately in respect of any such territory, and the provisions of Article 11 shall apply to any such denunciation.

> *Remarks*
>
> The delegations of Germany, Italy, the Netherlands and Salvador proposed that this article should be omitted.

Article 13. The High Contracting Parties agree that, at the conclusion of a period of three years from the coming into force of the present Convention under the terms of Article 15, this Convention shall be subject to revision upon the request of one-third of the said High Contracting Parties, which request shall be addressed to the Secretary-General of the League of Nations.

Article 14. The present Convention, of which the French and English texts are both authentic, is subject to ratification. It shall bear to-day's date.

Each Power shall address its ratification to the Secretary-General of the League of Nations, who will at once notify the deposit of such ratification to each of the other signatory Powers.

The instruments of ratification will remain in the archives of the Secretariat of the League of Nations.

Article 15. A first *procès-verbal* of the deposit of ratifications shall be drawn up by the Secretary-General of the League of Nations as soon as the present Convention shall have been ratified by the following Powers:

[Here follows the list of the principal producing Powers, to be drawn up by the Conference.]

The Convention shall come into force four months after the date of the notification of this *procès-verbal* by the Secretary-General of the League of Nations to all signatory Powers.

Subsequently, the Convention will come into force in respect of each High Contracting Party four months after the date on which its ratification or accession shall have been notified by the Secretary-General of the League of Nations to all signatory or acceding States.

Remarks

The delegations of Spain and Salvador recommended that the text of this article should correspond to that of Article 41 of the Convention for the Supervision of the International Trade in Arms and Ammunition and in Implements of War of June 17th, 1925, to the effect that the Convention should come into force after ratification by fourteen Powers.

Article 16. The High Contracting Parties agree to accept reservations which may be made by Estonia, Finland, Latvia, Poland and Roumania at the moment of their signature of the present Convention, and which shall suspend, until the accession of Russia to the present Convention under the same conditions as the said Powers, the application, in respect of those States, of Articles . . . of the present Convention.

[League of Nations, *Official Journal* (November 1929): 1601–1604]

Tripartite Arms Declaration (1950)

Tripartite Declaration Regarding Security in the Near East, 25 May 1950

The Governments of the United Kingdom, France, and the United States, having had occasion during the recent Foreign Ministers meeting in London to review certain questions affecting the peace and stability of the Arab states and of Israel, and particularly that of the supply of arms and war material to these states, have resolved to make the following statements:

1. The three Governments recognize that the Arab states and Israel all need to maintain a certain level of armed forces for the purposes of assuring their internal security and their legitimate self-defense and to permit them to play their part in the defense of the area as a whole. All applications for arms or war material for these countries will be considered in the light of these principles. In this connection the three Governments wish to recall and reaffirm the terms of the statements made by their representatives on the Security Council on August 4, 1949, in which they declared their opposition to the development of an arms race between the Arab states and Israel.

2. The three Governments declare that assurances have been received from all the states in question, to which they permit arms to be supplied from their countries, that the purchasing state does not intend to undertake any act of aggression against any other state. Similar assurances will be requested from any other state in the area to which they permit arms to be supplied in the future.

3. The three Governments take this opportunity of declaring their deep interest in and their desire to promote the establishment and maintenance of peace and stability in the area and their unalterable opposition to the use of force or threat of force between any of the states in that area. The three Governments, should they find that any of these states was preparing to violate frontiers or armistice lines, would, consistently with their obligations as members of the United Nations, immediately take action, both within and outside the United Nations, to prevent such violation.

[U.S. Department of State *Bulletin* (5 June 1950); S/RES/558 (1984)]

United Nations Security Council Resolutions on the Arms Embargo Against South Africa

Resolution 181 (1963)

Resolution 181 was adopted by the Security Council at its 1056th meeting, on 7 August 1963 (with voluntary compliance), by nine votes to none, with France and the United Kingdom abstaining.

The Security Council,

Having considered the question of race conflict in South Africa resulting from the policies of *apartheid* of the Government of the Republic of South Africa, as submitted by the thirty-two African Member States,

Recalling its resolution 134 (1960) of 1 April 1960,

Taking into account that world public opinion has been reflected in General Assembly resolution 1761 (XVII) of 6 November 1962, and particularly in its paragraphs 4 and 8,

Noting with appreciation the interim reports adopted on 6 May and 16 July 1963 by the Special Committee on the Policies of *apartheid* of the Government of the Republic of South Africa,

Noting with concern the recent arms build-up by the Government of South Africa, some of which arms are being used in furtherance of that Government's racial policies,

Regretting that some States are indirectly providing encouragement in various ways to the Government of South Africa to perpetuate, by force, its policy of *apartheid,*

Regretting the failure of the Government of South Africa to accept the invitation of the Security Council to delegate a representative to appear before it,

Being convinced that the situation in South Africa is seriously disturbing international peace and security,

1. *Strongly deprecates* the policies of South Africa in its perpetuation of racial discrimination as being inconsistent with the principles contained in the Charter of the United Nations and contrary to its obligations as a Member of the United Nations;

2. *Calls upon* the Government of South Africa to abandon the policies of *apartheid* and discrimination, as called for in Security Council resolution 134 (1960), and to liberate all persons imprisoned, interned or subjected to other restrictions for having opposed the policy of *apartheid;*

3. *Solemnly calls upon all* States to cease forthwith the sale and shipment of arms, ammunition of all types and military vehicles to South Africa;

4. *Requests* the Secretary-General to keep the situation in South Africa under observation and to report to the Security Council by 30 October 1963.

Resolution 182 (1963)

Resolution 182 was adopted unanimously by the Security Council at its 1078th meeting on 4 December 1963 (with voluntary compliance).

The Security Council,

Having considered the race conflict in South Africa resulting from the policies of *apartheid* of the Government of the Republic of South Africa,

Recalling previous resolutions of the Security Council and of the General Assembly which have dealt with the racial policies of the Government of the Republic of South Africa, and in particular Security Council resolution 181 (1963) of 7 August 1963,

Having considered the Secretary-General's report contained in document S/5438 and addenda,

Deploring the refusal of the Government of the Republic of South Africa, as confirmed in the reply of the Minister of Foreign Affairs of the Republic of South Africa to the Secretary-General received on 11 October 1963, to comply with Security Council resolution 181 (1963) and to accept the repeated recommendations of other United Nations organs,

Noting with appreciation the replies to the Secretary-General's communication to the Member States on the action taken and proposed to be taken by their Governments in the context of paragraph 3 of that resolution, and hoping that all the Member States as soon as possible will inform the Secretary-General about their willingness to carry out the provisions of that paragraph,

Taking note of the reports of the Special Committee on the Policies of *apartheid* of the Government of the Republic of South Africa,

Noting with deep satisfaction the overwhelming support for resolution 1881 (XVII) adopted by the General Assembly on 11 October 1963,

Taking into account the serious concern of the Member States with regard to the policy of *apartheid,* as expressed in the general debate in the General Assembly as well as in the discussions in the Special Political Committee,

Being strengthened in its conviction that the situation in South Africa is seriously disturbing international peace and security, and strongly deprecating the policies of the Government of South Africa in its perpetuation of racial discrimination as being inconsistent with the principles contained in the Charter of the United Nations and with its obligations as a Member of the United Nations,

Recognizing the need to eliminate discrimination in regard to basic human rights and fundamental freedoms for all individuals within the territory of the Republic of South Africa without distinction as to race, sex, language, or religion,

Expressing the firm conviction that the policies of *apartheid* and racial discrimination as practised by the Government of the Republic of South Africa are abhorrent to the conscience of mankind and that therefore a positive alternative to these policies must be found through peaceful means,

1. *Appeals* to all States to comply with the provisions of Security Council resolution 181 (1963) of 7 August 1963;

2. *Urgently requests* the Government of the Republic of South Africa to cease forthwith its continued imposition of discriminatory and repressive measures which are contrary to the principles and purposes of the Charter and which are in violation of its obligations as a Member of the United Nations and of the provisions of the Universal Declaration of Human Rights;

3. *Condemns* the non-compliance by the Government of the Republic of South Africa with the appeals contained in the above-mentioned resolutions of the General Assembly and the Security Council;

4. *Again calls upon* the Government of the Republic of South Africa to liberate all persons imprisoned, interned or subjected to other restrictions for having opposed the policy of *apartheid;*

5. *Solemnly calls upon* all States to cease forthwith the sale and shipment of equipment and materials for the manufacture and maintenance of arms and ammunition in South Africa;

6. *Requests* the Secretary-General to establish under his direction and reporting to him a small group of recognized experts to examine methods of resolving the present situation in South Africa through full, peaceful and orderly application of human rights and fundamental freedoms to all inhabitants of the territory as a whole, regardless of race, colour or creed, and to consider what part the United Nations might play in the achievement of that end;

7. *Invites* the Government of the Republic of South Africa to avail itself of the assistance of this group in order to bring about such peaceful and orderly transformation;

8. *Requests* the Secretary-General to continue to keep the situation under observation and to report to the Security Council such new developments as may occur and in any case, not later than 1 June 1964, on the implementation of the present resolution.

Resolution 418 (1977)

Resolution 418 was adopted by the Security Council at its 2046th meeting on 4 November 1977 (with mandatory compliance).

The Security Council,

Recalling its resolution 392 (1976) of 19 June 1976, strongly condemning the South African Government for its resort to massive violence against and killings of the African people, including school-children and students and others opposing racial discrimination, and calling upon that Government urgently to end violence against the African people and to take urgent steps to eliminate *apartheid* and racial discrimination,

Recognizing that the military build-up by South Africa and its persistent acts of aggression against the neighbouring States seriously disturb the security of those states,

Further recognizing that the existing arms embargo must be strengthened and universally applied, without any reservations or qualifications whatsoever, in order to prevent a further aggravation of the grave situation in South Africa,

Taking note of the Lagos Declaration for Action against *Apartheid,*

Gravely concerned that South Africa is at the threshold of producing nuclear weapons,

Strongly condemning the South African Government for its acts of repression, its defiant continuance of the system of *apartheid* and its attacks against neighbouring independent States,

Considering that the policies and acts of the South African Government are fraught with danger to international peace and security,

Recalling its resolution 181 (1963) of 7 August 1963 and other resolutions concerning a voluntary arms embargo against South Africa,

Convinced that a mandatory arms embargo needs to be universally applied against South Africa in the first instance,

Acting therefore under Chapter VII of the Charter of the United Nations,

1. *Determines,* having regard to the policies and acts of the South African Government, that the acquisition by South Africa of arms and related matériel constitutes a threat to the maintenance of international peace and security;

2. *Decides* that all States shall cease forthwith any provision to South Africa of arms and related matériel of all types, including the sale or transfer of weapons and ammunition, military vehicles and equipment, paramilitary police equipment; and spare parts for the aforementioned, and shall cease as well the provision of all types of equipment and supplies and grants of licensing arrangements for the manufacture and development of nuclear weapons;

3. *Calls upon* all States to review, having regard to the objectives of the present resolution, all existing contractual arrangements with and licenses granted to South Africa relating to the manufacture and maintenance of arms, ammunition of all types and military equipment and vehicles, with a view to terminating them;

4. Further decides that all States shall refrain from any co-operation with South Africa in the manufacture and development of nuclear weapons;

5. *Calls upon* all States, including States non-members of the United Nations, to act strictly in

accordance with the provisions of the present resolution;

6. *Requests* the Secretary-General to report to the Security Council on the progress of the implementation of the present resolution, the first report to be submitted not later than 1 May 1978;

7. *Decides* to keep this item on the agenda for further action, as appropriate, in the light of developments.

Resolution 558 (1984)

Resolution 558 was adopted unanimously by the Security Council at its 2564th meeting on 13 December 1984.

The Security Council,

Recalling its resolution 418 (1977) of 4 November 1977, in which it decided upon a mandatory arms embargo against South Africa,

Recalling its resolution 421 (1977) of 9 December 1977, by which it entrusted a Committee consisting of all its members with the task of, among other things, studying ways and means by which the mandatory arms embargo could be made more effective against South Africa and to make recommendations to the Council,

Taking note of the Committee's report to the Security Council contained in document S/14179 of 19 September 1980,

Recognizing that South Africa's intensified efforts to build up its capacity to manufacture armaments undermines the effectiveness of the mandatory arms embargo against South Africa,

Considering that no State should contribute to South Africa's arms production capability by purchasing arms manufactured in South Africa,

1. *Reaffirms* its resolution 418 (1977) and stresses the continuing need for the strict application of all its provisions;

2. *Requests* all States to refrain from importing arms, ammunition of all types and military vehicles produced in South Africa;

3. *Requests* all States, including States non-members of the United Nations to act strictly in accordance with the provisions of the present resolution;

4. *Requests* the Secretary-General to report to the Security Council Committee established by resolution 421 (1977) concerning the question of South Africa on the progress of the implementation of the present resolution before 31 December 1985.

Preventing Manufacture of Nuclear Weapons, 1968

Treaty on the Non-Proliferation of Nuclear Weapons (1968)

The NPT entered into force on 5 March 1970.

The States concluding this Treaty, hereinafter referred to as the "Parties to the Treaty",

Considering the devastation that would be visited upon all mankind by a nuclear war and the consequent need to make every effort to avert the danger of such a war and to take measures to safeguard the security of peoples,

Believing that the proliferation of nuclear weapons would seriously enhance the danger of nuclear war,

In conformity with resolutions of the United Nations General Assembly calling for the conclusion of an agreement on the prevention of wider dissemination of nuclear weapons,

Undertaking to cooperate in facilitating the application of International Atomic Energy Agency safeguards on peaceful nuclear activities,

Expressing their support for research, development and other efforts to further the application, within the framework of the International Atomic Energy Agency safeguards system, of the principle of safeguarding effectively the flow of source and special fissionable materials by use of instruments and other techniques at certain strategic points,

Affirming the principle that the benefits of peaceful applications of nuclear technology, including any technological by-products which may be derived by nuclear-weapon States from the development of nuclear explosive devices, should be available for peaceful purposes to all Parties of the Treaty, whether nuclear-weapon or non-nuclear weapon States,

Convinced that, in furtherance of this principle, all Parties to the Treaty are entitled to participate in the fullest possible exchange of scientific information for, and to contribute alone or in cooperation with other States to, the further development of the applications of atomic energy for peaceful purposes,

Declaring their intention to achieve at the earliest possible date the cessation of the nuclear arms race and to undertake effective measures in the direction of nuclear disarmament,

Urging the cooperation of all States in the attainment of this objective,

Recalling the determination expressed by the Parties to the 1963 Treaty banning nuclear weapon tests in the atmosphere, in outer space and under water in its Preamble to seek to achieve the discontinuance of all test explosions of nuclear weapons for all time and to continue negotiations to this end,

Desiring to further the easing of international tension and the strengthening of trust between States in order to facilitate the cessation of the manufacture of nuclear weapons, the liquidation of all their existing stockpiles, and the elimination from national arsenals of nuclear weapons and the means of their delivery pursuant to a treaty on general and complete disarmament under strict and effective international control,

Recalling that, in accordance with the Charter of the United Nations, States must refrain in their international relations from the threat or use of force against the territorial integrity or political independence of any State, or in any other manner inconsistent with the Purposes of the United Nations, and that the establishment and maintenance of international peace and security are to be promoted with the least diversion for armaments of the world's human and economic resources,

Have agreed as follows:

Article I. Each nuclear-weapon State Party to the Treaty undertakes not to transfer to any recipient whatsoever nuclear weapons or other nuclear explosive devices or control over such weapons or explosive devices directly, or indirectly; and not in any way to assist, encourage, or induce any non-nuclear-weapon State to manufacture or otherwise acquire nuclear weapons or other nuclear explosive devices, or control over such weapons or explosive devices.

Article II. Each non-nuclear-weapon State Party to the Treaty undertakes not to receive the transfer from any transferor whatsoever of nuclear weapons or other nuclear explosive devices or of control over such weapons or explosive devices directly, or indirectly; not to manufacture or otherwise acquire nuclear weapons or other nuclear explosive devices; and not to seek or receive any assistance in the manufacture of nuclear weapons or other nuclear explosive devices.

Article III

1. Each non-nuclear-weapon State Party to the Treaty undertakes to accept safeguards, as set forth in an agreement to be negotiated and concluded with the International Atomic Energy Agency in accordance with the Statute of the International Atomic Energy Agency and the Agency's safeguards system, for the exclusive purpose of verification of the fulfillment of its obligations assumed under this Treaty with a view to preventing diversion of nuclear energy from peaceful uses to nuclear weapons or other nuclear explosive devices. Procedures for the safeguards required by this article shall be followed with respect to source or special fissionable material whether it is being produced, processed or used in any principal nuclear facility or is outside any such facility. The safeguards required by this article shall be applied to all source or special fissionable material in all peaceful nuclear activities within the territory of such State, under its jurisdiction, or carried out under its control anywhere.

2. Each State Party to the Treaty undertakes not to provide: (a) source or special fissionable material, or (b) equipment or material especially designed or prepared for the processing, use or production of special fissionable material, to any non-nuclear-weapon State for peaceful purposes, unless the source or special fissionable material

shall be subject to the safeguards required by this article.

3. The safeguards required by this article shall be implemented in a manner designed to comply with article IV of this Treaty, and to avoid hampering the economic or technological development of the Parties or international cooperation in the field of peaceful nuclear activities, including the international exchange of nuclear material and equipment for the processing, use or production of nuclear material for peaceful purposes in accordance with the provisions of this article and the principle of safeguarding set forth in the Preamble of the Treaty.

4. Non-nuclear-weapon States Party to the Treaty shall conclude agreements with the International Atomic Energy Agency to meet the requirements of this article either individually or together with other States in accordance with the Statute of the International Atomic Energy Agency. Negotiation of such agreements shall commence within 180 days from the original entry into force of this Treaty. For States depositing their instruments of ratification or accession after the 180-day period, negotiation of such agreements shall commence not later than the date of such deposit. Such agreements shall enter into force not later than eighteen months after the date of initiation of negotiations.

Article IV

1. Nothing in this Treaty shall be interpreted as affecting the inalienable right of all the Parties to the Treaty to develop research, production and use of nuclear energy for peaceful purposes without discrimination and in conformity with articles I and II of this Treaty.

2. All the Parties to the Treaty undertake to facilitate, and have the right to participate in, the fullest possible exchange of equipment, materials and scientific and technological information for the peaceful uses of nuclear energy. Parties to the Treaty in a position to do so shall also cooperate in contributing alone or together with other States or international organizations to the further development of the applications of nuclear energy for peaceful purposes, especially in the territories of non-nuclear-weapon States Party to the Treaty, with due consideration for the needs of the developing areas of the world.

Article V. Each party to the Treaty undertakes to take appropriate measures to ensure that, in accordance with this Treaty, under appropriate international observation and through appropriate international procedures, potential benefits from any peaceful applications of nuclear explosions will be made available to non-nuclear-weapon States Party to the Treaty on a nondiscriminatory basis and that the charge to such Parties for the explosive devices used will be as low as possible and exclude any charge for research and development. Non-nuclear-weapon States Party to the Treaty shall be able to obtain such benefits, pursuant to a special international agreement or agreements, through an appropriate international body with adequate representation of non-nuclear-weapon States. Negotiations on this subject shall commence as soon as possible after the Treaty enters into force. Non-nuclear-weapon States Party to the Treaty so desiring may also obtain such benefits pursuant to bilateral agreements.

Article VI. Each of the Parties to the Treaty undertakes to pursue negotiations in good faith on effective measures relating to cessation of the nuclear arms race at an early date and to nuclear disarmament, and on a treaty on general and complete disarmament under strict and effective international control.

Article VII. Nothing in this Treaty affects the right of any group of States to conclude regional treaties in order to assure the total absence of nuclear weapons in their respective territories.

Article VIII

1. Any Party to the Treaty may propose amendments to this Treaty. The text of any proposed amendment shall be submitted to the Depositary Governments which shall circulate it to all Parties to the Treaty. Thereupon, if requested to do so by one-third or more of the Parties to the Treaty, the Depositary Governments shall convene a conference, to which they shall invite all the Parties to the Treaty, to consider such an amendment.

2. Any amendment to this Treaty must be approved by a majority of the votes of all the Parties to the Treaty, including the votes of all nuclear-weapon States Party to the Treaty and all other Parties which, on the date the amendment is circulated, are members of the Board of Governors of the International Atomic Energy Agency. The amendment shall enter into force for each Party that deposits its instrument of ratification of the amendment upon the deposit of such instruments of ratification by a majority of all the Parties, including the instruments of ratification of all nuclear-weapon States Party to the Treaty and all other Parties which, on the date the amendment is circulated, are members of the Board of Governors of the International Atomic Energy Agency. Thereafter, it shall enter into force for any other Party upon the deposit of its instrument of ratification of the amendment.

3. Five years after the entry into force of this Treaty, a conference of Parties to the Treaty shall be held in Geneva, Switzerland, in order to review the operation of this Treaty with a view to assuring that the purposes of the Preamble and the provisions of the Treaty are being realized. At intervals of five years thereafter, a majority of the Parties to the Treaty may obtain, by submitting a proposal to this effect to the Depositary Governments, the convening of further conferences with the same objective of reviewing the operation of the Treaty.

Article IX

1. This Treaty shall be open to all States for signature. Any State which does not sign the Treaty before its entry into force in accordance with paragraph 3 of this article may accede to it at any time.

2. This Treaty shall be subject to ratification by signatory States. Instruments of ratification and instruments of accession shall be deposited with the Governments of the United States of America, the United Kingdom of Great Britain and Northern Ireland and the Union of Soviet Socialist Republics, which are hereby designated the Depositary Governments.

3. This Treaty shall enter into force after its ratification by the States, the Governments of which are designated Depositaries of the Treaty, and forty other States signatory to this Treaty and the deposit of their instruments of ratification. For the purposes of this Treaty, a nuclear-weapon State is one which has manufactured and exploded a nuclear weapon or other nuclear explosive device prior to January 1, 1967.

4. For States whose instruments of ratification or accession are deposited subsequent to the entry into force of this Treaty, it shall enter into force on the date of the deposit of their instruments of ratification or accession.

5. The Depositary Governments shall promptly inform all signatory and acceding States of the date of each signature, the date of deposit of each instrument of ratification or of accession, the date of the entry into force of this Treaty, and the date of receipt of any requests for convening a conference or other notices.

6. This Treaty shall be registered by the Depositary Governments pursuant to article 102 of the Charter of the United Nations.

Article X

1. Each Party shall in exercising its national sovereignty have the right to withdraw from the Treaty if it decides that extraordinary events, related to the subject matter of this Treaty, have jeopardized the supreme interests of its country. It shall give notice of such withdrawal to all other Parties to the Treaty and to the United Nations Security Council three months in advance. Such notice shall include a statement of the extraordinary events it regards as having jeopardized its supreme interests.

2. Twenty-five years after the entry into force of the Treaty, a conference shall be convened to decide whether the Treaty shall continue in force indefinitely, or shall be extended for an additional fixed period or periods. This decision shall be taken by a majority of the Parties to the Treaty.

Article XI. [Deposit of Ratification]

DONE in triplicate, at the cities of Washington, London and Moscow, this first day of July one thousand nine hundred sixty-eight.

[U.S. Arms Control and Disarmament Agency, *Arms Control and Disarmament Agreements: Texts and Histories of the Negotiations,* 1982 ed. (Washington, D.C.), pp. 91–95]

International Atomic Energy Agency (IAEA)

United States "Atoms for Peace" Proposal (1953)

Address by President Eisenhower to the General Assembly, 8 December 1953

When Secretary General Hammarskjold's invitation to address this General Assembly reached me in Bermuda,[1] I was just beginning a series of conferences with the Prime Ministers and Foreign Ministers of Great Britain and of France. Our subject was some of the problems that beset our world.

During the remainder of the Bermuda Conference, I had constantly in mind that ahead of me lay a great honor. That honor is mine today as I stand here, privileged to address the General Assembly of the United Nations.

At the same time that I appreciate the distinction of addressing you, I have a sense of exhilaration as I look upon this Assembly.

Never before in history has so much hope for so many people been gathered together in a single organization. Your deliberations and decisions during these somber years have already realized part of those hopes.

But the great tests and the great accomplishments still lie ahead. And in the confident expectation of those accomplishments, I would use the office which, for the time being, I hold, to assure you that the Government of the United States will remain steadfast in its support of this body. This we shall do in the conviction that you will provide a great share of the wisdom, the courage, and the faith which can bring to this world lasting peace for all nations, and happiness and well being for all men.

Clearly, it would not be fitting for me to take this occasion to present to you a unilateral American report on Bermuda. Nevertheless, I assure you that in our deliberations on that lovely island we sought to invoke those same great concepts of universal peace and human dignity which are so cleanly etched in your Charter.

Neither would it be a measure of this great opportunity merely to recite, however hopefully, pious platitudes.

A Danger Shared by All

I therefore decided that this occasion warranted my saying to you some of the things that have been on the minds and hearts of my legislative and executive associates and on mine for a great many months—thoughts I had originally planned to say primarily to the American people.

I know that the American people share my deep belief that if a danger exists in the world, it is danger shared by all—and equally, that if hope exists in the mind of one nation, that hope should be shared by all.

Finally, if there is to be advanced any proposal designed to ease even by the smallest measure the tensions of today's world, what more appropriate audience could there be than the members of the General Assembly of the United Nations?

I feel impelled to speak today in a language that in a sense is new—one which I, who have spent so much of my life in the military profession, would have preferred never to use.

That new language is the language of atomic warfare.

The atomic age has moved forward at such a pace that every citizen of the world should have some comprehension, at least in comparative terms, of the extent of this development, of the utmost significance to every one of us. Clearly, if the peoples of the world are to conduct an intelligent search for peace, they must be armed with the significant facts of today's existence.

My recital of atomic danger and power is necessarily stated in United States terms, for these are the only incontrovertible facts that I know. I need hardly point out to this Assembly, however, that this subject is global, not merely national in character.

The Fearful Potentials

On July 16, 1945, the United States set off the world's first atomic explosion.

Since that date in 1945, the United States of America has conducted 42 test explosions.

Atomic bombs today are more than 25 times as powerful as the weapons with which the atomic age dawned, while hydrogen weapons are in the ranges of millions of tons of TNT equivalent.

Today, the United States' stockpile of atomic weapons, which, of course, increases daily, exceeds by many times the explosive equivalent of the total of all bombs and all shells that came from every plane and every gun in every theatre of war in all of the years of World War II.

A single air group, whether afloat or land-based, can now deliver to any reachable target a destructive cargo exceeding in power all the bombs that fell on Britain in all of World War II.

In size and variety, the development of atomic weapons has been no less remarkable. The development has been such that atomic weapons have virtually achieved conventional status within our armed services. In the United States, the Army, the Navy, the Air Force, and the Marine Corps are all capable of putting this weapon to military use.

But the dread secret, and the fearful engines of atomic might, are not ours alone.

In the first place, the secret is possessed by our friends and allies, Great Britain and Canada, whose scientific genius made a tremendous contribution to our original discoveries, and the designs of atomic bombs.

The secret is also known by the Soviet Union.

The Soviet Union has informed us that, over recent years, it has devoted extensive resources to atomic weapons. During this period, the Soviet Union has exploded a series of atomic devices, including at least one involving thermo-nuclear reactions.

No Monopoly of Atomic Power

If at one time the United States possessed what might have been called a monopoly of atomic power, that monopoly ceased to exist several years ago. Therefore, although our earlier start has permitted us to accumulate what is today a great quantitative advantage, the atomic realities of today comprehend two facts of even greater significance.

First, the knowledge now possessed by several nations will eventually be shared by others—possibly all others.

Second, even a vast superiority in numbers of weapons, and a consequent capability of devastating retaliation, is no preventive, of itself, against the fearful material damage and toll of human lives that would be inflicted by surprise aggression.

The free world, at least dimly aware of these facts, has naturally embarked on a large program of warning and defense systems. That program will be accelerated and expanded.

But let no one think that the expenditure of vast sums for weapons and systems of defense can guarantee absolute safety for the cities and citizens of any nation. The awful arithmetic of the atomic bomb does not permit of any such easy solution. Even against most powerful defense, an aggressor in possession of the effective minimum number of atomic bombs for a surprise attack could probably place a sufficient number of his bombs on the chosen targets to cause hideous damage.

Should such an atomic attack be launched against the United States, our reactions would be swift and resolute. But for me to say that the defense capabilities of the United States are such that they could inflict terrible losses upon an aggressor—for me to say that the retaliation capabilities of the United States are so great that such an aggressor's land would be laid waste—all this, while fact, is not the true expression of the purpose and the hope of the United States.

To pause there would be to confirm the hopeless finality of a belief that two atomic colossi are doomed malevolently to eye each other indefinitely across a trembling world. To stop there would be to accept helplessly the probability of civilization destroyed—the annihilation of the irreplaceable heritage of mankind handed down to us generation from generation—and the condemnation of mankind to begin all over again the age-old struggle upward from savagery toward decency, and right, and justice.

Surely no sane member of the human race could discover victory in such desolation. Could anyone wish his name to be coupled by history with such human degradation and destruction.

Occasional pages of history do record the faces of the "Great Destroyers" but the whole book of history reveals mankind's never-ending quest for peace, and mankind's God-given capacity to build.

It is with the book of history, and not with isolated pages, that the United States will ever wish to be identified. My country wants to be constructive, not destructive. It wants agreements, not wars, among nations. It wants itself to live in freedom, and in the confidence that the people of every other nation enjoy equally the right of choosing their own way of life.

No Idle Words or Shallow Visions

So my country's purpose is to help us move out of the dark chamber of horrors into the light, to find a way by which the minds of men, the hopes of men, the souls of men everywhere, can move forward toward peace and happiness and well being.

In this quest, I know that we must not lack patience.

I know that in a world divided, such as ours today, salvation cannot be attained by one dramatic act.

I know that many steps will have to be taken over many months before the world can look at itself one day and truly realize that a new climate of mutually peaceful confidence is abroad in the world.

But I know, above all else, that we must start to take these steps—NOW.

The United States and its allies, Great Britain and France, have over the past months tried to take some of these steps. Let no one say that we shun the conference table.

On the record has long stood the request of the United States, Great Britain, and France to negotiate with the Soviet Union the problems of a divided Germany.

On that record has long stood the request of the same three nations to negotiate an Austrian State Treaty.

On the same record still stands the request of the United Nations to negotiate the problems of Korea.

Most recently, we have received from the Soviet Union what is in effect an expression of willingness to hold a Four Power Meeting.[2] Along with our allies, Great Britain and France, we were pleased to see that this note did not contain the unacceptable pre-conditions previously put forward.

As you already know from our joint Bermuda communiqué, the United States, Great Britain, and France have agreed promptly to meet with the Soviet Union.

The Government of the United States approaches this conference with hopeful sincerity. We will bend every effort of our minds to the single purpose of emerging from that conference with tangible results toward peace—the only true way of lessening international tension.

We never have, we never will, propose or suggest that the Soviet Union surrender what is rightfully theirs.

We will never say that the peoples of Russia are an enemy with whom we have no desire ever to deal or mingle in friendly and fruitful relationship.

On the contrary, we hope that this Conference may initiate a relationship with the Soviet Union which will eventually bring about a free intermingling of the peoples of the East and of the West—the one sure, human way of developing the understanding required for confident and peaceful relations.

Instead of the discontent which is now settling upon Eastern Germany, occupied Austria, and the countries of Eastern Europe, we seek a harmonious family of free European nations, with none a threat to the other, and least of all a threat to the peoples of Russia.

Beyond the turmoil and strife and misery of Asia, we seek peaceful opportunity for these peoples to develop their natural resources and to elevate their lives.

These are not idle words or shallow visions. Behind them lies a story of nations lately come to independence, not as a result of war, but through free grant or peaceful negotiation. There is a record, already written, of assistance gladly given by nations of the West to needy peoples, and to those suffering the temporary effects of famine, drought, and natural disaster.

These are deeds of peace. They speak more loudly than promises or protestations of peaceful intent.

For the Benefit of Mankind

But I do not wish to rest either upon the reiteration of past proposals or the restatement of past deeds. The gravity of the time is such that every new avenue of peace, no matter how dimly discernible, should be explored.

There is at least one new avenue of peace which has not yet been well explored—an avenue now laid out by the General Assembly of the United Nations.

In its resolution of November 18th [*28*], 1953, this General Assembly suggested—and I quote—"that the Disarmament Commission study the desirability of establishing a sub-committee consisting of representatives of the Powers principally involved, which should seek in private an acceptable solution . . . and report on such a solution to the General Assembly and to the Security Council not later than 1 September 1954."[3]

The United States, heeding the suggestion of the General Assembly of the United Nations, is instantly prepared to meet privately with such other countries as may be "principally involved," to seek "an acceptable solution" to the atomic armaments race which overshadows not only the peace, but the very life, of the world.

We shall carry into these private or diplomatic talks a new conception.

The United States would seek more than the mere reduction or elimination of atomic materials for military purposes.

It is not enough to take this weapon out of the hands of the soldiers. It must be put into the hands of those who will know how to strip its military casing and adapt it to the arts of peace.

The United States knows that if the fearful trend of atomic military buildup can be reversed, this greatest of destructive forces can be developed into a great boon, for the benefit of all mankind.

The United States knows that peaceful power from atomic energy is no dream of the future. That capability, already proved, is here—now—today. Who can doubt, if the entire body of the world's scientists and engineers had adequate amounts of fissionable material with which to test and develop their ideas, that this capability would rapidly be transformed into universal, efficient, and economic usage.

To hasten the day when fear of the atom will begin to disappear from the minds of people, and the governments of the East and West, there are certain steps that can be taken now.

Proposal for Joint Atomic Contributions

I therefore make the following proposals:

The Governments principally involved, to the extent permitted by elementary prudence, to begin now and continue to make joint contributions from their stockpiles of normal uranium and fissionable materials to an International Atomic Energy Agency. We would expect that such an agency would be set up under the aegis of the United Nations.

The ratios of contributions, the procedures and other details would properly be within the scope of the "private conversations" I have referred to earlier.

The United States is prepared to undertake these explorations in good faith. Any partner of the United States acting in the same good faith will find the United States a not unreasonable or ungenerous associate.

Undoubtedly initial and early contributions to this plan would be small in quantity. However, the proposal has the great virtue that it can be undertaken without the irritations and mutual suspicions incident to any attempt to set up a completely acceptable system of world-wide inspection and control.

The Atomic Energy Agency could be made responsible for the impounding, storage, and protection of the contributed fissionable and other materials. The ingenuity of our scientists will provide special safe conditions under which such a bank of fissionable material can be made essentially immune to surprise seizure.

The more important responsibility of this Atomic Energy Agency would be to devise methods whereby this fissionable material would be allocated to serve the peaceful pursuits of mankind. Experts would be mobilized to apply atomic energy to the needs of agriculture, medicine, and other peaceful activities. A special purpose would be to provide abundant electrical energy in the power-starved areas of the world. Thus the contributing powers would be dedicating some of their strength to serve the needs rather than the fears of mankind.

The United States would be more than willing—it would be proud to take up with others "principally involved" the development of plans whereby such peaceful use of atomic energy would be expedited.

Of those "principally involved" the Soviet Union must, of course, be one.

Out of Fear and Into Peace

I would be prepared to submit to the Congress of the United States, and with every expectation of approval, any such plan that would:

First—encourage world-wide investigation into the most effective peacetime uses of fissionable material, and with the certainty that they had all the material needed for the conduct of all experiments that were appropriate;

Second—begin to diminish the potential destructive power of the world's atomic stockpiles;

Third—allow all peoples of all nations to see that, in this enlightened age, the great powers of the earth, both of the East and of the West, are interested in human aspirations first, rather than in building up the armaments of war;

Fourth—open up a new channel for peaceful discussion, and initiate at least a new approach to the many difficult problems that must be solved in both private and public conversations, if the world is to shake off the inertia imposed by fear, and is to make positive progress toward peace.

Against the dark background of the atomic bomb, the United States does not wish merely to present strength, but also the desire and the hope for peace.

The coming months will be fraught with fateful decisions. In this Assembly; in the capitals and military headquarters of the world; in the hearts of men everywhere, be they governors or governed, may they be the decisions which will lead this world out of fear and into peace.

To the making of these fateful decisions, the United States pledges before you—and therefore before the world—its determination to help solve the fearful atomic dilemma—to devote its entire heart and mind to find the way by which the miraculous inventiveness of man shall not be dedicated to his death, but consecrated to his life.

I again thank the delegates for the great honor they have done me, in inviting me to appear before them, and in listening to me so courteously.

Thank you.

[*Documents on Disarmament, 1945–1959,* vol. 1, doc. 92, "Atomic Power for Peace" (Department of State publication 5314; 1953)]

Notes

1. See communiqué of 7 December 1953 (*American Foreign Policy, 1950–1955: Basic Documents,* vol. 1, pp. 1468–1470).

2. Note of 26 November 1953, *Department of State Bulletin* (21 December 1953): 853–854.

3. *Documents on Disarmament, 1945–1959,* vol. 1, doc. 91.

IAEA Statute (1956)

Statute of the International Atomic Energy Agency, October 26, 1956

Article I. Establishment of the Agency

The Parties hereto establish an International Atomic Energy Agency (hereinafter referred to as "the Agency") upon the terms and conditions hereinafter set forth.

Article II. Objectives

The Agency shall seek to accelerate and enlarge the contribution of atomic energy to peace, health and prosperity throughout the world. It shall ensure, so far as it is able, that assistance provided by it or at its request or under its supervision or control is not used in such a way as to further any military purpose.

Article III. Functions

A. The Agency is authorized:

1. To encourage and assist research on, and development and practical application of, atomic energy for peaceful uses throughout the world; and, if requested to do so, to act as an intermediary for the purposes of securing the performance of services or the supplying of materials, equipment, or facilities by one member of the Agency for another; and to perform any operation or service useful in research on, or development or practical application of, atomic energy for peaceful purposes;

2. To make provision, in accordance with this Statute, for materials, services, equipment, and facilities to meet the needs of research on, and development and practical application of, atomic energy for peaceful purposes, including the production of electric power, with due consideration for the needs of the under-developed areas of the world;

3. To foster the exchange of scientific and technical information on peaceful uses of atomic energy;

4. To encourage the exchange and training of scientists and experts in the field of peaceful uses of atomic energy;

5. To establish and administer safeguards designed to ensure that special fissionable and other materials, services, equipment, facilities, and information made available by the Agency or at its request or under its supervision or control are not used in such a way as to further any military purpose; and to apply safeguards, at the request of the parties, to any bilateral or multilateral arrangement, or, at the request of a State, to any of that State's activities in the field of atomic energy;

6. To establish or adopt, in consultation and, where appropriate, in collaboration with the competent organs of the United Nations and with the specialized agencies concerned, standards of safety for protection of health and minimization of danger

to life and property (including such standards for labour conditions), and to provide for the application of these standards to its own operations as well as to the operations making use of materials, services, equipment, facilities, and information made available by the Agency or at its request or under its control or supervision; and to provide for the application of these standards, at the request of the parties, to operations under any bilateral or multilateral arrangement, or, at the request of a State, to any of that State's activities in the field of atomic energy;

7. To acquire or establish any facilities, plant and equipment useful in carrying out its authorized functions, whenever the facilities, plant, and equipment otherwise available to it in the area concerned are inadequate or available only on terms it deems unsatisfactory.

B. In carrying out its functions, the Agency shall:

1. Conduct its activities in accordance with the purposes and principles of the United Nations to promote peace and international cooperation, and in conformity with policies of the United Nations furthering the establishment of safeguarded worldwide disarmament and in conformity with any international agreements entered into pursuant to such policies;

2. Establish control over the use of special fissionable materials received by the Agency, in order to ensure that these materials are used only for peaceful purposes;

3. Allocate its resources in such a manner as to secure efficient utilization and the greatest possible general benefit in all areas of the world, bearing in mind the special needs of the underdeveloped areas of the world;

4. Submit reports on its activities annually to the General Assembly of the United Nations and, when appropriate, to the Security Council; if in connexion with the activities of the Agency there should arise questions that are within the competence of the Security Council, the Agency shall notify the Security Council, as the organ bearing the main responsibility for the maintenance of international peace and security, and may also take the measures open to it under this Statute, including those provided in paragraph C of article XII;

5. Submit reports to the Economic and Social Council and other organs of the United Nations on matters within the competence of these organs.

C. In carrying out its functions, the Agency shall not make assistance to members subject to any political, economic, military, or other conditions incompatible with the provisions of this Statute.

D. Subject to the provisions of this Statute and to the term of agreements concluded between a State or a group of States and the Agency which shall be in accordance with the provisions of the Statute, the activities of the Agency shall be carried out with due observance of the sovereign rights of States.

Article IV. Membership

A. The initial members of the Agency shall be those States Members of the United Nations or of any of the specialized agencies which shall have signed this Statute within ninety days after it is opened for signature and shall have deposited an instrument of ratification.

B. Other members of the Agency shall be those States, whether or not Members of the United Nations or of any of the specialized agencies, which deposit an instrument of acceptance of this Statute after their membership has been approved by the General Conference upon the recommendation of the Board of Governors. In recommending and approving a State for membership, the Board of Governors and the General Conference shall determine that the State is able and willing to carry out the obligations of membership in the Agency, giving due consideration to its ability and willingness to act in accordance with the purposes and principles of the Charter of the United Nations.

C. The Agency is based on the principle of the sovereign equality of all its members, and all members, in order to ensure to all of them the rights and benefits resulting from membership, shall fulfill in good faith the obligations assumed by them in accordance with this Statute.

Article V. General Conference

A. A General Conference consisting of representatives of all members shall meet in regular annual session and in such special sessions as shall be convened by the Director General at the request of the Board of Governors or of a majority of members. The sessions shall take place at the headquarters of the Agency unless otherwise determined by the General Conference.

B. At such sessions, each member shall be represented by one delegate who may be accompanied by alternates and by advisers. The cost of attendance of any delegation shall be borne by the member concerned.

C. The General Conference shall elect a President and such other officers as may be required at the beginning of each session. They shall hold office for the duration of the session. The General Conference, subject to the provisions of this Statute, shall adopt its own rules of procedure. Each member shall have one vote. Decisions pursuant to paragraph H of article XIV, paragraph C of article XVIII and paragraph B of article XIX shall be made by a two-thirds majority of the members present and voting. Decisions on other questions, including the determination of additional questions or categories of questions to be decided by a two-thirds majority, shall be made by a majority of the members present and voting. A majority of members shall constitute a quorum.

D. The General Conference may discuss any questions or any matters within the scope of this Statute or relating to the powers and functions of any organs provided for in this Statute, and may make recommendations to the membership of the Agency or to the Board of Governors or to both on any such questions or matters.

E. The General Conference shall:

1. Elect members of the Board of Governors in accordance with article VI;

2. Approve States for membership in accordance with article IV;

3. Suspend a member from the privileges and rights of membership in accordance with article XIX;

4. Consider the annual report of the Board;

5. In accordance with article XIV, approve the budget of the Agency recommended by the Board or return it with recommendations as to its entirety or parts to the Board, for resubmission to the General Conference;

6. Approve reports to be submitted to the United Nations as required by the relationship agreement between the Agency and the United Nations, except reports referred to in paragraph C of article XII, or return them to the Board with its recommendations;

7. Approve any agreement or agreements between the Agency and the United Nations and other organizations as provided in article XVI or return such agreements with its recommendations to the Board, for resubmission to the General Conference;

8. Approve rules and limitations regarding the exercise of borrowing powers by the Board, in accordance with paragraph G of article XIV; approve rules regarding the acceptance of voluntary contributions to the Agency; and approve, in accordance with paragraph F of article XIV, the manner in which the general fund referred to in that paragraph may be used;

9. Approve amendments to this Statute in accordance with paragraph C of article XVIII;

10. Approve the appointment of the Director General in accordance with paragraph A of article VII.

F. The General Conference shall have the authority:

1. To take decisions on any matter specifically referred to the General Conference for this purpose by the Board;

2. To propose matters for consideration by the Board and request from the Board reports on any matters relating to the functions of the Agency.

Article VI. Board of Governors

A. The Board of Governors shall be composed as follows:

1. The outgoing Board of Governors (or in the case of the first Board, the Preparatory Commission referred to in Annex I) shall designate for membership on the Board the five members most advanced in the technology of atomic energy including the production of source materials and the member most advanced in the technology of atomic energy including the production of source materials in each of the following areas not represented by the aforesaid five:

(1) North America
(2) Latin America
(3) Western Europe
(4) Eastern Europe
(5) Africa and the Middle East
(6) South Asia
(7) South East Asia and the Pacific
(8) Far East.

2. The outgoing Board of Governors (or in the case of the first Board, the Preparatory Commission referred to in Annex I) shall designate for membership on the Board two members from among the following other producers of source materials: Belgium, Czechoslovakia, Poland, and Portugal; and shall also designate for membership on the Board one other member as a supplier of technical assistance. No member in this category in any one year will be eligible for redesignation in the same category for the following year.

3. The General Conference shall elect ten members to membership on the Board of Governors, with due regard to equitable representation on the

Board as a whole of the members in the areas listed in sub-paragraph A-1 of this article, so that the Board shall at all times include in this category a representative of each of those areas except North America. Except for the five members chosen for a term of one year in accordance with paragraph D of this article, no member in this category in any one term of office will be eligible for re-election in the same category for the following term of office.

B. The designations provided for in subparagraphs A-1 and A-2 of this article shall take place not less than sixty days before each regular annual session of the General Conference. The elections provided for in sub-paragraph A-3 of this article shall take place at regular annual sessions of the General Conference.

C. Members represented on the Board of Governors in accordance with subparagraphs A-1 and A-2 of this article shall hold office from the end of the next regular annual session of the General Conference after their designation until the end of the following regular annual session of the General Conference.

D. Members represented on the Board of Governors in accordance with subparagraph A-3 of this article shall hold office from the end of the regular annual session of the General Conference at which they are elected until the end of the second regular annual session of the General Conference thereafter. In the election of these members for the first Board, however, five shall be chosen for a term of one year.

E. Each member of the Board of Governors shall have one vote. Decisions on the amount of the Agency's budget shall be made by a two-thirds majority of those present and voting, as provided in paragraph H of article XIV. Decisions on other questions, including the determination of additional questions or categories of questions to be decided by a two-thirds majority, shall be made by a majority of those present and voting. Two-thirds of all members of the Board shall constitute a quorum.

F. The Board of Governors shall have authority to carry out the functions of the Agency in accordance with this Statute, subject to its responsibilities to the General Conference as provided in this Statute.

G. The Board of Governors shall meet at such times as it may determine. The meetings shall take place at the headquarters of the Agency unless otherwise determined by the Board.

H. The Board of Governors shall elect a Chairman and other officers from among its members

and, subject to the provisions of this Statute, shall adopt its own rules of procedure.

I. The Board of Governors may establish such committees as it deems advisable. The Board may appoint persons to represent it in its relations with other organizations.

J. The Board of Governors shall prepare an annual report to the General Conference concerning the affairs of the Agency and any projects approved by the Agency. The Board shall also prepare for submission to the General Conference such reports as the Agency is or may be required to make to the United Nations or to any other organization the work of which is related to that of the Agency. These reports, along with the annual reports, shall be submitted to members of the Agency at least one month before the regular annual session of the General Conference.

Article VII. Staff

A. The staff of the Agency shall be headed by a Director General. The Director General shall be appointed by the Board of Governors with the approval of the General Conference for a term of four years. He shall be the chief administrative officer of the Agency.

B. The Director General shall be responsible for the appointment, organization, and functioning of the staff and shall be under the authority of and subject to the control of the Board of Governors. He shall perform his duties in accordance with regulations adopted by the Board.

C. The staff shall include such qualified scientific and technical and other personnel as may be required to fulfil the objectives and functions of the Agency. The Agency shall be guided by the principle that its permanent staff shall be kept to a minimum.

D. The paramount consideration in the recruitment and employment of the staff and in the determination of the conditions of service shall be to secure employees of the highest standards of efficiency, technical competence, and integrity. Subject to this consideration, due regard shall be paid to the contributions of members to the Agency and to the importance of recruiting the staff on as wide a geographical basis as possible.

E. The terms and conditions on which the staff shall be appointed, remunerated, and dismissed shall be in accordance with regulations made by the Board of Governors, subject to the provisions of this Statute and to general rules approved by the

General Conference on the recommendation of the Board.

F. In the performance of their duties, the Director General and the staff shall not seek or receive instructions from any source external to the Agency. They shall refrain from any action which might reflect on their position as officials of the Agency; subject to their responsibilities to the Agency, they shall not disclose any industrial secret or other confidential information coming to their knowledge by reason of their official duties for the Agency. Each member undertakes to respect the international character of the responsibilities of the Director General and the staff and shall not seek to influence them in the discharge of their duties.

G. In this article the term "staff" includes guards.

Article VIII. Exchange of Information

A. Each member should make available such information as would, in the judgment of the member, be helpful to the Agency.

B. Each member shall make available to the Agency all scientific information developed as a result of assistance extended by the Agency pursuant to article XI.

C. The Agency shall assemble and make available in an accessible form the information made available to it under paragraphs A and B of this article. It shall take positive steps to encourage the exchange among its members of information relating to the nature and peaceful uses of atomic energy and shall serve as an intermediary among its members for this purpose.

Article IX. Supplying of Materials

A. Members may make available to the Agency such quantities of special fissionable materials as they deem advisable and on such terms as shall be agreed with the Agency. The materials made available to the Agency may, at the discretion of the member making them available, be stored either by the member concerned or, with the agreement of the Agency, in the Agency's depots.

B. Members may also make available to the Agency source materials as defined in article XX and other materials. The Board of Governors shall determine the quantities of such materials which the Agency will accept under agreements provided for in article XIII.

C. Each member shall notify the Agency of the quantities, form, and composition of special fissionable materials, source materials, and other materials which that member is prepared, in conformity

with its laws, to make available immediately or during a period specified by the Board of Governors.

D. On request of the Agency a member shall, from the materials which it has made available, without delay deliver to another member or group of members such quantities of such materials as the Agency may specify, and shall without delay deliver to the Agency itself such quantities of such materials as are really necessary for operations and scientific research in the facilities of the Agency.

E. The quantities, form and composition of materials made available by any member may be changed at any time by the member with the approval of the Board of Governors.

F. An initial notification in accordance with paragraph C of this article shall be made within three months of the entry into force of this Statute with respect to the member concerned. In the absence of a contrary decision of the Board of Governors, the materials initially made available shall be for the period of the calendar year succeeding the year when this Statute takes effect with respect to the member concerned. Subsequent notifications shall likewise, in the absence of a contrary action by the Board, relate to the period of the calendar year following the notification and shall be made no later than the first day of November of each year.

G. The Agency shall specify the place and method of delivery and, where appropriate, the form and composition, of materials which it has requested a member to deliver from the amounts which that member has notified the Agency it is prepared to make available. The Agency shall also verify the quantities of materials delivered and shall report those quantities periodically to the members.

H. The Agency shall be responsible for storing and protecting materials in its possession. The Agency shall ensure that these materials shall be safeguarded against (1) hazards of the weather, (2) unauthorized removal or diversion, (3) damage or destruction, including sabotage, and (4) forcible seizure. In storing special fissionable materials in its possession, the Agency shall ensure the geographical distribution of these materials in such a way as not to allow concentration of large amounts of such materials in any one country or region of the world.

I. The Agency shall as soon as practicable establish or acquire such of the following as may be necessary:

1. Plant, equipment, and facilities for the receipt, storage, and issue of materials;

2. Physical safeguards;

3. Adequate health and safety measures;

4. Control laboratories for the analysis and verification of materials received;

5. Housing and administrative facilities for any staff required for the foregoing.

J. The materials made available pursuant to this article shall be used as determined by the Board of Governors in accordance with the provisions of this Statute. No member shall have the right to require that the materials it makes available to the Agency be kept separately by the Agency or to designate the specific project in which they must be used.

Article X. Services, equipment, and facilities. Members may make available to the Agency services, equipment, and facilities which may be of assistance in fulfilling the Agency's objectives and functions.

Article XI. Agency projects

A. Any member or group of members of the Agency desiring to set up any project for research on, or development or practical application of, atomic energy for peaceful purposes may request the assistance of the Agency in securing special fissionable and other materials, services, equipment, and facilities necessary for this purpose. Any such request shall be accompanied by an explanation of the purpose and extent of the project and shall be considered by the Board of Governors.

B. Upon request, the Agency may also assist any member or group of members to make arrangements to secure necessary financing from outside sources to carry out such projects. In extending this assistance, the Agency will not be required to provide any guarantees or to assume any financial responsibility for the project.

C. The Agency may arrange for the supplying of any materials, services, equipment, and facilities necessary for the project by one or more members or may itself undertake to provide any or all of these directly, taking into consideration the wishes of the member or members making the request.

D. For the purpose of considering the request, the Agency may send into the territory of the member or group of members making the request a person or persons qualified to examine the project. For this purpose the Agency may, with the approval of the member or group of members making the request, use members of its own staff or employ suitably qualified nationals of any member.

E. Before approving a project under this article, the Board of Governors shall give due consideration to:

1. The usefulness of the project, including its scientific and technical feasibility;

2. The adequacy of plans, funds, and technical personnel to assure the effective execution of the project;

3. The adequacy of proposed health and safety standards for handling and storing materials and for operating facilities;

4. The inability of the member or group of members making the request to secure the necessary finances, materials, facilities, equipment, and services;

5. The equitable distribution of materials and other resources available to the Agency;

6. The special needs of the under-developed areas of the world; and

7. Such other matters as may be relevant.

F. Upon approving a project, the Agency shall enter into an agreement with the member or group of members submitting the project, which agreement shall:

1. Provide for allocation to the project of any required special fissionable or other materials;

2. Provide for transfer of special fissionable materials from their then place of custody, whether the materials be in the custody of the Agency or of the member making them available for use in Agency projects, to the member or group of members submitting the project, under conditions which ensure the safety of any shipment required and meet applicable health and safety standards;

3. Set forth the terms and conditions, including charges, on which any materials, services, equipment, and facilities are to be provided by the Agency itself, and, if any such materials, services, equipment, and facilities are to be provided by a member, the terms and conditions as arranged for by the member or group of members submitting the project and the supplying member;

4. Include undertakings by the member or group of members submitting the project: (a) that the assistance provided shall not be used in such a way as to further any military purpose; and (b) that the project shall be subject to the safeguards provided for in article XII, the relevant safeguards being specified in the agreement;

5. Make appropriate provision regarding the rights and interests of the Agency and the member or members concerned in any inventions or dis-

coveries, or any patents therein, arising from the project;

6. Make appropriate provision regarding settlement of disputes;

7. Include such other provisions as may be appropriate.

G. The provisions of this article shall also apply where appropriate to a request for materials, services, facilities, or equipment in connexion with an existing project.

Article XII. Agency Safeguards

A. With respect to any Agency project, or other arrangement where the Agency is requested by the parties concerned to apply safeguards, the Agency shall have the following rights and responsibilities to the extent relevant to the project or arrangement:

1. To examine the design of specialized equipment and facilities including nuclear reactors, and to approve it only from the viewpoint of assuring that it will not further any military purpose, that it complies with applicable health and safety standards, and that it will permit effective application of the safeguards provided for in this article;

2. To require the observance of any health and safety measures prescribed by the Agency;

3. To require the maintenance and production of operating records to assist in ensuring accountability for source and special fissionable materials used or produced in the project or arrangement;

4. To call for and receive progress reports;

5. To approve the means to be used for the chemical processing of irradiated materials solely to ensure that this chemical processing will not lend itself to diversion of materials for military purposes and will comply with applicable health and safety standards; to require that special fissionable materials recovered or produced as a by-product be used for peaceful purposes under continuing Agency safeguards for research or in reactors, existing or under construction, specified by the member or members concerned; and to require deposit with the Agency of any excess of any special fissionable materials recovered or produced as a by-product over what is needed for the above-stated uses in order to prevent stockpiling of these materials, provided that thereafter at the request of the member or members concerned special fissionable materials so deposited with the Agency shall be returned promptly to the member or members concerned for use under the same provisions as stated above;

6. To send into the territory of the recipient State or States inspectors, designated by the Agency after consultation with the State or States concerned, who shall have access at all times to all places and data and to any person who by reason of his occupation deals with materials, equipment, or facilities which are required by this Statute to be safeguarded, as necessary to account for source and special fissionable materials supplied and fissionable products and to determine whether there is compliance with the undertaking against use in furtherance of any military purpose referred to in sub-paragraph F-4 of article XI, with the health and safety measures referred to in sub-paragraph A-2 of this article, and with any other conditions prescribed in the agreement between the Agency and the State or States concerned. Inspectors designated by the Agency shall be accompanied by representatives of the authorities of the State concerned, if that State so requests, provided that the inspectors shall not thereby be delayed or otherwise impeded in the exercise of their functions;

7. In the event of non-compliance and failure by the recipient State or States to take requested corrective steps within a reasonable time, to suspend or terminate assistance and withdraw any materials and equipment made available by the Agency or a member in furtherance of the project.

B. The Agency shall, as necessary, establish a staff of inspectors. The staff of inspectors shall have the responsibility of examining all operations conducted by the Agency itself to determine whether the Agency is complying with the health and safety measures prescribed by it for application to projects subject to its approval, supervision or control, and whether the Agency is taking adequate measures to prevent the source and special fissionable materials in its custody or used or produced in its own operations from being used in furtherance of any military purpose. The Agency shall take remedial action forthwith to correct any non-compliance or failure to take adequate measures.

C. The staff of inspectors shall also have the responsibility of obtaining and verifying the accounting referred to in sub-paragraph A-6 of this article and of determining whether there is compliance with the undertaking referred to in sub-paragraph F-4 of article XI, with the measures referred to in sub-paragraph A-2 of this article, and with all other conditions of the project prescribed in the agreement between the Agency and the State or States concerned. The inspectors shall report any non-compliance to the Director General who shall thereupon transmit the report to the Board of Governors. The Board shall call upon the recipient

State or States to remedy forthwith any non-compliance which it finds to have occurred. The Board shall report the non-compliance to all members and to the Security Council and General Assembly of the United Nations. In the event of failure of the recipient State or States to take fully corrective action within a reasonable time, the Board may take one or both of the following measures: direct curtailment or suspension of assistance being provided by the Agency or by a member, and call for the return of materials and equipment made available to the recipient member or group of members. The Agency may also, in accordance with article XIX, suspend any non-complying member from the exercise of the privileges and rights of membership.

Article XIII. Reimbursement of Members. Unless otherwise agreed upon between the Board of Governors and the member furnishing to the Agency materials, services, equipment, or facilities, the Board shall enter into an agreement with such member providing for reimbursement for the items furnished.

Article XIV. Finance

A. The Board of Governors shall submit to the General Conference the annual budget estimates for the expenses of the Agency. To facilitate the work of the Board in this regard, the Director General shall initially prepare the budget estimates. If the General Conference does not approve the estimates, it shall return them together with its recommendations to the Board. The Board shall then submit further estimates to the General Conference for its approval.

B. Expenditures of the Agency shall be classified under the following categories:

1. Administrative expenses: these shall include:

(a) Costs of the staff of the Agency other than the staff employed in connexion with materials, services, equipment, and facilities referred to in sub-paragraph B-2 below; costs of meetings; and expenditures required for the preparation of Agency projects and for the distribution of information;

(b) Costs of implementing the safeguards referred to in article XII in relation to Agency projects or, under sub-paragraph A-5 of article III, in relation to any bilateral or multilateral arrangement, together with the costs of handling and storage of special fissionable material by the Agency other than the storage and handling charges referred to in paragraph E below;

2. Expenses, other than those included in sub-paragraph 1 of this paragraph, in connexion with any materials, facilities, plant, and equipment acquired or established by the Agency in carrying out its authorized functions, and the costs of materials, services, equipment, and facilities provided by it under agreements with one or more members.

C. In fixing the expenditures under sub-paragraph B-1(b) above, the Board of Governors shall deduct such amounts as are recoverable under agreements regarding the application of safeguards between the Agency and parties to bilateral or multilateral arrangements.

D. The Board of Governors shall apportion the expenses referred to in sub-paragraph B-1 above, among members in accordance with a scale to be fixed by the General Conference. In fixing the scale the General Conference shall be guided by the principles adopted by the United Nations in assessing contributions of Member States to the regular budget of the United Nations.

E. The Board of Governors shall establish periodically a scale of charges, including reasonable uniform storage and handling charges, for materials, services, equipment, and facilities furnished to members by the Agency. The scale shall be designed to produce revenues for the Agency adequate to meet the expenses and costs referred to in sub-paragraph B-2 above, less any voluntary contributions which the Board of Governors may, in accordance with paragraph F, apply for this purpose. The proceeds of such charges shall be placed in a separate fund which shall be used to pay members for any materials, services, equipment, or facilities furnished by them and to meet other expenses referred to in sub-paragraph B-2 above which may be incurred by the Agency itself.

F. Any excess of revenues referred to in paragraph E over the expenses and costs there referred to, and any voluntary contributions to the Agency, shall be placed in a general fund which may be used as the Board of Governors, with the approval of the General Conference, may determine.

G. Subject to rules and limitations approved by the General Conference, the Board of Governors shall have the authority to exercise borrowing powers on behalf of the Agency without, however, imposing on members of the Agency any liability in respect of loans entered into pursuant to this authority, and to accept voluntary contributions made to the Agency.

H. Decisions of the General Conference on financial questions and of the Board of Governors on the amount of the Agency's budget shall require a two-thirds majority of those present and voting.

Article XV. Privileges and Immunities

A. The Agency shall enjoy in the territory of each member such legal capacity and such privileges and immunities as are necessary for the exercise of its functions.

B. Delegates of members together with their alternates and advisers, Governors appointed to the Board together with their alternates and advisers, and the Director General and the staff of the Agency, shall enjoy such privileges and immunities as are necessary in the independent exercise of their functions in connexion with the Agency.

C. The legal capacity, privileges, and immunities referred to in this article shall be defined in a separate agreement or agreements between the Agency, represented for this purpose by the Director General acting under instructions of the Board of Governors, and the members.

Article XVI. Relationship with Other Organizations

A. The Board of Governors, with the approval of the General Conference, is authorized to enter into an agreement or agreements establishing an appropriate relationship between the Agency and the United Nations and any other organizations the work of which is related to that of the Agency.

B. The agreement or agreements establishing the relationship of the Agency and the United Nations shall provide for:

1. Submission by the Agency of reports as provided for in sub-paragraphs B-4 and B-5 of article III;

2. Consideration by the Agency of resolutions relating to it adopted by the General Assembly or any of the Councils of the United Nations and the submission of reports, when requested, to the appropriate organ of the United Nations on the action taken by the Agency or by its members in accordance with this Statute as a result of such consideration.

Article XVII. Settlement of Disputes

A. Any question or dispute concerning the interpretation or application of this Statute which is not settled by negotiation shall be referred to the International Court of Justice in conformity with the Statute of the Court, unless the parties concerned agree on another mode of settlement.

B. The General Conference and the Board of Governors are separately empowered, subject to authorization from the General Assembly of the United Nations, to request the International Court of Justice to give an advisory opinion on any legal question arising within the scope of the Agency's activities.

Article XVIII. Amendments and Withdrawals

A. Amendments to this Statute may be proposed by any member. Certified copies of the text of any amendment proposed shall be prepared by the Director General and communicated by him to all members at least ninety days in advance of its consideration by the General Conference.

B. At the fifth annual session of the General Conference following the coming into force of this Statute, the question of a general review of the provisions of this Statute shall be placed on the agenda of that session. On approval by a majority of the members present and voting, the review will take place at the following General Conference. Thereafter, proposals on the question of a general review of this Statute may be submitted for decision by the General Conference under the same procedure.

C. Amendments shall come into force for all members when:

(i) Approved by the General Conference by a two-thirds majority of those present and voting after consideration of observations submitted by the Board of Governors on each proposed amendment, and

(ii) Accepted by two-thirds of all the members in accordance with their respective constitutional processes. Acceptance by a member shall be effected by the deposit of an instrument of acceptance with the depositary Government referred to in paragraph C of article XXI.

D. At any time after five years from the date when this Statute shall take effect in accordance with paragraph E of article XXI or whenever a member is unwilling to accept an amendment to this Statute, it may withdraw from the Agency by notice in writing to that effect given to the depositary Government referred to in paragraph C of article XXI, which shall promptly inform the Board of Governors and all members.

E. Withdrawal by a member from the Agency shall not affect its contractual obligations entered into pursuant to article XI or its budgetary obligations for the year in which it withdraws.

Article XIX. Suspension of Privileges

A. A member of the Agency which is in arrears in the payment of its financial contributions to the Agency shall have no vote in the Agency if the amount of its arrears equals or exceeds the amount of the contributions due from it for the preceding two years. The General Conference may, nevertheless, permit such a member to vote if it is satisfied that the failure to pay is due to conditions beyond the control of the member.

B. A member which has persistently violated the provisions of this Statute or of any agreement entered into by it pursuant to this Statute may be suspended from the exercise of the privileges and rights of membership by the General Conference acting by a two-thirds majority of the members present and voting upon recommendation by the Board of Governors.

Article XX. Definitions

As used in this Statute:

1. The term "special fissionable material" means plutonium-239; uranium-233; uranium enriched in the isotopes 235 or 233; any material containing one or more of the foregoing; and such other fissionable material as the Board of Governors shall from time to time determine; but the term "special fissionable material" does not include source material.

2. The term "uranium enriched in the isotopes 235 or 233" means uranium containing the isotopes 235 or 233 or both in an amount such that the abundance ratio of the sum of these isotopes to the isotope 238 is greater than the ratio of the isotope 235 to the isotope 238 occurring in nature.

[U.S. Senate, Hearings before the Committee on Foreign Relations, 10, 14, 15, and 20 May 1957 (85th Cong., 1st Sess.), *Statute of the International Atomic Energy Agency* (Washington, D.C.: G.P.O., 1957)]

The United States Adheres to IAEA (1980)

This agreement was signed at Vienna on 18 November 1977, and ratification was advised by the U.S. Senate on 2 July 1980. It was ratified by U.S. President Jimmy Carter on 31 July 1980, and it entered into force on 9 December 1980. Its official title is Agreement Between the United States of America and the International Atomic Energy Agency for the Application of Safeguards in the United States, proclaimed by U.S. President Jimmy Carter on 31 December 1980.

Whereas the United States of America (hereinafter referred to as the "United States") is a Party to the Treaty on the Non-Proliferation of Nuclear Weapons (hereinafter referred to as the "Treaty") which was opened for signature at London, Moscow and Washington on 1 July 1968 and which entered into force on 5 March 1970;[1]

Whereas States Parties to the Treaty undertake to co-operate in facilitating the application of International Atomic Energy Agency (hereinafter referred to as the "Agency") safeguards on peaceful nuclear activities;

Whereas non-nuclear-weapon States Parties to the Treaty under ake to accept safeguards, as set forth in an agreement to be negotiated and concluded with the Agency, on all source or special fissionable material in all their peaceful nuclear activities for the exclusive purpose of verification of the fulfillment of their obligations under the Treaty with a view to preventing diversion of nuclear energy from peaceful uses to nuclear weapons or other nuclear explosive devices;

Whereas the United States, a nuclear-weapon State as defined by the Treaty, has indicated that at such time as safeguards are being generally applied in accordance with paragraph 1 of Article III of the Treaty, the United States will permit the Agency to apply its safeguards to all nuclear activities in the United States—excluding only those with direct national security significance—by concluding a safeguards agreement with the Agency for that purpose;

Whereas the United States has made this offer and has entered into this agreement for the purpose of encouraging widespread adherence to the Treaty by demonstrating to non-nuclear-weapon States that they would not be placed at a commercial disadvantage by reason of the application of safeguards pursuant to the Treaty;

Whereas the purpose of a safeguards agreement giving effect to this offer by the United States would thus differ necessarily from the purposes of safeguards agreements concluded between the Agency and non-nuclear-weapon States Party to the Treaty;

Whereas it is in the interest of Members of the Agency, that, without prejudice to the principles and integrity of the Agency's safeguards system, the expenditure of the Agency's financial and other resources for implementation of such an agreement not exceed that necessary to accomplish the purpose of the Agreement;

Whereas the Agency is authorized, pursuant to Article III of the Statute of the International Atomic Energy Agency[2] (hereinafter referred to as the "Statute"), to conclude such a safeguards agreement;

Now, therefore, the United States and the Agency have agreed as follows:

PART I

Article 1

(a) The United States undertakes to permit the Agency to apply safeguards, in accordance with the terms of this Agreement, on all source or special fissionable material in all facilities within the United States, excluding only those facilities associated with activities with direct national security significance to the United States, with a view to enabling the Agency to verify that such material is not withdrawn, except as provided for in this Agreement, from activities in facilities while such material is being safeguarded under this Agreement.

(b) The United States shall, upon entry in force of this Agreement, provide the Agency with a list of facilities within the United States not associated with activities with direct national security significance to the United States and may, in accordance with the procedures set forth in Part II of this Agreement, add facilities to or remove facilities from that list as it deems appropriate.

(c) The United States may, in accordance with the procedures set forth in this Agreement, withdraw nuclear material from activities in facilities included in the list referred to in Article 1(b).

Article 2

(a) The Agency shall have the right to apply safeguards, in accordance with the terms of this Agreement, on all source or special fissionable material in all facilities within the United States, excluding only those facilities associated with activities with direct national security significance to the United

States, with a view to enabling the Agency to verify that such material is not withdrawn, except as provided for in this Agreement, from activities in facilities while such material is being safeguarded under this Agreement.

(b) The Agency shall, from time to time, identify to the United States those facilities, selected from the then current list provided by the United States in accordance with Article 1(b), in which the Agency wishes to apply safeguards, in accordance with the terms of this Agreement.

(c) In identifying facilities and in applying safeguards thereafter on source or special fissionable material in such facilities, the Agency shall proceed in a manner which the Agency and the United States mutually agree takes into account the requirement on the United States to avoid discriminatory treatment as between United States commercial firms similarly situated.

Article 3

(a) The United States and the Agency shall cooperate to facilitate the implementation of the safeguards provided for in this Agreement.

(b) The source or special fissionable material subject to safeguards under this Agreement shall be that material in those facilities which shall have been identified by the Agency at any given time pursuant to Article 2(b).

(c) The safeguards to be applied by the Agency under this Agreement on source or special fissionable material in facilities in the United States shall be implemented by the same procedures followed by the Agency in applying its safeguards on similar material in similar facilities in non-nuclear-weapon States under agreements pursuant to paragraph 1 of Article III of the Treaty.

Article 4. The safeguards provided for in this Agreement shall be implemented in a manner designed:

(a) To avoid hampering the economic and technological development of the United States or international co-operation in the field of peaceful nuclear activities, including international exchange of nuclear material;

(b) To avoid undue interference in peaceful nuclear activities of the United States and in particular in the operation of facilities; and

(c) To be consistent with prudent management practices required for the economic and safe conduct of nuclear activities.

Article 5

(a) The agency shall take every precaution to protect commercial and industrial secrets and other confidential information coming to its knowledge in the implementation of this Agreement.

(b) (i) The Agency shall not publish or communicate to any State, organization or person any information obtained by it in connection with the implementation of this Agreement, except that specific information relating to the implementation thereof may be given to the Board of Governors of the Agency (hereinafter referred to as "the Board") and to such Agency staff members as require such knowledge by reason of their official duties in connection with safeguards, but only to the extent necessary for the Agency to fulfill its responsibilities in implementing this Agreement.

(ii) Summarized information on nuclear material subject to safeguards under this Agreement may be published upon the decision of the Board if the United States agrees thereto.

Article 6

(a) The Agency shall, in implementing safeguards pursuant to this Agreement, take full account of technological developments in the field of safeguards, and shall make every effort to ensure optimum cost-effectiveness and the application of the principle of safeguarding effectively the flow of nuclear material subject to safeguards under this Agreement by use of instruments and other techniques at certain strategic points to the extent that present or future technology permits.

(b) In order to ensure optimum cost-effectiveness, use shall be made, for example, of such means as:

(i) Containment as a means of defining material balance areas for accounting purposes;

(ii) Statistical techniques and random sampling in evaluating the flow of nuclear material; and

(iii) Concentration of verification procedures on those stages in the nuclear fuel cycle involving the production, processing, use or storage of nuclear material from which nuclear weapons or other nuclear explosive devices could readily be made, and minimization of verification procedures in respect of other nuclear material, on condition that this does not hamper the Agency in applying safeguards under this Agreement.

Article 7

(a) The United States shall establish and maintain a system of accounting for and control of all nuclear material subject to safeguards under this Agreement.

(b) The Agency shall apply safeguards in accordance with Article 3(c) in such a manner as to enable the Agency to verify, in ascertaining that there has been no withdrawal of nuclear material, except as provided for in this Agreement, from activities in facilities while such material is being safeguarded under this Agreement, findings of the accounting and control system of the United States. The Agency's verification shall include, inter alia, independent measurements and observations conducted by the Agency in accordance with the procedures specified in Part II. The Agency, in its verification, shall take due account of the technical effectiveness of the system of the United States.

Article 8

(a) In order to ensure the effective implementation of safeguards under this Agreement, the United States shall, in accordance with the provisions set out in Part II, provide the Agency with information concerning nuclear material subject to safeguards under this Agreement and the features of facilities relevant to safeguarding such material.

(b) (i) The Agency shall require only the minimum amount of information and data consistent with carrying out its responsibilities under this Agreement.

(ii) Information pertaining to facilities shall be the minimum necessary for safeguarding nuclear material subject to safeguards under this Agreement.

(c) If the United States so requests, the Agency shall be prepared to examine on premises of the United States design information which the United States regards as being of particular sensitivity. Such information need not be physically transmitted to the Agency provided that it remains readily available for further examination by the Agency on premises of the United States.

Article 9

(a) (i) The Agency shall secure the consent of the United States to the designation of Agency inspectors to the United States.

(ii) If the United States, either upon proposal of a designation or at any other time after designation has been made, objects to the designation, the Agency shall propose to the United States an alternative designation or designations.

(iii) If, as a result of the repeated refusal of the United States to accept the designation of Agency inspectors, inspections to be conducted under this Agreement would be impeded, such refusal shall be considered by the Board, upon referral by the Director General of the Agency (hereinafter referred to as "the Director General") with a view to its taking appropriate action.

(b) The United States shall take the necessary steps to ensure that Agency inspectors can effectively discharge their functions under this Agreement.

(c) The visits and activities of Agency inspectors shall be so arranged as:

(i) To reduce to a minimum the possible inconvenience and disturbance to the United States and to the peaceful nuclear activities inspected; and

(ii) To ensure protection of industrial secrets or any other confidential information coming to the inspectors' knowledge.

Article 10. The provisions of the International Organizations Immunities Act of the United States of America[3] shall apply to Agency inspectors performing functions in the United States under this Agreement and to any property of the Agency used by them.

Article 11. Safeguards shall terminate on nuclear material upon determination by the Agency that the material has been consumed, or has been diluted in such a way that it is no longer usable for any nuclear activity relevant from the point of view of safeguards, or has become practically irrecoverable.

Article 12

(a) If the United States intends to exercise its right to withdraw nuclear material from activities in facilities identified by the Agency pursuant to Articles 2(b) and 39(b) other than those facilities removed, pursuant to Article 34(b)(i) from the list provided for by Article 1(b) and to transfer such material to a destination in the United States other than to a facility included in the list established and maintained pursuant to Articles 1(b) and 34, the United States shall notify the Agency in advance of such withdrawal. Nuclear material in respect of which such notification has been given shall cease to be subject to safeguards under this Agreement as from the time of its withdrawal.

(b) Nothing in this Agreement shall effect the right of the United States to transfer material subject to safeguards under this Agreement to destinations not within or under the jurisdiction of the United States. The United States shall provide the Agency with information with respect to such trans-

fers in accordance with Article 89. The Agency shall keep records of each such transfer and, where applicable, of the reapplication of safeguards to the transferred nuclear material.

Article 13. Where nuclear material subject to safeguards under this Agreement is to be used in non-nuclear activities, such as the production of alloys or ceramics, the United States shall agree with the Agency, before the material is so used, on the circumstances under which the safeguards on such material may be terminated.

Article 14. The United States and the Agency will bear the expenses incurred by them in implementing their respective responsibilities under this Agreement. However, if the United States or persons under its jurisdiction incur extraordinary expenses as a result of a specific request by the Agency, the Agency shall reimburse such expenses provided that it has agreed in advance to do so. In any case the Agency shall bear the cost of any additional measuring or sampling which inspectors may request.

Article 15. In carrying out its functions under this Agreement within the United States, the Agency and its personnel shall be covered to the same extent as nationals of the United States by any protection against third-party liability provided under the Price-Anderson Act,[4] including insurance or other indemnity coverage that may be required by the Price-Anderson Act with respect to nuclear incidents.

Article 16. Any claim by the United States against the Agency or by the Agency against the United States in respect of any damage resulting from the implementation of safeguards under this Agreement, other than damage arising out of a nuclear incident, shall be settled in accordance with international law.

Article 17. If the Board, upon report of the Director General, decides that an action by the United States is essential and urgent in order to ensure compliance with this Agreement, the Board may call upon the United States to take the required action without delay, irrespective of whether procedures have been invoked pursuant to Article 21 for the settlement of a dispute.

Article 18. If the Board, upon examination of relevant information reported to it by the Director General, determines there has been any non-compliance with this Agreement, the Board may call upon the United States to remedy forthwith such non-compliance. In the event there is a failure to take fully corrective action within a reasonable time, the Board may make the reports provided for in paragraph C of Article XII of the Statute and may also take, where applicable, the other measures provided for in that paragraph. In taking such action the Board shall take account of the degree of assurance provided by the safeguards measures that have been applied and shall afford the United States every reasonable opportunity to furnish the Board with any necessary reassurance.

Article 19. The United States and the Agency shall, at the request of either, consult about any question arising out of the interpretation or application of this Agreement.

Article 20. The United States shall have the right to request that any question arising out of the interpretation or application of this Agreement be considered by the Board. The Board shall invite the United States to participate in the discussion of any such question by the Board.

Article 21. Any dispute arising out of the interpretation or application of this Agreement, except a dispute with regard to a determination by the Board under Article 18 or an action taken by the Board pursuant to such a determination which is not settled by negotiation or another procedure agreed to by the United States and the Agency shall, at the request of either, be submitted to an arbitral tribunal composed as follows: The United States and the Agency shall each designate one arbitrator, and the two arbitrators so designated shall elect a third, who shall be the Chairman. If, within thirty days of the request for arbitration, either the United States or the Agency has not designated an arbitrator, either the United States or the Agency may request the President of the International Court of Justice to appoint an arbitrator. The same procedure shall apply if, within thirty days of the designation or appointment of the second arbitrator, the third arbitrator has not been elected. A majority of the members of the arbitral tribunal shall constitute a quorum, and all decisions shall require the concurrence of two arbitrators. The arbitral procedure shall be fixed by the tribunal. The decisions of the tribunal shall be binding on the United States and the Agency.

Article 22. The Parties shall institute steps to suspend the application of Agency safeguards in the United States under other safeguards agreements with the Agency while this Agreement is in force. However, the United States and the Agency shall ensure that nuclear material being safeguarded under this Agreement shall be at all times at least equivalent in amount and composition to that which would be subject to safeguards in the United States under the agreements in question. The detailed arrangements for the implementation of this provision shall be specified in the subsidiary arrangements provided for in Article 39, and shall reflect the nature of any undertaking given under such other safeguards agreements.

Article 23

(a) The United States and the Agency shall, at the request of either, consult each other on amendments to this Agreement.

(b) All amendments shall require the agreement of the United States and the Agency.

Article 24. This Agreement or any amendments thereto shall enter into force on the date on which the Agency receives from the United States written notification that statutory and constitutional requirements of the United States for entry into force have been met.[5]

Article 25. The Director General shall promptly inform all Member States of the Agency of the entry into force of this Agreement, or of any amendments thereto.

Article 26. The Agreement shall remain in force as long as the United States is a party to the Treaty except that the Parties to this Agreement shall, upon the request of either of them, consult and, to the extent mutually agreed, modify this Agreement in order to ensure that it continues to serve the purpose for which it was originally intended. If the Parties are unable after such consultation to agree upon necessary modifications, either Party may, upon six months' notice, terminate this Agreement.

PART II

Article 27. The purpose of this part of the Agreement is to specify the procedures to be applied in the implementation of the safeguards provisions of Part I.

Article 28. The objective of the safeguards procedures set forth in this part of the Agreement is the timely detection of withdrawal, other than in accordance with the terms of this Agreement, of significant quantities of nuclear material from activities in facilities while such material is being safeguarded under this Agreement.

Article 29. For the purpose of achieving the objective set forth in Article 28, material accountancy shall be used as a safeguards measure of fundamental importance, with containment and surveillance as important complementary measures.

Article 30. The technical conclusion of the Agency's verification activities shall be a statement, in respect of each material balance area, of the amount of material unaccounted for over a specific period, and giving the limits of accuracy of the amounts stated.

Article 31. Pursuant to Article 7, the Agency, in carrying out its verification activities, shall make full use of the United States' system of accounting for and control of all nuclear material subject to safeguards under this Agreement and shall avoid unnecessary duplication of the United States' accounting and control activities.

Article 32. The United States' system of accounting for and control of all nuclear material subject to safeguards under this Agreement shall be based on a structure of material balance areas, and shall make provision, as appropriate and specified in the Subsidiary Arrangements, for the establishment of such measures as:

(a) A measurement system for the determination of the quantities of nuclear material received, produced, shipped, lost or otherwise removed from inventory, and the quantities on inventory.

(b) The evaluation of precision and accuracy of measurements and the estimation of measurement uncertainty;

(c) Procedures for identifying, reviewing and evaluating differences in shipper/receiver measurements;

(d) Procedures for taking a physical inventory;

(e) Procedures for the evaluation of accumulations of unmeasured inventory and unmeasured losses;

(f) A system of records and reports showing, for each material balance area, the inventory of nuclear material and the changes in that inventory including receipts into and transfers out of the material balance area;

(g) Provisions to ensure that the accounting procedures and arrangements are being operated correctly; and

(h) Procedures for the provision of reports to the Agency in accordance with Articles 57 through 63 and 65 through 67.

Article 33. Safeguards under this Agreement shall not apply to material in mining or ore processing activities.

Article 34. The United States may, at any time, notify the Agency of any facility or facilities to be added to or removed from the list provided for in Article 1(b):

(a) In case of addition to the list, the notification shall specify the facility or facilities to be added to the list and the date upon which the addition is to take effect;

(b) In the case of removal from the list of a facility or facilities then currently identified pursuant to Articles 2(b) or 39(b):

(i) The Agency shall be notified in advance and the notification shall specify: the facility or facilities being removed, the date of removal, and the quantity and composition of the nuclear material contained therein at the time of notification. In exceptional circumstances, the United States may remove facilities without giving advance notification;

(ii) Any facility in respect of which notification has been given in accordance with sub-paragraph (i) shall be removed from the list and the nuclear material contained therein shall cease to be subject to safeguards under this Agreement in accordance with and at the time specified in the notification by the United States.

(c) In the case of removal from the list of a facility or facilities not then currently identified pursuant to Articles 2(b) or 39(b), the notification shall specify the facility or facilities being removed and the date of removal. Such facility or facilities shall be removed from the list at the time specified in the notification by the United States.

Article 35

(a) Safeguards shall terminate on nuclear material subject to safeguards under this Agreement, under the conditions set forth in Article 11. Where the conditions of that Article are not met, but the United States considers that the recovery of safeguarded nuclear material from residues is not for the time being practicable or desirable, the United States and the Agency shall consult on the appropriate safeguards measures to be applied.

(b) Safeguards shall terminate on nuclear material subject to safeguards under this Agreement, under the conditions set forth in Article 13, provided that the United States and the Agency agree that such nuclear material is practicably irrecoverable.

Article 36. At the request of the United States, the Agency shall exempt from safeguards nuclear material, which would otherwise be subject to safeguards under this Agreement, as follows:

(a) Special fissionable material, when it is used in gram quantities or less as a sensing component in instruments;

(b) Nuclear material, when it is used in non-nuclear activities in accordance with Article 13, if such nuclear material is recoverable; and

(c) Plutonium with an isotopic concentration of plutonium-238 exceeding 80%.

Article 37. At the request of the United States, the Agency shall exempt from safeguards nuclear material that would otherwise be subject to safeguards under this Agreement, provided that the total quantity of nuclear material which has been exempted in the United States in accordance with this Article may not at any time exceed:

(a) One kilogram in total of special fissionable material, which may consist of one or more of the following:

(i) Plutonium;

(ii) Uranium with an enrichment of 0.2 (20%) and above, taken account of by multiplying its weight by its enrichment; and

(iii) Uranium with an enrichment below 0.2 (20%) and above that of natural uranium, taken account of by multiplying its weight by five times the square of its enrichment;

(b) Ten metric tons in total of natural uranium and depleted uranium with an enrichment above 0.005 (0.5%);

(c) Twenty metric tons of depleted uranium with an enrichment of 0.005 (0.5%) or below; and

(d) Twenty metric tons of thorium; or such greater amounts as may be specified by the Board for uniform application.

Article 38. If exempted nuclear material is to be processed or stored together with nuclear material subject to safeguards under this Agreement, provision shall be made for the reapplication of safeguards thereto.

Article 39

(a) The United States and the Agency shall make Subsidiary Arrangements which shall:

(i) contain a current listing of those facilities identified by the Agency pursuant to Article 2(b) and thus containing nuclear material subject to safeguards under this Agreement; and

(ii) specify in detail, to the extent necessary to permit the Agency to fulfil its responsibilities under this Agreement in an effective and efficient manner, how the procedures laid down in this Agreement are to be applied.

(b) (i) After entry into force of this Agreement, the Agency shall identify to the United States, from the list provided in accordance with Article 1(b), those facilities to be included in the initial Subsidiary Arrangements listing;

(ii) The Agency may thereafter identify for inclusion in the Subsidiary Arrangements listing additional facilities from the list provided in accordance with Article 1(b) as that list may have been modified in accordance with Article 34.

(c) The Agency shall also designate to the United States those facilities to be removed from the Subsidiary Arrangements listing which have not otherwise been removed pursuant to notification by the United States in accordance with Article 34. Such facility or facilities shall be removed from the Subsidiary Arrangements listing upon such designation to the United States.

(d) The Subsidiary Arrangements may be extended or changed by agreement between the Agency and the United States without amendment to this Agreement.

Article 40

(a) With respect to those facilities which shall have been identified by the Agency in accordance with Article 39(b)(i), such Subsidiary Arrangements shall enter into force at the same time as, or as soon as possible after, entry into force of this Agreement. The United States and the Agency shall make every effort to achieve their entry into force within 90 days after entry into force of this Agreement; an extension of that period shall require agreement between the United States and the Agency.

(b) With respect to facilities which, after the entry into force of this Agreement, have been identified by the Agency in accordance with Article 39(b)(ii) for inclusion in the Subsidiary Arrangements listing, the United States and the Agency shall make every effort to achieve the entry into force of such Subsidiary Arrangements within ninety days following such identification to the United States; an extension of that period shall require agreement between the Agency and the United States.

(c) Upon identification of a facility by the Agency in accordance with Article 39(b), the United States shall provide the Agency promptly with the information required for completing the Subsidiary Arrangements, and the Agency shall have the right to apply the procedures set forth in this Agreement to the nuclear material listed in the inventory provided for in Article 41, even if the Subsidiary Arrangements have not yet entered into force.

Article 41. The Agency shall establish, on the basis of the initial reports referred to in Article 60(a) below, a unified inventory of all nuclear material in the United States subject to safeguards under this Agreement, irrespective of its origin, and shall maintain this inventory on the basis of subsequent reports concerning those facilities, of the initial reports referred to in Article 60(b), of subsequent reports concerning the facilities listed pursuant to Article 39(b)(ii), and of the results of its verification activities. Copies of the inventory shall be made available to the United States at intervals to be agreed.

Article 42. Pursuant to Article 8, design information in respect of facilities identified by the Agency in accordance with Article 39(b)(i) shall be provided to the Agency during the discussion of the Subsidiary Arrangements. The time limits for the provision of design information in respect of any facility which is identified by the Agency in accordance with Article 39(b)(ii) shall be specified in the Subsidiary Arrangements and such information shall be provided as early as possible after such identification.

Article 43. The design information to be provided to the Agency shall include, in respect of each facility identified by the Agency in accordance with Article 39(b), when applicable:

(a) The identification of the facility, stating its general character, purpose, nominal capacity and geographic location, and the name and address to be used for routine business purposes;

(b) A description of the general arrangement of the facility with reference, to the extent feasible, to the form, location and flow of nuclear material and to the general layout of important items of equipment which use, produce or process nuclear material;

(c) A description of features of the facility relating to material accountancy, containment and surveillance; and

(d) A description of the existing and proposed procedures at the facility for nuclear material accountancy and control, with special reference to material balance areas established by the operator, measurements of flow and procedures for physical inventory taking.

Article 44. Other information relevant to the application of safeguards shall also be provided to the Agency in respect of each facility identified by the Agency in accordance with Article 39(b), in particular on organizational responsibility for material accountancy and control. The United States shall provide the Agency with supplementary information on the health and safety procedures which the Agency shall observe and with which the inspectors shall comply at the facility.

Article 45. The Agency shall be provided with design information in respect of a modification relevant for safeguards purposes, for examination, and shall be informed of any change in the information provided to it under Article 44, sufficiently in advance for the safeguards procedures to be adjusted when necessary.

Article 46. The design information provided to the Agency shall be used for the following purposes:

(a) To identify the features of facilities and nuclear material relevant to the application of safeguards to nuclear material in sufficient detail to facilitate verification;

(b) To determine material balance areas to be used for Agency accounting purposes and to select those strategic points which are key measurement points and which will be used to determine flow and inventory of nuclear material; in determining such material balance areas the Agency shall, inter alia, use the following criteria:

(i) The size of the material balance area shall be related to the accuracy with which the material balance can be established;

(ii) In determining the material balance area, advantage shall be taken of any opportunity to use containment and surveillance to help ensure the completeness of flow measurements and thereby to simplify the application of safeguards and to concentrate measurement efforts at key measurement points;

(iii) A number of material balance areas in use at a facility or at distinct sites may be combined in one material balance area to be used for Agency accounting purposes when the Agency determines that this is consistent with its verification requirements; and

(iv) A special material balance area may be established at the request of the United States around a process step involving commercially sensitive information;

(c) To establish the nominal timing and procedures for taking of physical inventory of nuclear material for Agency accounting purposes;

(d) To establish the records and reports requirements and records evaluation procedures;

(e) To establish requirements and procedures for verification of the quantity and location of nuclear material; and

(f) To select appropriate combinations of containment and surveillance methods and techniques at the strategic points at which they are to be applied.

The results of the examination of the design information shall be included in the Subsidiary Arrangements.

Article 47. Design information shall be re-examined in the light of changes in operating conditions, of developments in safeguards technology or of experience in the application of verification procedures, with a view to modifying the action the Agency has taken pursuant to Article 46.

Article 48. The Agency, in co-operation with the United States, may send inspectors to facilities to verify the design information provided to the Agency pursuant to Article 42 through 45, for the purposes stated in Article 46.

Article 49. In establishing a national system of materials control as referred to in Article 7, the United States shall arrange that records are kept in respect of each material balance area determined in accordance with Article 46(b). The records to be kept shall be described in the Subsidiary Arrangements.

Article 50. The United States shall make arrangements to facilitate the examination of records referred to in Article 49 by inspectors.

Article 51. Records referred to in Article 49 shall be retained for at least five years.

Article 52. Records referred to in Article 49 shall consist, as appropriate, of:

(a) Accounting records of all nuclear material subject to safeguards under this Agreement; and

(b) Operating records for facilities containing such nuclear material.

Article 53. The system of measurements on which the records used for the preparation of reports are based shall either conform to the latest international standards or be equivalent in quality to such standards.

Article 54. The accounting records referred to in Article 52(a) shall set forth the following in respect of each material balance area determined in accordance with Article 46(b):

(a) All inventory changes, so as to permit a determination of the book inventory at any time;

(b) All measurement results that are used for determination of the physical inventory; and

(c) All adjustments and corrections that have been made in respect of inventory changes, book inventories and physical inventories.

Article 55. For all inventory changes and physical inventories the records referred to in Article 52(a) shall show, in respect of each batch of nuclear material: material identification, batch data and source data. The records shall account for uranium, thorium and plutonium separately in each batch of nuclear material. For each inventory change, the date of the inventory change and, when appropriate, the originating material balance area and the receiving material balance area or the recipient shall be indicated.

Article 56. The operating records referred to in Article 52(b) shall set forth, as appropriate, in respect of each material balance area determined in accordance with Article 46(b):

(a) Those operating data which are used to establish changes in the quantities and composition of nuclear material;

(b) The data obtained from the calibration of tanks and instruments and from sampling and analyses, the procedures to control the quality of measurements and the derived estimates of random and systematic error;

(c) A description of the sequence of the actions taken in preparing for, and in taking, a physical inventory, in order to ensure that it is correct and complete; and

(d) A description of the actions taken in order to ascertain the cause and magnitude of any accidental or unmeasured loss that might occur.

Article 57. The United States shall provide the Agency with reports as detailed in Articles 58 through 67 in respect of nuclear material subject to safeguards under this Agreement.

Article 58. Reports shall be made in English.

Article 59. Reports shall be based on the records kept in accordance with Articles 49 through 56 and shall consist, as appropriate, of accounting reports and special reports.

Article 60. The United States shall provide the Agency with an initial report on all nuclear material contained in each facility which becomes listed in the Subsidiary Arrangements in accordance with Article 39(b):

(a) With respect to those facilities listed pursuant to Article 39(b)(i), such reports shall be dispatched to the Agency within thirty days of the last day of the calendar month in which this Agreement enters into force, and shall reflect the situation as of the last day of that month.

(b) With respect to each facility listed pursuant to Article 39(b)(ii), an initial report shall be dispatched to the Agency within thirty days of the last day of the calendar month in which the Agency identifies the facility to the United States and shall reflect the situation as of the last day of that month.

Article 61. The United States shall provide the Agency with the following accounting reports for each material balance area determined in accordance with Article 46(b):

(a) Inventory change reports showing all changes in the inventory of nuclear material. The reports shall be dispatched as soon as possible and in any event within thirty days after the end of the month in which the inventory changes occurred or were established; and

(b) Material balance reports showing the material balance based on a physical inventory of nuclear material actually present in the material balance area. The reports shall be dispatched as soon as possible and in any event within thirty days after the physical inventory has been taken.

The reports shall be based on data available as of the date of reporting and may be corrected at a later date, as required.

Article 62. Inventory change reports submitted in accordance with Article 61(a) shall specify identification and batch data for each batch of nuclear material, the date of the inventory change, and, as appropriate, the originating material balance area and the receiving material balance area or the recipient. These reports shall be accompanied by concise notes:

(a) Explaining the inventory changes, on the basis of the operating data contained in the operating records provided for under Article 56(a); and

(b) Describing, as specified in the Subsidiary Arrangements, the anticipated operational programme, particularly the taking of a physical inventory.

Article 63. The United States shall report each inventory change, adjustment and correction, either periodically in a consolidated list or individually.

Inventory changes shall be reported in terms of batches. As specified in the Subsidiary Arrangements, small changes in inventory of nuclear materials, such as transfers of analytical samples, may be combined in one batch and reported as one inventory change.

Article 64. The Agency shall provide the United States with semi-annual statements of book inventory of nuclear material subject to safeguards under this Agreement, for each material balance area, as based on the inventory change reports for the period covered by each such statement.

Article 65. Material balance reports submitted in accordance with Article 61(b) shall include the following entries, unless otherwise agreed by the United States and the Agency:

(a) Beginning physical inventory;

(b) Inventory changes (first increases, then decreases);

(c) Ending book inventory;

(d) Shipper/receiver differences;

(e) Adjusted ending book inventory;

(f) Ending physical inventory; and

(g) Material unaccounted for.

A statement of the physical inventory, listing all batches separately and specifying material identification and batch data for each batch, shall be attached to each material balance report.

Article 66. The United States shall make special reports without delay:

(a) If any unusual incident or circumstances lead the United States to believe that there is or may have been loss of nuclear material subject to safeguards under this Agreement that exceeds the limits specified for this purpose in the Subsidiary Arrangements; or

(b) If the containment has unexpectedly changed from that specified in the Subsidiary Arrangements to the extent that unauthorized removal of nuclear material subject to safeguards under this Agreement has become possible.

Article 67. If the Agency so requests, the United States shall provide it with amplifications or clarifications of any report submitted in accordance with Articles 57 through 63, 65 and 66, in so far as relevant for the purpose of safeguards.

Article 68. The Agency shall have the right to make inspections as provided for in Articles 69 through 82.

Article 69. The Agency may make ad hoc inspections in order to:

(a) Verify the information contained in the initial reports submitted in accordance with Article 60;

(b) Identify and verify changes in the situation which have occurred since the date of the relevant initial report; and

(c) Identify and if possible verify the quantity and composition of the nuclear material subject to safeguards under this Agreement in respect of which the information referred to in Article 89(a) has been provided to the Agency.

Article 70. The Agency may make routine inspections in order to:

(a) Verify that reports submitted pursuant to Articles 57 through 63, 65 and 66 are consistent with records kept pursuant to Articles 49 through 56;

(b) Verify the location, identity, quantity and composition of all nuclear material subject to safeguards under this Agreement; and

(c) Verify information on the possible causes of material unaccounted for, shipper/receiver differences and uncertainties in the book inventory.

Article 71. Subject to the procedures laid down in Article 75, the Agency may make special inspections:

(a) In order to verify the information contained in special reports submitted in accordance with Article 66; or

(b) If the Agency considers that information made available by the United States, including explanations from the United States and information obtained from routine inspections, is not adequate for the Agency to fulfil its responsibilities under this Agreement.

An inspection shall be deemed to be special when it is either additional to the routine inspection effort provided for in Articles 76 through 80, or involves access to information or locations in addition to the access specified in Article 74 for ad hoc and routine inspections, or both.

Article 72. For the purposes specified in Articles 69 through 71, the Agency may:

(a) Examine the records kept pursuant to Articles 49 through 56;

(b) Make independent measurements of all nuclear material subject to safeguards under this Agreement;

(c) Verify the functioning and calibration of instruments and other measuring and control equipment;

(d) Apply and make use of surveillance and containment measures; and

(e) Use other objective methods which have been demonstrated to be technically feasible.

Article 73. Within the scope of Article 72, the Agency shall be enabled:

(a) To observe that samples at key measurement points for material balance accountancy are taken in accordance with procedures which produce representative samples, to observe the treatment and analysis of the samples and to obtain duplicates of such samples;

(b) To observe that the measurements of nuclear material at key measurement points for material balance accountancy are representative, and to observe the calibration of the instruments and equipment involved;

(c) To make arrangements with the United States that, if necessary:

(i) Additional measurements are made and additional samples taken for the Agency's use;

(ii) The Agency's standard analytical samples are analysed;

(iii) Appropriate absolute standards are used in calibrating instruments and other equipment; and

(iv) Other calibrations are carried out;

(d) To arrange to use its own equipment for independent measurement and surveillance, and if so agreed and specified in the Subsidiary Arrangements to arrange to install such equipment;

(e) To apply its seals and other identifying and tamper-indicating devices to containment, if so agreed and specified in the Subsidiary Arrangements; and

(f) To make arrangements with the United States for the shipping of samples taken for the Agency's use.

Article 74

(a) For the purposes specified in Article 69 (a) and (b) and until such time as the strategic points have been specified in the Subsidiary Arrangements, Agency inspectors shall have access to any location where the initial report or any inspections carried out therewith indicate that nuclear material subject to safeguards under this Agreement is present.

(b) For the purposes specified in Article 69(c), the inspectors shall have access to any facility identified pursuant to Articles 2(b) or 39(b) in which nuclear material referred to in Article 69(c) is located.

(c) For the purposes specified in Article 70 the inspectors shall have access only to the strategic points specified in the Subsidiary Arrangements and to the records maintained pursuant to Articles 49 through 56; and

(d) In the event of the United States concluding that any unusual circumstances require extended limitations on access by the Agency, the United States and the Agency shall promptly make arrangements with a view to enabling the Agency to discharge its safeguards responsibilities in the light of these limitations. The Director General shall report each such arrangement to the Board.

Article 75. In circumstances which may lead to special inspections for the purposes specified in Article 71 the United States and the Agency shall consult forthwith. As a result of such consultations the Agency may:

(a) Make inspections in addition to the routine inspection effort provided for in Articles 76 through 80; and

(b) Obtain access, in agreement with the United States, to information or locations in addition to those specified in Article 74. Any disagreement concerning the need for additional access shall be resolved in accordance with Articles 20 and 21; in case action by the United States is essential and urgent, Article 17 shall apply.

Article 76. The Agency shall keep the number, intensity and duration of routine inspections, applying optimum timing, to the minimum consistent with the effective implementation of the safeguards procedures set forth in this Agreement, and shall make the optimum and most economical use of inspection resources available to it.

Article 77. The Agency may carry out one routine inspection per year in respect of facilities listed in the Subsidiary Arrangements pursuant to Article 39 with a content or annual throughput, whichever is greater, of nuclear material not exceeding five effective kilograms.

Article 78. The number, intensity, duration, timing and mode of routine inspections in respect of facilities listed in the Subsidiary Arrangements pursuant to Article 39 with a content or annual throughput of nuclear material exceeding five effective kilograms shall be determined on the basis that in the maximum or limiting case the inspection regime shall be no more intensive than is necessary and sufficient to maintain continuity of knowledge of the flow and inventory of nuclear material, and the maximum routine inspection effort in respect of such facilities shall be determined as follows:

(a) For reactors and sealed storage installations the maximum total of routine inspection per year shall be determined by allowing one sixth of a man-year of inspection for each such facility;

(b) For facilities, other than reactors or sealed storage installations, involving plutonium or uranium enriched to more than 5%, the maximum total of routine inspection per year shall be determined by allowing for each such facility $30 \times \sqrt{E}$ man-days of inspection per year, where E is the inventory or annual throughput of nuclear material, whichever is greater, expressed in effective kilograms. The maximum established for any such facility shall not, however, be less than 1.5 man-years of inspection; and

(c) For facilities not covered by paragraphs (a) or (b), the maximum total of routine inspection per year shall be determined by allowing for each such facility one third of a man-year of inspection plus 0.4 x E man-days of inspection per year, where E is the inventory or annual throughput of nuclear material, whichever is greater, expressed in effective kilograms.

The United States and the Agency may agree to amend the figures for the maximum inspection effort specified in this Article, upon determination by the Board that such amendment is reasonable.

Article 79. Subject to Articles 76 through 78 the criteria to be used for determining the actual number, intensity, duration, timing and mode of routine inspections in respect of any facility listed in the Subsidiary Arrangements pursuant to Article 39 shall include:

(a) The form of the nuclear material, in particular, whether the nuclear material is in bulk form or contained in a number of separate items; its chemical composition and, in the case of uranium, whether it is of low or high enrichment; and its accessibility;

(b) The effectiveness of the United States' accounting and control system, including the extent to which the operators of facilities are functionally independent of the United States' accounting and control system; the extent to which the measures specified in Article 32 have been implemented by the United States; the promptness of reports provided to the Agency; their consistency with the Agency's independent verification; and the amount and accuracy of the material unaccounted for, as verified by the Agency;

(c) Characteristics of that part of the United States fuel cycle in which safeguards are applied under this Agreement, in particular, the number and types of facilities containing nuclear material subject to safeguards under this Agreement, the characteristics of such facilities relevant to safeguards, notably the degree of containment; the extent to which the design of such facilities facilitates verification of the flow and inventory of nuclear material; and the extent to which information from different material balance areas can be correlated;

(d) International interdependence, in particular the extent to which nuclear material, safeguarded under this Agreement, is received from or sent to other States for use or processing; any verification activities by the Agency in connection therewith; and the extent to which activities in facilities in which safeguards are applied under this Agreement are interrelated with those of other States; and

(e) Technical developments in the field of safeguards, including the use of statistical techniques and random sampling in evaluating the flow of nuclear material.

Article 80. The United States and the Agency shall consult if the United States considers that the inspection effort is being deployed with undue concentration on particular facilities.

Article 81. The Agency shall give advance notice to the United States of the arrival of inspectors at facilities listed in the Subsidiary Arrangements pursuant to Article 39, as follows:

(a) For ad hoc inspections pursuant to Article 69(c), at least 24 hours; for those pursuant to Article 69(a) and (b), as well as the activities provided for in Article 48, at least one week;

(b) For special inspections pursuant to Article 71, as promptly as possible after the United States and the Agency have consulted as provided for in Article 75, it being understood that notification of arrival normally will constitute part of the consultations; and

(c) For routine inspections pursuant to Article 70 at least twenty-four hours in respect of the facilities referred to in Article 78(b) and sealed storage installations containing plutonium or uranium enriched to more than 5% and one week in all other cases.

Such notice of inspections shall include the names of the inspectors and shall indicate the facilities to be visited and the periods during which they will be visited. If the inspectors are to arrive from outside the United States the Agency shall also give advance notice of place and time of their arrival in the United States.

Article 82. Notwithstanding the provisions of Article 81, the Agency may, as a supplementary measure, carry out without advance notification a portion of the routine inspections pursuant to Article 78 in accordance with the principle of random sampling. In performing any unannounced inspections, the Agency shall fully take into account any operational programme provided by the United States pursuant to Article 62(b). Moreover, whenever practicable, and on the basis of the operational programme, it shall advise the United States periodically of its general programme of announced and unannounced inspections, specifying the general periods when inspections are foreseen. In carrying out any unannounced inspections, the Agency shall make every effort to minimize any practical difficulties for the United States and facility operators bearing in mind the relevant provisions of Articles 44 and 87. Similarly the United States shall make every effort to facilitate the task of the inspectors.

Article 83. The following procedures shall apply to the designation of inspectors:

(a) The Director General shall inform the United States in writing of the name, qualifications, nationality, grade and such other particulars as may be relevant, of each Agency official he proposes for designation as an inspector for the United States;

(b) The United States shall inform the Director General within thirty days of the receipt of such a proposal whether it accepts the proposal;

(c) The Director General may designate each official who has been accepted by the United States as one of the inspectors for the United States, and shall inform the United States of such designations; and

(d) The Director General, acting in response to a request by the United States or on his own initiative, shall immediately inform the United States of the withdrawal of the designation of any official as an inspector for the United States.

However, in respect of inspectors needed for the activities provided for in Article 48 and to carry out ad hoc inspections pursuant to Article 69(a) and (b) the designation procedures shall be completed if possible within thirty days after the entry into force of this Agreement. If such designation appears impossible within this time limit, inspectors for such purposes shall be designated on a temporary basis.

Article 84. The United States shall grant or renew as quickly as possible appropriate visas, where required, for each inspector designated for United States.

Article 85. Inspectors, in exercising their functions under Article 48 and 69 to 73, shall carry out their activities in a manner designed to avoid hampering or delaying the construction, commissioning or operation of facilities, or affecting their safety. In particular inspectors shall not operate any facility themselves or direct the staff of a facility to carry out any operation. If inspectors consider that in pursuance of paragraphs 72 and 73, particular operations in a facility should be carried out by the operator, they shall make a request therefor.

Article 86. When inspectors require services available in the United States, including the use of equipment, in connection with the performance of inspections, the United States shall facilitate the procurement of such services and the use of such equipment by inspectors.

Article 87. The United States shall have the right to have inspectors accompanied during their inspections by its representatives, provided that inspectors shall not thereby be delayed or otherwise impeded in the exercise of their functions.

Article 88. The Agency shall inform the United States of:

(a) The results of inspections, at intervals to be specified in the Subsidiary Arrangements; and

(b) The conclusions it has drawn from its verification activities in the United States, in particular by means of statements in respect of each material balance area determined in accordance with Article 46(b) which shall be made as soon as possible after a physical inventory has been taken and verified by the Agency and a material balance has been struck.

Article 89

(a) Information concerning nuclear material exported from and imported into the United States shall be provided to the Agency in accordance with arrangements made with the Agency as, for example, those set forth in INFCIRC/207.

(b) In the case of international transfers to or from facilities identified by the Agency pursuant to Articles 2(b) and 39(b) with respect to which information has been provided to the Agency in accordance with arrangements referred to in paragraph (a), a special report, as envisaged in Article 66, shall be made if any unusual incident or circumstances

lead the United States to believe that there is or may have been loss of nuclear material, including the occurrence of significant delay, during the transfer.

DEFINITIONS

Article 90. For the purposes of this Agreement:

A. *Adjustment* means an entry into an accounting record or a report showing a shipper/receiver difference or material unaccounted for.

B. *Annual throughput* means, for the purposes of Articles 77 and 78, the amount of nuclear material transferred annually out of a facility working at nominal capacity.

C. *Batch* means a portion of nuclear material handled as a unit for accounting purposes at a key measurement point and for which the composition and quantity are defined by a single set of specifications or measurements. The nuclear material may be in bulk form or contained in a number of separate items.

D. *Batch data* means the total weight of each element of nuclear material and, in the case of plutonium and uranium, the isotopic composition when appropriate. The units of account shall be as follows:

(a) Grams of contained plutonium;

(b) Grams of total uranium and grams of contained uranium-235 plus uranium-233 for uranium enriched in these isotopes; and

(c) Kilograms of contained thorium, natural uranium or depleted uranium.

For reporting purposes the weights of individual items in the batch shall be added together before rounding to the nearest unit.

E. *Book inventory of a material balance area* means the algebraic sum of the most recent physical inventory of that material balance area and of all inventory changes that have occurred since that physical inventory was taken.

F. *Correction* means an entry into an accounting record or a report to rectify an identified mistake or to reflect an improved measurement of a quantity previously entered into the record or report. Each correction must identify the entry to which it pertains.

G. *Effective kilogram* means a special unit used in safeguarding nuclear material. The quantity in effective kilograms is obtained by taking:

(a) For plutonium, its weight in kilograms;

(b) For uranium with an enrichment of 0.01 (1%) and above, its weight in kilograms multiplied by the square of its enrichment;

(c) For uranium with an enrichment below 0.01 (1%) and above 0.005 (0.5%), its weight in kilograms multiplied by 0.0001; and

(d) For depleted uranium with an enrichment of 0.005 (0.5%) or below, and for thorium, its weight in kilograms multiplied by 0.00005.

H. *Enrichment* means the ratio of the combined weight of the isotopes uranium-233 and uranium-235 to that of the total uranium in question.

I. *Facility* means:

(a) A reactor, a critical facility, a conversion plant, a fabrication plant, a reprocessing plant, an isotope separation plant or a separate storage installation; or

(b) Any location where nuclear material in amounts greater than one effective kilogram is customarily used.

J. *Inventory change* means an increase or decrease, in terms of batches, of nuclear material in a material balance area; such a change shall involve one of the following:

(a) Increases:

(i) Import;

(ii) Domestic receipt: receipts from other material balance areas, receipts from a non-safeguarded activity or receipts at the starting point of safeguards;

(iii) Nuclear production: production of special fissionable material in a reactor; and

(iv) De-exemption: reapplication of safeguards on nuclear material previously exempted therefrom on account of its use or quantity.

(b) Decreases:

(i) Export;

(ii) Domestic shipment: shipments to other material balance areas or shipments for a non-safeguarded activity;

(iii) Nuclear loss: loss of nuclear material due to its transformation into other element(s) or isotope(s) as a result of nuclear reactions;

(iv) Measured discard: nuclear material which has been measured, or estimated on the basis of measurements, and disposed of in such a way that it is not suitable for further nuclear use;

(v) Retained waste: nuclear material generated from processing or from an operational accident, which is deemed to be unrecoverable for the time being but which is stored;

(vi) Exemption: exemption of nuclear material from safeguards on account of its use or quantity; and

(vii) Other loss: for example, accidental loss (that is, irretrievable and inadvertent loss of nuclear material as the result of an operational accident) or theft.

K. *Key measurement point* means a location where nuclear material appears in such a form that it may be measured to determine material flow or inventory. Key measurement points thus include, but are not limited to, the inputs and outputs (including measured discards) and storages in material balance areas.

L. *Man-year of inspection* means, for the purposes of Article 78, 300 man-days of inspection, a man-day being a day during which a single inspector has access to a facility at any time for a total of not more than eight hours.

M. *Material balance area* means an area in or outside of a facility such that:

(a) The quantity of nuclear material in each transfer into or out of each material balance area can be determined; and

(b) The physical inventory of nuclear material in each material balance area can be determined when necessary in accordance with specified procedures, in order that the material balance for Agency safeguards purposes can be established.

N. *Material unaccounted for* means the difference between book inventory and physical inventory.

O. *Nuclear material* means any source or any special fissionable material as defined in Article XX of the Statute. The term source material shall not be interpreted as applying to ore or ore residue. Any determination by the Board under Article XX of the Statute after the entry into force of this Agreement which adds to the materials considered to be source material or special fissionable material shall have effect under this Agreement only upon acceptance by the United States.

P. *Physical inventory* means the sum of all the measured or derived estimates of batch quantities of nuclear material on hand at a given time within a material balance area, obtained in accordance with specified procedures.

Q. *Shipper/receiver difference* means the difference between the quantity of nuclear material in a batch as stated by the shipping material balance area and as measured at the receiving material balance area.

R. *Source data* means those data, recorded during measurement or calibration or used to derive empirical relationships, which identify nuclear material and provide batch data. Source data may include, for example, weight of compounds, conversion factors to determine weight of element, specific gravity, element concentration, isotopic ratios, relationship between volume and manometer readings and relationship between plutonium produced and power generated.

S. *Strategic point* means a location selected during examination of design information where, under normal conditions and when combined with the information from all strategic points taken together, the information necessary and sufficient for the implementation of safeguards measures is obtained and verified; a strategic point may include any location where key measurements related to material balance accountancy are made and where containment and surveillance measures are executed.

[Signatures]

NOTES
1   TIAS 6839; 21 UST 483.
2   Done 26 October 1956. TIAS 3873, 5284, 7668; 8 UST 1095; 14 UST 135; 24 UST 1637.
3   59 Stat. 669; 22 U.S.C. § 288 note.
4   71 Stat. 576; 42 U.S.C. § 2210.
5   9 December 1980.
[TIAS stands for *Treaties and Other International Acts Series*; UST stands for *United States Treaties and Other International Acts.*]

Protocol to the Agreement Between the United States of America and the International Atomic Energy Agency for the Application of Safeguards in the United States

Article 1. This Protocol specifies the procedures to be followed with respect to facilities identified by the Agency pursuant to Article 2 of this Protocol.

Article 2

(a) The Agency may from time to time identify to the United States those facilities included in the list, established and maintained pursuant to Articles 1(b) and 34 of the Agreement, of facilities not associated with activities having direct national security significance to the United States, other than those which are then currently identified by the Agency pursuant to Articles 2(b) and 39(b) of the Agreement, to which the provisions of this Protocol shall apply.

(b) The Agency may also include among the facilities identified to the United States pursuant to the foregoing paragraph, any facility which had previously been identified by the Agency pursuant to Articles 2(b) and 39(b) of the Agreement but which had subsequently been designated by the Agency pursuant to Article 39(c) of the Agreement for removal from the Subsidiary Arrangements listing.

(c) In identifying facilities pursuant to the foregoing paragraphs and in the preparation of Transitional Subsidiary Arrangements pursuant to Article 3 of this Protocol, the Agency shall proceed in a manner which the Agency and the United States mutually agree takes into account the requirement on the United States to avoid discriminatory treatment as between United States commercial firms similarly situated.

Article 3. The United States and the Agency shall make Transitional Subsidiary Arrangements which shall:

(a) contain a current listing of those facilities identified by the Agency pursuant to Article 2 of this Protocol;

(b) specify in detail how the procedures set forth in this Protocol are to be applied.

Article 4

(a) The United States and the Agency shall make every effort to complete the Transitional Subsidiary Arrangements with respect to each facility identified by the Agency pursuant to Article 2 of this Protocol within ninety days following such identification to the United States.

(b) With respect to any facility identified pursuant to Article 2(b) of this Protocol, the information previously submitted to the Agency in accordance with Articles 42 through 45 of the Agreement, the results of the examination of the design information and other provisions of the Subsidiary Arrangements relative to such facility, to the extent that such information, results and provisions satisfy the provisions of this Protocol relating to the submission and examination of information and the preparation of Transitional Subsidiary Arrangements, shall constitute the Transitional Subsidiary Arrangements for such facility, until and unless the United States and the Agency shall otherwise complete Transitional Subsidiary Arrangements for such facility in accordance with the provisions of this Protocol.

Article 5. In the event that a facility currently identified by the Agency pursuant to Article 2(a) of this Protocol is identified by the Agency pursuant to Articles 2(b) and 39(b) of the Agreement, the Transitional Subsidiary Arrangements relevant to such facility shall, to the extent that such Transitional Subsidiary Arrangements satisfy the provisions of the Agreement, be deemed to have been made part of the Subsidiary Arrangements to the Agreement.

Article 6. Design information in respect of each facility identified by the Agency pursuant to Article 2 of this Protocol shall be provided to the Agency during the discussion of the relevant Transitional Subsidiary Arrangements. The information shall include, when applicable:

(a) The identification of the facility, stating its general character, purpose, nominal capacity and geographic location, and the name and address to be used for routine business purpose;

(b) A description of the general arrangement of the facility with reference, to the extent feasible, to the form, location and flow of nuclear material and to the general layout of important items of equipment which use, produce or process nuclear material;

(c) A description of features of the facility relating to material accountancy, containment and surveillance; and

(d) A description of the existing and proposed procedures at the facility for nuclear material accountancy and control, with special reference to material balance areas established by the operator, measurements of flow and procedures for physical inventory taking.

Article 7. Other information relevant to the application of the provisions of this Protocol shall also be provided to the Agency in respect of each facility identified by the Agency in accordance with Article 2 of this Protocol, in particular on organizational responsibility for material accountancy and control. The United States shall provide the Agency with supplementary information on the health and safety procedures which the Agency shall observe and with which inspectors shall comply when visiting the facility in accordance with Article 11 of this Protocol.

Article 8. The Agency shall be provided with design information in respect of a modification rele-

vant to the application of the provisions of this Protocol, for examination, and shall be informed of any change in the information provided to it under Article 7 of this Protocol, sufficiently in advance for the procedures under this Protocol to be adjusted when necessary.

Article 9. The design information provided to the Agency in accordance with the provisions of this Protocol, in anticipation of the application of safeguards under the Agreement, shall be used for the following purposes:

(a) To identify the features of facilities and nuclear material relevant to the application of safeguards to nuclear material in sufficient detail to facilitate verification;

(b) To determine material balance areas to be used for Agency accounting purposes and to select those strategic points which are key measurement points and which will be used to determine flow and inventory of nuclear material; in determining such material balance areas the Agency shall, inter alia, use the following criteria;

(i) The size of the material balance area shall be related to the accuracy with which the material balance can be established;

(ii) In determining the material balance area, advantage shall be taken of any opportunity to use containment and surveillance to help ensure the completeness of flow measurements and thereby to simplify the application of safeguards and to concentrate measurement efforts at key measurement points;

(iii) A number of material balance areas in use at a facility or at distinct sites may be combined in one material balance area to be used for Agency accounting purposes when the Agency determines that this is consistent with its verification requirements; and

(iv) A special material balance area may be established at the request of the United States around a process step involving commercially sensitive information;

(c) To establish the nominal timing and procedures for taking of physical inventory of nuclear material for Agency accounting purposes;

(d) To establish the records and reports requirements and records evaluation procedures;

(e) To establish requirements and procedures for verification of the quantity and location of nuclear material; and

(f) To select appropriate combinations of containment and surveillance methods and techniques and the strategic points at which they are to be applied.

The results of the examination of the design information shall be included in the relevant Transitional Subsidiary Arrangements.

Article 10. Design information provided in accordance with the provisions of this Protocol shall be re-examined in the light of changes in operating conditions, of developments in safeguards technology or of experience in the application of verification procedures, with a view to modifying the action taken pursuant to Article 9 of this Protocol.

Article 11

(a) The Agency, in co-operation with the United States, may send inspectors to facilities identified by the Agency pursuant to Article 2 of this Protocol to verify the design information provided to the Agency in accordance with the provisions of this Protocol, for the purposes stated in Article 9 of this Protocol or for such other purposes as may be agreed between the United States and the Agency.

(b) The Agency shall give notice to the United States with respect to each such visit at least one week prior to the arrival of inspectors at the facility to be visited.

Article 12. In establishing a national system of materials control as referred to in Article 7(a) of the Agreement, the United States shall arrange that records are kept in respect of each material balance area determined in accordance with Article 9(b) of this Protocol. The records to be kept shall be described in the relevant Transitional Subsidiary Arrangements.

Article 13. Records referred to in Article 12 of this Protocol shall be retained for at least five years.

Article 14. Records referred to in Article 12 of this Protocol shall consist, as appropriate, of:

(a) Accounting records of all nuclear material stored, processed, used or produced in each facility; and

(b) Operating records for activities within each facility.

Article 15. The system of measurements on which the records used for the preparation of reports are based shall either conform to the latest international standards or be equivalent in quality to such standards.

Article 16. The accounting records referred to in Article 14(a) of this Protocol shall set forth the following in respect of each material balance area determined in accordance with Article 9(b) of this Protocol:

(a) All inventory changes, so as to permit a determination of the book inventory at any time;

(b) All measurement results that are used for determination of the physical inventory; and

(c) All adjustments and corrections that have been made in respect of inventory changes, book inventories and physical inventories.

Article 17. For all inventory changes and physical inventories the records referred to in Article 14(a) of this Protocol shall show, in respect of each batch of nuclear material: material identification, batch data and source data. The records shall account for uranium, thorium and plutonium separately in each batch of nuclear material. For each inventory change, the date of the inventory change and, when appropriate, the originating material balance area and the receiving material balance area or the recipient, shall be indicated.

Article 18. The operating records referred to in Article 14(b) of this Protocol shall set forth, as appropriate, in respect of each material balance area determined in accordance with Article 9(b) of this Protocol:

(a) Those operating data which are used to establish changes in the quantities and composition of nuclear material;

(b) The data obtained from the calibration of tanks and instruments and from sampling and analyses, the procedures to control the quality of measurements and the derived estimates of random and systematic error;

(c) A description of the sequence of the actions taken in preparing for, and in taking, a physical inventory, in order to ensure that it is correct and complete; and

(d) A description of the actions taken in order to ascertain the cause and magnitude of any accidental or unmeasured loss that might occur.

Article 19. The United States shall provide the Agency with accounting reports as detailed in Articles 20 through 25 of this Protocol in respect of nuclear material in each facility identified by the Agency pursuant to Article 2 of this Protocol.

Article 20. The accounting reports shall be based on the records kept in accordance with Articles 12 to 18 to this Protocol. They shall be made in English.

Article 21. The United States shall provide the Agency with an initial report on all nuclear material in each facility identified by the Agency pursuant to Article 2 of this Protocol. Such report shall be dispatched to the Agency within thirty days of the last day of the calendar month in which the facility is identified by the Agency and shall reflect the situation as of the last day of that month.

Article 22. The United States shall provide the Agency with the following accounting reports for each material balance area determined in accordance with Article 9(b) of this Protocol:

(a) Inventory change reports showing all changes in the inventory of nuclear material. The reports shall be dispatched as soon as possible and in any event within thirty days after the end of the month in which the inventory changes occurred or were established; and

(b) Material balance reports showing the material balance based on a physical inventory of nuclear material actually present in the material balance area. The reports shall be dispatched as soon as possible and in any event within thirty days after the physical inventory has been taken.

The reports shall be based on data available as of the date of reporting and may be corrected at a later date, as required.

Article 23. Inventory change reports submitted in accordance with Article 22(a) of this Protocol shall specify identification and batch data for each batch of nuclear material, the date of the inventory change, and, as appropriate, the originating material balance area and the receiving material balance area or the recipient. These reports shall be accompanied by concise notes:

(a) Explaining the inventory changes, on the basis of the operating data contained in the operating records provided for in Article 18(a) of this Protocol; and

(b) Describing, as specified in the relevant Transitional Subsidiary Arrangements, the anticipated operational programme, particularly the taking of a physical inventory.

Article 24. The United States shall report each inventory change, adjustment and correction, either periodically in a consolidated list or individually. Inventory changes shall be reported in terms of batches. As specified in the relevant Transitional Subsidiary Arrangements, small changes in inventory of nuclear material, such as transfers of analytical samples, may be combined in one batch and reported as one inventory change.

Article 25. Material balance reports submitted in accordance with Article 22(b) of this Protocol shall include the following entries, unless otherwise agreed by the United States and the Agency:

(a) Beginning physical inventory;

(b) Inventory changes (first increases, then decreases);

(c) Ending book inventory;

(d) Shipper/receiver differences;

(e) Adjusted ending book inventory;

(f) Ending physical inventory; and

(g) Material unaccounted for.

A statement of the physical inventory, listing all batches separately and specifying material identification and batch data for each batch, shall be attached to each material balance report.

Article 26. The Agency shall provide the United States with semi-annual statements of book inventory of nuclear material in facilities identified pursuant to Article 2 of this Protocol, for each material balance area, as based on the inventory change reports for the period covered by each such statement.

Article 27

(a) If the Agency so requests, the United States shall provide it with amplifications or clarifications of any report submitted in accordance with Article 19 of this Protocol, in so far as consistent with the purpose of the Protocol.

(b) The Agency shall inform the United States of any significant observations resulting from its examination of reports received pursuant to Article 19 of this Protocol and from visits of inspectors made pursuant to Article 11 of this Protocol.

(c) The United States and the Agency shall, at the request of either, consult about any question arising out of the interpretation or application of this Protocol, including corrective action which, in the opinion of the Agency, should be taken by the United States to ensure compliance with its terms, as indicated by the Agency in its observations pursuant to paragraph (b) of this Article.

Article 28. The definitions set forth in Article 90 of the Agreement shall apply, to the extent relevant, to this Protocol.

DONE in Vienna on the eighteenth day of November 1977. . . .

[Signatures]

[U.S. Arms Control and Disarmament Agency, *Arms Control and Disarmament Agreements: Texts and Histories of the Negotiations,* 1982 ed. (Washington, D.C.), pp. 206–238]

Argentine-Brazilian Joint Declaration on Nuclear Policy (1990)

This declaration was issued at Foz do Iguaçú, Brazil, on 28 November 1990.

The President of the Argentine Republic, Mr. Carlos Saúl Menem, and the President of the Federative Republic of Brazil, Mr Fernando Collor, meeting at Foz do Iguaçú, Brazil,

CONSIDERING:

Their decision to advance the ongoing integration process;

The importance of the use of nuclear energy solely for peaceful purposes for the scientific, economic and social development of both countries;

The commitments made in the Joint Declarations on Nuclear Policy of Foz do Iguaçú (1985), Brasilia (1986), Viedma (1987), Iperó (1988) and Ezeiza (1988);

The reaffirmation of those commitments by both Presidents in the joint communiqué issued at Buenos Aires on 6 July 1990;

The progress achieved in bilateral nuclear co-operation as a result of joint efforts within the framework of the Agreement on Co-operation in the Peaceful Uses of Nuclear Energy;

NOTING:

The efforts made by the Permanent Bilateral Committee on Nuclear Co-operation to enhance the co-operation between the two countries in the areas of research, the exchange of information, industrial complementarity, the exchange of nuclear material, the development of joint projects and policy co-ordination;

The visits by the Presidents and technical experts of the two countries to each other's nuclear facilities, especially to the uranium enrichment plants at Pilcaniyeu and Iperó and the radiochemical process laboratories at Ezeiza, which are a clear indication of the level of mutual confidence achieved between Argentina and Brazil, and

TAKING INTO ACCOUNT:

The fact that the Permanent Committee has developed mechanisms for monitoring the two countries' nuclear activities which establish, *inter alia,* joint criteria for the classification of nuclear material and facilities and the determination of their importance, and provide for reciprocal inspections of all nuclear facilities,

HEREBY DECIDE:

1. To adopt the Joint Accounting and Control System agreed on by the Permanent Committee, which shall apply to all the nuclear activities of the two countries;

2. That, as an initial step, the following activities will be carried out within the next 45 days;

a. The exchange of the respective lists describing all their nuclear facilities;

b. The exchange of the statements of the initial inventories of nuclear material existing in each country;

c. The first reciprocal inspections of centralized records systems;

d. The presentation to the International Atomic Energy Agency (IAEA) of the records and reports system which is part of the Joint Accounting and Control System, with a view to bringing it into conformity with the records and reports which both countries submit to the Agency in accordance with the safeguards agreements in force;

3. To enter into negotiations with IAEA with a view to the conclusion of a joint safeguards agreement based on the Joint Accounting and Control System;

4. After the conclusion of the safeguards agreement with IAEA, to take appropriate action to permit the full entry into force for the two countries of the Treaty for the Prohibition of Nuclear Weapons in Latin America (Treaty of Tlatelolco), including action to update and improve its wording.

[*Disarmament: A Periodic Review by the United Nations* 14:1 (1991): 225–226]

Missile Technology Control Regime

Guidelines for Sensitive Missile-Relevant Transfers

1. The purpose of these Guidelines is to limit the risks of nuclear proliferation by controlling transfers that could make a contribution to nuclear weapons delivery systems other than manned aircraft. The Guidelines are not designed to impede national space programs or international cooperation in such programs as long as such programs could not contribute to nuclear weapons delivery systems. These guidelines, including the attached Annex, form the basis for controlling transfers to any destination beyond the Government's jurisdiction or control of equipment and technology relevant to missiles whose performance in terms of payload and range exceeds stated parameters. Restraint will be exercised in the consideration of all transfers of items contained within the Annex and all such transfers will be considered on a case-by-case basis. The Government will implement the Guidelines in accordance with national legislation.

2. The Annex consists of two categories of items, which term includes equipment and technology. Category I items, all of which are in Annex Items 1 and 2, are those items of greatest sensitivity. If a Category I item is included in a system, that system will also be considered as Category I, except when the incorporated item cannot be separated, removed or duplicated. Particular restraint will be exercised in the consideration of Category I transfers, and there will be a strong presumption to deny such transfers. Until further notice, the transfer of Category I production facilities will not be authorized. The transfer of other Category I items will be authorized only on rare occasions and where the Government (A) obtains binding government-to-government undertakings embodying the assurances from the recipient government called for in paragraph 5 of these Guidelines and (B) assumes responsibility for taking all steps necessary to ensure that the item is put only to its stated end-use. It is understood that the decision to transfer remains the sole and sovereign judgment of the United States Government.

3. In the evaluation of transfer applications for Annex items, the following factors will be taken into account:

A. Nuclear proliferation concerns;

B. The capabilities and objectives of the missile and space programs of the recipient state;

C. The significance of the transfer in terms of the potential development of nuclear weapons delivery systems other than manned aircraft;

D. The assessment of the end-use of the transfers, including the relevant assurances of the recipient states referred to in sub-paragraphs 5.A and 5.B below;

E. The applicability of relevant multilateral agreements.

4. The transfer of design and production technology directly associated with any items in the Annex will be subject to as great a degree of scrutiny and control as will the equipment itself, to the extent permitted by national legislation.

5. Where the transfer could contribute to a nuclear weapons delivery system, the Government will authorize transfers of items in the Annex only on receipt of appropriate assurances from the government of the recipient state that:

A. The items will be used only for the purpose stated and that such use will not be modified nor the items modified or replicated without the prior consent of the United States Government;

B. Neither the items nor replicas nor derivatives thereof will be retransferred without the consent of the United States Government.

6. In furtherance of the effective operation of the Guidelines, the United States Government will, as necessary and appropriate, exchange relevant information with other governments applying the same Guidelines.

7. The adherence of all States to these Guidelines in the interest of international peace and security would be welcome.

SUMMARY OF THE EQUIPMENT AND TECHNOLOGY ANNEX

(Only the full text of the Annex is authoritative, and it should be consulted for precise details.)

Category I

- Complete rocket systems (including ballistic missile systems, space launch vehicles, and sounding rockets) and unmanned air vehicle systems (including cruise missile systems, target drones, and reconnaissance drones) capable of delivering at least a 500 kg payload to a range of at least 300 km as well as the specially designed production facilities for these systems.
- Complete subsystems usable in the systems in Item 1, as follows, as well as the specially designed production facilities and production equipment therefor:
- Individual rocket stages;
- Re-entry vehicles;
- Solid or liquid fuel rocket engines;
- Guidance sets;
- Thrust vector controls;
- Warhead safing, arming, fuzing, and firing mechanisms.

Category II

- Propulsion components.
- Propellants and constituents.
- Propellant production technology and equipment.
- Missile structural composites: production technology and equipment.
- Pyrolytic deposition/densification technology and equipment.
- Structural materials.
- Flight instruments, inertial navigation equipment, software, and production equipment.
- Flight control systems.
- Avionics equipment.
- Launch/ground support equipment and facilities.
- Missile computers.
- Analog-to-digital converters.
- Test facilities and equipment.
- Software and related analog or hybrid computers.
- Reduced observable technology, materials, and devices.
- Nuclear effects protection.

EQUIPMENT AND TECHNOLOGY ANNEX

1. *Introduction*

(a) This annex consists of two categories of items, which term includes equipment and technology. Category I items, all of which are in Annex Items 1 and 2, are those items of greatest sensitivity. If a Category I item is included in a system, that system will also be considered as Category I, except when the incorporated item cannot be separated, removed or duplicated. Category II items are those items in the Annex not designated Category I.

(b) The transfer of design and production technology directly associated with any items in the Annex will be subject to as great a degree of scrutiny and control as will the equipment itself, to the extent permitted by national legislation.

2. *Definitions.* For the purpose of this Annex, the following definitions shall apply:

(a) The term *technology* means specific information which is required for the development, production or use of a product. The information may take the form of technical data or technical assistance.

(b) (1) *Development* is related to all stages prior to serial production such as

- design
- design research
- design analyses
- design concepts
- assembly and testing of prototypes
- pilot production schemes
- design data
- process of transforming design data into a product
- configuration design
- integration design
- layouts

(2) *Production* means all production stages such as

- production engineering
- manufacture
- integration
- assembly (mounting)
- inspection
- testing
- quality assurance

(3) *Use* means

- operation
- installation (including on-site installation)
- maintenance (checking)
- repair
- overhaul and refurbishing

(c) (1) *Technical data* may take forms such as blueprints, plans, diagrams, models, formulae, engineering designs and specifications, manuals and instructions written or recorded on other media or devices such as disk, tape, read-only memories.

(2) *Technical assistance* may take forms such as

- instruction
- skills
- training
- working knowledge
- consulting services

(d) NOTE: This definition of technology does not include *technology in the public domain* nor *basic scientific research.*

(1) *In the public domain* as it applies to this Annex means technology which has been made available without restrictions upon its further dissemination. (Copyright restrictions do not remove technology from being in the public domain.)

(2) *Basic scientific research* means experimental or theoretical work undertaken principally to acquire new knowledge of the fundamental principles of phenomena and observable facts, not primarily directed towards a specific practical aim or objective.

(e) The term *production facilities* means equipment and specially designed software therefor integrated into facilities for prototype development or for one or more stages of serial production.

(f) The term *production equipment* means tooling, templates, jigs, mandrels, moulds, dies, fixtures, alignment mechanisms, test equipment, other machinery and components thereof, limited to those specially designed or modified for prototype development or for one or more stages of serial production.

Item 1—Category I. Complete rocket systems (including ballistic missile systems, space launch vehicles, and sounding rockets) and unmanned air vehicle systems (including cruise missile systems, target drones, and reconnaissance drones) capable of delivering at least a 500 kg payload to a range of at least 300 km as well as specially designed production facilities for these systems.

Item 2—Category I. Complete subsystems usable in the systems in Item 1, as follows, as well as the specially designed production facilities and production equipment therefor:

(a) Individual rocket stages:

(b) Reentry vehicles, and specially designed equipment therefor, as follows, except as provided in note (1) below for those designed for non-weapons payloads:

(1) Heat shields and components thereof fabricated of ceramic or ablative materials;

(2) Heat sinks and components thereof fabricated of light-weight, high heat capacity materials;

(3) Electronic equipment specially designed or modified for reentry vehicles;

(c) Solid or liquid fuel rocket engines, having a total impulse capacity of 2.5×10^5 lb-sec or greater, except as provided in note (1) below for those specially designed or modified for orbital correction of satellites;

(d) Guidance sets capable of achieving system accuracy (CEP) of 10 km or less at a range of 300 km, except as provided in note (1) below for those designed for missiles with range under 300 km or manned aircraft;

(e) Thrust vector controls, except as provided in note (1) below for those designed for rocket systems with range under 300 km;

(f) Warhead safing, arming, fuzing, and firing mechanisms, except as provided in note (1) below for those designed for systems other than those in Item 1.

Notes to Item 2:

(1) The exceptions in (b), (c), (d), (e), and (f) above may be treated as Category II if the subsystem is exported subject to end use statements and quantity limits appropriate for the excepted end use stated above.

(2) CEP (circle of equal probability) is a measure of accuracy; the radius of the circle centered at the target, at a specific range, in which 50% of the payloads impact.

Item 3—Category II. Propulsion components and equipment usable in the systems in Item 1, as follows, as well as the specially designed production facilities therefor:

(a) Light-weight turbojet and turbofan engines (including turbocompound engines) that are small and fuel efficient;

(b) Ramjet/Scramjet engines, including devices to regulate combustion, and specially designed production equipment therefor;

(c) Rocket motor cases and specially designed production equipment therefor;

(d) Staging mechanisms and specially production equipment therefor;

(e) Liquid fuel control systems and components therefor, specially designed to operate in vibrating environments of more than 12 g rms between 20 Hz and 2000 Hz including;

(1) Servo valves designed for flow rates of 24 litres per minute or greater at a pressure of 250 bars, and having flow contact surfaces made of 90% or more tantalum, titanium or zirconium, either separately or combined, except when such surfaces are made of materials containing more than 97% and less than 99.7% titanium;

(2) Pumps (except vacuum pumps), having all flow contact surfaces made of 90% or more tantalum, titanium or zirconium, either separately or combined, except when such surfaces are made of materials containing more than 97% and less than 99.7% titanium.

Notes to Item 3:

(1) Item 3(a) engines may be exported as part of a manned aircraft or in quantities appropriate for replacement parts for manned aircraft.

(2) Item 3(e) systems and components may be exported as part of a satellite.

Item 4—Category II. Propellants and constituent chemicals for propellants as follows:

(a) Propulsive substances:

(1) Hydrazine with a concentration of more than 70%;

(2) Unsymmetric dimethylhydrazine (UDMH);

(3) Spherical ammonium perchlorate with particles of uniform diameter less than 500 microns;

(4) Spherical aluminium powder with particles of uniform diameter of less than 500 microns and an aluminium content of 97% or greater;

(5) Metal fuels in particle sizes less than 500 microns, whether spherical, atomized, spheroidal, flaked or ground, consisting of 97% or more of any of the following: zirconium, titanium, uranium, tungsten, boron, zinc, and alloys of these; magnesium; Misch metal;

(6) Nitro-amines (cyclotetramethylene-tetranitramine (HMX), cyclotetramethylenetrinitramine (RDX) when specially formulated as propulsive substances.

(b) Polymeric substances:

(1) Carboxy-terminated polybutadiene (CTPB);

(2) Hydroxy-terminated polybutadiene (HTPB);

(c) Composite propellants including moulded glue propellants and propellants with nitrated bonding and aluminum content in excess of 5%.

(d) Other high energy density fuels such as Boron Slurry, having an energy density of 40×10^6 joules/kg or greater.

Item 5—Category II. Production technology or production equipment specially designed or modified for production, handling, mixing, curing, casting, pressing, machining and acceptance testing of the liquid or solid propellants and propellant constituents as described in Item 4.

Item 6—Category II. Equipment, technical data and procedures for the production of structural composites usable in the systems in Item 1 as follows, and specially designed components and accessories and specially designed software therefor:

(a) Filament winding machines of which the motions for positioning, wrapping and winding fibres are coordinated and programmed in three or more axes, specially designed to fabricate composite structures or laminates from fibrous and filamentary materials; and coordinating and programming controls;

(b) Tape-laying machines of which the motions for positioning and laying tape and sheets are coordinated and programmed in two or more axes, specially designed for the manufacture of composite airframes and missile structures;

(c) Interlacing machines, including adapters and modification kits for weaving, interlacing or braiding fibers to fabricate composite structures, except textile machinery which has not been modified for the above end-uses;

(d) Specially designed or adapted equipment for the production of fibrous and filamentary materials as follows:

(1) Equipment for converting polymeric fibres (such as polyacrylonitrile, rayon, or polycarbosilane) including special provision to strain the fibre during heating;

(2) Equipment for the vapor deposition of elements or compounds on heated filamentary substrates; and

(3) Equipment for the wet-spinning of refractory ceramics (such as aluminum oxide);

(e) Specially designed or adapted equipment for special fiber surface treatment or for producing prepregs and preforms. NOTE: Equipment covered by this sub-item includes but is not limited to rollers, tension stretchers, coating equipment, cutting equipment, and clicker dies.

(f) Technical data (including processing conditions) and procedures for the regulation of temperature, pressures or atmosphere in autoclaves when used for the production of composites or partially processed composites.

Note to Item 6: Specially designed or adapted components and accessories for the machines covered by this entry include, but are not limited to, moulds, mandrels, dies, fixtures and tooling for the preform pressing, curing, casting, sintering or bonding of composite structures, laminates and manufactures thereof.

Item 7—Category II. Pyrolytic deposition and densification equipment and technology as follows:

(a) Technology for producing pyrolytically derived materials formed on a mould, mandrel or other substrate from precursor gases which decompose in the 1300 to 2900 degrees Celsius temperature range at pressures of 1 mm Hg to 150 mm Hg (including technology for the composition of precursor gases, flow-rates, and process control schedules and parameters);

(b) Specially designed nozzles for the above processes;

(c) Equipment and process controls, and specially designed software therefor, specially designed for densification and pyrolysis of structural composite rocket nozzles and reentry vehicle nose tips.

Item 8—Category II. Structural materials usable in the systems in Item 1, as follows:

(a) Composite structures, laminates, and manufactures thereof, including resin impregnated fiber prepregs and metal coated fiber preforms therefor, specially designed for use in the systems in Item 1 and the subsystems in Item 2 made either with an organic matrix or metal matrix utilizing fibrous or filamentary reinforcements having a specific tensile strength greater than 7.62×10^4 m (3×10^6 inches) and a specific modulus greater than 3.18×10^6 m (1.25×10^8 inches);

(b) Resaturated pyrolyzed (i.e., carbon-carbon) materials specially designed for rocket systems;

(c) Fine grain artificial graphites for rocket nozzles and re-entry vehicle nosetips having all of the following characteristics:

(1) Bulk density of 1.79 or greater (measured at 293K);

(2) Tensile strain to failure of 0.7 percent or greater (measured at 293K);

(3) Coefficient of thermal expansion of 2.75×10^6 or less per degree K (in the range of 293K to 1,255K);

(d) Ceramic composite materials specially designed for use in missile radomes.

Item 9—Category II. Compasses, gyroscopes, accelerometers and inertial equipment and specially designed software therefor, as follows; and specially designed components therefore usable in the systems in Item 1:

(a) Integrated flight instrument systems which include gyrostabilizers or automatic pilots and integration software therefor, specially designed or modified for use in the systems in Item 1;

(b) Gyro-astro compasses and other devices which derive position or orientation by means of automatically tracking celestial bodies;

(c) Accelerometers with a threshold of 0.005 g or less, or a linearity error within 0.25 percent of full scale output or both, which are designed for use in inertial navigation systems or in guidance systems of all types;

(d) Gyros with a rated free directional drift rate (rated free precession) of less than 0.5 degree (1 sigma or rms) per hour in a 1g environment;

(e) Continuous output accelerometers which utilize servo or force balance techniques and gyros, both specified to function at acceleration levels greater than 100 g;

(f) Inertial or other equipment using accelerometers described by subitems (c) and (e) above or gyros described by subitems (d) or (e) above, and systems incorporating such equipment, and specially designed integration software therefor;

(g) Specially designed test, calibration, and alignment equipment for the above;

(h) Specially designed production equipment for the above, including the following;

(1) For ring laser gyro equipment, the following equipment used to characterize mirrors, having the threshold accuracy shown or better:

(i) Rectilinear Scatterometer (10 ppm);

(ii) Polar Scatterometer (10ppm);

(iii) Reflectometer (50ppm);

(iv) Profilimeter (5 Angstroms);

(2) For other inertial equipment:

(i) Inertial Measurement Unit (IMU Module) Tester;

(ii) IMU Platform Tester;

(iii) IMU Stable Element Handling Fixture;

(iv) IMU Platform Balance Fixture;

(v) Gyro Tuning Test Station;

(vi) Gyro Dynamic Balance Station;

(vii) Gyro Run-In/Motor Test Station;

(viii) Gyro Evacuation and Fill Station;

(ix) Centrifuge Fixture for Gyro Bearings;

(x) Accelerometer Axis Align Station;

(xi) Accelerometer Test Station.

Note to Item 9: Items (a) through to (f) may be exported as part of a manned aircraft or satellite or in quantities appropriate for replacement parts for manned aircraft.

Item 10—Category II. Flight control systems usable in the systems in Item 1 as follows, as well as the specially designed test, calibration, and alignment equipment therefor:

(a) Hydraulic, mechanical, electro-optical, or electro-mechanical flight control systems (including fly-by-wire systems) specially designed or modified for the systems in Item 1;

(b) Attitude control equipment specially designed or modified for the systems in Item 1;

(c) Design technology for integration of air vehicle fuselage, propulsion system and lifting and control surfaces to optimize aerodynamic performance throughout the flight regime of an unmanned air vehicle;

(d) Design technology for integration of flight control, guidance, and propulsion data into a flight management system for optimization of rocket system trajectory.

Note to Item 10: Items (a) and (b) may be exported as part of a manned aircraft or satellite or in quantities appropriate for replacement parts for manned aircraft.

Item 11—Category II. Avionics equipment specially designed or modified for use in unmanned air vehicles or rockets systems and specially designed software and components therefor usable in the systems in Item 1, including but not limited to:

(a) Radar and laser radar systems, including altimeters;

(b) Passive sensors for determining bearing to specific electromagnetic sources (direction finding equipment) or terrain characteristics;

(c) Equipment specially designed for real-time integration, processing, and use of navigation information derived from an external source;

(d) Electronic assemblies and components specially designed for military use incorporating any of the following:

(1) Specially designed, integral structural supports;

(2) Techniques for conductive heat removal;

(3) Radiation hardening;

(4) Design for reliable short-term operation at temperatures in excess of 125 degrees Celsius;

(e) Design technology for protection of avionic and electrical subsystems against electromagnetic pulse (EMP) and electromagnetic interference (EMI) hazards from external sources, as follows:

(1) Technology for design of shielding systems;

(2) Technology for the configuration design of hardened electrical circuits and subsystems;

(3) Determination of hardening criteria for the above.

Notes to Item 11:

(1) Item 11 equipment may be exported as part of a manned aircraft or satellite or in quantities appropriate for replacement parts for manned aircraft.

(2) Examples of equipment included in this item:

- Terrain contour mapping equipment;
- Scene mapping and correlation (both digital and analog) equipment;
- Doppler navigation radar equipment;
- Passive interferometer equipment;
- Imaging sensor equipment (both active and passive).

Item 12—Category II. Launch and ground support equipment and facilities usable for the systems in Item 1, as follows:

(a) Apparatus and devices specially designed or modified for the handling, control, activation and launching of the systems in Item 1;

(b) Military vehicles specially designed or modified for the handling, control, activation and launching of the systems in Item 1;

(c) Gravity meters (gravimeters), gravity gradiometers, and specially designed components therefor, designed or modified for airborne or marine use, and having a static or operational accuracy of one milligal or better, with a time to steady-state registration of two minutes or less;

(d) Telemetering and telecontrol equipment suitable for use with unmanned air vehicles or rocket systems;

(e) Precision tracking systems:

(1) Tracking systems which use a translator installed on the rocket system or unmanned air vehicle in conjunction with either surface or airborne references or navigation satellite systems to provide real-time measurements of inflight position and velocity;

(2) Software systems which process recorded data for post-mission precision tracking enabling determination of vehicle position.

Item 13—Category II. Analog computers, digital computers, or digital differential analyzers specially designed or modified for use in air vehicles or rocket systems and usable in the systems in Item 1, having any of the following characteristics:

(a) Rated for continuous operation at temperatures from below − 45 degrees Celsius to above 55 degrees Celsius;

(b) Designed as ruggedized or radiation-hardened equipment and capable of meeting military specifications for ruggedized or radiation-hardened equipment; or,

(c) Modified for military use.

Note to Item 13: Item 13 equipment may be exported as part of a manned aircraft or satellite or in quantities appropriate for replacement parts for manned aircraft.

Item 14—Category II. Analog-to-digital converters, other than digital voltmeters or counters, usable in the systems in Item 1 and having any of the following characteristics: rated for continuous operation at temperatures from below − 45 degrees Celsius to above 55 degrees Celsius; designed to meet military specifications for ruggedized equipment, or modified for military use; or designed for radiation resistance, as follows:

(a) Electrical input type analog-to-digital converters having any of the following characteristics:

(1) A conversion rate of more than 200,000 complete conversions per second at rated accuracy;

(2) An accuracy in excess of 1 part in more than 10,000 of full scale over the specified operating temperature range;

(3) A figure of merit 1×10^8 or more (derived from the number of complete conversions per second divided by the accuracy).

(b) Analog-to-digital converter microcircuits having both of the following characteristics:

(1) A maximum conversion time to maximum resolution of less than 20 microseconds;

(2) A rated non-linearity of better than 0.025 percent of full scale over the specified operating temperature range.

Item 15—Category II. Test facilities and equipment usable for the systems in Item 1, as follows:

(a) Vibration test equipment using digital control techniques and specially designed ancillary equipment and software therefor capable of imparting forces of 100 kN (22,500 lbs) or greater;

(b) Supersonic (Mach 1.4 to Mach 5), hypersonic (Mach 5 to Mach 15), and hypervelocity (above Mach 15) wind tunnels, except those specially designed for educational purposes and having a test section size (measured internally) of less than 25 cm (10 inches);

(c) Test benches with the capacity to handle solid or liquid fuel rockets of more than 20,000 lbs of thrust, and capable of measuring the three thrust components.

Note to Item 15 (a): The term "digital control" refers to equipment, the functions of which are, partly or entirely, automatically controlled by stored and digitally coded electrical signals.

Item 16—Category II. Specially designed software, or specially designed software and related specially designed analog or hybrid (combined analog/digital) computers, for modeling, simulation, or design integration of rocket systems and unmanned air vehicle systems, usable for the systems in Item 1.

Item 17—Category II. Technology, materials, and devices for reduced observables such as radar reflectivity, optical/infrared signatures and acoustic signatures (i.e., stealth technology), for military application in rocket systems and unmanned air vehicles, and usable for the systems in Item 1, for example:

(a) Structural materials and coatings specially designed for reduced radar reflectivity;

(b) Optical coatings, including paints, specially designed or formulated for reduced optical reflection or emissivity, except when specially used for thermal control of satellites.

Item 18—Category II. Technology and devices specially designed for use in protecting rocket systems and unmanned air vehicles against nuclear effects (e.g., Electromagnetic Pulse (EMP), X-rays, combined blast and thermal effects), and usable for the systems in Item 1, for example:

(a) Hardened microcircuits and detectors specially designed to withstand radiation as follows:

(1) Neutron dosage of 1×10^{12} neutrons/cm^2 (single event);

(2) Gamma dose rate of 1×10^9 rads/sec;

(3) Total dose 1500 rads (single event).

(b) Radomes specially designed to withstand a combined thermal shock greater than 100 cal/cm^2 accompanied by a peak overpressure of greater than 7 pounds per square inch.

Note to Item 18(a): A microcircuit is defined as a device in which a number of passive and active circuit elements are considered as indivisibly associated on or within a continuous structure to perform the function of a circuit.

[Reprinted in Trevor Findlay, ed., *Chemical Weapons and Missile Proliferation: With Implications for the Asia/Pacific Region* (Boulder, Colo., 1991), pp. 150–161]

Big Five Initiative on Arms Transfer and Proliferation Restraints (1991)

Statement of the Five Countries, Paris, 9 July 1991

1. Representatives of the United States of America, the People's Republic of China, France, the United Kingdom, and the Union of Soviet Socialist Republics, met in Paris on the 8th and 9th of July to review issues related to conventional arms transfers and to the non-proliferation of weapons of mass destruction.

They noted with concern the dangers associated with the excessive buildup of military capabilities, and confirmed they would not transfer conventional weapons in circumstances which would undermine stability. They also noted the threats to peace and stability posed by the proliferation of nuclear weapons, chemical and biological weapons, and missiles, and undertook to seek effective measures of non-proliferation and arms control in a fair, reasonable, comprehensive and balanced manner on a global as well as on a regional basis.

2. They had a thorough and positive exchange of views on the basis of the arms control initiatives presented in particular by President Bush, President Mitterrand, Prime Minister Major and on other initiatives which address these problems globally and as a matter of urgency in the Middle East. They also agreed to support continued work in the United Nations on an arms transfers register to be established under the aegis of the UN Secretary General, on a non-discriminatory basis, as a step towards increased transparency on arms transfers and in general military matters.

They stressed that the ultimate response to the threat of proliferation is verifiable arms control and disarmament agreements amongst the parties concerned. They expressed strong support for full implementation of existing arms control regimes. For their part, they will contribute to this objective by developing and maintaining stringent national and, as far as possible, harmonized controls to ensure that weapons of mass destruction-related equipment and materials are transferred for permitted purposes only and are not diverted.

They also strongly supported the objective of establishing a weapons of mass destruction-free zone in the Middle East. They expressed their view that critical steps towards this goal include full implementation of UNSC [UN Security Council] resolution 687 and adoption by countries in the region of a comprehensive program of arms control for the region, including:

- a freeze and ultimate elimination of ground to ground missiles in the region;
- submission by all nations in the region of all of their nuclear activities to IAEA [International Atomic Energy Agency] safeguards;
- a ban on the importation and production of nuclear weapons usable materials;
- agreement by all states in the region to undertake to becoming parties to the CW [chemical weapons] Convention as soon as it is concluded in 1992.

3. They acknowledged that Article 51 of the UN Charter guarantees every state the right of self-defence. That right implies that states have also the right to acquire means with which to defend themselves. In this respect, the transfer of conventional weapons, conducted in a responsible manner, should contribute to the ability of states to meet their legitimate defence, security and national sovereignty requirements and to participate effectively in collective measures requested by the United Nations for the purpose of maintaining or restoring international peace and security.

They recognized that indiscriminate transfers of military weapons and technology contribute to regional instability. They are full conscious of the special responsibilities that are incumbent upon them to ensure that such risks be avoided, and of the special role they have to play in promoting greater responsibility, confidence and transparency in this field. They also recognize that a long term solution to this problem should be found in close consultation with recipient countries.

4. They expressed the intention that:

- when considering under their national control procedures conventional weapons transfers, they will observe rules of restraint. They will develop agreed guidelines on this basis;
- taking into account the special situation of the Middle East as a primary area of tension, they will develop modalities of consultation and of infor-

mation exchanges concerning arms transfers to this region as a matter of priority;

- a group of experts will meet in September with a view to reaching agreement on this approach;
- another plenary meeting will be held in October in London;
- further meetings will be held periodically to review these issues.

5. They expressed the conviction that this process of continuing cooperation will contribute to a worldwide climate of vigilance in this field which other countries share.

Communiqué of the Five Countries, London, 18 October 1991

1. In accordance with their agreement in Paris on 8 and 9 July 1991, representatives of the United States of America, the People's Republic of China, France, the United Kingdom of Great Britain and Northern Ireland, and the Union of Soviet Socialist Republics met in London on 17 and 18 October to take forward their discussion on issues related to conventional arms transfers and to the non-proliferation of weapons of mass destruction.

2. Recalling the statement which was issued in Paris on 9 July, they:

- agreed [on] common guidelines for the export of conventional weapons (annexed). They expressed the hope that other arms exporting countries will adopt similar guidelines of restraint;
- agreed to inform each other about transfers to the region of the Middle East, as a matter of priority, of tanks, armoured combat vehicles, artillery, military aircraft and helicopters, naval vessels, and certain missile systems, without prejudice to existing commitments to other governments;
- agreed to make arrangements to exchange information for the purpose of meaningful consultation, bearing in mind their shared concern to ensure the proper application of the agreed guidelines, and to continue discussions on how best to develop these arrangements on a global and regional basis in order to achieve this objective;
- welcomed work at the United Nations General Assembly on the early establishment of a UN register of conventional arms transfers, and supported the current consultations on this issue

between a wide range of UN members in which they are actively participating. They called for universal support of this work;

- noted the threats to peace and stability posed by the proliferation of nuclear weapons, chemical and biological weapons, missiles, etc, and undertook to seek effective measures of non-proliferation and arms control in a fair, reasonable, comprehensive and balanced manner on a global as well as on a regional basis. They reaffirmed the importance of maintaining stringent and, so far as possible, harmonized guidelines for exports in this area. They embarked on a comparison of their national export controls on equipment related to weapons of mass destruction and agreed to examine the scope for further harmonization of those controls. They agreed to pursue discussions at their next meeting on these subjects;
- agreed to continue discussing the possibilities for lowering tension and arms levels, including the development of further measures of restraint concerning arms transfers and ways of encouraging regional and global efforts towards arms control and disarmament;
- agreed to continue to give these efforts high priority and meet again in the next year in the United States to take forward their discussions, and to meet regularly thereafter at least once a year.

Guidelines for Conventional Arms Transfers

The People's Republic of China, the French Republic, the Union of Soviet Socialist Republics, the United Kingdom of Great Britain and Northern Ireland, and the United States of America,

- recalling and reaffirming the principles which they stated as a result of their meeting in Paris on 8 and 9 July 1991,
- mindful of the dangers to peace and stability posed by the transfer of conventional weapons beyond levels needed for defensive purposes,
- reaffirming the inherent right to individual or collective self-defense recognized in Article 51 of the Charter of the United Nations, which implies that states have the right to acquire means of legitimate self-defense,
- recalling that in accordance with the Charter of the United Nations, UN Member States have undertaken to promote the establishment and maintenance of international peace and security with the least diversion for armaments of the world's human and economic resources,

- seeking to ensure that arms transferred are not used in violations of the purposes and principles of the UN Charter,
- mindful of their special responsibilities for the maintenance of international peace and security,
- reaffirming their commitment to seek effective measures to promote peace, security, stability and arms control on a global and regional basis in a fair, reasonable, comprehensive and balanced manner,
- noting the importance of encouraging international commerce for peaceful purposes,
- determined to adopt a serious, responsible and prudent attitude of restraint regarding arms transfers,

declare that, when considering under their national control procedures conventional arms transfers, they intend to observe rules of restraint, and to act in accordance with the following guidelines:

1. They will consider carefully whether proposed transfers will:

a) promote the capabilities of the recipient to meet needs for legitimate self-defense;

b) serve as an appropriate and proportionate response to the security and military threats confronting the recipient country;

c) enhance the capability of the recipient to participate in regional or other collective arrangements or other measures consistent with the Charter of the United Nations or requested by the United Nations;

2. They will avoid transfers which would be likely to:

a) prolong or aggravate an existing armed conflict;

b) increase tension in a region or contribute to regional instability;

c) introduce destabilising military capabilities in a region;

d) contravene embargoes or other relevant internationally agreed restraints to which they are parties;

e) be used other than for the legitimate defense and security needs of the recipient state;

f) support or encourage international terrorism;

g) be used to interfere with the internal affairs of sovereign states;

h) seriously undermine the recipient state's economy.

[U.S. Arms Control and Disarmament Agency, *World Military Expenditures and Arms Transfers, 1990* (Washington, D.C., 1991), pp. 23–24-B]

Rules of War

——————————————————— ◯ ———————————————————

See also The Law of War *and* Medieval Peace Movements and the Western Quest for Peace.

The arms control technique of drafting rules of war seeks to limit the destructiveness of military violence should war break out. This technique has evolved from custom, historical precedent and, later, treaties, resolutions, and agreements, which together form the rules of war (or "law of war") and provide a large reservoir of legal and accepted practices.

The underlying rationale of the collective law of war as an important element of arms control is essentially (a) to outlaw weapons considered to cause unnecessary or disproportionate destruction and suffering; (b) to distinguish between combatants and civilians and to provide appropriate protections to each; and (c) to emphasize that it is vital that the demands of humanity and the environment must be accorded priority. Any broad definition of the law of war could incorporate a wide variety of treaties and agreements that, in this volume, have been assigned to other sections—including those seeking to outlaw chemical, bacteriological, and biological weapons, regulate submarine warfare, and restrict aerial bombing.

To accomplish all of these objectives, between 1581 and 1864 nations concluded more than 300 international agreements—291 for the purpose of protecting the lives of the wounded and sick. (Hans Morgenthau, *Politics Among Nations: The Struggle for Power and Peace* [New York, 1960]: 239.) In the aftermath of World War II—when military technology, especially weapons of mass destruction, appeared to have outstripped the law of war—many "realists" pessimistically concluded that the efforts of international law to deal with modern war were no longer relevant. Writing in the *Proceeding of the American Society of International Law*, Charles G. Fenwick argued this point: "The laws of war belong to a past age, and except for a few minor matters of no consequence, it is futile to attempt to revive them. . . . War has got beyond the control of law" (vol. 110, 1949, p. 43).

Other observers, viewing the widespread destruction of cities and the forty million or so casualties of World War II, concluded the opposite. Indeed, Major General J. F. C. Fuller denounced the new concept of total war:

> *To beget and build in order to kill and demolish is lunacy. And the more powerful becomes the war machine, the more certain is it that war will bring losses far in excess of gains, not only to the vanquished but also the victors. This is the*

uncontradictable fact the Second World War has revealed to all who still are sane. . . . The peoples of today and tomorrow will realize, as their ancestors did in the seventeenth and eighteenth centuries, that wars fought without rules restricting their ravages are absurdities which can only lead to victories of mutual ruin. (Armament and History: A Study of the Influence of Armament on History from the Dawn of Classical Warfare to the Second World War, New York, 1945, pp. 185, 195.)

Ancient Example

Oath of the Delphic Amphictyons (7th Century B.C.)

. . . I read their oaths, in which the men of ancient times swore that they would raze no city of the Amphictyonic states, nor shut them off from flowing water either in war or in peace; that if anyone should violate this oath, they would march against such an one and raze his cities; and if anyone should violate the shrine of the god or be accessory to such violation, or make any plot against the holy places, they would punish him with hand and foot and voice, and all their power. To the oath was added a mighty curse.

[*The Speeches of Aeschines*. Trans. by Charles Darwin Adams. (New York: G. P. Putnam's Sons, 1919), pp. 244–247]

Peace of God

The Peace and Truce of God and Peace of Lands is examined by Professor Heyn in his essay entitled "Medieval Peace Movements in Europe." In the Peace and Truce of God, armed forces began to distinguish between combatants and the protections due civilians.

Peace of God, Proclaimed in the Synod of Charroux (989)

Following the example of my predecessors, I, Gunbald, archbishop of Bordeaux, called together the bishops of my diocese in a synod at Charroux.... and we, assembled there in the name of God, made the following decrees:

1. Anathema against those who break into churches. If anyone breaks into or robs a church, he shall be anathema unless he makes satisfaction.

2. Anathema against those who rob the poor. If anyone robs a peasant or any other poor person of a sheep, ox, ass, cow, goat, or pig, he shall be anathema unless he makes satisfaction.

3. Anathema against those who injure clergymen. If anyone attacks, seizes, or beats a priest, deacon, or any other clergyman, who is not bearing arms (shield, sword, coat of mail, or helmet), but is going along peacefully or staying in the house, the sacrilegious person shall be excommunicated and cut off from the church, unless he makes satisfaction, or unless the bishop discovers that the clergyman brought it upon himself by his own fault.

[Oliver J. Thatcher and Edgar H. McNeal, *A Source Book for Medieval History: Selected Documents Illustrating the History of Europe in the Middle Ages* (New York, 1905), p. 412]

Peace of God, Proclaimed by Guy of Anjou, Bishop of Puy (990)

In the name of the divine, supreme, and undivided Trinity. Guy of Anjou, by the grace of God bishop [of Puy], greeting and peace to all who desire the mercy of God. Be it known to all the faithful subjects of God, that because of the wickedness that daily increases among the people, we have called together certain bishops [names], and many other bishops, princes, and nobles. And since we know that only the peaceloving shall see the Lord, we urge all men, in the name of the Lord, to be sons of peace.

1. From this hour forth, no man in the bishoprics over which these bishops rule, and in these counties, shall break into a church... except that the bishop may enter a church to recover the taxes that are due him from it.

2. No man in the counties or bishoprics shall seize a horse, colt, ox, cow, ass, or the burdens which it carries, or a sheep, goat, or pig, or kill any of them, unless he requires it for a lawful expedition. On an expedition a man may take what he needs to eat, but shall carry nothing home with

him; and no one shall take material for fortifying or besieging a castle except from his own lands or subjects.

3. Clergymen shall not bear arms; no one shall injure monks or any unarmed persons who accompany them; except that the bishop or the archdeacon may use such means as are necessary to compel them to pay the taxes which they owe them.

4. No one shall seize a peasant, man or woman, for the purpose of making him purchase his freedom, unless the peasant has forfeited his freedom. This is not meant to restrict the rights of a lord over the peasants living on his own lands or on lands which he claims.

5. From this hour forth no one shall seize ecclesiastical lands, whether those of a bishop, chapter, or monastery, and no one shall levy any unjust tax or toll from them; unless he holds them as *precaria* from the bishop or the brothers.

6. No one shall seize or rob merchants.

7. No layman shall exercise any authority in the matter of burials or ecclesiastical offerings; no priest shall take money for baptism, for it is the gift of the Holy Spirit.

8. If anyone breaks the peace and refuses to keep it, he shall be excommunicated and anathematized and cut off from the holy mother church, until he makes satisfaction; if he refuses to make satisfaction, no priest shall say mass or perform divine services for him, no priest shall bury him or permit him to be buried in consecrated ground; no priest shall knowingly give him communion; if any priest knowingly violates this decree he shall be deposed. [Oliver J. Thatcher and Edgar H. McNeal, *A Source Book for Medieval History: Selected Documents Illustrating the History of Europe in the Middle Ages* (New York, 1905), pp. 412–413]

Truce of God

According to Thatcher and McNeal, the earliest Truce of God extant is that made for the Archbishopric of Arles (except for the doubtful case of the council of Elne, 1027), and it exists in the form of a communication recommending it to the clergy of Italy.

Truce of God, Proclaimed in the Diocese of Elne (1027)

. . . And so the said bishops, with all the clergy and the faithful people, provided that—

[1] throughout the whole of the said country [Roussillon] and bishopric no one should attack his enemy from the ninth hour [counting from sunrise] on Saturday until the first hour [counting from sunrise] on Monday, so that everyone may perform his religious duties on Sunday.

[2] And none shall attack a monk or a clergyman who is unarmed, nor any man going to or coming from a church or a council, nor a man accompanied by a woman.

[3] And none shall dare to violate a church or the houses within thirty paces of a church. . . .

[6] No Christian should eat or drink with excommunicates, nor kiss them, nor talk with them, except about their repentance. If they die excommunicate, they shall not be buried at the church; nor should any cleric or faithful Christian pray for them. . . .

[R. G. D. Laffan, ed., *Select Documents of European History, 800–1492* (New York, 1929), pp. 19–20]

Truce of God, Made for the Archbishopric of Arles (1035–1041)

In the name of God, the omnipotent Father, Son, and Holy Spirit. Reginbald, archbishop of Arles, with Benedict, bishop of Avignon, Nithard, bishop of Nice, the venerable abbot Odilo [of Cluny], and all the bishops, abbots, and other clergy of Gaul, to all the archbishops, bishops, and clergy of Italy, grace and peace from God, the omnipotent Father, who is, was, and shall be.

1. For the salvation of your souls, we beseech all you who fear God and believe in him and have been redeemed by his blood, to follow the footsteps of God, and to keep peace one with another, that you may obtain eternal peace and quiet with Him.

2. This is the peace or truce of God which we have received from heaven through the inspiration of God, and we beseech you to accept it and observe it even as we have done; namely, that all Christians, friends and enemies, neighbors and strangers, should keep true and lasting peace one with another from vespers on Wednesday to sunrise on Monday, so that during these four days and five nights, all persons may have peace, and, trusting in this peace, may go about their business without fear of their enemies.

3. All who keep the peace and truce of God shall be absolved of their sins by God, the omnipotent Father, and His Son Jesus Christ, and the Holy

Spirit, and by St. Mary with the choir of virgins, and St. Michael with the choir of angels, and St. Peter with all the saints and all the faithful, now and forever.

4. Those who have promised to observe the truce and have wilfully violated it, shall be excommunicated by God the omnipotent Father, and His Son Jesus Christ, and the Holy Spirit, from the communion of all the saints of God, shall be accursed and despised here and in the future world, shall be damned with Dathan and Abiram and with Judas who betrayed his Lord, and shall be overwhelmed in the depths of hell, as was Pharaoh in the midst of the sea, unless they make such satisfaction as is described in the following:

5. If anyone has killed another on the days of the truce of God, he shall be exiled and driven from the land and shall make a pilgrimage to Jerusalem, spending his exile there. If anyone has violated the truce of God in any other way, he shall suffer the penalty prescribed by the secular laws and shall do double the penance prescribed by the canons.

6. We believe it is just that we should suffer both secular and spiritual punishment if we break the promise which we have made to keep the peace. For we believe that this peace was given to us from heaven by God; for before God gave it to his people, there was nothing good done among us. The Lord's Day was not kept, but all kinds of labor were performed on it.

7. We have vowed and dedicated these four days to God: Thursday, because it is the day of his ascension; Friday, because it is the day of his passion; Saturday, because it is the day in which he was in the tomb; and Sunday, because it is the day of his res-urrection; on that day no labor shall be done and no one shall be in fear of his enemy.

8. By the power given to us by God through the apostles, we bless and absolve all who keep the peace and truce of God; we excommunicate, curse, anathematize, and exclude from the holy mother church all who violate it.

9. If anyone shall punish violators of this decree and of the truce of God, he shall not be held guilty of a crime, but shall go and come freely with the blessing of all Christians, as a defender of the cause of God. But if anything has been stolen on other days, and the owner finds it on one of the days of the truce, he shall not be restrained from recovering it, lest thereby an advantage should be given to the thief.

10. In addition, brothers, we request that you observe the day on which the peace and truce was established by us, keeping it in the name of the holy Trinity. Drive all thieves out of your country, and curse and excommunicate them in the name of all the saints.

11. Offer your tithes and the first fruits of your labors to God, and bring offerings from your goods to the churches for the souls of the living and the dead, that God may free you from all evils in this world, and after this life bring you to the kingdom of heaven, through Him who lives and reigns with God the Father and the Holy Spirit, forever and ever. Amen.

[Oliver J. Thatcher and Edgar H. McNeal, *A Source Book for Medieval History: Selected Documents Illustrating the History of Europe in the Middle Ages* (New York, 1905), pp. 414–415]

Truce of God for the Archbishopric of Besançon and Vienne (ca. 1041)

1. We command all to keep the truce from sunset on Wednesday to sunrise on Monday, and from Christmas to the octave of [i.e., week after] Epiphany [January 6], and from Septuagesima Sunday [third Sunday before Lent] to the octave of Easter [the Sunday after Easter].

2. If anyone violates the truce and refuses to make satisfaction, after he has been admonished three times, the bishop shall excommunicate him and shall notify the neighboring bishops of his action by letter. No bishop shall receive the excommunicated person, but shall confirm the sentence of excommunication against him in writing. If any bishop violates this decree he shall be in danger of losing his rank.

3. And since a threefold cord is stronger and harder to break than a single one, we command bishops mutually to aid one another in maintaining this peace, having regard only to God and the salvation of their people, and not to neglect this through love or fear of anyone. If any bishop is negligent in this regard, he shall be in danger of losing his rank.

[Oliver J. Thatcher and Edgar H. McNeal, *A Source Book for Medieval History: Selected Documents Illustrating the History of Europe in the Middle Ages* (New York, 1905), pp. 416–417]

Truce for the Bishopric of Terouanne (1063)

Drogo, bishop of Terouanne, and count Baldwin [of Hainault] have established this peace with the cooperation of the clergy and people of the land.

Dearest brothers in the Lord, these are the conditions which you must observe during the time of the peace which is commonly called the truce of God, and which begins with sunset on Wednesday and lasts until sunrise on Monday.

1. During those four days and five nights no man or woman shall assault, wound, or slay another, or attack, seize, or destroy a castle, burg, or villa, by craft or by violence.

2. If anyone violates this peace and disobeys these commands of ours, he shall be exiled for thirty years as a penance, and before he leaves the bishopric he shall make compensation for the injury which he committed. Otherwise he shall be excommunicated by the Lord God and excluded from all Christian fellowship.

3. All who associate with him in any way, who give him advice or aid, or hold converse with him, unless it be to advise him to do penance and to leave the bishopric, shall be under excommunication until they have made satisfaction.

4. If any violator of the peace shall fall sick and die before he completes his penance, no Christian shall visit him or move his body from the place where it lay, or receive any of his possessions.

5. In addition, brethren, you should observe the peace in regard to lands and animals and all things that can be possessed. If anyone takes from another an animal, a coin, or a garment, during the days of the truce, he shall be excommunicated unless he makes satisfaction. If he desires to make satisfaction for his crime he shall first restore the thing which he stole or its value in money, and shall do penance for seven years within the bishopric. If he should die before he makes satisfaction and completes his penance, his body shall not be buried or removed from the place where it lay, unless his family shall make satisfaction for him to the person whom he injured.

6. During the days of the peace, no one shall make a hostile expedition on horseback, except when summoned by the count; and all who go with the count shall take for their support only as much as is necessary for themselves and their horses.

7. All merchants and other men who pass through your territory from other lands shall have peace from you.

8. You shall also keep this peace every day of the week from the beginning of Advent to the octave of

Epiphany and from the beginning of Lent to the octave of Easter, and from the feast of Rogations [the Monday before Ascension Day] to the octave of Pentecost.

9. We command all priests on feast days and Sundays to pray for all who keep the peace, and to curse all who violate it or support its violators.

10. If anyone has been accused of violating the peace and denies the charge, he shall take the communion and undergo the ordeal of hot iron. If he is found guilty, he shall do penance within the bishopric for seven years.

[Oliver J. Thatcher and Edgar H. McNeal, *A Source Book for Medieval History: Selected Documents Illustrating the History of Europe in the Middle Ages* (New York, 1905), pp. 417–418]

Peace of the Land

Peace of the Land for Elsass [Alsace] (1085–1103)

Be it known to all lovers of peace that the people of Elsass with their leaders have mutually sworn to maintain perpetual peace on the following terms:

1. All churches shall have peace always and everywhere. All clergy and women, merchants, hunters, pilgrims, and farmers while they work in the fields and on their way to and from their labor, shall have peace.

2. They have sworn to keep the peace especially on certain days and during certain seasons; namely, from vespers on Wednesday to sunrise on Monday or every week, on the vigils and feast days of the saints, on the four times of fast, from Advent to the octave of Epiphany, and from Septuagesima Sunday to the octave of Pentecost. In these times no one shall bear arms except those on journey. All public enemies of the royal majesty shall be excluded from the benefits of this peace.

3. If anyone of those who have sworn to maintain this peace shall commit any crime against one of the others, on one of these days, such as robbing, burning, seizing, or committing any other violence on his lands or in his house, or beating him so as to bring blood, he shall suffer capital punishment, if he is a freeman, and shall lose his hand, if he is a serf.

4. If anyone conceals a violator of the peace or aids him to escape, he shall suffer the penalty of the guilty person.

5. If anyone unjustly accuses one of those who have sworn to keep the peace of having violated it, or calls out the forces of the peace against him, through malice or anger, he shall suffer the penalty described above.

6. If anyone who dwells in the province has been accused of violating the peace, he shall clear himself inside of seven days by the testimony of seven of his peers, if he is a freeman or a ministerial; but if he belongs to a lower rank in the city or country, he shall clear himself by the ordeal of cold water. . . .

[Oliver J. Thatcher and Edgar H. McNeal, *A Source Book for Medieval History: Selected Documents Illustrating the History of Europe in the Middle Ages* (New York, 1905), pp. 420–421]

Peace of the Land Established by Henry IV (1103)

In the year of the incarnation of our Lord 1103, the emperor Henry established this peace at Mainz, and he and the archbishops and bishops signed it with their own signatures. The son of the king and the nobles of the whole kingdom, dukes, margraves, counts, and many others, swore to observe it. Duke Welf, duke Bertholf, and duke Frederick swore to keep the peace from that day to four years from the next Pentecost. They swore to keep peace with churches, clergy, monks, merchants, women, and Jews. This is the form of the oath which they swore:

No one shall attack the house of another or waste it with fire, or seize another for ransom, or strike, wound, or slay another. If anyone does any of these things he shall lose his eyes or his hand, and the one who defends him shall suffer the same penalty. If the violator flees into a castle, the castle shall be besieged for three days by those who have sworn to keep the peace, and if the violator is not given up it shall be destroyed. If the offender flees from justice out of the country, his lord shall take away his fief, if he has one, and his relatives shall take his patrimony. If anyone steals anything worth five solidi or more, he shall lose his eyes or his hand. If anyone steals anything worth less than five solidi, he shall be made to restore the theft, and shall lose his hair and be beaten with rods; if he has committed this smaller theft three times, he shall lose his eyes or his hand. If thou shalt meet thine enemy on the road and canst injure him, do so; but if he escapes to the house or castle of anyone, thou shalt let him remain there unharmed.

[Oliver J. Thatcher and Edgar H. McNeal, *A Source Book for Medieval History: Selected Documents Illustrating the History of Europe in the Middle Ages* (New York, 1905), p. 419]

Pre–World War I Examples

United States–Prussia Treaty (1785)

This treaty of "Amity and Commerce" included two articles unusual for the time— emphasizing the protections to be granted civilians and to prisoners of war—that clearly stemmed from medieval experiences.

Article XXIII. If war should arise between the two contracting parties, the merchants of either country, then residing in the other, shall be allowed to remain nine months to collect their debts and settle their affairs, and may depart freely, carrying off all their effects, without molestation or hindrance: And all women and children, scholars of every faculty, cultivators of the earth, artizans, manufacturers and fishermen unarmed and inhabiting unfortified towns, villages or places, and in general all others whose occupations are for the common subsistence and benefit of mankind, shall be allowed to continue their respective employments and shall not be molested in their persons, nor shall their houses or goods be burnt, or otherwise destroyed, nor their fields wasted by the armed force of the enemy, into whose power, by the events of war, they may happen to fall; but if any thing is necessary to be taken from them for the use of such armed force, the same shall be paid for at a reasonable price. And all merchants and trading vessels employed in exchanging the products of different places, and thereby rendering the necessaries, conveniences and comforts of human life more easy to be obtained, and more general, shall be allowed to pass free and unmolested; and neither of the contracting powers shall grant or issue any commission to any private armed vessels, empowering them to take or destroy such trading vessels or interrupt such commerce.

And to prevent the destruction of prisoners of war, by sending them into distant and inclement countries, or crowding them into close and noxious places, the two contracting parties solemnly pledge themselves to each other, and to the world, that they will not adopt any such practice; that neither will send the prisoners whom they may take from the other into the East-Indies, or any other parts of Asia or Africa, but that they shall be placed in some part of their dominions, in Europe or America, in wholesome situations; that they shall not be confined in dungeons, prison-ships, nor prisons, not be put into irons, not bound, nor otherwise restrained in the use of their limbs; that the officers shall be enlarged on their paroles within convenient districts, and have comfortable quarters, and the common men be disposed in cantonments open and extensive enough for air and exercise, and lodged in barracks as roomy and good as are provided by the party in whose power they are for their own troops; . . .

[Leon Friedman, ed., *The Law of War: A Documentary History* (New York, 1972), vol. 1, p. 150]

The Lieber Code (1863)

Washington, D.C., 24 April 1863. Instructions for the Government of Armies of the United States in the Field by Order of the Secretary of War

Section I. Martial Law—Military Jurisdiction— Military Necessity—Retaliation.

Article XIV. Military necessity, as understood by modern civilized nations, consists in the necessity of those measures which are indispensable for securing the ends of the war, and which are lawful according to the modern law and usages of law.

Article XV. Military necessity admits of all direct destruction of life or limb of *armed* enemies, and of other persons whose destruction is incidentally *unavoidable* in the armed contests of the war; it allows of the capturing of every armed enemy, and every enemy of importance to the hostile government, or of peculiar danger to the captor; it allows of all destruction of property, and obstruction of the ways and channels of traffic, travel, or communication, and of all withholding of sustenance or means of life from the enemy; of the appropriation of whatever an enemy's country affords necessary for the subsistence and safety of the army, and of such deception as does not involve the breaking of good faith either positively pledged, regarding agreements entered into during the war, or supposed by the modern law of war to exist. Men who take up arms against one another in public war do not cease on this account to be moral beings, responsible to one another and to God.

Article XVI. Military necessity does not admit of cruelty—that is, the infliction of suffering for the sake of suffering or for revenge, nor of maiming or wounding except in fight, nor of torture to extort confessions. It does not admit of the use of poison in any way, nor of the wanton devastation of a district. It admits of deception, but disclaims acts of perfidy; and, in general, military necessity does not include any act of hostility which makes the return to peace unnecessarily difficult.

Article XVII. War is not carried on by arms alone. It is lawful to starve the hostile belligerent, armed or unarmed, so that it leads to the speedier subjection of the enemy.

Article XVIII. When a commander of a besieged place expels the noncombatants, in order to lessen the number of those who consume his stock of provisions, it is lawful, though an extreme measure, to drive them back, so as to hasten on the surrender.

Article XIX. Commanders, whenever admissible, inform the enemy of their intention to bombard a place, so that the noncombatants, and especially the women and children, may be removed before the bombardment commences. But it is no infraction of the common law of war to omit thus to inform the enemy. Surprise may be a necessity.

Article XX. Public war is a state of armed hostility between sovereign nations or governments. It is a law and requisite of civilized existence that men live in political, continuous societies, forming organized units, called states or nations, whose constituents bear, enjoy, and suffer, advance and retrograde together, in peace and in war.

Article XXI. The citizen or native of a hostile country is thus an enemy, as one of the constituents of the hostile state or nation, and as such is subjected to the hardships of the war.

Article XXII. Nevertheless, as civilization has advanced during the last centuries, so has likewise steadily advanced, especially in war on land, the distinction between the private individual belonging to a hostile country and the hostile country itself, with its men in arms. The principle has been more and more acknowledged that the unarmed citizen is to be spared in person, property, and honor as much as the exigencies of war will admit.

Article XXIII. Private citizens are no longer murdered, enslaved, or carried off to distant parts, and the inoffensive individual is as little disturbed in his private relations as the commander of the hostile troops can afford to grant in the overruling demands of a vigorous war.

Article XXIV. The almost universal rule in remote times was, and continues to be with barbarous armies, that the private individual of the hostile country is destined to suffer every privation of liberty and protection, and every disruption of family ties. Protection was, and still is with uncivilized people, the exception.

Article XXV. In modern regular wars of the Europeans, and their descendants in other portions of the globe, protection of the inoffensive citizen of the hostile country is the rule; privation and disturbance of private relations are the exceptions.

Article XXVI. Commanding generals may cause the magistrates and civil officers of the hostile country to take the oath of temporary allegiance or an oath of fidelity to their own victorious government or rulers, and they may expel every one who declines to do so. But whether they do so or not, the people and their civil officers owe strict obedience to them as long as they hold sway over the district or country, at the peril of their lives.

Article XXVII. The law of war can no more wholly dispense with retaliation than can the law of nations, of which it is a branch. Yet civilized nations acknowledge retaliation as the sternest feature of war. A reckless enemy often leaves to his opponent no other means of securing himself against the repetition of barbarous outrage.

Article XXVIII. Retaliation will, therefore, never be resorted to as a measure of mere revenge, but only as a means of protective retribution, and moreover, cautiously and unavoidably; that is to say, retaliation shall only be resorted to after careful inquiry into the real occurrence, and the character of the misdeeds that may demand retribution.

Unjust or inconsiderate retaliation removes the belligerents farther and farther from the mitigating rules of regular war, and by rapid steps leads them nearer to the internecine wars of savages.

Article XXIX. Modern times are distinguished from earlier ages by the existence, at one and the same time, of many nations and great governments related to one another in close intercourse.

Peace is their normal condition; war is the exception. The ultimate object of all modern war is a renewed state of peace.

The more vigorously wars are pursued, the better it is for humanity. Sharp wars are brief.

Article XXX. Ever since the formation and coexistence of modern nations, and ever since wars have become great national wars, war has come to be acknowledged not to be its own end, but the means to obtain great ends of state, or to consist in defense against wrong; and no conventional restriction of the modes adopted to injure the enemy is any longer admitted; but the law of war imposes many limitations and restrictions on principles of justice, faith, and honor.

Section II. Public and Private Property of the Enemy—Protection of Persons, and Especially of Women; of Religion, the Arts and Sciences— Punishment of Crimes against the Inhabitants of Hostile Countries.

Article XXXI. A victorious army appropriates all public money, seizes all public movable property until further direction by its government, and sequesters for its own benefit or of that of its government all the revenues of real property belonging to the hostile government or nation. The title to such real property remains in abeyance during military occupation, and until the conquest is made complete.

Article XXXII. A victorious army, by the martial power inherent in the same, may suspend, change, or abolish, as far as the martial power extends, the relations which arise from the services due, according to the existing laws of the invaded country, from one citizen, subject, or native of the same to another.

The commander of the army must leave it to the ultimate treaty of peace to settle the permanency of this change.

Article XXXIII. It is no longer considered lawful—on the contrary, it is held to be a serious breach of the law of war—to force the subjects of the enemy into the service of the victorious government, except the latter should proclaim, after a fair and complete conquest of the hostile country or district, that it is resolved to keep the country, district, or place permanently as its own and make it a portion of its own country.

Article XXXIV. As a general rule, the property belonging to churches, to hospitals, or other establishments of an exclusively charitable character, to establishments of education, or foundations for the promotion of knowledge, whether public schools, universities, academies of learning or observatories, museums of the fine arts, or of a scientific character—such property is not to be considered public property in the sense of paragraph XXXI; but it may be taxed or used when the public service may require it.

Article XXXV. Classical works of art, libraries, scientific collections, or precious instruments, such as astronomical telescopes, as well as hospitals, must be secured against all avoidable injury, even when they are contained in fortified places whilst besieged or bombarded.

Article XXXVI. If such works of art, libraries, collections, or instruments belonging to a hostile nation or government can be removed without injury, the ruler of the conquering state or nation may order them to be seized and removed for the benefit of the said nation. The ultimate ownership is to be settled by the ensuing treaty of peace.

In no case shall they be sold or given away, if captured by the armies of the United States, nor shall they ever be privately appropriated, or wantonly destroyed or injured.

Article XXXVII. The United States acknowledge and protect, in hostile countries occupied by them, religion and mortality; strictly private property; the persons of the inhabitants, especially those of women; and the sacredness of domestic relations.

Offenses to the contrary shall be rigorously punished.

This rule does not interfere with the right of the victorious invader to tax the people or their property, to levy forced loans, to billet soldiers, or to appropriate property, especially houses, lands, boats or ships, and churches, for temporary and military uses.

[Leon Friedman, ed., *The Law of War: A Documentary History* (New York, 1972), vol. 1, pp. 158–165]

The Declaration of St. Petersburg (1868)

Declaration Renouncing the Use in War of Certain Explosive Projectiles, St. Petersburg, Russia, 11 December 1868

Upon the invitation of the Imperial Cabinet of Russia, an international military commission having been assembled at St. Petersburg in order to consider the desirability of forbidding the use of certain projectiles in time of war among civilized nations, and this commission having fixed by a common accord the technical limits within which the necessities of war ought to yield to the demands of humanity, the undersigned have been authorized by the orders of their Governments to declare as follows:

Considering that the progress of civilization should have the effect of alleviating, as much as possible the calamities of war:

That the only legitimate object which states should endeavor to accomplish during war is to weaken the military force of the enemy;

That for this purpose, it is sufficient to disable the greatest possible number of men;

That this object would be exceeded by the employment of arms which uselessly aggravate the sufferings of disabled men, or render their death inevitable;

That the employment of such arms would, therefore, be contrary to the laws of humanity;

The contracting parties engage, mutually, to renounce, in case of war among themselves, the employment, by their military or naval forces, of any projectile of less weight than four hundred grammes, which is explosive, or is charged with fulminating or inflammable substances.

They agree to invite all the state which have not taken part in the deliberations of the International Military Commission, assembled at St. Petersburg, by sending delegates thereto, to accede to the present engagement.

This engagement is obligatory only upon the contracting or acceding parties thereto, in case of war between two or more of themselves; it is not applicable with regard to non-contracting powers, or powers that shall not have acceded to it.

It will also cease to be obligatory from the moment when, in a war between contracting or acceding parties, a non-contracting party, or a non-acceding party, shall join one of the belligerents.

The contracting or acceding parties reserve to themselves the right to come to an understanding, hereafter, whenever a precise proposition shall be drawn up, in view of future improvements which may be effected in the armament of troops, in order to maintain the principles which they have established, and to reconcile the necessities of war with the laws of humanity.

[Leon Friedman, ed., *The Law of War: A Documentary History* (New York, 1972), vol. 1, pp. 192–193]

Declaration Concerning Expanding Bullets (1899)

This declaration was signed at The Hague on 29 July 1899.

Declaration IV, 3

The undersigned, plenipotentiaries of the Powers represented at the International Peace Conference at The Hague, duly authorized to that effect by their Governments, inspired by the sentiments which found expression in the Declaration of St. Petersburg of the 29th November (11th December), 1868,

Declare as follows:

The contracting Parties agree to abstain from the use of bullets which expand or flatten easily in the human body, such as bullets with a hard envelope which does not entirely cover the core or is pierced with incisions.

The present Declaration is only binding for the contracting Powers in the case of a war between two or more of them.

It shall cease to be binding from the time when, in a war between the contracting Powers, one of the belligerents is joined by a non-contracting Power.

The present Declaration shall be ratified as soon as possible.

The ratification shall be deposited at The Hague.

A *procès-verbal* shall be drawn up on the receipt of each ratification, a copy of which, duly certified, shall be sent through the diplomatic channel to all the contracting Powers.

The non-signatory Powers may adhere to the present Declaration. For this purpose they must make their adhesion known to the contracting Powers by means of a written notification addressed to the Netherland Government, and by it communicated to all the other contracting Powers.

In the event of one of the high contracting Parties denouncing the present Declaration, such denunciation shall not take effect until a year after the notification made in writing to the Netherland Government, and forthwith communicated by it to all the other contracting Powers.

This denunciation shall only affect the notifying Power.

In faith of which the plenipotentiaries have signed the present Declaration, and have affixed their seals thereto.

Done at The Hague, the 29th July, 1899, in a single copy, which shall be kept in the archives of the Netherland Government, and of which copies, duly certified, shall be sent through the diplomatic channel to the contracting Powers.

[Signatures]

[Leon Friedman, ed., *The Law of War: A Documentary History* (New York, 1972), vol. 1, pp. 247–248]

Convention Relative to the Laying of Automatic Submarine Contact Mines (1907)

This convention was ratified by the United States on 10 March 1908.

His Majesty the German Emperor, King of Prussia [and other heads of state]:

Inspired by the principle of the freedom of sea routes, the common highways of all nations;

Seeing that, although the existing position of affairs makes it impossible to forbid the employment of automatic submarine contact mines, it is nevertheless desirable to restrict and regulate their employment in order to mitigate the severity of war and to ensure, as far as possible, to peaceful navigation the security to which it is entitled, despite the existence of war;

Until such time as it is found possible to formulate rules on the subject which shall ensure to the interests involved all the guarantees desirable;

Have resolved to conclude a convention for this purpose, and have appointed the following as their plenipotentiaries:

[Names of plenipotentiaries]

Who, after having deposited their full powers, found in good and due form, have agreed upon the following provisions:

Article 1. It is forbidden:

1. To lay unanchored automatic contact mines, except when they are so constructed as to become harmless one hour at most after the person who laid them ceases to control them;

2. To lay anchored automatic contact mines which do not become harmless as soon as they have broken loose from their moorings;

3. To use torpedoes which do not become harmless when they have missed their mark.

Article 2. It is forbidden to lay automatic contact mines off the coast and ports of the enemy, with the sole object of intercepting commercial shipping.

Article 3. When anchored automatic contact mines are employed, every possible precaution must be taken for the security of peaceful shipping.

The belligerents undertake to do their utmost to render these mines harmless within a limited time, and, should they cease to be under surveillance, to notify the danger zones as soon as military exigencies permit, by a notice addressed to shipowners, which must also be communicated to the governments through the diplomatic channel.

Article 4. Neutral powers which lay automatic contact mines off their coasts must observe the same rules and take the same precautions as are imposed on belligerents.

The neutral power must inform shipowners, by a notice issued in advance, where automatic contact mines have been laid. This notice must be communicated at once to the governments through the diplomatic channel.

Article 5. At the close of the war, the contracting powers undertake to do their utmost to remove the mines which they had laid, each power removing its own mines.

As regards anchored automatic contact mines laid by one of the belligerents off the coast of the other, their position must be notified to the other party by the power which laid them, and each power must proceed with the least possible delay to remove the mines in its own waters.

Article 6. The contracting powers which do not at present own perfected mines of the pattern contemplated in the present convention, and which, consequently, could not at present carry out the rules laid down in Articles 1 and 3, undertake to convert the *matériel* of their mines as soon as possible, so as to bring it into conformity with the foregoing requirements.

Article 7. The provisions of the present convention do not apply except between contracting powers, and then only if all the belligerents are parties to the convention.

Article 8. [Ratification]

Article 9. Non-signatory powers may adhere to the present convention.

The power which desires to adhere notifies in writing its intention to the Netherland Government, transmitting to it the act of adhesion, which shall be deposited in the archives of the said Government. . . .

Article 10. [Ratification]

Article 11. [Denunciation]

Article 12. The contracting powers undertake to reopen the question of the employment of automatic contact mines six months before the expiration of the period contemplated in the first paragraph of the preceding article [seven years], in the event of the question not having been already reopened and settled by the Third Peace Conference.

If the contracting powers conclude a fresh convention relative to the employment of mines, the present convention shall cease to be applicable from the moment it comes into force.

[Signatures]

[James Brown Scott, *The Hague Peace Conferences of 1899 and 1907* (Baltimore, 1909), vol. 2: *Documents,* pp. 429–437]

Hague Conventions

Convention II (1899)

Section II.—On Hostilities

Chapter I.—On Means of Injuring the Enemy, Sieges, and Bombardments

Article 22. The right of belligerents to adopt means of injuring the enemy is not unlimited.

Article 23. Besides the prohibitions provided by special Conventions, it is especially prohibited—

(a.) To employ poison or poisoned arms;

(b.) To kill or wound treacherously individuals belonging to the hostile nation or army;

(c.) To kill or wound an enemy who, having laid down arms, or having no longer means of defence, has surrendered at discretion;

(d.) To declare that no quarter will be given;

(e.) To employ arms, projectiles, or material of a nature to cause superfluous injury;

(f.) To make improper use of a flag of truce, the national flag or military ensigns and uniform of the enemy, as well as the distinctive badges of the Geneva Convention;

(g.) To destroy or seize the enemy's property, unless such destruction or seizure be imperatively demanded by the necessities of war.

Article 24. Ruses of war and the employment of methods necessary to obtain information about the enemy and the country, are considered allowable.

Article 25. The attack or bombardment of towns, villages, habitations or buildings which are not defended, is prohibited.

Article 26. The commander of an attacking force, before commencing a bombardment, except in the case of an assault, should do all he can to warn the authorities.

Article 27. In sieges and bombardments all necessary steps should be taken to spare as far as possible edifices devoted to religion, art, science, and charity, hospitals, and places where the sick and wounded are collected, provided they are not used at the same time for military purposes.

The besieged should indicate these buildings or places by some particular and visible signs, which should previously be notified to the assailants.

Article 28. The pillage of a town or place, even when taken by assault, is prohibited.

Convention IV (1907)

Section II.—On Hostilities

Chapter I.—On Means of Injuring the Enemy, Sieges, and Bombardments

Article 22. The right of belligerents to adopt means of injuring the enemy is not unlimited.

Article 23. In addition to the prohibitions provided by special Conventions, it is especially forbidden—

(a.) To employ poison or poisoned weapons;

(b.) To kill or wound treacherously individuals belonging to the hostile nation or army;

(c.) To kill or wound an enemy who, having laid down his arms, or having no longer means of defence, has surrendered at discretion;

(d.) To declare that no quarter will be given;

(e.) To employ arms, projectiles, or material calculated to cause unnecessary suffering;

(f.) To make improper use of a flag of truce, of the national flag or of the military insignia and uni-

form of the enemy, as well as the distinctive badges of the Geneva Convention;

(g.) To destroy or seize the enemy's property, unless such destruction or seizure be imperatively demanded by the necessities of war;

(h.) To declare abolished, suspended, or inadmissible in a court of law the rights and actions of the nationals of the hostile party.

A belligerent is likewise forbidden to compel the nationals of the hostile party to take part in the operations of war directed against their own country, even if they were in the belligerent's service before the commencement of the war.

Article 24. Ruses of war and the employment of measures necessary for obtaining information about the enemy and the country are considered permissible.

Article 25. The attack or bombardment, *by whatever means,* of towns, villages, dwellings, or buildings which are undefended is prohibited.

Article 26. The officer in command of an attacking force must, before commencing a bombardment, except in cases of assault, do all in his power to warn the authorities.

Article 27. In sieges and bombardments all necessary steps must be taken to spare, as far as possible, buildings dedicated to religion, art, science, or charitable purposes, historic monuments, hospitals, and places where the sick and wounded are collected, provided they are not being used at the time for military purposes.

It is the duty of the besieged to indicate the presence of such buildings or places by distinctive and visible signs, which shall be notified to the enemy beforehand.

Article 28. The pillage of a town or place, even when taken by assault, is prohibited.

[James Brown Scott, *The Hague Conventions and Declarations of 1899 and 1907,* 3d ed. (New York, 1918), pp. 116–118]

Interwar Conventions, 1929–1935

Red Cross Convention (1929)

Convention for the Amelioration of the Condition of the Wounded and Sick of Armies in the Field, Geneva, 27 July 1929

Chapter I. The Wounded and Sick

Article I. Officers, soldiers, and other persons officially attached to the armies who are wounded or sick shall be respected and protected in all circumstances; they shall be humanely treated and cared for without distinction of nationality by the belligerent in whose power they are.

A belligerent, however, when compelled to leave his wounded or sick in the hands of his adversary, shall leave with them, so far as military exigencies permit, a portion of the personnel and matériel of his sanitary service to assist in caring for them.

Article II. Subject to the care that must be taken of them under the preceding article, the wounded and sick of an army who fall into the power of the other belligerent shall become prisoners of war, and the general rules of international law in respect to prisoners of war shall become applicable to them.

The belligerents shall remain free, however, to agree upon such clauses to the benefit of the wounded and sick prisoners as they may deem of value over and above already existing obligations.

Article III. After every engagement, the belligerent who remains in possession of the field of battle shall take measures to search for the wounded and the dead and to protect them from robbery and ill-treatment.

A local armistice or cessation of fire to enable the removal of wounded left between the lines shall be arranged whenever circumstances permit.

Article IV. Belligerents shall mutually forward to each other as soon as possible the names of the wounded, sick and dead taken in charge or discovered by them, as well as all indications which may serve for their identification.

They shall draw up and forward to each other death certificates.

They shall collect and likewise forward to each other all objects of personal use found on the field of battle or on the dead, especially one-half of their identity plaque, the other half remaining attached to the body.

They shall see that a careful examination, if possible, medical, is made of the bodies of the dead prior to their interment or cremation, with a view to verifying their death, establishing their identity, and in order to be able to furnish a report thereon.

They shall further see that they are honorably buried and that the graves are treated with respect and may always be found again.

For this purpose, and at the outbreak of hostilities, they shall officially organize a service of graves in order to render any later exhumation possible and to make certain of the identity of the bodies even though they may have been moved from grave to grave.

Upon the termination of hostilities, they shall exchange lists of graves and of dead buried in their cemeteries and elsewhere. . . .

[Leon Friedman, ed., *The Law of War: A Documentary History* (New York, 1972), vol. 1, pp. 476–477]

Convention on Treatment of Prisoners of War (1929)

Convention Relative to the Treatment of Prisoners of War, Geneva, 27 July 1929

Title I. General Provisions

Article I. The present Convention shall apply, without prejudice to the stipulations of Title VII:

(1) To all persons mentioned in Articles I, II and III of the Regulations annexed to the Hague Convention respecting the laws and customs of war on land, of October 18, 1907, and captured by the enemy.

(2) To all persons belonging to the armed forces of belligerent parties, captured by the enemy in the course of military operations at sea or in the air, except for such derogations as might be rendered inevitable by the conditions of capture. However, such derogations shall not infringe upon the fundamental principles of the present Convention; they shall cease from the moment when the persons captured have rejoined a prisoners-of-war camp.

Article II. Prisoners of war are in the power of the hostile Power, but not of the individuals or corps who have captured them.

They must at all times be humanely treated and protected, particularly against acts of violence, insults and public curiosity.

Measures of reprisal against them are prohibited.

Article III. Prisoners of war have the right to have their person and their honor respected. Women shall be treated with all the regard due to their sex.

Prisoners retain their full civil status.

Article IV. The Power detaining prisoners of war is bound to provide for their maintenance.

Difference in treatment among prisoners is lawful only when it is based on the military rank, state of physical or mental health, professional qualifications or sex of those who profit thereby.

Title II. Capture

Article V. Every prisoner of war is bound to give, if he is questioned on the subject, his true name and rank, or else his regimental number.

If he infringes this rule, he is liable to have the advantages given to prisoners of his class curtailed.

No coercion may be used on prisoners to secure information relative to the condition of their army or country. Prisoners who refuse to answer may not be threatened, insulted, or exposed to unpleasant or disadvantageous treatment of any kind whatever.

If, because of physical or mental condition, a prisoner is unable to identify himself, he shall be turned over to the medical corps.

Article VI. All effects and objects of personal use—except arms, horses, military equipment and military papers—shall remain in the possession of prisoners of war, as well as metal helmets and gas masks.

Money in the possession of prisoners of war may not be taken away from them except by order of an officer and after the amount has been determined. A receipt shall be given. Money thus taken away shall be entered to the account of each prisoner.

Identification documents, insignia of rank, decorations and objects of value may not be taken from prisoners.

Title III. Captivity

Section I. Evacuation of Prisoners of War

Article VII. Prisoners of war shall be evacuated within the shortest possible period after their capture, to depots located in a region far enough from the zone of combat for them to be out of danger.

Only prisoners who, because of wounds or sickness, would run greater risks by being evacuated than by remaining where they are may be temporarily kept in a dangerous zone.

Prisoners shall not be needlessly exposed to danger while awaiting their evacuation from the combat zone.

Evacuation of prisoners on foot may normally be effected only by stages of 20 kilometers a day, unless the necessity of reaching water and food depots requires longer stages.

Article VIII. Belligerents are bound mutually to notify each other of their capture of prisoners within the shortest period possible, through the intermediary of the information bureaus, such as are organized according to Article LXXVII. They are likewise bound to inform each other of the official addresses to which the correspondence of their families may be sent to prisoners of war.

As soon as possible, every prisoner must be enabled to correspond with his family himself, under the conditions provided in Articles XXXVI *et seq.*

As regards prisoners captured at sea, the provisions of the present article shall be observed as soon as possible after arrival at port.

Section II. Prisoners-of-War Camps

Article IX. Prisoners of war may be interned in a town, fortress, or other place, and bound not to go beyond certain fixed limits. They may also be interned in enclosed camps; they may not be confined or imprisoned except as an indispensable measure of safety or sanitation, and only while the circumstances which necessitate the measure continue to exist.

Prisoners captured in unhealthful regions, or where the climate is injurious for persons coming from temperate regions, shall be transported, as soon as possible, to a more favorable climate.

Belligerents shall, so far as possible, avoid assembling in a single camp prisoners of different races or nationalities.

No prisoner may, at any time, be sent into a region where he might be exposed to the fire of the combat zone, nor used to give protection from bombardment to certain points or certain regions by his presence.

Chapter I. Installation of Camps

Article X. Prisoners of war shall be lodged in buildings or in barracks affording all possible guarantees of hygiene and healthfulness.

The quarters must be fully protected from dampness, sufficiently heated and lighted. All precautions must be taken against danger of fire.

With regard to dormitories—the total surface, minimum cubic amount of air, arrangement and material of bedding—the conditions shall be the same as for the troops at base camps of the detaining Power.

Chapter II. Food and Clothing of Prisoners of War

Article XI. The food ration of prisoners of war shall be equal in quantity and quality to that of troops at base camps.

Furthermore, prisoners shall receive facilities for preparing, themselves, additional food which they might have.

A sufficiency of potable water shall be furnished them. The use of tobacco shall be permitted. Prisoners may be employed in the kitchens.

All collective disciplinary measures affecting the food are prohibited.

Article XII. Clothing, linen and footwear shall be furnished prisoners of war by the detaining Power. Replacement and repairing of these effects must be assured regularly. In addition, laborers must receive work clothes wherever the nature of the work requires it.

Canteens shall be installed in all camps where prisoners may obtain, at the local market price, food products and ordinary objects.

Profits made by the canteens for camp administrations shall be used for the benefit of prisoners.

. . . . .

Annexed Regulations [Footnote in the original]

Article I. The laws, rights, and duties of war apply not only to armies, but also to militia and volunteer corps fulfilling the following conditions:

1. To be commanded by a person responsible for his subordinates;

2. To have a fixed distinctive emblem recognizable at a distance;

3. To carry arms openly; and

4. To conduct their operations in accordance with the laws and customs of war.

In countries where militia or volunteer corps constitute the army, or form part of it, they are included under the denomination "army."

Article II. The inhabitants of a territory which has not been occupied, who, on the approach of the enemy, spontaneously take up arms to resist the invading troops without having had time to organize themselves in accordance with Article I, shall be regarded as belligerents if they carry arms openly and if they respect the laws and customs of war.

Article III. The armed forces of the belligerent parties may consist of combatants and non-combatants. In the case of capture by the enemy, both have a right to be treated as prisoners of war.

[Leon Friedman, ed., *The Law of War: A Documentary History* (New York, 1972), vol. 1, pp. 493–497]

Protection of Artistic and Scientific Institutions and Historic Monuments, Inter-American Agreement (1935)

The so-called Roerich Pact was signed at Washington on 15 April 1935. It entered into force on 26 August 1935.

The High Contracting Parties, animated by the purpose of giving conventional form to the postulates of the Resolution approved on December 16, 1933, by all the States represented at the Seventh International Conference of American States, held at Montevideo, which recommended to "the Governments of America which have not yet done so that they sign the 'Roerich Pact,' initiated by the Roerich Museum in the United States, and which has as its object, the universal adoption of a flag, already designed and generally known, in order thereby to preserve in any time of danger all nationally and privately owned immovable monuments which form the cultural treasure of peoples," have resolved to conclude a treaty with that end in view, and to the effect that the treasures of culture be respected and protected in time of war and in peace, have agreed upon the following articles:

Article I. The historic monuments, museums, scientific, artistic, educational and cultural institutions shall be considered as neutral and as such respected and protected by belligerents.

The same respect and protection shall be due to the personnel of the institutions mentioned above.

The same respect and protection shall be accorded to the historic monuments, museums, scientific, artistic, educational and cultural institutions in time of peace as well as in war.

Article II. The neutrality of, and protection and respect due to, the monuments and institutions mentioned in the preceding article, shall be recognized in the entire expanse of territories subject to the sovereignty of each of the signatory and acceding States, without any discrimination as to the State allegiance of said monuments and insti-

tutions. The respective Governments agree to adopt the measures of internal legislation necessary to insure said protection and respect.

Article III. In order to identify the monuments and institutions mentioned in article I, use may be made of a distinctive flag (red circle with a triple red sphere in the circle on a white background) in accordance with the model attached to this treaty.

Article IV. The signatory Governments and those which accede to this treaty, shall send to the Pan American Union, at the time of signature or accession, or at any time thereafter, a list of the monuments and institutions for which they desire the protection agreed to in this treaty.

The Pan American Union, when notifying the Governments of signatures or accessions, shall also send the list of monuments and institutions mentioned in this article, and shall inform the other Governments of any changes in said list.

Article V. The monuments and institutions mentioned in article I shall cease to enjoy the privileges recognized in the present treaty in case they are made use of for military purposes.

Article VI. The States which do not sign the present treaty on the date it is opened for signature, may sign or adhere to it at any time.

Article VII. [ratification]

Article VIII. [denunciation]

[Signatures]

[Charles I. Bevan, *Treaties and Other International Agreements of the United States of America, 1776–1947,* 4 vols. (Washington, D.C., 1968–1970), vol. 3, pp. 254–255]

Geneva Convention of 1949

Geneva Convention I (1949)

Convention for the Amelioration of the Condition of the Wounded and Sick in Armed Forces in the Field, Geneva, 12 August 1949

Chapter I. *General Provisions*

. . . .

Article III. In the case of armed conflict not of an international character occurring in the territory of one of the High Contracting Parties, each Party to the conflict shall be bound to apply, as a minimum, the following provisions:

1. Persons taking no active part in the hostilities, including members of armed forces who have laid down their arms and those placed *hors de combat* by sickness, wounds, detention, or any other cause, shall in all circumstances be treated humanely, without any adverse distinction founded on race, colour, religion or faith, sex, birth or wealth, or any other similar criteria.

To this end, the following acts are and shall remain prohibited at any time and in any place whatsoever with respect to the above-mentioned persons:

(a) violence to life and person, in particular murder of all kinds, mutilation, cruel treatment and torture;

(b) taking of hostages;

(c) outrages upon personal dignity, in particular humiliating and degrading treatment;

(d) the passing of sentences and the carrying out of executions without previous judgment pronounced by a regularly constituted court, affording all the judicial guarantees which are recognized as indispensable by civilized peoples.

2. The wounded and sick shall be collected and cared for.

An impartial humanitarian body, such as the International Committee of the Red Cross, may offer its services to the Parties to the conflict.

The Parties to the conflict should further endeavour to bring into force, by means of special agreements, all or part of the other provisions of the present Convention.

The application of the preceding provisions shall not affect the legal status of the Parties to the conflict. . . .

Chapter II. *Wounded and Sick*

Article XII. Members of the armed forces and other persons mentioned in the following Article, who are wounded or sick, shall be respected and protected in all circumstances.

They shall be treated humanely and cared for by the Party to the conflict in whose power they may be, without any adverse distinction founded on sex, race, nationality, religion, political opinions, or any other similar criteria. Any attempts upon their lives, or violence to their persons, shall be strictly prohibited; in particular, they shall not be murdered or exterminated, subjected to torture or to biological experiments; they shall not wilfully be left without medical assistance and care, nor shall conditions exposing them to contagion or infection be created.

Only urgent medical reasons will authorize priority in the order of treatment to be administered.

Women shall be treated with all consideration due to their sex.

The Party to the conflict which is compelled to abandon wounded or sick to the enemy shall, as far as military considerations permit, leave with them a part of its medical personnel and material to assist in their care.

Article XIII. The present Convention shall apply to the wounded and sick belonging to the following categories:

1. Members of the armed forces of a Party to the conflict, as well as members of militias or volunteer corps forming part of such armed forces.

2. Members of other militias and members of other volunteer corps, including those of organized resistance movements, belonging to a Party to the

conflict and operating in or outside their own territory, even if this territory is occupied, provided that such militias or volunteer corps, including such organized resistance movements, fulfill the following conditions:

(a) That of being commanded by a person responsible for his subordinates;

(b) That of having a fixed distinctive sign recognizable at a distance;

(c) That of carrying arms openly;

(d) That of conducting their operations in accordance with the laws and customs of war.

3. Members of regular armed forces who profess allegiance to a Government or an authority not recognized by the Detaining Power.

4. Persons who accompany the armed forces without actually being members thereof, such as civil members of military aircraft crews, war correspondents, supply contractors, members of labour units or of services responsible for the welfare of the armed forces, provided that they have received authorization from the armed forces which they accompany.

5. Members of crews, including masters, pilots and apprentices, of the merchant marine and the crews of civil aircraft of the Parties to the conflict, who do not benefit by more favourable treatment under any other provisions in international law.

6. Inhabitants of a non-occupied territory who, on approach of the enemy, spontaneously take up arms to resist the invading forces, without having had time to form themselves into regular armed units, provided they carry arms openly and respect the laws and customs of war. . . .

[Leon Friedman, ed., *The Law of War: A Documentary History* (New York, 1972), vol. 1, pp. 525–530]

Geneva Convention II (1949)

Convention for the Amelioration of the Condition of Wounded, Sick and Shipwrecked Members of Armed Forces at Sea, Geneva, 12 August 1949

Article III. In the case of armed conflict not of an international character occurring in the territory of one of the High Contracting Parties, each Party to the conflict shall be bound to apply, as a minimum, the following provisions:

1. Persons taking no active part in the hostilities, including members of the armed forces who have laid down their arms and those placed *hors de combat* by sickness, wounds, detention, or any other cause, shall in all circumstances be treated humanely, without any adverse distinction founded on race, colour, religion or faith, sex, or wealth, or any other similar criteria.

To this end, the following acts are and shall remain prohibited at any time and in any place whatsoever with respect to the above-mentioned persons:

(a) violence to life and person, in particular murder of all kinds, mutilation, cruel treatment and torture;

(b) taking of hostages;

(c) outrages upon personal dignity, in particular, humiliating and degrading treatment;

(d) the passing of sentences and the carrying out of executions without previous judgment pronounced by a regularly constituted court, affording all the judicial guarantees which are recognized as indispensable by civilized peoples.

2. The wounded, sick and shipwrecked shall be collected and cared for.

An impartial humanitarian body, such as the International Committee of the Red Cross, may offer its services to the Parties to the conflict.

The Parties to the conflict should further endeavor to bring into force, by means of special agreements, all or part of the other provisions of the present Convention.

The application of the preceding provisions shall not affect the legal status of the Parties to the conflict.

[Leon Friedman, ed., *The Law of War: A Documentary History* (New York, 1972), vol. 1, pp. 570–571]

Geneva Convention III (1949)

Convention Relative to the Treatment of Prisoners of War, Geneva, 12 August 1949

Article III. In the case of armed conflict not of an international character occurring in the territory of one of the High Contracting Parties, each Party to the conflict shall be bound to apply, as a minimum, the following provisions:

1. Persons taking no active part in the hostilities, including members of armed forces who have laid down their arms and those placed *hors de combat* by sickness, wounds, detention, or any other cause, shall in all circumstances be treated humanely, without any adverse distinction founded on race, colour, religion or faith, sex, birth or wealth, or any other similar criteria.

To this end the following acts are and shall remain prohibited at any time and in any place whatsoever with respect to the above-mentioned persons:

(a) violence to life and person, in particular murder of all kinds, mutilation, cruel treatment and torture;

(b) taking of hostages;

(c) outrages upon personal dignity, in particular, humiliating and degrading treatment;

(d) the passing of sentences and the carrying out of executions without previous judgment pronounced by a regularly constituted court affording all the judicial guarantees which are recognized as indispensable by civilized peoples.

2. The wounded and sick shall be collected and cared for.

An impartial humanitarian body, such as the International Committee of the Red Cross, may offer its services to the Parties to the conflict.

The Parties to the conflict should further endeavour to bring into force, by means of special agreements, all or part of the other provisions of the present Convention.

The application of the preceding provisions shall not affect the legal status of the Parties to the conflict.

Article IV

A. Prisoners of war, in the sense of the present Convention, are persons belonging to one of the following categories, who have fallen into the power of the enemy:

1. Members of the armed forces of a Party to the conflict, as well as members of militias or volunteer corps forming part of such armed forces.

2. Members of other militias and members of other volunteer corps, including those of organized resistance movements, belonging to a Party to the conflict and operating in or outside their own territory, even if this territory is occupied, provided that such militias or volunteer corps, including such organized resistance movements, fulfill the following obligations:

(a) that of being commanded by a person responsible for his subordinates;

(b) that of having a fixed distinctive sign recognizable at a distance;

(c) that of carrying arms openly;

(d) that of conducting their operations in accordance with the laws and customs of war.

3. Members of regular armed forces who profess allegiance to a government or an authority not recognized by the Detaining Power.

4. Persons who accompany the armed forces without actually being members thereof, such as civilian members of military aircraft crews, war correspondents, supply contractors, members of labour units or of services responsible for the welfare of the armed forces, provided that they have received authorization from the armed forces which they accompany, who shall provide them for that purpose with an identity card similar to the annexed model.

5. Members of crews, including masters, pilots and apprentices, of the merchant marine and the crews of civil aircraft of the Parties to the conflict, who do not benefit by more favourable treatment under any other provisions of international law.

6. Inhabitants of a non-occupied territory, who on the approach of the enemy spontaneously take up arms to resist the invading forces, without having had time to form themselves into regular armed units, provided they carry arms openly and respect the laws and customs of war. . . .

Part II. General Protection of Prisoners of War

Article XII. Prisoners of war are in the hands of the enemy Power, but not of the individuals or military units who have captured them. Irrespective of the individual responsibilities that may exist, the

Detaining Power is responsible for the treatment given them.

Prisoners of war may only be transferred by the Detaining Power to a Power which is a party to the Convention and after the Detaining Power has satisfied itself of the willingness and ability of such transferee Power to apply the Convention. When prisoners of war are transferred under such circumstances, responsibility for the application of the Convention rests on the Power accepting them while they are in its custody.

Nevertheless, if that Power fails to carry out the provisions of the Convention in any important respect, the Power to whom the prisoners of war were transferred shall, upon being notified by the Protecting Power, take effective measures to correct the situation or shall request the return of the prisoners of war. Such requests must be complied with.

Article XIII. Prisoners of war must at all times be humanely treated. Any unlawful act or omission by the Detaining Power causing death or seriously endangering the health of a prisoner of war in its custody is prohibited, and will be regarded as a serious breach of the present Convention. In particular, no prisoner of war may be subjected to physical mutilation or to medical or scientific experiments of any kind which are not justified by the medical, dental or hospital treatment of the prisoner concerned and carried out in his interest.

Likewise, prisoners of war must at all times be protected, particularly against acts of violence or intimidation and against insults and public curiosity.

Measures of reprisal against prisoners of war are prohibited.

Article XIV. Prisoners of war are entitled in all circumstances to respect for their persons and honour.

Women shall be treated with all the regard due to their sex and shall in all cases benefit by treatment as favourable as that granted to men.

Prisoners of war shall retain the full civil capacity which they enjoyed at the time of their capture. The Detaining Power may not restrict the exercise, either within or without its own territory, of the rights such capacity confers except in so far as the captivity requires.

Article XV. The Power detaining prisoners of war shall be bound to provide free of charge for their maintenance and for the medical attention required by their state of health.

Article XVI. Taking into consideration the provisions of the present Convention relating to rank and sex, and subject to any privileged treatment which may be accorded to them by reason of their state of health, age or professional qualifications, all prisoners of war shall be treated alike by the Detaining Power, without any adverse distinction based on race, nationality, religious belief or political opinions, or any other distinction founded on similar criteria.

Part III. Captivity

. . . .

Chapter II. *Quarters, Food and Clothing of Prisoners of War*

Article XXV. Prisoners of war shall be quartered under conditions as favourable as those for the forces of the Detaining Power who are billeted in the same area. The said conditions shall make allowance for the habits and customs of the prisoners and shall in no case be prejudicial to their health.

The foregoing provisions shall apply in particular to the dormitories of prisoners of war as regards both total surface and minimum cubic space, and the general installations, bedding and blankets.

The premises provided for the use of prisoners of war, individually or collectively, shall be entirely protected from dampness and adequately heated and lighted, in particular between dusk and lights out. All precautions must be taken against the danger of fire.

In any camps in which women prisoners of war, as well as men, are accommodated, separate dormitories shall be provided for them.

Article XXVI. The basic daily food rations shall be sufficient in quantity, quality and variety to keep prisoners of war in good health and to prevent loss of weight or the development of nutritional deficiencies. Account shall also be taken of the habitual diet of the prisoners.

The Detaining Power shall supply prisoners of war who work with such additional rations as are necessary for the labour on which they are employed.

Sufficient drinking water shall be supplied to prisoners of war. The use of tobacco shall be permitted.

Prisoners of war shall, as far as possible, be associated with the preparation of their meals; they may be employed for that purpose in the kitchens. Furthermore, they shall be given the means of preparing, themselves, the additional food in their possession.

Adequate premises shall be provided for messing.

Collective disciplinary measures affecting food are prohibited.

Article XXVII. Clothing, underwear and footwear shall be supplied to prisoners of war in sufficient quantities by the Detaining Power, which shall make allowance for the climate of the region where the prisoners are detained. Uniforms of enemy armed forces captured by the Detaining Power should, if suitable for the climate be made available to clothe prisoners of war.

The regular replacement and repair of the above articles shall be assured by the Detaining Power. In addition, prisoners of war who work shall receive appropriate clothing, wherever the nature of the work demands.

Article XXVIII. Canteens shall be installed in all camps, where prisoners of war may procure foodstuffs, soap and tobacco and ordinary articles in daily use. The tariff shall never be in excess of local market prices.

The profits made by canteens shall be used for the benefit of the prisoners; a special fund shall be created for this purpose. The prisoners' representative shall have the right to collaborate in the management of the canteen and of this fund.

When a camp is closed down, the credit balance of the special fund shall be handed to an international welfare organization, to be employed for the benefit of prisoners of war of the same nationality as those who have contributed to the fund. In case of a general repatriation, such profits shall be kept by the Detaining Power, subject to any agreement to the contrary between the Powers concerned.

Chapter III. *Hygiene and Medical Attention*

Article XXIX. The Detaining Power shall be bound to take all sanitary measures necessary to ensure the cleanliness and healthfulness of camps and to prevent epidemics.

Prisoners of war shall have for their use, day and night, conveniences which conform to the rules of hygiene and maintained in a constant state of cleanliness. In any camps in which women prisoners of war are accommodated, separate conveniences shall be provided for them.

Also, apart from the baths and showers with which the camps shall be furnished, prisoners of war shall be provided with sufficient water and soap for their personal toilet and for washing their personal laundry; the necessary installations, facilities and time shall be granted them for that purpose.

Article XXX. Every camp shall have an adequate infirmary where prisoners of war may have the attention they require, as well as appropriate diet. Isolation wards shall, if necessary, be set aside for cases of contagious or mental disease.

Prisoners of war suffering from serious disease, or whose condition necessitates special treatment, a surgical operation or hospital care, must be admitted to any military or civilian medical unit where such treatment can be given, even if their repatriation is contemplated in the near future. Special facilities shall be afforded for the care to be given to the disabled, in particular to the blind, and for their rehabilitation, pending repatriation.

Prisoners of war shall have the attention, preferably, of medical personnel of the Power on which they depend and, if possible, of their nationality.

Prisoners of war may not be prevented from presenting themselves to the medical authorities for examination. The detaining authorities shall, upon request, issue to every prisoner who has undergone treatment, an official certificate indicating the nature of his illness or injury, and the duration and kind of treatment received. A duplicate of this certificate shall be forwarded to the Central Prisoners of War Agency.

The costs of treatment, including those of any apparatus necessary for the maintenance of prisoners of war in good health, particularly dentures and other artificial appliances, and spectacles, shall be borne by the Detaining Power....

[Leon Friedman, ed., *The Law of War: A Documentary History* (New York, 1972), vol. 1, pp. 589–601]

Geneva Convention IV (1949)

Convention Relative to the Protection of Civilian Persons in Time of War, Geneva, 12 August 1949

Article III. In the case of armed conflict not of an international character occurring in the territory of one of the High Contracting Parties, each Party to the conflict shall be bound to apply, as a minimum, the following provisions:

1. Persons taking no active part in the hostilities, including members of armed forces who have laid down their arms and those placed *hors de combat* by sickness, wounds, detention, or any other cause, shall in all circumstances be treated humanely, without any adverse distinction founded on race, colour, religion or faith, sex, birth or wealth, or any other similar criteria.

To this end, the following acts are and shall remain prohibited at any time and in any place whatsoever with respect to the above-mentioned persons:

(a) violence to life and person, in particular murder of all kinds, mutilation, cruel treatment and torture;

(b) taking of hostages;

(c) outrages upon personal dignity, in particular humiliating and degrading treatment;

(d) the passing of sentences and the carrying out of executions without previous judgment pronounced by a regularly constituted court, affording all the judicial guarantees which are recognized as indispensable by civilized peoples.

2. The wounded and sick shall be collected and cared for.

An impartial humanitarian body, such as the International Committee of the Red Cross, may offer its services to the Parties of the conflict.

The Parties to the conflict should further endeavour to bring into force, by means of special agreements, all or part of the other provisions of the present Convention.

The application of the preceding provisions shall not affect the legal status of the Parties to the conflict.

Part II. *General Protection of Populations Against Certain Consequences of War*

Article XIII. The provisions of Part II cover the whole of the populations of the countries in conflict, without any adverse distinction based, in particular, on race, nationality, religion or political opinion, and are intended to alleviate the sufferings caused by war.

Article XIV. In time of peace, the High Contracting Parties and, after the outbreak of hostilities, the Parties thereto, may establish in their own territory and, if the need arises, in occupied areas, hospitals and safety zones and localities so organized as to protect from the effects of war, wounded, sick and aged persons, children under fifteen, expectant mothers and mothers of children under seven.

Upon the outbreak and during the course of hostilities, the Parties concerned may conclude agreements on mutual recognition of the zones and localities they have created. They may for this purpose implement the provisions of the Draft Agreement annexed to the present Convention, with such amendments as they may consider necessary.

The Protecting Powers and the International Committee of the Red Cross are invited to lend their good offices in order to facilitate the institution and recognition of these hospital and safety zones and localities.

Article XV. Any Party to the conflict may, either direct or through a neutral State or some humanitarian organization, propose to the adverse Party to establish, in the regions where fighting is taking place, neutralized zones intended to shelter from the effects of war the following persons, without distinction:

(a) wounded and sick combatants or non-combatants.

(b) civilian persons who take no part in hostilities, and who, while they reside in the zones, perform no work of a military character.

When the Parties concerned have agreed upon the geographical position, administration, food supply and supervision of the proposed neutralized zone, a written agreement shall be concluded and signed by the representatives of the Parties to the conflict. The agreement shall fix the beginning and the duration of the neutralization of the zone.

Article XVI. The wounded and sick, as well as the infirm, and expectant mothers, shall be the object of particular protection and respect.

As far as military considerations allow, each Party to the conflict shall facilitate the steps taken to search for the killed and wounded, to assist the shipwrecked and other persons exposed to grave danger, and to protect them against pillage and ill-treatment. . . .

Article XVIII. Civilian hospitals organized to give care to the wounded and sick, the infirm and maternity cases, may in no circumstances be the object of attack, but shall at all times be respected and protected by the Parties to the conflict.

States which are Parties to a conflict shall provide all civilian hospitals with certificates showing that they are civilian hospitals and that the buildings which they occupy are not used for any purpose which would deprive these hospitals of protection in accordance with Article XIX.

Civilian hospitals shall be marked by means of the emblem provided for in Article XXVIII of the Geneva Convention for the Amelioration of the Condition of the Wounded and Sick in Armed Forces in the Field of August 12, 1949, but only if so authorized by the State.

The Parties to the conflict shall, in so far as military considerations permit, take the necessary steps to make the distinctive emblems indicating civilian hospitals clearly visible to the enemy land, air and naval forces in order to obviate the possibility of any hostile action.

In view of the dangers to which hospitals may be exposed by being close to military objectives, it is recommended that such hospitals be situated as far as possible from such objectives.

Article XIX. The protection to which civilian hospitals are entitled shall not cease unless they are used to commit, outside their humanitarian duties acts harmful to the enemy. Protection may, however, cease only after due warning has been given, naming, in all appropriate cases, a reasonable time limit, and after such warning has remained unheeded.

The fact that sick or wounded members of the armed forces are nursed in these hospitals, or the presence of small arms and ammunition taken from such combatants and not yet handed to the proper service, shall not be considered to be acts harmful to the enemy.

Part III. *Status and Treatment of Protected Persons*

Section I. Provisions Common to the Territories of the Parties to the Conflict and to Occupied Territories

Article XXVII. Protected persons are entitled, in all circumstances, to respect for their persons, their honour, their family rights, their religious convictions and practices, and their manners and customs. They shall at all times be humanely treated, and shall be protected especially against all acts of violence or threats thereof and against insults and public curiosity.

Women shall be especially protected against any attack on their honour, in particular against rape, enforced prostitution, or any form of indecent assault.

Without prejudice to the provisions relating to their state of health, age and sex, all protected persons shall be treated with the same consideration by the Party to the conflict in whose power they are, without any adverse distinction based, in particular, on race, religion or political opinion.

Article XXVIII. The presence of a protected person may not be used to render certain points or areas immune from military operations.

Article XXIX. The Party to the conflict in whose hands protected persons may be, is responsible for the treatment accorded to them by its agents, irrespective of any individual responsibility which may be incurred.

[Leon Friedman, ed., *The Law of War: A Documentary History* (New York, 1972), vol. 1]

U.S. Department of the Army Field Manual
FM 27–10

The Law of Land Warfare (1956)

Section III. FORBIDDEN MEANS
OF WAGING WARFARE

33. Means of Injuring the Enemy Limited

a. *Treaty Provision.* The right of belligerents to adopt means of injuring the enemy is not unlimited. *(HR, art. 22)*[1]

b. The means employed are definitely restricted by international declarations and conventions and by the laws and usages of war.

34. Employment of Arms Causing Unnecessary Injury

a. *Treaty Provision.* It is especially forbidden . . . to employ arms, projectiles, or material calculated to cause unnecessary suffering. *(HR, art. 23, par. (e).)*

b. *Interpretation.* What weapons cause "unnecessary injury" can only be determined in light of the practice of States in refraining from the use of a given weapon because it is believed to have that effect. The prohibition certainly does not extend to the use of explosive contained in artillery projectiles, mines, rockets, or hand grenades. Usage has, however, established the illegality of the use of lances with barbed heads, irregular-shaped bullets, and projectiles filled with glass, the use of any substance on bullets that would tend unnecessarily to inflame a wound inflicted by them, and the scoring of the surface or the filing off of the ends of the hard cases of bullets.

35. Atomic Weapons. The use of explosive "atomic weapons," whether by air, sea, or land forces, cannot as such be regarded as violative of international law in the absence of any customary rule of international law or international convention restricting their employment.

36. Weapons Employing Fire. The use of weapons which employ fire, such as tracer ammunition, flame-throwers, napalm and other incendiary agents, against targets requiring their use is not violative of international law. They should not, however, be employed in such a way as to cause unnecessary suffering to individuals.

37. Poison

a. *Treaty Provision.* It is especially forbidden . . . to employ poison or poisoned weapons. *(HR, art. 23, par. (a).)*

b. *Discussion of Rule.* The foregoing rule does not prohibit measures being taken to dry up springs, to divert rivers and aqueducts from their courses, or to destroy, through chemical or bacterial agents harmless to man, crops intended solely for consumption by the armed forces (if that fact can be determined).

38. Gases, Chemicals, and Bacteriological Warfare. The United States is not a party to any treaty, now in force, that prohibits or restricts the use in warfare of toxic or nontoxic gases, of smoke or incendiary materials, or of bacteriological warfare. A treaty signed at Washington, 6 February 1922, on behalf of the United States, the British Empire, France, Italy, and Japan *(3 Malloy, Treaties 3116)* contains a provision (art. V) prohibiting "The use in war of asphyxiating, poisonous or other gases, and all analogous liquids, materials, or devices," but that treaty was expressly conditioned to become effective only upon ratification by all of the signatory powers, and, not having been ratified by all of the signatories, has never become effective. The Geneva Protocol "for the prohibition of the use in war of asphyxiating, poisonous, or other gases, and of bacteriological methods of warfare," signed on 17 June 1925, on behalf of the United States and many other powers (94 *League of Nations Treaty Series* 65), has been ratified or adhered to by and is now effective between a considerable number of

States. However, the United States Senate has refrained from giving its advice and consent to the ratification of the Protocol by the United States, and it is accordingly not binding on this country.

Section IV. BOMBARDMENTS, ASSAULTS, AND SIEGES

39. Bombardment of Undefended Places Forbidden. The attack or bombardment, by whatever means, of towns, villages, dwellings, or buildings which are undefended is prohibited. *(HR, art. 25.)*

40. Defended Place Defined. Investment, bombardment, assault, and siege have always been recognized as legitimate means of land warfare. Defended places in the sense of Article 25, HR, include:

a. A fort or fortified place.

b. A city or town surrounded by detached defense positions, which is considered jointly with such defense positions as an indivisible whole.

c. A place which is occupied by a combatant military force or through which such a force is passing. The occupation of such a place by medical units alone is not sufficient to make it a defended place.

Factories producing munitions and military supplies, military camps, warehouses storing munitions and military supplies, ports and railroads being used for the transportation of military supplies, and other places devoted to the support of military operations or the accommodation of troops may also be attacked and bombarded even though they are not defended.

41. Unnecessary Killing and Devastation. Particularly in the circumstances referred to in the preceding paragraph, loss of life and damage to property must not be out of proportion to the military advantage to be gained. Once a fort or defended locality has surrendered, only such further damage is permitted as is demanded by the exigencies of war, such as the removal of fortifications, demolition of military buildings, and destruction of stores *(GC, art. 147;* par. 502 herein).[2]

42. Aerial Bombardment. There is no prohibition of general application against bombardment from the air of combatant troops, defended places, or other legitimate military objectives.

NOTES

1. Annex to Hague Convention No. IV, 18 October 1907, embodying the Regulations Respecting the Laws and Customs of War on Land.

2. Geneva Convention Relative to the Protection of Civilian Persons in Time of War [12 August 1949].

U.N. Resolutions and Treaty

U.N. Resolution on Nuclear Weapons (1961)

General Assembly Resolution 1653, United Nations, 24 November 1961

THE GENERAL ASSEMBLY,

Mindful of its responsibility under the Charter of the United Nations in the maintenance of international peace and security, as well as in the consideration of principles governing disarmament,

Gravely concerned that, while negotiations on disarmament have not so far achieved satisfactory results, the armaments race, particularly in the nuclear and thermo-nuclear fields, has reached a dangerous stage requiring all possible precautionary measures to protect humanity and civilization from the hazard of nuclear and thermo-nuclear catastrophe,

Recalling that the use of weapons of mass destruction, causing unnecessary human suffering, was in the past prohibited, as being contrary to the laws of humanity and to the principles of international law, by international declarations and binding agreements, such as the Declaration of St. Petersburg of 1868, the Declaration of the Brussels Conference of 1874, the Conventions of The Hague Peace Conferences of 1899 and 1907, and the Geneva Protocol of 1925, to which the majority of nations are still parties,

Considering that the use of nuclear and thermo-nuclear weapons would bring about indiscriminate suffering and destruction to mankind and civilization to an even greater extent than the use of those weapons declared by the aforementioned international declarations and agreements to be contrary to the laws of humanity and a crime under international law,

Believing that the use of weapons of mass destruction, such as nuclear and thermo-nuclear weapons, is a direct negation of the high ideals and objectives which the United Nations has been established to achieve through the protection of succeeding generations from the scourge of war and through the preservation and promotion of their cultures,

1. *Declares* that:

(a) The use of nuclear and thermo-nuclear weapons is contrary to the spirit, letter and aims of the United Nations and, as such, a direct violation of the Charter of the United Nations;

(b) The use of nuclear and thermo-nuclear weapons would exceed even the scope of war and cause indiscriminate suffering and destruction to mankind and civilization and, as such, is contrary to the rules of international law and to the laws of humanity;

(c) The use of nuclear and thermo-nuclear weapons is a war directed not against an enemy or enemies alone but also against mankind in general, since the peoples of the world not involved in such a war will be subjected to all the evils generated by the use of such weapons;

(d) Any State using nuclear and thermo-nuclear weapons is to be considered as violating the Charter of the United Nations, as acting contrary to the laws of humanity and as committing a crime against mankind and civilization;

2. *Requests* the Secretary-General to consult the Governments of Member States to ascertain their views on the possibility of convening a special conference for signing a convention on the prohibition of the use of nuclear and thermo-nuclear weapons for war purposes and to report on the results of such consultation to the General Assembly at its seventeenth session.

[Leon Friedman, ed., *The Law of War: A Documentary History* (New York, 1972), vol. 1, pp. 697–698]

U.N. Resolution on Human Rights (1968)

General Assembly Resolution 2444, United Nations, 19 December 1968

THE GENERAL ASSEMBLY,

Recognizing the necessity of applying basic humanitarian principles in all armed conflicts,

Taking note of resolution XXIII on human rights in armed conflicts, adopted on 12 May 1968 by the International Conference on Human Rights,

Affirming that the provisions of that resolution need to be implemented effectively as soon as possible,

1. *Affirms* resolution XXVIII of the XXth International Conference of the Red Cross held at Vienna in 1965, which laid down, *inter alia,* the following principles for observance by all governmental and other authorities responsible for action in armed conflicts:

(a) That the right of the parties to a conflict to adopt means of injuring the enemy is not unlimited;

(b) That it is prohibited to launch attacks against the civilian populations as such;

(c) That distinction must be made at all times between persons taking part in the hostilities and members of the civilian population to the effect that the latter be spared as much as possible;

2. *Invites* the Secretary-General, in consultation with the International Committee of the Red Cross and other appropriate international organizations, to study:

(a) Steps which could be taken to secure the better application of existing humanitarian international conventions and rules in all armed conflicts;

(b) The need for additional humanitarian international conventions or for other appropriate legal instruments to ensure the better protection of civilians, prisoners and combatants in all armed conflicts and the prohibition and limitation of the use of certain methods and means of warfare;

3. *Requests* the Secretary-General to take all other necessary steps to give effect to the provisions of the present resolution and to report to the General Assembly at its twenty-fourth session on the steps he has taken;

4. *Further requests* Member States to extend all possible assistance to the Secretary-General in the preparation of the study requested in paragraph 2 above;

5. *Calls upon* all States which have not yet done so to become parties to the Hague Conventions of 1899 and 1907, the Geneva Protocol of 1925 and the Geneva Conventions of 1949.

[Leon Friedman, ed., *The Law of War: A Documentary History* (New York, 1972), vol. 1, pp. 699–700]

U.N. Resolution on Protection of Civilians (1970)

General Assembly Resolution 2675, United Nations, 9 December 1970

THE GENERAL ASSEMBLY,

Noting that in the present century the international community has accepted an increased role and new responsibilities for the alleviation of human suffering in any form and in particular during armed conflicts,

Recalling that to this end a series of international instruments has been adopted, including the four Geneva Conventions of 1949,

Recalling further its resolution 2444 (XXIII) of 19 December 1968 on respect for human rights in armed conflicts,

Bearing in mind the need for measures to ensure the better protection of human rights in armed conflicts of all types,

Noting with appreciation the work that is being undertaken in this respect by the International Committee of the Red Cross,

Noting with appreciation the reports of the Secretary-General on respect for human rights in armed conflicts,

Convinced that civilian populations are in special need of increased protection in time of armed conflicts,

Recognizing the importance of the strict application of the Geneva Convention relative to the Protection of Civilian Persons in Time of War, of 12 August 1949,

Affirms the following basic principles for the protection of civilian populations in armed conflicts, without prejudice to their future elaboration within the framework of progressive development of the international law of armed conflict:

1. Fundamental human rights, as accepted in international law and laid down in international instruments, continue to apply fully in situations of armed conflict.

2. In the conduct of military operations during armed conflicts, a distinction must be made at all times between persons actively taking part in the hostilities and civilian populations.

3. In the conduct of military operations, every effort should be made to spare civilian populations from the ravages of war, and all necessary precautions should be taken to avoid injury, loss or damage to civilian populations.

4. Civilian populations as such should not be the object of military operations.

5. Dwellings and other installations that are used only by civilian populations should not be the object of military operations.

6. Places or areas designated for the sole protection of civilians, such as hospital zones or similar refuges, should not be the object of military operations.

7. Civilian populations, or individual members thereof, should not be the object of reprisals, forcible transfers or other assaults on their integrity.

8. The provision of international relief to civilian populations is in conformity with the humanitarian principles of the Charter of the United Nations, the Universal Declaration of Human Rights and other international instruments in the field of human rights. The Declaration of Principles for International Humanitarian Relief to the Civilian Population in Disaster Situations, as laid down in resolution XXVI adopted by the twenty-first International Humanitarian Relief to the Civilian Population in Disaster conflict, and all parties to a conflict should make every effort to facilitate this application.

[Leon Friedman, ed., *The Law of War: A Documentary History* (New York, 1972), vol. 1, pp. 755–756]

Restricting Excessively Injurious or Indiscriminate Conventional Weapons (1981)

This United Nations convention was adopted on 10 April 1981, and it entered into force on 2 December 1983.

Convention on Prohibitions or Restrictions, on the Use of Certain Conventional Weapons Which May Be Deemed to Be Excessively Injurious or to Have Indiscriminate Effects

The High Contracting Parties,

Recalling that every State has the duty, in conformity with the Charter of the United Nations, to refrain in its international relations from the threat or use of force against the sovereignty, territorial integrity or political independence of any State, or in any other manner inconsistent with the purposes of the United Nations,

Further recalling the general principle of the protection of the civilian population against the effects of hostilities,

Basing themselves on the principle of international law that the right of the parties to an armed conflict to choose methods or means of warfare is not unlimited, and on the principle that prohibits the employment in armed conflicts of weapons, projectiles and material and methods of warfare of a nature to cause superfluous injury or unnecessary suffering,

Also recalling that it is prohibited to employ methods or means of warfare which are intended, or may be expected, to cause widespread, long-term and severe damage to the natural environment,

Confirming their determination that in cases not covered by this Convention and its annexed Protocols or by other international agreements, the civilian population and the combatants shall at all times remain under the protection and authority of the principles of international law derived from established custom, from the principles of humanity and from the dictates of public conscience,

Desiring to contribute to international detente, the ending of the arms race and the building of confidence among States, and hence to the realization of the aspiration of all peoples to live in peace,

Recognizing the importance of pursuing every effort which may contribute to progress towards general and complete disarmament under strict and effective international control,

Reaffirming the need to continue the codification and progressive development of the rules of international law applicable in armed conflict,

Wishing to prohibit or restrict further the use of certain conventional weapons and believing that the positive results achieved in this area may facilitate the main talks on disarmament with a view to putting an end to the production, stockpiling and proliferation of such weapons,

Emphasizing the desirability that all States become parties to this Convention and its annexed Protocols, especially the militarily significant States,

Bearing in mind that the General Assembly of the United Nations and the United Nations Disarmament Commission may decide to examine the question of a possible broadening of the scope of the prohibitions and restrictions contained in this Convention and its annexed Protocols,

Further bearing in mind that the Committee on Disarmament may decide to consider the question of adopting further measures to prohibit or restrict the use of certain conventional weapons,

Have agreed as follows:

Article 1. SCOPE OF APPLICATION. This Convention and its annexed Protocols shall apply in the situations referred to in Article 2 common to the Geneva Conventions of 12 August 1949 for the Protection of War Victims, including any situation described in paragraph 4 of Article 1 of Additional Protocol I to these Conventions.

Article 2. RELATIONS WITH OTHER INTERNATIONAL AGREEMENTS. Nothing in this Convention or its an-

nexed Protocols shall be interpreted as detracting from other obligations imposed upon the High Contracting Parties by international humanitarian law applicable in armed conflict.

Article 3. [Signature]

Article 4. [Ratification]

Article 5. [Entry into force]

Article 6. Dissemination. The High Contracting Parties undertake, in time of peace as in time of armed conflict, to disseminate this Convention and those of its annexed Protocols by which they are bound as widely as possible in their respective countries and, in particular, to include the study thereof in their programmes of military instruction, so that those instruments may become known to their armed forces.

Article 7. TREATY RELATIONS UPON ENTRY INTO FORCE OF THIS CONVENTION

1. When one of the parties to a conflict is not bound by an annexed Protocol, the parties bound by this Convention and that annexed Protocol shall remain bound by them in their mutual relations.

2. Any High Contracting Party shall be bound by this Convention and any Protocol annexed thereto which is in force for it, in any situation contemplated by Article 1, in relation to any State which is not a party to this Convention or bound by the relevant annexed Protocol, if the latter accepts and applies this Convention or the relevant Protocol, and so notifies the Depositary.

3. The Depositary shall immediately inform the High Contracting Parties concerned of any notification received under paragraph 2 of this Article.

4. This Convention, and the annexed Protocols by which a High Contracting Party is bound, shall apply with respect to an armed conflict against that High Contracting Party of the type referred to in Article 1, paragraph 4, of Additional Protocol I to the Geneva Conventions of 12 August 1949 for the Protection of War Victims:

(a) where the High Contracting Party is also a party to Additional Protocol I and an authority referred to in Article 96, paragraph 3, of that Protocol has undertaken to apply the Geneva Conventions and Additional Protocol I in accordance with Article 96, paragraph 3, of the said Protocol, and undertakes to apply this Convention and the relevant annexed Protocols in relation to that conflict; or

(b) where the High Contracting Party is not a party to Additional Protocol I and an authority of the type referred to in subparagraph (a) above accepts and applies the obligations of the Geneva Conventions and of this Convention and the relevant annexed Protocols in relation to that conflict. Such an acceptance and application shall have in relation to that conflict the following effects:

(i) the Geneva Conventions and this Convention and its relevant annexed Protocols are brought into force for the parties to the conflict with immediate effect;

(ii) the said authority assumes the same rights and obligations as those which have been assumed by a High Contracting Party to the Geneva Conventions, this Convention and its relevant annexed Protocols; and

(iii) the Geneva Conventions, this Convention and its relevant annexed Protocols are equally binding upon all parties to the conflict.

The High Contracting Party and the authority may also agree to accept and apply the obligations of Additional Protocol I to the Geneva Conventions on a reciprocal basis.

Article 8. REVIEW AND AMENDMENTS

1. (a) At any time after the entry into force of this Convention any High Contracting Party may propose amendments to this Convention or any annexed Protocol by which it is bound. Any proposal for an amendment shall be communicated to the Depositary, who shall notify it to all the High Contracting Parties and shall seek their views on whether a conference should be convened to consider the proposal. If a majority, that shall not be less than eighteen of the High Contracting Parties, so agree, he shall promptly convene a conference to which all High Contracting Parties shall be invited. States not parties to this Convention shall be invited to the conference as observers.

(b) Such a conference may agree upon amendments which shall be adopted and shall enter into force in the same manner as this Convention and the annexed Protocols, provided that amendments to this Convention may be adopted only by the High Contracting Parties and that amendments to a specific annexed Protocol may be adopted only by the High Contracting Parties which are bound by that Protocol.

2. (a) At any time after the entry into force of this Convention any High Contracting Party may propose additional protocols relating to other categories of conventional weapons not covered by the existing annexed Protocols. Any such proposal for an additional protocol shall be communicated to the Depositary, who shall notify it to all the High Contracting Parties in accordance with subparagraph 1 (a) of this Article. If a majority, that shall not be less than eighteen of the High Contracting Parties, so agree, the Depositary shall promptly convene a conference to which all States shall be invited.

(b) Such a conference may agree, with the full participation of all States represented at the conference, upon additional protocols which shall be adopted in the same manner as this Convention, shall be annexed thereto and shall enter into force as provided in paragraphs 3 and 4 of Article 5 of this Convention.

3. (a) If, after a period of ten years following the entry into force of this Convention, no conference has been convened in accordance with subparagraph 1 (a) or 2 (a) of this Article, any High Contracting Party may request the Depositary to convene a conference to which all High Contracting Parties shall be invited to review the scope and operation of this Convention and the Protocols annexed thereto and to consider any proposal for amendments of this Convention or of the existing Protocols. States not parties to this Convention shall be invited as observers to the conference. The conference may agree upon amendments which shall be adopted and enter into force in accordance with subparagraph 1 (b) above.

(b) At such conference consideration may also be given to any proposal for additional protocols relating to other categories of conventional weapons not covered by the existing annexed Protocols. All States represented at the conference may participate fully in such consideration. Any additional protocols shall be adopted in the same manner as this Convention, shall be annexed thereto and shall enter into force as provided in paragraphs 3 and 4 of Article 5 of this Convention.

(c) Such a conference may consider whether provision should be made for the convening of a further conference at the request of any High Contracting Party if, after a similar period to that referred to in subparagraph 3 (a) of this Article, no conference has been convened in accordance with subparagraph 1 (a) or 2 (a) of this Article.

Article 9. DENUNCIATION

1. Any High Contracting Party may denounce this Convention or any of its annexed Protocols by so notifying the Depositary.

2. Any such denunciation shall only take effect one year after receipt by the Depositary of the no-

tification of denunciation. If, however, on the expiry of that year the denouncing High Contracting Party is engaged in one of the situations referred to in Article 1, the Party shall continue to be bound by the obligations of this Convention and of the relevant annexed Protocols until the end of the armed conflict or occupation and, in any case, until the termination of operations connected with the final release, repatriation or reestablishment of the person protected by the rules of international law applicable in armed conflict, and in the case of any annexed Protocol containing provisions concerning situations in which peace-keeping, observation or similar functions are performed by United Nations forces or missions in the area concerned, until the termination of those functions.

3. Any denunciation of this Convention shall be considered as also applying to all annexed Protocols by which the denouncing High Contracting Party is bound.

4. Any denunciation shall have effect only in respect of the denouncing High Contracting Party.

5. Any denunciation shall not affect the obligations already incurred, by reason of an armed conflict, under this Convention and its annexed Protocols by such denouncing High Contracting Party in respect of any act committed before this denunciation becomes effective.

Article 10. [Depositary]

Article 11. [Transmittal]

Protocol on Non-Detectable Fragments (Protocol I)

It is prohibited to use any weapon the primary effect of which is to injure by fragments which in the human body escape detection by X-rays.

Protocol on Prohibitions or Restrictions on the Use of Mines, Booby-Traps and Other Devices (Protocol II)

Article 1. MATERIAL SCOPE OF APPLICATION. This Protocol relates to the use on land of the mines, booby-traps and other devices defined herein, including mines laid to interdict beaches, waterway crossings or river crossings, but does not apply to the use of antiship mines at sea or in inland waterways.

Article 2. DEFINITIONS. For the purpose of this Protocol:

1. "Mine" means any munition placed under, on or near the ground or other surface area and de-signed to be detonated or exploded by the presence, proximity or contact of a person or vehicle, and "remotely delivered mine" means any mine so defined delivered by artillery, rocket, mortar or similar means or dropped from an aircraft.

2. "Booby-trap" means any device or material which is designed, constructed or adapted to kill or injure and which functions unexpectedly when a person disturbs or approaches an apparently harmless object or performs an apparently safe act.

3. "Other devices" means manually-emplaced munitions and devices designed to kill, injure or damage and which are actuated by remote control or automatically after a lapse of time.

4. "Military objective" means, so far as objects are concerned, any object which by its nature, location, purpose or use makes an effective contribution to military action and whose total or partial destruction, capture or neutralization, in the circumstances ruling at the time, offers a definite military advantage.

5. "Civilian objects" are all objects which are not military objectives as defined in paragraph 4.

6. "Recording" means a physical, administrative and technical operation designed to obtain, for the purpose of registration in the official records, all available information facilitating the location of minefields, mines and booby-traps.

Article 3. GENERAL RESTRICTIONS ON THE USE OF MINES, BOOBY-TRAPS AND OTHER DEVICES

1. This Article applies to:

(a) mines;

(b) booby-traps; and

(c) other devices.

2. It is prohibited in all circumstances to direct weapons to which this Article applies, either in offence, defence or by way of reprisals, against the civilian population as such or against individual civilians.

3. The indiscriminate use of weapons to which this Article applies is prohibited. Indiscriminate use is any placement of such weapons:

(a) which is not on, or directed at, a military objective; or

(b) which employs a method or means of delivery which cannot be directed at a specific military objective; or

(c) which may be expected to cause incidental loss of civilian life, injury to civilians, damage to civilian objects, or a combination thereof, which would be excessive in relation to the concrete and direct military advantage anticipated.

4. All feasible precautions shall be taken to protect civilians from the effects of weapons to which this Article applies. Feasible precautions are those precautions which are practicable or practically possible taking into account all circumstances ruling at the time, including humanitarian and military considerations.

Article 4. RESTRICTIONS ON THE USE OF MINES OTHER THAN REMOTELY DELIVERED MINES, BOOBY-TRAPS AND OTHER DEVICES IN POPULATED AREAS

1. This Article applies to:

(a) mines other than remotely delivered mines;

(b) booby-traps; and

(c) other devices.

2. It is prohibited to use weapons to which this Article applies in any city, town, village or other area containing a similar concentration of civilians in which combat between ground forces is not taking place or does not appear to be imminent, unless either:

(a) they are placed on or in the close vicinity of a military objective belonging to or under the control of an adverse party; or

(b) measures are taken to protect civilians from their effects, for example, the posting of warning signs, the posting of sentries, the issue of warnings or the provision of fences.

Article 5. RESTRICTIONS ON THE USE OF REMOTELY DELIVERED MINES

1. The use of remotely delivered mines is prohibited unless such mines are only used within an area which is itself a military objective or which contains military objectives, and unless:

(a) their location can be accurately recorded in accordance with Article 7(1)(a); or

(b) an effective neutralizing mechanism is used on each such mine, that is to say, a self-actuating mechanism which is designed to render a mine harmless or cause it to destroy itself when it is anticipated that the mine will no longer serve the military purpose for which it was placed in position, or a remotely-controlled mechanism which is designed to render harmless or destroy a mine when the mine no longer serves the military purpose for which it was placed in position.

2. Effective advance warning shall be given of any delivery or dropping of remotely delivered mines which may affect the civilian population, unless circumstances do not permit.

Article 6. PROHIBITION ON THE USE OF CERTAIN BOOBY-TRAPS

1. Without prejudice to the rules of international law applicable in armed conflict relating to treachery and perfidy, it is prohibited in all circumstances to use:

(a) any booby-trap in the form of an apparently harmless portable object which is specifically designed and constructed to contain explosive material and to detonate when it is disturbed or approached; or

(b) booby-traps which are in any way attached to or associated with:

(i) internationally recognized protective emblems, signs or signals;

(ii) sick, wounded or dead persons;

(iii) burial or cremation sites or graves;

(iv) medical facilities, medical equipment, medical supplies or medical transportation;

(v) children's toys or other portable objects or products specially designed for the feeding, health, hygiene, clothing or education of children;

(vi) food or drink;

(vii) kitchen utensils or appliances except in military establishments, military locations or military supply depots;

(viii) objects clearly of a religious nature;

(ix) historic monuments, works of art or places of worship which constitute the cultural or spiritual heritage of peoples;

(x) animals or their carcasses.

2. It is prohibited in all circumstances to use any booby-trap which is designed to cause superfluous injury or unnecessary suffering.

Article 7. RECORDING AND PUBLICATION OF THE LOCATION OF MINEFIELDS, MINES AND BOOBY-TRAPS

1. The parties to a conflict shall record the location of:

(a) all pre-planned minefields laid by them; and

(b) all areas in which they have made large-scale and pre-planned use of booby-traps.

2. The parties shall endeavour to ensure the recording of the location of all other minefields, mines and booby-traps which they have laid or placed in position.

3. All such records shall be retained by the parties who shall:

(a) immediately after the cessation of active hostilities:

(i) take all necessary and appropriate measures, including the use of such records, to protect civilians from the effects of minefields, mines and booby-traps; and either

(ii) in cases where the forces of neither party are in the territory of the adverse party, make available to each other and to the Secretary-General of the United Nations all information in their possession concerning the location of minefields, mines and booby-traps in the territory of the adverse party; or

(iii) once complete withdrawal of the forces of the parties from the territory of the adverse party has taken place, make available to the adverse party and to the Secretary-General of the United Nations all information in their possession concerning the location of minefields, mines and booby-traps in the territory of the adverse party;

(b) when a United Nations force or mission performs functions in any area, make available to the authority mentioned in Article 8 such information as is required by that Article;

(c) whenever possible, by mutual agreement, provide for the release of information concerning the location of minefields, mines and boobytraps, particularly in agreements governing the cessation of hostilities.

Article 8. PROTECTION OF UNITED NATIONS FORCES AND MISSIONS FROM THE EFFECTS OF MINEFIELDS, MINES AND BOOBY-TRAPS

1. When a United Nations force or mission performs functions of peace-keeping, observation or similar functions in any area, each party to the conflict shall, if requested by the head of the United Nations force or mission in that area, as far as it is able:

(a) remove or render harmless all mines or booby-traps in that area;

(b) take such measures as may be necessary to protect the force or mission from the effects of minefields, mines and booby-traps while carrying out its duties; and

(c) make available to the head of the United Nations force or mission in that area, all information in the party's possession concerning the location of minefields, mines and booby-traps in that area.

2. When a United Nations fact-finding mission performs functions in any area, any party to the conflict concerned shall provide protection to that mission except where, because of the size of such mission, it cannot adequately provide such protection. In that case it shall make available to the head of the mission the information in its possession concerning the location of minefields, mines and booby-traps in that area.

Article 9. INTERNATIONAL CO-OPERATION IN THE REMOVAL OF MINEFIELDS, MINES AND BOOBY-TRAPS. After the cessation of active hostilities, the parties shall endeavour to reach agreement, both among themselves and, where appropriate, with other States and with international organizations, on the provision of information and technical and material assistance—including, in appropriate circumstances, joint operations—necessary to remove or otherwise render ineffective minefields, mines and booby-traps placed in position during the conflict.

Technical Annex to the Protocol on Prohibitions or Restrictions on the Use of Mines, Booby-Traps and Other Devices (Protocol II)

GUIDELINES ON RECORDING

Whenever an obligation for the recording of the location of minefields, mines and booby-traps arises under the Protocol, the following guidelines shall be taken into account.

1. With regard to pre-planned minefields and large-scale and pre-planned use of booby-traps:

(a) maps, diagrams or other records should be made in such a way as to indicate the extent of the minefield or booby-trapped area; and (b) the location of the minefield or booby-trapped area should be specified by relation to the coordinates of a single reference point and by the estimated dimensions of the area containing mines and booby-traps in relation to that single reference point.

2. With regard to other minefields, mines and booby-traps laid or placed in position:

In so far as possible, the relevant information specified in paragraph 1 above should be recorded so as to enable the areas containing minefields, mines and booby-traps to be identified.

Protocol on Prohibitions or Restrictions on the Use of Incendiary Weapons (Protocol III)

Article 1. DEFINITIONS. For the purpose of this Protocol:

1. "Incendiary weapon" means any weapon or munition which is primarily designed to set fire to objects or to cause burn injury to persons through the action of flame, heat, or a combination thereof, produced by a chemical reaction of a substance delivered on the target.

(a) Incendiary weapons can take the form of, for example, flame throwers, fougasses, shells, rockets, grenades, mines, bombs and other containers of incendiary substances.

(b) Incendiary weapons do not include:

(i) Munitions which may have incidental incendiary effects, such as illuminants, tracers, smoke or signalling systems;

(ii) Munitions designed to combine penetration, blast or fragmentation effects with an additional incendiary effect, such as armour-piercing projectiles, fragmentation shells, explosive bombs and similar combined-effects munitions in which the incendiary effect is not specifically designed to cause burn injury to persons, but to be used against military objectives, such as armoured vehicles, aircraft and installations or facilities.

2. "Concentration of civilians" means any concentration of civilians, be it permanent or temporary, such as in inhabited parts of cities, or inhabited towns or villages, or as in camps or columns of refugees or evacuees, or groups of nomads.

3. "Military objective" means, so far as objects are concerned, any object which by its nature, location, purpose or use makes an effective contribution to military action and whose total or partial destruction, capture or neutralization, in the circumstances ruling at the time, offers a definite military advantage.

4. "Civilian objects" are all objects which are not military objectives as defined in paragraph 3.

5. "Feasible precautions" are those precautions which are practicable or practically possible taking into account all circumstances ruling at the time, including humanitarian and military considerations.

Article 2. PROTECTION OF CIVILIANS AND CIVILIAN OBJECTS

1. It is prohibited in all circumstances to make the civilian population as such, individual civilians or civilian objects the object of attack by incendiary weapons.

2. It is prohibited in all circumstances to make any military objective located within a concentration of civilians the object of attack by air-delivered incendiary weapons.

3. It is further prohibited to make any military objective located within a concentration of civilians the object of attack by means of incendiary weapons other than air-delivered incendiary weapons, except when such military objective is clearly separated from the concentration of civilians and all feasible precautions are taken with a view to limiting the incendiary effects to the military objective and to avoiding, and in any event to minimizing,

incidental loss of civilian life, injury to civilians and damage to civilian objects.

4. It is prohibited to make forests or other kinds of plant cover the object of attack by incendiary weapons except when such natural elements are used to cover, conceal or camouflage combatants or other military objectives, or are themselves military objectives.

Resolution on Small-Calibre Weapon Systems

[Adopted by the conference at its 7th plenary meeting, 23 September 1979]

The United Nations Conference on Prohibitions or Restrictions of Use of Certain Conventional Weapons,

Recalling the United Nations General Assembly resolution 32/152 of 19 December 1977,

Aware of the continuous development of small-calibre weapon systems (i.e., arms and projectiles),

Anxious to prevent an unnecessary increase of the injurious effects of such weapon systems,

Recalling the agreement embodied in The Hague Declaration of 29 July 1899, to abstain, in international armed conflict, from the use of bullets which expand or flatten easily in the human body,

Convinced that it is desirable to establish accurately the wounding effects of current and new generations of small-calibre weapon systems including the various parameters that affect the energy transfer and the wounding mechanism of such systems,

1. Takes note with appreciation of the intensive research carried out nationally and internationally in the area of wound ballistics, in particular relating to small-calibre weapon systems, as documented during the Conference;

2. Considers that this research and the international discussion on the subject has led to an increased understanding of the wounding effects of small-calibre weapon systems and of the parameters involved;

3. Believes that such research, including testing of small-calibre weapon systems, should be continued with a view to developing standardized assessment methodology relative to ballistic parameters and medical effects of such systems;

4. Invites Governments to carry out further research, jointly or individually, on the wounding effects of small-calibre weapon systems and to communicate, where possible, their findings and conclusions;

5. Welcomes the announcement that an international scientific symposium on wound ballistics will be held in Gothenburg, Sweden, in late 1980 or in 1981, and hopes that the results of the symposium will be made available to the United Nations Disarmament Commission, the Committee on Disarmament and other interested fora;

6. Appeals to all Governments to exercise the utmost care in the development of small-calibre weapon systems, so as to avoid an unnecessary escalation of the injurious effects of such systems.

[*Final Report of the United Nations Conference on Prohibitions or Restrictions of Use of Certain Conventional Weapons Which May Be Deemed to Be Excessively Injurious or to Have Indiscriminate Effects* (A/CONF.95/15 and Corr.2, annex)]

Stabilizing the
International Environment

◯

See also Preventing Accidental War. *Entries that are the subjects of essays in Volume I or II are marked with asterisks.*

The Turkish Straits

During the nineteenth and twentieth centuries the major powers have made repeated attempts to control the Turkish Straits connecting the Black Sea to the Mediterranean Sea. The Treaty of Lausanne (1923) demilitarized the straits; however, by 1936, Turkey was given the right to fortify certain portions of the straits and was required to monitor the passage of warships.

The Montreux Convention (1936)

Convention Regarding the Regime of the Straits, 20 July 1936

Desiring to regulate transit and navigation in the Straits of the Dardanelles, the Sea of Marmora and the Bosphorus comprised under the general term "Straits" in such manner as to safeguard, within the framework of Turkish security and of the security, in the Black Sea, of the riparian States, the principle enshrined in article 23 of the Treaty of Peace signed at Lausanne on July 24th, 1923.

SECTION I. MERCHANT VESSELS

Article 4. In time of war, Turkey not being belligerent, merchant vessels, under any flag or with any kind of cargo, shall enjoy freedom of transit and navigation in the Straits subject to the provisions of articles 2 and 3.

Pilotage and towage remain optional.

Article 5. In time of war, Turkey being belligerent, merchant vessels not belonging to a country at war with Turkey shall enjoy freedom of transit and navigation in the Straits on condition that they do not in any way assist the enemy.

Such vessels shall enter the Straits by day and their transit shall be effected by the route which shall in each case be indicated by the Turkish authorities.

SECTION II. VESSELS OF WAR

Article 8. For the purposes of the present Convention, the definitions of vessels of war and of their specification together with those relating to the calculation of tonnage shall be as set forth in Annex II to the present Convention.

Article 9. Naval auxiliary vessels specifically designed for the carriage of fuel, liquid or non-liquid, shall not be subject to the provisions of article 13 regarding notification, nor shall they be counted for the purpose of calculating the tonnage which is subject to limitation under articles 14 and 18, on condition that they shall pass through the Straits singly. They shall, however, continue to be on the same footing as vessels of war for the purposes of the remaining provisions governing transit.

The auxiliary vessels specified in the preceding paragraph shall only be entitled to benefit by the exceptional status therein contemplated if their armament does not include: for use against floating targets, more than two guns of a maximum calibre of 105 millimetres; for use against aerial targets, more than two guns of a maximum calibre of 75 millimetres.

Article 10. In time of peace, light surface vessels, minor war vessels and auxiliary vessels, whether belonging to Black Sea or non-Black-Sea Powers, and whatever their flag, shall enjoy freedom of transit through the Straits without any taxes or charges whatever, provided that such transit is begun during daylight and subject to the conditions laid down in article 13, and the articles following thereafter.

Vessels of war other than those which fall within the categories specified in the preceding paragraph shall only enjoy a right of transit under the special conditions provided by articles 11 and 12.

Article 11. Black Sea Powers may send through the Straits capital ships of a tonnage greater than that laid down in the first paragraph of article 14, on condition that these vessels pass through the Straits singly, escorted by not more than two destroyers.

Article 12. Black Sea Powers shall have the right to send through the Straits, for the purpose of rejoining their base, submarines constructed or purchased outside the Black Sea, provided that adequate notice of the laying down or purchase of such submarines shall have been given to Turkey.

Submarines belonging to the said Powers shall also be entitled to pass through the Straits to be repaired in dockyards outside the Black Sea on condition that detailed information on the matter is given to Turkey.

In either case, the said submarines must travel by day and on the surface, and must pass through the Straits singly.

Article 13. The transit of vessels of war through the Straits shall be preceded by a notification given to the Turkish Government through the diplomatic channel. The normal period of notice shall be eight days; but it is desirable that in the case of non-Black-Sea Powers this period should be increased to fifteen days. The notification shall specify the destination, name, type and number of the vessels, as also the date of entry for the outward passage and, if necessary, for the return journey. Any change of date shall be subject to three days' notice..

Entry into the Straits for the outward passage shall take place within a period of five days from the date given in the original notification. After the expiry of this period, a new notification shall be given under the same conditions as for the original notification.

When effecting transit, the commander of the naval force shall, without being under any obligation to stop, communicate to a signal station at the entrance to the Dardanelles or the Bosphorus the exact composition of the force under his orders.

Article 14. The maximum aggregate tonnage of all foreign naval forces which may be in course of transit through the Straits shall not exceed 15,000 tons, except in the cases provided for in article 11 and in Annex III to the present Convention.

The forces specified in the preceding paragraph shall not, however, comprise more than nine vessels.

Vessels, whether belonging to Black Sea or non-Black-Sea Powers, paying visits to a port in the Straits, in accordance with the provisions of article 17, shall not be included in this tonnage.

Neither shall vessels of war which have suffered damage during their passage through the Straits be included in this tonnage: such vessels, while undergoing repair, shall be subject to any special provisions relating to security laid down by Turkey.

Article 15. Vessels of war in transit through the Straits shall in no circumstances make use of any aircraft which they may be carrying.

Article 16. Vessels of war in transit through the Straits shall not, except in the event of damage or peril of the sea, remain therein longer than is necessary for them to effect the passage.

Article 17. Nothing in the provisions of the preceding articles shall prevent a naval force of any tonnage or composition from paying a courtesy visit of limited duration to a port in the Straits, at the invitation of the Turkish Government. Any such force must leave the Straits by the same route as that by which it entered, unless it fulfils the conditions required for passage in transit through the Straits as laid down by articles 10, 14 and 18.

Article 18

(1) The aggregate tonnage which non-Black-Sea Powers may have in that sea in time of peace shall be limited as follows:

(a) Except as provided in paragraph (b) below, the aggregate tonnage of the said Powers shall not exceed 30,000 tons;

(b) If at any time the tonnage of the strongest fleet in the Black Sea shall exceed by at least 10,000 tons the tonnage of the strongest fleet in that sea at the date of the signature of the present Convention, the aggregate tonnage of 30,000 tons mentioned in paragraph (a) shall be increased by the same amount, up to a maximum of 45,000 tons. For this purpose, each Black Sea Power shall, in conformity with Annex IV to the present Convention, inform the Turkish Government, on January 1st and July 1st of each year, of the total tonnage of its fleet in the Black Sea; and the Turkish Government shall transmit this information to the other High Contracting Parties and to the Secretary-General of the League of Nations.

(c) The tonnage which any one non-Black-Sea Power may have in the Black Sea shall be limited to two thirds of the aggregate tonnage provided for in paragraphs (a) and (b) above;

(d) In the event, however, of one or more non-Black-Sea Powers desiring to send naval forces into the Black Sea, for a humanitarian purpose, the said forces, which shall in no case exceed 8,000 tons altogether, shall be allowed to enter the Black Sea without having to give the notification provided for in article 13 of the present Convention, provided an authorisation is obtained from the Turkish Government in the following circumstances: if the figure of the aggregate tonnage specified in paragraphs (a) and (b) above has not been reached and will not be exceeded by the despatch of the forces which it is desired to send, the Turkish Government shall grant the said authorisation within the shortest possible time after receiving the request which has been addressed to it; if the said figure has already been reached or if the despatch of the forces which it is desired to send will cause it to be exceeded, the Turkish Government will immediately inform the other Black Sea Powers of the request for authorisation, and if the said Powers make no objection within twenty-four hours of having received this information, the Turkish Government shall, within forty-eight hours at the latest, inform the interested Powers of the reply which it has decided to make to their request.

Any further entry into the Black Sea of naval forces of non-Black-Sea Powers shall only be effected within the available limits of the aggregate tonnage provided for in paragraphs (a) and (b) above.

(2) Vessels of war belonging to non-Black-Sea Powers shall not remain in the Black Sea more than twenty-one days, whatever be the object of their presence there.

Article 19. In time of war, Turkey not being belligerent, warships shall enjoy complete freedom of transit and navigation through the Straits under the same conditions as those laid down in articles 10 to 18.

Vessels of war belonging to belligerent Powers shall not, however, pass through the Straits except in cases arising out of the application of article 25 of the present Convention, and in cases of assistance rendered to a State victim of aggression in virtue of a treaty of mutual assistance binding Turkey, concluded within the framework of the Covenant of the League of Nations, and registered and published in accordance with the provisions of article 18 of the Covenant.

In the exceptional cases provided for in the preceding paragraph, the limitations laid down in articles 10 to 18 of the present Convention shall not be applicable.

Notwithstanding the prohibition of passage laid down in paragraph 2 above, vessels of war belonging to belligerent Powers, whether they are Black Sea Powers or not, which have become separated from their bases, may return thereto.

Vessels of war belonging to belligerent Powers shall not make any capture, exercise the right of visit and search, or carry out any hostile act in the Straits.

Article 20. In time of war, Turkey being belligerent, the provisions of articles 10 to 18 shall not be applicable; the passage of warships shall be left entirely to the discretion of the Turkish Government.

Article 21. Should Turkey consider herself to be threatened with danger of war, she shall have the right to apply the provisions of article 20 of the present Convention.

Vessels which have passed through the Straits before Turkey has made use of the powers conferred upon her by the preceding paragraph, and which thus find themselves separated from their bases, may return thereto. It is, however, understood that Turkey may deny this right to vessels of war belonging to the State whose attitude has given rise to the application of the present article.

Should the Turkish Government make use of the powers conferred by the first paragraph of the present article, a notification to that effect shall be addressed to the High Contracting Parties and to the Secretary-General of the League of Nations.

If the Council of the League of Nations decide by a majority of two-thirds that the measures thus taken by Turkey are not justified, and if such should also be the opinion of the majority of the High Contracting Parties signatories to the present Convention, the Turkish Government undertakes to discontinue the measures in question as also any measures which may have been taken under article 6 of the present Convention. . . .

SECTION III. AIRCRAFT

Article 23. In order to assure the passage of civil aircraft between the Mediterranean and the Black Sea, the Turkish Government will indicate the air routes available for this purpose, outside the forbidden zones which may be established in the Straits. Civil aircraft may use these routes provided that they give the Turkish Government, as regards occasional flights, a notification of three days, and as regards flights on regular services, a general notification of the dates of passage.

The Turkish Government moreover undertake, notwithstanding any remilitarisation of the Straits, to furnish the necessary facilities for the safe passage of civil aircraft authorised under the air regulations in force in Turkey to fly across Turkish territory between Europe and Asia. The route which is to be followed in the Straits zone by aircraft which have obtained an authorisation shall be indicated from time to time.

SECTION IV. GENERAL PROVISIONS

Article 24. The functions of the International Commission set up under the Convention relating to the regime of the Straits of July 24th, 1923, are hereby transferred to the Turkish Government.

The Turkish Government undertake to collect statistics and to furnish information concerning the application of articles 11, 12, 14 and 18 of the present Convention.

They will supervise the execution of all the provisions of the present Convention relating to the passage of vessels of war through the Straits.

As soon as they have been notified of the intended passage through the Straits of a foreign naval force, the Turkish Government shall inform the representatives at Angora of the High Contracting Parties of the composition of that force, its tonnage, the date fixed for its entry into the Straits, and, if necessary, the probable date of its return.

The Turkish Government shall address to the Secretary-General of the League of Nations and to the High Contracting Parties an annual report giving details regarding the movements of foreign vessels of war through the Straits and furnishing all information which may be of service to commerce and navigation, both by sea and by air, for which provision is made in the present Convention.

Article 25. Nothing in the present Convention shall prejudice the rights and obligations of Turkey, or of any of the other High Contracting Parties Members of the League of Nations, arising out of the Covenant of the League of Nations. . . .

Article 28. The present Convention shall remain in force for twenty years from the date of its entry into force. . . .

Article 29. At the expiry of each period of five years from the date of the entry into force of the present Convention each of the High Contracting Parties shall be entitled to initiate a proposal for amending one or more of the provisions of the present Convention.

[Signatures]

[U.S. Senate. Subcommittee on Disarmament. *Disarmament and Security: A Collection of Documents, 1919–1955* (Washington, D.C., 1956), pp. 57–64]

"Open Skies" Proposals and Agreements

Eisenhower's "Open Skies" Proposal (1955)

Following is the text of a statement made by President Eisenhower at the Geneva Conference of Heads of Government on 21 July 1955.

Aerial Inspection and Exchange of Military Blueprints

Disarmament is one of the most important subjects on our agenda. It is also extremely difficult. In recent years the scientists have discovered methods of making weapons many, many times more destructive of opposing armed forces—but also of homes, and industries and lives—than ever known or even imagined before. These same scientific discoveries have made much more complex the problems of limitation and control and reduction of armament.

After our victory as Allies in World War II, my country rapidly disarmed. Within a few years our armament was at a very low level. Then events occurred beyond our borders which caused us to realize that we had disarmed too much. For our own security and to safeguard peace we needed greater strength. Therefore we proceeded to rearm and to associate with others in a partnership for peace and for mutual security.

The American people are determined to maintain and if necessary increase this armed strength for as long a period as is necessary to safeguard peace and to maintain our security.

But we know that a mutually dependable system for less armament on the part of all nations would be a better way to safeguard peace and to maintain our security.

It would ease the fears of war in the anxious hearts of people everywhere. It would lighten the burdens upon the backs of the people. It would make it possible for every nation, great and small, developed and less developed, to advance the standards of living of its people, to attain better food, and clothing, and shelter, more of education and larger enjoyments of life.

Therefore the United States Government is prepared to enter into a sound and reliable agreement making possible the reduction of armament. I have directed that an intensive and thorough study of this subject be made within our own government. From these studies, which are continuing, a very important principle is emerging to which I referred in my opening statement on Monday.

No sound and reliable agreement can be made unless it is completely covered by an inspection and reporting system adequate to support every portion of the agreement.

The lessons of history teach us that disarmament agreements without adequate reciprocal inspection increase the dangers of war and do not brighten the prospects of peace.

Thus it is my view that the priority attention of our combined study of disarmament should be upon the subject of inspection and reporting.

Questions suggest themselves.

How effective an inspection system can be designed which would be mutually and reciprocally acceptable within our countries and the other nations of the world? How would such a system operate? What could it accomplish?

Is certainty against surprise aggression attainable by inspection? Could violations be discovered promptly and effectively counteracted?

We have not as yet been able to discover any scientific or other inspection method which would make certain of the elimination of nuclear weapons. So far as we are aware no other nation has made such a discovery. Our study of this problem is continuing. We have not as yet been able to discover any accounting or other inspection method of being certain of the true budgetary facts of total expenditures for armament. Our study of this problem is continuing. We by no means exclude the possibility of finding useful checks in these fields.

As you can see from these statements, it is our impression that many past proposals of disarmament are more sweeping than can be insured by effective inspection.

Gentlemen, since I have been working on this memorandum to present to this Conference, I have been searching my heart and mind for something that I could say here that could convince everyone of the great sincerity of the United States in approaching this problem of disarmament.

I should address myself for a moment principally to the Delegates from the Soviet Union, because our two great countries admittedly possess new and terrible weapons in quantities which do give rise in other parts of the world, or reciprocally, to the fears and dangers of surprise attack.

I propose, therefore, that we take a practical step, that we begin an arrangement, very quickly, as between ourselves—immediately. These steps would include:

To give to each other a complete blueprint of our military establishments, from beginning to end, from one end of our countries to the other; lay out the establishments and provide the blueprints to each other.

Next, to provide within our countries facilities for aerial photography to the other country—we to provide you the facilities within our country, ample facilities for aerial reconnaissance, where you can make all the pictures you choose and take them to your own country to study, you to provide exactly the same facilities for us and we to make these examinations, and by this step to convince the world that we are providing as between ourselves against

the possibility of great surprise attack, thus lessening danger and relaxing tension. Likewise we will make more easily attainable a comprehensive and effective system of inspection and disarmament, because what I propose, I assure you, would be but a beginning.

Now from my statements I believe you will anticipate my suggestion. It is that we instruct our representatives in the Subcommittee on Disarmament in discharge of their mandate from the United Nations to give priority effort to the study of inspection and reporting. Such a study could well include a step by step testing of inspection and reporting methods.

The United States is ready to proceed in the study and testing of a reliable system of inspections and reporting, and when that system is proved, then to reduce armaments with all others to the extent that the system will provide assured results.

The successful working out of such a system would do much to develop the mutual confidence which will open wide the avenues of progress for all our peoples.

The quest for peace is the statesman's most exacting duty. Security of the nation entrusted to his care is his greatest responsibility. Practical progress to lasting peace is his fondest hope. Yet in pursuit of his hope he must not betray the trust placed in him as guardian of the people's security. A sound peace—with security, justice, well-being, and freedom for the people of the world—*can* be achieved, but only by patiently and thoughtfully following a hard and sure and tested road.

[*The Geneva Conference of Heads of Government, July 18–23, 1955,* in *Documents on Disarmament, 1945–1959,* vol. 1, Doc. 120. (Department of State publication 6046, 1955), pp. 56–59]

Hungary-Romania "Open Skies" Regime (1991)

The Hungary-Romania "Open Skies" agreement was signed at Bucharest on 11 May 1991.

Agreement between the Government of Hungary and the Government of Romania on the Establishment of an Open Skies Regime

The Government of the Republic of Hungary and the Government of Romania, hereinafter referred to as the Parties;

Recalling their commitments in the Conference on Security and Cooperation in Europe to promoting greater openness and transparency of their military activities and to enhancing security by means of confidence and security building measures;

Seeking to implement in their bilateral relations in addition to the provisions of the 1990 Vienna Document of the Negotiations on Confidence- and Security-Building Measures, further cooperative confidence and security building measures;

Reaffirming their desire to further contribute to the successful conclusion of the negotiations of the Open Skies Conference, as expressed in the Charter of Paris for a New Europe;

Convinced that a successful bilateral Open Skies regime provides valuable experience for the elaboration of an Open Skies Treaty, and the simultaneous functioning of the two regimes will lead to enhanced confidence and security;

Noting that an Open Skies regime and its successful implementation would encourage reciprocal openness on the part of the States Parties, enhance the predictability of their military activities and strengthen confidence between them;

Convinced that the Open Skies regime will be implemented on a reciprocal and equitable basis which will protect the interest of each State Party;

Noting the possibility of employing the results of such overflights to improve openness and transparency, to enhance confidence and security building, and to improve the monitoring of, and thus promote compliance with, current or future arms control measures;

Noting that the operation of an Open Skies regime will be without prejudice to States not parties to this Agreement;

Believing that an effective Open Skies regime would serve to consolidate improved goodneighbourly relations between the States Parties;

Have agreed as follows:

Article I. Definitions. For the purposes of this Agreement and its Annexes:

1. The term "Aircrew Member" means an individual from any of the two Parties who has been designated and accepted in accordance with Article XIX. of this Agreement, and who performs duties associated with the operation or maintenance of the Observation Aircraft or its sensors, and who participates as a member of the aircrew of the Observation Aircraft during the Observation Flight, or who is an Inspector Escort.

2. The term "Observation Crew Member" means an individual from the Observing Party who has been designated and accepted in accordance with Article XIX. of this Agreement, and who performs duties associated with the operation of the sensors of the Observation Aircraft of the Observed Party and who participates as an Aircrew Member of the Observation Aircraft of the Observed Party during the Observation Flight.

3. The term "Flight Monitor" means an individual designated by the Observed Party to be on board the Observation Aircraft during the Observation Flight and who performs duties in accordance with Annex D.

4. The term "Flight Plan" means a flight plan of the Observing Party meeting the requirements of Article VI.

5. The term "Hazardous Airspace" means areas of an Observed Party in which there are invisible or unusual dangers to the safety of the aircraft. Hazardous airspace include prohibited areas, restricted areas and danger areas, established in the interest of flight safety, public safety and environmental protection and published by the Observed Party in accordance with ICAO rules in the Aeronautical Information Publication (AIP).

6. The term "Inspector" means an individual who is designated by the Observed Party or Observing Party to conduct inspections of the Observation Air-

craft, its equipment, its sensors in accordance with Article IX. and Annex C.

7. The term "Inspection Team" means the group of inspectors designated by the Observed Party or Observing Party to conduct the inspection of the Observation Aircraft, its equipment and its sensors in accordance with Article IX. and Annex C.

8. The term "Inspector Escort" means a designated representative of the Observing Party or the Observed Party who has been authorized to monitor all activities of Inspectors and the Inspection Team during inspections and perform other specified duties in accordance with Article IX. and Annex C.

9. The term "Inspection" means that activity described in and performed pursuant to Article IX. and Annex C.

10. The term "Period of Inspection" means the period of time during which the Inspection Team inspects the Observation Aircraft, its equipment and its sensors in accordance with Article IX. and Annex C.

11. The term "Observation Aircraft" means an unarmed, fixed wing aircraft, capable of carrying two Observed Party Flight Monitors in addition to its Aircrew Members. An aircraft is considered unarmed when it is not carrying any armament (munitions) of any type or equipment dedicated to armament operations.

12. The term "Observation Flight" means a flight and any accompanying refueling stops, conducted in accordance with the provisions and restrictions of this Agreement by an Observation Aircraft over the Territory of an Observed Party.

13. The term "Observed Party" means a Party over whose Territory an Observation Flight is conducted.

14. The term "Observing Party" means a Party conducting an Observation Flight.

15. The term "Point of Entry" means the Airfield(s) in the Territory of each Party that are designated in Annex B. for the departure of the Observation Aircraft from the Observed Party's Territory.

16. The term "Point of Exit" means the Airfield(s) in the Territory of each Party that are designated in Annex B. for the departure of the Observation Aircraft from the Observed Party's Territory.

17. The term "Permitted Observation Equipment" means on-board observation equipment of the Observation Aircraft as described in Annex E.

18. The term "Quota" means the number of Observation Flights that each Party undertakes to accept annually ("Passive Quota") and also the number of Observation Flights each Party shall have the right to conduct annually ("Active Quota"), as set forth in Annex A.

19. The term "Arrival Fix" means the compulsory reporting point specified and promulgated by the Observed Party in Annex B. through which the Observation Aircraft shall enter the territorial airspace of the Observed Party.

20. The term "Departure Fix" means the compulsory reporting point specified and promulgated by the Observed Party in Annex B. through which the Observation Aircraft shall depart the territorial airspace of the Observed Party.

21. The "ATS" Route means a specified route designed for channelling the flow of traffic as necessary for the provisions of Air Traffic Services.

Article II. Basic Rights and Obligations of the Parties

1. Each Party shall have the right to conduct Observation Flights in accordance with the provisions of this Agreement.

2. Each Party undertakes to permit Observation Flights over its Territory in accordance with the provisions of this Agreement.

3. Each Party may conduct Observation Flights with its own Observation Aircraft or the Observation Aircraft of the other Party.

4. Areas with Hazardous Airspace are excepted in accordance with the provisions of Articles I., VIII., and Annex G.

Article III. Quotas of Observation Flights

1. For the purposes of fulfilling objectives of this Agreement, each Party shall have the right to conduct and undertakes the obligation to accept an agreed number of Observation Flights in accordance with Annex A.

2. The number of Observation Flights a Party shall be allowed to conduct shall be equal to the number of overflights it shall be required to accept.

Article IV. Observation Aircraft. While conducting flights under this Agreement the Observation Aircraft shall comply with the provisions of this Agreement.

Unless inconsistent with the provisions of this Agreement, the Observation Aircraft shall also comply with:

a. the published standards and recommended practice of ICAO;

b. published national air traffic control rules, procedures and guidelines on flight safety of the Observed Party; and

c. the instructions of the ATC authorities and the ground control services.

Article V. Pre- and Post-Observation Flight Procedures

1. Upon entry into force of this Agreement, each Party shall provide the other Party with the following information:

a. emergency airfields between its Arrival Fixes and Points of Entry and between its Points of Exit and its Departure Fixes;

b. instrument arrival and departure procedures:

—for its Points of Entry and Exit;

—for its alternate airfields near its Points of Entry and Exit;

—for suitable airfields along the route of flight which may be used in an emergency.

2. Each Party shall promptly notify the other Party of any updates and amendments to such information.

3. A Party may change the location of its Points of Entry and/or Exit upon three months prior notification to the other Party.

4. In order to conduct an Observation Flight, the Observing Party shall notify the Observed Party of the estimated time of arrival of its Observation Aircraft at the Observed Party's Point of Entry. Such notice shall be given not less than 24 hours in advance of the estimated time of arrival.

5. The notification to the Observed Party shall also indicate the type and model of the incoming aircraft, its registration number and call sign, as well as the names, passport types and numbers and functions of each Aircrew Member.

6. In case the Observing Party intends to use the Observation Aircraft of the Observed Party, it shall submit its request to do so 7 days in advance of the proposed time of the commencement of the Observation Flight.

7. Upon completion of the Observation Flight, the Observation Aircraft shall depart the Territory of the Observed Party from the Point of Exit. The departure flight from the Point of Exit shall commence not later than 24 hours following the completion of the Observation Flight, unless weather conditions or the airworthiness of the Observation Aircraft do not permit.

Article VI. Flight Plans and Conduct of Observation Flights

1. Within six hours following the arrival of the Observation Aircraft or the Observation Crew at the Point of Entry, the Observing Party shall submit a Flight Plan for the Proposed Observation Flight to the Observed Party. The Observed Party shall as soon as possible review and approve or amend and approve the proposed Flight Plan in accordance with the provisions of this Agreement.

2. The Observation Flight shall be conducted in accordance with the approved Flight Plan and in accordance with clearances and instructions from the Observed Party's air traffic controllers.

3. The Flight Plan shall have the content according to Annex 2 to the Convention on International Civil Aviation, signed in Chicago, 1944, and be in the format specified by ICAO Document 4444-RAC/ 501, Rules of the Air and Air Traffic Services, as amended or revised.

4. The Flight Plan shall provide and require that:

a. the planned duration of the Observation Flight shall not exceed the duration of Observation Flights that is set forth in Annex A;

b. the Observation Flight commences not earlier than 16 hours and not later than 48 hours after delivery of the Flight Plan to the Observed Party,

c. the Observation Aircraft shall fly a direct route between the coordinates or navigation fixes designated in the Flight Plan, and shall visit each coordinate or navigation fix in the declared sequence set forth in the Flight Plan; and

d. the Observation Aircraft shall not hold over, delay departure from or otherwise loiter at any point of its approved Flight Plan route nor otherwise unreasonably disrupt the normal flow of air traffic except:

—as allowed for in the approved flight plan;

—as necessary for the purposes of arrival or departure at designated airfields when executing published procedures or the instructions of air traffic control;

—as instructed by air traffic control;

—as required for reasons of flight safety;

—flight tracks shall be permitted to intersect provided that no point of intersection is crossed more than once on any observation flight.

5. The Observed Party shall ensure that Aircrew Members are given the Observed Party's most recent weather and safety information pertaining to

the Flight Plan for each Observation Flight, including Notices to Airmen, IFR procedures and information about alternate and emergency airfields along the flight route stated in the approved Flight Plan.

6. All Observation Flights shall be carried out in compliance with the provisions of this Agreement and ICAO standards and recommended practice, and with due regard for differences existing in national rules and regulations, published in AIP or in accordance with national flight and air traffic control requirements of which the Observation Aircraft's Aircrew shall be informed.

7. In the event that the Observation Aircraft makes a deviation from the Flight Plan, as permitted under Article XIII. of this Agreement, the additional flight time arising from such deviation shall not count against the duration specified in Annex A.

Article VII. Sensors

1. Each Party may use during Observation Flights any sensor that is necessary for reaching the objectives of this Agreement listed in Annex E. Sensors not listed in Annex E are prohibited and shall not be on board of the Observation Aircraft.

2. The Parties undertake to use the same types of sensors of comparable capability and to this end to facilitate access to such sensors for use by the other Party.

3. The Observation Aircraft shall be equipped with the same sensors, when used upon request by the other Party.

4. Data acquired by sensors during Observation Flights will remain encapsulated on board the Observation Aircraft until the termination of the Observation Flight. Sensor data link operations of any kind are prohibited.

5. As provided in Paragraph 4, of Article XVI. of this Agreement, a Party may utilize a type or model of sensor not listed in Annex E for or in connection with an Observation Flight upon:

a. receiving the approval of the Hungarian-Romanian Open Skies Consultative Commission (HROSCC), and

b. making a representative type or model of such sensor available for pre-flight examination by the other Party in accordance with the provisions of Annex E.

6. Any Party operating an Observation Aircraft will ensure that the sensors function to specifications and also that their specifications conform with agreed requirements.

Article VIII. Hazardous Airspace

1. Observation Aircraft may conduct Observation Flights anywhere over the Territory of the Observed Party in accordance with Article II and Article VI.

2. Hazardous Airspace must be publicly announced. Such public announcements must specify the dangers to the Observation Aircraft and Aircrew Members. Each Party shall ensure that such public announcements of Hazardous Airspace are promptly provided to the Other Party by the source designated by the Party in Annex H.

3. Particular Hazardous Airspace announced in Annex H must be taken into account by the Observing Party when preparing an Observation Flight Plan.

4. Each Party may introduce amendments and additions to Annex H, giving notice thereof to the other Party.

5. In case of need, the Observed Party shall inform the Aircrew Members during preparations for the Observation Flight of the new particular Hazardous Airspace, indicating the causes for the restrictions introduced.

6. In the event that the Flight Plan of the Observing Party requests overflight of Hazardous Airspace of the Observed Party, the Observed Party shall approve the Flight Plan if it conforms with Article VI., but may amend it to specify the minimum safe altitude over the Hazardous Airspace. This minimum safe altitude shall be made part of the Flight Plan. If there is no minimum safe altitude available consistent with air safety requirements, the Observed Party shall propose an alternative flight routing as near to the Hazardous Airspace as is permitted by air safety requirements. Alternatively the Observed Party may propose that the time of arrival of the Observation Aircraft over the Hazardous Airspace be amended to a time consistent with flight safety requirements. Such alternative flight routing or timing shall be incorporated in a revised Flight Plan and approved by the Observed Party.

7. The Observing Party may elect either to conduct the Observation Flight on the basis of an amended Flight Plan, avoiding the particular Hazardous Airspace, or to cancel the Observation Flight. In that latter event, the Observation Aircraft or the Observation Crew shall depart the Territory of the Observed Party in accordance with Article V. and no overflight shall be recorded against the Quota of either Party.

8. In the event the Observing Party informs the Observed Party that denial of access to any portion of the Hazardous Airspace of the Observed Party was not justified on the basis of air safety considerations and in a further event that the matter is not resolved through diplomatic channels, the Observing Party may raise the matter for consideration in the Hungarian-Romanian Open Skies Consultative Commission pursuant to Article XVI. of this Agreement.

Article IX. Aircraft and Sensor Inspections. When an Observation Flight is conducted using an Observation Aircraft of the Observing Party, upon delivery of the Flight Plan, unless otherwise mutually agreed to by the Observed and the Observing Party, the Inspection Team of the Observed Party may inspect the Observation Aircraft, accompanied by Inspector Escorts of the Observing Party, to determine whether there is any Prohibited Equipment on the Observation Aircraft. Such inspection shall terminate no later than three hours prior to the scheduled commencement of the Observation Flight set forth in the Flight Plan. All such inspections shall be conducted in accordance with Annex C.

Article X. Flight Monitors on Observation Aircraft. The Observed Party shall have the right to have two Flight Monitors on board the Observation Aircraft during each Observation Flight in accordance with Annex D. Such Flight Monitors shall have the right of access to all areas of the Observation Aircraft during the Observation Flight. Flight Monitors have the rights and obligations specified in Annex D. In discharging their functions, Flight Monitors shall not interfere with the activities of the Aircrew Members. . . .

Article XII. Prohibition, Correction or Curtailment of Observation Flights. The Observed Party, by notifying the Observing Party, may prohibit prior to its commencement, or correct or curtail in a nonharmful manner subsequent to its commencement, any Observation Flight:

a. that is not permitted by the terms of Annex A;

b. for which a Flight Plan has not been filed in accordance with this Agreement;

c. that arrives at the Point of Entry less than 24 hours after the notification required by Article V. of this Agreement;

d. that fails to arrive at the Point of Entry within 6 hours of the estimated time of arrival set forth in said notification;

e. that deviates from the Flight Plan, except as permitted by Article XIII. of this Agreement;

f. that is conducted by an aircraft other than an Observation Aircraft; or

g. that is otherwise in non-compliance with the terms, conditions, provisions and restrictions of this Agreement.

2. The Observed Party may correct or curtail in its territorial airspace a flight to a Point of Entry or from a Point of Exit that deviates from the direct route required by Article VI.

3. When an Observed Party prohibits, corrects or curtails an Observation Flight in accordance with this Article, it must provide in writing to the Observing Party through routine diplomatic channels an explanation for its action.

4. An Observation Flight that has been prohibited shall not be recorded against the Quota of the Observed Party. A proposed Observation Flight that has been corrected or curtailed shall not be recorded against the Quota of the Observed Party.

5. Disputes bearing on this Article may be submitted to the Hungarian-Romanian Open Skies Consultative Commission for resolution as stipulated in Article XVI. of this Agreement. . . .

Article XV. Use of Information

1. Information acquired through Observation Flights shall be used exclusively for the attainment of the purpose of this Treaty.

2. Both the Observing and the Observed Parties shall receive complete set of the data obtained as a result of the processing of observation materials.

3. Observation materials obtained as a result of an Observation Flight shall be processed in accordance with Annex H.

4. Information obtained by a Party as a result of Observation Flights must not be used to the detriment of the other Party's security or other interests and must not be transferred to any third State.

Article XVI. Hungarian-Romanian Open Skies Consultative Commission

1. To promote the objectives and implementation of the provisions of this Agreement, the Parties hereby establish the Hungarian-Romanian Open Skies Consultative Commission (hereinafter referred to as "the Commission").

2. The Commission shall make decisions and undertake actions on the basis of agreement of the Parties.

3. Each Party may raise before the Commission any issues concerning compliance with the obligations of this Agreement.

4. The Parties shall meet within the framework of the Commission to:

a. agree upon such technical and administrative measures, consistent with this Agreement, as may be necessary to ensure the viability and effectiveness of this Agreement;

b. consider questions relating to compliance with the obligations assumed under this Agreement;

c agree on updates to the Annexes that so provide; and

d. consider and act upon all matters referred to it by a Party pursuant to this Agreement.

5. General provisions for the operation of the Commission are set forth in Annex F. . . .

Article XIX. Aircrew Members and Inspection Crew Members

1. Aircrew Members and Inspection Crew Members shall be designated by each Party in the following manner:

a. Within 30 days after signature of this Agreement each Party shall provide to the other Party for its review a list of proposed Aircrew Members and Inspection Crew Members who will conduct Observation Flights for that Party. This list shall not exceed 30 persons and shall contain the name, birth date, rank, function and passport type for each person on the list. Each Party shall have the right to amend its list of Aircrew Members and Inspection Crew Members. Each Party shall have to provide to the other Party its amended list of Aircrew Members and Inspection Crew Members.

b. If any person on the original or amended list is unacceptable to the other Party, it shall, within 14 days, notify the Party providing the list that such persons will not be accepted as Aircrew Members and Inspection Crew Members. Persons not declared unacceptable within 14 days are deemed accepted as Aircrew Members and Inspection Crew Members. In the event that a Party subsequently determines that an Aircrew Member or an Inspection Crew Member is unacceptable, the Party shall so notify the Party that designated the Aircrew Member or Inspection Crew Member, which shall, not later than two working days thereafter, strike such person from its Aircrew Member and Inspection Crew Member list.

2. In order to exercise their functions effectively, for the purpose of implementing the Agreement, Aircrew Members and Inspection Crew Members shall be accorded the inviolability and immunities as specified in Articles 29, 30, paragraph 2 with respect to papers and correspondence and 31 of the Convention on Diplomatic Relations done in Vienna on 18 April 1961. Such inviolability and immunities shall be accorded for the entire period from the arrival of the Aircrew Members or Inspection Crew Members to the Territory of the Observed Party until their departure from it, and thereafter with respect to acts previously performed in the exercise of their official functions as Aircrew Members or Inspection Crew Members. The immunity from jurisdiction may be waived by the Observing Party in those cases when it is of the opinion that immunity would impede the course of justice and that it can be waived without prejudice to the Agreement. Such waiver must always be express. Without prejudice to their inviolability and immunities or to the rights of the Observing Party under this Agreement, it is the duty of Aircrew Members and Inspection Crew Members to respect the laws and regulations of the Observed Party.

3. Aircrew Members and Inspection Crew Members of a Party shall be permitted to bring into the Territory of the Observed Party, without payment of any customs duties or related charges, articles for their personal use, with the exception of articles the import or export of which is prohibited by law or controlled by quarantine regulations.

4. In the event that either the Observing Party or the Observed Party considers that there has been a violation or an abuse of the inviolability or immunities accorded under this Article, that party may forward a report specifying the nature of the issue to the Commission for consideration.

[Signatures]

[*Disarmament, A Periodic Review by the United Nations* 14, no. 4 (1991): 163–185]

Treaty on Open Skies (1992)

*This agreement between twenty-five nations to open their skies to short-notice,
unarmed surveillance flights was signed on 25 March 1992*

The States concluding this Treaty, hereinafter referred to collectively as the States Parties or individually as a State Party,

Recalling the commitments they have made in the Conference on Security and Co-operation in Europe to promoting greater openness and transparency in their military activities and to enhancing security by means of confidence- and security-building measures,

Welcoming the historic events in Europe which have transformed the security situation from Vancouver to Vladivostok,

Wishing to contribute to the further development and strengthening of peace, stability and co-operative security in that area by the creation of an Open Skies regime for aerial observation,

Recognizing the potential contribution which an aerial observation regime of this type could make to security and stability in other regions as well,

Noting the possibility of employing such a regime to improve openness and transparency, to facilitate the monitoring of compliance with existing or future arms control agreements and to strengthen the capacity for conflict prevention and crisis management in the framework of the Conference on Security and Co-operation in Europe and in other relevant international institutions,

Envisaging the possible extension of the Open Skies regime into additional fields, such as the protection of the environment,

Seeking to establish agreed procedures to provide for aerial observation of all the territories of States Parties, with the intent of observing a single State Party or groups of States Parties, on the basis of equity and effectiveness while maintaining flight safety,

Noting that the operation of such an Open Skies regime will be without prejudice to States not participating in it,

Have agreed as follows:

Article I. GENERAL PROVISIONS

1. This Treaty establishes the regime, to be known as the Open Skies regime, for the conduct of observation flights by States Parties over the territories of other States Parties, and sets forth the rights and obligations of the States Parties relating thereto. . . .

Article III. QUOTAS

SECTION I. GENERAL PROVISIONS

1. Each State Party shall have the right to conduct observation flights in accordance with the provisions of this Treaty.

2. Each State Party shall be obliged to accept observation flights over its territory in accordance with the provisions of this Treaty.

3. Each State Party shall have the right to conduct a number of observation flights over the territory of any other State Party equal to the number of observation flights which that other State Party has the right to conduct over it.

4. The total number of observation flights that each State Party is obliged to accept over its territory is the total passive quota for that State Party. The allocation of the total passive quota to the States Parties is set forth in Annex A, Section I to this Treaty.

5. The number of observation flights that a State Party shall have the right to conduct each year over the territory of each of the other States Parties is the individual active quota of that State Party with respect to that other State Party. The sum of the individual active quotas is the total active quota of that State Party. The total active quota of a State Party shall not exceed its total passive quota.

6. The first distribution of active quotas is set forth in Annex A, Section II to this Treaty

7. After entry into force of this Treaty, the distribution of active quotas shall be subject to an annual review for the following calendar year within the framework of the Open Skies Consultative Commission. In the event that it is not possible during the annual review to arrive within three weeks at agreement on the distribution of active quotas with respect to a particular State Party, the previous year's distribution of active quotas with respect to that State Party shall remain unchanged.

8. Except as provided for by the provisions of Article VIII, each observation flight conducted by a State Party shall be counted against the individual and total active quotas of that State Party.

9. Notwithstanding the provisions of paragraphs 3 and 5 of this Section, a State Party to which an active quota has been distributed may, by agreement with the State Party to be overflown, transfer a part or all of its total active quota to other States Parties and shall promptly notify all other States Parties and the Open Skies Consultative Commission thereof. Paragraph 10 of this Section shall apply.

10. No State Party shall conduct more observation flights over the territory of another State Party than a number equal to 50 per cent, rounded up to the nearest whole number, of its own total active quota, or of the total passive quota of that other State Party, whichever is less.

11. The maximum flight distances of observation flights over the territories of the States Parties are set forth in Annex A, Section III to this Treaty.

SECTION II. PROVISIONS FOR A GROUP OF STATES PARTIES

1. (A) Without prejudice to their rights and obligations under this Treaty, two or more States Parties which hold quotas may form a group of States Parties at signature of this Treaty and thereafter. For a group of States Parties formed after signature of this Treaty, the provisions of this Section shall apply no earlier than six months after giving notice to all other States Parties, and subject to the provisions of paragraph 6 of this Section.

(B) A group of States Parties shall co-operate with regard to active and passive quotas in accordance with the provisions of either paragraph 2 or 3 of this Section.

2. (A) The members of a group of States Parties shall have the right to redistribute amongst themselves their active quotas for the current year, while retaining their individual passive quotas. Notification of the redistribution shall be made immediately to all third States Parties concerned.

(B) An observation flight shall count as many observation flights against the individual and total active quotas of the observing Party as observed Parties belonging to the group are overflown. It shall count one observation flight against the total passive quota of each observed Party.

(C) Each State Party in respect of which one or more members of a group of States Parties hold active quotas shall have the right to conduct over the territory of any member of the group 50 per cent more observation flights, rounded up to the nearest whole number, than its individual active quota in respect of that member of the group or to conduct two such overflights if it holds no active quota in respect of that member of the group.

(D) In the event that it exercises this right the State Party concerned shall reduce its active quotas in respect of other members of the group in such a way that the total sum of observation flights it conducts over their territories shall not exceed the sum of the individual active quotas that the State Party holds in respect of all the members of the group in the current year.

(E) The maximum flight distances of observation flights over the territories of each member of the group shall apply. In case of an observation flight conducted over several members, after completion of the maximum flight distance for one member all sensors shall be switched off until the observation aircraft reaches the point over the territory of the next member of the group of States Parties where the observation flight is planned to begin. For such follow-on observation flight the maximum flight distance related to the Open Skies airfield nearest to this point shall apply.

3. (A) A group of States Parties shall, at its request, be entitled to a common total passive quota which shall be allocated to it and common individual and total active quotas shall be distributed in respect of it.

(B) In this case, the total passive quota is the total number of observation flights that the group of States Parties is obliged to accept each year. The total active quota is the sum of the number of observation flights that the group of States Parties has the right to conduct each year. Its total active quota shall not exceed the total passive quota.

(C) An observation flight resulting from the total active quota of the group of States Parties shall be carried out on behalf of the group.

(D) Observation flights that a group of States Parties is obliged to accept may be conducted over the territory of one or more of its members.

(E) The maximum flight distances of each group of States Parties shall be specified pursuant to Annex A, Section III and Open Skies airfields shall be designated pursuant to Annex E to this Treaty.

4. In accordance with the general principles set out in Article X, paragraph 3 any third State Party that considers its rights under the provisions of Sec-

tion I, paragraph 3 of this Article to be unduly restricted by the operation of a group of States Parties may raise this problem before the Open Skies Consultative Commission.

5. The group of States Parties shall ensure that procedures are established allowing for the conduct of observation flights over the territories of its members during one single mission, including refuelling if necessary. In the case of a group of States Parties established pursuant to paragraph 3 of this Section, such observation flights shall not exceed the maximum flight distance applicable to the Open Skies airfields at which the observation flights commence.

6. No earlier than six months after notification of the decision has been provided to all other States Parties:

(A) a group of States Parties established pursuant to the provisions of paragraph 2 of this Section may be transformed into a group of States Parties pursuant to the provisions of paragraph 3 of this Section;

(B) a group of States Parties established pursuant to the provisions of paragraph 3 of this Section may be transformed into a group of States Parties pursuant to the provisions of paragraph 2 of this Section;

(C) a State Party may withdraw from a group of States Parties; or

(D) a group of States Parties may admit further States Parties which hold quotas.

7. Following entry into force of this Treaty, changes in the allocation or distribution of quotas resulting from the establishment of or an admission to or a withdrawal from a group of States Parties according to paragraph 3 of this Section shall become effective on 1 January following the first annual review within the Open Skies Consultative Commission occurring after the six-month notification period. When necessary, new Open Skies airfields shall be designated and maximum flight distances established accordingly.

Article IV. SENSORS

1. Except as otherwise provided for in paragraph 3 of this Article, observation aircraft shall be equipped with sensors only from amongst the following categories: (A) optical panoramic and framing cameras; (B) video cameras with real-time display; (C) infra-red line-scanning devices; and (D) sideways-looking synthetic aperture radar.

2. A State Party may use, for the purposes of conducting observation flights, any of the sensors specified in paragraph 1 above, provided that such sensors are commercially available to all States Parties, subject to the following performance limits:

(A) in the case of optical panoramic and framing cameras, a ground resolution of no better than 30 centimetres at the minimum height above ground level determined in accordance with the provisions of Annex D, Appendix 1, obtained from no more than one panoramic camera, one vertically-mounted framing camera and two obliquely-mounted framing cameras, one on each side of the aircraft, providing coverage, which need not be continuous, of the ground up to 50 kilometres of each side of the flight path of the aircraft;

(B) in the case of video cameras, a ground resolution of no better than 30 centimetres determined in accordance with the provisions of Annex D, Appendix 1;

(C) in the case of infra-red line-scanning devices, a ground resolution of no better than 50 centimetres at the minimum height above ground level determined in accordance with the provisions of Annex D, Appendix 1, obtained from a single device; and

(D) in the case of sideways-looking synthetic aperture radar, a ground resolution of no better than three metres calculated by the impulse response method, which, using the object separation method, corresponds to the ability to distinguish on a radar image two corner reflectors, the distance between the centres of which is no less than five metres, over a swath width of no more than 25 kilometres, obtained from a single radar unit capable of looking from either side of the aircraft, but not both simultaneously.

3. The introduction of additional categories and improvements to the capabilities of existing categories of sensors provided for in this Article shall be addressed by the Open Skies Consultative Commission pursuant to Article X of this Treaty.

4. All sensors shall be provided with aperture covers or other devices which inhibit the operation of sensors so as to prevent collection of data during transit flights or flights to points of entry or from points of exit over the territory of the observed Party. Such covers or such other devices shall be removable or operable only from outside the observation aircraft.

5. Equipment that is capable of annotating data collected by sensors in accordance with Annex B,

Section II shall be allowed on observation aircraft. The State Party providing the observation aircraft for an observation flight shall annotate the data collected by sensors with the information provided for in Annex B, Section II to this Treaty.

6. Equipment that is capable of displaying data collected by sensors in real-time shall be allowed on observation aircraft for the purposes of monitoring the functioning and operation of the sensors during the conduct of an observation flight.

7. Except as required for the operation of the agreed sensors, or as required for the operation of the observation aircraft, or as provided for in paragraphs 5 and 6 of this Article, the collection, processing, retransmission or recording of electronic signals from electro-magnetic waves are prohibited on board the observation aircraft and equipment for such operations shall not be on that observation aircraft.

8. In the event that the observation aircraft is provided by the observing Party, the observing Party shall have the right to use an observation aircraft equipped with sensors in each sensor category that do not exceed the capability specified in paragraph 2 of this Article.

9. In the event that the observation aircraft used for an observation flight is provided by the observed Party, the observed Party shall be obliged to provide an observation aircraft equipped with sensors from each sensor category specified in paragraph 1 of this Article, at the maximum capability and in the numbers specified in paragraph 2 of this Article, subject to the provisions of Article XVIII, Section II, unless otherwise agreed by the observing and observed Parties. The package and configuration of such sensors shall be installed in such a way so as to provide coverage of the ground provided for in paragraph 2 of this Article. In the event that the observation aircraft is provided by the observed Party, the latter shall provide a sideways-looking synthetic aperture radar with a ground resolution of no worse than six metres, determined by the object separation method.

10. When designating an aircraft as an observation aircraft pursuant to Article V of this Treaty, each State Party shall inform all other States Parties of the technical information on each sensor installed on such aircraft as provided for in Annex B to this Treaty.

11. Each State Party shall have the right to take part in the certification of sensors installed on observation aircraft in accordance with the provisions

of Annex D. No observation aircraft of a given type shall be used for observation flights until such type of observation aircraft and its sensors has been certified in accordance with the provisions of Annex D to this Treaty.

12. A State Party designating an aircraft as an observation aircraft shall, upon 90-day prior notice to all other States Parties and subject to the provisions of Annex D to this Treaty, have the right to remove, replace or add sensors, or amend the technical information it has provided in accordance with the provisions of paragraph 10 of this Article and Annex B to this Treaty. Replacement and additional sensors shall be subject to certification in accordance with the provisions of Annex D to this Treaty prior to their use during an observation flight.

13. In the event that a State Party or group of States Parties, based on experience with using a particular observation aircraft, considers that any sensor or its associated equipment installed on an aircraft does not correspond to those certified in accordance with the provisions of Annex D, the interested States Parties shall notify all other States Parties of their concern. The State Party that designated the aircraft shall:

(A) take the steps necessary to ensure that the sensor and its associated equipment installed on the observation aircraft correspond to those certified in accordance with the provisions of Annex D, including, as necessary, repair, adjustment or replacement of the particular sensor or its associated equipment; and

(B) at the request of an interested State Party, by means of a demonstration flight set up in connection with the next time that the aforementioned observation aircraft is used, in accordance with the provisions of Annex F, demonstrate that the sensor and its associated equipment installed on the observation aircraft correspond to those certified in accordance with the provisions of Annex D. Other States Parties that express concern regarding a sensor and its associated equipment installed on an observation aircraft shall have the right to send personnel to participate in such a demonstration flight.

14. In the event that, after the steps referred to in paragraph 13 of this Article have been taken, the States Parties remain concerned as to whether a sensor or its associated equipment installed on an observation aircraft correspond to those certified in accordance with the provisions of Annex D, the issue may be referred to the Open Skies Consultative Commission. . . .

Article VI. CHOICE OF OBSERVATION AIRCRAFT, GENERAL PROVISIONS FOR THE CONDUCT OF OBSERVATION FLIGHTS, AND REQUIREMENTS FOR MISSION PLANNING

SECTION I. CHOICE OF OBSERVATION AIRCRAFT AND GENERAL PROVISIONS FOR THE CONDUCT OF OBSERVATION FLIGHTS

1. Observation flights shall be conducted using observation aircraft that have been designated by a State Party pursuant to Article V. Unless the observed Party exercises its right to provide an observation aircraft that it has itself designated, the observing Party shall have the right to provide the observation aircraft. In the event that the observing Party provides the observation aircraft, it shall have the right to provide an aircraft that it has itself designated or an aircraft designated by another State Party. In the event that the observed Party provides the observation aircraft, the observing Party shall have the right to be provided with an aircraft capable of achieving a minimum unrefuelled range, including the necessary fuel reserves, equivalent to one-half of the flight distance, as notified in accordance with paragraph 5, subparagraph (G) of this Section. . . .

5. The observing Party shall notify the observed Party of its intention to conduct an observation flight, no less than 72 hours prior to the estimated time of arrival of the observing Party at the point of entry of the observed Party. States Parties providing such notifications shall make every effort to avoid using the minimum pre-notification period over weekends. Such notification shall include:

(A) the desired point of entry and, if applicable, Open Skies airfield where the observation flight shall commence;

(B) the date and estimated time of arrival of the observing Party at the point of entry and the date and estimated time of departure for the flight from the point of entry to the Open Skies airfield, if applicable, indicating specific accommodation needs;

(C) the location, specified in Annex E, Appendix 1, where the conduct of the pre-flight inspection is desired and the date and start time of such pre-flight inspection in accordance with the provisions of Annex F;

(D) the mode of transport and, if applicable, type and model of the transport aircraft used to travel to the point of entry in the event that the observation aircraft used for the observation flight is provided by the observed Party;

(E) the diplomatic clearance number for the observation flight or for the flight of the transport aircraft used to bring the personnel in and out of the territory of the observed Party to conduct an observation flight;

(F) the identification of the observation aircraft, as specified in Annex C;

(G) the approximate observation flight distance; and

(H) the names of the personnel, their gender, date and place of birth, passport number and issuing State Party, and their function. . . .

13. The observed Party shall provide the flight crew, upon its arrival at the point of entry or at the Open Skies airfield where the observation flight commences, with the most recent weather forecast and air navigation information and information on flight safety, including Notices to Airmen. Updates of such information shall be provided as requested. Instrument procedures, and information about alternate airfields along the flight route, shall be provided upon approval of the mission plan in accordance with the requirements of Section II of this Article.

14. While conducting observation flights pursuant to this Treaty, all observation aircraft shall be operated in accordance with the provisions of this Treaty and in accordance with the approved flight plan. Without prejudice to the provisions of Section II, paragraph 2 of this Article, observation flights shall also be conducted in compliance with:

(A) published ICAO standards and recommended practices; and

(B) published national air traffic control rules, procedures and guidelines on flight safety of the State Party whose territory is being overflown.

15. Observation flights shall take priority over any regular air traffic. The observed Party shall ensure that its traffic control authorities facilitate the conduct of observation flights in accordance with this Treaty. . . .

21. The observing Party shall compile a mission report of the observation flight using the appropriate format developed by the Open Skies Consultative Commission. The mission report shall contain pertinent data on the date and time of the observation flight, its route and profile, weather conditions, time and location of each observation period for each sensor, the approximate amount of data collected by sensors, and the result of inspection of covers for sensor apertures or other devices that inhibit the operation of sensors in accordance with

Article VII and Annex E. The mission report shall be signed by the observing and observed Parties at the point of exit and shall be provided by the observing Party to all other States Parties within seven days after departure of the observing Party from the point of exit.

SECTION II. REQUIREMENTS FOR MISSION PLANNING

1. Unless otherwise agreed, the observing Party shall, after arrival at the Open Skies airfield, submit to the observed Party a mission plan for the proposed observation flight that meets the requirements of paragraphs 2 and 4 of this Section.

2. The mission plan may provide for an observation flight that allows for the observation of any point on the entire territory of the observed Party, including areas designated by the observed Party as hazardous airspace in the source specified in Annex I. The flight path of an observation aircraft shall not be closer than, but shall be allowed up to, ten kilometres from the border with an adjacent State that is not a State Party.

3. The mission plan may provide that the Open Skies airfield where the observation flight terminates, as well as the point of exit, may be different from the Open Skies airfield where the observation flight commences or the point of entry. The mission plan shall specify, if applicable, the commencement time of the observation flight, the desired time and place of planned refuelling stops or rest periods, and the time of continuation of the observation flight after a refuelling stop or rest period within the 96-hour period specified in Section I, paragraph 9 of this Article....

5. In the event that the mission plan filed by the observing Party provides for flights through hazardous airspace, the observed Party shall:

(A) specify the hazard to the observation aircraft;

(B) facilitate the conduct of the observation flight by co-ordination or suppression of the activity specified pursuant to subparagraph (A) of this paragraph; or

(C) propose an alternative flight altitude, route, or time.

6. No later than four hours after submission of the mission plan, the observed Party shall accept the mission plan or propose changes to it in accordance with Article VIII, Section I, paragraph 4 and paragraph 5 of this Section. Such changes shall not preclude observation of any point on the entire territory of the observed Party, including areas designated by the observed Party as hazardous airspace in the source specified in Annex I to this Treaty. Upon agreement, the mission plan shall be signed by the observing and observed Parties. In the event that the Parties do not reach agreement on the mission plan within eight hours of the submission of the original mission plan, the observing Party shall have the right to decline to conduct the observation flight in accordance with the provisions of Article VIII of this Treaty....

Article VIII. PROHIBITIONS, DEVIATIONS FROM FLIGHT PLANS AND EMERGENCY SITUATIONS

SECTION I. PROHIBITION OF OBSERVATION FLIGHTS AND CHANGES TO MISSION PLANS

1. The observed Party shall have the right to prohibit an observation flight that is not in compliance with the provisions of this Treaty....

4. The observed Party shall have the right to propose changes to the mission plan as a result of any of the following circumstances:

(A) the weather conditions affect flight safety;

(B) the status of the Open Skies airfield to be used, alternate airfields, or refuelling airfields prevents their use; or

(C) the mission plan is inconsistent with Article VI, Section II, paragraphs 2 and 4....

SECTION II. DEVIATIONS FROM THE FLIGHT PLAN

1. Deviations from the flight plan shall be permitted during the observation flight if necessitated by: (A) weather conditions affecting flight safety; (B) technical difficulties relating to the observation aircraft; (C) a medical emergency of any person on board; or (D) air traffic control instructions related to circumstances brought about by *force majeure*.

2. In addition, if weather conditions prevent effective use of optical sensors and infra-red line-scanning devices, deviations shall be permitted, provided that: (A) flight safety requirements are met; (B) in cases where national rules so require, permission is granted by air traffic control authorities; and (C) the performance of the sensors does not exceed the capabilities specified in Article IV, paragraph 2, unless otherwise agreed....

Article IX. SENSOR OUTPUT FROM OBSERVATION FLIGHTS

SECTION I. GENERAL PROVISIONS

1. For the purposes of recording data collected by sensors during observation flights, the following recording media shall be used: (A) in the case of optical panoramic and framing cameras, black and white photographic film; (B) in the case of video cameras, magnetic tape; (C) in the case of infrared line-scanning devices, black and white photographic film or magnetic tape; and (D) in the case of sideways-looking synthetic aperture radar, magnetic tape.

The agreed format in which such data is to be recorded and exchanged on other recording media shall be decided within the Open Skies Consultative Commission during the period of provisional application of this Treaty.

2. Data collected by sensors during observation flights shall remain on board the observation aircraft until completion of the observation flight. The transmission of data collected by sensors from the observation aircraft during the observation flight is prohibited.

3. Each roll of photographic film and cassette or reel of magnetic tape used to collect data by a sensor during an observation flight shall be placed in a container and sealed in the presence of the States Parties as soon as is practicable after it has been removed from the sensor.

4. Data collected by sensors during observation flights shall be made available to States Parties in accordance with the provisions of this Article and shall be used exclusively for the attainment of the purposes of this Treaty.

5. In the event that, on the basis of data provided pursuant to Annex B, Section I to this Treaty, a data recording medium to be used by a State Party during an observation flight is incompatible with the equipment of another State Party for handling that data recording medium, the States Parties involved shall establish procedures to ensure that all data collected during observation flights can be handled, in terms of processing, duplication and storage, by them.

SECTION II. OUTPUT FROM SENSORS THAT USE PHOTOGRAPHIC FILM

1. In the event that output from duplicate optical cameras is to be exchanged, the cameras, film and film processing shall be of an identical type.

2. Provided that the data collected by a single optical camera is subject to exchange, the States Parties shall consider, within the Open Skies Consultative Commission during the period of provisional application of this Treaty, the issue of whether the responsibility for the development of the original film negative shall be borne by the observing Party or by the State Party providing the observation aircraft. The State Party developing the original film negative shall be responsible for the quality of processing the original negative film and producing the duplicate positive or negative. In the event that States Parties agree that the film used during the observation flight conducted on an observation aircraft provided by the observed Party shall be processed by the observing Party, the observed Party shall bear no responsibility for the quality of the processing of the original negative film.

3. All the film used during the observation flight shall be developed:

(A) in the event that the original film negative is developed at a film processing facility arranged for by the observed Party, no later than three days, unless otherwise agreed, after the arrival of the observation aircraft at the point of exit; or

(B) in the event that the original film negative is developed at a film processing facility arranged for by the observing Party, no later than ten days after the departure of the observation aircraft from the territory of the observed Party.

4. The State Party that is developing the original film negative shall be obliged to accept at the film processing facility up to two officials from the other State Party to monitor the unsealing of the film cassette or container and each step in the storage, processing, duplication and handing of the original film negative, in accordance with the provisions of Annex K, Section II to this Treaty. The State Party monitoring the film processing and duplication shall have the right to designate such officials from among its nationals present on the territory on which the film processing facility arranged for by the other State Party is located, provided that such individuals are on the list of designated personnel in accordance with Article XIII, Section I of this Treaty. The State Party developing the film shall assist the officials of the other State Party in their functions provided for in this paragraph to the maximum extent possible.

5. Upon completion of an observation flight, the State Party that is to develop the original film neg-

ative shall attach a 21-step sensitometric test strip of the same film type used during the observation flight or shall expose a 21-step optical wedge onto the leader or trailer of each roll of original film negative used during the observation flight. After the original film negative has been processed and duplicate film negative or positive has been produced, the States Parties shall assess the image quality of the 21-step sensitometric test strips or images of the 21-step optical wedge against the characteristics provided for that type of original film negative or duplicate film negative or positive in accordance with the provisions of Annex K, Section I to this Treaty.

6. In the event that only one original film negative is developed:

(A) the observing Party shall have the right to retain or receive the original film negative; and

(B) the observed Party shall have the right to select and receive a complete first generation duplicate or part thereof, either positive or negative, of the original film negative. Unless otherwise agreed, such duplicate shall be: (1) of the same format and film size as the original film negative; (2) produced immediately after development of the original film negative; and (3) provided to the officials of the observed Party immediately after the duplicate has been produced.

7. In the event that two original film negatives are developed:

(A) if the observation aircraft is provided by the observing Party, the observed Party shall have the right, at the completion of the observation flight, to select either of the two original film negatives, and the original film negative not selected shall be retained by the observing Party; or

(B) if the observation aircraft is provided by the observed Party, the observing Party shall have the right to select either of the original film negatives, and the original film negative not selected shall be retained by the observed Party....

SECTION IV. ACCESS TO SENSOR OUTPUT

Each State Party shall have the right to request and receive from the observing Party copies of data collected by sensors during an observation flight. Such copies shall be in the form of first generation duplicates produced from the original data collected by sensors during an observation flight. The State Party requesting copies shall also notify the observed Party. A request for duplicates of data shall include the following information: (A) the ob-

serving Party; (B) the observed Party; (C) the date of the observation flight; (D) the sensor by which the data was collected; (E) the portion or portions of the observation period during which the data was collected; and (F) the type and format of duplicate recording medium, either negative or positive film, or magnetic tape.

Article X. OPEN SKIES CONSULTATIVE COMMISSION

1. In order to promote the objectives and facilitate the implementation of the provisions of this Treaty, the States Parties hereby establish an Open Skies Consultative Commission.

2. The Open Skies Consultative Commission shall take decisions or make recommendations by consensus. Consensus shall be understood to mean the absence of any objection by any State Party to the taking of a decision or the making of a recommendation.

3. Each State Party shall have the right to raise before the Open Skies Consultative Commission, and have placed on its agenda, any issue relating to this Treaty, including any issue related to the case when the observed Party provides an observation aircraft.

4. Within the framework of the Open Skies Consultative Commission the States Parties to this Treaty shall: (A) consider questions relating to compliance with the provisions of this Treaty; (B) seek to resolve ambiguities and differences of interpretation that may become apparent in the way this Treaty is implemented; (C) consider and take decisions on applications for accession to this Treaty; and (D) agree as to those technical and administrative measures, pursuant to the provisions of this Treaty, deemed necessary following the accession to this Treaty by other States.

5. The Open Skies Consultative Commission may propose amendments to this Treaty for consideration and approval in accordance with Article XVI. The Open Skies Consultative Commission may also agree on improvements to the viability and effectiveness of this Treaty, consistent with its provisions. Improvements relating only to modification of the annual distribution of active quotas pursuant to Article III and Annex A, to updates and additions to the categories or capabilities of sensors pursuant to Article IV, to revision of the share of costs pursuant to Annex L, Section I, paragraph 9, to arrangements for the sharing and availability of data pursuant to

Article IX, Sections III and IV and to the handling of mission reports pursuant to Article VI, Section I, paragraph 21, as well as to minor matters of an administrative or technical nature, shall be agreed upon within the Open Skies Consultative Commission and shall not be deemed to be amendments to this Treaty.

6. The Open Skies Consultative Commission shall request the use of the facilities and administrative support of the Conflict Prevention Centre of the Conference on Security and Co-operation in Europe, or other existing facilities in Vienna, unless it decides otherwise.

7. Provisions for the operation of the Open Skies Consultative Commission are set forth in Annex L to this Treaty.

Article XI. NOTIFICATIONS AND REPORTS

The States Parties shall transmit notifications and reports required by this Treaty in written form. The States Parties shall transmit such notifications and reports through diplomatic channels or, at their choice, through other official channels, such as the communications network of the Conference on Security and Co-operation in Europe.

. . . . .

ANNEX L. OPEN SKIES CONSULTATIVE COMMISSION

SECTION I. GENERAL PROVISIONS

Procedures and other provisions relating to the Open Skies Consultative Commission are established in this Annex pursuant to Article X of the Treaty.

1. The Open Skies Consultative Commission shall be composed of representatives designated by each State Party. Alternates, advisers and experts of a State Party may take part in the proceedings of the Open Skies Consultative Commission as deemed necessary by that State Party.

2. The initial session of the Open Skies Consultative Commission shall open within 60 days of the signature of the Treaty. The Chairman of the opening meeting shall be the representative of Canada.

3. The Open Skies Consultative Commission shall meet for no fewer than four regular sessions per calendar year unless it decides otherwise. Extraordinary sessions shall be convened at the request of one or more States Parties by the Chairman of the Open Skies Consultative Commission, who

shall promptly inform all other States Parties of the request. Such sessions shall open no later than 15 days after receipt of such a request by the Chairman.

4. Sessions of the Open Skies Consultative Commission shall last no longer than four weeks, unless it decides otherwise.

5. States Parties shall assume in rotation, determined by alphabetical order in the French language, the chairmanship of the Open Skies Consultative Commission. Each Chairman shall serve from the opening of a session until the opening of the following session, unless otherwise agreed.

6. Representatives at meetings shall be seated in alphabetical order of the States Parties in the French language.

7. The working languages of the Open Skies Consultative Commission shall be English, French, German, Italian, Russian and Spanish.

8. The proceedings of the Open Skies Consultative Commission shall be confidential, unless otherwise agreed. The Open Skies Consultative Commission may agree to make its proceedings or decisions public.

9. During the period of provisional application, and prior to 30 June 1992, the Open Skies Consultative Commission shall settle the distribution of costs arising under the Treaty. It shall also settle as soon as possible the scale of distribution for the common expenses associated with the operation of the Open Skies Consultative Commission.

10. During the period of provisional application of the Treaty the Open Skies Consultative Commission shall develop a document relating to notifications and reports required by the Treaty. Such document shall list all such notifications and reports and shall include appropriate formats as necessary.

11. The Open Skies Consultative Commission shall work out or revise, as necessary, its rules of procedure and working methods.

SECTION II. ANNUAL REVIEW OF ACTIVE QUOTAS

Procedures for the annual review of active quotas as foreseen in Article III, Section I, paragraph 7 of the Treaty shall be as follows:

1. States Parties wishing to modify all or part of the past year's distribution with respect to their active quota shall notify all other States Parties and the Open Skies Consultative Commission, by 1 October of each year, of those States Parties over which they wish to conduct their observation flights during the

next calendar year. Such proposed modifications shall be considered by the States Parties during this review, according to the rules set forth in the following paragraphs of this Section.

2. If the requests for observation flights over the territory of any given State Party do not exceed its passive quota, then the distribution shall be established as requested, and presented to the Open Skies Consultative Commission for approval.

3. If the requests for observation flights over the territory of any given State Party exceed its passive quota, then the distribution shall be established by general agreement among the interested States Parties, and presented to the Open Skies Consultative Commission for approval.

SECTION III. EXTRAORDINARY OBSERVATION FLIGHTS

1. The Open Skies Consultative Commission shall consider requests from the bodies of the Conference on Security and Cooperation in Europe authorized to deal with respect to conflict prevention and crisis management and from other relevant international organizations to facilitate the organization and conduct of extraordinary observation flights over the territory of a State Party with its consent

2. The data resulting from such observation flights shall be made available to the bodies and organizations concerned.

3. Notwithstanding any other provision of the Treaty, States Parties may agree on a bilateral and voluntary basis to conduct observation flights over the territory of each other following the procedures regarding the conduct of observation flights. Unless otherwise agreed by the States Parties concerned, the data resulting from such observation flights shall be made available to the Open Skies Consultative Commission.

4. Observation flights conducted under the provisions of this Section shall not be counted against the active or passive quotas of the States Parties involved.

SECTION IV. ADDITIONAL FIELDS FOR THE USE OF THE OPEN SKIES REGIME

1. States Parties may raise for consideration in the Open Skies Consultative Commission proposals for the use of the Open Skies regime in additional specific fields, such as the environment.

2. The Open Skies Consultative Commission may take decisions on such proposals or, if necessary, may refer them to the first and subsequent conferences called to review the implementation of the Treaty, in accordance with the provisions of Article XVI, paragraph 3 of the Treaty.

[U.S. Arms Control and Disarmament Agency, *Treaty on Open Skies* (Washington, D.C., 1992)]

Banning Nuclear Tests

Proposal to End Nuclear Weapons Tests (1956)

India introduced the Proposal for the Cessation of Nuclear Weapons Tests in the Disarmament Commission on 12 July 1956.

1. Cessation of all explosions of nuclear and other weapons of mass destruction.

This proposal is advanced for the following reasons:

(a) It is universally admitted that the effects of experimental explosions are incalculable in their consequences. Many authorities are apprehensive that the continuance of these explosions would constitute a grave danger to the health and well-being of both the present and future generations. The consequences of the release of strontium 90 into the upper atmosphere are particularly menacing. They are long-lasting, uncontrollable and tend to spread even to areas remote from the scene of explosion. While there may be certain authorities who may not feel fully convinced that experimental explosions on the present scale will cause serious danger to humanity, it is evident that no risks should be taken when the health, well-being and even survival of the human race are at stake. The responsible opinion of those who believe that nuclear tests do constitute a serious danger to human welfare and survival must, therefore, be decisive in such a context.

(b) The cessation of explosions would serve as an important initial step in nuclear disarmament which might make subsequent steps less difficult.

(c) The cessation of explosions would have a profound political effect and a deep impact on world opinion in general, and particularly in Asia and the Pacific area where opinion is strongly in favour of a cessation of these tests and apprehensive of the consequences of continued explosions.

(d) In a measure, international tensions will thereby be relaxed and suspicions diminished.

(e) Other countries would thus be prevented from acquiring the facilities for establishing, through tests, the production of nuclear weapons. The diffusion of the capabilities for testing such weapons can only increase world-wide insecurity.

(f) Both international law and international morality are violated by the pollution of oceans and of the atmosphere consequent on such explosions.

(g) Contrary to all past practice, these war preparations affect neutrals and consequently offend against the accepted canons of international law.

(h) Since the existing stockpiles of weapons of mass destruction are sufficient to destroy the world there would seem to be no utility even from the military point of view, in further experimental explosions.

(i) The prohibition of further explosions would be to a large extent self-enforcing. The question of controls and of national sovereignty would not be involved at this stage, and the available evidence indicates that with proper utilization of monitoring devices no evasion of significance would be possible.

The Government of India further proposes that the following initial steps in nuclear disarmament be taken:

2. Prohibition of the further use of fissionable material for military purposes.

3. Prohibition of the transfer of fissionable material from civilian to military stocks.

4. An agreement by those powers most advanced in the production of weapons of mass destruction to dismantle in public, as a token of their will towards disarmament, a limited number of atomic or hydrogen bombs and to make available for peaceful purposes the fissionable material contained in these weapons.

These proposals, if adopted, would lead to the reversing of the nuclear armaments race and make a profound impact upon world public opinion. These measures are immediately possible.

In addition to the cessation of explosions and the initial measures for nuclear disarmament proposed above, the Government of India further proposes that the following steps should be taken to halt competitive armament:

5. The military budgets of all countries should be reduced even if the reductions are initially small.

6. There should be voluntary submission to the United Nations of details of armament expenditure so that such information could be internationally held.

7. There should be no export or conveying of nuclear weapons to other countries by those countries at present manufacturing such weapons.

8. With reference to the Disarmament Commission itself the Government of India proposes that the Commission and its Sub-Committee be reconstituted and enlarged to make them more representative of the world both geographically and politically, thus providing more facilities for adjustment of major differences. The Government of India also holds the view that the work of the Commission would be facilitated if the two principal nuclear powers were to enter into direct talks without prejudice to the functions of the Commission or its Subcommittee.
[*Documents on Disarmament, 1945–1959*, vol. 1, Doc. 172. U.N. doc. DC/98, 31 July 1956, in Disarmament Commission *Official Records: Supplement for January to December 1956*, pp. 52–54]

Limited Nuclear Test Ban (1963)

The LTBT *was signed at Moscow on 5 August 1963, and it entered into force on 10 October 1963.*

Treaty Banning Nuclear Weapon Tests in the Atmosphere, in Outer Space and Under Water

The Governments of the United States of America, the United Kingdom of Great Britain and Northern Ireland, and the Union of Soviet Socialist Republics, hereinafter referred to as the "Original Parties,"

Proclaiming as their principal aim the speediest possible achievement of an agreement on general and complete disarmament under strict international control in accordance with the objectives of the United Nations which would put an end to the armaments race and eliminate the incentive to the production and testing of all kinds of weapons, including nuclear weapons.

Seeking to achieve the discontinuance of all test explosions of nuclear weapons for all time, determined to continue negotiations to this end, and desiring to put an end to the contamination of man's environment by radioactive substances,

Have agreed as follows:

Article I

1. Each of the Parties to this Treaty undertakes to prohibit, to prevent, and not to carry out any nuclear weapon test explosion, or any other nuclear explosion, at any place under its jurisdiction or control:

(a) in the atmosphere; beyond its limits, including outer space; or under water, including territorial waters or high seas; or

(b) in any other environment if such explosion causes radioactive debris to be present outside the territorial limits of the State under whose jurisdiction or control such explosion is conducted. It is understood in this connection that the provisions of this subparagraph are without prejudice to the conclusion of a treaty resulting in the permanent banning of all nuclear test explosions, including all such explosions underground, the conclusion of which, as the Parties have stated in the Preamble to this Treaty, they seek to achieve.

2. Each of the Parties to this Treaty undertakes furthermore to refrain from causing, encouraging, or in any way participating in, the carrying out of any nuclear weapon test explosion, or any other nuclear explosion, anywhere which would take place in any of the environments described, or have the effect referred to, in paragraph 1 of this Article.

Article II

1. Any Party may propose amendments to this Treaty. The text of any proposed amendment shall be

submitted to the Depository Governments which shall circulate it to all Parties to this Treaty. Thereafter, if requested to do so by one-third or more of the Parties, the Depository Governments shall convene a conference, to which they shall invite all the Parties, to consider such amendment.

2. Any amendment to this Treaty must be approved by a majority of the votes of all the Parties to this Treaty, including the votes of all of the Original Parties. The amendment shall enter into force for all Parties upon the deposit of instruments of ratification by a majority of all the Parties, including the instruments of ratification of all of the Original Parties.

Article III

1. This Treaty shall be open to all States for signature. Any State which does not sign this Treaty before its entry into force in accordance with paragraph 3 of this Article may accede to it at any time.

2. This Treaty shall be subject to ratification by signatory States. Instruments of ratification and instruments of accession shall be deposited with the Governments of the Original Parties—the United States of America, the United Kingdom of Great Britain and Northern Ireland, and the Union of Soviet Socialist Republics—which are hereby designated the Depository Governments.

3. This Treaty shall enter into force after its ratification by all the Original Parties and the deposit of their instruments of ratification.

4. For States whose instruments of ratification or accession are deposited subsequent to the entry into force of this Treaty, it shall enter into force on the date of the deposit of their instruments of ratification or accession.

5. The Depository Governments shall promptly inform all signatory and acceding States of the date of each signature, the date of deposit of each instrument of ratification of and accession to this Treaty, the date of its entry into force, and the date of receipt of any requests for conferences or other notices.

6. This Treaty shall be registered by the Depositary Governments pursuant to Article 102 of the Charter of the United Nations.

Article IV. This Treaty shall be of unlimited duration.

Each Party shall in exercising its national sovereignty have the right to withdraw from the Treaty if it decides that extraordinary events, related to the subject matter of this Treaty, have jeopardized the supreme interests of its country. It shall give notice of such withdrawal to all other Parties to the Treaty three months in advance.

Article V. [*Deposit of Ratification*]

[Signature]

[U.S. Arms Control and Disarmament Agency, *Arms Control and Disarmament Agreements: Texts and Histories of the Negotiations* (Washington, D.C., 1990), pp. 45–47]

Threshold Test Ban Treaty (1974)

This treaty was signed at Moscow on 3 July 1974.

Treaty Between the United States of America and the Union of Soviet Socialist Republics on the Limitation of Underground Nuclear Weapon Tests

The United States of America and the Union of Soviet Socialist Republics, hereinafter referred to as the Parties,

Declaring their intention to achieve at the earliest possible date the cessation of the nuclear arms race and to take effective measures toward reductions in strategic arms, nuclear disarmament, and

general and complete disarmament under strict and effective international control,

Recalling the determination expressed by the Parties to the 1963 Treaty Banning Nuclear Weapon Tests in the Atmosphere, in Outer Space and Under Water in its Preamble to seek to achieve the discontinuance of all test explosions of nuclear weapons for all time, and to continue negotiations to this end,

Noting that the adoption of measures for the further limitation of underground nuclear weapon tests would contribute to the achievement of these objectives and would meet the interests of strengthening peace and the further relaxation of international tension,

Reaffirming their adherence to the objectives and principles of the Treaty Banning Nuclear Weapon Tests in the Atmosphere, in Outer Space and Under Water and of the Treaty on the Non-Proliferation of Nuclear Weapons,

Have agreed as follows:

Article I

1. Each Party undertakes to prohibit, to prevent, and not to carry out any underground nuclear weapon test having a yield exceeding 150 kilotons at any place under its jurisdiction or control, beginning March 31, 1976.

2. Each Party shall limit the number of its underground nuclear weapon tests to a minimum.

3. The Parties shall continue their negotiations with a view toward achieving a solution to the problem of the cessation of all underground nuclear weapon tests.

Article II

1. For the purpose of providing assurance of compliance with the provisions of this Treaty, each Party shall use national technical means of verification at its disposal in a manner consistent with the generally recognized principles of international law.

2. Each Party undertakes not to interfere with the national technical means of verification of the other Party operating in accordance with paragraph 1 of this Article.

3. To promote the objectives and implementation of the provisions of this Treaty the Parties shall, as necessary, consult with each other, make inquiries and furnish information in response to such inquiries.

Article III. The provisions of this Treaty do not extend to underground nuclear explosions carried out by the Parties for peaceful purposes. Underground nuclear explosions for peaceful purposes shall be governed by an agreement which is to be negotiated and concluded by the Parties at the earliest possible time.

Article IV. This Treaty shall be subject to ratification in accordance with the constitutional procedures of each Party. This Treaty shall enter into force on the day of the exchange of instruments of ratification.

Article V

1. This Treaty shall remain in force for a period of five years. Unless replaced earlier by an agree-

ment in implementation of the objectives specified in paragraph 3 of Article I of this Treaty, it shall be extended for successive five-year periods unless either Party notifies the other of its termination no later than six months prior to the expiration of the Treaty. Before the expiration of this period the Parties may, as necessary, hold consultations to consider the situation relevant to the substance of this Treaty and to introduce possible amendments to the text of the Treaty.

2. Each Party shall, in exercising its national sovereignty, have the right to withdraw from this Treaty if it decides that extraordinary events related to the subject matter of this Treaty have jeopardized its supreme interests. It shall give notice of its decision to the other Party six months prior to withdrawal from this Treaty. Such notice shall include a statement of the extraordinary events the notifying Party regards as having jeopardized its supreme interests.

3. This Treaty shall be registered pursuant to Article 102 of the Charter of the United Nations.

DONE at Moscow on July 3, 1974,

[Signatures]

Protocol to the Treaty Between the United States of America and the Union of Soviet Socialist Republics on the Limitation of Underground Nuclear Weapon Tests.

The United States of America and the Union of Soviet Socialist Republics, hereinafter referred to as the Parties,

Having agreed to limit underground nuclear weapon tests,

Have agreed as follows:

1. For the Purpose of ensuring verification of compliance with the obligations of the Parties under the Treaty by national technical means, the Parties shall, on the basis of reciprocity, exchange the following data:

a. The geographic coordinates of the boundaries of each test site and of the boundaries of the geophysically distinct testing areas therein.

b. Information on the geology of the testing areas of the sites (the rock characteristics of geological formations and the basic physical properties of the rock, i.e., density, seismic velocity, water saturation, porosity and the depth of water table).

c. The geographic coordinates of underground nuclear weapon tests, after they have been conducted.

d. Yield, date, time, depth and coordinates for two nuclear weapon tests for calibration purposes from each geophysically distinct testing area where underground nuclear weapon tests have been and are to be conducted. In this connection the yield of such explosions for calibration purposes should be as near as possible to the limit defined in Article I of the Treaty and not less than one-tenth of that limit. In the case of testing areas where data are not available on two tests for calibration purposes, the data pertaining to one such test shall be exchanged, if available, and the data pertaining to the second test shall be exchanged as soon as possible after the second test having a yield in the above-mentioned range. The provisions of this Protocol shall not require the Parties to conduct tests solely for calibration purposes.

2. The Parties agree that the exchange of data pursuant to subparagraphs a, b, and d of paragraph 1 shall be carried out simultaneously with the exchange of instruments of ratification of the Treaty, as provided in Article IV of the Treaty, having in mind that the Parties shall, on the basis of reciprocity, afford each other the opportunity to familiarize themselves with these data before the exchange of instruments of ratification.

3. Should a Party specify a new test site or testing area after the entry into force of the Treaty, the data called for by subparagraphs a and b of paragraph l shall be transmitted to the other Party in advance of use of that site or area. The data called for by subparagraph d of paragraph 1 shall also be transmitted in advance of use of that site or area if they are available; if they are not available, they shall be transmitted as soon as possible after they have been obtained by the transmitting Party.

4. The Parties agree that the test sites of each Party shall be located at places under its jurisdiction or control and that all nuclear weapon tests shall be conducted solely within the testing areas specified in accordance with paragraph 1.

5. For the purposes of the Treaty, all underground nuclear explosions at the specified test sites shall be considered nuclear weapon tests and shall be subject to all the provisions of the Treaty relating to nuclear weapon tests. The provisions of Article III of the Treaty apply to all underground nuclear explosions conducted outside of the specified test sites, and only to such explosions.

This Protocol shall be considered an integral part of the Treaty.

DONE at Moscow on July 3, 1974.

[Signatures]

[U.S. Arms Control and Disarmament Agency, *Arms Control and Disarmament Agreements: Texts and Histories of the Negotiations* (Washington, D.C., 1990), pp. 187–190]

Direct Communication Agreements, or Hot Lines

United States—USSR "Hot Line" Treaty (1963)

The United States–Soviet hot line agreement was signed at Geneva on 20 June 1963, and it entered into force the same day.

Memorandum of Understanding Between the United States of America and the Union of Soviet Socialist Republics Regarding the Establishment of a Direct Communications Link

For use in time of emergency the Government of the United States of America and the Government of the Union of Soviet Socialist Republics have agreed to establish as soon as technically feasible a direct communications link between the two Governments.

Each Government shall be responsible for the arrangements for the link on its own territory. Each Government shall take the necessary steps to ensure continuous functioning of the link and prompt delivery to its head of government of any communications received by means of the link from the head of government of the other party.

Arrangements for establishing and operating the link are set forth in the Annex which is attached hereto and forms an integral part hereof.

[Signatures]

Annex to the Memorandum of Understanding Between the United States of America and the Union of Soviet Socialist Republics Regarding the Establishment of a Direct Communications Link

The direct communications link between Washington and Moscow established in accordance with the Memorandum, and the operation of such link, shall be governed by the following provisions:

1. The direct communications link shall consist of:

a. Two terminal points with telegraph-teleprinter equipment between which communications shall be directly exchanged;

b. One full-time duplex wire telegraph circuit, routed Washington-London-Copenhagen-Stockholm-Helsinki-Moscow, which shall be used for the transmission of messages;

c. One full-time duplex radiotelegraph circuit, routed Washington-Tangier-Moscow, which shall be used for service communications and for coordination of operations between the two terminal points.

If experience in operating the direct communications link should demonstrate that the establishment of an additional wire telegraph circuit is advisable, such circuit may be established by mutual agreement between authorized representatives of both Governments.

2. In case of interruption of the wire circuit, transmission of messages shall be effected via the radio circuit, and for this purpose provision shall be made at the terminal points for the capability of prompt switching of all necessary equipment from one circuit to another.

3. The terminal points of the link shall be so equipped as to provide for the transmission and reception of messages from Moscow to Washington in the Russian language and from Washington to Moscow in the English language. In this connection, the USSR shall furnish the United States four sets of telegraph terminal equipment, including page printers, transmitters, and reperforators, with one year's supply of spare parts and all necessary special tools, test equipment, operating instructions, and other technical literature, to provide for transmission and reception of messages in the Russian language.

The United States shall furnish the Soviet Union four sets of telegraph terminal equipment, including page printers, transmitters, and reperforators, with one year's supply of spare parts and all necessary special tools, test equipment, operating instructions and other technical literature, to provide for transmission and reception of messages in the English language.

The equipment described in this paragraph shall be exchanged directly between the parties without any payment being required therefor.

4. The terminal points of the direct communications link shall be provided with encoding equipment. For the terminal point in the USSR, four sets of such equipment (each capable of simplex operation), with one year's supply of spare parts, with all necessary special tools, test equipment, operating instructions and other technical literature, and with all necessary blank tape, shall be furnished by the United States to the USSR against payment of the cost thereof by the USSR.

The USSR shall provide for preparation and delivery of keying tapes to the terminal point of the link in the United States for reception of messages from the USSR. The United States shall provide for the preparation and delivery of keying tapes to the terminal point of the link in the USSR for reception of messages from the United States. Delivery of prepared keying tapes to the terminal points of the link shall be effected through the Embassy of the USSR in Washington (for the terminal of the link in the USSR) and through the Embassy of the United States in Moscow (for the terminal of the link in the United States).

5. The United States and the USSR shall designate the agencies responsible for the arrangements regarding the direct communications link, for its technical maintenance, continuity and reliability, and for the timely transmission of messages.

Such agencies may, by mutual agreement, decide matters and develop instructions relating to the technical maintenance and operation of the direct communications link and effect arrangements to improve the operation of the link.

6. The technical parameters of the telegraph circuits of the link and of the terminal equipment, as well as the maintenance of such circuits and equipment, shall be in accordance with CCITT and CCIR recommendations.

Transmission and reception of messages over the direct communications link shall be effected in accordance with applicable recommendations of international telegraph and radio communications regulations, as well as with mutually agreed instructions.

7. The costs of the direct communications link shall be borne as follows:

a. The USSR shall pay the full cost of leasing the portion of the telegraph circuit from Moscow to Helsinki and 50% of the cost of leasing the portion of the telegraph circuit from Helsinki to London. The United States shall pay the full cost of leasing the portion of the telegraph circuit from Washington to London and 50% of the cost of leasing the portion of the telegraph circuit from London to Helsinki.

b. Payment of the cost of leasing the radio telegraph circuit between Washington and Moscow shall be effected without any transfer of payments between the parties. The USSR shall bear the expenses relating to the transmission of messages from Moscow to Washington. The United States shall bear the expenses relating to the transmission of messages from Washington to Moscow.

[U.S. Arms Control and Disarmament Agency, *Arms Control and Disarmament Agreements: Texts and Histories of the Negotiations* (Washington, D.C., 1990), pp. 34–36]

United States–USSR "Hot Line" Treaty (1971)

This agreement was signed at Washington, D.C., on 30 September 1971, and it entered into force the same day.

Agreement Between the United States of America and the Union of Soviet Socialist Republics on Measures To Improve the USA-USSR Direct Communications Link

The United States of America and the Union of Soviet Socialist Republics, hereinafter referred to as the Parties,

Noting the positive experience gained in the process of operating the existing Direct Communications Link between the United States of America and the Union of Soviet Socialist Republics, which was established for use in time of emergency pursuant to the Memorandum of Understanding Regarding the Establishment of a Direct Communications Link, signed on June 20, 1963,

Having examined, in a spirit of mutual understanding, matters relating to the improvement and modernization of the Direct Communications Link,

Having agreed as follows:

Article 1

1. For the purpose of increasing the reliability of the Direct Communications Link, there shall be established and put into operation the following:

(a) two additional circuits between the United States of America and the Union of Soviet Socialist Republics each using a satellite communications system, with each Party selecting a satellite communications system of its own choice,

(b) a system of terminals (more than one) in the territory of each Party for the Direct Communications Link, with the locations and number of terminals in the United States of America to be determined by the United States side, and the locations and number of terminals in the Union of Soviet Socialist Republics to be determined by the Soviet side.

2. Matters relating to the implementation of the aforementioned improvements of the Direct Communications Link are set forth in the Annex which is attached hereto and forms an integral part hereof.

Article 2. Each Party confirms its intention to take all possible measures to assure the continuous and reliable operation of the communications circuits and the system of terminals of the Direct Communications Link for which it is responsible in accordance with this Agreement and the Annex hereto, as well as to communicate to the head of its Government any messages received via the Direct Communications Link from the head of Government of the other Party.

Article 3. The Memorandum of Understanding Between the United States of America and the Union of Soviet Socialist Republics Regarding the Establishment of a Direct Communications Link, signed on June 20, 1963, with the Annex thereto, shall remain in force, except to the extent that its provisions are modified by this Agreement and Annex hereto.

Article 4. The undertakings of the Parties hereunder shall be carried out in accordance with their respective Constitutional processes.

Article 5. This Agreement, including the Annex hereto, shall enter into force upon signature.

[Signatures]

Annex to the Agreement Between the United States of America and the Union of Soviet Socialist Republics on Measures To Improve the USA-USSR Direct Communications Link

Improvements to the USA-USSR Direct Communications Link shall be implemented in accordance with the provisions set forth in this Annex.

1. CIRCUITS

(a) Each of the original circuits established pursuant to paragraph 1 of the Annex to the Memorandum of Understanding, dated June 20, 1963, shall continue to be maintained and operated as part of the Direct Communications Link until such time, after the satellite communications circuits provided for herein become operational, as the agencies designated pursuant to paragraph III (hereinafter referred to as the "designated agencies") mutually agree that such original circuit is no longer necessary. The provisions of paragraph 7 of the Annex to the Memorandum of Understanding, dated June 20, 1963, shall continue to govern the allocation of the costs of maintaining and operating such original circuits.

(b) Two additional circuits shall be established using two satellite communications systems. Taking into account paragraph 1 (e) below, the United States side shall provide one circuit via the Intelsat system and the Soviet side shall provide one circuit via the Molniya II system. The two circuits shall be duplex telephone band-width circuits conforming to CCITT standards, equipped for secondary telegraphic multiplexing. Transmission and reception of messages over the Direct Communications Link shall be effected in accordance with applicable recommendations of international communications regulations, as well as with mutually agreed instructions.

(c) When the reliability of both additional circuits has been established to the mutual satisfaction of the designated agencies, they shall be used as the primary circuits of the Direct Communications Link for transmission and reception of teleprinter messages between the United States and the Soviet Union.

(d) Each satellite communications circuit shall utilize an earth station in the territory of the United States, a communications satellite transponder, and an earth station in the territory of the Soviet Union. Each Party shall be responsible for linking the earth stations in its territory to its own terminals of the Direct Communications Link.

(e) For the circuits specified in paragraph 1 (b):

—The Soviet side will provide and operate at least one earth station in its territory for the satellite communications circuit in the Intelsat system, and will also arrange for the use of suitable earth station facilities in its territory for the satellite communications circuit in the Molniya II system. The United States side, through a governmental agency or other United States legal entity, will make appropriate arrangements with Intelsat with regard to access for the Soviet Intelsat earth station to the Intelsat space segment, as well as for the use of the applicable portion of the Intelsat space segment.

—The United States side will provide and operate at least one earth station in its territory for the satellite communications circuit in the Molniya II system, and will also arrange for the use of suitable earth station facilities in its territory for the satellite communications circuit in the Intelsat system.

(f) Each earth station shall conform to the performance specifications and operating procedures at the corresponding satellite communications system and the ratio of antenna gain to the equivalent noise temperature should be no less than 31 decibels. Any deviation from these specifications and procedures which may be required in any unusual situation shall be worked out and mutually agreed upon by the designated agencies of both Parties after consultation.

(g) The operational commissioning dates for the satellite communications circuits based on the Intelsat and Molniya II systems shall be as agreed upon by the designated agencies of the Parties through consultations.

(h) The United States side shall bear the costs of: (1) providing and operating the Molniya II earth station in its territory; (2) the use of the Intelsat earth station in its territory; and (3) the transmission of messages via the Intelsat system. The Soviet side shall bear the costs of: (1) providing and operating the Intelsat earth station in its territory; (2) the use of the Molniya II earth station in its territory; and (3) the transmission of messages via the Molniya II system. Payment of the costs of the satellite communications circuits shall be effected without any transfer of payments between the Parties.

(i) Each Party shall be responsible for providing to the other Party notification of any proposed modification or replacement of the communications satellite system containing the circuit provided by it that might require accommodation by earth stations using that system or otherwise affect the maintenance or operation of the Direct Communications Link. Such notification should be given sufficiently in advance to enable the designated agencies to consult and to make, before the modification or replacement is effected, such preparation as may be agreed upon for accommodation by the affected earth stations.

II. TERMINALS

(a) Each Party shall establish a system of terminals in its territory for the exchange of messages with the other Party, and shall determine the locations and number of terminals in such a system. Terminals of the Direct Communications Link shall be designated "USA" and "USSR."

(b) Each Party shall take necessary measures to provide for rapidly switching circuits among terminal points in such a manner that only one terminal location is connected to the circuits at any one time.

(c) Each Party shall use teleprinter equipment from its own sources to equip the additional terminals for the transmission and reception of messages from the United States to the Soviet Union in the English language and from the Soviet Union to the United States in the Russian language.

(d) The terminals of the Direct Communications Link shall be provided with encoding equipment. One-time tape encoding equipment shall be used for transmissions via the Direct Communications Link. A mutually agreed quantity of encoding equipment of a modern and reliable type selected by the United States side, with spares, test equipment, technical literature and operating supplies, shall be furnished by the United States side to the Soviet side against payment of the cost thereof by the Soviet side; additional spares for the encoding equipment supplied will be furnished as necessary.

(e) Keying tapes shall be supplied in accordance with the provisions set forth in paragraph 4 of the Annex to the Memorandum of Understanding, dated June 20, 1963. Each Party shall be responsible for reproducing and distributing additional keying tapes for its system of terminals and for implementing procedures which ensure that the re-

quired synchronization of encoding equipment can be effected from any one terminal at any time.

III. OTHER MATTERS

Each Party shall designate the agencies responsible for arrangements regarding the establishment of the additional circuits and the systems of terminals provided for in this Agreement and Annex, for their operation and for their continuity and reliability. These agencies shall, on the basis of direct contacts:

(a) arrange for the exchange of required performance specifications and operating procedures for the earth stations of the communications systems using Intelsat and Molniya II satellites;

(b) arrange for testing, acceptance and commissioning of the satellite circuits and for operation of these circuits after commissioning; and,

(c) decide matters and develop instructions relating to the operation of the secondary teleprinter multiplex system used on the satellite circuits.

[U.S. Arms Control and Disarmament Agency, *Arms Control and Disarmament Agreements: Texts and Histories of the Negotiations* (Washington, D.C., 1990), pp. 124–128]

United States–USSR Memorandum of Understanding (1984)

This memorandum was signed at Washington, D.C., on 17 July 1984, and it entered into force the same day.

Memorandum of Understanding Between the United States of America and the Union of Soviet Socialist Republics on the U.S.–U.S.S.R. Direct Communications Link

The Department of State, referring to the Memorandum of Understanding between the United States of America and the Union of Soviet Socialist Republics regarding the Establishment of a Direct Communications Link, signed June 20, 1963; to the Agreement on Measures to improve the Direct Communications Link, signed September 30, 1971; and to the exchange of views between the two parties in Moscow and Washington during which it was deemed desirable to arrange for facsimile communication in addition to the current teletype Di-

rect Communications Link, proposes that for this purpose the parties shall:

1. Establish and maintain three transmission links employing INTELSAT and STATSIONAR satellites and cable technology with secure orderwire circuit for operational monitoring. In this regard:

(a) Each party shall provide communications circuits capable of simultaneously transmitting and receiving 4800 bits per second.

(b) Operation of facsimile communication shall begin with the test operation over the INTELSAT satellite channel as soon as development, procurement and delivery of the necessary equipment by the sides are completed.

(c) Facsimile communication via STATSIONAR shall be established after transition of the Direct Communications Link teletype circuit from MOLNIYA to STATSIONAR using mutually agreeable transition procedures and after successful tests of facsimile communication via INTELSAT and cable.

2. Employ agreed-upon information security devices to assure secure transmission of facsimile materials. In this regard:

(a) The information security devices shall consist of microprocessors that will combine the digital facsimile output with buffered random data read from standard 5¼-inch floppy disks. The American side shall provide a specification describing the key data format and necessary keying material resident on a floppy disk for both parties until such time as the Soviet side develops this capability. Beyond that time, each party shall provide necessary keying material to the other.

(b) The American side shall provide to the Soviet side the floppy disk drives integral to the operation of the microprocessor.

(c) The necessary security devices as well as spare parts for the said equipment shall be provided by the American side to the Soviet side in return for payment of costs thereof by the Soviet side.

3. Establish and maintain at each operating end of the Direct Communications Link facsimile terminals of the same make and model. In this regard:

(a) Each party shall be responsible for the acquisition, installation, operation and maintenance of its own facsimile machines, the related information security devices, and local transmission circuits appropriate to the implementation of this understanding, except as otherwise specified.

(b) A Group III facsimile unit which meets CCITT Recommendations T.4 and T.30 and operates at 4800 bits per second shall be used for this purpose.

(c) The necessary facsimile equipment as well as spare parts for the said equipment shall be provided to the Soviet side by the American side in return for payment of costs thereof by the Soviet side.

4. Establish and maintain secure orderwire communications necessary for coordination of facsimile operation. In this regard:

(a) The orderwire terminals used with the information security devices described in Paragraph 2(a) shall incorporate standard USSR Cyrillic and United States Latin keyboards and cathode ray tube displays to permit telegraphic exchange of information between operators. The specific layout of the Cyrillic keyboard shall be as specified by the Soviet side.

(b) To coordinate the work of the facsimile equipment operators, an orderwire shall be configured so as to permit, prior to the transmission and reception of facsimile messages, the exchange of all information pertinent to the coordination of such messages.

(c) Orderwire messages concerning facsimile transmissions shall be encoded using the same information security devices specified in Paragraph 2(a).

(d) The orderwire shall use the same modem and communications link as used for facsimile transmission.

(e) A printer shall be included to provide a record copy of all information exchanged on the orderwire.

(f) The necessary orderwire equipment as well as spare parts for the said equipment shall be provided by the American side to the Soviet side, in return for payment of costs thereof by the Soviet side.

5. Ensure the exchange of information necessary for the operation and maintenance of the facsimile system.

6. Take all possible measures to assure the continuous, secure and reliable operation of the facsimile equipment, information security devices and communications links including orderwire, for which each party is responsible in accordance with this agreement.

The Department of State also proposes that the parties, in consideration of the continuing advances in information and communications technology, conduct reviews as necessary regarding questions concerning improvement of the Direct Communications Link and its technical maintenance.

It is also proposed to note that the Memorandum of Understanding between the United States of America and the Union of Soviet Socialist Republics regarding the Establishment of a Direct Communications Link, signed on June 20, 1963, with the Annex thereto; the Agreement between the United States of America and the Union of the Soviet Socialist Republics on Measures to Improve the Direct Communications Link, with the Annex thereto, signed on September 30, 1971; those Understandings, with Attached Annexes, reached between the United States and Union of Soviet Socialist Republics delegations of technical specialists and experts signed on September 11, 1972, December 10, 1973, March 22, 1976, and the exchange of notes at Moscow on March 20 and April 29, 1975, constituting an Agreement Amending the Agreement of September 30, 1971, remain in force, except to the extent that their provisions are modified by this agreement.

If the foregoing is acceptable to the Soviet side, it is proposed that this note, together with the reply of the Embassy of the Union of Soviet Socialist Republics, shall constitute an agreement, effective on the date of the Embassy's reply.

[U.S. Arms Control and Disarmament Agency, *Arms Control and Disarmament Agreements: Texts and Histories of the Negotiations* (Washington, D.C., 1990), pp. 316–318]

United Kingdom–USSR Direct Communication Link Pact (1967)

This agreement was signed at London on 25 August 1967, and it entered into force the same day.

The Establishment of a Direct Communication Link between the Residence of the Prime Minister of the United Kingdom in London and the Kremlin

The Government of the United Kingdom of Great Britain and Northern Ireland and the Government of the Union of Soviet Socialist Republics;

Having in mind the agreement concerning the establishment of a direct communication link between the Residence of the Prime Minister of the United Kingdom in London and the Kremlin;

Have agreed on the following:

Article 1. The direct communication link between the Residence of the Prime Minister of the United Kingdom and the Kremlin shall be organised from the following component parts:

a) Two terminal communication points equipped with telegraphic printing apparatus, between which the exchange of communications will be carried out directly.

b) One duplex cable telegraph channel with round-the-clock operation, organised by agreement with the respective countries, along the route United Kingdom, Holland, Denmark, Poland, USSR.

c) One duplex radio telegraph channel with round-the-clock operation, organised between London and Moscow.

The radio telegraph channel shall be equipped with apparatus for automatic error correction.

Article 2

1. The terminal communication points shall be equipped with apparatus securing the transmission and reception of communications from Moscow to London in the Russian language and from London to Moscow in the English language.

2. In connexion with this, the Soviet Union shall deliver to the United Kingdom six complete sets of terminal telegraph equipment, including three-register (Russian and Latin scripts and figures) page teleprinters with spare parts for one year's use and with all necessary special instruments, measuring devices, instructions for use, and other technical literature.

3. The United Kingdom shall deliver to the Soviet Union six complete sets of terminal telegraph equipment including double-register (Latin script and figures), page teleprinters with spare parts for one years's use with all necessary special instruments, measuring devices, instructions for use and other technical literature.

4. The equipment mentioned in this Article shall be delivered by the Contracting Parties by direct mutual exchange without payment.

Article 3

1. The terminal points of the direct communication link shall be equipped with encyphering apparatus provided by the United Kingdom, using a one-time cypher tape.

2. The United Kingdom shall deliver to the Soviet Union six sets of the above-mentioned apparatus

for the terminal communication point in the Soviet Union with spare parts for one year's use, with all necessary instructions and other technical literature, with payment by the Soviet Union of the cost of its delivery.

Article 4

1. The Soviet Union shall ensure the preparation and the delivery of cypher tape to the terminal communication point in the United Kingdom for the reception of communications from the Soviet Union.

2. The United Kingdom shall secure the preparation and delivery of cypher tape to the terminal communication point in the Soviet Union for the reception of communications from the United Kingdom.

3. The transfer of the prepared cypher tapes to the terminal points of communication shall be carried out through the Embassy of the Soviet Union in London (for the communication point in the Soviet Union) and through the British Embassy in Moscow (for the communication point in the United Kingdom).

Article 5

1. Each Contracting Party shall determine which authorities shall be responsible for the organization of the direct communication link, its technical maintenance, the continuity and reliability of operation, and the timely transmission of communications.

2. The operation of the direct communication link will be carried out on the basis of Recommendations signed by the representatives of the authorities of the Contracting Parties which are responsible for the technical organisation of this link.

3. These authorities by mutual agreement may make necessary alterations and additions to the Recommendations; they will take measures for improving the quality of the signals operation.

Article 6

1. The technical parameters of the telegraph channels and the terminal equipment and also their technical maintenance must correspond to the recommendations of the Consultative Committees of the International Telecommunications Union.

2. The transmissions and reception of communications on the direct communication link shall be carried out in accordance with the appropriate provisions of the international Telegraph and Radio Regulations and also in accordance with mutually agreed instructions.

Article 7. Expenses for the direct communication link shall be shared in the following way:

a) The sectors of the line on the territory from Moscow to the State frontier of the Soviet Union and from London to the State frontier of the United Kingdom shall be paid for respectively by each Contracting Party.

b) the international sector of the line from the State frontier of the Soviet Union to the State frontier of the United Kingdom shall be paid for by each Contracting Party equally, 50% each.

c) Expenses relating to the setting up and use of the radio telegraph channel London-Moscow shall be paid for by each Contracting Party on its own territory.

Article 8. The Contracting Parties shall take measures to ensure that the direct communication link Residence of the Prime Minister—Kremlin shall be opened as soon as possible after the signing of the present Agreement.

Article 9. The present Agreement shall enter into force from the date of its signature.

[Signatures]

[*Treaty Series No. 91* (London, HMSO, November 1967), Cmnd. 3462]

United Kingdom–USSR Improvement of Direct Communications Link (1987)

This agreement was signed at Moscow on 31 March 1987, and it entered into force the same day.

Agreement on the Improvement of the Direct Communications Link between the Residence of the Prime Minister of the United Kingdom in London and the Kremlin

The Government of the United Kingdom of Great Britain and Northern Ireland and the Government of the Union of Soviet Socialist Republics;

Noting the positive experience gained in the process of operating the existing Direct Communications Link between the residence of the Prime Minister of the United Kingdom in London and the Kremlin, which was established in accordance with the Agreement on the Establishment of a Direct Communications Link signed on 25 August 1967;[1]

Taking into account the obligations set out in Article I of the Agreement on the Prevention of Accidental Nuclear War, signed on 10 October 1977;[2]

Having examined in a spirit of mutual understanding, matters relating to the improvement of the Direct Communications Link;

Have agreed as follows:

Article I. For the purpose of increasing the quality and speed of operation of direct communications between the Governments, meanwhile ensuring their continued reliability, the Contracting Parties shall establish and bring into operation an encrypted facsimile link which shall be based on the utilization of mutually agreed satellite and cable channels.

Article II

1. For the purpose of establishing, bringing into operation and subsequent utilization of the encrypted facsimile link, the Contracting Parties shall designate the agencies which will be responsible for arrangements regarding the link, its technical maintenance, continuity and reliability, and for its further improvement. These agencies shall by mutual agreement:

(a) determine the configuration and technical parameters of the link and channels of communication and the specific types of equipment to be used, and shall work out the technical solutions, mea-

sures and plans on the basis of which the improved link shall be established;

(b) work out recommendations and rules in accordance with which the operation of the link shall be carried out;

(c) as necessary consider and resolve questions relating to the carrying out of possible changes in the configuration, in the hardware and software and in the working procedures of the Direct Communications Link in the future.

2. Measures for the establishment, operation and further improvement of the link shall be undertaken on the basis of decisions, minutes or other concluding documents of meetings of technical experts signed by representatives of the above mentioned agencies of the Contracting Parties.

Article III

1. The Contracting Parties shall take measures to ensure that the encrypted facsimile link is established in the shortest possible time after signature of the present Agreement.

2. Each of the Contracting Parties shall acquire the equipment which has been agreed for use on the encrypted facsimile link and the spare parts and materials necessary for their operation and shall carry out independently the technical decisions which have been worked out.

3. By agreement of the agencies of the Contracting Parties, elements of the hardware and software of the link may be developed by one of the Contracting Parties and delivered to the other Contracting party just as equipment, spare parts and materials which one of the Contracting Parties may have available can be delivered to the other Contracting Party if this is necessary.

Article IV. Transmission and reception of messages over the encrypted facsimile link from London to Moscow shall be carried out in the English language and from Moscow to London in the Russian language subject to observance of the relevant provisions of international regulations and agreed recommendations and rules.

Article V. Expenditure on the establishment and operation of the encrypted facsimile link shall be based on the principle that the cost of equipment and sectors of the lines within territorial boundaries shall be paid for respectively by each Contracting Party and that the costs of the international sectors of the link shall be shared equally. The costs of any adaptation of the terminal equipment shall also be shared equally. The detailed division of costs and expenses shall be settled by mutual agreement between the agencies of the Contracting Parties designated in Article II of the present Agreement.

Article VI. After the entry into operation of the encrypted facsimile link, by mutual agreement of the agencies of the Contracting Parties, the present direct communications teleprinter link shall be closed without mutual accounting between the Contracting Parties.

Article VII. The present Agreement shall enter into force on the date of signature.

In witness whereof the representatives of the two Governments have signed the present Agreement.

Done in duplicate at Moscow this 31st day of March 1987 in the English and Russian languages, both texts being equally authoritative.

[Signature]

[*Treaty Series No. 34* (London, HMSO, 31 March 1987), Cm. 190]

Notes

1 Treaty Series No. 91 (1967), Cmnd. 3462.
2 Treaty Series No. 10 (1978), Cmnd. 7072.

Reduction of Nuclear War Risk

United States–USSR Nuclear War Risk Reduction Agreement (1971)

This agreement was signed at Washington, D.C., on 30 September 1971, and it entered into force the same day.

Agreement on Measures To Reduce the Risk of Outbreak of Nuclear War Between the United States of America and the Union of Soviet Socialist Republics

The United States of America and the Union of Soviet Socialist Republics, hereinafter referred to as the Parties:

Taking into account the devastating consequences that nuclear war would have for all mankind, and recognizing the need to exert every effort to avert the risk of outbreak of such a war, including measures to guard against accidental or unauthorized use of nuclear weapons,

Believing that agreement on measures for reducing the risk of outbreak of nuclear war serves the interests of strengthening international peace and security, and is in no way contrary to the interests of any other country,

Bearing in mind that continued efforts are also needed in the future to seek ways of reducing the risk of outbreak of nuclear war,

Have agreed as follows:

Article 1. Each Party undertakes to maintain and to improve, as it deems necessary, its existing organizational and technical arrangements to guard against the accidental or unauthorized use of nuclear weapons under its control.

Article 2. The Parties undertake to notify each other immediately in the event of an accidental, unauthorized or any other unexplained incident involving a possible detonation of a nuclear weapon which could create a risk of outbreak of nuclear war. In the event of such an incident, the Party whose nuclear weapon is involved will immediately make every effort to take necessary measures to render harmless or destroy such weapon without its causing damage.

Article 3. The Parties undertake to notify each other immediately in the event of detection by missile warning systems of unidentified objects, or in the event of signs of interference with these systems or with related communications facilities, if such occurrences could create a risk of outbreak of nuclear war between the two countries.

Article 4. Each Party undertakes to notify the other Party in advance of any planned missile launches if such launches will extend beyond its national territory in the direction of the other Party.

Article 5. Each Party, in other situations involving unexplained nuclear incidents, undertakes to act in such a manner as to reduce the possibility of its actions being misinterpreted by the other Party. In any such situation, each Party may inform the other Party or request information when, in its view, this is warranted by the interests of averting the risk of outbreak of nuclear war.

Article 6. For transmission of urgent information, notifications and requests for information in situations requiring prompt clarification, the Parties shall make primary use of the Direct Communications Link between the Governments of the United States of America and the Union of Soviet Socialist Republics.

For transmission of other information, notifications and requests for information, the Parties, at their own discretion, may use any communications facilities, including diplomatic channels, depending on the degree of urgency.

Article 7. The Parties undertake to hold consultations, as mutually agreed, to consider questions relating to implementation of the provisions of this Agreement, as well as to discuss possible amendments thereto aimed at further implementation of the purposes of this Agreement.

Article 8. This Agreement shall be of unlimited duration.

Article 9. This Agreement shall enter into force upon signature.

[Signatures]

[U.S. Arms Control and Disarmament Agency, *Arms Control and Disarmament Agreements: Texts and Histories of the Negotiations* (Washington, D.C., 1990), pp. 120–121]

United States–USSR Prevention of Nuclear War Agreement (1973)

This agreement was signed at Washington, D.C., on 22 June 1973, and it entered into force the same day.

Agreement Between the United States of America and the Union of Soviet Socialist Republics on the Prevention of Nuclear War

The United States of America and the Union of Soviet Socialist Republics, hereinafter referred to as the Parties,

Guided by the objectives of strengthening world peace and international security,

Conscious that nuclear war would have devastating consequences for mankind,

Proceeding from the desire to bring about conditions in which the danger of an outbreak of nuclear war anywhere in the world would be reduced and ultimately eliminated,

Proceeding from their obligations under the Charter of the United Nations regarding the maintenance of peace, refraining from the threat or use of force, and the avoidance of war, and in conformity with the agreements to which either Party has subscribed,

Proceeding from the Basic Principles of Relations between the United States of America and the Union of Soviet Socialist Republics signed in Moscow on May 29, 1972,

Reaffirming that the development of relations between the United States of America and the Union of Soviet Socialist Republics is not directed against other countries and their interests,

Have agreed as follows:

Article I. The United States and the Soviet Union agree that an objective of their policies is to remove the danger of nuclear war and of the use of nuclear weapons.

Accordingly, the Parties agree that they will act in such a manner as to prevent the development of situations capable of causing a dangerous exacerbation of their relations, as to avoid military confrontations, and as to exclude the outbreak of nuclear war between them and between either of the Parties and other countries.

Article II. The Parties agree, in accordance with Article I and to realize the objective stated in that Article, to proceed from the premise that each Party will refrain from the threat or use of force against the other Party, against the allies of the other Party and against other countries, in circumstances which may endanger international peace and security. The Parties agree that they will be guided by these considerations in the formulation of their foreign policies and in their actions in the field of international relations.

Article III. The Parties undertake to develop their relations with each other and with other countries in a way consistent with the purposes of this Agreement.

Article IV. If at any time relations between the Parties or between either Party and other countries appear to involve the risk of a nuclear conflict, or if relations between countries not parties to this Agreement appear to involve the risk of nuclear war between the United States of America and the Union of Soviet Socialist Republics or between either Party and other countries, the United States and the Soviet Union, acting in accordance with the provisions of this Agreement, shall immediately enter into urgent consultations with each other and make every effort to avert this risk.

Article V. Each Party shall be free to inform the Security Council of the United Nations, the Secretary General of the United Nations and the Governments of allied or other countries of the progress and outcome of consultations initiated in accordance with Article IV of this Agreement.

Article VI. Nothing in this Agreement shall affect or impair:

(a) the inherent right of individual or collective self-defense as envisaged by Article 51 of the Charter of the United Nations,

(b) the provisions of the Charter of the United Nations, including those relating to the maintenance or restoration of international peace and security, and

(c) the obligations undertaken by either Party towards its allies or other countries in treaties, agreements, and other appropriate documents.

Article VII. This Agreement shall be of unlimited duration.

[Signatures]

[U.S. Arms Control and Disarmament Agency, *Arms Control and Disarmament Agreements: Texts and Histories of the Negotiations* (Washington, D.C., 1990), pp. 179–180

United Kingdom–USSR Prevention of Accidental Nuclear War (1977)

This agreement was signed at Moscow on 10 October 1977, and it entered into force the same day.

United Kingdom of Great Britain and Northern Ireland and the Union of Soviet Socialist Republics Agreement on the Prevention of Accidental Nuclear War

The Government of the United Kingdom of Great Britain and Northern Ireland and the Government of the Union of Soviet Socialist Republics:

Conscious of the devastating results of any nuclear war, and of the special responsibilities incumbent upon the United Kingdom and the Soviet Union as nuclear powers to do everything possible to avoid the risk of outbreak of such a war:

Have agreed as follows:

Article I. Each party undertakes to maintain and, whenever it believes it is necessary, to improve its existing organisational and technical arrangements for guarding against the accidental or unauthorized use of nuclear weapons under its control.

Article II. The two Parties undertake to notify each other immediately of any accident or other unexplained or unauthorized incident which could result in the explosion of one of their nuclear weapons or could otherwise create the risk of outbreak of nuclear war. In the event of such an incident, the Party whose nuclear weapon is involved will immediately make every effort to take necessary measures to render harmless or destroy such weapon without its causing damage.

Article III. In the event of the occurrence of an incident of the type referred to in Article II of this Agreement each Party undertakes to act in such a manner as to reduce the possibilities of its action being misinterpreted by the other Party. In such circumstances each Party should provide to, or request from, the other such information as it considers necessary.

Article IV. The Parties shall use the direct communications link between their Governments for transmission of, or requests for, urgent information in situations requiring prompt clarification.

Article V. The Agreement shall enter into force on the day of signature.

In witness whereof the undersigned, being duly authorised thereto by their respective Governments, have signed this Agreement.

[Signatures]

[London, Her Majesty's Stationery Office, *Treaty Series 10 (1978)*. Cmnd. 7072]

United States–USSR Nuclear Risk Reduction Centers (1987)

This agreement was signed at Washington, D.C., on 15 September 1987, and it entered into force the same day.

Agreement Between the United States of America and the Union of Soviet Socialist Republics on the Establishment of Nuclear Risk Reduction Centers

The United States of America and the Union of Soviet Socialist Republics, hereinafter referred to as the Parties,

Affirming their desire to reduce and ultimately eliminate the risk of outbreak of nuclear war, in particular, as a result of misinterpretation, miscalculation, or accident,

Believing that a nuclear war cannot be won and must never be fought,

Believing that agreement on measures for reducing the risk of outbreak of nuclear war serves the interests of strengthening international peace and security,

Reaffirming their obligations under the Agreement on Measures to Reduce the Risk of Outbreak of Nuclear War between the United States of America and the Union of Soviet Socialist Republics of September 30, 1971, and the Agreement between the Government of the United States of America and the Government of the Union of Soviet Socialist Republics on the Prevention of Incidents on and over the High Seas of May 25, 1972,

Have agreed as follows:

Article 1. Each Party shall establish, in its capital, a national Nuclear Risk Reduction Center that shall operate on behalf of and under the control of its respective Government.

Article 2. The Parties shall use the Nuclear Risk Reduction Centers to transmit notifications identified in Protocol I which constitutes an integral part of this Agreement.

In the future, the list of notifications transmitted through the Centers may be altered by agreement between the Parties, as relevant new agreements are reached.

Article 3. The Parties shall establish a special facsimile communications link between their national Nuclear Risk Reduction Centers in accordance with Protocol II which constitutes an integral part of this Agreement.

Article 4. The Parties shall staff their national Nuclear Risk Reduction Centers as they deem appropriate, so as to ensure their normal functioning.

Article 5. The Parties shall hold regular meetings between representatives of the Nuclear Risk Reduction Centers at least once each year to consider matters related to the functioning of such Centers.

Article 6. This Agreement shall not affect the obligations of either Party under other agreements.

Article 7. This Agreement shall enter into force on the date of its signature. The duration of this Agreement shall not be limited. This Agreement may be terminated by either Party upon 12 months written notice to the other Party.

[Signatures]

Protocol I to the Agreement Between the United States of America and the Union of Soviet Socialist Republics on the Establishment of Nuclear Risk Reduction Centers

Pursuant to the provisions and in implementation of the Agreement between the United States of America and the Union of Soviet Socialist Republics on the Establishment of Nuclear Risk Reduction Centers, the Parties have agreed as follows:

Article 1. The Parties shall transmit the following types of notifications through the Nuclear Risk Reduction Centers:

(a) notifications of ballistic missile launches under Article 4 of the Agreement on Measures to Reduce the Risk of Outbreak of Nuclear War between the United States of America and the Union of Soviet Socialist Republics of September 30, 1971;

(b) notifications of ballistic missile launches under paragraph 1 of Article VI of the Agreement between the Government of the United States of America and the Government of the Union of Soviet Socialist Republics on the Prevention of Incidents on and over the High Seas of May 25, 1972.

Article 2. The scope and format of the information to be transmitted through the Nuclear Risk Reduction Centers shall be agreed upon.

Article 3. Each Party also may, at its own discretion as a display of good will and with a view to building confidence, transmit through the Nuclear Risk Reduction Centers communications other than those provided for under Article 1 of this Protocol.

Article 4. Unless the Parties agree otherwise, all communications transmitted through and communications procedures of the Nuclear Risk Reduction Centers' communication link will be confidential.

Article 5. This Protocol shall enter into force on the date of its signature and shall remain in force as long as the Agreement between the United States of America and the Union of Soviet Socialist Republics on the Establishment of Nuclear Risk Reduction Centers of September 15, 1987, remains in force.

Done at Washington on September 15, 1987, in two copies, each in the English and Russian languages, both texts being equally authentic.

Protocol II to the Agreement Between the United States of America and the Union of Soviet Socialist Republics on the Establishment of Nuclear Risk Reduction Centers

Pursuant to the provisions and in implementation of the Agreement Between the United States of America and the Union of Soviet Socialist Republics on the Establishment of Nuclear Risk Reduction Centers, the Parties have agreed as follows:

Article 1. To establish and maintain for the purpose of providing direct facsimile communications between their national Nuclear Risk Reduction Centers, established in accordance with Article 1 of this Agreement, hereinafter referred to as the national Centers, an INTELSAT satellite circuit and a STATSIONAR satellite circuit, each with a secure orderwire communications capability for operational monitoring. In this regard:

(a) There shall be terminals equipped for communication between the national Centers;

(b) Each Party shall provide communications circuits capable of simultaneously transmitting and receiving 4800 bits per second;

(c) Communication shall begin with test operation of the INTELSAT satellite circuit, as soon as purchase, delivery and installation of the necessary equipment by the Parties are completed. Thereafter, taking into account the results of test operations, the Parties shall agree on the transition to a fully operational status;

(d) To the extent practicable, test operation of the STATSIONAR satellite circuit shall begin simultaneously with test operation of the INTELSAT satellite circuit. Taking into account the results of test operations, the Parties shall agree on the transition to a fully operational status.

Article 2. To employ agreed-upon information security devices to assure secure transmission of facsimile messages. In this regard:

(a) The information security devices shall consist of microprocessors that will combine the digital message output with buffered random data read from standard 5¼ inch floppy disks;

(b) Each Party shall provide, through its Embassy, necessary keying material to the other.

Article 3. To establish and maintain at each operating end of the two circuits, facsimile terminals of the same make and model. In this regard:

(a) Each party shall be responsible for the purchase, installation, operation and maintenance of its own terminals, the related information security devices, and local transmission circuits appropriate to the implementation of this Protocol;

(b) A Group III facsimile unit which meets CCITT Recommendations T.4 and T.30 and operates at 4800 bits per second shall be used;

(c) Direct facsimile messages from the USSR national Center to the U.S. national Center shall be transmitted and received in the Russian language, and from the U.S. national Center to the USSR national Center in the English language;

(d) Transmission and operating procedures shall be in conformity with procedures employed on the Direct Communications Link and adapted as necessary for the purpose of communications between the national Centers.

Article 4. To establish and maintain a secure orderwire communications capability necessary to coordinate facsimile operation. In this regard:

(a) The orderwire terminals used with the information security devices described in paragraph (a) of Article 2 shall incorporate standard USSR Cyrillic and United States Latin keyboards and cathode ray tube displays to permit the exchange of messages between operators. The specific layout of the Cyrillic keyboard shall be as specified by the Soviet side;

(b) To coordinate the work of operators, the orderwire shall be configured so as to permit, prior to the transmission and reception of messages, the exchange of all information pertinent to the coordination of such messages;

(c) Orderwire messages concerning transmissions shall be encoded using the same information security devices specified in paragraph (a) of Article 2;

(d) The orderwire shall use the same modem and communications link as used for facsimile message transmission;

(e) A printer shall be included to provide a record copy of all information exchanged on the orderwire.

Article 5. To use the same type of equipment and the same maintenance procedures as currently in use for the Direct Communications Link for the establishment of direct facsimile communications between the national Centers. The equipment, security devices, and spare parts necessary for telecommunications links and the orderwire shall be provided by the United States side to the Soviet side in return for payment of costs thereof by the Soviet side.

Article 6. To ensure the exchange of information necessary for the operation and maintenance of the telecommunication system and equipment configuration.

Article 7. To take all possible measures to assure the continuous, secure and reliable operation of the equipment and communications link, including the orderwire, for which each Party is responsible in accordance with this Protocol.

Article 8. To determine, by mutual agreement between technical experts of the Parties, the distribution and calculation of expenses for putting into operation the communication link, its maintenance and further development.

Article 9. To convene meetings of technical experts of the Parties in order to consider initially questions pertaining to the practical implementation of the activities provided for in this Protocol and, thereafter, by mutual agreement and as necessary for the purpose of improving telecommunications and information technology in order to achieve the mutually agreed functions of the national Centers.

Article 10. This Protocol shall enter into force on the date of its signature and shall remain in force as long as the agreement between the United States of America and the Union of Soviet Socialist Republics on the Establishment of Nuclear Risk Reduction Centers of September 15, 1987, remains in force.

DONE at Washington on September 15, 1987, in two copies, each in the English and Russian languages, both texts being equally authentic.

[Signatures]

[U.S. Arms Control and Disarmament Agency, *Arms Control and Disarmament Agreements: Texts and Histories of the Negotiations* (Washington, D.C., 1990), pp. 338–344]

Indian-Pakistani Agreement Not to Attack Nuclear Installations (1988)

This agreement was signed at Islamabad on 31 December 1988.

Agreement on the Prohibition of Attack Against Nuclear Installations and Facilities Between the Republic of India and the Islamic Republic of Pakistan

The Government of the Republic of India and the Government of the Islamic Republic of Pakistan, hereinafter referred to as the Contracting parties,

Reaffirming their commitment to durable peace and the development of friendly and harmonious bilateral relations;

Conscious of the role of confidence building measures in promoting such bilateral relations based on mutual trust and goodwill;

Have agreed as follows:

Article I

1. Each party shall refrain from undertaking, encouraging or participating in, directly or indirectly, any action aimed at causing the destruction of, or damage to, any nuclear installation or facility in the other country.

2. The term "nuclear installation or facility" includes nuclear power and research reactors, fuel fabrication, uranium enrichment, isotopes separation and reprocessing facilities as well as any other installations with fresh or irradiated nuclear fuel and materials in any form and establishments storing significant quantities of radio-active materials.

Article II. Each Contracting Party shall inform the other on 1st January of each calendar year of the latitude and longitude of its nuclear installations and facilities and whenever there is any change.

Article III. This Agreement is subject to ratification. It shall come into force with effect from the date on which the Instruments of Ratification are exchanged.

[Signatures]

[PPNN (Programme for Promoting Nuclear Non-Proliferation) *Newsbrief* [Centre for International Policy Studies, Department of Politics, University of South Hampton, U.K.], no. 6 (July 1989): 12]

Prevention of Dangerous Military Incidents

United States–USSR Prevention of Incidents at Sea Treaty (1972)

This treaty was signed at Moscow on 25 May 1972.

Agreement Between the Government of the United States of America and the Government of the Union of Soviet Socialist Republics on the Prevention of Incidents On and Over the High Seas

The Government of the United States of America and the Government of the Union of Soviet Socialist Republics,

Desiring to assure the safety of navigation of the ships of their respective armed forces on the high seas and flight of their military aircraft over the high seas, and

Guided by the principles and rules of international law,

Have decided to conclude the Agreement and have agreed as follows:

Article I. For the purpose of this Agreement, the following definitions shall apply:

1. "Ship" means:

(a) A warship belonging to the naval forces of the Parties bearing the external marks distinguishing warships of its nationality, under the command of an officer duly commissioned by the government and whose name appears in the Navy list, and manned by a crew who are under regular naval discipline;

(b) Naval auxiliaries of the Parties, which include all naval ships authorized to fly the naval auxiliary flag where such a flag has been established by either Party.

2. "Aircraft" means all military manned heavier-than-air and lighter-than-air craft, excluding space craft.

3. "Formation" means an ordered arrangement of two or more ships proceeding together and normally maneuvered together.

Article II. The Parties shall take measures to instruct the commanding officers of their respective ships to observe strictly the letter and spirit of the International Regulations for Preventing Collisions at Sea, hereinafter referred to as the Rules of the Road. The Parties recognize that their freedom to conduct operations on the high seas is based on the principles established under recognized international law and codified in the 1958 Geneva Convention on the High Seas.

Article III

1. In all cases ships operating in proximity to each other, except when required to maintain course and speed under the Rules of the Road, shall remain well clear to avoid risk of collision.

2. Ships meeting or operating in the vicinity of a formation of the other Party shall, while conforming to the Rules of the Road, avoid maneuvering in a manner which would hinder the evolutions of the formation.

3. Formations shall not conduct maneuvers through areas of heavy traffic where internationally recognized traffic separation schemes are in effect.

4. Ships engaged in surveillance of other ships shall stay at a distance which avoids the risk of collision and also shall avoid executing maneuvers embarrassing or endangering the ships under surveillance. Except when required to maintain course and speed under the Rules of the Road, a surveillant shall take positive early action so as, in the exercise of good seamanship, not to embarrass or endanger ships under surveillance.

5. When ships of both Parties maneuver in sight of one another, such signals (flag, sound, and light) as are prescribed by the Rules of the Road, the International Code of Signals, or other mutually

agreed signals, shall be adhered to for signalling operations and intentions.

6. Ships of the Parties shall not simulate attacks by aiming guns, missile launchers, torpedo tubes, and other weapons in the direction of a passing ship of the other Party, not launch any object in the direction of passing ships of the other Party, and not use searchlights or other powerful illumination devices to illuminate the navigation bridges of passing ships of the other Party.

7. When conducting exercises with submerged submarines, exercising ships shall show the appropriate signals prescribed by the International Code of Signals to warn ships of the presence of submarines in the area.

8. Ships of one Party when approaching ships of the other Party conducting operations as set forth in Rule 4 (c) of the Rules of the Road, and particularly ships engaged in launching or landing aircraft as well as ships engaged in replenishment underway, shall take appropriate measures not to hinder maneuvers of such ships and shall remain well clear.

Article IV. Commanders of aircraft of the Parties shall use the greatest caution and prudence in approaching aircraft and ships of the other Party operating on and over the high seas, in particular, ships engaged in launching or landing aircraft, and in the interest of mutual safety shall not permit: simulated attacks by the simulated use of weapons against aircraft and ships, or performance of various aerobatics over ships, or dropping various objects near them in such a manner as to be hazardous to ships or to constitute a hazard to navigation.

Article V

1. Ships of the Parties operating in sight of one another shall raise proper signals concerning their intent to begin launching aircraft.

2. Aircraft of the Parties flying over the high seas in darkness or under instrument conditions shall, whenever feasible, display navigation lights.

Article VI. Both Parties shall:

1. Provide through the established system of radio broadcasts of information and warning to mariners, not less than 3 to 5 days in advance as a rule, notification of actions on the high seas which represent a danger to navigation or to aircraft in flight.

2. Make increased use of the informative signals contained in the International Code of Signals to signify the intentions of their respective ships when maneuvering in proximity to one another. At night, or in conditions of reduced visibility, or under conditions of lighting and such distances when signal flags are not distinct, flashing light should be used to inform ships of maneuvers which may hinder the movements of others or involve a risk of collision.

3. Utilize on a trial basis signals additional to those in the International Code of Signals, submitting such signals to the Intergovernmental Maritime Consultative Organization for its consideration and for the information of other States.

Article VII. The parties shall exchange appropriate information concerning instances of collision, incidents which result in damage, or other incidents at sea between ships and aircraft of the Parties. The United States Navy shall provide such information through the Soviet Naval Attache in Washington and the Soviet Navy shall provide such information through the United States Naval Attache in Moscow.

Article VIII. This Agreement shall enter into force on the date of its signature and shall remain in force for a period of three years. It will thereafter be renewed without further action by the Parties for successive periods of three years each.

This Agreement may be terminated by either Party upon six months written notice to the other Party.

Article IX. The Parties shall meet within one year after the date of the signing of this Agreement to review the implementation of its terms. Similar consultations shall be held thereafter annually, or more frequently as the Parties may decide.

Article X. The Parties shall designate members to form a Committee which will consider specific measures in conformity with this Agreement. The Committee will, as a particular part of its work, consider the practical workability of concrete fixed distances to be observed in encounters between ships, aircraft, and ships and aircraft. The Committee will meet within six months of the date of signature of this Agreement and submit its recommendations for decision by the Parties during the consultations prescribed in Article IX.

[Signatures]

[U.S. Arms Control and Disarmament Agency, *Arms Control and Disarmament Agreements: Texts and Histories of the Negotiations,* 1982 ed. (Washington, D.C., 1982), pp. 144–146]

United Kingdom–USSR Prevention of Incidents at Sea Treaty (1986)

This agreement was signed at London on 15 July 1986, and it entered into force the same day.

Agreement Between the Government of the United Kingdom of Great Britain and Northern Ireland and the Government of the Union of Soviet Socialist Republics Concerning the Prevention of Incidents at Sea Beyond the Territorial Sea

The Government of the United Kingdom of Great Britain and Northern Ireland and the Government of the Union of Soviet Socialist Republics;

Desiring to ensure the safety of navigation of the ships of their respective armed forces, and of the fight of their military aircraft beyond the territorial sea;

Acknowledging that actions prohibited by this Agreement should also not be taken against non-military ships of the Parties;

Guided by the principles and rules of international law;

Have agreed as follows:

Article I. For the purposes of this Agreement the following definitions shall apply:

1. "ship" means:

(a) a warship belonging to the armed forces of the Parties bearing the external marks distinguishing warships of its nationality, under the command of an officer duly commissioned by the Government and whose name appears in the appropriate service list or its equivalent, and manned by a crew who are under regular armed forces discipline; and

(b) auxiliary ships belonging to the armed forces of the Parties, which include all ships authorised to fly the auxiliary ship flag where such a flag has been established by either Party;

2. "aircraft" means all military manned heavier-than-air and lighter-than air craft, excluding space craft;

3. "formation" means an ordered arrangement of two or more ships proceeding in company and normally manoeuvring together.

This Agreement shall apply to ships and aircraft operating beyond the territorial sea.

Article II. The Parties shall take measures to instruct the Commanding Officers of their respective ships to observe strictly the letter and spirit of the 1972 International Regulations for Preventing Collisions at Sea,[1] hereinafter referred to as "the 1972 Collision Regulations". The Parties recognise that their freedom to conduct operations beyond the territorial sea is based on the principles established under recognised international law and codified in the 1958 Geneva Convention on the High Seas.[2]

Article III

1. In all cases ships of the Parties operating in proximity to each other, except when required to maintain course and speed under the 1972 Collision Regulations, shall remain well clear to avoid risk of collision.

2. Ships meeting or operating in the vicinity of a formation of the other Party shall, while conforming to the 1972 Collision Regulations, avoid manoeuvring in a manner which would hinder the evolutions of the formation.

3. Formations shall not conduct manoeuvres through areas of heavy traffic where internationally recognised traffic separation schemes are in effect.

4. Ships engaged in surveillance of ships of the other Party shall stay at a distance which avoids the risk of collision and shall also avoid executing manoeuvres embarrassing or endangering the ships under surveillance. Except when required to maintain course and speed under the 1972 Collision Regulations, a surveillant shall take positive early action so as, in the exercise of good seamanship, not to embarrass or endanger ships under surveillance.

5. When ships of both Parties manoeuvre in sight of one another, such signals, (flag, sound and light) as are prescribed by the 1972 Collision Regulations, the International Code of Signals and the Table of Special Signals set forth in the Annex to this Agreement shall be adhered to for signalling operations and intentions. At night or in conditions of reduced visibility, or under conditions of lighting and at such distances when signal flags are not distinct, flashing light or Very High Frequency Radio Channel 16 (156.8 Mhz) should be used.

6. Ships of the Parties shall not simulate attacks by aiming guns, missile launchers, torpedo tubes and other weapons in the direction of passing ships of the other Party; nor launch any object in the direction of passing ships of the other Party in such a manner as to hazardous to those ships or to constitute a hazard to navigation; nor use searchlights or other powerful illumination devices for the purpose of illuminating the navigation bridges of passing ships of the other Party.

Such actions shall also not be taken by ships of each Party against non-military ships of the other Party.

7. When conducting exercises with submerged submarines, supporting ships shall show the appropriate signals prescribed by the International Code of Signals, or in the Table of Special Signals set forth in the Annex to this Agreement, to warn ships of the presence of submarines in the area.

8. Ships of one Party when approaching ships of the other Party conducting operations which in accordance with Rule 3(g) of the 1972 Collision Regulations are restricted in their ability to manoeuvre, and particularly ships engaged in launching or landing aircraft as well as ships engaged in replenishment underway, shall take appropriate measures not to hinder manoeuvres of such ships and shall remain well clear.

Article IV

1. Commanders of aircraft of the Parties shall use the greatest caution and prudence in approaching aircraft and ships of the other Party, in particular ships engaged in launching or landing aircraft, and, in the interest of mutual safety, shall not permit simulated attacks by the simulated use of weapons against aircraft and ships of the other Party, or the performance of aerobatics over ships of the other Party, or dropping objects near them in such a manner as to be hazardous to ships or to constitute a hazard to navigation.

Such actions shall also not be taken by aircraft of each Party against non-military ships of the other Party.

2. Aircraft of the Parties flying in darkness or under instrument conditions shall, whenever feasible, display navigation lights.

Article V. The Parties shall take measures to notify the non-military ships of each Party about the provisions of this Agreement directed at securing mutual safety.

Article VI. The Parties shall provide through the established system of radio broadcasts of information and warning to mariners, normally not less than three to five days in advance, notification of actions beyond the territorial sea which represent a danger to navigation or to aircraft in flight.

Article VII. The Parties shall exchange in a timely manner appropriate information concerning instances of collisions, incidents which result in damage, and other incidents as sea between ships and aircraft of the Parties. The Royal Navy shall provide such information through the Soviet Naval or other Military Attaché in London and the Soviet Navy shall provide such information through the British Naval or other Military Attaché in Moscow.

Article VIII. This Agreement shall enter into force on the date of its signature. It may be terminated by either Party giving six months' written notice of termination to the other Party.

Article IX. Representatives of the Parties shall meet within one year after the date of the signing of this Agreement to review the implementation of its terms, as well as possible ways of promoting a higher level of safety of navigation of their ships and flight of their aircraft beyond the territorial sea. Similar consultations shall be held thereafter annually, or more frequently as the Parties may decide.

[Signatures]

[London, Her Majesty's Stationery Office (January 1987), Cm. 57]

Notes

1. Treaty Series No. 77 (1977), Cmnd. 6962 as amended by Treaty Series No. 68 (1984), Cmnd. 9340.
2. Treaty Series No. 5 (1963), Cmnd. 1929.

United States–USSR Agreement on the Prevention of Dangerous Military Activities (1989)

The Government of the United States of America and the Government of the Union of Soviet Socialist Republics, hereinafter referred to as the Parties,

Confirming their desire to improve relations and deepen mutual understanding,

Convinced of the necessity to prevent dangerous military activities, and thereby to reduce the possibility of incidents arising between their armed forces,

Committed to resolving expeditiously and peacefully any incident between their armed forces which my arise as a result of dangerous military activities,

Desiring to ensure the safety of the personnel and equipment of their armed forces when operating in proximity to one another during peacetime, and

Guided by generally recognized principles and rules of international law,

Have agreed as follows:

Article I. For the purposes of this Agreement:

1. "Armed forces" means, for the United States of America: the armed forces of the United States, including the United States Coast Guard; for the Union of Soviet Socialist Republics: the armed forces of the USSR, and the Border Troops of the USSR.

2. "Personnel" means any individual, military or civilian, who is serving in or is employed by the armed forces of the Parties.

3. "Equipment" means any ship, aircraft, or ground hardware of the armed forces of the Parties.

4. "Ship" means any warship or auxiliary ship of the armed forces of the Parties.

5. "Aircraft" means any military aircraft of the armed forces of the Parties, excluding spacecraft.

6. "Ground hardware" means any material of the armed forces of the Parties designed for use on land.

7. "Laser" means any source of intense, coherent highly directional electromagnetic radiation in the visible, infrared, or ultraviolet regions that is based on the stimulated radiation of electrons, atoms, or molecules.

8. "Special Caution Area" means a region, designated mutually by the parties, in which personnel and equipment of their armed forces are present and, due to circumstances in the region, in which special measures shall be undertaken in accordance with this Agreement.

9. "Interference with command and control networks" means actions that hamper, interrupt or limit the operation of the signals and information transmission means and systems providing for the control of personnel and equipment of the armed forces of a Party.

Article II

1. In accordance with the provisions of this Agreement, each Party shall take necessary measures directed toward preventing dangerous military activities, which are the following activities of personnel and equipment of its armed forces when operating in proximity to personnel and equipment of the armed forces of the other Party during peacetime:

(a) Entering by personnel and equipment of the armed forces of one Party into the national territory of the other Party owing to circumstances brought about by *force majeure,* or as a result of unintentional actions by such personnel;

(b) Using a laser in such a manner that its radiation could cause harm to personnel or damage to equipment of the armed forces of the other Party;

(c) Hampering the activities of the personnel and equipment of the armed forces of the other party in a Special Caution Area in a manner which could cause harm to personnel or damage to equipment; and

(d) Interfering with command and control networks in a manner which could cause harm to personnel or damage to equipment of the armed forces of the other Party.

2. The Parties shall take measures to ensure expeditious termination and resolution by peaceful means, without resort to the threat or use of force, of any incident which may arise as a result of dangerous military activities.

3. Additional provisions concerning prevention of dangerous military activities and resolution of any incident which may arise as a result of those activities are contained in Articles III, IV, V, and VI of this Agreement and the Annexes thereto.

Article III

1. In the interest of mutual safety, personnel of the armed forces of the Parties shall exercise great caution and prudence while operating near the national territory of the other Party.

2. If, owing to circumstances brought about by force majeure or as a result of unintentional actions, as set forth in Article II, subparagraph 1(a) of this Agreement, personnel and equipment of the armed forces of one Party enter into the national territory of the other Party, such personnel shall adhere to the procedures set forth in Annexes 1 and 2 to this Agreement.

Article IV

1. When personnel of the armed forces of one Party, in proximity to personnel and equipment of the armed forces of the other party, intend to use a laser and that use could cause harm to personnel or damage to equipment of the armed forces of that other Party, the personnel of the armed forces of the Party intending such use of a laser shall attempt to notify the relevant personnel of the armed forces of the other Party. In any case, personnel of the armed forces of the Party intending use of a laser shall follow appropriate safety measures.

2. If personnel of the armed forces of one Party believe that personnel of the armed forces of the other Party are using a laser in a manner which could cause harm to them or damage to their equipment, they shall immediately attempt to establish communications to seek termination of such use. If the personnel of the armed forces of the Party having received such notification are actually using a laser in proximity to the area indicated in the notification, they shall investigate the relevant circumstances. If their use of a laser could in fact cause harm to personnel or damage to equipment of the armed forces of the other Party, they shall terminate such use.

3. Notifications with respect to the use of a laser shall be made in the manner provided for in Annex 1 to this Agreement.

Article V

1. Each Party may propose to the other Party that the Parties agree to designate a region as a Special Caution Area. The other Party may accept or decline the proposal. Either Party also has the right to request that a meeting of the Joint Military Commission be convened, in accordance with Article IX of this Agreement, to discuss such a proposal.

2. Personnel of the armed forces of the Parties present in a designated Special Caution Area shall establish and maintain communications, in accordance with Annex 1 to this Agreement, and undertake other measures as may be later agreed upon by the Parties, in order to prevent dangerous military activities and to resolve any incident which may arise as a result of such activities.

3. Each Party has the right to terminate an arrangement with respect to a designated Special Caution Area. The Party intending to exercise this right shall provide timely notification of such intent to the other Party, including the date and time of termination of such an arrangement, through use of the communications channel set forth in paragraph 3 of Article VII of this Agreement.

Article VI

1. When personnel of the armed forces of one Party, in proximity to personnel and equipment of the armed forces of the other Party, detect interference with their command and control networks which could cause harm to them or damage to their equipment, they may inform the relevant personnel for the armed forces of the other Party if they believe that the interference is being caused by such personnel and equipment of the armed forces of that Party.

2. If the personnel of the armed forces of the Party having received such information establish that this interference with the command and control networks is being caused by their activities, they shall take expeditious measures to terminate the interference.

Article VII

1. For the purpose of preventing dangerous military activities, and expeditiously resolving any incident which may arise as a result of such activities, the armed forces of the Parties shall establish and maintain communications as provided for in Annex 1 to this Agreement.

2. The Parties shall exchange appropriate information on instances of dangerous military activities or incidents which may arise as a result of such activities, as well as on other issues related to this Agreement.

3. The Chairman of the Joint Chiefs of Staff of the United States shall convey information referred to in paragraph 2 of this Article through the Defense Attache of the Union of Soviet Socialist Republics in Washington, D.C. The Chief of the

General Staff of the Armed Forces of the Union of Soviet Socialist Republics shall convey such information through the Defense Attache of the United States in Moscow.

Article VIII

1. This Agreement shall not affect the rights and obligations of the Parties under other international agreements and arrangements in force between the Parties, and the flights of individual or collective self-defense and of navigation and overflight, in accordance with international law. Consistent with the foregoing, the Parties shall implement the provisions of this Agreement, taking into account the sovereign interests of both Parties.

2. Nothing in this Agreement shall be directed against any Third Party. Should an incident encompassed occur in the territory of an ally of a Party, that Party shall have the right to consult with its ally as to appropriate measures to be taken.

Article IX

1. To promote the objectives and implementation of the provisions of this Agreement, the Parties hereby establish a Joint Military Commission. Within the framework of the commission, the Parties shall consider:

(a) Compliance with the obligations assumed under this Agreement;

(b) Possible ways to ensure a higher level of safety for the personnel and equipment of their armed forces; and

(c) Other measures as may be necessary to improve the viability and effectiveness of this Agreement.

2. Meetings of the Joint Military Commission shall be convened annually or more frequently as may be agreed upon by the Parties.

Article X

1. This Agreement, including its Annexes, which form an integral part thereof, shall enter into force on January 1, 1990.

2. This Agreement may be terminated by either Party six months after written notice is given to the other Party.

3. This Agreement shall be registered in accordance with Article 102 of the Charter of the United Nations.

DONE at Moscow on the twelfth of June, 1989. . . . [Signatures]

ANNEX 1
PROCEDURES FOR ESTABLISHING AND MAINTAINING COMMUNICATIONS

SECTION I: Communications Channels

For the purpose of implementing this Agreement, the armed forces of the Parties shall provide for establishing and maintaining, as necessary, communication at the following levels:

(a) The Task Force Commander of the armed forces of one Party present in a Special Caution Area and the Task Force Commander of the armed forces of the other Party in the same Area;

(b) Commander* of a ship, aircraft, ground vehicle or ground unit of the armed forces of one Party and the Commander* of a ship, aircraft, ground vehicle or ground unit of the armed forces of the other Party; and

(c) Commander* of an aircraft of the armed forces of one Party and an air traffic control or monitoring facility of the other Party.

[*"Commander" means the individual with authority to command or lead a ship, aircraft, ground vehicle, or ground unit.]

SECTION II: Radio Frequencies

1. To establish radio communication, as necessary, the following frequencies shall be used: [section omitted]

2. The Parties agree to conduct necessary testing to ensure reliability of the communications channels agreed by the Parties.

SECTION III: Signals and Phrases

1. The Parties recognize that the lack of radio communication can increase the danger to the personnel and equipment of their armed forces involved in any incident which may arise as a result of dangerous military activities. Personnel of the armed forces of the Parties involved in such incidents who are unable to establish radio communication, or who establish radio communication but cannot be understood, shall try to communicate using those signals referred to in this section. In addition, such personnel shall attempt to establish communications with other personnel of their armed forces, who in turn shall take measures to resolve the incident through communications channels set forth in this Agreement.

2. Ship-to-ship and ship-to-shore communications shall be conducted using signals and phrases as set forth in the International Code of Signals of

1965 and the Special Signals developed in accordance with the Agreement between the Government of the United States of America and the Government of the Union of Soviet Socialist Republics on the Prevention of Incidents On and Over the High Seas of 1972. Aircraft-to-aircraft communications shall be conducted using signals and phrases for intercepting and intercepted aircraft contained in Rules of the Air, Annex 2 to the 1944 Convention on International Civil Aviation (Chicago Convention). The additional signals and phrases contained in paragraph 4 of this Section may also be used.

3. Whenever aircraft of the parties come into visual contact with each other, their aircrews shall monitor the frequency 121.5 MHz or 243.0 MHz. If it is necessary to exchange information, but communications in a common language are not possible, attempts shall be made to convey essential information and acknowledgement of instructions by using phrases referred to in paragraphs 2 and 4 of this Section. If radio communication is not possible, then visual signals shall be used.

4. The following table contains additional signals and phrases for communications between aircraft, ships, ground vehicles, or ground units, in accordance with the Agreement: [table omitted]

ANNEX 2:
PROCEDURES FOR THE RESOLUTION OF INCIDENTS RELATED TO ENTERING INTO NATIONAL TERRITORY

This annex sets forth the procedures for the expeditious resolution, by peaceful means, of any incident which may arise during entry being made by personnel and equipment of the armed forces on one Party into the national territory of the other Party owing to circumstances brought about by *force majeure* or as a result of unintentional actions, as set forth in Article II, subparagraph 1(a) of this Agreement.

SECTION I: Entering into National Territory Owing to Circumstances Brought About by *Force Majeure*

1. When personnel of the armed forces of one Party are aware that, owing to circumstances brought about by *force majeure,* they may enter or have entered into the national territory of the other party, they shall continuously attempt to establish and maintain communications with personnel of the armed forces of the other Party, as provided for in Annex 1 to this Agreement.

2. Upon receiving a communication from personnel of the armed forces of a Party who are aware that they may enter or have entered into the national territory of the other Party, personnel of the armed forces of that other Party shall provide them appropriate instructions as to subsequent actions, and assistance to the extent of existing capabilities.

3. If personnel and equipment of the armed forces of a Party enter into the national territory of the other party, the personnel shall take into consideration any instructions received from the personnel of the armed forces of the other Party that are appropriate to the existing circumstances and, subject to the provisions of Article VIII, paragraph 1 of this Agreement, shall either depart the national territory or proceed to a designated location.

4. Personnel of the armed forces of a Party having entered into the national territory of the other Party, upon arrival at the location designated by personnel of the armed forces of that other party, shall be:

(a) Accorded an opportunity to contact their Defense Attache or consular authorities as soon as possible.

(b) Cared for properly and their equipment protected; and

(c) Assisted in repairing their equipment in order to facilitate their departure from the national territory, and in departing at the earliest opportunity.

SECTION II: Entering into National Territory As a Result of Unintentional Actions of Personnel

1. When the personnel of the armed forces of one Party establish that personnel and equipment of the armed forces of the other Party may enter into their national territory as a result of unintentional actions or that such an entry has already taken place, the personnel who have made this determination shall continuously attempt to establish and maintain communications with the personnel of the armed forces of that other Party, as provided for in Annex 1 to this Agreement. The purpose of such communications is: to alert personnel of the armed forces of that other Party of the possibility of entry or the fact of entry into national territory; to clarify the reasons for and circumstances of their actions; to recommend that they take measures to prevent such an entry, if possible; or, to render them assistance as appropriate.

2. Personnel of the armed forces of a Party, having been alerted that they may enter into the na-

tional territory of the other Party, shall, if possible, undertake measures so that their actions do not result in such an entry.

3. If personnel and equipment of the armed forces of a Party enter into the national territory of the other party, the personnel shall take into consideration any instructions received from the personnel of the armed forces of the other Party that are appropriate to the existing circumstances and, subject to the provisions of Article VIII, paragraph 1 of this Agreement, shall either depart the national territory or proceed to a designated location. With respect to personnel and equipment which have arrived at a designated location, the procedures provided for in Section 1, paragraph 4 of this Annex shall be applicable.

AGREED STATEMENTS

In connection with the Agreement Between the Government of the United States of America and the Government of the Union of Soviet Socialist Republics on the Prevention of Dangerous Military Activities, the Parties have agreed as follows:

First agreed statement. In the case of any entry by personnel and equipment of the armed forces of one Party into the national territory of the other Party owing to circumstances brought about by *force majeure* or as a result of unintentional actions by such personnel, as set forth in Article II, subparagraph 1(a) of the Agreement Between the Government of the United States of America and the Government of the Union of Soviet Socialist Republics on the Prevention of Dangerous Military Activities, the procedures set forth in Annexes 1 and 2 to this Agreement shall apply regardless of whether that other party has been made aware of the circumstances of such entry.

Second agreed statement. As indicated in Article VIII of the Agreement Between the Government of the United States of America and the Government of the Union of Soviet Socialist Republics on the Prevention of Dangerous Military Activities, this Agreement does not affect the rights of navigation under international law, including the right of warships to exercise innocent passage.

[*Arms Control Today* 19, no. 7 (August 1989): 15–17]

United States–USSR Agreement on Notification of Strategic Exercises (1989)

This agreement was signed at Jackson Hole, Wyoming, on 23 September 1989, and it entered into force on 1 January 1990.

Agreement Between the Government of the Union of Soviet Socialist Republics and the Government of the United States of America on Reciprocal Advance Notification of Major Strategic Exercises

The Government of the Union of Soviet Socialist Republics and the Government of the United States of America, hereinafter referred to as the Parties,

Affirming their desire to reduce and ultimately eliminate the risk of outbreak of nuclear war, in particular as a result of misinterpretation, miscalculation, or accident,

Believing that a nuclear war cannot be won and must never be fought,

Recognizing the necessity to promote the increase of mutual trust and the strengthening of strategic stability,

Acknowledging the importance of exchanging advance notification of major strategic exercises on the basis of reciprocity,

Reaffirming their obligations under the Agreement between the United States of America and the Union of Soviet Socialist Republics on the Establishment of Nuclear Risk Reduction Centers of September 15, 1987,

Have agreed as follows:

Article I. On the basis of reciprocity, each Party shall notify the other Party no less than 14 days in advance about the beginning of one major strategic forces exercise which includes the participation of heavy bomber aircraft to be held during each calendar year.

Article II

1. Each Party shall provide to the other Party the notifications required by Article I through the Nuclear Risk Reduction Centers established by the Agreement between the United States of America and the Union of Soviet Socialist Republics on the Establishment of Nuclear Risk Reduction Centers of September 15, 1987.

2. The notifications required by Article I shall be provided no less than 14 days prior to the date in Coordinated Universal Time (UTC) during which the relevant exercise will commence.

Article III. The Parties shall undertake to hold consultations, as mutually agreed, to consider questions relating to implementation of the provisions of this Agreement, as well as to discuss possible amendments thereto aimed at furthering the implementation of the objectives of this Agreement. Amendments shall enter into force in accordance with procedures to be agreed upon.

Article IV. This Agreement shall not affect the obligations of either Party under other agreements.

Article V

1. This Agreement shall be of unlimited duration.

2. This Agreement may be terminated by either Party upon 12 months written notice to the other Party.

Article VI. This Agreement shall enter into force on January 1, 1990, and notifications pursuant to this Agreement shall commence with the calendar year 1990.

[Signatures]

[Reprinted in *Arms Control Today,* October 1989, p. 25]

Environmental Modification Treaty (1977)

This treaty was signed at Geneva on 18 May 1977, and it entered into force on 5 October 1978.

Convention on the Prohibition of Military or Any Other Hostile Use of Environmental Modification Techniques

The States Parties to this Convention,

Guided by the interest of consolidating peace, and wishing to contribute to the cause of halting the arms race, and of bringing about general and complete disarmament under strict and effective international control, and of saving mankind from the danger of using new means of warfare,

Determined to continue negotiations with a view to achieving effective progress towards further measures in the field of disarmament,

Recognizing that scientific and technical advances may open new possibilities with respect to modification of the environment,

Recalling the Declaration of the United Nations Conference on the Human Environment adopted at Stockholm on 16 June 1972,

Realizing that the use of environmental modification techniques for peaceful purposes could improve the interrelationship of man and nature and contribute to the preservation and improvement of the environment for the benefit of present and future generations,

Recognizing, however, that military or any other hostile use of such techniques could have effects extremely harmful to human welfare,

Desiring to prohibit effectively military or any other hostile use of environmental modification techniques in order to eliminate the dangers to mankind from such use, and affirming their willingness to work towards the achievement of this objective,

Desiring also to contribute to the strengthening of trust among nations and to the further improvement of the international situation in accordance with the purposes and principles of the Charter of the United Nations,

Have agreed as follows:

Article I

1. Each State Party to this Convention undertakes not to engage in military or any other hostile use of environmental modification techniques having widespread, long-lasting or severe effects as the means of destruction, damage or injury to any other State Party.

2. Each State Party to this Convention undertakes not to assist, encourage or induce any State, group of States or international organization to engage in activities contrary to the provisions of paragraph 1 of this article.

Article II. As used in Article I, the term "environmental modification techniques" refers to any technique for changing—through the deliberate manipulation of natural processes—the dynamics, composition or structure of the Earth, including its biota, lithosphere, hydrosphere and atmosphere, or of outer space.

Article III

1. The provisions of this Convention shall not hinder the use of environmental modification techniques for peaceful purposes and shall be without prejudice to the generally recognized principles and applicable rules of international law concerning such use.

2. The States Parties to this Convention undertake to facilitate, and have the right to participate in, the fullest possible exchange of scientific and technological information on the use of environmental modification techniques for peaceful purposes. States Parties in a position to do so shall contribute,

alone or together with other States or international organizations, to international economic and scientific cooperation in the preservation, improvement, and peaceful utilization of the environment, with due consideration for the needs of the developing areas of the world.

Article IV. Each State Party to this Convention undertakes to take any measures it considers necessary in accordance with its constitutional processes to prohibit and prevent any activity in violation of the provisions of the Convention anywhere under its jurisdiction or control.

Article V

1. The States Parties to this Convention undertake to consult one another and to cooperate in solving any problems which may arise in relation to the objectives of, or in the application of the provisions of, the Convention. Consultation and cooperation pursuant to this article may also be undertaken through appropriate international procedures within the framework of the United Nations and in accordance with its Charter. These international procedures may include the services of appropriate international organizations, as well as of a Consultative Committee of Experts as provided for in paragraph 2 of this article.

2. For the purposes set forth in paragraph 1 of this article, the Depositary shall, within one month of the receipt of a request from any State Party to this convention, convene a Consultative Committee of Experts. Any State Party may appoint an expert to the Committee whose functions and rules of procedure are set out in the annex, which constitutes an integral part of this Convention. The Committee shall transmit to the Depositary a summary of its findings of fact, incorporating all views and information presented to the Committee during its proceedings. The Depositary shall distribute the summary to all States Parties.

3. Any State Party to this Convention which has reason to believe that any other State Party is acting in breach of obligations deriving from the provisions of the Convention may lodge a complaint with the Security Council of the United Nations. Such a complaint should include all relevant information as well as all possible evidence supporting its validity.

4. Each State Party to this Convention undertakes to cooperate in carrying out any investigation which the Security Council may initiate, in accordance with the provisions of the Charter of the United Nations, on the basis of the complaint received by the Council. The Security Council shall inform the States Parties of the results of the investigation.

5. Each State Party to this Convention undertakes to provide or support assistance, in accordance with the provisions of the Charter of the United Nations, to any State Party which so requests, if the Security Council decides that such Party has been harmed or is likely to be harmed as a result of violation of the Convention.

Article VI

1. Any State Party to this Convention may propose amendments to the Convention. The text of any proposed amendment shall be submitted to the Depositary who shall promptly circulate it to all States Parties.

2. An amendment shall enter into force for all States Parties to this Convention which have accepted it, upon the deposit with the Depositary of instruments of acceptance by a majority of States Parties. Thereafter it shall enter into force for any remaining State Party on the date of deposit of its instrument of acceptance.

Article VII. This Convention shall be of unlimited duration.

Article VIII

1. Five years after the entry into force of this Convention, a conference of the States Parties to the Convention shall be convened by the Depositary at Geneva, Switzerland. The conference shall review the operation of the Convention with a view to ensuring that its purposes and provisions are being realized, and shall in particular examine the effectiveness of the provisions of paragraph 1 of Article I in eliminating the dangers of military or any other hostile use of environmental modification techniques.

2. At intervals of not less than five years thereafter, a majority of the States Parties to the Convention may obtain, by submitting a proposal to this effect to the Depositary, the convening of a conference with the same objectives.

3. If no conference has been convened pursuant to paragraph 2 of this article within ten years following the conclusion of a previous conference, the Depositary shall solicit the views of all States Parties to the Convention, concerning the convening of such a conference. If one third or ten of the States

Parties, whichever number is less, respond affirmatively, the Depositary shall take immediate steps to convene the conference.

Article IX [Ratification]
[Signatures]

Annex to the Convention

Consultative Committee of Experts

1. The Consultative Committee of Experts shall undertake to make appropriate findings of fact and provide expert views relevant to any problem raised pursuant to paragraph 1 of Article V of this Convention by the State Party requesting the convening of the Committee.

2. The work of the Consultative Committee of Experts shall be organized in such a way as to permit it to perform the functions set forth in paragraph 1 of this annex. The Committee shall decide procedural questions relative to the organization of its work, where possible by consensus, but otherwise by a majority of those present and voting. There shall be no voting on matters of substance.

3. The Depositary or his representative shall serve as the Chairman of the Committee.

4. Each expert may be assisted at meetings by one or more advisers.

5. Each expert shall have the right, through the Chairman, to request from States, and from international organizations, such information and assistance as the expert considers desirable for the accomplishment of the Committee's work.

Understandings Regarding the Convention
[*These are not incorporated into the Convention but are part of the negotiating record and were included in the report transmitted by the CCD to the U.N. General Assembly in September 1976.*]

Understanding Relating to Article I

It is the understanding of the Committee that, for the purposes of this Convention, the terms, "widespread" "long-lasting" and "severe" shall be interpreted as follows:

(a) "widespread": encompassing an area on the scale of several hundred square kilometres;

(b) "long-lasting" lasting for a period of months, or approximately a season;

(c) "severe": involving serious or significant disruption or harm to human life, natural and economic resources or other assets.

It is further understood that the interpretation set forth above is intended exclusively for this Convention and is not intended to prejudice the interpretation of the same or similar terms if used in connexion with any other international agreement.

Understanding Relating to Article II

It is the understanding of the Committee that the following examples are illustrative of phenomena that could be caused by the use of environmental modification techniques as defined in Article II of be Convention: earthquakes; tsunamis; an upset in the ecological balance of a region; changes in weather patterns (clouds, precipitation, cyclones of various types and tornadic storms); changes in climate patterns; changes in ocean currents; changes in the state of the ozone layer; and changes in the state of the ionosphere.

It is further understood that all the phenomena listed above, when produced by military or any other hostile use of environmental modification techniques, would result, or could reasonably be expected to result, in widespread, long-lasting or severe destruction, damage or injury. Thus, military any other hostile use of environmental modification techniques as defined in Article II, so as to cause those phenomena as a means of destruction, damage or injury to another State Party, would be prohibited.

It is recognized, moreover, that the list of examples set out above is not exhaustive. Other phenomena which could result from the use of environmental modification techniques as defined in Article II could also be appropriately included. The absence of such phenomena from the list does not in any way imply that the undertaking contained in Article I would not be applicable to those phenomena, provided the criteria set out in that article were met.

Understanding Relating to Article III

It is the understanding of the Committee that this Convention does not deal with the question whether or not a given use of environmental modification techniques for peaceful purposes is in accordance with generally recognized principles and applicable rules of international law.

Understanding Relating to Article VIII

It is the understanding of the Committee that a proposal to amend the Convention may also be considered at any conference of Parties held pursuant to Article VIII. It is further understood that any proposed amendment that is intended for such consideration should, if possible, be submitted to the Depositary no less than 90 days before the commencement of the conference.

[U.S. Arms Control and Disarmament Agency, *Arms Control and Disarmament Agreements: Texts and Histories of the Negotiations* (Washington, D.C., 1990), pp. 214–219]

Convention on the Physical Protection of Nuclear Material (1980)

This agreement was signed at New York on 3 March 1980, and it was ratified by U.S. President Ronald Reagan on 4 September 1981.

The States Parties to This Convention,

Recognizing the right of all States to develop and apply nuclear energy for peaceful purposes and their legitimate interests in the potential benefits to be derived from the peaceful application of nuclear energy,

Convinced of the need for facilitating international cooperation in the peaceful application of nuclear energy,

Desiring to avert the potential dangers posed by the unlawful taking and use of nuclear material,

Convinced that offenses relating to nuclear material are a matter of grave concern and that there is an urgent need to adopt appropriate and effective measures to ensure the prevention, detection and punishment of such offenses,

Aware of the Need for international cooperation to establish, in conformity with the national law of each State Party and with this Convention, effective measures for the physical protection of nuclear material,

Convinced that this Convention should facilitate the safe transfer of nuclear material,

Stressing also the importance of the physical protection of nuclear material in domestic use, storage and transport,

Recognizing the importance of effective physical protection of nuclear material used for military purposes, and understanding that such material is and will continue to be accorded stringent physical protection,

Have Agreed as follows:

Article 1. For the purposes of this Convention:

(a) "nuclear material" means plutonium except that with isotopic concentration exceeding 80% in plutonium-238; uranium-233; uranium enriched in the isotopes 235 or 233; uranium containing the mixture of isotopes as occurring in nature other than in the form of ore or ore-residue; any material containing one or more of the foregoing;

(b) "uranium enriched in the 235 or 233" means uranium containing the isotopes 235 or 233 or both in an amount such that the abundance ratio of the sum of these isotopes to the isotope 238 is greater than the ratio of the isotope 235 to the isotope 238 occurring in nature;

(c) "international nuclear transport" means the carriage of a consignment of nuclear material by any means of transportation intended to go beyond the territory of the State where the shipment originates beginning with the departure from a facility of the shipper in that State and ending with the arrival at a facility of the receiver within the State of ultimate destination.

Article 2

1. The Convention shall apply to nuclear material used for peaceful purposes while in international nuclear transport.

2. With the exception of articles 3 and 4 and paragraph 3 of article 5, this Convention shall also apply to nuclear material used for peaceful purposes while in domestic use, storage and transport.

3. Apart from the commitments expressly undertaken by States Parties in the articles covered by paragraph 2 with respect to nuclear material used for peaceful purposes while in domestic use, storage and transport, nothing in this Convention shall be interpreted as affecting the sovereign rights of a State regarding the domestic use, storage and transport of such nuclear material.

Article 3. Each State Party shall take appropriate steps within the framework of its national law and consistent with international law to ensure as far as practicable that, during international nuclear transport, nuclear material within its territory, or on board a ship or aircraft under its jurisdiction insofar as such ship or aircraft is engaged in the transport to or from that State, is protected at the levels described in Annex 1.

Article 4

1. Each State Party shall not export or authorize the export of nuclear material unless the State Party has received assurances that such material will be protected during the international nuclear transport at the levels described in Annex I.

2. Each State Party shall not import or authorize the import of nuclear material from a State not party to this Convention unless the State Party has received assurances that such material will during the international nuclear transport be protected at the levels described in Annex I.

3. A State Party shall not allow the transit of its territory by land or internal waterways or through its airports or seaports of nuclear material between States that are not parties to this Convention unless the State Party has received assurances as far as practicable that this nuclear material will be protected during international nuclear transport at the levels described in Annex I.

4. Each State Party shall apply within the framework of its national law the levels of physical protection described in Annex I to nuclear material being transported from a part of that State to another part of the same State through international waters or airspace.

5. The State Party responsible for receiving assurances that the nuclear material will be protected at the levels described in Annex I according to paragraphs 1 to 3 shall identify and inform in advance States which the nuclear material is expected to transit by land or internal waterways, or whose airports or seaports it is expected to enter.

6. The responsibility for obtaining assurances referred to in paragraph 1 may be transferred, by mutual agreement, to the State Party involved in the transport as the importing State.

7. Nothing in this article shall be interpreted as in any way affecting the territorial sovereignty and jurisdiction of a State, including that over its airspace and territorial sea.

Article 5

1. States Parties shall identify and make known to each other directly or through the International Atomic Energy Agency their central authority and point of contact having responsibility for physical protection of nuclear material and for coordinating recovery and response operations in the event of any unauthorized removal, use or alteration of nuclear material or in the event of credible threat thereof.

2. In the case of theft, robbery or any other unlawful taking of nuclear material or of credible threat thereof, States Parties shall, in accordance with their national law, provide cooperation and assistance to the maximum feasible extent in the recovery and protection of such material to any State that so requests. In particular:

(a) a State Party shall take appropriate steps to inform as soon as possible other States, which appear to it to be concerned, of any theft, robbery or other unlawful taking of nuclear material or credible threat thereof and to inform, where appropriate, international organizations;

(b) as appropriate, the States Parties concerned shall exchange information with each other or international organizations with a view to protecting threatened nuclear material, verifying the integrity of the shipping container, or recovering unlawfully taken nuclear material and shall:

(i) coordinate their efforts through diplomatic and other agreed channels;

(ii) render assistance, if requested;

(iii) ensure the return of nuclear material stolen or missing as a consequence of the above-mentioned events.

The means of implementation of this cooperation shall be determined by the States Parties concerned.

3. States Parties shall cooperate and consult as appropriate, with each other directly or through international organizations, with a view to obtaining guidance on the design, maintenance and improvement of systems of physical protection of nuclear material in international transport.

Article 6

1. States Parties shall take appropriate measures consistent with their national law to protect the confidentiality of any information which they receive in confidence by virtue of the provisions of this Convention from another State Party or through participation in an activity carried out for the im-

plementation of this Convention. If States Parties provide information to international organizations in confidence, steps shall be taken to ensure that the confidentiality of such information is protected.

2. States Parties shall not be required by this Convention to provide any information which they are not permitted to communicate pursuant to national law or which would jeopardize the security of the State concerned or the physical protection of nuclear material.

Article 7

1. The intentional commission of:

(a) an act without lawful authority which constitutes the receipt, possession, use, transfer, alteration, disposal or dispersal of nuclear material and which causes or is likely to cause death or serious injury to any person or substantial damage to property;

(b) a theft or robbery of nuclear material:

(c) an embezzlement or fraudulent obtaining of nuclear material;

(d) an act constituting a demand for nuclear material by threat or use of force or by any other form of intimidation;

(e) a threat:

(i) to use nuclear material to cause death or serious injury to any person or substantial property damage, or

(ii) to commit an offense described in subparagraph (b) in order to compel a natural or legal person, international organization or State to do or to refrain from doing any act;

(f) an attempt to commit any offense described in paragraphs (a), (b) or (c); and

(g) an act which constitutes participation in any offense described in paragraphs

(a) to (f) shall be made a punishable offense by each State Party under its national law.

2. Each State Party shall make the offenses described in this article punishable by appropriate penalties which take into account their grave nature.

Article 8

1. Each State Party shall take such measures as may be necessary to establish its jurisdiction over the offenses set forth in article 7 in the following cases:

(a) when the offense is committed in the territory of that State or on board a ship or aircraft registered in that State;

(b) when the alleged offender is a national of that State.

2. Each State Party shall likewise take such measures as may be necessary to establish its jurisdiction over these offenses in cases where the alleged offender is present in its territory and it does not extradite him pursuant to article 11 to any of the States mentioned in paragraph 1.

3. This Convention does not exclude any criminal jurisdiction exercised in accordance with national law.

4. In addition to the State Parties mentioned in paragraphs 1 and 2, each State Party may, consistent with international law, establish its jurisdiction over the offenses set forth in article 7 when it is involved in international nuclear transport as the exporting or importing State.

Article 9. Upon being satisfied that the circumstances so warrant, the State Party in whose territory the alleged offender is present shall take appropriate measures, including detention, under its national law to ensure his presence for the purpose of prosecution or extradition. Measures taken according to this article shall be notified without delay to the States required to establish jurisdiction pursuant to article 8 and, where appropriate, all other States concerned.

Article 10. The State Party in whose territory the alleged offender is present shall, if it does not extradite him, submit, without exception whatsoever and without undue delay, the case to its competent authorities for the purpose of prosecution, through proceedings in accordance with the laws of that State.

Article 11

1. The offenses in article 7 shall be deemed to be included as extraditable offenses in any extradition treaty existing between States Parties. States Parties undertake to include those offenses as extraditable offenses in every future extradition treaty to be concluded between them.

2. If a State Party which makes extradition conditional on the existence of a treaty receives a request for extradition from another State Party with which it has no extradition treaty, it may at its option consider this Convention as the legal basis for extradition in respect of those offenses. Extradition shall be subject to the other conditions provided by the law of the requested State.

3. States Parties which do not make extradition conditional on the existence of a treaty shall recog-

nize those offenses as extraditable offenses between themselves subject to the conditions provided by the law of the requested State.

4. Each of the offenses shall be treated, for the purpose of extradition between States Parties, as if it had been committed not only in the place in which it occurred but also in the territories of the States Parties required to establish their jurisdiction in accordance with paragraph 1 of article 8.

Article 12. Any person regarding whom proceedings are being carried out in connection with any of the offenses set forth in article 7 shall be guaranteed fair treatment at all stages of the proceedings.

Article 13

1. States Parties shall afford one another the greatest measure of assistance in connection with criminal proceedings brought in respect of the offenses set forth in article 7, including the supply of evidence at their disposal necessary for the proceedings. The law of the State requested shall apply in all cases.

2. The provisions of paragraph 1 shall not affect obligations under any other treaty, bilateral or multilateral, which governs or will govern, in whole or in part, mutual assistance in criminal matters.

Article 14

1. Each State Party shall inform the depositary of its laws and regulations which give effect to this Convention. The depositary shall communicate such information periodically to all States Parties.

2. The State Party where an alleged offender is prosecuted shall, wherever practicable, first communicate the final outcome of the proceedings to the States directly concerned. The State Party shall also communicate the final outcome to the depositary who shall inform all States.

3. Where an offense involves nuclear material used for peaceful purposes in domestic use, storage or transport, and both the alleged offender and the nuclear material remain in the territory of the State Party in which the offense was committed, nothing in this Convention shall be interpreted as requiring that State Party to provide information concerning criminal proceedings arising out of such an offense.

Article 15. The Annexes constitute an integral part of this Convention.

Article 16

1. A conference of States Parties shall be convened by the depositary five years after the entry into force of this Convention to review the implementation of the Convention and its adequacy as concerns the preamble, the whole of the operative part and the annexes in the light of the then prevailing situation.

2. At intervals of not less than five years thereafter, the majority of States Parties may obtain, by submitting a proposal to this effect to the depositary, the convening of further conferences with the same objective.

Article 17

1. In the event of a dispute between two or more States Parties concerning the interpretation or application of this Convention, such States Parties shall consult with a view to the settlement of the dispute by negotiation, or by any other peaceful means of settling disputes acceptable to all parties to the dispute.

2. Any dispute of this character which cannot be settled in the manner prescribed in paragraph 1 shall, at the request of any party to such dispute, be submitted to arbitration or referred to the International Court of Justice for decision. Where a dispute is submitted to arbitration, if, within six months from the date of the request, the parties to the dispute are unable to agree on the organization of the arbitration, a party may request the President of the International Court of Justice or the Secretary-General of the United Nations to appoint one or more arbitrators. In case of conflicting requests by the parties to the dispute, the request to the Secretary-General of the United Nations shall have priority.

3. Each State Party may at the time of signature, ratification, acceptance or approval of this Convention or accession thereto declare that it does not consider itself bound by either or both of the dispute settlement procedures provided for in paragraph 2. The other States Parties shall not be bound by a dispute settlement procedure provided for in paragraph 2, with respect to a State Party which has made a reservation to that procedure.

4. Any State Party which has made a reservation in accordance with paragraph 3 may at any time withdraw that reservation by notification to the depositary.

Article 18. [Ratification]

Article 19. [Ratification]

Article 20.

1. Without prejudice to article 16 a State Party may propose amendments to this Convention. The proposed amendment shall be submitted to the de-

pository who shall circulate it immediately to all States Parties. If a majority of States Parties request the depositary to convene a conference to consider the proposed amendments, the depositary shall invite all States Parties to attend such a conference to begin not sooner than thirty days after the invitations are issued. Any amendment adopted at the conference by a two-thirds majority of all States Parties shall be promptly circulated by the depositary to all States Parties.

2. The amendment shall enter into force for each State Party that deposits its instrument of ratification, acceptance or approval of the amendment on the thirtieth day after the date on which two thirds of the States Parties have deposited their instruments of ratification, acceptance or approval with the depositary. Thereafter, the amendment shall enter into force for any other State Party on the day on which that State Party deposits its instrument of ratification, acceptance or approval of the amendment.

Article 21. [Ratification]
Article 22. [Ratification]

Annex I

Levels of Physical Protection to Be Applied in International Transport of Nuclear Material as Categorized in Annex II.

1. Levels of physical protection for nuclear material during storage incidental to international nuclear transport include:

(a) For Category III materials, storage within an area to which access is controlled;

(b) For Category II materials, storage within an area under constant surveillance by guards or electronic devices, surrounded by a physical barrier with a limited number of points of entry under ap-

propriate control or any area with an equivalent level of physical protection;

(c) For Category I material, storage within a protected area as defined for Category II above, to which, in addition, access is restricted to persons whose trustworthiness has been determined, and which is under surveillance by guards who are in close communication with appropriate response forces. Specific measures taken in this context should have as their object the detection and prevention of any assault, unauthorized access or unauthorized removal of material.

2. Levels of physical protection for nuclear material during international transport include:

(a) For Category II and III materials, transportation shall take place under special precautions including prior arrangements among sender, receiver, and carrier, and prior agreement between natural or legal persons subject to the jurisdiction and regulation of exporting and importing States, specifying time, place and procedures for transferring transport responsibility;

(b) For Category I materials, transportation shall take place under special precautions identified above for transportation of Category II and III materials, and in addition, under constant surveillance by escorts and under conditions which assure close communication with appropriate response forces;

(c) For natural uranium other than in the form of ore or ore-residue, transportation protection for quantities exceeding 500 kilograms U shall include advance notification of shipment specifying mode of transport, expected time of arrival and confirmation of receipt of shipment.

[Signatures]

[Annex II follows on the facing page.]

[U.S. Arms Control and Disarmament Agency, *Arms Control and Disarmament Agreements: Texts and Histories of the Negotiations* (Washington, D.C., 1990), pp. 302–313]

Annex II

Table: Categorization of Nuclear Material

Material	Form	Category I	Category II	Category III[3]
1. Plutonium[1]	Unirradiated[2]	2 kg or more	Less than 2 kg but more than 500 g	500 g or less but more than 15 g
2. Uranium-235	Unirradiated[2]: uranium enriched to 20% U^{235} or more	5 kg or more	Less than 5 kg but more than 1 kg.	1 kg or less but more than 15 g
	uranium enriched to 10% U^{235} but less than 20%		10 kg or more	Less than 10 kg but more than 1 kg.
	uranium enriched above natural, but less than 10% U^{235}			10 kg or more
3. Uranium-233	Unirradiated[2]	2 kg or more	Less than 2 kg but more than 500 g	500 g or less but more than 15 g
4. Irradiated fuel			Depleted or natural uranium, thorium or low-enriched fuel (less than 10% fissile content).[4] [5]	

1. All plutonium except that with isotopic concentration exceeding 80% in plutonium-238.
2. Material not irradiated in a reactor or material irradiated in a reactor but with a radiation level equal to or less than 100 rads/hour at one metre unshielded.
3. Quantities not falling in Category III and natural uranium should be protected in accordance with prudent management practice.
4. Although this level of protection is recommended, it would be open to States, upon evaluation of the specific circumstances, to assign a different category of physical protection.
5. Other fuel which by virtue of its original fissile material contents is classified as Category I and II before irradiation may be reduced one category level while the radiation level from the fuel exceeds 100 rads/hour at one metre unshielded.

Confidence- and Security-Building Measures in Europe (1986)

The Stockholm CSCE *document was signed on 19 September 1986.*

Document of the Stockholm Conference on Confidence- and Security-Building Measures and Disarmament in Europe Convened in Accordance With the Relevant Provisions of the Concluding Document of the Madrid Meeting of the Conference on Security and Cooperation in Europe

(1) The representatives of the participating States of the Conference on Security and Co-operation in Europe (CSCE), Austria, Belgium, Bulgaria, Canada, Cyprus, Czechoslovakia, Denmark, Finland, France, the German Democratic Republic, the Federal Republic of Germany, Greece, the Holy See, Hungary, Iceland, Ireland, Italy, Liechtenstein, Luxembourg, Malta, Monaco, the Netherlands, Norway, Poland, Portugal, Romania, San Marino, Spain, Sweden, Switzerland, Turkey, the Union of Soviet Socialist Republics, the United Kingdom, the United States of America and Yugoslavia, met in Stockholm from 17 January 1984 to 19 September 1986, in accordance with the provisions relating to the Conference on Confidence- and Security-Building Measures and Disarmament in Europe contained in the Concluding Document of the Madrid Followup Meeting of the CSCE.

. . . .

(5) Contributions were made by the following non-participating Mediterranean States: Algeria, Egypt, Israel, Lebanon, Libya, Morocco, Syria and Tunisia.

(6) The participating States recalled that the aim of the Conference on Confidence- and Security-Building Measures and Disarmament in Europe is, as a substantial and integral part of the multilateral process initiated by the Conference on Security and Cooperation in Europe, to undertake, in stages, new, effective and concrete actions designed to make progress in strengthening confidence and security and in achieving disarmament, so as to give effect and expression to the duty of States to refrain from the threat or use of force in their mutual relations as well as in their international relations in general.

(7) The participating States recognized that the set of mutually complementary confidence- and security-building measures which are adopted in the present document and which are in accordance with the Madrid mandate serve by their scope and nature and by their implementation to strengthen confidence and security in Europe and thus to give effect and expression to the duty of States to refrain from the threat or use of force.

(8) Consequently the participating States have declared the following:

REFRAINING FROM THE THREAT OR USE OF FORCE

(9) The participating States, recalling their obligation to refrain, in their mutual relations as well as in their international relations in general, from the threat or use of force against the territorial integrity or political independence of any State, or in any other manner inconsistent with the purposes of the United Nations, accordingly reaffirm their commitment to respect and put into practice the principle of refraining from the threat or use of force, as laid down in the Final Act.

(10) No consideration may be invoked to serve to warrant resort to the threat or use of force in contravention of this principle.

(11) They recall the inherent right of individual or collective self-defence if an armed attack occurs, as set forth in the Charter of the United Nations.

(12) They will refrain from any manifestation of force for the purpose of inducing any other State to renounce the full exercise of its sovereign rights.

(13) As set forth in the Final Act, no occupation or acquisition of territory resulting from the threat or use of force in contravention of international law, will be recognized as legal.

(14) They recognize their commitment to peace and security. Accordingly they reaffirm that they will refrain from any use of armed forces inconsistent with the purposes and principles of the Charter of the United Nations and the provisions of the Declaration on Principles Guiding Relations between Participating States, against another participating State, in particular from invasion of or attack on its territory.

(15) They will abide by their commitment to refrain from the threat or use of force in their rela-

tions with any State, regardless of that State's political, social, economic, or cultural system and irrespective of whether or not they maintain with that State relations of alliance.

(16) They stress that non-compliance with the obligation of refraining from the threat or use of force, as recalled above, constitutes a violation of international law.

(17) They stress their commitment to the principle of peaceful settlement of disputes as contained in the Final Act, convinced that it is an essential complement to the duty of States to refrain from the threat or use of force, both being essential factors for the maintenance and consolidation of peace and security. They recall their determination and the necessity to reinforce and to improve the methods at their disposal for the peaceful settlement of disputes. They reaffirm their resolve to make every effort to settle exclusively by peaceful means any dispute between them.

(18) The participating States stress their commitment to the Final Act and the need for full implementation of all its provisions which will further the process of improving security and developing co-operation in Europe, thereby contributing to international peace and security in the world as a whole.

(19) They emphasize their commitment to all the principles of the Declaration on Principles Guiding Relations between Participating States and declare their determination to respect and put them into practice irrespective of their political, economic or social systems as well as of their size, geographical location or level of economic development.

(20) All these ten principles are of primary significance and, accordingly, they will be equally and unreservedly applied, each of them being interpreted taking into account the others.

(21) Respect for and the application of these principles will enhance the development of friendly relations and co-operation among the participating States in all fields covered by the provisions of the Final Act.

(22) They reconfirm their commitment to the basic principle of the sovereign equality of States and stress that all States have equal rights and duties within the framework of international law.

(23) They reaffirm the universal significance of human rights and fundamental freedoms. Respect for and the effective exercise of these rights and freedoms are essential factors for international peace, justice and security, as well as for the devel-

opment of friendly relations and co-operation among themselves as among all States, as set forth in the Declaration on Principles Guiding Relations between Participating States.

(24) They reaffirm that, in the broader context of world security, security in Europe is closely linked with security in the Mediterranean area as a whole; in this context, they confirm their intention to develop good neighbourly relations with all States in the region, with due regard to reciprocity, and in the spirit of the principles contained in the Declaration on Principles Guiding Relations between Participating States, so as to promote confidence and security and make peace prevail in the region in accordance with the provisions contained in the Mediterranean chapter of the Final Act.

(25) They emphasize the necessity to take resolute measures to prevent and to combat terrorism, including terrorism in international relations. They express their determination to take effective measures, both at the national level and through international co-operation, for the prevention and suppression of all acts of terrorism. They will take all appropriate measures in preventing their respective territories from being used for the preparation, organization or commission of terrorist activities. This also includes measures to prohibit on their territories illegal activities, including subversive activities, of persons, groups and organizations that instigate, organize or engage in the perpetration of acts of terrorism, including those directed against other States and their citizens.

(26) They will fulfil in good faith their obligations under international law; they also stress that strict compliance with their commitments within the framework of the CSCE is essential for building confidence and security;

(27) The participating States confirm that in the event of a conflict between the obligations of the members of the United Nations under the Charter of the United Nations and their obligations under any treaty or other international agreement, their obligations under the Charter will prevail, in accordance with Article 103 of the Charter of the United Nations.

(28) The participating States have adopted the following measures:

PRIOR NOTIFICATION OF CERTAIN MILITARY ACTIVITIES

(29) The participating States will give notification in writing through diplomatic channels in an

agreed form of content, to all other participating States 42 days or more in advance of the start of notifiable[1] military activities in the zone of application for confidence- and security-building measures (CSBMS).[2]

(30) Notification will be given by the participating State on whose territory the activity in question is planned to take place even if the forces of that State are not engaged in the activity or their strength is below the notifiable level. This will not relieve other participating States of their obligation to give notification, if their involvement in the planned military activity reaches the notifiable level.

(31) Each of the following military activities in the field conducted as a single activity in the zone of application for CSBMS, at or above the levels defined below, will be notified.

(31.1) The engagement of formations of land forces[3] of the participating States in the same exercise activity conducted under a single operational command independently or in combination with any possible air or naval components.

(31.1.1) This military activity will be subject to notification whenever it involves at any time during the activity:

- at least 13,000 troops, including support troops, or
- at least 300 battle tanks

if organized into a divisional structure or at least two brigades/regiments, not necessarily subordinate to the same division.

(31.1.2) The participation of air forces of the participating States will be included in the notification if it is foreseen that in the course of the activity 200 or more sorties by aircraft, excluding helicopters, will be flown.

(31.2) The engagement of military forces either in an amphibious landing or in a parachute assault by airborne forces in the zone of application for CSBMS.

(31.2.1) These military activities will be subject to notification whenever the amphibious landing involves at least 3,000 troops or whenever the parachute drop involves at least 3,000 troops.

(31.3) The engagement of formations of land forces of the participating States in a transfer from outside the zone of application for CSBMS to arrival points in the zone, or from inside the zone of application for CSBMS to points of concentration in the zone, to participate in a notifiable exercise activity or to be concentrated.

(31.3.1) The arrival or concentration of these forces will be subject to notification whenever it involves, at any time during the activity:

- at least 13,000 troops, including support troops, or
- at least 300 battle tanks

if organized into a divisional structure or at least two brigades/regiments, not necessarily subordinate to the same division.

(31.3.2) Forces which have been transferred into the zone will be subject to all provisions of agreed CSBMS when they depart their arrival points to participate in a notifiable exercise activity or to be concentrated within the zone of application for CSBMS.

(32) Notifiable military activities carried out without advance notice to the troops involved are exceptions to the requirement for prior notification to be made 42 days in advance.

(32.1) Notification of such activities, above the agreed thresholds, will be given at the time the troops involved commence such activities.

(33) Notification will be given in writing of each notifiable military activity in the following agreed form:

(34) **A—General Information**

(34.1) The designation of the military activity;

(34.2) The general purpose of the military activity;

(34.3) The names of the States involved in the military activity;

(34.4) The level of organizing and commanding the military activity;

(34.5) The start and end dates of the military activity.

(35) **B—Information on different types of notifiable military activities**

(35.1) The engagement of land forces of the participating States in the same exercise activity conducted under a single operational command independently or in combination with any possible air or naval components;

(35.1.1) The total number of troops taking part in the military activity (i.e., ground troops, amphibious troops, airmobile and airborne troops) and the number of troops participating for each State involved, if applicable

(35.1.2) Number and type of divisions participating for each State;

(35.1.3) The total number of battle tanks for each State and the total number of anti-tank guided missile launchers mounted on armoured vehicles;

(35.1.4) The total number of artillery pieces and multiple rocket launchers (100 mm calibre or above);

(35.1.5) The total number of helicopters, by category;

(35.1.6) Envisaged number of sorties by aircraft, excluding helicopters;

(35.1.7) Purpose of air missions;

(35.1.8) Categories of aircraft involved;

(35.1.9) The level of command, organizing and commanding the air force participation;

(35.1.10) Naval ship-to-shore gunfire;

(35.1.11) Indication of other naval ship-to-shore support;

(35.1.12) The level of command, organizing and commanding the naval force participation.

(35.2) The engagement of military forces either in an amphibious landing or in a parachute assault by airborne forces in the zone of application for CSBMS;

(35.2.1) The total number of amphibious troops involved in notifiable amphibious landings, and/or the total number of airborne troops involved in notifiable parachute assaults;

(35.2.2) In the case of a notifiable amphibious landing, the point or points of embarkation, if in the zone of application for CSBMS.

(35.3) The engagement of formations of land forces of the participating States in a transfer from outside the zone of application for CSBMS to arrival points in the zone, or from inside the zone of application for CSBMS to points of concentration in the zone, to participate in a notifiable exercise activity or to be concentrated:

(35.3.1) The total number of troops transferred;

(35.3.2) Number and type of divisions participating in the transfer;

(35.3.3) The total number of battle tanks participating in a notifiable arrival of concentration;

(35.3.4) Geographical coordinates for the points of arrival and for the points of concentration.

(36) **C—The envisaged area and timeframe of the activity**

(36.1) The area of the military activity delimited by geographic coordinates, as appropriate;

(36.2) The start and end dates of each phase (transfers, deployment, concentration of forces, active exercise phase, recovery phase) of activities in the zone of application for CSBMS of participating formations, the tactical purpose and corresponding geographical areas (delimited by geographical coordinates) for each phase;

(36.3) Brief descriptions of each phase.

(37) **D—Other information**

(37.1) Changes, if any, in relation to information provided in the annual calendar regarding the activity;

(37.2) Relationship of the activity to other notifiable activities.

OBSERVATION OF CERTAIN MILITARY ACTIVITIES

(38) The participating States will invite observers from all other participating States to the following notifiable military activities:

(38.1) • The engagement of formations of land force[3] of the participating States in the same exercise activity conducted under a single operational command independently or in combination with any possible air or naval components;

(38.2) • The engagement of military forces either in an amphibious landing or in a parachute assault by airborne forces in the zone of application for CSBMS;

(38.3) • In the case of the engagement of formations of land forces of the participating States in a transfer from outside the zone of application for CSBMS to arrival points in the zone, or from inside the zone of application for CSBMS to points of concentration in the zone, to participate in a notifiable exercise activity or to be concentrated, the concentration of these forces. Forces which have been transferred into the zone will be subject to all provisions of agreed confidence- and security-building measures when they depart their arrival points to participate in a notifiable exercise activity or to be concentrated within the zone of application for CSBMS.

(38.4) • The above-mentioned activities will be subject to observation whenever the number of troops engaged meets or exceeds 17,000 troops, except in the case of either an amphibious landing or a parachute assault by airborne forces, which will be subject to observation whenever the number of troops engaged meets or exceeds 5,000 troops.

(39) The host State will extend the invitations in writing through diplomatic channels to all other participating States at the time of notification. The host State will be the participating State on whose territory the notified activity will take place.

(40) The host State may delegate some of its responsibilities as host to another participating State engaged in the military activity on the territory of the host State. In such cases, the host State will specify the allocation of responsibilities in its invitation to observe the activity.

(41) Each participating State may send up to two observers to the military activity to be observed.

(42) The invited State may decide whether to send military and/or civilian observers, including members of its personnel accredited to the host State. Military observers will, normally, wear their uniforms and insignia while performing their tasks.

(43) Replies to the invitation will be given in writing not later than 21 days after the issue of the invitation.

(44) The participating State accepting an invitation will provide the names and ranks of their observers in their reply to the invitation. If the invitation is not accepted in time, it will be assumed that no observers will be sent.

(45) Together with the invitation the host State will provide a general observation programme, including the following information:

(45.1) • the date, time and place of assembly of observers;

(45.2) • planned duration of the observation programme;

(45.3) • languages to be used in interpretation and/or translation;

(45.4) • arrangements for board, lodging and transportation of the observers;

(45.5) • arrangements for observation equipment which will be issued to the observers by the host State;

(45.6) • possible authorization by the host State of the use of special equipment that the observers may bring with them;

(45.7) • arrangements for special clothing to be issued to the observers because of weather or environmental factors.

(46) The observers may make requests with regard to the observation programme. The host State will, if possible, accede to them.

(47) The host State will determine a duration of observation which permits the observers to observe a notifiable military activity from the time that agreed thresholds for observation are met or exceeded until, for the last time during the activity, the thresholds for observation are no longer met.

(48) The host State will provide the observers with transportation to the area of the notified activity and back. This transportation will be provided from either the capital or another suitable location to be announced in the invitation, so that the observers are in position before the start of the observation programme.

(49) The invited State will cover the travel expenses for its observers to the capital, or another suitable location specified in the invitation, of the host State, and back.

(50) The observers will be provided equal treatment and offered equal opportunities to carry out their functions.

(51) The observers will be granted, during their mission, the privileges and immunities accorded to diplomatic agents in the Vienna Convention on Diplomatic Relations.

(52) The host State will not be required to permit observation of restricted locations, installations or defence sites.

(53) In order to allow the observers to confirm that the notified activity is non-threatening in character and that it is carried out in conformity with the appropriate provisions of the notification, the host State will:

(53.1) • at the commencement of the observation programme give a briefing on the purpose, the basic situation, the phases of the activity and possible changes as compared with the notification and provide the observers with a map of the area of the military activity with a scale of 1 to not more than 500,000 and an observation programme with a daily schedule as well as a sketch indicating the basic situation;

(53.2) • provide the observers with appropriate observation equipment; however, the observers will be allowed to use their personal binoculars, which will be subject to examination and approval by the host State;

(53.3) • in the course of the observation programme give the observers daily briefings with the help of maps on the various phases of the military activity and their development and inform the observers about their positions geographically; in the case of a land force activity conducted in combination with air or naval components, briefings will be given by representatives of these forces;

(53.4) • provide opportunities to observe directly forces of the State/States engaged in the military activity so that the observers get an impression of the flow of the activity; to this end, the observers will be given the opportunity to observe major combat units of the participating formations of a divisional or equivalent level and, whenever possible, to visit some units and communicate with commanders and troops; commanders or other senior personnel of participating formations as well as of the visited units will inform the observers of the mission of their respective units;

(53.5) • guide the observers in the area of the military activity; the observers will follow the instructions issued by the host State in accordance with the provisions set out in this document;

(53.6) • provide the observers with appropriate means of transportation in the area of the military activity;

(53.7) • provide the observers with opportunities for timely communication with their embassies or other official missions and consular posts; the host State is not obligated to cover the communication expenses of the observers;

(53.8) • provide the observers with appropriate board and lodging in a location suitable for carrying out the observation programme and, when necessary, medical care.

(54) The participating States need not invite observers to notifiable military activities which are carried out without advance notice to the troops involved unless these notifiable activities have a duration of more than 72 hours. The continuation of these activities beyond this time will be subject to observation while the agreed thresholds for observation are met or exceeded. The observation programme will follow as closely as practically possible all the provisions for observation set out in this document.

ANNUAL CALENDARS

(55) Each participating State will exchange, with all other participating States, an annual calendar of its military activities subject to prior notification,[4] within the zone of application for csbms, forecast for the subsequent calendar year. It will be transmitted every year, in writing, through diplomatic channels, not later than 15 November for the following year.

(56) Each participating State will list the above-mentioned activities chronologically and will provide information on each activity in accordance with the following model:

(56.1) • type of military activity and its designation;

(56.2) • general characteristics and purpose of the military activity;

(56.3) • States involved in the military activity;

(56.4) • area of the military activity, indicated by appropriate geographic features and/or defined by geographic co-ordinates;

(56.5) • planned duration of the military activity and the 14-day period, indicated by dates, within which it is envisaged to start;

(56.6) • the envisaged total number of troops engaged in the military activity;

(56.7) • the types of armed forces involved in the military activity;

(56.8) • the envisaged level of command, under which the military activity will take place;

(56.9) • the number and type of divisions whose participation in the military activity is envisaged;

(56.10) • any additional information concerning, *inter alia,* components of armed forces, which the participating State planning the military activity considers relevant.

(57) Should changes regarding the military activities in the annual calendar prove necessary, they will be communicated to all other participating States no later than in the appropriate notification.

(58) Information on military activities subject to prior notification not included in an annual calendar will be communicated to all participating States as soon as possible, in accordance with the model provided in the annual calendar.

CONSTRAINING PROVISIONS

(59) Each participating State will communicate, in writing, to all other participating States, by 15 November each year, information concerning military activities subject to prior notification[4] involving more than 40,000 troops, which it plans to carry out in the second subsequent calendar year. Such communication will include preliminary information on each activity, as to its general purpose, time-frame and duration, area, size and States involved.

(60) Participating States will not carry out military activities subject to prior notification involving more than 75,000 troops, unless they have been the object of communication as defined above.

(61) Participating States will not carry out military activities subject to prior notification involving more than 40,000 troops unless they have been included in the annual calendar, not later than 15 November each year.

(62) If military activities subject to prior notification are carried out in addition to those contained in the annual calendar, they should be as few as possible.

COMPLIANCE AND VERIFICATION

(63) According to the Madrid Mandate, the confidence- and security-building measures to be agreed upon "will be provided with adequate forms of verification which correspond to their content."

(64) The participating States recognize that national technical means can play a role in monitoring compliance with agreed confidence- and security-building measures.

(65) In accordance with the provisions contained in this document each participating State has the right to conduct inspections on the territory of any other participating State within the zone of application for CSBMS.

(66) Any participating State will be allowed to address a request for inspection to another participating State on whose territory, within the zone of application for CSBMS, compliance with the agreed confidence- and security-building measures is in doubt.

(67) No participating State will be obliged to accept on its territory, within the zone of application for CSBMS, more than three inspections per calendar year.

(68) No participating State will be obliged to accept more than one inspection per calendar year from the same participating State.

(69) An inspection will not be counted if, due to *force majeure,* it cannot be carried out.

(70) The participating State which requests an inspection will state the reasons for such a request.

(71) The participating State which has received such a request will reply in the affirmative to the request within the agreed period of time, subject to the provisions contained in paragraphs (67) and (68).

(72) Any possible dispute as to the validity of the reasons for a request will not prevent or delay the conduct of an inspection.

(73) The participating State which requests an inspection will be permitted to designate for inspection on the territory of another State, within the zone of application for CSBMS, a specific area. Such an area will be referred to as the "specified area." The specified area will comprise terrain where notifiable military activities are conducted or where another participating State believes a notifiable military activity is taking place. The specified area will be defined and limited by the scope and scale of notifiable military activities but will not exceed that required for an army level military activity.

(74) In the specified area the representatives of the inspecting State accompanied by the representatives of the receiving State will be permitted access, entry and unobstructed survey, except for areas or sensitive points to which access is normally denied or restricted, military and other defence installations, as well as naval vessels, military vehicles and aircraft. The number and extent of the restricted areas should be as limited as possible. Areas where notifiable military activities can take place will not be declared restricted areas, except for certain permanent or temporary military installations which, in territorial terms, should be as small as possible, and consequently those areas will not be used to prevent inspection of notifiable military activities. Restricted areas will not be employed in a way inconsistent with the agreed provisions on inspection.

(75) Within the specified area, the forces of participating States other than the receiving State will also be subject to the inspection conducted by the inspecting State.

(76) Inspection will be permitted on the ground, from the air or both.

(77) The representatives of the receiving State will accompany the inspection team, including when it is in land vehicles and an aircraft from the time of their first employment until the time they are no longer in use for the purposes of inspection.

(78) In its request, the inspecting State will notify the receiving State of:

(78.1) • the reasons for the request;

(78.2) • the location of the specified area defined by geographical co-ordinates;

(78.3) • the preferred point(s) of entry for the inspection team;

(78.4) • mode of transport to and from the point(s) of entry and, if applicable, to and from the specified area;

(78.5) • where in the specified area the inspection will begin;

(78.6) • whether the inspection will be conducted from the ground, from the air or both simultaneously

(78.7) • whether aerial inspection will be conducted using an airplane, a helicopter or both;

(78.8) • whether the inspection team will use land vehicles provided by the receiving State or, if mutually agreed, its own vehicles;

(78.9) • information for the issuance of diplomatic visas to inspectors entering the receiving State.

(79) The reply to the request will be given in the shortest possible period or time, but within not more than twenty-four hours. Within thirty-six hours after the issuance of the request, the inspection team will be permitted to enter the territory of the receiving State.

(80) Any request for inspection as well as the reply thereto will be communicated to all participating States without delay.

(81) The receiving State should designate the point(s) of entry as close as possible to the specified area. The receiving State will ensure that the inspection team will be able to reach the specified area without delay from the point(s) of entry.

(82) All participating States will facilitate the passage of the inspection teams through their territory.

(83) Within 48 hours after the arrival of the inspection team at the specified area, the inspection will be terminated.

(84) There will be no more than four inspectors in an inspection team. While conducting the inspection the inspection team may divide into two parts.

(85) The inspectors and, if applicable, auxiliary personnel, will be granted during their mission the privileges and immunities in accordance with the Vienna Convention on Diplomatic Relations.

(86) The receiving State will provide the inspection team with appropriate board and lodging in a location suitable for carrying out the inspection, and, when necessary, medical care; however this does not exclude the use by the inspection team of its own tents and rations.

(87) The inspection team will have use of its own maps, own photo cameras, own binoculars and own dictaphones, as well as own aeronautical charts.

(88) The inspection team will have access to appropriate telecommunications equipment of the receiving State, including the opportunity for continuous communication between the members of an inspection team in an aircraft and those in a land vehicle employed in the inspection.

(89) The inspecting State will specify whether aerial inspection will be conducted using an airplane a helicopter or both. Aircraft for inspection will be chosen by mutual agreement between the inspecting and receiving States. Aircraft will be chosen which provide the inspection team a continuous view of the ground during the inspection.

(90) After the flight plan, specifying, *inter alia,* the inspection team's choice of flight path, speed and altitude in the specified area, has been filed with the competent air traffic control authority the inspection aircraft will be permitted to enter the specified area without delay. Within the specified area, the inspection team will, at its request, be permitted to deviate from the approved flight plan to make specific observations provided such deviation is consistent with paragraph (74) as well as flight safety and air traffic requirements. Directions to the crew will be given through a representative of the receiving State on board the aircraft involved in the inspection.

(91) One member of the inspection team will be permitted, if such a request is made, at any time to observe data on navigational equipment of the aircraft and to have access to maps and charts used by the flight crew for the purpose of determining the exact location of the aircraft during the inspection flight.

(92) Aerial and ground inspectors may return to the specified area as often as desired within the 48-hour inspection period.

(93) The receiving State will provide for inspection purposes land vehicles with cross country capability. Whenever mutually agreed taking into account the specific geography relating to the area to be inspected, the inspecting State will be permitted to use its own vehicles.

(94) If land vehicles or aircraft are provided by the inspecting State, there will be one accompanying driver for each land vehicle, or accompanying aircraft crew.

(95) The inspecting State will prepare a report of its inspection and will provide a copy of that report to all participating States without delay.

(96) The inspection expenses will be incurred by the receiving State except when the inspecting State uses its own aircraft and/or land vehicles. The travel expenses to and from the point(s) of entry will be borne by the inspecting State.

(97) Diplomatic channels will be used for communications concerning compliance and verification.

(98) Each participating State will be entitled to obtain timely clarification from any other participating State concerning the application of agreed confidence- and security-building measures. Com-

munications in this context will, if appropriate, be transmitted to all other participating States.

(99) The participating States stress that these confidence- and security-building measures are designed to reduce the dangers of armed conflict and misunderstanding or miscalculation of military activities and emphasize that their implementation will contribute to these objectives.

(100) Reaffirming the relevant objectives of the Final Act, the participating States are determined to continue building confidence, to lessen military confrontation and to enhance security for all. They are also determined to achieve progress in disarmament.

(101) The measures adopted in this document are politically binding and will come into force on 1 January 1987.

(102) The Government of Sweden is requested to transmit the present document to the follow-up meeting of the CSCE in Vienna and to the Secretary-General of the United Nations. The Government of Sweden is also requested to transmit the present document to the Governments of the non-participating Mediterranean States.

(103) The text of this document will be published in each participating State, which will disseminate it and make it known as widely as possible.

(104) The representatives of the participating States express their profound gratitude to the Government and people of Sweden for the excellent arrangements made for the Stockholm Conference and the warm hospitality extended to the delegations which participated in the Conference.

ANNEX I

Under the terms of the Madrid mandate, the zone of application for CSBMS is defined as follows:

On the basis of equality of rights, balance and reciprocity, equal respect for the security interests of all CSCE participating States, and of their respective obligations concerning confidence- and security-building measures and disarmament in Europe, these confidence- and security-building measures will cover the whole of Europe as well as the adjoining sea area[5] and air space. They will be of military significance and politically binding and will be provided with adequate forms of verification which correspond to their content.

As far as the adjoining sea area[5] and air space is concerned, the measures will be applicable to the military activities of all the participating States taking place there whenever these activities affect security in Europe as well as constitute a part of activities taking place within the whole of Europe as referred to above, which they will agree to notify. Necessary specifications will be made through the negotiations on the confidence- and security-building measures at the Conference.

Nothing in the definition of the zone given above will diminish obligations already undertaken under the Final Act. The confidence- and security-building measures to be agreed upon at the Conference will also be applicable in all areas covered by any of the provisions in the Final Act relating to confidence-building measures and certain aspects of security and disarmament.

ANNEX II

Chairman's Statement

It is understood that, taking into account the agreed date of entry into force of the agreed confidence- and security-building measures and the provisions contained in them concerning the time-frames of certain advance notifications, and expressing their interest in an early transition to the full implementation of the provisions of this document, the participating States agree to the following:

The annual calendars concerning military activities subject to prior notification and forecast for 1987 will be exchanged not later than 15 December 1986.

Communications, in accordance with agreed provisions, concerning military activities involving more than 40,000 troops planned for the calendar year 1988 will be exchanged by 15 December 1986. Participating States may undertake activities involving more than 75,000 troops during the calendar year 1987 provided that they are included in the annual calendar exchanged by 15 December 1986.

Activities to begin during the first 42 days after 1 January 1987 will be subject to the relevant provisions of the Final Act of the CSCE. However, the participating States will make every effort to apply to them the provisions of this document to the maximum extent possible.

This statement will be an annex to the Document of the Stockholm Conference and will be published with it.

ANNEX III

Chairman's Statement

It is understood that each participating State can raise any question consistent with the mandate of the Conference on Confidence- and Security-Building Measures and Disarmament in Europe at any stage subsequent to the Vienna CSCE Follow-up Meeting.

This statement will be an annex to the Document of the Stockholm Conference and will be published with it.

ANNEX IV

Chairman's Statement

It is understood that the participating States recall that they have the right to belong or not to belong to international organizations, to be or not to be a party to bilateral or multilateral treaties including the right to be or not to be a party to treaties of alliance; they also have the right of neutrality. In this context, they will not take advantage of these rights to circumvent the purposes of the system of inspection, and in particular the provision that a participating State will be obliged to accept on its territory within the zone of application for CSBMS, more than three inspections per calendar year.

Appropriate understandings between participating States on this subject will be expressed in inter-pretative statements to be included in the journal of the day.

The statement will be an annex to the Document of the Stockholm Conference and will be published with it.

Notes

1. In this document, the term notifiable means subject to notification.

2. See Annex I.

3. In this context, the term land forces includes amphibious, airmobile, and airborne forces.

4. As defined in the provisions on Prior Notification of Certain Military Activities.

5. "In this context, the notion of adjoining sea area is understood to refer also to ocean areas adjoining Europe" [quoted text in original]. Whenever the term "the zone of application for CSBMS" is used in this document, the above definition will apply.

[U.S. Arms Control and Disarmament Agency, *Arms Control and Disarmament Agreements: Texts and Histories of the Negotiations* (Washington, D.C., 1990), pp. 323–335]

CONTRIBUTORS

Richard Dean Burns, *Editor in Chief.* Professor, Chair of History, and Director of the Center for the Study of Armament and Disarmament, California State University, Los Angeles. Coauthor of *Disarmament in Perspective: An Analysis of Selected Arms Control and Disarmament Agreements Between the World Wars 1919–1939;* editor of *A Guide to American Foreign Relations Since 1700* and *Arms Control and Disarmament: A Bibliography;* general editor of the *War/Peace Bibliography Series* and the *Twentieth-Century Presidential (Bibliographical) Series.* An Introduction to Arms Control and Disarmament; The United States

Eric H. Arnett. Senior Program Associate, Program on Science and International Security, American Association for the Advancement of Science. Director, Project on Advanced Weaponry in the Developing World. Author of *Sea-Launched Cruise Missiles and U.S. Security.* Science, Technology, and Arms Control

Detlef Bald. Scientific Director, sowi. Lecturer, Munich University. Author of *Der deutsche Offizier: Sozial- und Bildungsgeschichte im 20. Jahrhundert; Tradition und Reform im militärischen Bildungswesen: Eine Dokumentation, 1810–1985;* and *The Bundeswehr, The Military, and German Society: 1945–1990.* Germany

Nicole Ball. Davidson Sommers Fellow, Overseas Development Council (Washington). Author of *Pressing for Peace: Can Aid Induce Reform?; Security and Economy in the Third World;* and many articles on the link between development and se-

curity in the developing world. Disarmament and Development in the Third World

Joseph Preston Baratta. Historian of the world federalist movement and of international organization. Compiler of *Strengthening the United Nations: A Bibliography on U.N. Reform and World Federalism.* Author of monographs on international verification, peacekeeping, arbitration, and human rights for the U.S. Institute of Peace. The Kellogg-Briand Pact and the Outlawry of War

James Barros. Professor of Political Science, University of Toronto. Author of numerous studies dealing with the politics of interwar and postwar international organizations, including a three-volume study of the secretaries-general of the League of Nations and the United Nations. The League of Nations and Disarmament

Jurgen Brauer. Assistant Professor of Economics, School of Business Administration, Augusta College (Augusta, Ga.). Coeditor of *Economic Issues of Disarmament* and author of articles on the economics of third-world military spending. Economic Consequences of Arms Control and Disarmament

Lester H. Brune. John and Augusta Oglesby Professor of American Heritage, Bradley University. Author of *Chronological History of United States Foreign Relations,* 3 volumes; *Origins of U.S. National Security Policy, 1900–1941;* and *The Missile Crisis of October 1962.* Regulating Aerial Bombing: 1919–1945

Thomas H. Buckley. Professor of American History, University of Tulsa. Author of *The United States and the Washington Conference, 1921–1922; American Foreign and National Security Policies, 1914–1945;* and articles on the Washington Naval Conference. THE WASHINGTON NAVAL LIMITATION SYSTEM: 1921–1939

George Bunn. Lawyer; former arms control negotiator. Member, Center for International Security and Arms Control, Stanford University. Former general counsel for the U.S. Arms Control and Disarmament Agency and U.S. ambassador to the Geneva disarmament conference. Author of *Arms Control by Committee: Managing Negotiations with the Russians.* NEGOTIATING ARMS CONTROL AND DISARMAMENT AGREEMENTS

Matthew Bunn. Editor, *Arms Control Today;* Associate Director for Publications, Arms Control Association. Author of *Foundation for the Future: The* ABM *Treaty and National Security.* THE ANTI-BALLISTIC MISSILE TREATY: 1972 TO THE PRESENT

Sammy Kum Buo. Senior Political Affairs Officer, Office of Disarmament Affairs, U.N. Secretariat. Secretary-General, Third Review Conference of the Biological Weapons Convention, 1991. Director, United Nations Regional Centre for Peace and Disarmament in Africa, 1986–1989. Author of articles on African political and security issues. AFRICA

Susan M. Burns. Former Graduate Fellow, RAND Corporation. Author of "Preventing Nuclear War: Arms Management Measures" and "Arms Limitations," two chapters in a study of South Asian arms control sponsored by the U.S. Department of Energy and Los Alamos National Laboratory. SOUTH ASIA: INDIA AND PAKISTAN

Stanley M. Burstein. Professor of History, California State University (Los Angeles). Editor and translator of *On the Erythraean Sea,* by Agatharchides of Cnidus. Author of *Outpost of Hellenism: The Emergence of Heraclea on the Black Sea; The Babyloniaca of Berossus; The Hellenistic Age: From the Battle of Ipsos to the Death of Kleopatra VII;* and articles on ancient Greek and Near Eastern history. ARMS CONTROL IN ANTIQUITY

Dan Caldwell. Professor of Political Science and Chairman of the Council on International Studies, Pepperdine University. Coeditor, with Michael Krepon, of *The Politics of Arms Control Treaty Ratification.* Author of *The Dynamics of Domestic Politics and Arms Control: The* SALT II *Treaty Ratification Debate.* FROM SALT TO START: LIMITING STRATEGIC NUCLEAR WEAPONS

Walter C. Clemens, Jr. Professor of Political Science, Boston University. Fellow, Harvard University Center for Science and International Affairs. Member, International Institute for Strategic Studies and the Arms Control Association. Author of *The Arms Race and Sino-Soviet Relations; Can Russia Change?; Baltic Independence and Russian Empire;* and articles in *Asian Survey, China Quarterly,* and *Journal of International Affairs.* CHINA

Sandi E. Cooper. Professor of History, College of Staten Island and at the Graduate Center, City University of New York. Coeditor of the *Garland Library of War and Peace.* Editor for western Europe in Harold Josephson, ed., *Biographical Dictionary of Modern Peace Leaders.* Author of *Patriotic Pacifism: Waging War on War in Europe, 1815–1914* and of numerous articles and essays on peace movements. TRANSNATIONAL PEACE MOVEMENTS AND ARMS CONTROL: THE NINETEENTH AND TWENTIETH CENTURIES

Alessandro Corradini. Consultant for disarmament affairs, United Nations. Former Director and Deputy to the Assistant Secretary-General for Disarmament. Contributor to several books on security, arms control, and disarmament. Author of many articles on international organization, peace, and disarmament. GENERAL AND COMPLETE DISARMAMENT PROPOSALS

Neta C. Crawford. Visiting Professor of Political Science, Clark University (Worcester, Mass.). Author of *Soviet Military Aircraft; Force-Prone States: Sources of Highly Militarized Foreign Policy* (forthcoming); and articles on problems of international relations. RESTRAINING VIOLENCE IN EARLY SOCIETIES

Richard P. Cronin. Specialist in Asian Affairs, Congressional Research Service, Library of Congress. Author of *Japan, the United States, and Prospects for the Asia-Pacific Century: Three Scenarios for the Future* and numerous CRS reports, articles, and book chapters on Asian security and foreign policy issues. JAPAN

Gloria Charmian Duffy. President, Global Outlook research institute. Author and editor, *Compliance and the Future of Arms Control; International Arms Control: Issues and Agreements;* and articles on international security and the Soviet Union. ARMS CONTROL TREATY COMPLIANCE

William Epstein. Senior Fellow, United Nations Institute for Training and Research. Represented Secretary-General at the negotiations for the Partial Test Ban Treaty, the Treaty of Tlatelolco, and the Nuclear Non-Proliferation Treaty and all its review conferences. Author of several books, including *The Last Chance: Nuclear Proliferation and Arms Control* and *The Prevention of Nuclear War: A U.N. Perspective.* THE NON-PROLIFERATION TREATY AND THE REVIEW CONFERENCES: 1965 TO THE PRESENT

Andrew D. Farrand. Senior Development Officer, Claremont Graduate School (Claremont, Calif.). Author of "The Development of Imperial Ideologies Before the Mexican-American War" in *Proceedings of the 1978 Meeting of the Rocky Mountain Council on Latin American Studies.* CHILE AND ARGENTINA: ENTENTE AND NAVAL LIMITATION, 1902

Ann Florini. Senior Researcher, Center for International Relations, University of California, Los Angeles. Author of "The Opening Skies: Third-Party Imaging Satellite and U.S. Security" (*International Security,* Fall 1988) and numerous publications on Open Skies and on the relationship between civil and military uses of space technology. THE OPEN SKIES NEGOTIATIONS

Charles C. Flowerree. Foreign Service Officer (retired); U.S. Ambassador to the Conference on Disarmament, 1980–1981. Member, Executive Council of the Committee for National Security. Coauthor of the *International Handbook on Chemical Weapons Proliferation* and author of articles on arms control subjects. CHEMICAL AND BIOLOGICAL WEAPONS AND ARMS CONTROL

Raymond L. Garthoff. Senior Fellow, Brookings Institution (Washington); Foreign Service officer (retired). Author of many studies, including *Détente and Confrontation: American-Soviet Relations from Nixon to Reagan* and *The Great Transition: American-Soviet Relations and the End of the Cold War* (forthcoming). THE OUTER SPACE TREATY: 1967 TO THE PRESENT

Curt Gasteyger. Professor of international relations and director, Programme for Strategic and International Security Studies, Graduate Institute of International Studies (Geneva). Author of *Searching for World Security* and *Europe in World Politics* (forthcoming). SWITZERLAND

Toby Trister Gati. Senior Vice President, United Nations Association of the United States of America (UNA-USA). THE UNITED NATIONS AND DISARMAMENT

Charles R. Gellner. Director, International Security Analyses. Consultant and publisher of newsletter, "Choice Bits: A Commentary on International Security Affairs." THE UNITED STATES ARMS CONTROL AND DISARMAMENT AGENCY

Patrick Glynn. Resident Scholar, American Enterprise Institute for Public Policy Research. Special Assistant to the Director of the U.S. Arms Control and Disarmament Agency, 1986–1987. Author of *Closing Pandora's Box: Arms Races, Arms Control, and the History of the Cold War* and many articles on foreign policy, defense, and arms control. CRITICS OF ARMS CONTROL AND DISARMAMENT

Fen Osler Hampson. Associate Professor of International Affairs and Director, Program in International Security, Carleton University (Ontario). Coeditor of *Securing Europe's Future; The Allies and Arms Control; Managing Regional Conflict;* and *Canada Among Nations* (vols. 7–9). Author of *Forming Economic Policy: The Case of Energy in Canada and Mexico; Unguided Missiles: How America Buys Its Weapons;* and *Multilateral Negotiation: Lessons from Arms Control, Trade, and the Environment* (forthcoming). "NO-FIRST-USE" NUCLEAR POLICY

Udo Heyn. Professor of History, California State University, Los Angeles. Editor, book reviewer; author of *Private Banking and Industrialization: The Case of Frankfurt am Main, 1825–1875* and internationally published articles on economic and war/peace issues. MEDIEVAL ARMS CONTROL MOVEMENTS AND THE WESTERN QUEST FOR PEACE

Laura S. Hayes Holgate. Project Coordinator, Center for Science and International Affairs, John F. Kennedy School of Government, Harvard University. Coordinator, Chemical and Biological Weapons Colloquium, Harvard University. Coauthor of conference presentations and book chapters; participant in research projects on topics such as the United Nations, humanitarianism and war, and population and national security. PREVENTING ACCIDENTAL WAR

Elaine Holoboff. Lecturer in Soviet military and security policy, Department of War Studies, King's College London. Author of *The Crisis in Soviet Military Reform* and articles on Soviet arms control and disarmament policy. RUSSIA AND THE SOVIET UNION

P. Terrence Hopmann. Professor of Political Science and Director of the International Relations Program, Brown University. Coauthor of *Unity and Disintegration in International Alliances;* coeditor of *Rethinking the Nuclear Weapons Dilemma in Europe.* Author of *Resolving International Conflicts: The Negotiation Process* and *Negotiating Security in Europe: The CSCE and Arms Control in Europe, 1973–1992* (both forthcoming). FROM MBFR TO CFE: NEGOTIATING CONVENTIONAL ARMS CONTROL IN EUROPE

Robert C. Johansen. Director of Graduate Studies, Kroc Institute for International Peace Studies, University of Notre Dame. Visiting Scholar, Center for International Affairs, Harvard University. Board of Directors, U.S. Arms Control Association. Contributing editor, *World Policy Journal.* Author of *The National Interest and the Human Interest: An Analysis of U.S. Foreign Policy.* UNILATERAL INITIATIVES

Christopher C. Joyner. Professor of Political Science and International Affairs, George Washington University. Editor of *The Antarctic Legal Regime; The Persian Gulf War: Lessons for Strategy, Law, and Diplomacy;* and *International Law of the Sea and the Future of Deep Seabed Mining.* Author of *Antarctica and the Law of the Sea; Antarctica as a Global Commons: Law, Politics and Environmental Priorities* (forthcoming); and more than 250 journal articles on international law and world politics. THE ANTARCTIC STATE TREATY: 1959 TO THE PRESENT

Jeffrey Kimball. Professor of History, Miami University. Executive Committee member, *Peace and Change: A Journal of Peace Research in History.* Editor and contributor, *To Reason Why: The Debate About the Causes of American Involvement in the Vietnam War.* Author of articles on foreign relations, war, and peace history. THE UNITED STATES

Allan S. Krass. Professor of Physics and Science Policy, Hampshire College (Amherst, Mass.). Visiting researcher, Stockholm International Peace Research Institute, 1980–1981, 1983–1984. Senior Arms Analyst, Union of Concerned Scientists, 1985–1990. Author of *Verification: How Much is Enough?* and *Uranium Enrichment and Nuclear Weapon Proliferation.* ARMS CONTROL TREATY VERIFICATION

Keith Krause. Associate Professor of Political Science and Deputy Director, Centre for International and Strategic Studies at York University (Toronto). Author of *Arms and the State: Patterns of Military Production and Trade* as well as articles and chapters on international arms transfers. CONTROLLING THE ARMS TRADE SINCE 1945; REGULATING ARMS SALES THROUGH WORLD WAR II

Steven Kull. Senior scholar, Center for International Security Studies, University of Maryland. Senior research associate, Global Outlook (Palo Alto, Calif.). Author of *Minds at War: Nuclear Reality and the Inner Conflicts of Defense Policymakers* and *Burying Lenin: The Revolution in Soviet Ideology and Foreign Policy.* PSYCHOLOGICAL DIMENSIONS OF NUCLEAR ARMS CONTROL

John M. Lamb. Executive Director and founder, Canadian Centre for Global Security (formerly the Canadian Centre for Arms Control and Disarmament). Specialist in Canadian foreign policy, arms control, and the arms trade. CANADA

Thomas M. Leonard. Professor of History, University of North Florida. Author of *Central America and the United States: The Search for Stability; The United States and Central America, 1944–1949: Perceptions of Political Dynamics;* and *Panama and the United States: A Guide to Issues and Sources* (forthcoming). LATIN AMERICA

Benjamin S. Loeb. Retired from government service relating to nuclear energy. Coauthor, with Glenn T. Seaborg, of *Kennedy, Khrushchev, and the Test Ban* and *Stemming the Tide: Arms Control in the Johnson Years.* Author of articles and book reviews on arms control history. TEST BAN PROPOSALS AND AGREEMENTS: THE 1950S TO THE PRESENT

Mary E. Lord. Executive Director, ACCESS, a nonprofit information clearinghouse on world affairs that tracks organizations and experts working on peace, security, and international relations worldwide. Contributor to ACCESS directories and guides to organizations, issues, and foundations. NONGOVERNMENT ORGANIZATIONS IN ARMS CONTROL AND DISARMAMENT

Mary K. MacDonald. University Research Fellow, St. Francis Xavier University (Antigonish, Nova Scotia). Completed dissertation, "An Arms Control Phoenix: Building Transparency Through an Arms Trade Register" at Queen's University (Kingston, Ontario). REGULATING ARMS SALES THROUGH WORLD WAR II

James Macintosh. Senior Research Associate, York University Centre for International and Strategic Studies (Toronto). Author of *Confidence (and Security) Building Measures and the Arms Control Process: A Canadian Perspective* as well as articles and chapters on confidence building, verification, and European arms control. CONFIDENCE-BUILDING MEASURES IN EUROPE: 1975 TO THE PRESENT

John B. A. Macleod. Staff researcher, Canadian Centre for Arms Control and Disarmament (Ottawa). CANADA

Kerry Stephen McNamara. Executive Director, Civic Education Project. Former fellow, Center for Science and International Affairs, Harvard University. Consultant to a variety of educational and training programs in east central Europe and the former Soviet Union. FRANCE

Robert Karl Manoff. Director, Center for War, Peace, and the News Media, New York University. Coeditor, *Reading the News.* Author of articles on arms control and nuclear issues in *Harper's, Bulletin of the Atomic Scientists, Journal of Communication,* and the *New York Times.* THE MEDIA AND ARMS CONTROL AND DISARMAMENT

Janet M. Manson. Visiting Assistant Professor of History, Clemson University. Author of *Diplomatic Ramifications of Unrestricted Submarine Warfare, 1939–1941;* coauthor of "Carte and Tierce: Leonard, Virginia Woolf, and War for Peace," in *Virginia Woolf and War: Fiction, Reality, and Myth;* coeditor of *Peace, Politics, and Women Around Bloomsbury* (forthcoming). REGULATING SUBMARINE WARFARE: 1919–1945

John Tepper Marlin. President, JTM Reports; Director, Conversion Information Center, Council on Economic Priorities (New York). Coauthor of *Building a Peace Economy; Soviet Conversion 1991;* and articles on the economics of military spending and conversion. ECONOMIC CONSEQUENCES OF ARMS CONTROL AND DISARMAMENT

Frank A. Mayer. Professor of History, California State University, Los Angeles, specializing in Atlantic Studies 1945–1990 and Conflict Resolution. Fellow, Consortium for Atlantic Studies. Member, American Council on Germany. Author of *Crossroads: Kennedy and Adenauer; A Study in German-American Relations, 1961–1963* (forthcoming). THE DISARMING AND REARMING OF GERMANY

Mike M. Mochizuki. Associate Professor of International Relations, University of Southern California. Author of *Ruling Japan: Conservative Hegemony in the Postwar Era* and articles on Japanese politics and foreign policy, U.S.-Japanese relations, and East Asian security issues. THE DISARMING AND REARMING OF JAPAN

John Ellis van Courtland Moon. Professor of History, Fitchburg State College (Fitchburg, Mass.). Author of *Confines of Concept: American Strategy in World War II* and articles on chemical- and biological-warfare policy, preparedness, and disarmament. CONTROLLING CHEMICAL AND BIOLOGICAL WEAPONS THROUGH WORLD WAR II

Allan S. Nanes. Specialist in U.S. Foreign Policy, Congressional Research Service, Library of Congress (retired). Coeditor of three books, including *The United States and Iran: A Documentary History.* Author of many articles on various aspects of international affairs. DEMILITARIZATION AND NEUTRALIZATION THROUGH WORLD WAR II

Janne E. Nolan. Senior Fellow, Brookings Institution (Washington, D.C.). Author of *Trappings of Power: Ballistic Missiles in the Third World* and *Guardians of the Arsenal: The Politics of Nuclear Strategy.* THE INF TREATY: ELIMINATING INTERMEDIATE-RANGE NUCLEAR MISSILES, 1987 TO THE PRESENT

Ronald O'Rourke. Specialist in National Defense, Congressional Research Service, Library of Congress. Author of numerous CRS reports and articles on naval affairs, including a CRS overview issue brief, *Naval Arms Control,* and a CRS report, *Naval Arms Control: A Bilateral Limit on Attack Submarines?* NAVAL ARMS CONTROL SINCE WORLD WAR II

W. Hays Parks.   Chief, International Law Branch, International and Operational Law Division; Special Assistant for Law of War Matters, Office of The Judge Advocate General of the Army (Washington, D.C.). Adjunct Professor of International Law, George Washington University National Law Center. THE LAW OF WAR

Neal H. Petersen.   Historical Consultant specializing in diplomatic history and intelligence. Former Deputy Historian, Department of State, and consultant, U.S. Arms Control and Disarmament Agency. THE VERSAILLES TREATY: 1919–1936

Edmund T. Piasecki.   Former Research Associate for Policy Studies, United Nations Association of the United States of America (UNA-USA). The United Nations and Disarmament

John Pike.   Director, Space Policy Project, Federation of American Scientists (FAS), coordinating research, analysis, and advocacy on military and civilian space policy. Former political consultant and science writer; author of over 170 studies and articles on space and national security. Coauthor of *The Impact of U.S. and Soviet Ballistic Missile Defense Programs on the ABM Treaty*. ARMS CONTROL AND ANTI-SATELLITE WEAPONS

Ron Purver.   Senior Research Fellow, Canadian Institute for International Peace and Security. Author of *Arms Control: A Regional Approach; Arms Control in the North; Arctic Arms Control: Constraints and Opportunities;* and articles on maritime arms control and Arctic security. THE RUSH-BAGOT AGREEMENT: DEMILITARIZING THE GREAT LAKES, 1817 TO THE PRESENT

Bennett Ramberg.   Senior Research Associate, Center for International Relations, University of California, Los Angeles. Coeditor of *Globalism vs. Realism: International Relations' Third Debate* and *Energy and Security in the Industrializing World*. Author of *Nuclear Power Plants as Weapons for the Enemy; Global Nuclear Energy Risks: The Search for Preventive Medicine; Destruction of Nuclear Energy Facilities in War;* and *The Seabed Arms Control Negotiations*. THE SEABED TREATY: 1971 TO THE PRESENT

John R. Redick.   Associate Professor, Division of Continuing Education, and Lecturer, Humanities Division, University of Virginia. Consultant to foundations working in the arms control and disarmament field and specialist on nuclear proliferation with an emphasis on Latin America. Author of *Argentina and Brazil: An Evolving Nuclear Relationship*. LATIN AMERICA; NUCLEAR WEAPON-FREE ZONES

David Robertson.   Fellow and Tutor in Politics, St. Hugh's College (Oxford). Author of *Enhancing European Security; The Penguin Dictionary of Politics;* and *Class and the British Electorate*. GREAT BRITAIN

James A. Schear.   United Nations Office for Disarmament Affairs. Coeditor of *Seeking Stability in Space* and *On the Defensive: The Future of SDI*. Author of articles on contemporary problems of international security and arms control. POLITICAL ASPECTS OF ARMS CONTROL AND DISARMAMENT

Lawrence Scheinman.   Professor of Government, Cornell University. Former senior official, U.S. Department of State; former Special Assistant to Director General of the International Atomic Energy Agency. Member, Council on Foreign Relations. Author of *The International Atomic Energy Agency and World Nuclear Order* and *Atomic Energy Policy in France Under the Fourth Republic*. THE INTERNATIONAL ATOMIC ENERGY AGENCY AND ARMS CONTROL

R. Michael Schiffer.   Director of international security programs, Center for War, Peace, and the News Media, New York University. Adjunct professor, George Washington University. Frequent commentator on major news programs and in magazines regarding the media and U.S. foreign policy. Editor of *The War in the Gulf and the War in the Press; Reconstructing Europe;* and *Europe's New Architecture: European Perspectives on Security in the 1990s*. Author of articles in *Journal of International Affairs* and *World Observer*. THE MEDIA AND ARMS CONTROL AND DISARMAMENT

Joseph M. Siracusa.   Reader in Diplomacy, University of Queensland (Australia). Author of *Australian-American Relations Since 1945; A History of United States Foreign Policy;* and *The Changing of America*. AUSTRALIA AND NEW ZEALAND

E. Timothy Smith.   Associate Professor of History, Barry University (Miami). Author of *The United States, Italy, and NATO, 1947–1952* and several articles on United States policy toward Italy in the post–World War II era. THE DISARMING AND REARMING OF ITALY

Leonard S. Spector. Senior Associate and Director, Nuclear Non-Proliferation Project, Carnegie Endowment for International Peace (Washington, D.C.). Coauthor, with Jacqueline R. Smith, of *Nuclear Ambitions: The Spread of Nuclear Weapons, 1989–1990* and author of other books and articles on nuclear proliferation. THE PROLIFERATION OF NUCLEAR WEAPONS

Eric Stambler. Research Analyst, Space Policy Project, Federation of American Scientists (FAS). Former researcher, Committee for National Security and the Institute for Peace and International Security. ARMS CONTROL AND ANTI-SATELLITE WEAPONS

Cherie J. Steele. Ph.D. candidate, University of California, Los Angeles. Fellow, Center for International Relations. BUDGETARY LIMITATIONS ON MILITARY EXPENDITURES

Gerald M. Steinberg. Department of Political Studies and Research Director, Center for Strategic Studies, Bar-Ilan University (Ramat Gan, Israel). Consultant on arms control, Israeli Foreign Ministry. Author of *Satellite Reconnaissance: The Role of Informal Bargaining* and *Deterrence, Defense, or Arms Control? Israeli Perceptions and Responses for the 1990s.* THE MIDDLE EAST

Webster A. Stone. Writer specializing in popular fiction and nonfiction projects related to terrorism, counterterrorism, and special warfare. Author of "Moscow Still Holding" for the *New York Times Magazine.* Creator of the bestseller *Rogue Warrior* by Richard Marcinko. THE HOT LINE: WASHINGTON-MOSCOW DIRECT COMMUNICATIONS LINK, 1963 TO THE PRESENT

Phillip R. Trimble. Professor of Law, University of California, Los Angeles. Former staff member, Senate Foreign Relations Committee and State Department lawyer, diplomat, and consultant to the Arms Control and Disarmament Agency. Author of books and articles on arms control and on international law. LEGAL DIMENSIONS OF ARMS CONTROL AND DISARMAMENT

Douglas C. Waller. National security correspondent, *Newsweek.* Former legislative assistant to Sen. William Proxmire. Coauthor of *Nuclear Peril: The Politics of Proliferation* and *The Strategic Defense Initiative: Progress and Challenge.* Author of *Congress and the Nuclear Freeze: An Inside Look at the Politics of a Mass Movement* and *The Operators* (forthcoming). THE STRATEGIC DEFENSE INITIATIVE AND ARMS CONTROL

Arthur H. Westing. Ecologist and conservationist, Westing Associates (Putney, Vt.). Specialist in environmental security and the effects of military activities on the environment. Consultant, U.N. Environment Program and the U.N. Institute for Disarmament Research. THE ENVIRONMENTAL MODIFICATION CONVENTION: 1977 TO THE PRESENT

Håkan Wiberg. Director, Center for Peace and Conflict Research (Copenhagen). President, European Peace Research Association. Former Professor of Sociology, Lund University (Sweden). Coauthor of *Arms Races* and *Norden, Europe, and the Near Future.* Editor of *Images of the World in the Year 2000* and *Inadvertent Nuclear War.* SCANDINAVIA

Lawrence S. Wittner. Professor of History, State University of New York, Albany. Author of *Rebels Against War, Cold War America,* and *American Intervention in Greece.* Currently writing a trilogy on the history of the world nuclear disarmament movement. TRANSNATIONAL PEACE MOVEMENTS AND ARMS CONTROL IN THE NINETEENTH AND TWENTIETH CENTURIES

Leneice N. Wu. Coordinator of Division Research, Foreign Affairs and National Defense Division, Congressional Research Service, Library of Congress. Author and contributor to various congressional publications on arms control. Coordinator of House Foreign Affairs Committee Print, "Fundamentals of Nuclear Arms Control." THE BARUCH PLAN: 1946–1949

Stephen Young. Legislative Co-Director, 20/20 VISION, a national grass-roots lobbying organization on military and environmental issues. Author of articles on conventional arms transfers, the European Community, and the START Treaty. THE AUSTRIAN STATE TREATY: 1955 TO THE PRESENT

ACRONYMS

ABM   Anti-Ballistic Missile
ACDA   Arms Control and Disarmament Agency
ALCM   air-launched cruise missile
ALMV   air-launched miniature vehicle
ASAT   anti-satellite weapon
ASW   anti-submarine warfare
ATBM   anti-tactical ballistic missile
ATS   advanced technology submarine
AWACS   airborne warning and control system

BAMBI   Ballistic Missile Interrupt
BWC   Biological and Toxin Weapons
(or BW)   Convention

CAT   conventional arms transfer
CCD   Conference of the Committee on
           Disarmament
CD   Conference on Disarmament
CDE   Conference on Disarmament in Europe
CCSBMDE   Conference on Confidence- and Security-
           Building Measures and Disarmament in
           Europe
CENTO   Central Treaty Organization
CEP   circular error probable
CFE   conventional forces in Europe
CSBM   confidence- and security-building
           measures
CSCE   Conference on Security and Cooperation
           in Europe
CTB   comprehensive test ban
CWC   chemical weapons convention

DOD   Department of Defense (U.S.)

EDC   European Defense Community
ENDC   Eighteen Nation Disarmament
           Conference
ERIS   exo-atmospheric reentry vehicle
           interception system
ERW   enhanced radiation weapon

FROD   functionally related observable
           differences

GCD   general and complete disarmament
GLCM   ground-launched cruise missile

HUMINT   human intelligence

IAEA   International Atomic Energy Agency
ICBM   intercontinental ballistic missile
INF   intermediate-range nuclear forces

LTBT   limited test ban treaty

MAD   mutual assured destruction
MARV   maneuverable reentry vehicle
MBFR   mutual (and balanced) force reduction
           (talks)
MHV   miniature homing vehicle
MIRV   multiple independently targetable reentry
           vehicle
MTCR   Missile Technology Control Regime

NATO   North Atlantic Treaty Organization
NFZ   nuclear-free zone
NGO   nongovernment organization
NNA (or   neutral nonaligned
NN)
NPT   non-proliferation treaty
NSA   National Security Agency (U.S.)
NTM   national technical means
NWFZ   nuclear-weapon-free zone

OAS   Organization of American States
OPANAL   Agency for the Prohibition of Nuclear
           Weapons in Latin America

PNE   peaceful nuclear explosion
R & D   research and development

SALT   Strategic Arms Limitation Talks (Treaty)
SLBM   submarine-launched ballistic missile
SLCM   sea-launched cruise missile
SSM   Sinai Support Mission
SSOD   Special Session on Disarmament
START   Strategic Arms Reduction Talks (Treaty)

TTBT   Threshold Test Ban Treaty

U.N.   United Nations

WEU   Western European Union
WTO   Warsaw Pact

1613

INDEX

*Arabic numbers printed in bold-faced type refer to extended treatment
of a subject or to a treaty excerpt included in Volume III.*

A

Aaron, David, in China, 905
Aberdeen, George Hamilton-Gordon, earl of, Rush-
    Bagot Agreement and, 584–585
Aboukir (ship), 740
Abrahamson, James, on strategic-defense deployment,
    1126
"Abrazo del Estrecho" (1899), 598
ACCESS (organization), organizational databases of,
    420–422
Accidental war, preventing, **1093–1100**
    effectiveness of agreements, 1100
    "Rules of the Road," 1095
    U.N. efforts, 1099–1100
Accidents Measures Agreement (1971), 1094–1095
Accounting units. *See* Units of account
Acheson, Dean
    committee to develop atomic safeguards, 774
    on H-bomb development, 1071
    on negative aspects of disarmament, 271
    on Pacific Island fortifications, 653
    Reagan negotiation strategies and, 399
Achieving Effective Arms Control, 398
Actium, Battle of, 557
Act of Paris (1815), Swiss neutrality and, 677
Adams, Charles Francis, Rush-Bagot Agreement and, 586
Adams, Gordon, on impact of defense spending, 346
Adams, John, Great Lakes demilitarization and, 581
Adams, John Quincy, Great Lakes demilitarization and,
    582, 583, 688
Addams, Jane, Women's International League for Peace
    and Freedom and, 411
Adelman, Kenneth
    ACDA and, 527
    on effective verification measures, 298
    on Soviet prestige, 473

Adenauer, Konrad
    agreement to WEU supervision, 97
    Austrian neutrality and, 812
    Austrian State Treaty and, 790
    disarmament policy, 102
    elected chancellor, 786
    European-army concept and, 788
    Stalin and, 789
    West German rearmament and, 787
Adherence to and Compliance with Agreements, 532
Aegean islands, Montreux convention on, 683
Aeneid. See Virgil (Publius Vergilius Maro)
Aerial bombing, **725–736, 1371–1388**
    opposition to, 498
Aerial inspection
    Antarctic Treaty on, 820
    Open Skies on, 1114, 1115–1116
    Soviet plans for, 192
    Stockholm Document on, 938
    Vienna confidence-building negotiations proposal on,
        942
Afghanistan
    chemical warfare agents, 1003
    Soviet invasion of
        effect on India and Pakistan, 235
        Helsinki consultation follow-up meetings and, 934,
            935
        and hot line, 851
        SALT II and, 907
Africa, **15–29**. *See also* Horn of Africa
    arms control and disarmament, 19–20
        colonial areas, 714, 717
        confidence-building measures, 27–28
        democratization and, 28
        diplomatic initiatives, 1980s, 21–22
        economic development and, 23–24
        economic factors, 20–21, 23–25

1615

B

C

D

E

G

H

J

K

M

Q

R

U

W

X

Y